SCHAUM'S OUTLINE OF

THEORY AND PROBLEMS

OF

PROGRAMMING
with
ADVANCED
STRUCTURED COBOL

with
**File Processing,
Structured Systems Development,
and Interactive Considerations**

•

LAWRENCE R. NEWCOMER, M.S.

*Assistant Professor of Computer Science
The Pennsylvania State University
York Campus*

SCHAUM'S OUTLINE SERIES
McGRAW-HILL BOOK COMPANY

*New York   St. Louis   San Francisco   Auckland   Bogotá   Hamburg   Johannesburg
London   Madrid   Mexico   Milan   Montreal   New Delhi   Panama   Paris
São Paulo   Singapore   Sydney   Tokyo   Toronto*

LAWRENCE R. NEWCOMER is an Assistant Professor of Computer Science at Pennsylvania State University/York Campus. He holds a B.A. in English from Wesleyan University (Conn.), an M.S. in Psychology from Millersville State University, and an M.S. in Computer Science from the Pennsylvania State University.

In addition to teaching computer science business applications, Professor Newcomer is the author of *Schaum's Outline of Programming with Structured COBOL*. He has also published articles on computer science education, produced several licensed program products, and served as a data processing consultant to business and industry.

Schaum's Outline of Theory and Problems of
PROGRAMMING WITH ADVANCED STRUCTURED COBOL

1 2 3 4 5 6 7 8 9 10 11 12 13 14 15 16 17 18 19 20 SHP SHP 8 9 8 7

ISBN 0-07-037999-8

Production Manager, Nick Monti
Sponsoring Editor, John Aliano
Editing Supervisor, Marthe Grice

Library of Congress Cataloging-in-Publication Data

Newcomer, Lawrence R.
    Schaum's outline of theories and problems of
programming with advanced structured COBOL with
file processing structured systems development
and interactive considerations.

    (Schaum's outline series)
    Includes index.
    1. COBOL (Computer program language)   2. Structured
programming.   I. Title.
QA76.73.C25N47 1986   005.13'3   86-2847
ISBN 0-07-037999-8

To my mother,
my brother and his family,
and Deirdre and Caitlin,
and
in memory of my father

Preface

This Outline is designed to cover those aspects of COBOL not treated in *Schaum's Outline of Programming with Structured COBOL* (McGraw-Hill, 1984). In particular, attention is paid to the processing of files on direct access storage devices, the use of the COBOL COPY library, the use of external subprograms (i.e., CALL rather than PERFORM), interactive program design considerations, and other advanced topics.

Chapters 1–4 expand on material directly relevant to the professional practice of programming. These topics include (1) the systems development process (with the structured methodologies of structured analysis, structured design, and structured programming), (2) COBOL coding standards, and (3) program testing and debugging.

Since this Outline deals with advanced COBOL topics, it is assumed throughout that the reader is already familiar with the material covered in *Schaum's Outline of Programming with Structured COBOL*.

Most COBOL syntax in this Outline adheres to the 1974 ANSI standard. Where extensions to ANSI COBOL are presented they are extensions supported by IBM OS/VS COBOL compilers and are clearly identified as such. Changes to the COBOL language defined by ANSI COBOL-85 are discussed in Chapter 13.

I would like to thank the administration and the Advisory Board of the Pennsylvania State University/York Campus for supporting me in this task. Without their assistance I would not have been able to complete this project in the time allotted. Special thanks are due to Oscar Fox and Frank Miller for their support in scheduling my teaching duties, and to Marge Johnson for her cheerful handling of messages and materials.

As usual, the entire staff at McGraw-Hill was helpful, competent, and friendly. Special thanks are due to John Aliano and Marthe Grice for their invaluable contributions to this project.

I am also indebted to the following people (in alphabetical order) for their ideas and writings on structured methodology: L. Constantine, T. DeMarco, M. Page-Jones, V. Weinberg, and E. Yourdon. Chapters 1–3 are a simplified encapsulation of their ideas which I hope does justice to the original works. The reader is urged to pursue these topics further by consulting the aforementioned authors.

I would like to thank my students for enduring various early versions of the text, particularly the class of 1986 who diligently located many errors in the original manuscript. Thanks are also due to Linda Collision, WesLee Johnson, Sue Schneider, and Marci Shaffer for contributing to the solved problems, and to Dr. Russell Etter for his patience and support. Ken Watkins deserves particular thanks for his friendship, personal support, and insights into the difficult process of writing a book. Deep appreciation is due to my parents for their support of my own education. Finally, I would like to thank my wife for her many helpful comments and suggestions which greatly improved the manuscript, and both my wife and daughter for their patience, support, and involvement in this book.

Lawrence R. Newcomer

Contents

CONTENTS

Chapter 1

The Systems Development Process: Where Programming Fits In

Every COBOL programmer is part of a web of interactions affecting his or her whole organization. To illuminate the context in which the COBOL programmer works, this chapter investigates the life cycle of a typical business computer system. The systems development process for a typical *business application system* (a collection of computer programs working together to solve a particular business problem) depends on whether the organization follows the classical approach to systems development or the newer structured methodologies.

1.1 Classical Versus Structured Systems Development

Similarities between Classical and Structured Methods

Classical methodology and structured methodology both organize the systems development process into a set of orderly phases. Although details may vary, there is general agreement that systems development should consist of the following three *major* steps:

Step	Name	Carried Out By
1	Systems analysis	Systems analysts
2	Systems design	Systems analysts or systems designers
3	Implementation	Systems analysts and programmers

The main goals of both classical and structured *analysis* are to (1) identify the problem causing the need for systems development, (2) analyze the current system to determine how things are being done now, (3) determine objectives for the new system to be developed, (4) propose a general solution to the stated problem which will meet the stated objectives, and (5) specify the requirements for the new system in a form suitable for use in systems design.

The main goals of both classical and structured *design* are to (1) accept the requirements specification produced during systems analysis as the major input to the design process, (2) produce a physical design for the new system which meets these requirements, and (3) document the design in a form suitable for use in implementation.

The main goals of both classical and structured *implementation* are to (1) accept the physical design from the previous step, (2) design, code, test, and document the individual modules which make up the system, (3) install any new hardware, (4) train users, (5) test the entire system, and (6) install the system.

It should be noted that although some organizations may rush through systems analysis and design in order to begin implementation as soon as possible, there is growing recognition of the importance of the two preparatory steps in minimizing the total lifetime costs of computer systems.

Differences between Classical and Structured Methods

Classical and structured methodologies differ in three major ways. Two of these are quantitative: Structured methodology places more explicit emphasis on (1) determining system objectives before doing any kind of design (arguing that it is impossible to design without goals) and on (2) specifying the logical requirements of the system (called "logical design") before attempting to design the actual details of the system as it will eventually be implemented (called "physical design").

1

The third major difference is qualitative: Structured methodology introduces several new graphic tools for analysis and design, offering significant improvements over the tools traditionally used in systems development.

Traditional Systems Development Tools

Classical analysis relies mainly on English narrative (ordinary written English) and systems flowcharts to document the requirements specification, which is the major output of the analysis step. However, experience has shown that there are major drawbacks to both these tools. English narrative documentation is typically lengthy and laced with technical jargon. Users have difficulty determining whether their objectives are accurately captured in the requirements, and designers are slowed down in their attempts to comprehend design parameters. Systems flowcharts are slanted toward physical specifications and therefore are not well-adapted to expressing the user's *logical* requirements.

EXAMPLE 1.1 A *systems flowchart* is a graphic tool for depicting the documents and files in a system and the manual procedures and/or computer programs which act on them. Typical symbols used in systems flowcharts are shown in Fig. 1-1. Other system flowcharting symbols indicating specialized types of input and output are beyond the scope of this Outline.

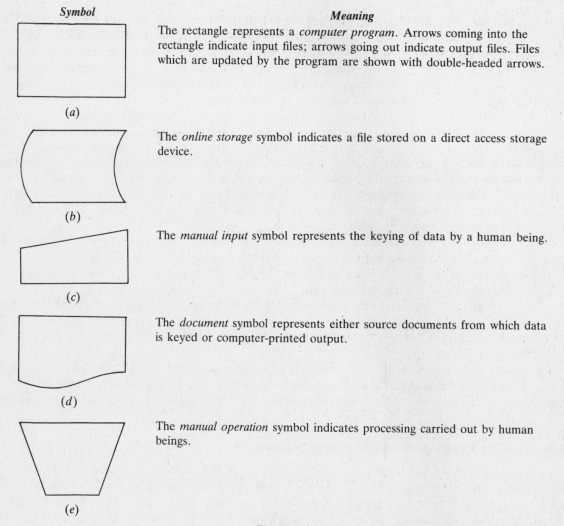

Symbol	Meaning
(a)	The rectangle represents a *computer program*. Arrows coming into the rectangle indicate input files; arrows going out indicate output files. Files which are updated by the program are shown with double-headed arrows.
(b)	The *online storage* symbol indicates a file stored on a direct access storage device.
(c)	The *manual input* symbol represents the keying of data by a human being.
(d)	The *document* symbol represents either source documents from which data is keyed or computer-printed output.
(e)	The *manual operation* symbol indicates processing carried out by human beings.

Fig. 1-1

EXAMPLE 1.2   A sample systems flowchart is shown in Fig. 1-2.

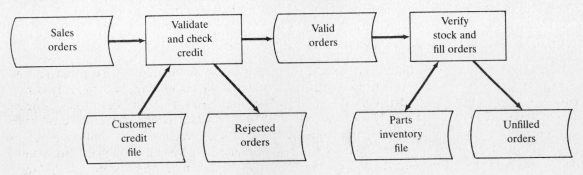

Fig. 1-2

The primary tools of classical design are English narrative program specifications, systems flowcharts, program flowcharts, and sometimes pseudocode and hierarchy charts. The difficulties with these tools include the following: (1) English narrative specifications tend to be unwieldy and ambiguous, (2) systems flowcharts are good for documenting current operating procedures but not particularly good for design purposes, (3) program flowcharts are difficult to draw and keep up to date, (4) both program flowcharts and pseudocode tend to include too many implementation details and thus have the systems designer intruding on what should be the work of the programmer, and (5) there is no well-defined method for producing traditional hierarchy charts, so that the important goals of top-down modular design are left too much to chance. For a discussion of traditional top-down modular design, see *Schaum's Outline of Programming with Structured COBOL* (McGraw-Hill, 1984).

EXAMPLE 1.3   Although systems flowcharts use the same symbols as program flowcharts, the two serve totally different purposes. *Systems flowcharts* show the relationships between the files and programs in a system, whereas *program flowcharts* show the internal logic of a single program or module (see Section 3.2). Contrast Fig. 1-2 with the segment of a program flowchart shown in Fig. 1-3.

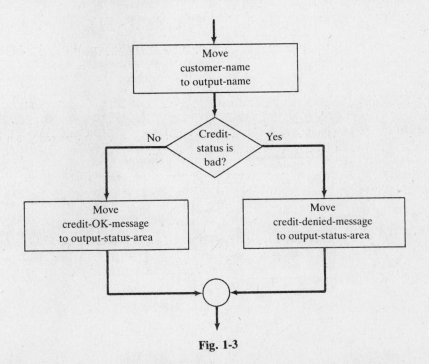

Fig. 1-3

As of this writing, both the classical and structured approaches to systems development tend to use the techniques of structured programming for the systems implementation step. See Chapter 3 for a review of these important techniques.

1.2 Tools of Structured Methodology

Structured methodology is a collection of tools and techniques for improving the entire systems development process. It consists of the interrelated areas of structured analysis, structured design, and structured programming. Historically, the structured programming techniques were developed first, and their great success in improving programmer productivity provided the motivation to create similar techniques for improving the productivity of systems analysts and systems designers. This section discusses the major tools of structured analysis and structured design.

EXAMPLE 1.4 Structured analysis does not totally discard classical analysis tools. English narrative might be used in the analysis of a current university student registration system to help describe the processing of student schedules:

A student picks up a student schedule form from the academic affairs office. After selecting a preliminary schedule by consulting the course offerings listing, the student contacts an academic advisor for approval. The advisor adds any required courses the student may have missed, removes any courses for which the

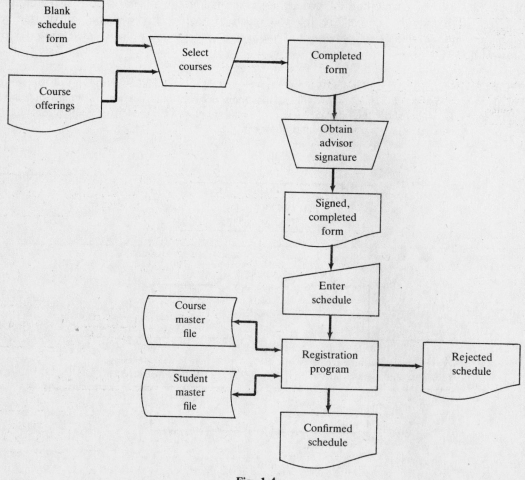

Fig. 1-4

student does not have the prerequisites, and then signs the completed schedule form. The student then takes the signed form to administrative data processing, where the approved schedule is keyed into the computer system. Each course is checked against the course master file to ensure that there is room available. If all desired courses have room available, the student is registered and both the course master file and the student master file are updated and a schedule confirmation is printed. If any desired course is closed, the student is not registered and is given a rejection notice and sent back to the advisor to choose a new schedule.

EXAMPLE 1.5 Structured analysis recognizes the worth of the traditional systems flowchart when its use is restricted to illustrating the physical flow of data between programs and files. The analysis of the university student registration system might include a systems flowchart depicting the physical flow of information required to register a student. See Fig. 1-4.

Data Flow Diagrams

The main tool of structured analysis is the *data flow diagram* (*DFD*). A data flow diagram graphically depicts the logical flow of data through a system, along with the transformations which are applied to that data.

EXAMPLE 1.6 A data flow diagram for the registration system is given in Fig. 1-5.

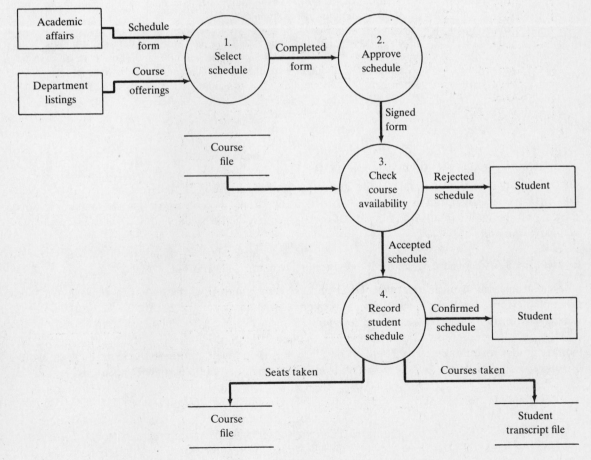

Fig. 1-5

EXAMPLE 1.7 The meanings of graphic symbols used in DFDs are shown in Fig. 1-6.

Symbol	*Meaning*
Student *(a)*	A rectangular box represents a source or sink. A *source* supplies input data to the DFD; it is where the data processed by the DFD comes from. A *sink* is the ultimate destination for data; it is where the data processed within the DFD goes.
Signed form *(b)*	A labeled arrow represents a *data flow*. The direction of the arrow shows the direction of data movement. The label should give a precise name to the piece of data involved. The whole point of a DFD is to give a picture of the data flows within a system.
Approve schedule *(c)*	A labeled circle signifies a *transform*. It represents the processing or transformation of data. A transform does not have to change data physically. It can also increase the amount of information in data, as when a transform validates a piece of data. Raw data flows in and valid data flows out. Physically the raw data and valid data are the same, but the valid data contains more information because we know that the valid data is valid (whereas the raw data may or may not be valid). Each transform should be labeled with a name that clearly identifies the function of the transform. The best names consist of a precise transitive verb followed by a singular object, e.g., "edit inquiry" or "update customer balance". Transforms in DFDs are sometimes called "bubbles".
Course file *(d)*	A pair of labeled parallel lines signifies a *data store*. A data store has the characteristics of a file; it can retain data over time and allow it to be accessed and/or updated more than once. The name of the data store is written between the parallel lines. It should be both concise and descriptive.

Fig. 1-6

Each DFD should be small enough to fit on a single page. Complex systems can be depicted by a set of leveled data flow diagrams. The entire system under study is first pictured by an overview DFD. The overview DFD is sometimes deliberately drawn to consist of just a single transform showing all the major inputs and outputs of the system under study. Such an overview DFD is called a *context diagram*.

EXAMPLE 1.8 A context diagram for the registration system is shown in Fig. 1-7.

The transform(s) in an overview DFD will be very general processes which represent a large amount of work. Each such transform is broken down into a separate DFD showing the internal details of the transform. This is called *leveling*.

If a bubble numbered "x" is to be leveled, the new "child" DFD showing the internal details of x would number its bubbles x.1, x.2, etc. If bubble x.2 is then leveled in turn, the child diagram would use numbers x.2.1, x.2.2, x.2.3, etc. It is best if the "parent" bubble spawns no more than seven "children".

Leveling can be repeated as often as necessary to reach the desired amount of detail. A good guideline is to stop when the bottom-level transformations (called *functional primitives*) can each be described in one page of documentation. The leveled set of DFDs thus produced forms a *hierarchy* with the overview DFD at the top. The bubble numbering scheme not only uniquely identifies each bubble but also reflects this hierarchical structure.

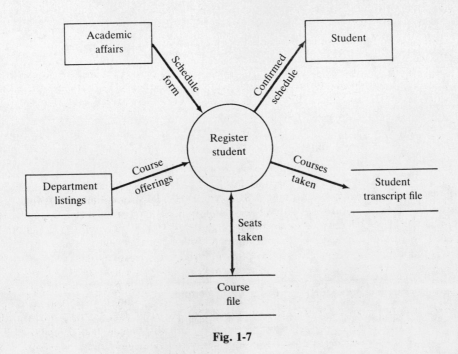

Fig. 1-7

EXAMPLE 1.9   Figure 1-8 shows the leveling of bubble 2 from the DFD of Fig. 1-5.

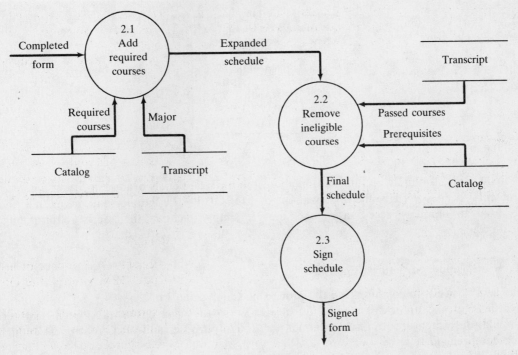

Fig. 1-8

During leveling, the input and output data flows of a parent bubble should match the input and output flows of its lower-level DFD. The child DFD may of course show internal details (such as data flows, transforms, and data stores) not present in the higher-level diagram.

EXAMPLE 1.10 "Completed form" is the sole input to bubble 2 in Fig. 1-5; "Signed form" is its sole output. These data flows are the input to and output from the entire leveling diagram shown in Fig. 1-8. Since Fig. 1-8 shows the internal details of bubble 2, it includes new data flows and transforms (e.g., "Major", "Expanded schedule", "Add required courses") which are not present in the overview DFD of Fig. 1-5.

Data Structure Diagrams

Structured analysis uses *data structure diagrams* (*DSD*) to show the logical relationships among data items in a system. The DSD is a useful tool for showing the user's *logical data access requirements*.

EXAMPLE 1.11 There are many ways to draw DSD's. Figure 1-9 illustrates one format with a DSD for the student registration system. The arrows indicate the relationships between records. For example, if a program accesses a particular STUDENT record, it may also need to access COURSE records to get information about the courses taken by the student. Once COURSE information has been retrieved, it may also be necessary to access FACULTY information, etc.

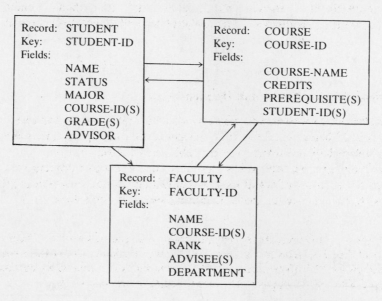

Fig. 1-9

A DSD gives absolutely *no* information about the physical details of implementing the indicated requirements. It does *not* give file organizations or COBOL PICTUREs for data items, tell *how* the key is used to uniquely access a record, etc. It simply pictures the user's requirements for information.

Process Specification: Structured English

The analyst needs to communicate the processing requirements of a new system to the users (for their verification and approval) and to the designers (so they can design the system). Structured English is a tool which is both precise enough for design purposes and yet nontechnical enough for users to comprehend readily.

Structured English is a form of pseudocode (see Section 3.2) which combines clear and precise descriptions of processing actions (expressed in the vocabulary of the users) with the three fundamental logic structures of structured programming. Whereas pseudocode usually shows both what must be done and how to do it, structured English concerns itself strictly with *what* must be done to the input in order to produce the output.

EXAMPLE 1.12 The following program segment shows the structured English for internal processing requirements of bubble 2.2 of Example 1.9 (Fig. 1-8). Note the emphasis on *what* must be done rather than the details of *how* it is done.

```
dowhile there are unprocessed courses on expanded schedule
    list prerequisites for course (found in catalog)
    check transcript to ensure that all prerequisites
        were taken and passed
    if any prerequisites are not satisfied then
        remove course from expanded schedule
    endif
endwhile
```

Structured English, like pseudocode, uses only the three basic logic structures of sequence, selection (decision), and iteration (repetition). Example 1.12 illustrates a popular scheme in which selection is indicated with "if . . . then . . . else . . . endif" and "if . . . then . . . endif", while iteration is indicated with "dowhile . . . endwhile". The dashed lines and indentation enhance the clarity of the logic.

Process Specification: Decision Tables and Decision Trees

Structured English for processes which involve complicated decisions can result in many nested if constructs which are difficult for users and designers to follow. In such cases, the processing requirements are better depicted using decision tables or decision trees.

A *decision table* is a graphic tool which identifies the conditions pertinent to a problem and the actions to be taken for each set of conditions. An advantage of decision tables is that they keep the analyst (and users) from overlooking possible combinations of conditions.

EXAMPLE 1.13 Here is a decision table showing processing requirements for the "Check course availability" transform (bubble 3 of Fig. 1-5). The *condition stub* lists three conditions. All possible combinations of these conditions are indicated by "Y" (Yes) and "N" (No) table entries. Action(s) to be taken for each set of conditions are marked with an "*" opposite the corresponding *action stub* entry.

Student is senior	Y	Y	Y	Y	N	N	N	N
Course required for major	Y	Y	N	N	Y	Y	N	N
Course filled	Y	N	Y	N	Y	N	Y	N
Allow student in	*	*	*	*	*	*		*
Get department approval			*		*			

A disadvantage of decision tables is that analysts sometimes have trouble drawing them and users sometimes have trouble interpreting them. *Decision trees* present the same information in a format which is both easy to draw and self-explanatory.

EXAMPLE 1.14 Figure 1-10 shows a decision tree for the logic of Example 1.13.

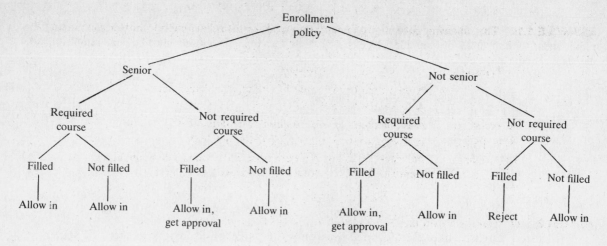

Fig. 1-10

Data Dictionary

Data flow diagrams, data structure diagrams, structured English, and decision tables/trees all refer to data items and the processes applied to them. The value of these graphic tools is greatly enhanced if the terms which appear in them are defined in a data dictionary.

The *data dictionary* is a central repository for all the information produced during systems development. During structured analysis, it serves to define data items in terms of their information content, and processes in terms of their inputs, outputs, and the DFDs, structured English, etc., which refer to them. Later, structured design adds details regarding the physical implementation of data items and processes. This information not only eliminates confusion and duplication of effort during systems development but also becomes an invaluable tool for later systems maintenance.

EXAMPLE 1.15 Here is a sample data dictionary definition of a data element. The notation used is explained below. All data items and processes referred to in this entry would be defined in their own separate data dictionary entries.

Name: STUDENT-TRANSCRIPT
Description: Holds all academic information regarding a student
Aliases: STUTRANS
Composition: STUDENT-TRANSCRIPT =
                            STUDENT-NAME +
                            STUDENT-ID   +
                            STATUS   +
                            MAJOR   +
                            {COURSE-INFORMATION} +
                            [ADVISOR | PERCENT-FULL-TIME] +
                            GRADUATING-YEAR

Processes using
this data element:

Process Name	*DFD Transform Number*
RECORD-STUDENT-SCHEDULE	Bubble 4 (Fig. 1-5)
ADD-REQUIRED-COURSES	Bubble 2.1 (Fig. 1-8)
REMOVE-INELIGIBLE-COURSES	Bubble 2.2 (Fig. 1-8)

EXAMPLE 1.16   The following table shows the notation used for data description in a data dictionary:

Notation	Meaning
=	A data item is composed of one or more other items.
A = B + C	A is composed of B and C.
A = {B}	A is composed of one or more repetitions of B.
A = [B | C]	A is composed of either B or C but not both.
Underlining	Indicates the *key field* in a record, i.e., a field which uniquely identifies the record and is used for record retrieval.

EXAMPLE 1.17   Here is a data dictionary entry for a process or transform:

Name:	REMOVE-INELIGIBLE-COURSES
DFD number:	Bubble 2.2 (see Fig. 1-8)
Description:	Removes courses from student's expanded schedule for which (1) student has not passed the prerequisites or (2) there is no room in course and course is not necessary for student in this semester
Inputs:	EXPANDED-SCHEDULE
	STUDENT-TRANSCRIPT
	COURSE-CATALOG
Outputs:	FINAL-SCHEDULE
Related specifications:	Structured English in Example 1.12

Structure Charts

Just as the data flow diagram is the main tool of structured analysis, so the structure chart is the main tool of structured design. Structured design takes the data flow diagrams describing the logical requirements for a new system and turns them into a physical design showing how these requirements can be implemented.

Structured design uses the black-box concept of a module to construct the physical design of a system. A module will eventually be implemented as a PERFORMed paragraph (or SECTION) or a separately compiled external subprogram invoked with the CALL statement (see Chapter 10). For purposes of design, however, modules are thought of as black boxes which transform inputs to outputs in well-defined ways but whose internal workings are unknown. The designer is only concerned with a module's *input*, *output*, and *function*.

A *structure chart* graphically depicts the physical design of a system in terms of (1) its functional decomposition into a hierarchy of black-box modules, (2) the major flows of data and control information between modules, and (3) the major decisions and loops in the system. See Chapter 2 for a discussion of how to create good structure charts.

EXAMPLE 1.18   Figure 1-11 shows a partial structure chart for the registration system. See Example 1.19 for an explanation of the notation used.

EXAMPLE 1.19   Symbols used in drawing structure charts are shown in Fig. 1-12.

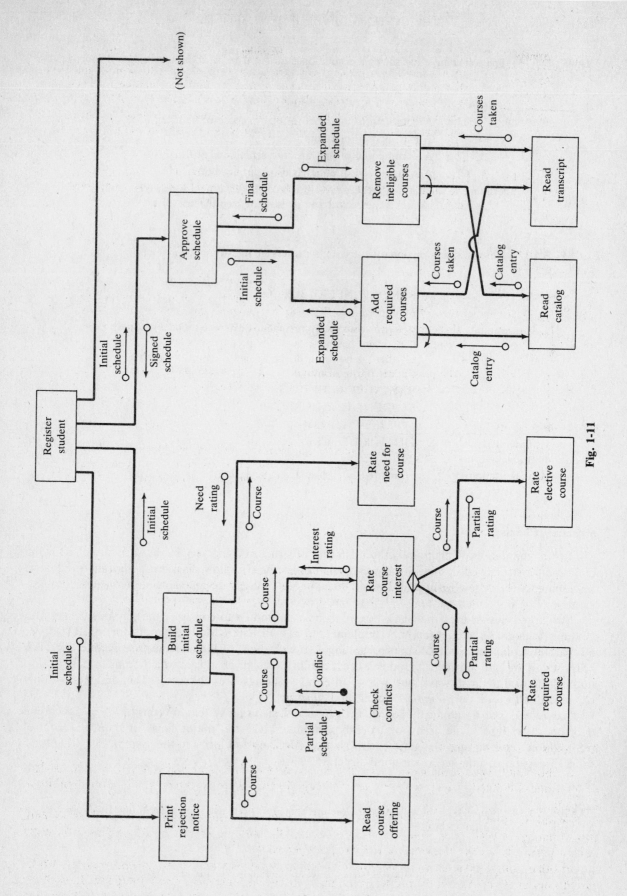

Fig. 1-11

Symbol	Meaning

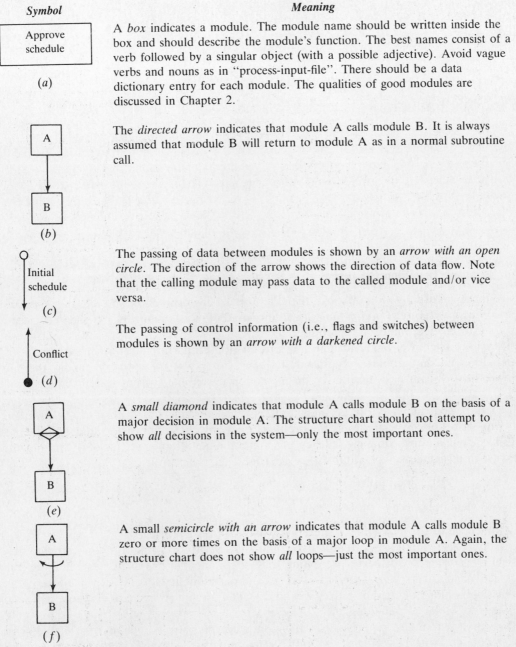

Symbol

(a) Approve schedule

A *box* indicates a module. The module name should be written inside the box and should describe the module's function. The best names consist of a verb followed by a singular object (with a possible adjective). Avoid vague verbs and nouns as in "process-input-file". There should be a data dictionary entry for each module. The qualities of good modules are discussed in Chapter 2.

(b) A → B

The *directed arrow* indicates that module A calls module B. It is always assumed that module B will return to module A as in a normal subroutine call.

(c) Initial schedule

The passing of data between modules is shown by an *arrow with an open circle*. The direction of the arrow shows the direction of data flow. Note that the calling module may pass data to the called module and/or vice versa.

(d) Conflict

The passing of control information (i.e., flags and switches) between modules is shown by an *arrow with a darkened circle*.

(e) A ◇ → B

A *small diamond* indicates that module A calls module B on the basis of a major decision in module A. The structure chart should not attempt to show *all* decisions in the system—only the most important ones.

(f) A → B

A small *semicircle with an arrow* indicates that module A calls module B zero or more times on the basis of a major loop in module A. Again, the structure chart does not show *all* loops—just the most important ones.

Fig. 1-12

The Roles of the Programmer/Analyst and Systems Designer

Traditionally, systems analysts carry out the processes of systems analysis and systems design (steps 1 and 2 in Section 1.1), while programmers and analysts are both involved in implementation (step 3).

However, some data processing departments combine the functions of systems analysis and programming. In such cases, one person carries out all the steps in the systems development process. Such a person is usually referred to as a *programmer/analyst*.

In other shops, systems analysis is carried out by specialists known as *systems analysts*, while systems design is carried out by a separate group of specialists known as *systems designers*. In such an environment, *programmers* restrict their activities to the implementation phase of systems development.

1.3   Systems Development with Structured Methodology

Structured methodology organizes systems analysis, design, and implementation into the following 10 phases. The activities within each phase are iterative; i.e., they should be repeated as often as needed to successfully complete the phase.

Phase 1—Problem Recognition and Initial Request (Analysis)

Data processing (DP) systems are created to fill a perceived need within the organization. Initially, someone who recognizes a need makes a request for a new data processing service or the modification of an existing service. This could be done by anyone within the organization (from the chief executive officer on down). Motivation for change can also come from outside the organization (e.g., from a customer or government agency). Sometimes requests arise from within the data processing department itself when the DP staff sees the need to create or improve services. The initial request is usually presented to the data processing manager in writing.

Phase 2—Problem Definition (Analysis)

Since there are usually more requests than data processing can handle, the DP manager (often in conjunction with a *computer policy committee*, composed of other managers and users) decides which requests are to receive immediate attention.

An analyst or team of analysts then develops an English-narrative report presenting a preliminary definition of the problem. The analyst(s) may interview the person making the request, interview other relevant persons, study documentation describing current systems and procedures, etc.

The report also discusses the problem *context* by identifying the history of the problem, the departments or people associated with the problem area, any constraints associated with the problem (such as laws, regulations, company policies, etc.), and the quantitative effects of the problem on the business (such as needless expenditures, lost revenues, etc.).

Phase 3—Review Current System (Analysis)

The objective of this phase is to determine what system currently exists and what is wrong with it. The analysts also identify several tentative approaches to problem solutions and estimate the costs and benefits associated with each, presenting their recommendations as part of their report. The analysts may conduct interviews, send out surveys and questionnaires, study existing documentation, carry out observations of current procedures and work flow, interview vendors, research available literature, visit similar installations, etc.

Although much of the report will be English narrative, structured analysis supplements the classical techniques with new *graphic tools* for documenting the existing system. Data flow diagrams, data structure diagrams, structured English, decision tables, decision trees, and structure charts can all be used to graphically describe the current system. Such tools not only facilitate precision, but they more conveniently summarize the current system for the users, who can thus more easily verify that it is being described accurately.

Phase 4—Determine Objectives for New/Modified System (Analysis)

In this phase the analysts turn from the study of the current system and its problems to the determination of the requirements for the new system. This necessitates careful solicitation of the users' objectives and priorities for the proposed system and the statement of these objectives and priorities in precise, measurable terms. The users' logical requirements can be depicted by means of data flow diagrams and data structure diagrams, which can give an overview of the goals for the new system. One of the major advantages of structured analysis is that user requirements are expressed in these compact, graphic forms, which more conveniently present user objectives to the users themselves, who can thus verify that their objectives are correctly expressed.

Phase 5—Determine Best Approach to Physical Implementation (Analysis)

In this phase the analysts consider, in the light of user objectives, the possible alternatives for implementing the new system. Should it be all manual, part manual and part automated, or all automated? Should the automated portions be batch or interactive or a combination of both? Should data base management and/or data communications technology be used? The analysts must determine to what extent each possibility meets user requirements and what costs and benefits are associated with each, so that a final recommendation can be made.

Phase 6—Logical Systems Design (Analysis)

The logical design phase is the major step in structured analysis. The output of this phase is called a *structured specification*, which consists of:

(1) An English-narrative summary of the current system and its problems

(2) A narrative list of objectives for the new system

(3) A leveled set of data flow diagrams describing the logical requirements for the new/modified system

(4) A data structure diagram depicting logical data access requirements

(5) A minispecification (using structured English, decision tables and/or decision trees) to depict processing requirements for each bottom-level bubble (functional primitive) in the leveled DFD

(6) A data dictionary defining every data item and process appearing anywhere within the structured specification

The minispecification should use English narrative and/or structured English, decision tables, and decision trees to explain *what* each bottom-level transform does; i.e., it should give the *rules by which the process transforms its inputs to its outputs*. The determination of *how* processing is to be done is left to the implementation phase of systems development.

Phase 7—Develop a Top-Down Implementation Plan (Analysis)

The purpose of this phase is to *plan* the structured design and implementation phases which follow. If the project is large, it is probably best to implement and deliver it to the users in stages (a process known as *versioned implementation*). This makes the users happy, gives them early experience with the system, and allows unexpected problems to surface quickly.

EXAMPLE 1.20   Below is a versioned implementation plan for the registration system:

System Version	Delivered Capabilities (Cumulative)
1	Enter and validate student transcript information.
2	Inquire and update against student transcript file.
3	Enter and validate student schedule information.
4	All functions for creating and maintaining master course file.
Final	All functions for entire registration system.

The implementation plan should identify what needs to be done during structured design and implementation and assign personnel to each task. The *sequence in which modules will be coded and tested* must be determined. Procedures for creation of test data, actual testing, user training, and final system conversion and acceptance should also be defined.

Phase 8—Physical Systems Design (Design)

The purpose of *structured design* is to take the structured specification produced during analysis and create from it a sufficiently detailed *physical design* to allow implementation of the system.

The main tool of structured design is the *structure chart*. Structured design provides (1) explicit guidelines for turning the data flow diagram of the structured specification into an initial version of a structure chart, (2) a set of criteria for evaluating modules which allows the designer to improve the initial structure chart to create a final design, and (3) the graphic tools of structured English, decision tables, and decision trees to document *what* each module is supposed to do (i.e., a *functional specification* for each module). Since these techniques of structured systems design can also be applied to the design of individual programs during implementation, they are presented separately in Chapter 2.

In addition to developing a structure chart, the systems designer must also decide (1) how to package the structure chart modules into separate computer programs and (2) how to package the data flows and other data elements in the data dictionary into records and files (or physical data base specifications). Fully detailed specifications for all input records, output records, auxiliary storage files, video screen formats, etc., are developed. These are often documented using special preprinted *record layout forms*, *printer spacing charts*, and *screen format charts*.

During the entire physical design phase, the designer should also document all design decisions by filling in details of the appropriate data dictionary entries, thus producing an expanded data dictionary.

Phase 9—Implementation

This is the phase in which the COBOL programmer finally enters the picture. Programmers are assigned to design, code, test, and document the individual modules which make up the system. Since the structured design module specifications indicate only *what* to do, not *how* to do it, the programmer is left to complete the module designs.

Structured programming techniques should, of course, be used to design and code each module. These methods are fully discussed in *Schaum's Outline of Programming with Structured COBOL* (McGraw-Hill, 1984) and are reviewed here in Chapter 3.

During implementation, systems analysts are responsible for (1) installation of any new hardware, (2) training of personnel, (3) creation of any new files, (4) conversion of existing files to new devices and/or file organizations, (5) completion of all system documentation (including operations and user documentation as well as program documentation), and (6) system testing.

Implementation should proceed in a top-down fashion, with the implementation plan serving as a guide. In particular, coding and testing of modules should be done *incrementally*; the module(s) at the top of the structure chart should be coded and debugged first and the remaining modules should be coded and debugged in a top-down fashion. Thus the system is built by continued addition of new modules to an already working subset which constantly expands.

When all coding and testing are successfully completed, the organization is ready to convert to the new or modified system. *Conversion* (or *installation*) entails ceasing to do things the "old" way and starting to use the new (or modified) system.

Phase 10—Acceptance and Evaluation

When conversion has been completed, management formally accepts the system and it *goes into production* (i.e., the organization uses the system in day-to-day operations). At this point and at regular intervals for the rest of its useful life, the system is evaluated by systems analysts to determine whether it is meeting its stated goals effectively or whether it should be changed or updated. A request to modify the system causes the entire development cycle to resume again at the beginning.

Review Questions

1.1   List the three major steps in systems development.

1.2   What are the major goals of structured analysis? structured design? implementation?

1.3   What personnel are responsible for each step of systems development?

1.4   Explain the roles of (1) the traditional analyst, (2) the programmer/analyst, and (3) the systems designer.

1.5   What are the three major differences between classical and structured methodologies?

1.6   Explain some disadvantages of traditional analysis tools.

1.7   Explain some disadvantages of traditional design tools.

1.8   Explain the differences between systems flowcharts and program flowcharts.

1.9   Discuss the symbols used in data flow diagrams.

1.10   What is a context diagram?

1.11   Explain the concept of leveling.

1.12   Explain the use of data structure diagrams.

1.13   Explain structured English. What are its advantages?

1.14   What are decision tables? When should they be used?

1.15   What are decision trees? When should they be used?

1.16   Why is the term "data dictionary" a misnomer?

1.17   Give a sample data element description from a data dictionary.

1.18   Give a sample process description from a data dictionary.

1.19   How are structure charts used in systems design?

1.20   Explain the notation used in drawing structure charts.

1.21   Describe the major activities in each phase of structured systems development.

1.22   What is the structured specification? How is it used?

1.23   Explain the use of a minispecification.

1.24   What is the purpose of a top-down implementation plan?

1.25   What is meant by versioned implementation?

1.26 What activities are carried out during structured design?

1.27 What are the programmers' responsibilities during implementation?

1.28 What are the analysts' responsibilities during implementation?

Solved Problems

1.29 The main output from the analysis phase of systems development is a *requirements specification*. What form does the requirements specification take when structured analysis is used?

The requirements specification produced by structured analysis is called a *structured specification*. It describes the logical requirements for the new system with three major tools:

(1) A leveled set of data flow diagrams for the new system.

(2) A minispecification for each bottom-level bubble of the data flow diagram. The minispecs describe *what* processing each bottom-level bubble must carry out in order to transform the input of the bubble to its output. Minispecifications may use any combination of structured English, decision tables, decision trees, and English narrative.

(3) The beginnings of a data dictionary, with an entry for every data flow and transform in the data flow diagram.

1.30 What form does system design take when structured design methodology is used?

The main output of structured design is:

(1) A structure chart for the new system.

(2) A functional specification for each module in the structure chart. The module specifications unambiguously define *what* each module does to its input in order to produce its output.

1.31 Why can it be said that the implementation phase involves the whole organization?

Implementation involves (1) programmers—who design, code, test, and document the individual modules in the system design; (2) analysts—who oversee the building and testing of the entire system as modules are put together, oversee the production of user and operations documentation, oversee the installation of new equipment and software, and oversee the training of all personnel affected by the change; (3) operations personnel—who help install and test new equipment and programs, enter data for the new system, and carry out any necessary file conversions; and (4) all users—who are involved with learning to use new equipment and new procedures required by the new system.

1.32 Give some advantages and disadvantages of using programmer/analysts to carry out all phases of systems development.

Advantages of having one person work on all phases of systems development include (1) efficiency, since there will be minimal duplication of effort; (2) lack of communications problems between separate analysts, designers, and programmers; (3) better continuity in achieving major systems goals; and (4) design advantages which might accrue from one person having an overview of the entire system and its development. Disadvantages would include (1) inability to carry out tasks in parallel; (2) greater vulnerability to continuity of the system if key personnel leave the project; and (3) poorer performance of analysis, design, and programming tasks owing to lack of specialization.

1.33   Is structured systems development totally different from traditional systems development?

> No. Structured methodology is best viewed as an *extension* of traditional methodology. It adds new graphic tools to the systems development tool chest and refines the goals and methods of analysis, design, and programming.

1.34   Imagine that you are the new registrar of COBOL U. Would you prefer to have COBOL's student registration system explained to you using the English narrative description in Example 1.4 or the data flow diagrams in Figs. 1-7, 1-5, and 1-8?

> As systems become larger and more complex, the graphic tools of structured analysis become an ever more convenient and efficient way to describe systems to both data processing professionals and users.

1.35   Draw a context DFD for a simplified payroll system.

> See Fig. 1-13 for a solution.

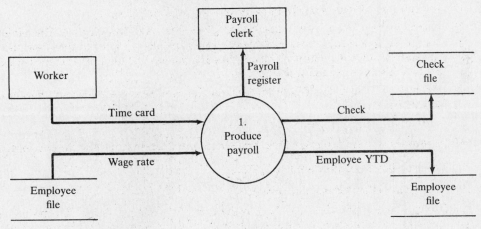

Fig. 1-13

1.36   Level the context diagram from Problem 1.35 (Fig. 1-13).

> See Fig. 1-14 for a solution.

1.37   Draw an overview DFD for producing monthly enrollment and attendance reports for a school district.

> See Fig. 1-15 for a solution.

1.38   Level bubble 3 from Problem 1.37 (Fig. 1-15).

> See Fig. 1-16 for a solution.

1.39   Draw an overview DFD for building a snowman.

> See Fig. 1-17 for a solution.

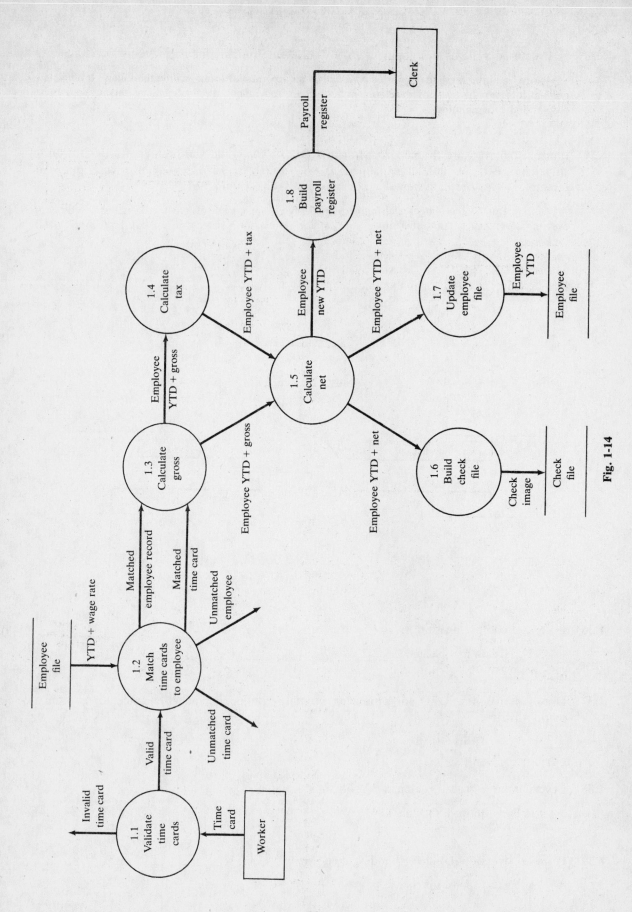

Fig. 1-14

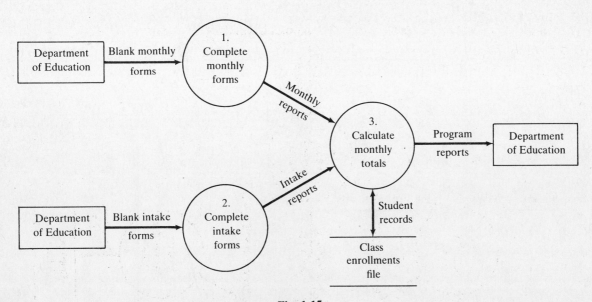

Fig. 1-15

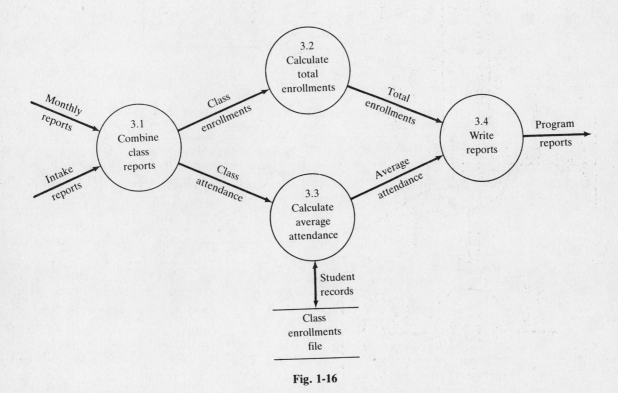

Fig. 1-16

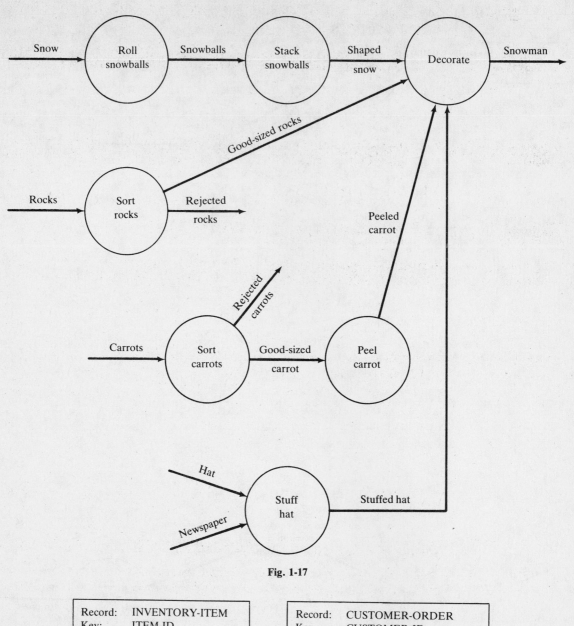

Fig. 1-17

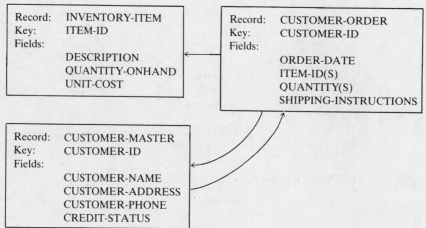

Record:	INVENTORY-ITEM
Key:	ITEM-ID
Fields:	
	DESCRIPTION
	QUANTITY-ONHAND
	UNIT-COST

Record:	CUSTOMER-ORDER
Key:	CUSTOMER-ID
Fields:	
	ORDER-DATE
	ITEM-ID(S)
	QUANTITY(S)
	SHIPPING-INSTRUCTIONS

Record:	CUSTOMER-MASTER
Key:	CUSTOMER-ID
Fields:	
	CUSTOMER-NAME
	CUSTOMER-ADDRESS
	CUSTOMER-PHONE
	CREDIT-STATUS

Fig. 1-18

1.40 Draw a data structure diagram (DSD) showing the data access requirements for a customer order entry system.

>   See Fig. 1-18 for a solution.

1.41 Give a minispecification for bubble 1.2 of Problem 1.36 (Fig. 1-14) using structured English.

```
if time-card-id matches employee-id
     create a payroll record
     get a new time card record
     get a new employee record
else if time-card-id is less than employee-id
     log an error for an unmatched time card
     get a new time card record
else
     log an error for an unmatched employee record
     get a new employee record
endif
```

1.42 Give a minispecification for a DFD bubble which determines insurance premiums. Use a decision table.

Age group	A1	A1	A1	A2	A2	A2
Accidents	0	1	>1	0	1	>1
Group A premium		×	×			
Group B premium	×			×	×	×
Apply surcharge			×			×

Note this decision table has entries which are not of the form true/false or yes/no. In this case, all possible conditions can be *coded* as above and explained in an attached table as follows:

(1) Age group: A1—under 23 years; A2—23 years or older.
(2) Number of accidents: 0—no accidents; 1—exactly one accident within past year; >1—more than one accident within past year.

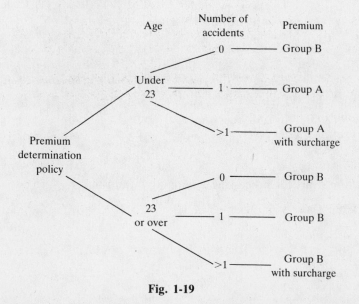

Fig. 1-19

1.43 Redo Problem 1.42 using a decision tree.

  See Fig. 1-19 for a solution.

1.44 Give a sample data dictionary entry for an employee file record from Problems 1.35 (Fig. 1-13) and 1.36 (Fig. 1-14).

Name:	EMPLOYEE-RECORD
Description:	Holds payroll information for each wage employee
Aliases:	None
Composition:	EMPLOYEE-RECORD =
	EMPLOYEE-ID +
	NAME +
	PAY-RATE +
	YTD-GROSS +
	YTD-FICA

Processes using
this data item:

Process Name	DFD Transform Number
Match time cards to employee	1.2
Update employee file	1.7

1.45 Give a sample data dictionary entry for a data element called WAREHOUSE-LOCATION.

Name:	WAREHOUSE-LOCATION
Description:	Code indicating which warehouse holds an item or employs a person
Aliases:	LOCATION
Composition:	WAREHOUSE-REGION + WAREHOUSE-NUMBER
Associated files:	INVENTORY-MASTER, EMPLOYEE-MASTER, and INTER-COMPANY-TRANSFER

Associated
processes:

Name	DFD Bubble	Structure Chart Module
CREATE-INVENTORY-RPT	9.3	26
SORT-COMPANY-MAIL	10.5	31
STOCK-TRANSFER	11.2	34

1.46 Draw a structure chart for processing a winning lottery ticket.

  See Fig. 1-20 for a solution.

1.47 Draw a structure chart for the DFDs in Problems 1.37 (Fig. 1-15) and 1.38 (Fig. 1-16).

  See Fig. 1-21 for a solution.

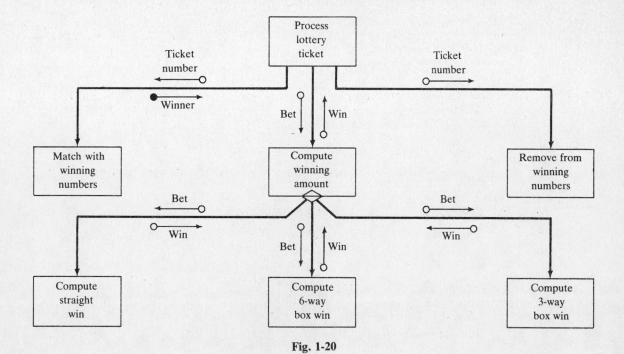

Fig. 1-20

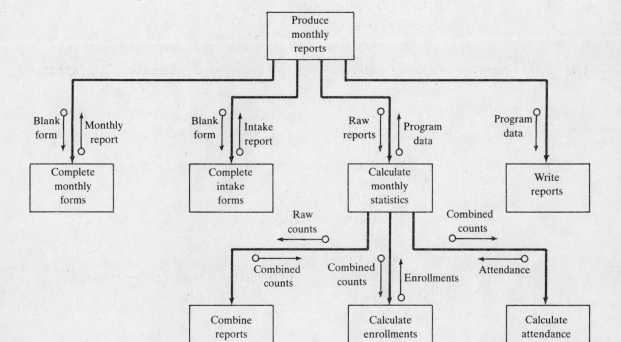

Fig. 1-21

1.48 Why are DFDs, DSDs, structured English, decision trees, and decision tables tools of analysis as well as design?

These graphic tools of structured methodology can be used to *describe the current system* as well as to *design the new one*.

1.49 What details should be specified in the implementation plan for a new student registration system?

The implementation plan should include details of:

(1) Testing procedures to be used
(2) Preparation of test data
(3) Sequence in which modules are to be coded and tested
(4) Installation and testing of any new equipment
(5) Installation and testing of any purchased software
(6) User training and practice
(7) Assignment of data processing personnel to tasks
(8) Entry of new data into the system
(9) Conversion of existing files to new forms
(10) Completion of system documentation

Chapter 2

Structured Design
Tools and Techniques

The input to structured design consists of the *structured specification* produced during structured analysis. The output of structured design is a *physical systems design* consisting of (1) structure chart(s) and (2) module specifications for each module in the structure chart(s). Although structured design deals with designing entire systems, the design tools presented below can be profitably adapted by the programmer to help design individual programs.

2.1 Steps in Structured Design

The major steps in structured design are:

(1) *Package* (i.e., break up) the data flow diagram into separate jobs and programs within jobs. Techniques of packaging are beyond the scope of this Outline.

(2) For each DFD piece (from step 1) which is transaction-centered, apply transaction analysis to partition the DFD by transaction (see Section 2.2). If transaction analysis is not appropriate, go on to step 3.

(3) For each transaction processing part of the DFD (or the original DFD, if transaction analysis was not appropriate), apply transform analysis to produce a structure chart (see Section 2.3).

(4) Improve the structure chart(s) according to the design criteria in Section 2.4.

(5) Produce module specifications for each structure chart module (see Section 2.5).

(6) Repackage modules into programs and jobs to meet performance requirements and limitations imposed by available hardware and operating systems (beyond the scope of this Outline).

2.2 Producing a Structure Chart: Transaction Analysis

Transaction analysis can be used to produce a "first-draft" structure chart for *transaction-centered* systems in which each type of input is identified by a *transaction code* which dictates the type of processing required. The DFD for a transaction-centered system will usually have one transform (called the *transaction center*) which receives an incoming transaction, identifies its transaction code, and routes it to an appropriate transform for processing.

EXAMPLE 2.1 A file update problem is transaction-centered. Normally there are at least three types of transactions:

Transaction Code	*Processing Required*
A	Add a new record to the file (new key field should not duplicate any already there).
C	Change some or all fields in an already existing record.
D	Delete an already existing record from the file.

EXAMPLE 2.2 The transaction center bubble for a file update problem is shown in Fig. 2-1.

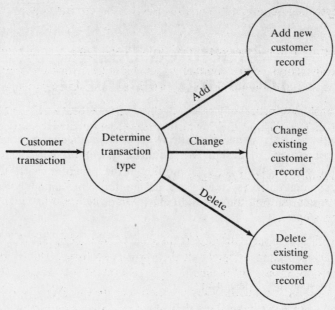

Fig. 2-1

Transaction analysis can be applied to DFDs with a transaction center to produce a structure chart as follows:

(1) Identify the transaction center on the DFD.

(2) Create a structure chart module which serves as a transaction center, i.e., which determines the type of each transaction (by transaction code) and calls the corresponding processing module. The structure chart should show a major decision in the transaction center module.

(3) Under the transaction center module, draw a separate module for processing each type of transaction.

(4) Apply transform analysis (Section 2.3) to derive the rest of the structure chart below each transaction processing module. Similarities in processing requirements for different transaction types will be reflected in the sharing of lower-level modules as top-down design progresses.

EXAMPLE 2.3 The beginning of the structure chart for the transaction center in Fig. 2-1 is shown in Fig. 2-2. The "change" transaction illustrated here is a customer payment.

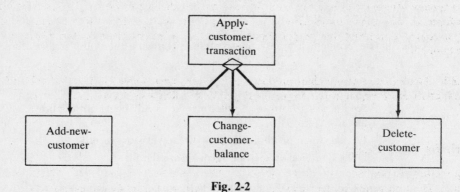

Fig. 2-2

Transaction analysis can be applied to any transaction processing system to derive a *good* design with:

(1)   A separate transaction processing module for each type of transaction

(2)   A special transaction center module which identifies transaction type (by inspecting the transaction code) and then calls the appropriate transaction processing module

The design for the transaction processing modules themselves is best arrived at by applying transform analysis to each part of the original DFD which processes a particular transaction.

2.3   Producing a Structure Chart: Transform Analysis

Transform analysis can be used to produce a first-draft structure chart for part or all of a DFD. It involves the following steps:

(1)   Follow each major input data flow (called an *afferent* data flow) to the point in the DFD where it reaches its most logical, highly processed form. This is the point where input ceases to be pure input and begins to be transformed into output.

(2)   Follow each major output data flow (called an *efferent* data flow) backward to the point where it no longer can be considered pure output (i.e., where input is still in the process of being converted to output).

(3)   Mark the points identified in steps 1 and 2 above and connect them with a closed curve. The bubbles which lie *inside* the curve just drawn make up the *central transform*.

(4)   Imagine that the data flows connecting the DFD bubbles are strings and cut each string at the points marked in 1 and 2 above. Draw the top-level module of a structure chart, and hang each major input and output "string" cut from the DFD from it; then hang a module called "central transform" from it as well. If the central transform in the DFD consists of more than one bubble, hang these bubbles from the newly created CENTRAL-TRANS-FORM module.

(5)   Redraw the DFD transform bubbles (now hanging from the top of the structure chart) as structure chart modules and fix up all arrows to show direction of call. It may also be necessary to *rename* some modules so that the final module name sums up the function of the module, together with all its subordinates.

(6)   Factor the modules in the initial chart by breaking them into subfunctions. The leveling diagrams for DFD bubbles should give good clues for when and how factoring should be done. Factoring may be repeated as often as needed to obtain the characteristics of a good design discussed in Section 2.4 below.

EXAMPLE 2.4   Figure 2-3 shows a portion of a DFD for CHANGE-CUSTOMER-BALANCE module (see Fig. 2-1 from Examples 2.2 and 2.3 above) after application of steps 1 to 3. The central transform has been identified by tracing afferent and efferent data flows in toward the center of the diagram. Determining the central transform involves some subjectivity (e.g., some people would include "Record credit" and "Delete invoice" in the central transform), but proper application of the design criteria in Section 2.4 should result in a good design either way.

EXAMPLE 2.5   The initial structure chart produced by applying steps 4 and 5 to Fig. 2-3 is shown in Fig. 2-4. This first-draft chart could be improved by applying the design criteria in Section 2.4.

2.4   Criteria for Good Design

The purpose of this section is to sensitize the systems designer and programmer to the characteristics of a good design. Any design (and especially an initial design produced by transaction

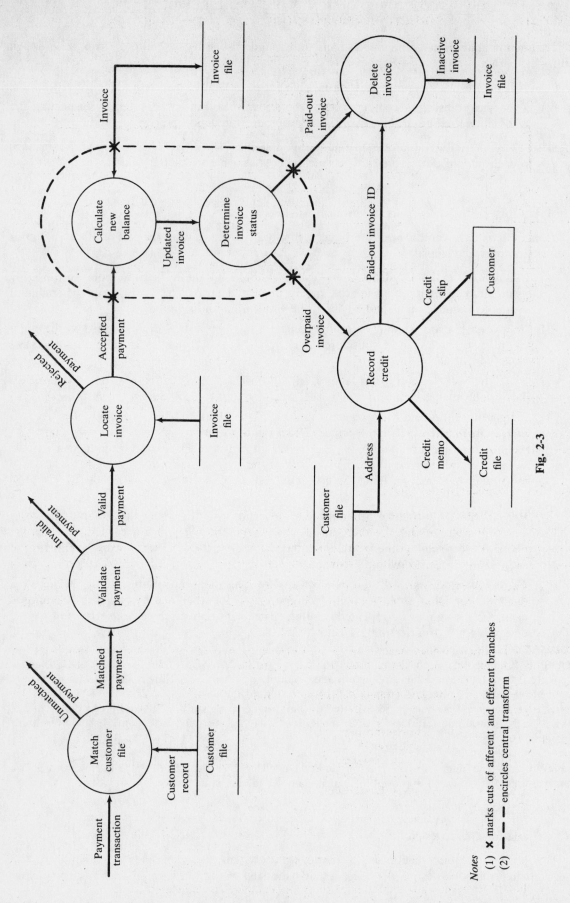

Fig. 2-3

Notes

(1) ✗ marks cuts of afferent and efferent branches

(2) - - - encircles central transform

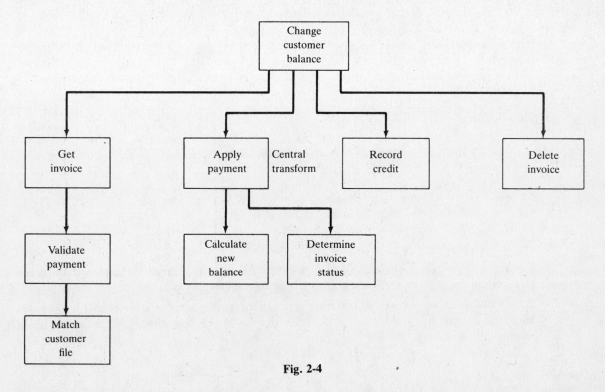

Fig. 2-4

analysis or transform analysis) can and should be improved by modifying it to meet the criteria discussed below.

Factoring or Partitioning of Modules

One way to improve a design is to *factor* or *partition* any or all modules in the system. Factoring refers to the act of removing a function from a module and placing it in a new module which the original module then calls to perform the function. This is the principal tool of traditional *top-down design*. The designer or programmer should observe the following principles of factoring:

(1) Factor to limit the size of a module to less than 50 lines of COBOL code (i.e., one page of listing). If a module becomes too large, simply move some of the code into another module.

EXAMPLE 2.6 The statements denoted by "∗∗∗" carry out a function within module A (implemented as a COBOL paragraph). Module A can be reduced in size by moving this function into its own paragraph ("B").

Module A *before Factoring*:	Module A *after Factoring*:

```
A.                                A.
    statement-1                       statement-1
    statement-2                       statement-2
      ∗∗∗ statement-3                 PERFORM B
      ∗∗∗ statement-4                 statement-7
      ∗∗∗ statement-5
      ∗∗∗ statement-6             B.
    statement-7                         ∗∗∗ statement-3
                                        ∗∗∗ statement-4
                                        ∗∗∗ statement-5
                                        ∗∗∗ statement-6
```

(2) Factor to make systems easier to read, understand, and maintain.

EXAMPLE 2.7 A change to the function carried out by statements 3–6 in Example 2.6 would be easier to implement in the factored version since that function is *isolated* in paragraph B.

(3) Factor to save memory and simplify maintenance by fostering the sharing of functions between modules.

EXAMPLE 2.8 Suppose module C also needs to carry out the function represented by statements 3–6 in Example 2.6. In the unfactored approach, module C would have to include duplicates of these statements, thus wasting memory and requiring modifications to *both* versions in case of change. With the factored approach, module C could simply PERFORM paragraph B when needed.

(4) Do *not* factor when a module consists of only *one* function. This is a good indication that factoring has gone as far as is desirable.

(5) Do *not* factor just any set of statements from a module. Only statements contributing to a single, well-defined function should be factored out of a module.

(6) Do *not* factor when the parent module would have to pass a large amount of data to the factored-out module (i.e., when the call becomes overly complex).

(7) It is better to err on the side of too much factoring (resulting in more numerous but smaller and simpler modules) than too little (resulting in fewer but larger and more complex modules).

Cohesion

Cohesion is a measure of how closely related the statements in a module are to one another. Highly cohesive modules tend to minimize both development and maintenance costs, and hence are most desirable.

The reader should understand, however, that perfection of an actual design is unlikely. The goal is to have as many highly cohesive modules as possible and to avoid the lower types of cohesion. Following is a list of the types of cohesion to look for in a system, from *high* (most desirable) to *low* (least desirable).

(1) *Functionally cohesive* modules carry out a single, well-defined function, and *each statement* in the module directly contributes to that function.

EXAMPLE 2.9 The module below is functionally cohesive since each statement directly contributes to the calculation of net pay. Note that the module is highly factored, with subfunctions removed to their own modules.

```
CALCULATE-NET-PAY.
    PERFORM CALCULATE-GROSS-PAY
    PERFORM CALCULATE-TAX
    SUBTRACT WS-TAX FROM WS-GROSS-PAY GIVING WS-NET-PAY
```

(2) *Sequentially cohesive* modules contain statements which must be carried out in a specific sequence because the "output" of each statement in the sequence becomes the "input" to the next. Note that this does not guarantee that each statement contributes to carrying out the same function; hence sequential cohesion is not as desirable as functional cohesion.

EXAMPLE 2.10 The following module is *not* functionally cohesive, since it carries out four separate functions: (1) calculate grade-point average, (2) determine type of honors, (3) format an output line, and (4) print the output line. It *is* sequentially cohesive, since the *sequence* of the statements cannot be changed without disrupting the correctness of the module (note how each statement generates data which is used by the next statement).

```
CALC-GPA-AND-PRINT-DEANS-LIST.
    DIVIDE TOTAL-CREDITS INTO TOTAL-GRADE-POINTS
        GIVING GPA
    IF GPA GREATER THAN 3.85
        MOVE 1 TO TYPE-OF-HONORS
    ELSE IF GPA GREATER THAN 3.65
        MOVE 2 TO TYPE-OF-HONORS
    ELSE
        MOVE 3 TO TYPE-OF-HONORS

    MOVE DEANS-LIST-MESSAGE (TYPE-OF-HONORS) TO OUTPUT-MESSAGE
    WRITE OUTPUT-MESSAGE-LINE
```

(3)   A module exhibits *communicational* (or *data-related*) cohesion if the statements in it are related simply because they manipulate the *same data item(s)*.

EXAMPLE 2.11   Consider the following module:

```
READ-AND-MAKE-COPIES.
    READ INPUT-FILE AT END ...
    MOVE INPUT-RECORD TO DISK-RECORD
    WRITE DISK-RECORD
    MOVE INPUT-RECORD TO PRINT-RECORD-AREA
    WRITE PRINT-LINE
```

It is not functionally cohesive, since it performs three different functions, or sequentially cohesive, since there are several permutations of the statements which are still correct. It *is* communicationally cohesive, since all statements manipulate INPUT-RECORD (or a copy of it). The statements here are not as strongly related as with functional or sequential cohesion.

(4)   A module exhibits *procedural* cohesion if it consists of statements which implement program control structures, notably *selection* (decision) and *iteration* (repetition).

EXAMPLE 2.12   A module which *decides* whether a customer is regular or past due and includes within the module all the statements needed to process both cases is procedurally cohesive. The common bond between the statements in the module is that they are all part of a decision structure. This example also illustrates that as cohesion decreases, it becomes more and more difficult to give a good descriptive name to a module.

```
PROCEDURAL-MODULE.
    IF DAYS-PAST-DUE LESS THAN 30
        MOVE "YES" TO CREDIT-OK-SW
        ADD BALANCE-DUE TO TOTAL-BALANCE-DUE
        PERFORM MAIL-SALES-FLYER
    ELSE
        PERFORM CALCULATE-LATE-FEE
        ADD LATE-FEE TO BALANCE-DUE
        PERFORM SEND-REMINDER
```

EXAMPLE 2.13   The module in Example 2.12 could be improved by having a separate decision module, together with modules for processing regular and overdue accounts:

```
CHOOSE-CUSTOMER-OPTIONS.
    IF DAYS-PAST-DUE LESS THAN 30
        PERFORM REGULAR-OPTIONS
    ELSE
        PERFORM OVERDUE-OPTIONS
```

(5) A module is *temporally* cohesive if the statements in it are related by the need to be executed at the same *time*.

EXAMPLE 2.14   Many programs have initialization and termination modules containing code which is executed at the beginning (end) of the program. Such modules do a variety of tasks such as opening (closing) files, printing headers (footers), initializing (printing) totals, etc. Although such temporally cohesive modules have an undesirably low level of cohesion, most programmers tolerate them because of their convenience. The "need" for temporally cohesive initialization and termination modules can be minimized, however, if the following principles are observed (see Problem 2.29 for an application): (1) *Delay initialization* tasks as long as possible and (2) Carry out *termination* tasks as *early* as possible.

(6) A module has *logical* (or *class-oriented*) cohesion if it contains statements that fall into the same *class* of actions.

EXAMPLE 2.15   Logically cohesive modules often select one of a set of similar actions, depending on the value of a flag passed to the module. The statements in the module below are related primarily because they are all WRITE statements. Evidently the programmer sought to "organize" the program by collecting all WRITE statements together, producing a module with unacceptably low cohesion. The design would be improved by eliminating the flag (OUTPUT-TYPE) and having a separate paragraph for each WRITE statement (to be PERFORMed as needed).

```
WRITE-ALL-OUTPUT.
    IF OUTPUT-TYPE = 1
        WRITE OUTPUT-LINE FROM TITLE-AREA AFTER ...
    ELSE IF OUTPUT-TYPE = 2
        WRITE OUTPUT-LINE FROM DETAIL-AREA AFTER ...
    ELSE IF OUTPUT-TYPE = 3
        WRITE NEW-MASTER-RECORD FROM MASTER-WORK-AREA
    ELSE IF OUTPUT-TYPE = 4
        WRITE HISTORY-RECORD FROM SUMMARY-WORK-AREA
```

(7) *Coincidental* cohesion is created by grouping totally unrelated statements together. Such a module appears to be a collection of random statements and is impossible to name.

EXAMPLE 2.16   Coincidentally cohesive modules are sometimes created when a module is arbitrarily broken into pieces to accommodate physical size restrictions (e.g., every group of 15 lines becomes a separate module). Although the original module may have had high cohesion, its dissection into 15-line pieces will probably produce modules which appear to contain unrelated statements.

Coupling

Whereas cohesion measures the relatedness of statements *within* a module, *coupling* measures the relationships *between modules*. Two or more modules can be related by the need to share data items. The more sharing of data between modules in a system, the more difficult it is to develop and maintain the system (since the action of one module on a data item can affect all other modules using that data item). Thus while good designs result in *high cohesion*, they also result (at the same time) in *low coupling*.

Coupling manifests itself in *arguments* passed between modules. Obviously it is not possible to eliminate coupling in a system (some data items must always be passed between modules), but the designer and programmer should both aim to minimize coupling. The following lists six common types of coupling to look for in a system, in order from *lowest* (most desirable) to *highest* (least desirable).

(1) *Data coupling* occurs when two or more modules refer to the same *nonglobal data element*.
     "Element" here implies that the item is, in COBOL terms, an elementary item, while
     "nonglobal" means that the item is accessible only to the modules which actually need and
     use it. Note that data coupling cannot be implemented within a COBOL PROCEDURE
     DIVISION since the entire DATA DIVISION is accessible to all statements in the program
     (i.e., the whole DATA DIVISION is global to the PROCEDURE DIVISION).

EXAMPLE 2.17 Data coupling is only possible in COBOL when *external subprograms* are used (i.e.,
when a module is separately compiled and called with the CALL statement rather than implemented as a
PERFORMed paragraph—see Chapter 10 for a discussion of external subprograms). In this case, the data
items passed as arguments are nonglobal. Thus the lowest type of coupling occurs in COBOL when an external
subprogram is CALLed, passing elementary items as arguments:

```
CALLING-MODULE.
    CALL "CHANGE" USING TRANSACTION-FIELD-1
                        TRANSACTION-FIELD-2
                        MASTER-FIELD-1
                        MASTER-FIELD-2
```

(2) *Stamp coupling* occurs when two modules share the same *nonglobal data structure* (i.e.,
     group item). Since the only nonglobal data in COBOL is data passed between external
     subprograms with the CALL statement (see Chapter 10), this form of coupling can only be
     implemented with external subprograms.

EXAMPLE 2.18 If in Example 2.17 *records* (group items) were passed between calling and called modules, this
would result in stamp coupling:

```
CALLING-MODULE.
    CALL "CHANGE" USING TRANSACTION-RECORD
                        MASTER-RECORD
```

Note that stamp coupling may pass parts of a group item which are not needed by the called module. If the
description of the group item changes, the called module will have to be changed even though it does not use the
fields in question. This is a disadvantage of stamp coupling.

(3) *Control coupling* occurs when one module passes a flag or switch to another with the
     purpose of controlling its internal logic. Note the distinction between a *control flag*, which
     tells another module *what to do* about an event occurring, and a *descriptive flag*, which
     simply tells another module *that the event has occurred*. The distinction between control and
     descriptive flags centers on the intended purpose of the flag and is usually reflected in the
     type of data name used. Names for control flags include verbs dictating actions, while
     names for descriptive flags consist of adjectives describing data items or program events.
     Descriptive flags will be necessary in almost every design; control flags should be avoided.

EXAMPLE 2.19 The following program segment illustrates control coupling by passing a control flag. Note the
verb in the data name "ORDER-MORE-ITEMS-SW".

```
CHECK-INVENTORY.
    IF QUANTITY-ONHAND LESS THAN REORDER-POINT
        MOVE "YES" TO ORDER-MORE-ITEMS-SW
```

By definition, a control flag *dictates* that the receiving module take certain prescribed action(s). Thus the use of a
control flag assumes knowledge of the internal workings of the calling module, e.g., that it can and should
"order more items". This increases the likelihood that change in one module will necessitate change in others.
Control coupling in which a called module tells the calling module what to do is known as *inversion of authority*.

EXAMPLE 2.20 This example is the same as Example 2.19 but uses a descriptive rather than a control flag. Descriptive flags are a more desirable form of control coupling since they make no assumption about what the calling module will do with the information returned (i.e., they do not *require* certain actions). Note the adjectival form of the data name "LOW-STOCK-SW".

```
CHECK-INVENTORY.
    IF QUANTITY-ONHAND LESS THAN REORDER-POINT
        MOVE "YES" TO LOW-STOCK-SW
    .
```

(4) *External coupling* occurs when two modules reference the same *global* data *element*. This is the type of coupling shared by all PROCEDURE DIVISION paragraphs which access the same elementary item in the DATA DIVISION (in COBOL the entire DATA DIVISION is global to the entire PROCEDURE DIVISION).

EXAMPLE 2.21 In a single COBOL program, the paragraphs VALIDATE-EMPLOYEE-HOURS and CALCULATE-GROSS-PAY may both access the elementary item EMPLOYEE-HOURS-WORKED.

(5) *Common coupling* occurs when two modules reference the same *global* data *structure*. In a COBOL PROCEDURE DIVISION, this is the type of coupling shared by all paragraphs which access the same group item.

EXAMPLE 2.22 In a traditional sequential file update, the paragraphs READ-OLD-MASTER-RECORD and WRITE-NEW-MASTER-RECORD may both access the group item WS-MASTER-WORK-AREA.

(6) *Content coupling* occurs when one module directly references or modifies something inside another. This highest (and therefore worst) form of coupling is actually difficult to program in COBOL.

EXAMPLE 2.23 Content coupling in COBOL occurs only when:

(1) A GO TO statement in one paragraph branches to another paragraph (thus directly referencing the start of the paragraph).
(2) A PERFORM statement performs a paragraph that is already part of a PERFORM . . . THRU . . . , thus referencing the inside of the "module" defined by PERFORM . . . THRU.
(3) The ALTER statement is used (*never* do this). If the reader has never heard of the ALTER statement, so much the better.

It is possible for two modules to be coupled in more than one way via different shared data items. In this case, the modules should be characterized according to the *worst* (highest) type of coupling exhibited.

Fan-Out

Fan-out refers to the number of immediate subordinates a module has (i.e., the number of modules it *calls*). Experiments in psychology have shown that humans have trouble dealing with more than about seven simultaneous mental activities; hence a good rule of thumb is to limit fan-out to no more than *seven* in order to keep the system understandable.

If fan-out for a module is too high, factoring can be used to introduce intermediate-level modules with lower fan-out.

EXAMPLE 2.24 In Fig. 2-5, the "Boss" module's fan-out exceeds seven.

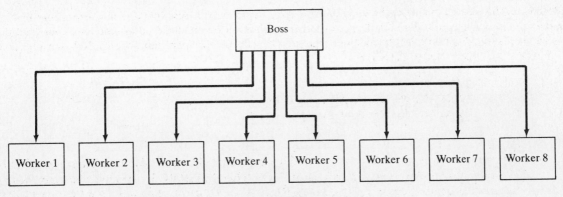

Fig. 2-5

EXAMPLE 2.25   In Fig. 2-6 the fan-out of "Boss" module in Fig. 2-5 is reduced from eight to four by factoring two supervisory functions out of "Boss".

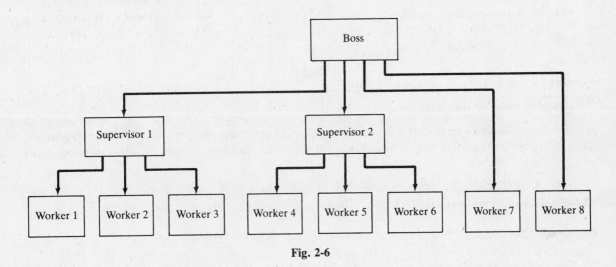

Fig. 2-6

Fan-In

Fan-in is the number of modules which *call* a given module. A good designer will be alert for a subfunction which is part of many higher-level functions and factor it to a module with high fan-in. This saves memory and eliminates having to make the same changes to duplicated parts of a program during maintenance (see Example 2.8 and Problems 2.20 and 2.37); it also saves duplication of effort during program coding and testing.

EXAMPLE 2.26   Structure chart notation for modules with fan-in greater than one varies. One method is to show *all* arrows from all calling modules. This can result in crossing lines in the chart, which are drawn with the *bridge* symbol to avoid ambiguity. The bridge (shown in Fig. 2-7) is illustrated in Fig. 1-11, where ADD-REQUIRED-COURSES and REMOVE-INELIGIBLE-COURSES both call READ-TRANSCRIPT.

Fig. 2-7   Bridge symbol

EXAMPLE 2.27 Another way to show fan-in is to *repeat* the module everywhere it is called, and then *mark* it with a special symbol (e.g., shade the upper right-hand corner of the rectangle) to indicate that it is repeated. With this approach, modules subordinate to a repeated module are drawn only once, as shown in Fig. 2-8.

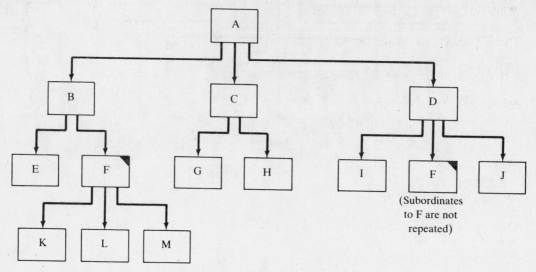

Fig. 2-8

2.5 Module Specification Techniques

Once the final structure chart has been completed, the systems designer must specify the function of each module in sufficient detail to allow a programmer to actually code it. This can be done in several ways:

(1)   A *module interface specification* gives the programmer the input to the module, the output from the module, and a simple statement of what function the module performs.

EXAMPLE 2.28 The module interface specification for GET-SHIPPING-RATE follows:

Module name:	GET-SHIPPING-RATE
Input:	SHIPPING-CLASS, SHIPPING-WEIGHT
Output:	SHIPPING-RATE
Function:	Determines shipping rate according to policy B27.1.
	See Decision Table A17.5. (Not shown)

(2)   When a structure chart module corresponds to a data flow diagram bubble, the minispecification for the bubble (part of the structured specification) is often enough for the programmer and thus can directly serve as a module specification (see Section 1.3).

(3)   If it is desired to provide the programmer with more detail, the module specifications can be written as pseudocode (in which case the programmer's job is made easier since the design of internal module logic is done for him or her—see Section 3.2).

Review Questions

2.1   What are the major steps in structured design?

2.2   Define transaction-centered system.

2.3   Explain the individual steps in transaction analysis.

2.4   What is the central transform?

2.5   Explain the individual steps in transform analysis.

2.6   What is factoring? Give some guidelines for factoring.

2.7   What is meant by cohesion?

2.8   Define each type of cohesion and give an example of each.

2.9   What is meant by coupling?

2.10 Define each type of coupling and give an example of each.

2.11 Why should module fan-out generally be limited to seven?

2.12 Explain how to decrease a module's fan-out.

2.13 What is module fan-in? How can high fan-in improve a design?

2.14 Explain the use of a module interface specification.

2.15 Discuss two other alternatives for documenting module specifications during design.

Solved Problems

2.16 Apply transaction analysis to produce a structure chart from the data flow diagram in Fig. 2-9.

See Fig. 2-10 for a solution.

2.17 Identify the central transform in the data flow diagram of Problem 1.36 (Fig. 1-14).

The central transform would consist of three bubbles: 1.3 Calculate gross, 1.4 Calculate tax, and 1.5 Calculate net.

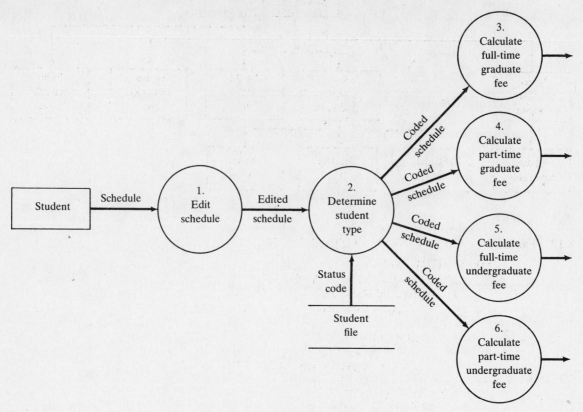

Fig. 2-9

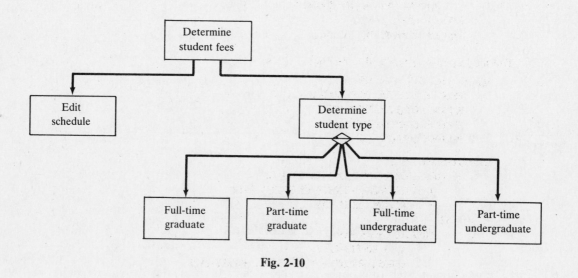

Fig. 2-10

2.18 Use transform analysis to produce a first-draft structure chart for the DFD in Problem 1.36
(use the results of Problem 2.17).

See Fig. 2-11 for a solution.

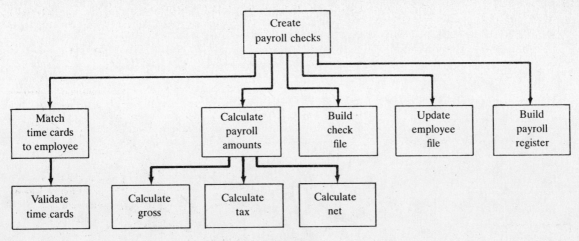

Fig. 2-11

2.19 Factor the following module to reduce its size:

```
ORIGINAL-LARGE-MODULE.
    IF HOURS-WORKED NOT GREATER THAN 40
        MULTIPLY HOURS-WORKED BY HOURLY-RATE
            GIVING GROSS-PAY
    ELSE
        COMPUTE GROSS-PAY =
            40 * HOURLY-RATE    +
            (HOURS-WORKED - 40) * 1.5 * HOURLY-RATE
    .
    IF GROSS-PAY LESS THAN 1000
        MOVE .03 TO INSURANCE-RATE
    ELSE
        MOVE .04 TO INSURANCE-RATE
    .
    MULTIPLY INSURANCE-RATE BY GROSS-PAY
        GIVING INSURANCE-DEDUCTION
    PERFORM COMPUTE-FICA
    PERFORM COMPUTE-TAX
    .
```

The module can be factored as follows:

```
SMALLER-FACTORED-VERSION.
    PERFORM COMPUTE-GROSS-PAY
    PERFORM COMPUTE-INSURANCE
    PERFORM COMPUTE-FICA
    PERFORM COMPUTE-TAX
    .
COMPUTE-GROSS-PAY.
    IF HOURS-WORKED NOT GREATER THAN 40
        MULTIPLY HOURS-WORKED BY HOURLY-RATE
            GIVING GROSS-PAY
    ELSE
        COMPUTE GROSS-PAY =
            40 * HOURLY-RATE    +
            (HOURS-WORKED - 40) * 1.5 * HOURLY-RATE
    .
COMPUTE-INSURANCE.
    IF GROSS-PAY LESS THAN 1000
        MOVE .03 TO INSURANCE-RATE
    ELSE
        MOVE .04 TO INSURANCE-RATE
    .
    MULTIPLY INSURANCE-RATE BY GROSS-PAY
        GIVING INSURANCE-DEDUCTION
```

2.20 Identify the shared function in the following two modules; then factor them to remove the shared function to its own module. The new module should exhibit increased fan-in.

```
MODULE-A.
    IF USER-CODE NOT EQUAL AUTHORIZATION-CODE
        MOVE "YES" TO ABORT-SW
    .
    IF TRANSACTION-TYPE EQUAL "A" OR "C" OR "D"
        MOVE "YES" TO TRANSACTION-CODE-OK-SW
    ELSE
        MOVE "NO" TO TRANSACTION-CODE-OK-SW
    .
    IF CUSTOMER-ID NOT NUMERIC
        MOVE "YES" TO ID-INVALID-SW
    .
MODULE-B.
    IF INVOICE-AMOUNT NOT NUMERIC
        MOVE "YES" TO INVALID-AMOUNT-SW
    .
    IF TRANSACTION-TYPE EQUAL "A" OR "C" OR "D"
        MOVE "YES" TO TRANSACTION-CODE-OK-SW
    ELSE
        MOVE "NO" TO TRANSACTION-CODE-OK-SW
    .
```

The shared function can be factored as follows:

```
FACTORED-MODULE-A.
    IF USER-CODE NOT EQUAL AUTHORIZATION-CODE
        MOVE "YES" TO ABORT-SW
    .
    PERFORM VALIDATE-TRANSACTION-CODE
    IF CUSTOMER-ID NOT NUMERIC
        MOVE "YES" TO ID-INVALID-SW
    .
FACTORED-MODULE-B.
    IF INVOICE-AMOUNT NOT NUMERIC
        MOVE "YES" TO INVALID-AMOUNT-SW
    .
    PERFORM VALIDATE-TRANSACTION-CODE
    .
VALIDATE-TRANSACTION-CODE.
    IF TRANSACTION-TYPE EQUAL "A" OR "C" OR "D"
        MOVE "YES" TO TRANSACTION-CODE-OK-SW
    ELSE
        MOVE "NO" TO TRANSACTION-CODE-OK-SW
    .
```

2.21 How are cohesion and coupling related in a design?

Good designs which tend to exhibit *high cohesion* also tend to exhibit *low coupling*. Similarly, poor designs with *low cohesion* also tend to have *high coupling*.

2.22 Classify the following module with respect to cohesion:

```
A-MODULE.
    MOVE HIGH-VALUES TO DELETE-FLAG
    PERFORM WRITE-CHECK-IMAGE
    ADD 1 TO INPUT-RECORD-COUNTER
    PERFORM CALCULATE-SALES-TAX
```

The module consists of unrelated statements and therefore exhibits *coincidental* cohesion.

2.23   Classify with respect to cohesion:

```
A-MODULE.
      OPEN INPUT TRANSACTION-FILE
      OPEN I-O   MASTER-FILE
      MOVE "YES" TO MORE-RECORDS-SW
      MOVE ZERO TO TRANSACTION-COUNTER
```

The module appears to be designed as an initialization module and exhibits *temporal* cohesion.

2.24   Classify with respect to cohesion:

```
A-MODULE.
      IF FLAG EQUAL "A"
            READ INVENTORY-MASTER-FILE
      ELSE IF FLAG EQUAL "B"
            READ CUSTOMER-MASTER-FILE
      ELSE IF FLAG EQUAL "C"
            READ INVOICE-MASTER-FILE

            .
```

The module is designed to contain all READ statements and therefore exhibits *logical* or *class-oriented* cohesion.

2.25   Classify with respect to cohesion:

```
PERFORM A-MODULE UNTIL EOF-SW EQUAL "YES"
. . . . . . . . . . . . . . . . . . . .
A-MODULE.
      READ RAW-TRANSACTION-FILE
            AT END MOVE "YES" TO EOF-SW

            .
      IF GOT-A-TRANSACTION
            PERFORM EDIT-A-TRANSACTION

            .
      IF TRANSACTION-IS-GOOD
            RELEASE SORTED-TRANSACTION
                  FROM RAW-TRANSACTION

            .
```

These statements are grouped together because they need to be executed repeatedly (i.e., they implement an iteration control structure); hence they exhibit *procedural* cohesion.

2.26   Classify with respect to cohesion:

```
A-MODULE.
      MOVE "NO" TO INVALID-SW
      IF REGULAR-HOURS NOT NUMERIC
            MOVE "YES" TO INVALID-SW

            .
      IF OVERTIME-HOURS NOT NUMERIC
            MOVE "YES" TO INVALID-SW

            .
      IF FIELDS-ARE-VALID
            MOVE REGULAR-HOURS  TO REGULAR-OUTPUT
            MOVE OVERTIME-HOURS TO OVERTIME-OUTPUT
            ADD  OVERTIME-HOURS REGULAR-HOURS
                  GIVING TOTAL-HOURS
```

This module performs several functions, for each of which the order of some of the statements could be rearranged. The only common bond between statements is that they manipulate REGULAR- and OVERTIME-HOURS; hence the module exhibits *communicational* or *data-related* cohesion.

2.27 Classify with respect to cohesion:

```
A-MODULE.
      MULTIPLY CREDITS BY GRADE-VALUE
          GIVING GRADE-POINTS
      ADD GRADE-POINTS TO TOTAL-GRADE-POINTS
      DIVIDE TOTAL-GRADE-POINTS BY TOTAL-CREDITS
          GIVING GPA
```

Each statement in the module contributes directly to the single function of calculating the grade-point average; hence the module is *functionally* cohesive.

2.28 Classify with respect to cohesion:

```
A-MODULE.
      IF INPUT-CODE NUMERIC
          MOVE SHIPPING-RATE (INPUT-CODE) TO BASE-RATE
      ELSE
          MOVE ZERO TO BASE-RATE
      .
      DIVIDE BASE-RATE BY 100 GIVING BASE-CODE
      ADD INDEX-ADJUST-VALUE TO BASE-CODE
          GIVING BASE-INDEX
      MOVE SHIPPING-TERMS (BASE-INDEX) TO OUTPUT-TERMS
      PERFORM PRINT-SHIPPING-TERMS
```

Each statement in this module produces output which is used by the next statement. Further, the module appears to carry out more than one function, and thus is only *sequentially* cohesive.

2.29 Show how temporally cohesive initialization and termination modules can be eliminated from the following code by postponing initialization and terminating promptly.

```
PROCEDURE DIVISION.
      PERFORM INITIALIZATION-ROUTINE
      SORT ANY-SORT-FILE
          ASCENDING KEY SOME-KEY-FIELD
          INPUT PROCEDURE PRE-PROCESS-RAW-RECORDS
          OUTPUT PROCEDURE PROCESS-SORTED-RECORDS
      PERFORM TERMINATION-ROUTINE
      STOP RUN
      .
PRE-PROCESS-RAW-RECORDS SECTION.
      PERFORM GET-A-TRANSACTION
      PERFORM PRE-PROCESS-THEN-RELEASE
          UNTIL NO-MORE-TRANSACTIONS
      .
PROCESS-SORTED-RECORDS SECTION.
      PERFORM RETURN-A-SORTED-TRANSACTION
      PERFORM DO-MAIN-PROCESSING
          UNTIL NO-MORE-SORTED-TRANSACTIONS
      .
```

```
            PERFORMED-MODULES SECTION.
            INITIALIZATION-ROUTINE.
                OPEN INPUT     RAW-TRANSACTIONS
                     I-O       MASTER-FILE
                     OUTPUT    REPORT-FILE
                MOVE "YES" TO MORE-TRANSACTIONS-SW
                             MORE-SORTED-RECORDS-SW
                MOVE ZERO  TO NUMBER-SORTED-RECORDS
                .
            TERMINATION-ROUTINE.
                PERFORM WRITE-FINAL-TOTALS
                CLOSE   RAW-TRANSACTIONS
                        MASTER-FILE
                        REPORT-FILE
                .
```

The PROCEDURE DIVISION can be rewritten to OPEN files as late as possible and CLOSE them as soon as possible. Likewise, initializing data items can be done just before the item is actually needed, and termination activities like printing final totals can be done as soon as the data is available. Note how the statements from INITIALIZATION-ROUTINE and TERMINATION-ROUTINE are incorporated into the INPUT and OUTPUT procedures below:

```
            PROCEDURE DIVISION.
                SORT ANY-SORT-FILE
                    ASCENDING KEY SOME-KEY-FIELD
                    INPUT PROCEDURE PRE-PROCESS-RAW-RECORDS
                    OUTPUT PROCEDURE PROCESS-SORTED-RECORDS
                STOP RUN
                .
            PRE-PROCESS-RAW-RECORDS SECTION.
                OPEN INPUT     RAW-TRANSACTIONS
                     OUTPUT    REPORT-FILE
                MOVE "YES" TO MORE-TRANSACTIONS-SW
                PERFORM GET-A-TRANSACTION
                PERFORM PRE-PROCESS-THEN-RELEASE
                    UNTIL NO-MORE-TRANSACTIONS
                CLOSE     RAW-TRANSACTIONS
                .
            PROCESS-SORTED-RECORDS SECTION.
                OPEN I-O       MASTER-FILE
                MOVE ZERO  TO NUMBER-SORTED-RECORDS
                MOVE "YES" TO MORE-SORTED-RECORDS-SW
                PERFORM RETURN-A-SORTED-TRANSACTION
                PERFORM DO-MAIN-PROCESSING
                    UNTIL NO-MORE-SORTED-TRANSACTIONS
                CLOSE     MASTER-FILE
                PERFORM WRITE-FINAL-TOTALS
                CLOSE     REPORT-FILE
```

2.30   What type of coupling exists between the following modules:

```
            A-MODULE.
                PERFORM B-MODULE
                IF PRINT-ERROR-MSG EQUALS "YES"
                    PERFORM PRINT-ERROR-MESSAGE
                .
```

```
B-MODULE.
    IF SOME-FIELD IS NOT NUMERIC
        MOVE "YES" TO PRINT-ERROR-MSG
    ELSE
        MOVE "NO" TO PRINT-ERROR-MSG
    .
```

The above modules illustrate *control* coupling since B-MODULE sets a flag which controls the internal logic of A-MODULE. Since B-MODULE is subordinate to A, this also illustrates *inversion of authority*. Note that this is not just a descriptive flag, since it tells the calling module *what* to do about nonnumeric data (the tip-off is that the name of the flag involves a verb: PRINT-ERROR-MSG).

2.31 What type of coupling exists between the following modules:

```
A-MODULE.
    PERFORM GET-A-TRANSACTION
    ADD 1 TO INQUIRY-COUNTER
    PERFORM CALCULATE-CURRENT-BALANCE
    .
B-MODULE.
    PERFORM FORMAT-RESPONSE
    PERFORM SEND-TO-TERMINAL
    ADD 1 TO INQUIRY-COUNTER
    .
```

The above modules illustrate *external* coupling, since they both refer to the same global data element (i.e., INQUIRY-COUNTER). The reader will recall that everything in the DATA DIVISION is global to the entire PROCEDURE DIVISION.

2.32 What type of coupling exists between the following modules:

```
A-MODULE.
    MOVE SPACES TO WS-DETAIL-LINE
    MOVE ZERO   TO OUT-OF-STOCK-COUNT
    PERFORM GENERATE-REORDER-FORM
    .
B-MODULE.
    ADD 1 TO PAGE-COUNTER
    MOVE SPACES TO WS-DETAIL-LINE
    PERFORM WRITE-HEADINGS
    .
```

The above modules illustrate *common* coupling, since they both refer to the same global data structure (i.e., WS-DETAIL-LINE, which is presumably a group item). The reader will recall that everything in the DATA DIVISION is global to the entire PROCEDURE DIVISION.

2.33 Classify with respect to coupling:

```
A-MODULE.
    CALL "B-MODULE" USING   WS-TRANSACTION-RECORD
                            WS-DETAIL-LINE
```

Since data items are passed between modules with the CALL statement, they are nonglobal. Since data structures (i.e., group items) are being passed, this illustrates *stamp* coupling.

2.34 Classify with respect to coupling:

```
A-MODULE.
      PERFORM GET-A-TRANSACTION
      IF TRANSACTION-CODE EQUAL "X"
            GO TO B-MODULE
            .
      PERFORM DO-SOMETHING-ELSE
            .
B-MODULE.
      PERFORM DO-SOMETHING
      PERFORM OUTPUT-SOMETHING
            .
```

Since the GO TO statement in A-MODULE directly refers to B-MODULE, this is an example of *content* coupling. Any use of GO TO or ALTER in COBOL results in content coupling.

2.35 Classify with respect to coupling:

```
A-MODULE.
      CALL "B-MODULE" USING      CURRENT-NET-PAY
                                 CURRENT-GROSS-PAY
                                 YTD-NET-PAY
                                 YTD-GROSS-PAY
```

Since the CALL statement is used, all data items are nonglobal. Since they are also elementary items, this illustrates *data* coupling. Data coupling is generally the most desirable form of coupling.

2.36 Use factoring to reduce the fan-out of the following module to no more than seven (it is currently eight; count the PERFORMs):

```
STUDENT-BILLING-MODULE.
      IF GRADUATE-STUDENT
            IF TEACHING-ASSISTANT
                  PERFORM BILL-T-A                        (1)
            ELSE IF FULL-TIME
                  PERFORM BILL-FULL-GRAD                  (2)
            ELSE
                  PERFORM BILL-PART-GRAD                  (3)
      ELSE IF UNDERGRADUATE
            IF DEGREE-STUDENT
                  IF FULL-TIME
                        PERFORM BILL-UNDER-DEGREE-FULL    (4)
                  ELSE
                        PERFORM BILL-UNDER-DEGREE-PART    (5)
            ELSE IF NON-DEGREE
                  IF FULL-TIME
                        PERFORM BILL-NON-DEGREE-FULL      (6)
                  ELSE
                        PERFORM BILL-NON-DEGREE-PART      (7)
            ELSE IF NON-CREDIT
                  PERFORM BILL-NON-CREDIT                 (8)
```

Fan-out can be reduced by factoring as follows:

```
FACTORED-BILLING-MODULE.
     IF GRADUATE-STUDENT
          PERFORM BILL-GRADUATE-STUDENT              (1)
     ELSE IF UNDERGRADUATE
          IF DEGREE-STUDENT
               PERFORM BILL-DEGREE-STUDENT           (2)
          ELSE IF NON-DEGREE
               PERFORM BILL-NON-DEGREE-STUDENT       (3)
          ELSE IF NON-CREDIT
               PERFORM BILL-NON-CREDIT               (4)
     .
BILL-GRADUATE-STUDENT.
     IF TEACHING-ASSISTANT
          PERFORM BILL-T-A
     ELSE IF FULL-TIME
          PERFORM BILL-FULL-GRAD
     ELSE
          PERFORM BILL-PART-GRAD
     .
BILL-DEGREE-STUDENT.
     IF FULL-TIME
          PERFORM BILL-UNDER-DEGREE-FULL
     ELSE
          PERFORM BILL-UNDER-DEGREE-PART
     .
BILL-NON-DEGREE-STUDENT.
     IF FULL-TIME
          PERFORM BILL-NON-DEGREE-FULL
     ELSE
          PERFORM BILL-NON-DEGREE-PART
     .
```

Note that the factored version has reduced fan-out from eight to four.

2.37 Why is high fan-in desirable?

High fan-in saves computer memory by eliminating repetition of code (a module appears only once in a program but is called from several places). It also reduces maintenance costs since changes to the module need be done in only one place (whereas if code is repeated in several different modules, it must be changed in each case). Development costs are also reduced since repetitive coding and testing are eliminated.

2.38 Give module interface specifications for the CALCULATE-NET and CALCULATE-TAX modules of Problem 2.18 (Fig. 2-11).

Module name:	CALCULATE-NET
Input:	WS-GROSS-PAY, WS-TAX-AMOUNT
Output:	WS-NET-PAY
Function:	Compute net pay as gross pay minus tax amount, rounded to nearest cent.
Module name:	CALCULATE-TAX
Input:	WS-GROSS-PAY, TAX-TABLE
Output:	WS-TAX-AMOUNT
Function:	Search TAX-TABLE for first entry less than WS-GROSS-PAY. Obtain TAX-RATE from this TAX-TABLE entry. Tax amount is gross pay multiplied by tax rate. Round to nearest cent.

Chapter 3

Structured Programming
and COBOL Coding Standards

The structure chart and module specifications from structured design become the input to the programmer during implementation. Using these tools, the programmer must (1) design the internal logic of each module, (2) code the module, (3) test the module, and (4) document the module. *Structured programming* is a set of tools and techniques for accomplishing these tasks in such a way that both development and maintenance costs are reduced.

3.1 Structured Programming Concepts

Structured programming is based on the *structure theorem* of Bohm and Jacopini which states that any program can be written using only the three basic logic structures of *sequence*, *selection*, and *iteration*. Since each of these structures is entered at the top and exited at the bottom, a program or module built by combining the three basic structures will have one entry point and one exit and will read from top to bottom.

In addition to specifying that modules should be coded using only the three fundamental logic structures, structured programming provides (1) techniques for the design of internal module logic and (2) guidelines (often called *coding standards*) for program style and typography.

Structured programming in COBOL is thoroughly covered in *Schaum's Outline of Programming with Structured COBOL* (McGraw-Hill, 1984). This chapter provides a brief survey of (1) the graphic tools used to design module logic, (2) the technique of stepwise refinement which guides the application of those tools, (3) coding standards to be followed when implementing module logic in a programming language, and (4) module documentation. Module testing is covered separately in Chapter 4.

3.2 Tools for Designing Internal Module Logic

Like structured analysis and structured design, structured programming is a *top-down* methodology. This means that internal module logic must be designed *before* coding can begin. Following are three common logic design tools which can be used for this purpose. The programmer should choose the tool which best fits his or her personal cognitive style.

Structured Flowcharts

Structured flowcharting is an older module logic design tool which has fallen out of favor because of the time involved in drawing and modifying the diagrams. Further, it is easy to abuse flowcharts by including logic structures other than the basic structures of sequence, selection, and iteration. Nevertheless, some people prefer flowcharting as a design tool because of its strong pictorial quality. For a discussion of structured flowcharting see Chapter 7 of *Schaum's Outline of Programming with Structured COBOL* (McGraw-Hill, 1984).

EXAMPLE 3.1 In order to keep flowcharts structured, they must be built by combining the three basic logic structures in Fig. 3-1. The type of iteration structure shown here is called a DOWHILE.

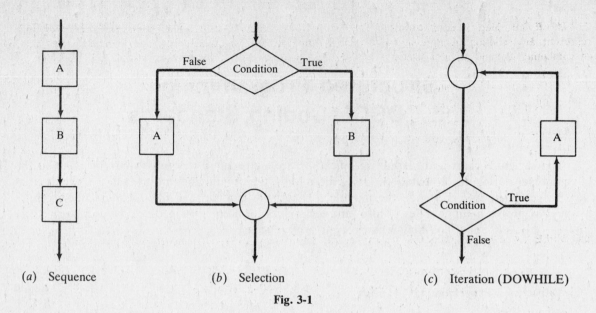

(a) Sequence   (b) Selection   (c) Iteration (DOWHILE)

Fig. 3-1

EXAMPLE 3.2 For convenience, structured programming also allows the variations on the iteration and selection structures shown in Fig. 3-2. Note that a DOWHILE loop may not be executed at all (i.e., zero times), whereas a DOUNTIL loop is always executed at least once. The *case* structure is useful when coding a transaction center (i.e., when a data item can take on several different values, each one of which dictates different processing).

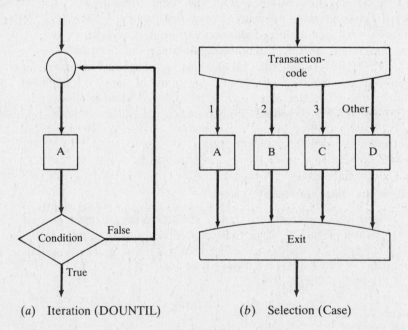

(a) Iteration (DOUNTIL)   (b) Selection (Case)

Fig. 3-2

Pseudocode

Pseudocode is currently favored as a logic design tool because it is easy to create and modify. It is a design language *made up* by the programmer, the only rule being that it must be able to express the three fundamental logic structures of structured programming.

Pseudocode differs from structured English in that it shows the details of *how* processing is to be accomplished, not just *what* is to be done. For a discussion of pseudocode as a module design tool see Chapter 7 of *Schaum's Outline of Programming with Structured COBOL* (McGraw-Hill, 1984).

EXAMPLE 3.3 Here is an illustration of the basic logic structures in "typical" pseudocode. "Condition" represents any valid logical expression and "process" indicates any valid structured programming construct built by combining sequence and/or selection and/or iteration structures:

Sequence	*Selection*	*Iteration (DOWHILE)*
process A	IF condition	WHILE condition
process B	process A	process A
process C	process B	process B
	ELSE	process C
	process C	ENDWHILE
	process D	
	ENDIF	

EXAMPLE 3.4 Here is another illustration of the supplementary logic structures in pseudocode:

Iteration (DOUNTIL)	*Case Structure (Selection)*
DOUNTIL condition	DOCASE on data-item
process A	CASE data-item = "a"
process B	process A
process C	process B
ENDUNTIL	CASE data-item = "b"
	process C
	CASE data-item = "c"
	process D
	process E
	CASE other
	process F
	ENDCASE

Nassi-Shneiderman Charts

Nassi-Shneiderman charts diagram a module as a rectangular box, showing the internal logic of the module as special shapes within the box. The logic is always read top to bottom and can consist of only sequence, selection, and iteration constructs, thus nicely *enforcing* the rules of structured programming (which flowcharting does not). Nassi-Shneiderman charts preserve the pictorial quality of flowcharts, but are easier to draw and are not susceptible to nonstructured deformations.

EXAMPLE 3.5 Figure 3-3 shows the sequence structure as drawn in Nassi-Shneiderman charts.

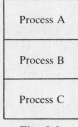

Fig. 3-3

Iteration is shown in Nassi-Shneiderman charts with an "L" shape. The horizontal bar of the L contains the condition controlling repetition, while the vertical bar indicates the *scope* of the structure, i.e., which processes are to be repeated.

EXAMPLE 3.6 The DOWHILE structure in Nassi-Shneiderman form is shown in Fig. 3-4. The horizontal bar with the condition for loop exit is drawn at the top of the set of statements to be repeated. The length of the vertical bar determines the number of statements involved in the DOWHILE.

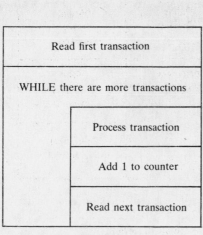

Fig. 3-4

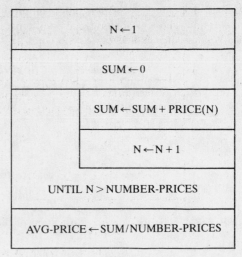

Fig. 3-5

EXAMPLE 3.7 The DOUNTIL structure in Nassi-Shneiderman form is shown in Fig. 3-5. The horizontal bar with the condition for loop repetition is drawn at the bottom of the set of statements to be repeated. The length of the vertical bar again determines the scope of the DOUNTIL (in this case the two statements "SUM ← SUM + PRICE(N)" and "N ← N + 1").

The selection structure is drawn by showing the condition to be tested in a horizontal block, along with two triangles which represent the true and false values of the condition. The actions to be carried out if the condition is true are aligned under the "true" triangle; the actions to be carried out if the condition is false are aligned under the "false" triangle.

EXAMPLE 3.8 Figure 3-6 shows the selection structure in Nassi-Shneiderman form.

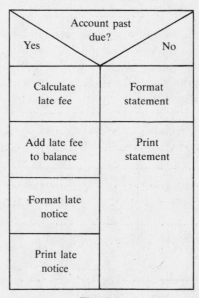

Fig. 3-6

EXAMPLE 3.9 Figure 3-7 shows the case structure in Nassi-Shneiderman form. Note that this is a generalization of the selection diagram.

EXAMPLE 3.10 Figure 3-8 shows a Nassi-Shneiderman chart illustrating the combination of logic structures. The algorithm balances a checkbook. Note the null entry under the "NO" triangle of "NEW-BALANCE < 0". This indicates a missing "ELSE" clause (i.e., an "IF . . . ENDIF" structure).

Case TRANSACTION-CODE is			
1	2	3	Other
Add new record	Change existing record	Delete existing record	Format error message
Increment number added	Increment number changed	Increment number deleted	Print error message
			Increment number errors

Fig. 3-7

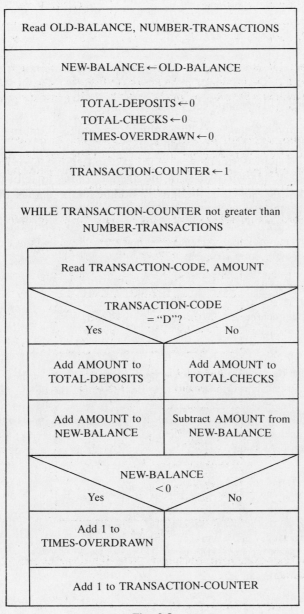

Read OLD-BALANCE, NUMBER-TRANSACTIONS

NEW-BALANCE ← OLD-BALANCE

TOTAL-DEPOSITS ← 0
TOTAL-CHECKS ← 0
TIMES-OVERDRAWN ← 0

TRANSACTION-COUNTER ← 1

WHILE TRANSACTION-COUNTER not greater than NUMBER-TRANSACTIONS

Read TRANSACTION-CODE, AMOUNT

TRANSACTION-CODE = "D"?
Yes / No

Add AMOUNT to TOTAL-DEPOSITS / Add AMOUNT to TOTAL-CHECKS

Add AMOUNT to NEW-BALANCE / Subtract AMOUNT from NEW-BALANCE

NEW-BALANCE < 0
Yes / No

Add 1 to TIMES-OVERDRAWN

Add 1 to TRANSACTION-COUNTER

Fig. 3-8

EXAMPLE 3.11   Below is the pseudocode equivalent of the Nassi-Shneiderman chart in Example 3.10:

```
read old-balance, #-transactions
set new-balance to old-balance
set total-deposits, total-checks, times-overdrawn to zero
set transaction-counter to 1
DOWHILE transaction-counter not greater than #-transactions
     read transaction-code, amount
     IF transaction-code = "D"
          add amount to total-deposits, new-balance
     ELSE
          add amount to total-checks
          subtract amount from new-balance
     ENDIF
     IF new-balance less than zero
          add 1 to times-overdrawn
     ENDIF
     add 1 to transaction-counter
ENDWHILE
```

3.3   Stepwise Refinement: A Technique for Logic Design

Stepwise refinement applies top-down philosophy to the design of internal module logic. It can be adapted for use with any of the design tools discussed in Section 3.2.

The central concept of stepwise refinement is to take an iterative approach to designing internal logic. The first attempt at design will deal with the *overall general* logic of the module in question. Each successive attempt will *refine* the design by adding more details of logic and processing. Eventually, all details are filled in and a finished design is created.

EXAMPLE 3.12   The following program segment is the first cut at designing the internal logic of REMOVE-INELIGIBLE-COURSES module from Example 1.17.

```
set course-count to 1
DOWHILE course-count not greater than #-courses-on-schedule
     process current course
     add 1 to course-count
ENDWHILE
```

Note that the first approximation deals only with the overall, controlling logic of the module. Having determined the overall logic, the programmer is now in a better position to refine the design to include more detail.

EXAMPLE 3.13   Below is the first stepwise refinement of the design in Example 3.12. "Process current course" is replaced by expanded pseudocode giving more details. Further refinement is still necessary, however, since detail is not yet sufficient to allow coding.

```
set course-count to 1
DOWHILE course-count not greater than #-courses-on-schedule

     determine if current course is eligible
     IF current course is not eligible
          remove current course from schedule
     ENDIF

     add 1 to course-count
ENDWHILE
```

EXAMPLE 3.14 Following is the second stepwise refinement of the design in Example 3.12. "Determine if current course is eligible" is replaced by pseudocode filling in details of that process.

```
set course-count to 1
DOWHILE course-count not greater than #-courses-on-schedule

    ┌──────────────────────────────────────────────────────┐
    │ read prerequisite-list from catalog                  │
    │ read courses-passed-list from student-transcript     │
    │ determine if all courses in prerequisite-list are    │
    │     also in courses-passed-list                      │
    └──────────────────────────────────────────────────────┘

    IF current course is not eligible
        remove current course from schedule
    ENDIF
    add 1 to course-count
ENDWHILE
```

Stepwise refinement should continue until the programmer can easily code each pseudocode statement in COBOL. In Example 3.14, the two "read" statements probably do not require further refinement. However, "determine if all courses in prerequisite-list are also in courses-passed-list" should be broken down into its constituent steps.

EXAMPLE 3.15 Here is the third stepwise refinement of REMOVE-INELIGIBLE-COURSES. The level of detail begins to approach that required for coding, and experienced programmers may stop stepwise refinement at this point. Others may wish to design the details of finding a prerequisite in the list of passed courses *before* starting to code (see Problem 3.17).

```
set course-count to 1
DOWHILE course-count not greater than #-courses-on-schedule
    read prerequisite-list for current course from catalog
    read courses-passed-list from student-transcript

    ┌──────────────────────────────────────────────────────┐
    │ set eligible-sw "on"                                 │
    │ set prerequisite-counter to 1                        │
    │ DOWHILE prerequisite-counter not greater than        │
    │         #-prerequisites AND eligible-sw is "on"      │
    │     IF current course from prerequisite-list is      │
    │             not in courses-passed-list               │
    │         set eligible-sw "off"                        │
    │     ENDIF                                            │
    │     add 1 to prerequisite-counter                    │
    │ ENDWHILE                                             │
    │ IF eligible-sw is "off"                              │
    │     set schedule-status for current course           │
    │         to "not scheduled"                           │
    │ ENDIF                                               │
    └──────────────────────────────────────────────────────┘

    add 1 to course-count
ENDWHILE
```

3.4 COBOL Coding Standards

Coding standards are rules for programming in a particular language which are not dictated by the syntax of the language itself. They are inspired, rather, by the need to reduce development and (especially) maintenance costs.

COBOL coding standards are thoroughly discussed in *Schaum's Outline of Programming with Structured COBOL* (McGraw-Hill, 1984). The following sections present a brief review of the major standards for (1) data names, (2) procedure names, (3) program structure, and (4) program typography.

Coding Standards: Data Names

(1) Keep names *descriptive*. Avoid ambiguous names such as TOTAL, COUNTER, or (inexcusable!) X, I, N, etc. Remember, there are 30 characters to work with.

(2) Give names of items which are part of a group item the same prefix (or suffix) which abbreviates the name of the group item, i.e., *CUSTOMER-MASTER*-ID, *CUSTOMER-MASTER*-NAME, *CUSTOMER-MASTER*-BALANCE-DUE.

(3) When possible, indicate the function of a data item in its name; e.g., all switches end in "-SW", all counters end in "-COUNT", all indexes with "-INDEX", etc.

Coding Standards: Procedure Names

(1) In COBOL, a module can be implemented as a paragraph, a SECTION, or a program. Paragraph names, SECTION names, and PROGRAM-IDs should all describe the function of the module in question.

(2) Sequence paragraph and SECTION headers by attaching a prefix or suffix to the name (and keep them in order).

Coding Standards: Program Structure

(1) Always include IDENTIFICATION DIVISION entries; they present information useful for program maintenance.

(2) End the IDENTIFICATION DIVISION with a set of comments giving an overview of what the program is all about.

(3) Increment DATA DIVISION level numbers by more than 1, e.g., 01, 05, 10, 15, etc. This makes structural changes easier.

(4) Code SELECT statements in some standard order (e.g., input files first, then I-O files, then output files). Use the same order for the corresponding file description entries (FDs).

(5) Do not use level-77 items in WORKING-STORAGE; instead, group items into meaningful categories and subordinate them to a level-01 name which describes the category.

(6) Use a standard order for coding WORKING-STORAGE items (e.g., program flags and switches, then program constants, then counters, then total areas, then subscripts, then tables, then working copies of logical records from files—in the same order as the SELECTs and FDs). For print files, define heading lines first, body lines next, then total and footing lines last.

(7) Avoid unnecessary (1) commas, (2) periods, and (3) SECTIONs.

(8) Use only *one* STOP RUN statement per program.

(9) Use literals and figurative constants in the PROCEDURE DIVISION only if they will *never* have to be changed. Otherwise, use a data item (called a *program constant*) initialized to the desired value with the VALUE clause.

(10) Keep program structure as simple as possible.

Coding Standards: Program Typography

(1) Keep the appearance of the program as simple and readable as possible.

(2) Place paragraph and SECTION headers alone on their own lines.

(3) Use *structured periods* (periods standing alone on a line) everywhere in the PROCE-DURE DIVISION (except after paragraph/SECTION headers) and in other DIVISIONs when entries have several clauses (e.g., SELECT, FD, SPECIAL-NAMES, etc.).

(4) Always indent to show the structure of data items.

(5) So far as possible, align PIC, USAGE, SYNC, and VALUE clauses in columns.

(6) Use special compiler features (such as EJECT, SKIP1, SKIP2, and SKIP3 in IBM OS/VS COBOL) to ensure that each DIVISION and SECTION begins on a new page of the source listing and that paragraphs are at least separated from one another by blank lines (if they are not on separate pages).

(7) Type only *one* PROCEDURE DIVISION verb per line.

(8) Indent to show the continuation of a statement over more than one line and/or to clarify relationships among statements. This is critical for IF statements and for statements with special clauses (such as READ . . . AT END . . . , and PERFORM . . . UNTIL . . .).

(9) Break long statements at the start of a clause and indent the next line.

(10) Vertically align similar statements or parts of statements for readability.

3.5 Module Documentation

Documentation is often thought of as something that is done *after* coding and testing are completed. However, when structured methodology is used, documentation is an ongoing process which is almost completed *before* coding begins (since the material produced during structured analysis, structured design, and the logic design phase of structured programming serves as excellent program documentation). The programmer's main responsibility, then, is to see to it that changes made during testing and debugging are reflected in this documentation.

In addition to keeping *systems documentation* (used by programmers and analysts) up to date, programmers are sometimes asked to write special documentation such as (1) *user documentation*—which tells users how to enter data, interpret output, etc.—and (2) *operator documentation*—which tells computer operators how to actually run programs (i.e., what tapes, disks, special forms, etc., will be needed; what job control or command language statements are required; what error messages might be produced and how to respond to them; what steps to take if the program ABENDS; etc.). Producing good documentation requires that the programmer have good technical writing skills.

Review Questions

3.1   What are the programmer's responsibilities during implementation?

3.2   What is the structure theorem?

3.3   What are the major guidelines of structured programming?

3.4   Explain how to draw structured flowcharts.

3.5   Show how the basic logic structures are represented in pseudocode.

3.6   Explain how to draw Nassi-Shneiderman charts.

3.7   Give advantages and disadvantages of the three logic design tools discussed in the text.

3.8   Explain how to carry out stepwise refinement.

3.9   How far should stepwise refinement be taken?

3.10   What is meant by coding standards?

3.11   Give an example of how to apply each coding standard discussed in this Outline.

3.12   Why is documentation an ongoing process throughout systems development when structured methodology is used?

3.13   Explain the differences between systems, user, and operations documentation.

Solved Problems

3.14   Design the internal logic for module CALCULATE-TAX of Problems 2.38 and 2.18. Use structured flowcharting.

      See Fig. 3-9 for a possible solution.

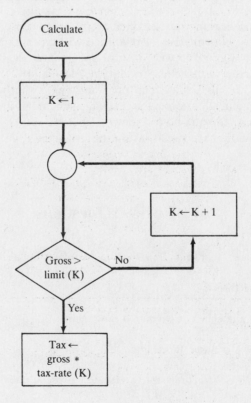

Fig. 3-9

3.15 Repeat Problem 3.14 using pseudocode.

```
set k to 1        /* k is index into tax-table */
dowhile ws-gross-pay not greater than tax-limit(k)
        add 1 to k
endwhile
ws-tax-amount = ws-gross-pay * tax-rate(k)
```

3.16 Repeat Problem 3.14 using Nassi-Shneiderman charts.

See Fig. 3-10 for a possible solution.

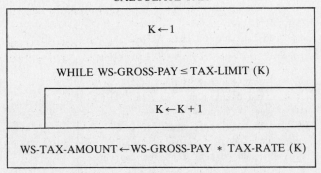

CALCULATE-TAX

Fig. 3-10

3.17 Finish the stepwise refinement of Example 3.15.

```
set course-count to 1
DOWHILE course-count not greater than #-courses-on-schedule
        read prerequisite-list for current course from catalog
        read courses-passed-list from student-transcript
        set eligible-sw "on"
        set prerequisite-counter to 1
        DOWHILE prerequisite-counter not greater than
                #-prerequisites AND eligible-sw is "on"

            set courses-passed-counter to 1
            set eligible-sw "off"
            DOWHILE courses-passed-counter not greater
                    than #-courses-passed
              AND   eligible-sw is "off"
                    IF current course from prerequisite-list
                      matches current course from
                      courses-passed-list
                        set eligible-sw "on"
                    ELSE
                        add 1 to courses-passed-counter
                    ENDIF
            ENDWHILE

            add 1 to prerequisite-counter
        ENDWHILE
        IF eligible-sw is "off"
            set schedule-status for current course
                to "not scheduled"
        ENDIF
        add 1 to course-count
ENDWHILE
```

3.18   Use stepwise refinement and pseudocode to design the internal module logic for transform
bubble 2.1 of Example 1.9.

Initial Version

```
read major from transcript-file
read required-courses for this major from catalog-file
read scheduled-courses from schedule form
add missing required-courses to scheduled-courses
```

First Refinement

```
read major from transcript-file
read required-courses for this major from catalog-file
read scheduled-courses from schedule form
```

```
set required-counter to 1
DOWHILE required-counter not greater than
          #-required-courses
    IF current required-course not in
        scheduled-courses
            add current required-course to
                    scheduled-courses
    ENDIF
    add 1 to required-counter
ENDWHILE
```

Second Refinement

```
read major from transcript-file
read required-courses for this major from catalog-file
read scheduled-courses from schedule form
set required-counter to 1
DOWHILE required-counter not greater than
          #-required-courses
```

```
    set scheduled-counter to 1
    set requirement-met "off"
    DOWHILE scheduled-counter not greater than
              #-scheduled-courses
      AND    requirement-met is "off"
          IF current required-course matches
              current scheduled-course
                  set requirement-met "on"
          ELSE
              add 1 to scheduled-counter
          ENDIF
    ENDWHILE
    IF requirement-met is "off"
        add current required-course to
            scheduled-courses
    ENDIF
```

```
    add 1 to required-counter
ENDWHILE
```

Third Refinement

"add current required-course to scheduled-courses" can be refined as follows:

```
add 1 to #-scheduled-courses
insert current required-course into list of
        scheduled-courses
```

The refinement of the "insert" operation is left as an exercise for the student.

3.19   Criticize the COBOL program in Fig. 3-11 with respect to structured programming coding standards.

```
00001              IDENTIFICATION DIVISION.
00002
00003              PROGRAM-ID.  NON-STRUCTURED-COBOL.
00004
00005              AUTHOR. LARRY NEWCOMER.
00006              INSTALLATION. PENN STATE UNIVERSITY -- YORK CAMPUS.
00007              SECURITY.  NONE.
00008
00009              ENVIRONMENT DIVISION.
00010
00011              CONFIGURATION SECTION.
00012              SOURCE-COMPUTER.   IBM-3081.
00013              OBJECT-COMPUTER.   IBM-3081.
00014
00015              INPUT-OUTPUT SECTION.
00016              FILE-CONTROL.
00017
00018                  SELECT TERMS-FILE
00019                      ASSIGN TO TERMS
00020                      ORGANIZATION IS SEQUENTIAL
00021                      ACCESS IS SEQUENTIAL
00022                      .
00023                  SELECT PAYMENT-REPORT
00024                      ASSIGN TO PAYMENTS
00025                      ORGANIZATION IS SEQUENTIAL
00026                      ACCESS IS SEQUENTIAL
00027                      .
00028
00029              DATA DIVISION.
00030
00031              FILE SECTION.
00032
00033              FD   TERMS-FILE
00034                   RECORD CONTAINS 80 CHARACTERS
00035                   LABEL RECORDS ARE OMITTED
00036                   .
00037
00038              01   TERMS-RECORD.
00039                   05   TERMS-PRINCIPAL        PIC S9(7)V99.
00040                   05   TERMS-INTEREST-RATE    PIC SV999.
00041                   05   TERMS-PAYMENT          PIC S9(5)V99.
00042                   05   FILLER                 PIC X(61).
00043
00044              FD   PAYMENT-REPORT
00045                   RECORD CONTAINS 132 CHARACTERS
00046                   LABEL RECORDS ARE OMITTED
00047                       LINAGE IS 60
00048                           WITH FOOTING AT 60
00049                           LINES AT TOP 3
00050                           LINES AT BOTTOM 3
00051                   .
00052
00053              01   PAYMENT-RECORD             PIC X(132).
00054
00055              WORKING-STORAGE SECTION.
```

Fig. 3-11

```
00056
00057          77  WS-INTEREST-AMOUNT             PIC S9(5)V99    COMP-3.
00058          77  WS-PAYMENT-AMOUNT              PIC S9(5)V99    COMP-3.
00059          77  WS-BALANCE                     PIC S9(7)V99    COMP-3.
00060          77  WS-PAYMENT-NUMBER              PIC S9(3)       COMP-3.
00061          77  WS-INTEREST-RATE               PIC SV999       COMP-3.
00062          77  WS-PRINCIPAL-AMOUNT            PIC S9(5)V99    COMP-3.
00063          77  WS-PAGE-NUMBER                 PIC S999        COMP-3.
00064
00065      01  WS-DATE.
00066          05  SYSTEM-YY                      PIC 99.
00067          05  SYSTEM-MM                      PIC 99.
00068          05  SYSTEM-DD                      PIC 99.
00069
00070      01  WS-HEADING-LINE-1.
00071          05  FILLER                         PIC X(10)       VALUE SPACES.
00072          05  FILLER                         PIC X(17)
00073                                             VALUE "MORTGAGE PAYMENTS".
00074          05  FILLER                         PIC X(1)        VALUE SPACES.
00075          05  WS-HEADING-MM                  PIC Z9.
00076          05  FILLER                         PIC X           VALUE "/".
00077          05  WS-HEADING-DD                  PIC 99.
00078          05  FILLER                         PIC X           VALUE "/".
00079          05  WS-HEADING-YY                  PIC 99.
00080          05  FILLER                         PIC X(4)        VALUE SPACES.
00081          05  FILLER                         PIC X(5)        VALUE "PAGE ".
00082          05  WS-HEADING-PAGE-NO             PIC ZZ9.
00083          05  FILLER                         PIC X(94)       VALUE SPACES.
00084
00085      01  WS-HEADING-LINE-2.
00086          05  FILLER                         PIC X(10)
00087                                             VALUE "PAYMENT #".
00088          05  FILLER                         PIC X(2)        VALUE SPACES.
00089          05  FILLER                         PIC X(15)
00090                                             VALUE "OLD BALANCE".
00091          05  FILLER                         PIC X(2)        VALUE SPACES.
00092          05  FILLER                         PIC X(10)
00093                                             VALUE "PAYMENT".
00094          05  FILLER                         PIC X(2)        VALUE SPACES.
00095          05  FILLER                         PIC X(10)
00096                                             VALUE "PRINCIPAL".
00097          05  FILLER                         PIC X(2)        VALUE SPACES.
00098          05  FILLER                         PIC X(10)
00099                                             VALUE "INTEREST".
00100          05  FILLER                         PIC X(2)        VALUE SPACES.
00101          05  FILLER                         PIC X(12)
00102                                             VALUE "NEW BALANCE".
00103          05  FILLER                         PIC X(55)       VALUE SPACES.
00104
00105      01  WS-DETAIL-LINE.
00106          05  FILLER                         PIC X(3)        VALUE SPACES.
00107          05  WS-DETAIL-NUMBER               PIC Z9.
00108          05  FILLER                         PIC X(7)        VALUE SPACES.
00109          05  WS-DETAIL-OLD-BAL              PIC Z,ZZZ,ZZZ.99.
00110          05  FILLER                         PIC X(5)        VALUE SPACES.
00111          05  WS-DETAIL-PAYMENT              PIC ZZ,ZZZ.99.
00112          05  FILLER                         PIC X(3)        VALUE SPACES.
00113          05  WS-DETAIL-PRINCIPAL            PIC ZZ,ZZZ.99.
00114          05  FILLER                         PIC X(3)        VALUE SPACES.
00115          05  WS-DETAIL-INTEREST             PIC ZZ,ZZZ.99.
00116          05  FILLER                         PIC X(3)        VALUE SPACES.
00117          05  WS-DETAIL-NEW-BAL              PIC Z,ZZZ,ZZZ.99.
00118          05  FILLER                         PIC X(55)       VALUE SPACES.
00119
00120      PROCEDURE DIVISION.
00121
00122          OPEN    INPUT    TERMS-FILE
00123                  OUTPUT   PAYMENT-REPORT
00124          READ TERMS-FILE
00125              AT END
00126                  DISPLAY "*** EMPTY TERMS FILE ***"
00127                  GO TO 300-END-RUN.
00128          ACCEPT WS-DATE FROM DATE
00129          MOVE SYSTEM-YY  TO WS-HEADING-YY
00130          MOVE SYSTEM-MM  TO WS-HEADING-MM
00131          MOVE SYSTEM-DD  TO WS-HEADING-DD
```

Fig. 3-11 (*cont.*)

```
00132                              MOVE ZERO TO WS-PAYMENT-NUMBER
00133                              MOVE TERMS-PRINCIPAL TO WS-BALANCE
00134                              MOVE TERMS-INTEREST-RATE TO WS-INTEREST-RATE
00135                              MOVE TERMS-PAYMENT TO WS-PAYMENT-AMOUNT WS-DETAIL-PAYMENT
00136                              MOVE 1 TO WS-PAGE-NUMBER  WS-HEADING-PAGE-NO
00137                              WRITE PAYMENT-RECORD
00138                                  FROM WS-HEADING-LINE-1
00139                                  AFTER ADVANCING PAGE
00140                              WRITE PAYMENT-RECORD
00141                                  FROM WS-HEADING-LINE-2
00142                                  AFTER ADVANCING 2 LINES.
00143
00144                          100-COMPUTE-NEXT-PAYMENT.
00145
00146                              ADD 1 TO WS-PAYMENT-NUMBER
00147                              MOVE WS-BALANCE TO WS-DETAIL-OLD-BAL
00148                              MOVE WS-PAYMENT-NUMBER TO WS-DETAIL-NUMBER
00149                              COMPUTE WS-INTEREST-AMOUNT =
00150                                  (WS-BALANCE * WS-INTEREST-RATE) / 12
00151                              SUBTRACT WS-INTEREST-AMOUNT FROM WS-PAYMENT-AMOUNT
00152                                  GIVING WS-DETAIL-PRINCIPAL  WS-PRINCIPAL-AMOUNT
00153                              IF WS-PRINCIPAL-AMOUNT NOT LESS THAN WS-BALANCE
00154                                  GO TO 200-PRINT-FINAL-PAYMENT.
00155                              MOVE WS-INTEREST-AMOUNT TO WS-DETAIL-INTEREST
00156                              SUBTRACT WS-PRINCIPAL-AMOUNT FROM WS-BALANCE
00157                                  GIVING WS-BALANCE WS-DETAIL-NEW-BAL
00158
00159                              WRITE PAYMENT-RECORD
00160                                  FROM WS-DETAIL-LINE
00161                                  AFTER ADVANCING 2 LINES
00162                                  AT END-OF-PAGE
00163                                      ADD 1 TO WS-PAGE-NUMBER
00164                                      MOVE WS-PAGE-NUMBER TO WS-HEADING-PAGE-NO
00165                                      WRITE PAYMENT-RECORD
00166                                          FROM WS-HEADING-LINE-1
00167                                          AFTER ADVANCING PAGE
00168                                      WRITE PAYMENT-RECORD
00169                                          FROM WS-HEADING-LINE-2
00170                                          AFTER ADVANCING 2 LINES.
00171                              GO TO 100-COMPUTE-NEXT-PAYMENT.
00172
00173                          200-PRINT-FINAL-PAYMENT.
00174
00175                              MOVE WS-BALANCE TO WS-DETAIL-PRINCIPAL
00176                              MOVE WS-INTEREST-AMOUNT TO WS-DETAIL-INTEREST
00177                              MOVE ZERO TO WS-DETAIL-NEW-BAL
00178                              ADD WS-INTEREST-AMOUNT WS-BALANCE GIVING WS-DETAIL-PAYMENT
00179                              WRITE PAYMENT-RECORD
00180                                  FROM WS-DETAIL-LINE
00181                                  AFTER ADVANCING 2 LINES.
00182
00183                          300-END-RUN.
00184
00185                              CLOSE TERMS-FILE
00186                                      PAYMENT-REPORT
00187                              STOP RUN.
```

Fig. 3-11 (*cont.*)

The following weaknesses are found in Fig. 3-11:

(1) Lines 1–8: Some IDENTIFICATION DIVISION entries are missing, and there is no set of comments giving an overview of what the program does.

(2) Lines 57–63: Level-77 items are used in WORKING-STORAGE, and there appears to be no standard order for listing these items.

(3) Lines 142, 150, 161, 163, 170, 181: Literals which *might* at some time have to be changed appear in the PROCEDURE DIVISION.

(4) PROCEDURE DIVISION does not use structured periods.

(5) PROCEDURE DIVISION makes significant use of the GO TO statement, and therefore is not coded using only the three fundamental logic structures of structured programming. Figure 3-11 provides an example of relatively clean nonstructured logic; in the "real" world, nonstructured code is often horribly difficult to understand and modify.

Chapter 4

Coding, Testing, and Debugging

Chapter 3 discussed techniques for individual module design and coding. This chapter places these activities in the context of the *implementation phase* of a project. During implementation, the programmer is assigned responsibility for one or more modules. He or she must then:

(1) Plan how to design the internal logic of the assigned modules.

(2) Carry out the design of internal module logic (using the techniques from Chapter 3).

(3) Plan how to code and test the assigned modules.

(4) Design and obtain test data needed to carry out the coding/testing plan.

(5) Code each module according to the sequence determined by the coding/testing plan (using the techniques in Chapter 3).

(6) Test and debug each module as per the coding/testing plan.

(7) Complete all module documentation.

The fundamentals of program coding, testing, and debugging are thoroughly covered in Chapters 8 and 9 of *Schaum's Outline of Programming with Structured COBOL* (McGraw-Hill, 1984). The reader should master this material before going on to the topics below.

4.1 Planning/Designing Internal Module Logic

If the systems designer has created good module specifications, the programmer may elect to design, code, and test one module at a time. With this "design-as-you-go" approach, the internal logic of each module is designed just before it is coded and tested. Thus some modules are not even designed until after other modules have been completely finished (i.e., coded, tested, and debugged).

In most cases, however, the programmer should design *all* the modules for which he or she is responsible *before* any modules are coded and tested. This gives the programmer the best chance to detect design flaws before any code is actually written (when it is much cheaper to make changes to the design).

See Chapters 2 and 3 for a discussion of how to design internal module logic.

4.2 Planning for Program Coding and Testing

Once module logic has been designed, the programmer must plan the order in which to code and test. Coding and testing of modules should be done *top-down* with respect to the structure chart developed by the systems designer. This means that no module should be coded until all modules between it and the top-level module have already been coded *and debugged*.

EXAMPLE 4.1 The module RATE-REQUIRED-COURSE from Example 1.18 (Fig. 1-11) should not be coded until after REGISTER-STUDENT, BUILD-INITIAL-SCHEDULE, and RATE-COURSE-INTEREST have been coded and fully debugged.

Top-down coding and testing usually require the use of *program stubs* to represent lower-level modules called by the module being tested. A program stub should perform the minimum activities required to allow the testing of the calling module to proceed correctly. Often program stubs can consist of just a paragraph name and a statement printing a message that the stub has been called. Sometimes stubs may also need to initialize data items or set switches used by the calling module.

EXAMPLE 4.2 In order to test the RATE-COURSE-INTEREST module below, *some* version of the RATE-REQUIRED-COURSE and RATE-ELECTIVE-COURSE modules must be coded (otherwise the PERFORM statements in RATE-COURSE-INTEREST will cause syntax errors). The needed modules are shown coded as minimal program stubs. Note that both stubs must place a value in INTEREST-RATING to fulfill the needs of the calling module. The constants "10" and "7" are arbitrarily chosen for debugging purposes.

```
RATE-COURSE-INTEREST.
    IF COURSE-TYPE EQUAL REQUIRED-COURSE-CODE
        PERFORM RATE-REQUIRED-COURSE
        ADD 15 TO INTEREST-RATING
    ELSE
        PERFORM RATE-ELECTIVE-COURSE
        SUBTRACT 2 FROM INTEREST-RATING
        .
RATE-REQUIRED-COURSE.
    DISPLAY "RATE-REQUIRED-COURSE CALLED FOR "
        COURSE-ID COURSE-TYPE
    MOVE 10 TO INTEREST-RATING
        .
RATE-ELECTIVE-COURSE.
    DISPLAY "RATE-ELECTIVE-COURSE CALLED FOR "
        COURSE-ID COURSE-TYPE
    MOVE 7 TO INTEREST-RATING
        .
```

Clearly the "top-down" rule permits many different sequences in which the modules of a structure chart can be coded and tested. Consider a "typical" structure chart produced by transform analysis. It will consist of afferent branches, efferent branches, and a central transform (see Section 2.3). Following are three common top-down sequences in which to code and test the modules of such a structure chart.

EXAMPLE 4.3 Figure 4-1 shows a typical structure chart produced by transform analysis.

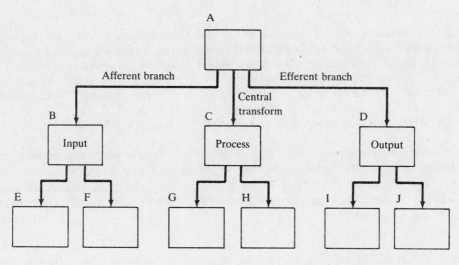

Fig. 4-1

EXAMPLE 4.4 The *horizontal* approach to top-down coding and testing works through the structure chart in a level-by-level fashion. The modules in Example 4.3 (Fig. 4-1) would be coded and tested in the sequence A, B, C, D, E, F, G, H, I, J. Note that with this approach, the lowest-level input and output modules are coded near the end. This can be a disadvantage since the users (and the developers) can not work with actual input and output until late in the implementation. This makes testing more difficult (since there are no lowest-level input modules to provide test data) and creates the risk of discovering user dissatisfaction with input/output functions relatively late in the development cycle (when changes are costly).

EXAMPLE 4.5 The *vertical* approach to top-down coding and testing works through the structure chart as follows: (1) code and test the highest-level module, (2) apply the vertical sequence to the subchart formed by the *leftmost* called module and all its children, (3) apply the vertical sequence to the subchart formed by the next leftmost called module and all its children, (4) continue until all subcharts (and thus the whole structure) have been coded and tested. The modules in Example 4.3 would be coded and tested in the sequence:

Module	Reason for Position in Sequence
A	Start with the topmost module.
B	Continue with leftmost module called by A.
E	Now process the subchart with B at the top; start with the leftmost module called by B.
F	Now process the next leftmost module called by B.
C	Since the subchart starting with B is done, continue with the next leftmost module called by A.
G	Now process the subchart with C at the top; start with the leftmost module called by C.
H	Now process the next leftmost module called by C.
D	Since the subchart starting with C is done, continue with the next leftmost module called by A.
I	Now process the subchart with D at the top; start with the leftmost module called by D.
J	Now process the next leftmost module called by D.

In the terminology of abstract data structures, the vertical approach follows a *preorder* (NLR-type) traversal of the structure chart "tree". It has the advantage of developing all input modules early but the disadvantage of developing output modules late. Since users do not get to see and approve actual output until late in the implementation, any requested changes will be expensive to make.

EXAMPLE 4.6 The third approach to top-down coding and testing implements the afferent and efferent branches of the chart first, and then tackles the central transform last. This allows users to experience actual input and output modules as early as possible and hence request changes at a time when they are least expensive to make. Using this approach, the modules in Example 4.3 could be coded and tested in the sequence: A, B, E, F, D, I, J, C, G, H (afferent branches, then efferent branches, then central transform). If it is desired to show users the output facilities (e.g., screen and report formats) first, the sequence A, D, I, J, B, E, F, C, G, H (efferent branches, then afferent branches, then central transform) could also be used.

The programmer may choose to invent still other top-down coding and testing sequences, depending on the needs of the application, but in all cases the coding/testing plan should be developed and written down before any modules are coded. The plan should specify (1) the sequence in which modules will be developed, (2) what stubs are needed at each stage, and (3) what test data will be used at each stage.

EXAMPLE 4.7 Here is a sample coding/testing plan for modules in Example 4.3, following the afferent/efferent/central transform sequence from Example 4.6:

Module(s)	Stubs Required	Test Data Required
A	B, C, D	One or two records without errors
B	E, F	Records of all types but without errors
E, F	None	Records of all types with errors of all types
D	I, J	Records of all types but without errors
I, J	None	Records of all types with errors of all types
C	G, H	One or two records without errors
G	H	Records of all types but without errors
H	None	Records of all types with errors of all types

4.3   Designing and Obtaining Test Data

Designing Test Data

Test data should be designed *before* any coding and testing are done. This helps eliminate any (possibly unconscious) biases or omissions in the test data.

As was illustrated in Example 4.7, test data should also start out simple and increase in complexity. If complex test data is used too early, debugging is made more difficult (since complex data will trigger all program bugs simultaneously, making them harder to isolate and identify). Bugs are more readily dispatched if they show up one at a time and have clearly identifiable causes.

The final test data, however, should exercise all possible logic paths through all modules being developed; i.e., *there should be no untested code*. Before a module is pronounced "debugged", there should be enough test data to ensure that every selection structure has been sent through both its "true" path and its "false" path and that every case structure has had each possible case tested. It is also recommended that each iteration structure be tested for zero, one, and the maximum number of repetitions.

Since it is not always easy to identify all the logic paths through a module, the programmer may find it helpful to draw a decision tree showing all decisions made within the module. Test data can then be constructed to take the module through each path (see Chapter 8 of *Schaum's Outline of Programming with Structured COBOL*, McGraw-Hill, 1984).

EXAMPLE 4.8   See Fig. 4-2 for a decision tree showing all possible logic paths through the module in Example 3.10 (Fig. 3-8). Note that both iteration and selection structures are represented in the decision tree. As indicated, the tree helps identify six different possibilities which should be tested in order to thoroughly evaluate the module.

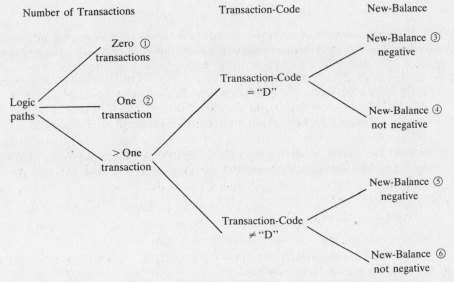

Fig. 4-2

Sources of Test Data

Depending on the particular system, test data can be obtained from the following sources:

(1) If the current project is a modification of an existing system, adequate test data may be on file from the time of the system's initial development.

(2) The programmer may use an interactive text editor (if one is available) to create test data files.

(3) The programmer may use operating system utility programs to generate test data files of the desired content, file organization, etc.

(4) The installation may have purchased or written software for the specific purpose of generating test data files. If such specialized programs are available, they can automate the production of large amounts of test data, with minimal effort on the programmer's part.

(5) The programmer may use utility programs to copy actual *live* data from existing applications. This copy of actual data can then be used in program testing and debugging. *Under no circumstances should live data files themselves be used for testing purposes.*

4.4 Module Testing and Debugging

Testing and Debugging Procedures

Testing refers to the process of detecting errors in a module by executing the module (along with any needed higher-level modules and lower-level stubs) with sample test data and checking the results against the already known, correct results. *Debugging* refers to the process of identifying the causes of program errors and correcting them. Testing and debugging are iterative processes in which the following cycle is repeated until all known bugs have been removed:

(1) Compile the (modified) source program.

(2) Make a test run with appropriate test data.

(3) Check the output of the program against the known, correct results.

(4) Identify the cause(s) of any error(s).

(5) Modify the source program to correct the error(s), and/or increase the complexity of the test data.

Types of Program Errors

There are two types of errors which occur during debugging:

(1) *Syntax errors* are caused by illegal statements in the COBOL source program. They are detected by the compiler during compilation and are flagged on the source listing.

(2) *Logic errors* occur during program execution. There are two types:

   (a) *Fatal logic errors* cause the program to *ABEND* (i.e., be prematurely terminated by the operating system before normal execution of a STOP RUN). Fatal logic errors are caused by either (1) the hardware encountering invalid instructions or data during the execution of the object program or (2) the operating system encountering an invalid request for system services issued by the executing object program. In both cases, the operating system takes over control of the hardware and terminates the user object program.

   (b) *Nonfatal logic errors* are caused by bugs which allow a program to execute a normal STOP RUN without producing correct output. Observe that whereas syntax and fatal logic errors are detected *automatically* by system hardware or software, nonfatal logic errors *must be detected by the programmer during program testing*. The programmer should always carefully examine all test output to ensure that results are indeed correct.

Information Needed to Detect and Identify Errors

Syntax errors are the easiest to debug since the COBOL compiler prints *diagnostic error messages*, which identify each error and the statement in which it occurs. Syntax errors are usually just typographic or spelling errors or inconsistencies in the naming of data items. At worst, the programmer must look up the correct COBOL syntax in the appropriate vendor manual.

As for logic errors, there are two basic kinds of information used to detect and identify both types:

(1) *Memory dump* information shows the contents of memory locations holding data items and/or machine language instructions. There are two types of dumps:

    (a) *Termination dumps* are printed by the operating system when a fatal logic error occurs, causing a program to ABEND. They show the contents of memory at the time of the fatal error. Usually, termination dumps are optional and must be requested by the programmer via operating system job control/command language statements. Termination dumps can be in the form of either standard operating system (hexadecimal) dumps or COBOL symbolic dumps.

    (b) *Dynamic dumps* are printed during program execution and do not interfere with the operation of program logic. They provide *snapshots* of memory at selected points during program execution. The programmer must supply COBOL and/or job control/command language statements to cause the printing of dynamic dump information. Dynamic dumps allow the programmer to trace the changes occurring to a data item as the program executes.

(2) *Program trace* information provides a recorded history showing the sequence in which the computer actually executed the instructions in a program. For example, the compiler-generated line number for each statement could be printed just before the machine language translation of the statement is executed. Trace information is particularly useful when debugging faulty selection and iteration structures. To cause the printing of trace information, the programmer must supply COBOL and/or job control/command language statements.

4.5 Introduction to Debugging Tools and Techniques

The debugging tools available to the COBOL programmer can be categorized as (1) features of the COBOL language itself which are specifically designed for use when debugging, (2) options which can be specified to the COBOL compiler to provide information useful for debugging, and (3) facilities for printing termination (ABEND) and dynamic dumps.

Since many debugging features either directly involve the operating system or are provided as vendor-specific *extensions* to ANSI standard COBOL, a universally applicable discussion of debugging tools is impossible. This Outline presents material pertinent to debugging COBOL programs for IBM 370-family computers running OS/VS-type operating systems. Unless identified as "ANSI standard", features should be considered as IBM extensions to ANSI COBOL.

4.6 COBOL Language Features Designed for Debugging

The following COBOL facilities are thoroughly discussed in Chapter 9 of *Schaum's Outline of Programming with Structured COBOL* (McGraw-Hill, 1984).

Debugging Lines (ANSI Standard)

It is often helpful to place extra statements in a program while it is being debugged. Once debugging is completed, these special *debugging statements* can be removed. ANSI COBOL provides a way to *logically* remove such statements without having to *physically* remove them from the source program.

When debugging statements are added to a program, they should be typed with a "D" in column 7. This identifies them to the compiler as *debugging lines*. The fate of debugging lines depends on the SOURCE-COMPUTER paragraph. If the "WITH DEBUGGING MODE" clause is specified in SOURCE-COMPUTER, then all debugging lines are translated into the object program, just like any other statements in the program. If "WITH DEBUGGING MODE" is omitted from the SOURCE-COMPUTER paragraph, then all debugging lines are treated as comments and are *not* translated into the object program.

EXAMPLE 4.9 This example illustrates the use of WITH DEBUGGING MODE and debugging lines. Since debugging lines will eventually be logically removed from the program, care must be taken to make the program syntactically correct both *with* and *without* the debugging lines (e.g., the period required for the debugging IF statement below is itself a debugging line). Assume TIMES-THROUGH is initially 1.

```
          SOURCE-COMPUTER.  IBM-3081 WITH DEBUGGING MODE.
                .
                .
                .
          XYZ-PARAGRAPH.
     D        IF TIMES-THROUGH EQUAL 1
     D            DISPLAY "FIRST TIME ENTERING XYZ-PARAGRAPH"
     D        ELSE
     D            DISPLAY "ENTERING XYZ-PARAGRAPH AGAIN"
     D        .
     D        ADD 1 TO TIMES-THROUGH
              PERFORM THIS-IS-A-NORMAL-STATEMENT
              PERFORM SO-IS-THIS
                .
     column 7-'
```

DISPLAY Statement (ANSI Standard)

Example 4.9 illustrates how the DISPLAY statement can be used to create dynamic trace output giving a history of the sequence in which program statements were executed. DISPLAY can also be used to produce dynamic dump output as follows:

EXAMPLE 4.10 DISPLAY can be used to print the contents of data items during execution:

```
          SOURCE-COMPUTER.  IBM-3081 WITH DEBUGGING MODE.
          . . . . .
          XYZ-PARAGRAPH.
              PERFORM GET-VALID-TRANSACTION
     D        DISPLAY "TRANSACTION-CODE IS " TRANSACTION-CODE
              IF TRANSACTION-CODE EQUAL SHIPMENT-CODE
                  PERFORM PROCESS-SHIPMENT ...
```

READY/RESET TRACE (Nonstandard)

Dynamic program trace information can be printed on the special IBM OS/VS COBOL system output file SYSOUT by using the READY TRACE statement. Once READY TRACE is executed, every time a paragraph (SECTION) is entered, the paragraph (SECTION) name is printed before the first statement in the paragraph (SECTION) is executed. A compiler option allows the compiler-generated line number of the paragraph (SECTION) header to be printed instead of the name.

Since loops can produce a large quantity of trace output, there is a companion statement, RESET TRACE, which turns the trace feature off.

A disadvantage of READY TRACE is that it is not very fine-grained; i.e., although it indicates *which* paragraphs are executed, it does not give any information about what happens *inside* each paragraph. If needed, such information can be obtained by using the DISPLAY statement as in Section 4.6 above. The use of both READY TRACE and DISPLAY requires a special job control language statement to define the file on which debugging information is to be printed (consult an instructor or vendor manual).

EXAMPLE 4.11   The trace is turned on by the first, third, and fifth executions of paragraph XYZ, and is turned off otherwise. Assume TIMES-THROUGH is initially 1.

```
     SOURCE-COMPUTER.  IBM-3081 WITH DEBUGGING MODE.
     . . . . .
     XYZ-PARAGRAPH.
D        IF TIMES-THROUGH EQUAL 1 OR 3 OR 5
D            READY TRACE
D        ELSE
D            RESET TRACE
D        .
D        ADD 1 TO TIMES-THROUGH
         PERFORM THIS-IS-A-NORMAL-STATEMENT ...
```

ON Statement (Nonstandard)

The ON statement is a powerful tool for limiting the amount of debugging output from a test run. It automates the function carried out by the TIMES-THROUGH counter in Example 4.11 above.

EXAMPLE 4.12   Here is the revised version of Example 4.11 with an ON statement replacing the manual TIMES-THROUGH counter:

```
     SOURCE-COMPUTER.  IBM-3081 WITH DEBUGGING MODE.
     . . . . .
     XYZ-PARAGRAPH.
D        ON 1 AND EVERY 2 UNTIL 5
D            READY TRACE
D        ELSE
D            RESET TRACE
D        .
         PERFORM THIS-IS-A-NORMAL-STATEMENT ...
```

The ON statement has the general form:

```
ON numeric-item [AND EVERY numeric-item] [UNTIL numeric-item]
     imperative-statement(s)
[ELSE imperative-statement(s)].
```

EXHIBIT Statement (Nonstandard)

The EXHIBIT statement provides a convenient way to produce dynamic dump output as a program executes.

EXAMPLE 4.13   The EXHIBIT statement has the three variations illustrated below. Assume DELETE-COUNTER PIC S9(4) contains the value + 0012. Note that EXHIBIT (unlike DISPLAY) does *not* remove the operational sign from numeric items. Thus " + 0012" prints as "001B" on IBM systems (see Chapter 5 of *Schaum's Outline of Programming with Structured COBOL*, McGraw-Hill, 1984).

(1)   EXHIBIT NAMED DELETE-COUNTER prints "DELETE-COUNTER = 001B" on the special system file SYSOUT. The COBOL name is printed, followed by "space = space current-value". A job control language statement is required to define the SYSOUT file when EXHIBIT is used. Consult an instructor or vendor manual.

(2)   EXHIBIT CHANGED NAMED DELETE-COUNTER produces the same output as #1 above, but only if the value of DELETE-COUNTER has changed since the last execution of this particular EXHIBIT statement. If the value has not changed, nothing is printed.

(3)   EXHIBIT CHANGED DELETE-COUNTER prints *only* the current value (i.e., "001B" without the COBOL name), but only if the current value has changed since the last execution of this particular EXHIBIT statement.

EXAMPLE 4.14   If desired, literals may also be included in EXHIBIT statements to help identify debugging output:

```
EXHIBIT NAMED DELETE-COUNTER
     " BEFORE NEXT TRANSACTION IS INPUT"
```

"USE FOR DEBUGGING" DECLARATIVES (ANSI Standard)

Debugging declaratives are perhaps the most useful COBOL source-level debugging tool for obtaining dynamic dump and trace information. They are written at the beginning of the PROCEDURE DIVISION in a special DECLARATIVES section and are executed automatically whenever certain events (defined within each debugging declarative itself) occur during program execution.

Debugging declaratives are only translated into the object program when WITH DEBUGGING MODE is in effect. The event(s) which trigger a debugging declarative during execution are defined with the USE FOR DEBUGGING statement, which has the form:

```
USE FOR DEBUGGING ON
    {    record-identifier
         ALL REFERENCES OF identifier
         file-name
         procedure-name
         ALL PROCEDURES      } . . .
```

EXAMPLE 4.15   The following program segment illustrates the correct syntax for a debugging declarative:

```
PROCEDURE DIVISION.
DECLARATIVES.
DEBUG-DELETIONS SECTION.
     USE FOR DEBUGGING ON
          ALL REFERENCES OF TRANSACTION-CODE
          ALL REFERENCES OF DELETE-COUNTER
                .
* THE FOLLOWING STATEMENT(S) ARE TO BE EXECUTED ACCORDING
* TO THE CONDITIONS DEFINED BY THE PRECEDING USE STATEMENT.
* ALTHOUGH ONLY A DISPLAY STATEMENT IS SHOWN, ANY NUMBER OF
* STATEMENTS COULD BE USED HERE:

     DISPLAY "DEBUG-ITEM IS " DEBUG-ITEM
                .
END DECLARATIVES.
* NORMAL PROCEDURE DIVISION STATEMENTS FOLLOW . . .
```

The USE FOR DEBUGGING ON ... options activate the debugging declarative statement(s) as follows:

(1) ON record-identifier. Declarative is executed *before* each WRITE statement for the file.

(2) ON ALL REFERENCES OF identifier. Declarative is executed *before* any WRITE statement using "identifier" and *after* any other statement referring to "identifier".

(3) ON file-name. Declarative is executed *after* OPEN, CLOSE, or READ.

(4) ON procedure-name. Declarative is executed *before* each execution of the indicated paragraph or SECTION.

(5) ON ALL PROCEDURES. Declarative is executed *before* each execution of any paragraph or SECTION.

In all cases, debugging declaratives are activated only when WITH DEBUGGING MODE is specified in the SOURCE-COMPUTER paragraph.

When a debugging declarative is activated during program execution, the system places valuable debugging information in a special data area named DEBUG-ITEM. DEBUG-ITEM (a reserved word) is *not* defined by the programmer. It is a part of the COBOL language and represents an area with the following contents:

```
01   DEBUG-ITEM.
     05    DEBUG-LINE     PIC X(6).
     05    FILLER         PIC X     VALUE SPACES.
     05    DEBUG-NAME     PIC X(30).
     05    FILLER         PIC X     VALUE SPACES.
     05    DEBUG-SUB-1    PIC S9(4) SIGN IS LEADING SEPARATE CHARACTER.
     05    FILLER         PIC X     VALUE SPACES.
     05    DEBUG-SUB-2    PIC S9(4) SIGN IS LEADING SEPARATE CHARACTER.
     05    FILLER         PIC X     VALUE SPACES.
     05    DEBUG-SUB-3    PIC S9(4) SIGN IS LEADING SEPARATE CHARACTER.
     05    FILLER         PIC X     VALUE SPACES.
     05    DEBUG-CONTENTS PIC X(n).
```

DEBUG-LINE contains the compiler-generated line number of the statement causing the DECLARATIVE to be activated; DEBUG-NAME contains the first 30 characters of the name of the item causing the DECLARATIVE to be activated; DEBUG-SUB-n contain the current subscript value(s) for the DEBUG-NAME data item (if applicable); and DEBUG-CONTENTS contains the current contents of DEBUG-NAME (if it is the name of a data item) or a short phrase describing how the procedure is being executed (if it is the name of a procedure). DEBUG-ITEM contains so much useful information that often all a DEBUGGING DECLARATIVE need do is simply DISPLAY or EXHIBIT the contents of DEBUG-ITEM (see Example 4.15 above).

EXAMPLE 4.16 Figure 4-3 shows an actual DEBUGGING DECLARATIVE, along with the output produced by displaying DEBUG-ITEM.

4.7 Compiler Options for Debugging (Nonstandard)

Each vendor supports a unique set of *compiler options*, which request optional compiler services to be performed during the translation of the source program to machine language. Usually these options are specified by the job control or command language statements which invoke the compiler.

Often full use of these options requires advanced knowledge of operating system facilities and/or assembler language programming. The intent of this Outline is to acquaint the reader with the type of debugging features available, so that the reader can better judge when further study of vendor manuals and supporting topics in computer science is warranted.

```
00010              SOURCE-COMPUTER. IBM-3081 WITH DEBUGGING MODE.
     .                    .
     .                    .
     .                    .
00052          PROCEDURE DIVISION.
00053
00054          DECLARATIVES.
00055
00056          MONITOR-SALES-RECORDS SECTION.
00057
00058              USE FOR DEBUGGING ON
00059                  ALL REFERENCES OF SALES-RECORD-NAME
00060                  ALL REFERENCES OF QUARTERLY-TOTAL
00061              .
00062              DISPLAY "DEBUG-ITEM CONTAINS: " DEBUG-ITEM
00063              .
00064          END DECLARATIVES.
00065
00066          010-PRODUCE-QUARTERLY-REPORT.
00067
00068              OPEN  INPUT  SALES-FILE
00069                    OUTPUT QUARTERLY-REPORT
00070              MOVE "NO" TO SALES-FILE-END
00071              PERFORM 020-READ-SALES-FILE
00072              PERFORM 030-PRINT-REPORT-LINES
00073                  UNTIL SALES-FILE-END = "YES"
00074              CLOSE  SALES-FILE
00075                     QUARTERLY-REPORT
00076              STOP RUN
00077              .
00078
00079          020-READ-SALES-FILE.

00080              READ SALES-FILE
00081                  AT END
00082                      MOVE "YES" TO SALES-FILE-END
00083              .
00084
00085          030-PRINT-REPORT-LINES.

00086              MOVE SALES-RECORD-NAME TO WORKING-NAME
00087              COMPUTE QUARTERLY-TOTAL =   SALES-RECORD-MONTH-1-SALES
00088                                      + SALES-RECORD-MONTH-2-SALES
00089                                      + SALES-RECORD-MONTH-3-SALES
00090              MOVE QUARTERLY-TOTAL TO WORKING-TOTAL
00091              MOVE SALES-RECORD-QUOTA TO WORKING-QUOTA
00092              WRITE QUARTERLY-REPORT-LINE
00093                  FROM WORKING-REPORT-LINE
00094              PERFORM 020-READ-SALES-FILE
00095              .

-------------  ACTUAL OUTPUT FOLLOWS --------------

DEBUG-ITEM CONTAINS: 000086 SALES-RECORD-NAME        CONVERSE
DEBUG-ITEM CONTAINS: 000087 QUARTERLY-TOTAL          066666F
DEBUG-ITEM CONTAINS: 000090 QUARTERLY-TOTAL          066666F
DEBUG-ITEM CONTAINS: 000086 SALES-RECORD-NAME        FLECKSTEINER
DEBUG-ITEM CONTAINS: 000087 QUARTERLY-TOTAL          077788H
DEBUG-ITEM CONTAINS: 000090 QUARTERLY-TOTAL          077788H
DEBUG-ITEM CONTAINS: 000086 SALES-RECORD-NAME        GETZ
DEBUG-ITEM CONTAINS: 000087 QUARTERLY-TOTAL          099999I
DEBUG-ITEM CONTAINS: 000090 QUARTERLY-TOTAL          099999I
```

Fig. 4-3

This section presents a few of the more important compiler options available with IBM OS/VS COBOL. They can be considered typical of the features available on large systems. Options which require knowledge of topics beyond COBOL itself are indicated as such.

Since details vary, depending on the hardware and operating system involved, the reader should consult an appropriate instructor or vendor manual to determine (1) *what* options are available and (2) *how* these options can be invoked.

Cross-Reference Listings (XREF)
(Background Needed: COBOL Only)

Most compilers provide the capability to print sorted and/or unsorted cross-reference listings as part of the compiler output. A *cross-reference listing* (XREF) is simply a list of all programmer-defined names used in a program, together with (1) the compiler-generated line number on which the name is defined and (2) the compiler-generated line number(s) for all statement(s) in which the name appears (is *referenced*). A sorted listing is alphabetical by programmer-defined name; an unsorted listing is printed in the order in which the names first appear in the program.

EXAMPLE 4.17 A cross-reference can be an invaluable debugging tool. If something is wrong with the field WORKING-TOTAL, for example, a cross-reference can allow the programmer to quickly locate the statement in which WORKING-TOTAL is defined, together with *all* statements that manipulate WORKING-TOTAL. Without a cross-reference listing, the programmer would have to manually scan the source listing, looking for all such references. This would be tedious, time-consuming, and error-prone.

EXAMPLE 4.18 Figure 4-4 shows a sorted cross-reference listing produced by an IBM OS/VS COBOL compiler. Note how data names and procedure names are listed separately. The data item QUARTERLY-TOTAL is defined on line 43 of the program and referenced on lines 75 and 78.

```
                                       CROSS-REFERENCE DICTIONARY

          DATA NAMES                   DEFN      REFERENCE


          QUARTERLY-REPORT             000016    000056   000062   000080
          QUARTERLY-REPORT-LINE        000037    000080
          QUARTERLY-TOTAL              000043    000075   000078
          SALES-FILE                   000015    000056   000062   000068
          SALES-FILE-END               000042    000058   000060   000070
          SALES-RECORD                 000025
          SALES-RECORD-MONTH-1-SALES   000027    000075
          SALES-RECORD-MONTH-2-SALES   000028    000075
          SALES-RECORD-MONTH-3-SALES   000029    000075
          SALES-RECORD-NAME            000026    000074
          SALES-RECORD-QUOTA           000030    000079
          SWITCHES-AND-TOTALS          000041
          WORKING-NAME                 000045    000074
          WORKING-QUOTA                000049    000079
          WORKING-REPORT-LINE          000044    000080
          WORKING-TOTAL                000047    000078


          PROCEDURE NAMES              DEFN      REFERENCE

          010-PRODUCE-QUARTERLY-REPORT 000054
          020-READ-SALES-FILE          000067    000059   000082
          030-PRINT-REPORT-LINES       000073    000060
```

Fig. 4-4

Data Division Maps (DMAP)
(Background Needed: Assembler Language)

When available, *data division maps* (DMAP) provide information about how DATA DIVISION items are translated into the object program. This includes such things as the *address* assigned to the data item within the object program, the *length* of the item in bytes, and the *type of data* to be placed in the item. Such information is needed when interpreting a standard operating system termination dump. Often a rudimentary knowledge of assembler language programming is necessary to make full use of a data division map. If the reader's background does not permit understanding of some of the material which follows, be assured that it is usually a "nice-to-know" rather than a "need-to-know" topic (the symbolic dump facility described in Section 4.8 provides an alternative debugging tool for programmers with no knowledge of assembler language techniques).

EXAMPLE 4.19 Figure 4-5 shows a data division map produced by an IBM OS/VS COBOL compiler:

(1) "INTRNL NAME" is the name used *within* the compiler itself to refer to a data item. Since it is this "internal name" which appears in syntax error messages on the source listing, the DMAP is useful when deciphering these messages.

(2) "LVL" is the "level number" of the data item, *normalized* to count 01, 02, 03, etc., regardless of the original numbering scheme. Original DATA DIVISION levels 01, 05, 10, 15 would appear as 01, 02, 03, 04 in the DMAP.

(3) "SOURCE NAME" is the COBOL name for the data item.

(4) The "BASE" and "DISPL" columns give information which allows the programmer to determine the execution-time address of a data item. Thus the programmer can locate any data item in a standard operating system termination dump. An IBM COBOL object program has a 4-byte *base locator* ("BL") field for every 4096 bytes of object code. Each base locator contains the address of the beginning of its 4096-byte block. The "DISPL" field tells how many bytes *beyond* a given base locator address a given data item lies. In Fig. 4-5, SALES-RECORD is "000" bytes beyond the address in the first base locator ("BL = 1"); WORKING-NAME is "008" bytes beyond the address in the third base locator ("BL = 3"); etc. Note that the displacements are given in hexadecimal (base 16) notation. The actual address assigned to any data item can be found by adding the contents of its base locator to its displacement. Unfortunately, the contents of the base locators themselves must be found by looking up the base locators in a standard operating system termination dump (see Problem 4.40). Hence the BASE and DISPL columns are of little use to programmers with no knowledge of such dumps.

(5) "DEFINITION" is the definition of the item as it would appear in an assembler language program. It gives the length of the item and the type of data stored there.

(6) "USAGE" gives the usage of the data item in COBOL terms. The abbreviations can be looked up in the appropriate vendor manual (e.g., "DISPL-NM" stands for "display numeric"; "NM-EDIT" stands for "numeric edited"; etc.).

(7) The "R", "O", "Q", "M" fields provide information regarding variable-length data items, file organization, type of records, etc. They are beyond the scope of this Outline.

INTRNL NAME	LVL	SOURCE NAME	BASE	DISPL	INTRNL NAME	DEFINITION	USAGE	R	O	Q	M
DNM=1-122	FD	SALES-FILE	DCB=01		DNM=1-122		QSAM				
DNM=1-146	01	SALES-RECORD	BL=1	000	DNM=1-146	DS 0CL80	GROUP				F
DNM=1-171	02	SALES-RECORD-NAME	BL=1	000	DNM=1-171	DS 15C	DISP				
DNM=1-198	02	SALES-RECORD-MONTH-1-SALES	BL=1	00F	DNM=1-198	DS 6C	DISP-NM				
DNM=1-234	02	SALES-RECORD-MONTH-2-SALES	BL=1	015	DNM=1-234	DS 6C	DISP-NM				
DNM=1-270	02	SALES-RECORD-MONTH-3-SALES	BL=1	01B	DNM=1-270	DS 6C	DISP-NM				
DNM=1-306	02	SALES-RECORD-QUOTA	BL=1	021	DNM=1-306	DS 7C	DISP-NM				
DNM=1-334	02	FILLER	BL=1	028	DNM=1-334	DS 40C	DISP				
DNM=1-345	FD	QUARTERLY-REPORT	DCB=02		DNM=1-345		QSAM				F
DNM=1-375	01	QUARTERLY-REPORT-LINE	BL=2	000	DNM=1-375	DS 132C	DISP				
DNM=1-406	01	SWITCHES-AND-TOTALS	BL=3	000	DNM=1-406	DS 0CL7	GROUP				
DNM=1-438	02	SALES-FILE-END	BL=3	000	DNM=1-438	DS 3C	DISP				
DNM=1-462	02	QUARTERLY-TOTAL	BL=3	003	DNM=1-462	DS 4P	COMP-3				
DNM=2-000	01	WORKING-REPORT-LINE	BL=3	008	DNM=2-000	DS 0CL139	GROUP				
DNM=2-032	02	WORKING-NAME	BL=3	008	DNM=2-032	DS 15C	DISP				
DNM=2-054	02	FILLER	BL=3	017	DNM=2-054	DS 5C	DISP				
DNM=2-068	02	WORKING-TOTAL	BL=3	01C	DNM=2-068	DS 10C	NM-EDIT				
DNM=2-104	02	FILLER	BL=3	026	DNM=2-104	DS 5C	DISP				
DNM=2-118	02	WORKING-QUOTA	BL=3	02B	DNM=2-118	DS 10C	NM-EDIT				
DNM=2-154	02	FILLER	BL=3	035	DNM=2-154	DS 94C	DISP				

Fig. 4-5

Condensed Listings (CLIST)
(Background Needed: Assembler Language)

A *condensed listing* (CLIST) is useful when a programmer with knowledge of assembler language is attempting to locate a particular PROCEDURE DIVISION statement in a standard operating system termination dump (programmers with no knowledge of assembler can use the symbolic dump described in Section 4.8). The condensed listing gives the address within the object program for each PROCEDURE DIVISION verb.

EXAMPLE 4.20   Figure 4-6 shows a condensed listing produced by an IBM OS/VS COBOL compiler. It gives the compiler-generated line number, the verb name, and the object program address for each verb in the PROCEDURE DIVISION. The addresses are given in hexadecimal. The object program address for the COMPUTE verb on line 75 is 00086C (hexadecimal).

```
                                 CONDENSED LISTING

     56   OPEN      000662        58   MOVE      0006D0        59   PERFORM   0006DA
     60   PERFORM   0006F2        62   CLOSE     000718        64   STOP      00080E
     68   READ      000824        70   MOVE      000850        74   MOVE      000866
     75   COMPUTE   00086C        78   MOVE      000890        79   MOVE      0008AC
     80   WRITE     0008CE        82   PERFORM   000916
```

Fig. 4-6

4.8   Facilities for Termination and Dynamic Dumps (Nonstandard)

There are two types of dumps available for debugging in an IBM OS/VS COBOL environment: (1) standard operating system termination dumps and (2) COBOL *symbolic dumps*, which can be obtained either as termination dumps or dynamically. Standard operating system dumps require a rudimentary knowledge of hexadecimal notation and assembler language for their use. Symbolic dumps are designed for use by the COBOL programmer with little or no knowledge of assembler language topics.

The intent of this Outline is to acquaint the reader with the types of facilities available. Consult an appropriate instructor or vendor manual for details on how to obtain and use the various dumps available for your system.

Symbolic Dumps
(Background Needed: COBOL Only)

Symbolic dumps are designed for COBOL programmers with no knowledge of assembler language. Unlike standard operating system dumps, they can be printed if the program ABENDS or during normal program execution. Unfortunately, symbolic dumps are not available on all systems (in which case the COBOL programmer is forced to work with standard operating system termination dumps). When available, the programmer can request a symbolic dump by specifying the proper job control or command language statements. Consult an instructor and/or vendor manual for details. IBM OS/VS COBOL symbolic dumps provide the following information in a form readily interpreted by the COBOL programmer: (1) the compiler-generated line number of the statement which caused the ABEND, (2) a trace of the last few paragraphs executed just prior to the ABEND (the actual number of paragraphs traced can range from 1 to 99), and (3) the contents of the entire DATA DIVISION at the time the ABEND occurred. The DATA DIVISION contents are printed in DISPLAY form (as normal alphanumeric characters) and are labeled with their COBOL data names for easy identification.

When working with IBM OS/VS COBOL, care must be taken to recognize that specifying WITH DEBUGGING MODE in the SOURCE-COMPUTER paragraph *disables* the symbolic dump feature. WITH DEBUGGING MODE should not be specified if a dump is desired.

EXAMPLE 4.21   Figure 4-7 shows that portion of an IBM OS/VS COBOL symbolic dump which identifies the statement causing the ABEND. "CARD NUMBER" is the compiler-generated line number of this last statement executed. Since COBOL allows more than one verb per statement, "VERB NUMBER" indicates the particular verb within the statement. Thus "CARD NUMBER 000075/VERB NUMBER 01" identifies the *first* verb on line number 75 as the verb which caused the error.

```
    LAST CARD NUMBER/VERB NUMBER EXECUTED -- CARD NUMBER 000075/VERB NUMBER 01.
```

Fig. 4-7

```
                                           FLOW TRACE

DEBUGGIN 000067 000073 000067 000073 000067 000073 000067 000073 000067 000073
```

Fig. 4-8

EXAMPLE 4.22 Figure 4-8 shows that portion of an IBM OS/VS COBOL symbolic dump which gives a trace of the paragraphs executed just prior to the ABEND. In this case, the programmer has specified job control language statements requesting a trace of the last *10* paragraphs executed. The paragraphs are identified by the compiler-generated line number of the paragraph header. The last paragraph entered before the ABEND (which would be the last one appearing in the trace) begins on line 73; the paragraph executed prior to the last one begins on line 67; etc.

```
                         TYPE CODES USED IN SYMDMP OUTPUT
                CODE    MEANING
                A     = ALPHABETIC
                AN    = ALPHANUMERIC
                ANE   = ALPHANUMERIC EDITED
                D     = DISPLAY (STERLING NONREPORT)
                DE    = DISPLAY EDITED (STERLING REPORT)
                F     = FLOATING POINT (COMP-1/COMP-2)
                FD    = FLOATING POINT DISPLAY (EXTERNAL FLOATING POINT)
                NB    = NUMERIC BINARY UNSIGNED (COMP)
                NB-S  = NUMERIC BINARY SIGNED
                ND    = NUMERIC DISPLAY UNSIGNED (EXTERNAL DECIMAL)
                ND-OL = NUMERIC DISPLAY OVERPUNCH SIGN LEADING
                ND-OT = NUMERIC DISPLAY OVERPUNCH SIGN TRAILING
                ND-SL = NUMERIC DISPLAY SEPARATE SIGN LEADING
                ND-ST = NUMERIC DISPLAY SEPARATE SIGN TRAILING
                NE    = NUMERIC EDITED
                NP    = NUMERIC PACKED DECIMAL UNSIGNED (COMP-3)
                NP-S  = NUMERIC PACKED DECIMAL SIGNED
                *     = SUBSCRIPTED
```

```
                                 DATA DIVISION DUMP OF DEBUGGIN
      LOC     CARD   LV NAME                      TYPE    VALUE
              000015 FD SALES-FILE                QSAM    FILE: OPEN    ORGANIZATION: PHYSICAL SEQUENTIAL
                                                          LAST SUCCESSFUL I/O STMT: READ      FILE STATUS: 00
    10C184                              DCB       00000000 00000000 00000000 00000000   00000000 0510F6D0 00504000 0010FB20
    10C1A4                                        4610E44A 8010C14C 01084800 00717150   129AF18C 009AD000 00000001 08090050
    10C1C4                                        00000000 0010F9D0 0010F728 0010F6D8   00000050 00000000 00000000 00000000
              000025 01 SALES-RECORD
    10F6D8    000026 02 SALES-RECORD-NAME         AN      SMITH
    10F6E7    000027 02 SALES-RECORD-MONTH-1-SALES  ND-OT 3000.3*
                                                   (HEX)  F3F0F0F0 F340
    10F6ED    000028 02 SALES-RECORD-MONTH-2-SALES  ND-OT +****.*2
                                                   (HEX)  4040C7C1 D9C2
    10F6F3    000029 02 SALES-RECORD-MONTH-3-SALES  ND-OT +****.*5
                                                   (HEX)  C1C7C540 40F5
    10F6F9    000030 02 SALES-RECORD-QUOTA        ND-OT   +10000.00
    10F700    000031 02 FILLER                    AN
              000016 FD QUARTERLY-REPORT          QSAM    FILE: OPEN    ORGANIZATION: PHYSICAL SEQUENTIAL
                                                          LAST SUCCESSFUL I/O STMT: WRITE      FILE STATUS: 00
    10C2A0                              DCB       00000000 00000000 00000000 00000000   00000000 01104140 00844000 0010F9B8
    10C2C0                                        4610E44A 8010C268 00F40048 007170D0   929AF198 00000000 00000001 08090084
    10C2E0                                        00000000 0010F868 001041CC 001041CC   00000084 00000000 00000000 00000000
    104148    000037 01 QUARTERLY-REPORT-LINE     AN      JONES           $4,001.00       $60,000.00

              000041 01 SWITCHES-AND-TOTALS
    10C0B0    000042 02 SALES-FILE-END            AN      NO
    10C0B3    000043 02 QUARTERLY-TOTAL           NP-S    +04001.00
              000044 01 WORKING-REPORT-LINE
    10C0B8    000045 02 WORKING-NAME              AN      SMITH
    10C0C7    000046 02 FILLER                    AN
    10C0CC    000047 02 WORKING-TOTAL             NE      $4,001.00
    10C0D6    000048 02 FILLER                    AN
    10C0DB    000049 02 WORKING-QUOTA             NE      $60,000.00
    10C0E5    000050 02 FILLER                    AN

              END OF COBOL DIAGNOSTIC AIDS
```

Fig. 4-9

EXAMPLE 4.23 Figure 4-9 shows that portion of an IBM OS/VS COBOL symbolic dump which lists the contents of all DATA DIVISION items. The first part of the dump is a legend explaining abbreviations used to indicate the *type of data* stored in each data item. In this case, "A" indicates "alphabetic" data, "ANE" indicates "alphanumeric edited" data, etc. This is followed by a list of each DATA DIVISION item, along with its contents. The columns in the symbolic dump present the following information:

Column Heading	Information Given
LOC	The actual execution time address of the data item in memory (given in hexadecimal).
CARD	The compiler-generated line number of the statement where the data item was defined (in the original COBOL program).
LV	The level number of the item in the original COBOL program, but normalized to go 01, 02, 03, 04, etc. Thus original level numbers 01, 05, 10, 15 would appear as 01, 02, 03, 04 in the dump.
NAME	The name of the data item in the COBOL source program.
TYPE	The type of data stored in the data item. These abbreviations are explained in the legend which prefaces this part of the dump.
VALUE	The contents of the item at the time the fatal error occurred: (1) For *files*, the dump indicates whether the file is open or closed, the file organization, the last successfully executed I/O statement, and the FILE STATUS value associated with the file at the time of the error. The symbolic dump also includes operating system tables of information about the file (the "DCB"). This information is presented in hexadecimal notation, and a knowledge of advanced assembler language is required to make use of it. (2) For *data items*, the dump prints the contents of the item. If the current contents are valid for a particular data item, they are printed in an easy-to-read edited format. If the current contents are invalid, asterisks are printed in the invalid character positions and the data value is also shown in hexadecimal notation.

EXAMPLE 4.24 The following information about DATA DIVISION items can be obtained from the symbolic dump in Fig. 4-9:

SALES-FILE is a file (level "FD") defined on line 15 ("CARD 000015") of the COBOL program. In IBM OS/VS operating system terminology, it is a "QSAM" file ("TYPE" is "QSAM"). The file is currently "OPEN", and the file organization is "PHYSICAL SEQUENTIAL". The last successful I/O statement executed for the file was a "READ", and the FILE STATUS area for the file currently contains "00". The "DCB" information consists of a hexadecimal display of the "data control block" table, in which the operating system keeps much important information about the file. Interpretation of the DCB information requires an advanced knowledge of assembler language programming. DCB information is usually not needed to debug a COBOL program.

SALES-RECORD-NAME is an alphanumeric data item ("TYPE" is "AN") defined on line 26 of the COBOL program ("CARD" is "000026"). Its level number is immediately subordinate to SALES-RECORD ("LV" is "02", just below "01" for SALES-RECORD). It was located at memory address 10F6D8 (hexadecimal) within the executing object program (see "LOC" column in dump). At the time of the error, SALES-RECORD-NAME contained "SMITH" (see "VALUE" column).

WORKING-TOTAL is a numeric edited ("NE") item defined on line 47 of the COBOL program and assigned memory location 10C0CC (hexadecimal) at execution time. It is at (normalized) level 02, immediately subordinate to WORKING-REPORT-LINE. At the time of the error, it contained valid data equal to "$4,001.00".

SALES-RECORD-MONTH-2–SALES is a "numeric display overpunch sign trailing" item (see legend for TYPE "ND-OT"). It is defined on line 28 of the COBOL program and was assigned address 10F6ED (hexadecimal) during execution. It is immediately subordinate to SALES-RECORD. At the time of the error, it contained invalid data. This is indicated in the symbolic dump by the asterisks in " + * * * * . * 2". Since the data is invalid, the contents of the item are repeated (immediately below in the VALUE column) in hexadecimal notation: "4040C7C1 D9C2".

Standard Operating System Termination Dumps
(Background Needed: Assembler Language)

Standard IBM OS/VS operating system termination dumps are printed in hexadecimal notation and require at least a rudimentary knowledge of assembler language to read. The information in a condensed listing (CLIST) and data division map (DMAP) helps the programmer to relate the COBOL source program PROCEDURE DIVISION and DATA DIVISION items (respectively) to the information presented in the dump (see Problems 4.40 and 4.41).

When symbolic dumps are available, they are easier to use and hence make more productive debugging tools. If symbolic debugging aids are not provided, however, the programmer may be forced to learn how to use standard operating system dumps.

EXAMPLE 4.25 Figure 4-10 shows a portion of an IBM OS/VS operating system standard termination (ABEND) dump for a COBOL program. Addresses and memory contents are given in hexadecimal notation. A dump of this type requires use of a condensed listing and a data division map for proper interpretation. Methods for debugging COBOL programs using standard operating system dumps are beyond the scope of this Outline. Consult an appropriate instructor or vendor manual for details on your system.

```
(DUMP STARTS AT 10C010 -- NOT SHOWN) ...

10C080   00000000 00000000 00000000 00000000     00000000 00000000 F2F14BF4 F24BF0F4    *........................21.42.04*
10C0A0   C6C5C240 F1F76B40 F1F9F8F5 00000000     D5D64004 00100C00 E2D4C9E3 C8404040    *FEB 17. 1985....NO .....SMITH   *
10C0C0   40404040 40404040 40404040 405BF46B     F0F0F14B F0F04040 4040405B F6F06BF0    *          .4.001.00    .60.0*
10C0E0   F0F04BF0 F0404040 40404040 40404040     40404040 40404040 40404040 40404040    *00.00                          *
  .           .
  .           .
  .           .
10C560   00000000 00000000 00000000 00000000     00000000 00000000 00000000 00000000    *................................*
10C580   00104A30 001049A0 0010C0B0 00000000     00000000 0007192C 00000000 03000304    *................................*
10C5A0   405BF6F0 6BF0F0F0 4BF0F000 00000000     00000000 00000000 0010C85C 0010C928    * .60.000.00..............H...I.*
  .           .
  .           .
  .           .
10C6E0   6000C083 92406002 5800D244 5000D238     5800C024 5000D244 5810C018 07F15800    *..... ....K...K.......K......1..*
10C700   D2385000 D2445800 D24C5000 D23C5800     C0285000 D24C5820 C02CD502 6000C085    *K...K...K...K.......K.....N.....*
10C720   07825810 C01C07F1 5800D23C 5000D24C     5810C054 91101030 05504780 501AD501    *........1..K...K..............N.*
```

Fig. 4-10

Review Questions

4.1 List seven steps the programmer should carry out in order to implement the modules assigned to him or her.

4.2 Discuss two approaches to designing the internal logic of modules assigned to a programmer.

4.3 What is meant by top-down coding and testing?

4.4 Explain the use of program stubs.

4.5 Discuss three different sequences for top-down coding and testing.

4.6 When should test data be designed?

4.7 Give some guidelines for designing test data.

4.8 List five possible sources for test data.

4.9 Differentiate between testing and debugging.

4.10 Give a five-step procedure for testing/debugging.

4.11 Differentiate between syntax and logic errors.

4.12 Describe the two types of logic errors.

4.13 What two basic kinds of information are used to debug logic errors?

4.14 Differentiate between termination dumps and dynamic dumps.

4.15 Discuss the use of the following COBOL language features for debugging: (1) debugging lines, (2) DISPLAY, (3) READY/RESET TRACE, (4) ON, (5) EXHIBIT, and (6) USE FOR DEBUGGING DECLARATIVES.

4.16 What is meant by compiler options?

4.17 Discuss the use of the following compiler options for debugging: (1) cross-reference listings, (2) data division maps, and (3) condensed listings.

4.18 Explain the differences between standard operating system termination dumps and COBOL symbolic dumps.

4.19 What information is provided in IBM OS/VS COBOL symbolic dumps?

4.20 What type of skills/information are needed to make use of a standard operating system termination dump?

Solved Problems

4.21 Why must the programmer plan the design of internal module logic?

Just as modules can be coded and tested in different sequences, so they can be designed in different sequences. If the programmer is assigned modules A, B, and C, some of the possibilities are:

(1) Design, code and test A; then design, code, and test B; then design, code, and test C (design as you go).

(2) Design A, B, and C; then code and test A; then code and test B; then code and test C (design first, then code).

(3) Design A and B; then code and test A; then code and test B; then design, code, and test C (nothing wrong with this if it makes sense for the application).

The programmer should choose the approach which best fits the needs of the particular application.

4.22 Which of the following sequences for coding and testing the modules in Fig. 4-1 (Example 4.3) violate the top-down rule that no module should be coded until all modules on the path between it and the top-level module have been coded and debugged:

(1) A, B, E, C, G, F, H, D, I, J

(2) A, C, E, G, H, D, I, J, B, F

(3) A, B, E, F, C, I, J, G, H, D

(4) A, C, G, H, B, D, E, I, J, F

Sequences (1) and (4) obey the rule. Sequence (2) codes module E *before* module B, and thereby violates the rule. Sequence (3) codes modules I and J *before* module D, and thereby violates the rule.

4.23 Refer to sequence (4) from Problem 4.22. What program stubs (if any) would be needed for the coding and testing of each module in the list?

Module	Stub(s) Needed
A	B, C, D
C	G, H
G	H (since C calls both G and H)
H	None
B	E, F
D	I, J
E	F (since B calls both E and F)
I	J (since D calls both I and J)
J	None
F	None

4.24   Make up enough sets of test data to test all six logic paths through the module in Fig. 3-8 (Example 3.10). Use the decision tree from Fig. 4-2 (Example 4.8). Identify *which* path in Fig. 4-2 is being tested by each transaction.

Set 1 (tests path # 1):

```
OLD-BALANCE = 0, #-TRANSACTIONS = 0
```

Set 2 (tests path # 2):

```
OLD-BALANCE = 100.00, #-TRANSACTIONS = 1
TRANSACTION-CODE = "D", AMOUNT = 50.00
```

Set 3 (Tests paths # 3–6):

```
OLD-BALANCE = 100.00, #-TRANSACTIONS = 4
TRANSACTION-CODE = "D", AMOUNT = 50.00       (path # 4)
TRANSACTION-CODE = "C", AMOUNT = 100.00      (path # 6)
TRANSACTION-CODE = "C", AMOUNT = 150.00      (path # 5)
TRANSACTION-CODE = "D", AMOUNT = 50.00       (path # 3)
```

4.25   Comment on the following scenario: Wily Programmer was assigned to write a completely new version of an existing master-file update program (the changes were so major that the existing program could not be revised). Wily was quite pleased to realize that he need not design and create test data for this project. He was able to save time (which could better be spent on coding and debugging) by simply copying a "live" transaction file from the existing system to use for testing the modules in the new program.

Instead of saving time, Wily has caused himself needless difficulties. He should indeed make use of the live test data available, but at the *end* of the debugging process, not at the *beginning*. Test data should start out simple and slowly increase in complexity. When a module is able to handle simple test data, then and only then should more complicated test data be "thrown" at it. This allows debugging to proceed more efficiently, because bugs are more likely to pop up one at a time (which makes them easier to deal with) rather than all at once (which makes them harder to identify and correct). Time spent in carefully planning and creating test data is amply repaid in shorter debugging time. Testing with copies of live data is usually done in the final stages of implementation.

4.26   Give two examples of a fatal logic error detected by *hardware*.

(1)   Suppose a COBOL program overflows a table area (and destroys some machine language instructions which just happen to follow the table in memory). When the hardware attempts to execute these instructions (which have been erased), it is likely to encounter invalid machine language operation codes and/or operand addresses, and thus abort the user program.

(2) Suppose a COBOL program inputs data into a numeric field but does not bother to edit the field. If the input value is not a valid number, the machine language instructions which manipulate the field will attempt to process invalid data. Some hardware systems will detect this condition and abort the user program.

4.27 Give two examples of a fatal logic error detected by the *operating system*.

(1) Suppose a COBOL program attempts to READ from a file which was OPENed for OUTPUT only. The READ statement is actually translated into a call on the operating system for input services. The operating system would detect the contradiction and abort the program.

(2) Suppose a COBOL program attempts to READ from an input file which has already encountered the end-of-file (AT END) condition. When the machine language version of the READ statement calls the operating system for input services, the system will detect the error and abort the user program.

4.28 What type(s) of information would be most useful for debugging the two errors in Problem 4.26?

(1) A memory dump of the table and the areas following it in memory

(2) A memory dump of the field in question

4.29 What type of information would be most useful for debugging the two errors in Problem 4.27?

(1) A program trace showing what statements were executed (i.e., OPEN . . . OUTPUT and READ), together with a memory dump showing the status of the file in question (i.e., that it is opened for output only).

(2) Program trace information would show that the program attempted to execute a READ *after* the AT END routine was already invoked. A dump of FILE STATUS information might also be helpful.

4.30 What, if anything, is wrong with the following code?

```
      SOURCE-COMPUTER.  IBM-3081 WITH DEBUGGING MODE.
             .
             .
             .
      NOT-DEBUGGED-PARA.
            ADD 1 TO RECORDS-INPUT-COUNT
            READ SOME-INPUT-FILE
                AT END
                    MOVE "YES" TO END-INPUT-FILE-SW
D                   DISPLAY "JUST HIT END OF FILE WITH"
D                   DISPLAY "RECORDS-INPUT-COUNT= "
D                       RECORDS-INPUT-COUNT.
            IF A-RECORD-WAS-INPUT
                PERFORM EDIT-INPUT-RECORD
                PERFORM PROCESS-EDITED-RECORD
                PERFORM OUTPUT-RESULTS
             .
```

The difficulty here is that the period which marks the termination of the AT END clause of the READ statement is on a debugging line ("D" in column 7). When the program *appears* to be debugged and "WITH DEBUGGING MODE" is removed from the SOURCE-COMPUTER paragraph, the line

```
      "D ... RECORDS-INPUT-COUNT."
```

will no longer be considered part of the program (it will be treated as a comment). This causes the AT END clause to *include* the IF statement at the end of the paragraph, producing a syntax error since AT END clauses may only contain *imperative* statements. Moral: Make sure your program is correct both with and without all debugging lines.

4.31 Show how the DISPLAY statement can be used to trace what happens *inside* a paragraph.

```
        SOURCE-COMPUTER.   IBM-3081 WITH DEBUGGING MODE.
        .
        .
        .
        NOT-DEBUGGED-PARA.
    D       DISPLAY "ENTERING NOT-DEBUGGED-PARA"
            ADD 1 TO RECORDS-INPUT-COUNT
    D       DISPLAY "AFTER INCREMENTING RECORDS-INPUT-COUNT"
            READ SOME-INPUT-FILE
                AT END
                    MOVE "YES" TO END-INPUT-FILE-SW
    D                   DISPLAY "JUST HIT END OF FILE"
                .
    D       DISPLAY "AFTER READ STATEMENT"
            IF A-RECORD-WAS-INPUT
    D           DISPLAY "INSIDE IF STATEMENT—CALLING EDIT"
                PERFORM EDIT-INPUT-RECORD
    D           DISPLAY "BACK FROM EDIT—CALLING PROCESS"
                PERFORM PROCESS-EDITED-RECORD
    D               DISPLAY "BACK FROM PROCESS—CALLING OUTPUT"
                PERFORM OUTPUT-RESULTS
    D           DISPLAY "BACK FROM OUTPUT—END OF PARAGRAPH"
                .
```

4.32 Modify the IBM OS/VS COBOL input paragraph below so that a program trace of record processing is produced for every *fifth* record input.

```
        GET-NEXT-RECORD.
            READ INPUT-FILE
                AT END
                    MOVE "YES" TO END-FILE-SW
            .
```

The modified paragraph is shown below.

```
        MODIFIED-GET-NEXT-RECORD.
    D       ON 1 AND EVERY 5
    D           READY TRACE
    D       ELSE
    D           RESET TRACE
    D       .
            READ INPUT-FILE
                AT END
                    MOVE "YES" TO END-FILE-SW
            .
```

4.33	Show how the EXHIBIT statement could be used to dump the changes to the data items in the IBM OS/VS COBOL paragraph below:

```
NOT-DEBUGGED-PARA.
      ADD 1 TO RECORDS-INPUT-COUNT
      READ SOME-INPUT-FILE
          AT END
                MOVE "YES" TO END-INPUT-FILE-SW
          .
      IF A-RECORD-WAS-INPUT
          PERFORM EDIT-INPUT-RECORD
          PERFORM PROCESS-EDITED-RECORD
          PERFORM OUTPUT-RESULTS
          .
```

The dump is shown below.

```
  DUMP-NOT-DEBUGGED-PARA.
          ADD 1 TO RECORDS-INPUT-COUNT
D     EXHIBIT NAMED RECORDS-INPUT-COUNT
      READ SOME-INPUT-FILE
          AT END
                MOVE "YES" TO END-INPUT-FILE-SW
          .
D     EXHIBIT NAMED SOME-INPUT-RECORD END-INPUT-FILE-SW
      IF A-RECORD-WAS-INPUT
          PERFORM EDIT-INPUT-RECORD
          PERFORM PROCESS-EDITED-RECORD
          PERFORM OUTPUT-RESULTS
          .
```

4.34	In debugging a payoll program, it is discovered that the field YTD-FICA contains incorrect values for many records in the test data. Write a debugging DECLARATIVE which might help illuminate the source of the errors.

```
SOURCE-COMPUTER.  IBM-3081 WITH DEBUGGING MODE.
    .
    .
PROCEDURE DIVISION.
DECLARATIVES.
MONITOR-YTD-FICA SECTION.
      USE FOR DEBUGGING ON
          ALL REFERENCES OF YTD-FICA
      .
      DISPLAY "MONITORING YTD-FICA, DEBUG-ITEM IS "
              DEBUG-ITEM
      .
END DECLARATIVES.
```

4.35	The first run of a student's programming assignment appeared to get hung up in an infinite loop. Write a debugging DECLARATIVE which will help the student locate the problem.

```
SOURCE-COMPUTER.  IBM-3081 WITH DEBUGGING MODE.
        .
        .
        .
PROCEDURE DIVISION.
DECLARATIVES.
TRACE-EXECUTION SECTION.
        USE FOR DEBUGGING ON
                ALL PROCEDURES
            .
        DISPLAY "MONITOR EXECUTION OF EACH PARAGRAPH "
                DEBUG-ITEM
            .
END DECLARATIVES.
        .
        .
        .
```

4.36   Show what the debugging output from the DECLARATIVE in Problem 4.35 would look like.

See Fig. 4-11 for actual IBM OS/VS COBOL output.

```
00010           SOURCE-COMPUTER. IBM-3081 WITH DEBUGGING MODE.
   .               .
   .               .
00052           PROCEDURE DIVISION.
00053
00054           DECLARATIVES.
00055
00056           TRACE-EXECUTION SECTION.
00057
00058               USE FOR DEBUGGING ON
00059                   ALL PROCEDURES
00060                 .
00061               DISPLAY "MONITOR EXECUTION OF EACH PARAGRAPH"
00062                       DEBUG-ITEM
00063                 .
00064           END DECLARATIVES.
00065
00066           010-PRODUCE-QUARTERLY-REPORT.
00067
00068               OPEN  INPUT  SALES-FILE
00069                     OUTPUT QUARTERLY-REPORT
00070               MOVE "NO" TO SALES-FILE-END
00071               PERFORM 020-READ-SALES-FILE
00072               PERFORM 030-PRINT-REPORT-LINES
00073                   UNTIL SALES-FILE-END = "YES"
00074               CLOSE  SALES-FILE
00075                      QUARTERLY-REPORT
00076               STOP RUN
00077                 .
00078
00079           020-READ-SALES-FILE.

00080               READ SALES-FILE
00081                   AT END
00082                       MOVE "YES" TO SALES-FILE-END
00083                 .
00084
00085           030-PRINT-REPORT-LINES.

00086               MOVE SALES-RECORD-NAME TO WORKING-NAME
00087               COMPUTE QUARTERLY-TOTAL =     SALES-RECORD-MONTH-1-SALES
00088                                         +   SALES-RECORD-MONTH-2-SALES
00089                                         +   SALES-RECORD-MONTH-3-SALES
00090               MOVE QUARTERLY-TOTAL TO WORKING-TOTAL
00091               MOVE SALES-RECORD-QUOTA TO WORKING-QUOTA
00092               WRITE QUARTERLY-REPORT-LINE
00093                   FROM WORKING-REPORT-LINE
00094                 .

---------------- ACTUAL OUTPUT FOLLOWS -----------------

MONITOR EXECUTION OF EACH PARAGRAPH000068 010-PRODUCE-QUARTERLY-REPORT          START PROGRAM
MONITOR EXECUTION OF EACH PARAGRAPH000071 020-READ-SALES-FILE                   PERFORM LOOP
MONITOR EXECUTION OF EACH PARAGRAPH000072 030-PRINT-REPORT-LINES                PERFORM LOOP
MONITOR EXECUTION OF EACH PARAGRAPH000072 030-PRINT-REPORT-LINES                PERFORM LOOP
MONITOR EXECUTION OF EACH PARAGRAPH000072 030-PRINT-REPORT-LINES                PERFORM LOOP
MONITOR EXECUTION OF EACH PARAGRAPH000072 030-PRINT-REPORT-LINES                PERFORM LOOP
MONITOR EXECUTION OF EACH PARAGRAPH000072 030-PRINT-REPORT-LINES                PERFORM LOOP
MONITOR EXECUTION OF EACH PARAGRAPH000072 030-PRINT-REPORT-LINES                PERFORM LOOP
MONITOR EXECUTION OF EACH PARAGRAPH000072 030-PRINT-REPORT-LINES                PERFORM LOOP
MONITOR EXECUTION OF EACH PARAGRAPH000072 030-PRINT-REPORT-LINES                PERFORM LOOP
```

Fig. 4-11

4.37 Write debugging DECLARATIVE(s) for a master-file update program which (1) is not correctly counting the number of delete transactions processed and (2) appears to be adding a (new) record to the file when it should be changing an existing record.

```
            SOURCE-COMPUTER.   IBM-3081 WITH DEBUGGING MODE.
            .
            .
            .
            PROCEDURE DIVISION.
            DECLARATIVES.
            MONITOR-DELETE-COUNT SECTION.
                 USE FOR DEBUGGING ON
                      ALL REFERENCES OF DELETED-RECORDS-COUNTER
                 .
                 DISPLAY "MONITORING DELETED-RECORDS-COUNTER: "
                      DEBUG-ITEM
                 .
            MONITOR-WRONG-ADDS SECTION.
                 USE FOR DEBUGGING ON
                      ADD-NEW-RECORD-PARA
                 .
                 DISPLAY "MONITORING PROCESSING OF RECORD ADDITIONS: "
                 EXHIBIT NAMED  TRANSACTION-RECORD
                                TRANSACTION-CODE
                 DISPLAY "DEBUG-ITEM IS " DEBUG-ITEM
                 .
            END DECLARATIVES.
            .
            .
            .
```

4.38 Show the portions of a cross-reference listing which may be relevant to the bugs in Problem 4.37.

A cross-reference listing makes it easy to locate the COBOL statements in which data items and/or paragraphs are defined and referenced. This can save time and help eliminate oversights during debugging. The cross-reference entries below indicate that DELETED-RECORDS-COUNTER is defined on line 75 and referenced on lines 150, 273, 381, and 569, while ADD-NEW-RECORD-PARA is defined on line 240 and referenced on lines 188, 391, and 407.

```
            DATA NAMES              DEFN      REFERENCE
            . . .                   . . .     . . .
            DELETED-RECORDS-COUNTER 0075       0150   0273   0381   0569
            .                       .          .
            .                       .          .
            .                       .          .
            PROCEDURE NAMES         DEFN      REFERENCE
            . . .                   . . .     . . .
            ADD-NEW-RECORD-PARA     0240      0188   0391   0407
```

4.39 Refer to the data division map in Fig. 4-5 to answer the following questions:

(*a*) What is the internal name for QUARTERLY-TOTAL?

(*b*) What is its normalized level number?

(*c*) What item(s) is it subordinate to?

(*d*)   Which base locator has been assigned to QUARTERLY-TOTAL?

(*e*)   What displacement is associated with QUARTERLY-TOTAL?

(*f*)   How would QUARTERLY-TOTAL be defined in assembler language terms?

(*g*)   What usage is associated with QUARTERLY-TOTAL?

(*a*)   "DNM = 1-462" is the internal name by which QUARTERLY-TOTAL is referred to within the compiler and in syntax error messages.

(*b*)   The normalized level number is "02".

(*c*)   QUARTERLY-TOTAL at normalized level number 02 is subordinate to SWITCHES-AND-TOTALS at normalized level number 01.

(*d*)   The "BASE" column for QUARTERLY-TOTAL reads "BL = 3", indicating that it has been assigned the *third* base locator in the program.

(*e*)   The "DISPL" column shows a value of "003". This means that QUARTERLY-TOTAL is located 3 bytes (character positions) beyond the address in base locator three.

(*f*)   The DEFINITION column indicates that QUARTERLY-TOTAL would be defined as "DS 4P". This indicates a "4-byte packed decimal" field in IBM 370-type assembler language.

(*g*)   The USAGE for QUARTERLY-TOTAL is "COMP-3" (i.e., packed decimal in IBM OS/VS COBOL).

4.40   *The following problem requires the ability to interpret IBM OS/VS termination dumps.* Show how to find a data item in a standard IBM OS/VS termination dump by locating WORKING-NAME using Figs. 4-5, 4-10, and 4-12.

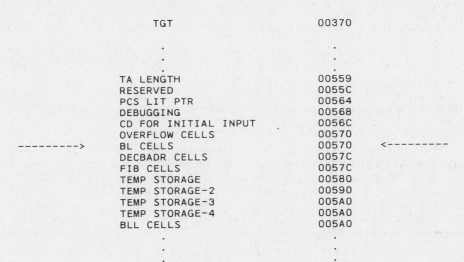

```
                    TGT                      00370

                     .                        .
                     .                        .
                     .                        .
                    TA LENGTH                 00559
                    RESERVED                  0055C
                    PCS LIT PTR               00564
                    DEBUGGING                 00568
                    CD FOR INITIAL INPUT      0056C
                    OVERFLOW CELLS            00570
        --------->  BL CELLS                  00570   <---------
                    DECBADR CELLS             0057C
                    FIB CELLS                 0057C
                    TEMP STORAGE              00580
                    TEMP STORAGE-2            00590
                    TEMP STORAGE-3            005A0
                    TEMP STORAGE-4            005A0
                    BLL CELLS                 005A0
                     .                        .
                     .                        .
                     .                        .
```

Fig. 4-12

In addition to the dump itself, one needs the task global table (TGT) portion of a data division map (DMAP) as shown in Fig. 4-12. The following procedure assumes that the reader is capable of interpreting OS/VS termination dumps:

(1)   Determine the relocation factor from the dump (the relocation factor for the dump partially depicted in Fig. 4-10 is 10C010 hexadecimal).

(2)   Locate the "BL CELLS" in the TGT portion of the DMAP. The BL CELLS are marked with an arrow in Fig. 4-12. Remember the DMAP address assigned to the BL CELLS (00570 in Fig. 4-12).

(3)   Locate the SOURCE NAME for the data item in the DMAP. Remember the base locator ("BASE") and displacement ("DISPL") assigned to the item (WORKING-NAME is assigned base locator 3 [BL = 3] and displacement 008 in Fig. 4-5).

(4) Multiply the base locator number (from step 3) by 4, then subtract 4 from the product; e.g., if "BL = 01", compute (01 ∗ 4) − 4 = 0; if "BL = 02", compute (02 ∗ 4) − 4 = 4; etc. (since BL = 03 for WORKING-NAME, compute [03 ∗ 4] − 4 = 8 decimal).

(5) Add the product (from step 4) to the address of the BL CELLS (from step 2). This gives the DMAP address of the desired base locator (for WORKING-NAME, add decimal 8 to hexadecimal 00570, giving 00578 hexadecimal).

(6) Add the DMAP address of the desired base locator (from step 5) to the relocation factor (from step 1). This gives the dump address for the needed base locator (for WORKING-NAME, add hexadecimal 00578 to hexadecimal 10C010, giving hexadecimal 10C588).

(7) Find the base locator in the termination dump (it will be a 4-byte field) and remember its contents (the 4-byte field at address 10C588 in Fig. 4-10 contains 0010C0B0).

(8) Add the contents of the desired base locator (from step 7) to the DMAP displacement assigned to the data item (from step 3). This sum is the dump address for the actual data item (add hexadecimal 10C0B0 from step 7 to displacement 8 from step 3, giving 10C0B8 hexadecimal).

(9) Using the address from step 8, find the data item in the dump. Note that if the length of the data item is not already known, it can be determined either from the DMAP or from the definition of the item in the COBOL program (Fig. 4-5 indicates that WORKING-NAME is a 15-byte item; locating the 15 bytes at 10C0B8 in the dump, we find E2D4C9E3 C8404040 40404040 404040, which is the EBCDIC code representation for "SMITH").

4.41 *The following problem requires the ability to interpret IBM OS/VS termination dumps.* Show how to locate a PROCEDURE DIVISION statement in an IBM OS/VS termination dump by finding the PERFORM statement on line 60 of the program whose condensed listing is shown in Fig. 4-6. Use the dump in Fig. 4-10.

In addition to the dump itself, one needs a condensed listing (CLIST) as shown in Fig. 4-6.

(1) Locate the desired statement in the condensed listing. Remember the CLIST address assigned to the item (the PERFORM statement on line 60 is assigned address 0006F2 hexadecimal).

(2) Determine the relocation factor from the dump (the relocation factor for the partial dump in Fig. 4-10 is 10C010 hexadecimal).

(3) Add the CLIST address (from step 1) to the relocation factor (from step 2). This gives the dump address for the desired statement (adding 0006F2 hexadecimal to 10C010 hexadecimal gives 10C702 hexadecimal).

(4) Using the address from step 3, locate the desired statement in the dump (the translation of the PERFORM statement begins . . . 5000 D2445800 D24C5000 etc.).

4.42 Refer to the DATA DIVISION and IBM OS/VS COBOL symbolic dump shown in Fig. 4-13 to answer the following questions:

(a) What is the PROGRAM-ID of the program in Fig. 4-13?

(b) What *verb* in the original COBOL source program caused the fatal error which initiated the dump?

(c) What are the line numbers of the last three paragraphs executed prior to the fatal error (ABEND)?

(d) Was PRINT-FILE open at the time of the ABEND?

(e) What was the last successful I/O statement for CARD-FILE?

(f) What are the contents of the FILE-STATUS area for PRINT-FILE?

(g) What address was assigned to LISTING-SALES-ID for this program run?

(h) In what line of the program is LISTING-SALES-ID defined?

(i) What is the level number of LISTING-SALES-ID in the original COBOL program?

(j) What is the normalized level number shown for LISTING-SALES-ID in the dump?

```
00021          DATA DIVISION.

00023          FILE SECTION.

00025      FD  CARD-FILE
00026          RECORD CONTAINS 80 CHARACTERS
00027          LABEL RECORDS ARE OMITTED
00028          .
00029
00030      01  SALES-CARD-INPUT        PIC X(80).
00032      FD  PRINT-FILE
00033          RECORD CONTAINS 132 CHARACTERS
00034          LABEL RECORDS ARE OMITTED
00035          .
00036
00037      01  PRINT-LINE              PIC X(132).

00039          WORKING-STORAGE SECTION.

00041      01  END-OF-CARDS-SWITCH     PIC X(3).

00043      01  WORKING-SALES-CARD.
00044
00045          05  WORKING-SALES-ID       PIC X(4).
00046          05  WORKING-CUSTOMER-ID    PIC X(5).
00047          05  WORKING-SALES-AMOUNT   PIC 9(5).
00048          05  FILLER                 PIC X(66).

00050      01  SALES-LISTING-LINE.
00051
00052          05  LISTING-SALES-ID       PIC X(4).
00053          05  FILLER                 PIC X(5)      VALUE SPACES.
00054          05  LISTING-CUSTOMER-ID    PIC X(5).
00055          05  FILLER                 PIC X(5)      VALUE SPACES.
00056          05  LISTING-SALES-AMOUNT   PIC 9(5).
00057          05  FILLER                 PIC X(108)    VALUE SPACES.

00059      01  SALES-TOTAL-LINE.
00060
00061          05  FILLER                 PIC X(18)
00062                                     VALUE "TOTAL SALES IS".
00063          05  TOTAL-SALES            PIC 9(6).
00064          05  FILLER                 PIC X(108)    VALUE SPACES.


------------------ ACTUAL SYMBOLIC DUMP OUTPUT ----------------

                     COBOL ABEND DIAGNOSTIC AIDS

PROGRAM        SALELIST
LAST PSW BEFORE ABEND = FF850007D010C986     SYSTEM COMPLETION CODE = 0C7
LAST CARD NUMBER/VERB NUMBER EXECUTED -- CARD NUMBER 000097/VERB NUMBER 01.
                              FLOW TRACE
SALELIST 000087 000095 000087 000095 000087 000095 000087 000095
                         TYPE CODES USED IN SYMDMP OUTPUT
                CODE      MEANING
                A       = ALPHABETIC
                AN      = ALPHANUMERIC
                ANE     = ALPHANUMERIC EDITED
                D       = DISPLAY (STERLING NONREPORT)
                DE      = DISPLAY EDITED (STERLING REPORT)
                F       = FLOATING POINT (COMP-1/COMP-2)
                FD      = FLOATING POINT DISPLAY (EXTERNAL FLOATING POINT)
                NB      = NUMERIC BINARY UNSIGNED (COMP)
                NB-S    = NUMERIC BINARY SIGNED
                ND      = NUMERIC DISPLAY UNSIGNED (EXTERNAL DECIMAL)
                ND-OL   = NUMERIC DISPLAY OVERPUNCH SIGN LEADING
                ND-OT   = NUMERIC DISPLAY OVERPUNCH SIGN TRAILING
                ND-SL   = NUMERIC DISPLAY SEPARATE SIGN LEADING
                ND-ST   = NUMERIC DISPLAY SEPARATE SIGN TRAILING
                NE      = NUMERIC EDITED
                NP      = NUMERIC PACKED DECIMAL UNSIGNED (COMP-3)
                NP-S    = NUMERIC PACKED DECIMAL SIGNED
                *       = SUBSCRIPTED
                         DATA DIVISION DUMP OF SALELIST

                         DATA DIVISION DUMP OF SALELIST
 LOC      CARD   LV NAME                     TYPE    VALUE
          000018 FD CARD-FILE                QSAM    FILE: OPEN    ORGANIZATION: PHYSICAL SEQUENTIAL
                                                     LAST SUCCESSFUL I/O STMT: READ     FILE STATUS: 00
10C254                               DCB     00000000 00000000 00000000 00000000    00000000 0510F6D0 00504000 0010FB20
10C274                                       4610E512 8010C21C 00CC4800 00715150    129AF18C 009AD000 00000001 08090050
10C294                                       00000000 0010F9D0 0010F728 0010F6D8    00000050 00000000 00000000 00000000
10F6D8    000030 01 SALES-CARD-INPUT         AN      2222CCCCCBAD

          000019 FD PRINT-FILE               QSAM    FILE: OPEN    ORGANIZATION: PHYSICAL SEQUENTIAL
                                                     LAST SUCCESSFUL I/O STMT: WRITE     FILE STATUS: 00
10C370                               DCB     00000000 00000000 00000000 00000000    00000000 01104140 00844000 0010F9B8
10C390                                       4610E512 8010C338 00E00048 007150D0    929AF198 00000000 00000001 08090084
10C3B0                                       00000000 0010F868 001041CC 001041CC    00000084 00000000 00000000 00000000
104148    000037 01 PRINT-LINE               AN      2222    AAAAA    00300


10C0B0    000041 01 END-OF-CARDS-SWITCH      AN      NO
          000043 01 WORKING-SALES-CARD
10C0B8    000045 02 WORKING-SALES-ID         AN      2222
10C0BC    000046 02 WORKING-CUSTOMER-ID      AN      CCCCC
10C0C1    000047 02 WORKING-SALES-AMOUNT     ND      *****
                                            (HEX)    C2C1C440 40
10C0C6    000048 02 FILLER                   AN

          000050 01 SALES-LISTING-LINE
10C108    000052 02 LISTING-SALES-ID         AN      2222
10C10C    000053 02 FILLER                   AN
10C111    000054 02 LISTING-CUSTOMER-ID      AN      AAAAA
10C116    000055 02 FILLER                   AN
10C11B    000056 02 LISTING-SALES-AMOUNT     ND      00300
10C120    000057 02 FILLER                   AN

          000059 01 SALES-TOTAL-LINE
10C190    000061 02 FILLER                   AN      TOTAL SALES IS
10C1A2    000063 02 TOTAL-SALES              ND      000600
10C1A8    000064 02 FILLER                   AN


                     END OF COBOL DIAGNOSTIC AIDS
```

Fig. 4-13

90

(k)   According to the dump, what type of data is contained in LISTING-SALES-AMOUNT?

(l)   What were the contents of LISTING-SALES-ID at the time of the error?

(m)   What were the contents of TOTAL-SALES at the time of the error?

(n)   Did any data item(s) contain *invalid* data at the time of the error? If so, give the contents of the item(s) in hexadecimal notation.

(o)   The dump indicates that the cause of the fatal error was "SYSTEM COMPLETION CODE = 0C7". Given that on IBM OS/VS systems "0C7" indicates an attempt to manipulate an invalid numeric field, what is the probable cause of the error and how could it be corrected?

(a)   The PROGRAM-ID is given at the beginning of the symbolic dump. In Fig. 4-13 it is SALELIST.

(b)   The "LAST CARD NUMBER/VERB NUMBER EXECUTED" indicates that the *first* verb ("VERB NUMBER 01") on line number 97 ("CARD NUMBER 000097") is the one causing the error.

(c)   The "FLOW TRACE" indicates the line numbers of the paragraphs executed just prior to the fatal error. In Fig. 4-13, the *last* paragraph entered begins on line 95, the *next to last* on line 87, and the *third* prior to the error was again on line 95.

(d)   The dump indicates that PRINT-FILE was *open* at the time of the fatal error ("FILE: OPEN").

(e)   The last successful I/O statement for CARD-FILE was a READ.

(f)   The FILE STATUS area for PRINT-FILE contains "00".

(g)   LISTING-SALES-ID was assigned address 10C108 (hexadecimal); see the "LOC" column in the dump.

(h)   LISTING-SALES-ID is defined on line 52 of the original program.

(i)   On line 52 of the original program, the level number for LISTING-SALES-ID is 05.

(j)   In the dump, the normalized level number for LISTING-SALES-ID is 02. Normalized means that the level numbers are adjusted to count by 1, i.e., 01, 02, 03, etc.

(k)   The TYPE column for LISTING-SALES-AMOUNT is "ND". The meaning of this code is given in the legend near the beginning of the dump (labeled "TYPE CODES USED IN SYMDMP OUTPUT"). "ND" abbreviates "NUMERIC DISPLAY UNSIGNED (EXTERNAL DECIMAL)".

(l)   LISTING-SALES-ID contained "2222" at the time of the error. This is shown in the "VALUE" column of the dump.

(m)   According to the VALUE column, TOTAL-SALES contained "000600" at the time of the error.

(n)   The contents of WORKING-SALES-AMOUNT appear in the dump as "* * * * * *". Since the asterisks are used to mark *invalid data*, this field must have been invalid at the time of the error. The actual contents of the field appear (in hexadecimal) immediately below the asterisks in the value column. WORKING-SALES-AMOUNT contained "C2C1C440 40" (hexadecimal).

(o)   Since WORKING-SALES-AMOUNT contains invalid numeric data, any use of it in the program (e.g., in the calculation of TOTAL-SALES) would result in an "0C7" fatal error. The real question is how it is possible for WORKING-SALES-AMOUNT to contain invalid data without the program being aware of it. The program should be rewritten to validate its input so that invalid data is detected and screened from processing. If a COBOL program is carefully designed to validate all input fields which might contain invalid data, it is impossible for the program to ABEND because of faulty data.

Chapter 5

Auxiliary Storage Devices
and File Processing

The main memory of a computer system cannot be used to permanently store data which is not currently being processed because (1) main memory is *volatile* (i.e., contents are lost if power is interrupted) and (2) main memory is never large enough to hold all the data for even small businesses. *Auxiliary storage devices* provide large-capacity, permanent storage for information *outside* of processor memory. Since auxiliary storage devices are attached to the computer system's processor as input/output devices, they provide the capability to (1) *input* information needed for processing from auxiliary storage into main memory (where it can be manipulated) and then (2) *output* any modified information from main memory back to auxiliary storage for permanent keeping.

The type of auxiliary storage device chosen to hold the information in a given file will help determine what kind of processing is possible for that file. There are two major types of auxiliary storage device in use today: tape and disk. We first describe how these devices are attached to the computer system.

5.1 Relation Between Auxiliary Storage Devices and the Processor

In medium- to large-scale systems, I/O devices are usually not directly attached to the processor. Typically, several I/O devices are attached to a control unit. The *control unit* oversees device operation and handles such functions as error detection/correction, etc. While one device is carrying out an order issued to it by the control unit, the control unit is often free to issue orders to still other attached devices, thus allowing *overlap* of device function.

Control units, in turn, are attached to channels. *Channels*, sometimes called "I/O processors", are small, special-purpose computers which handle the task of moving data into and out of the processor's main memory. Several control units are typically attached to each channel, and the channel is usually capable of operating more than one of these simultaneously, again providing overlap of input/output functions.

Each channel operates independently of the CPU, allowing I/O activity to proceed simultaneously with the execution of instructions by the CPU. This *I/O-compute overlap* allows the system as a whole to process more work. If a channel and the CPU need simultaneous access to main memory, the channel is given priority. This is called *cycle stealing* (the channel "steals a memory cycle" from the CPU).

The complex operation of channels, control units, and devices is ultimately controlled by the *operating system software* running in the processor. The machine language translations of COBOL "READ" and "WRITE" statements do *not* directly manipulate channels, etc. In reality, these statements call the operating system to *request* the needed I/O services, and the operating system carries them out. The COBOL programmer might think of the OPEN, CLOSE, READ, WRITE, and REWRITE statements as super-sophisticated PERFORM statements which call operating system routines to carry out I/O services. The operating system software automatically handles all the details.

EXAMPLE 5.1 Figure 5-1 diagrams the relationships between the hardware and software elements involved in large-system input/output.

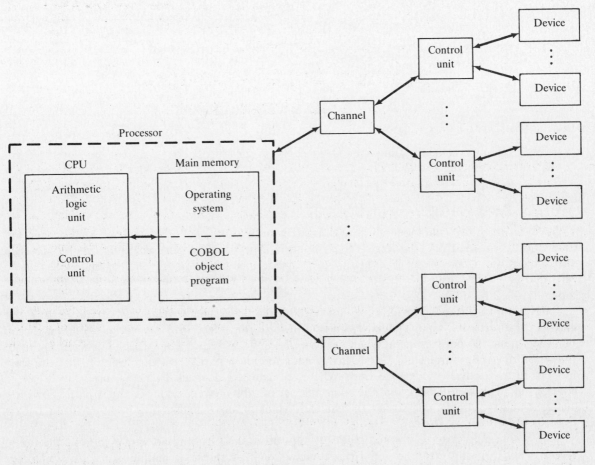

Fig. 5-1

5.2 Auxiliary Storage: Sequential Access Devices—Magnetic Tape

Magnetic tape used for auxiliary storage comes packaged in a variety of forms analogous to those found in home audio recording (e.g., reels, cartridges, and cassettes). Information (encoded in a binary form) is recorded on the tape magnetically, with selected spots on the tape representing either a binary 1 or 0, depending on the magnetic state of the spot. Unless the tape is physically destroyed or magnetically erased, it will retain this information indefinitely.

Information is read or written on the tape by a special device called a *tape drive*, the exact form of which depends on the type of tape to be used (e.g., reel or cartridge). The tape drive is typically attached to the computer system as an input/output device.

The generic term for a reel of tape (or cassette, etc.) is a *volume*. Note that a single drive can have different volumes mounted on it at different times. Thus one drive can accommodate many volumes, so long as it is not necessary to access more than one volume at a time. If *simultaneous* access is needed, then multiple drives are required (simultaneous access to three different volumes requires three tape drives, etc.).

Limitations on Processing Magnetic-Tape Files

Because of the design of magnetic-tape media, it is only practical to process tape files *sequentially*. This means that the records in a file must be processed in the order in which they are physically placed on the tape (first record first, second record second, etc.). While it is possible to program the tape drive to search for desired records in a random order, this would take much too long for almost all applications.

Since tape is restricted to *sequential access*, it is unsuitable for use in applications which require interactive, real-time, or transaction-oriented processing. Its low cost, however, still makes tape attractive for (1) applications which require only sequential processing (e.g., most payroll systems) and (2) making *backup copies* of files on other types of auxiliary storage devices. Backup is fast becoming the major use for tape in modern data processing.

Characteristics of Magnetic Tape

This Outline presents the fundamental concepts of reel-to-reel tape systems. Characteristics for cartridges and cassettes are analogous.

Track and Parity Concepts

Data is recorded on tape a byte (character) at a time. The bits in each given byte are magnetically encoded on a vertical "slice" of tape. The positions for recording bits within each vertical section of tape are called *tracks*. Most tapes today are *9-track*, meaning that 9 bits can be recorded in each vertical slice. Earlier tapes were 7-track, allowing 7 bits in each vertical section of tape.

Modern 9-track tapes provide room for an 8-bit data character (byte), plus a ninth *parity bit* in each vertical section of tape. The parity bit is used for error detection. Either *even* or *odd* parity can be used. In an odd parity system, when an 8-bit data byte is output from the processor to the tape, the tape drive (or control unit) automatically adds the ninth parity bit in such a way that the total number of 1 bits in all 9 tracks is odd. Whenever data is read back from the tape, the drive (or control unit) checks to ensure that the total number of 1 bits remains odd. If not, a *parity error* has occurred and the control unit signals the channel, which in turn signals the processor that the data is in error.

Most operating systems will automatically reposition the tape and attempt to reread the faulty record when a parity error occurs. Errors due to dust or transient malfunctions are sometimes automatically corrected in this manner. Automatic retry of failed I/O operations is carried out by the operating system and is transparent to the COBOL program.

In addition to the *vertical parity bit* described above, most tape drives also append a *horizontal parity bit* on each track at the end of a record. These 9 parity bits form an extra parity byte (character) which is tacked onto the end of the data. Horizontal parity enhances error-detection capabilities, making the probability of an undetected error extremely low.

EXAMPLE 5.2   Figure 5-2 shows how data could be recorded on a 9-track tape using EBCDIC code and odd parity. The ninth track here is used for vertical parity. Note also the horizontal parity bits forming an extra byte at the end of the data area.

| | Characters Represented | | | | | | | | Horizontal parity bits |
Track Number	A	1	B	2	C	3	D	4	
1	1	1	1	1	1	1	1	1	1
2	1	1	1	1	1	1	1	1	1
3	0	1	0	1	0	1	0	1	1
4	0	1	0	1	0	1	0	1	1
5	0	0	0	0	0	0	0	0	1
6	0	0	0	0	0	0	1	1	1
7	0	0	1	1	1	1	0	0	1
8	1	1	0	0	1	1	0	0	1
9	0	0	0	0	1	1	0	0	1

← Vertical parity bits

Fig. 5-2

Density and Data Transfer Rate

Tape drives differ in the *density* at which they can record data along the length of the tape. Density is measured in *bytes per inch* (*BPI*). Since one EBCDIC or ASCII character can be recorded in an 8-bit byte (9 with parity), bytes per inch is equivalent to *characters per inch* (*CPI*).

As tape technology improves, commercially available densities constantly increase. Drives in common use today operate at 800, 1600, and 6250 BPI. Often a given drive can be programmed to operate at different densities, depending on the needs of the application.

The recording density, together with the speed at which the tape moves past the read/write heads, determines the rate at which data can be read or written on the tape. The *data transfer rate* varies depending on drive model, but is on the order of 320 to 1250 bytes per millisecond (ms) for current drives.

Tape-Drive Operation and Interrecord Gaps

The following scenario describes the transfer of 100 bytes of data from the processor to the tape:

(1)   Since tape motion stops between operations, initially the tape is stopped in the drive.

(2)   At the start of the output operation, the drive must first bring the tape up to writing speed. The time required to do this depends on the particular model of tape drive. The distance traveled before the tape is up to proper speed forms a blank area on the tape known as a *gap*.

(3)   The 100 bytes of data are now magnetically encoded on the tape at the current density. Vertical and horizontal parity bits are also automatically encoded on the tape.

(4)   At the end of the write operation, the tape mechanism must stop the tape in the drive. The distance traveled during braking forms a blank area following the data.

(5)   The tape is now stopped and is ready for the next write operation.

The blank area produced between data areas is known as an *interrecord gap* (*IRG*) or *interblock gap* (*IBG*). The exact size of the gap varies with the drive model, but is on the order of 0.5 in.

The total time spent in (1) starting the tape prior to writing or reading a record and then (2) stopping it after the data transfer is complete is known as the *start/stop time*. It, too, varies with drive model, but is on the order of 1.5 ms.

Some companies manufacture tape drives which are designed solely to back up other types of auxiliary storage devices. Such *streamer tapes* do *not* start and stop during normal operation.

Blocking

In order to minimize (1) space wasted in interrecord gaps, and (2) start/stop time during file processing, records are usually recorded on tape in a *blocked* format. In an *unblocked* file, each record is separated from the other records in the file by interrecord gaps. This means that the tape must be started, then stopped, to read or write *each* record in the file.

EXAMPLE 5.3   Calculate the length of tape required to hold a file of five thousand 200-byte records at 1600 BPI density, if the file is unblocked:
At 1600 BPI, a 200-byte record requires 200/1600 or 0.125 in of tape. In an unblocked file, each such record will be followed by an IRG. Assuming a gap size of 0.5 in, the space required for a record and its gap is (0.5 + 0.125) or 0.625 in. Thus 5000 such records would require (5000 * 0.625) or 3125 in (260.4 ft) of tape.

EXAMPLE 5.4   Calculate the time required to read the entire file in Example 5.3:
Assume the data transfer rate is 320 bytes per ms and the start/stop time is 1.5 ms. It requires 200/320 = 0.625 ms to actually transfer one 200-byte record, and 1.5 ms to start and stop the tape before and after the transfer. The total time for one record is thus (0.625 + 1.5) or 2.125 ms. The time required for all 5000 records is then (5000 * 2.125) or 10,625 ms (*10.625 s*).

Blocking refers to the practice of placing more than one record (now called a *logical record*) between gaps. The *blocking factor* is the number of logical records in a block (or *physical record*).

The operating system automatically handles the assembling (blocking) of logical records into physical records (blocks) during output, and the disassembling (deblocking) of physical records (blocks) into separate logical records during input. Thus COBOL programs are always written to process *logical* records (i.e., a READ always inputs a logical record and a WRITE always outputs a logical record), and blocking is transparent to the COBOL program. Blocking/deblocking requirements are specified to the operating system via job control or command language statements.

EXAMPLE 5.5   Figure 5-3 contrasts blocked and unblocked tape files.

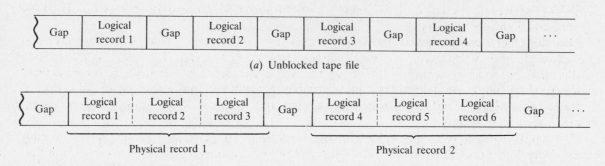

(*a*) Unblocked tape file

(*b*) Blocked file with blocking factor of 3

Fig. 5-3

Increasing the blocking factor decreases the number of interblock gaps required for a given file, thus saving space on the tape. Similarly, increasing the blocking factor decreases the number of tape start/stops required to process all logical records, thus decreasing the total time required to process the file.

EXAMPLE 5.6   Calculate the length of tape required for the file in Example 5.3 if a blocking factor of 10 is used:

With 10 logical records per block, each block is (10 * 200) or 2000 bytes. At 1600 BPI density, each block requires 2000/1600 or 1.25 in of tape. Further, each block will have a 0.5-in gap following it, for a total of (1.25 + 0.5) or 1.75 in per block. However, since there are 10 logical records per block, a file of 5000 logical records will consist of only 5000/10 or 500 blocks. Thus the total length of tape required is (500 * 1.75) or 875 in (73 ft) of tape, a savings of 2250 in (188 ft, or 72 percent) over the unblocked file.

EXAMPLE 5.7   Calculate the time required to process the file from Example 5.6.

Since each block is now 2000 bytes long, it takes 2000/320 or 6.25 ms to transfer one block, plus 1.5 ms for start/stop time, giving a total of (6.25 + 1.5) or 7.75 ms per block. With 500 blocks in the file, the total time for the entire file is (500 * 7.75) or 3875 ms (*3.875 s*), a savings of 6.75 s (64 percent) over the unblocked case.

Since tape drives are only capable of inputting or outputting an entire block (physical record) at a time, the operating system must have enough memory available to hold at least one entire block for each open file. The amount of available memory thus limits the blocking factor which can be used for a given application.

5.3   Auxiliary Storage: Direct Access Storage Devices—Magnetic Disk

Direct access storage devices (DASD) are a class of auxiliary storage devices which permit *both* sequential and random processing within an acceptable time limit. The ability to retrieve and update data in a matter of milliseconds makes direct access devices ideal for interactive, real-time, or transaction-oriented applications, as well as traditional batch systems. This Outline describes magnetic disk storage devices, currently the most popular form of direct access storage.

Magnetic Disk Concepts

There are two main types of magnetic disk: (1) hard disks and (2) floppy disks. Both types come in a variety of packages and sizes, but in all cases data is recorded magnetically in a binary format on the disk surface.

The hard-disk medium is usually called a *disk pack* and consists of one or more oxide-coated, rigid aluminum platters stacked next to one another on a central spindle (like a stack of phonograph records). The number and size of the platters varies from model to model, as does the speed of operation and storage capacity.

The floppy-disk medium consists of a single oxide-coated, nonrigid plastic platter enclosed in a protective plastic envelope. The two most popular sizes for floppy disks are 8 in and 5.25 in (the smaller disks are sometimes referred to as *minifloppies*). Depending on the model, floppy disks may be *double sided* (both sides of the plastic platter used to record data) or *single sided* (only one surface available for data recording), and recording can be done at *single* or *double density*, thus affecting storage speed and capacity.

The actual device which reads and writes data is known as a *disk drive*. There are many different types, depending on the disk medium used, etc. Unlike tape, the disk does not start and stop in the drive. During normal operation, the disk medium (pack or floppy) is constantly rotating. An *access mechanism* housing a set of *read/write heads* (typically one for each surface) moves in and out along the surfaces of the medium. The generic term for a disk pack, floppy disk, or its equivalent is a *volume*.

Magnetic Disk Operation

Each surface of a disk platter (i.e., top and bottom) is divided into concentric circles called *tracks*. Data (encoded in a binary form) is magnetically recorded around each track, with selected spots on the track representing either a binary 1 or 0, depending on the magnetic state of the spot. Unless a volume is physically destroyed or magnetically erased, it will retain its information indefinitely. As with tape, physical records are separated from one another on a track by IRGs.

A set of tracks immediately above and below one another forms a *cylinder*. Single-sided floppy disks have one track per cylinder; double-sided floppies have two tracks per cylinder (the track from the top surface and the corresponding track from the bottom surface); hard disks have a varying number of platters and therefore a varying number of tracks per cylinder. For reasons indicated below, space for disk files is allocated in terms of cylinders [rather than from tracks along the same surface(s)].

EXAMPLE 5.8   Figure 5-4 illustrates track and cylinder concepts for a typical hard-disk pack.

Most disk drives include a movable access mechanism, which contains one read/write head for every surface. The access mechanism is capable of positioning the read/write heads to any cylinder. Note well that the read/write heads always move together, so that if head 0 is positioned to track 7 of its surface, all other heads are simultaneously positioned to track 7 of their respective surfaces. This means that if *one* head is positioned to a track in a given cylinder, *all* heads are simultaneously positioned to that cylinder. Thus the remaining tracks in the cylinder can be accessed without further movement. This is why disk space is always organized in terms of cylinders rather than surfaces.

EXAMPLE 5.9   Figure 5-5 shows a *post-type* access mechanism in relation to its disk pack. The post-type mechanism moves laterally in and out between the surfaces. Some disks use a *swing-type* access mechanism, which pivots the read/write heads in to the desired track position. Regardless of the details, the purpose of the access mechanism is to position the read/write heads to the desired cylinder.

(a)   Top view of disk surface showing tracks

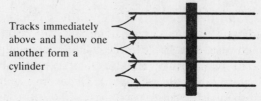

Tracks immediately
above and below one
another form a
cylinder

(b)   Side view of disk pack showing cylinder concept

Fig. 5-4

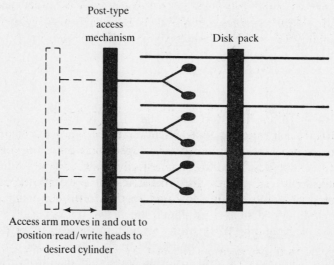

Access arm moves in and out to
position read/write heads to
desired cylinder

Fig. 5-5

In order to access a physical record on disk, the following hardware operations must take place:

(1)   The access mechanism must be moved to the cylinder containing the desired record. The *access time* varies from 0 ms (if the access mechanism is already at the desired cylinder) to the maximum time required to move from one edge of the pack to the opposite edge. Typically, an average figure is used for timing estimates. For example, an IBM 3350 disk has an average access time of 25 ms, while an IBM 3380 has an average access time of 16 ms. Access time is often called *seek* time (after the channel command used to program a disk to move the access mechanism). Note that the operating system must *know* the desired cylinder in order to initiate the seek operation.

(2)   The proper read/write head must be switched on. *Head switching* takes place at electronic speeds and is usually ignored in timing estimates. Note, however, that the operating system must *know* which head (track) of the cylinder contains the desired record.

(3)   The disk must now wait for the desired record to spin under the read/write head (the reader will recall that the disk pack is constantly rotating inside the drive). *Rotational delay* can range from 0 ms (if the desired record happens to be right under the head when it is switched on) to an entire rotation. Again, an average figure is used for timing estimates. An IBM 3350 disk has an average access time of 8.4 ms, while an IBM 3380 disk has an average access time of 8.3 ms. Note that the operating system (and the drive) must be able to identify *which* record on the track is to be accessed. Rotational delay is often called *search* time (after the channel command used to program this operation on a disk).

(4)   After the desired physical record has been located, actual data transfer can occur. The data transfer rate of an IBM 3350 is 1198 bytes/ms, while that of an IBM 3380 is 3000 bytes/ms. The *data transfer time* depends on the size of the physical record being read or written.

When making timing estimates in a multiprogramming environment, the phenomenon of head interference must be taken into account. *Head interference* occurs when two different programs in the multiprogramming mix are both accessing the same disk and are "interfering" with one another with respect to the positioning of the access mechanism. When head interference is a possibility, it is usually best to use average figures for timing estimates. Head interference can often be minimized by careful planning when assigning files to disks.

EXAMPLE 5.10   Suppose program A accesses file X and program B accesses file Y, and that programs A and B are run (i.e., multiprogrammed) at the same time. Head interference is *maximized* if files X and Y are located far from one another on the *same* disk. Head interference is *minimized* if files X and Y are placed on *separate* disks. The same considerations can be applied to the assignment of control units and channels (i.e., files X and Y might be assigned different control units and/or channels to minimize interference and thereby optimize throughput/response).

Types of Hard Disk

The most important variations in hard disks are described below:

(1)   Removable disk packs: *Removable disks* permit the current pack to be removed from the disk drive and replaced with a different pack. This allows one drive to accommodate many different packs, so long as simultaneous access is not needed. The current trend is away from removable packs, since they can not be engineered to the capacities and speeds of other types of hard disk and their exposure to the environment during removal reduces reliability.

(2)   Removable data modules: *Data modules* consist of a disk pack together with an access mechanism sealed in a plastic case to protect them from the environment. A data module can be removed from a given drive and replaced with another module. Manufacturers offer a variety of sealed media, providing a compromise between reliability, capacity, speed, and removability.

(3)   Fixed disk: With *fixed-disk* technology, the recording medium is *permanently* built into the disk drive and can not be removed. Fixed-disk engineering can provide faster access speeds and larger capacity, as well as increased reliability over removable media. Fixed disks can not be removed and replaced with other packs, but in a modern environment where many files need to be constantly online, this becomes relatively unimportant. The current trend is away from removable media in favor of fixed disks.

(4)   Fixed head disks: *Fixed head disks* are fixed (i.e., nonremovable) disks with a *permanent read/write head built over every track*, thus eliminating the typical movable access mechanism. Since access mechanism movement is the slowest part of accessing a disk record, fixed head disks are much faster than other types of disks. The engineering of a permanent read/write head for every track (rather than one movable head for every surface which can move to any desired track on that surface) does, however, increase the cost of this type of disk.

(5) Combination of fixed and movable heads: Some manufacturers provide a compromise between speed and cost by offering nonremovable disks with fixed heads for some of the tracks and a movable access mechanism for the remaining tracks. Files with very fast access requirements can be placed on the fixed head portion of the pack (e.g., heavily used disk-resident portions of the operating system).

Track Formats and Capacity

Track format refers to the way in which data is organized on a track. There are currently two important track formats: (1) sector (or fixed-block) architecture and (2) conventional (or variable-block) architecture.

Fixed-block architecture divides each track into a fixed number of fixed-size areas called *sectors*. The operating system must then "package" logical records into physical records equal to the sector size. This can result in some wasted space at the end of each sector if the operating system does not permit logical records to be split between sectors.

Fixed-block disks can be either *hard-* or *soft*-sectored. Hard-sectored disks *physically* mark sector locations on each track, thus permanently fixing the sector size. Soft-sectored disks *magnetically* mark sector locations, thus allowing the sector size to be changed by operating system programming. In either case, the sector size determines a fixed maximum capacity which is independent of the size of the physical records placed on the disk.

Sectors are sometimes identified (addressed) by assigning each sector on the pack a unique number (starting with 0). In other schemes, each cylinder is assigned a unique address (starting with 0), each read/write head is assigned a unique address (starting with 0), and the sectors on each track are numbered (starting with 0). Sectors are then identified by specifying the *combination* of cylinder number, (read/write) head number, and sector number.

Conventional architecture allows each track to be divided into a variable number of areas of variable size. This requires extra information to indicate the size of each physical record. In such designs, the maximum capacity of a disk depends on the size of the physical records placed on it.

A common track format for conventional architecture is count-data/count-key-data format. In this format, each physical record is preceded on the track by a *count field* and an (optional) *key field*. The count contains information about the size of the physical record, and the key contains data which uniquely identifies it on the track.

EXAMPLE 5.11 Following is a layout of a track using *count-data* format:

$$\langle IP \rangle \; G \; \langle HA \rangle \; G \; \underbrace{\langle count \rangle \; G \; \langle data \rangle}_{Record\ 0} \; G \; \underbrace{\langle A \rangle \; G \; \langle count \rangle \; G \; \langle data \rangle}_{Record\ 1} \; G \ldots$$

Explanation of areas:

(1) $\langle IP \rangle$ is the *index point*, a physical marker (e.g., a hole) indicating the beginning of each track.

(2) G indicates a *gap*. Gaps separate the various areas on the track and provide time for necessary hardware functions. The sizes of the gaps vary, depending on the function of the gap (i.e., a gap following a count area is different in size from a gap following a data area).

(3) $\langle HA \rangle$ is the *home address*. It contains the address of the track (in the form cylinder number/head number, written CCHH) and a flag indicating whether the track is operational or defective. Disks usually include "extra" cylinders which can be used to assign *alternate tracks* if a track becomes defective (see below).

(4) Under IBM OS/VS systems, "record 0", also known as the *track descriptor record* ($R0$), is used for two purposes: (1) if a track is defective, R0 of the defective track contains the address (CCHH) of the alternate track assigned to replace the defective one; (2) if a track is operational, R0 contains information indicating the amount of free space remaining on the track. R0 is written and maintained by the operating system and is not available for user data.

(5) ⟨A⟩ indicates the *address marker*, which precedes each count area (except R0). Address markers allow the control unit to locate the beginning of each count-data group on the track.

(6) A *count area* precedes each physical record on the track. It consists of (1) the record *identifier* (*ID*), which contains a cylinder number, head number, and record number, written CCHHR (record numbers start with 0); (2) the *key length*, which indicates the length of the optional key area (always 0 for count-data format); and (3) the *data length*, which indicates the length in bytes of the data area following the count area.

(7) The *data area* holds an actual physical record. If the file is unblocked, the data area holds *one* logical record; if the file is blocked, the data area holds *several* logical records.

EXAMPLE 5.12 Here is the layout of a track using *count-key-data* format:

$$⟨IP⟩ \; G \; ⟨HA⟩ \; G \; \underbrace{⟨count⟩ \; G \; ⟨data⟩}_{\text{Record 0}} \; G \; \underbrace{⟨A⟩ \; G \; ⟨count⟩ \; G \; ⟨key⟩ \; G \; ⟨data⟩}_{\text{Record 1}} \; G \ldots$$

The index point, home address, record 0, gaps, and address markers are the same in both count-data and count-key-data formats. In count-*key*-data format, however, user record areas (beginning with record 1) have an additional *key* field between the count and data areas. The key field is used to hold values which uniquely identify the contents of each data area. The exact definition of the key depends on the particular file, e.g., an account number, employee number, customer number, part number, etc.—The important thing is that it be able to uniquely identify logical records.

When the file is *unblocked*, each key area contains the identifying key value (e.g., account number) for the logical record in the data area it precedes. When the file is *blocked*, each key area usually contains the highest key value among the logical records in the block.

The "key length" field in the count area is nonzero in count-key-data format. It contains the length (in bytes) of the key area.

Error checking on disk is done using error detection/correction codes known as *cyclic check codes*. This scheme not only provides more sophisticated error detection than the parity systems used with tape but actually allows certain data errors to be corrected. In the case of an uncorrectable data error, most operating systems will automatically retry the operation several times before giving up.

EXAMPLE 5.13 The home address, count, key, and data areas in Examples 5.11 and 5.12 all end with several bytes of *cyclic check characters*, which are used for error detection/correction. Whenever data is being written, the control unit automatically calculates the cyclic check bytes and appends them to the end of the area in question. When an area is input later on, the control unit recalculates the cyclic check value from the input bits and compares the result with the cyclic check characters read from the disk. If the two values agree, no error is detected. If they disagree, the control unit *may* be able to correct the error; if not, it signals the channel (which in turn signals the CPU) that an error has occurred.

Physical records in conventional track formats can be located (addressed) by either:

(1) Cylinder number/head number/record number (available with both count-data and count-key-data formats, written CCHHR). To access the record, the access mechanism must first move to the indicated cylinder (this relatively time-consuming step is unnecessary for fixed head disks) and then switch on the indicated head. The disk then orients itself by locating the next address marker to spin under the head. As each count area spins under the head, its record identifier (containing a CCHHR value) is compared to the specified CCHHR. When a match is found, the corresponding data area can be read or written.

(2) Cylinder number/head number/key (available only with count-key-data format, written CCHH-key). In this case, the access mechanism must first move to the indicated cylinder (this relatively time-consuming step is unnecessary for fixed head disks) and then switch on the indicated head. The disk then orients itself by locating the next address marker to spin under the head. As each key area spins under the head, it is compared to the specified key value. When a match is found, the corresponding data area can be read or written.

In both cases (1) and (2), an entire physical record is always transferred between memory and the disk. When input records are blocked, the operating system must search the *physical* record just input to locate the desired *logical* record.

Count-data format is normally used for files which will only be accessed sequentially. Once the starting CCHHR is known, all physical records can easily be retrieved by incrementing the record number (and head number and cylinder number) until the end of the file is reached. There is thus no need for key areas and their attendant gaps.

Count-key-data format is normally used for files which are sometimes accessed randomly. In this case, the operating system must know the (1) cylinder number, (2) head number, and (3) key for the desired physical record. Since user input usually supplies the key value, the system need only determine the cylinder and head numbers. If count-data format were used, the operating system would have to determine the cylinder number, head number, and record number for the key given by the user—a more formidable task.

Disk Timing and Storage Calculations

Most business programs require far more time for I/O than for executing instructions in the CPU; i.e., they are *I/O bound*. The total I/O time is thus a good estimate of the *run time* for a typical batch business program. Likewise, the I/O time required to process a transaction is a good estimate of the *response time* in an interactive environment. The ability to estimate I/O time is thus important to the business programmer/analyst.

It is also important to be able to calculate how much disk space is needed to hold a given file; in real life, auxiliary storage is an expensive resource which must be allocated effectively. This section illustrates timing and storage calculations for typical disk processing. Observe the effects of blocking on time and space requirements for disk files.

EXAMPLE 5.14   Calculate the number of tracks required to hold a file of 8000 unblocked 300-byte records on an IBM 3350 disk. The file is formatted in count-key-data format with 8-byte keys.

According to IBM specifications, the number of count-key-data physical records per 3350 track is $19,254/(185 + 82 + KL + DL)$, where 19,254 is the track capacity, $(185 + 82)$ accounts for gaps, KL is the key length, and DL is the data length (i.e., the length of a physical record). For this file, $KL = 8$ and $DL = 300$; thus

$$\text{Number-physical-records-per-track} = \frac{19,254}{185 + 82 + 8 + 300} = 33.49$$

Since records are usually not split between tracks, this result must be *truncated* to 33 physical records per track. With an unblocked file there is one logical record per physical record, thus the number of tracks required is $8000/33 = 242.4$. Since a track is usually not shared between files, this number must be *rounded up* to *243 complete tracks* (with 30 tracks per cylinder on a 3350, this is $243/30 = 8.1$, which must be rounded up to 9 cylinders).

EXAMPLE 5.15   Illustrate how blocking can save disk space by recalculating Example 5.14 for a blocking factor of 10.

With a blocking factor of 10, each physical record is $(300 * 10) = 3000$ bytes. Thus there will be $19,254/(185 + 82 + 8 + 3000) = 5.9$, truncated to 5 physical records per track. Each physical record holds 10 logical records, so there are $5 * 10 = 50$ logical records per track. Thus 8000 logical records require $8000/50 = 160$ *tracks* (or $160/30 = 5.3$, rounded to 6 cylinders), a savings of 83 tracks (3 cylinders, or 34 percent).

EXAMPLE 5.16   Illustrate the importance of choosing a good blocking factor by improving the blocking factor in Example 5.15.

The blocking factor of 10 in Example 5.15 "wastes" 0.9 of a physical record at the end of each track. An optimum blocking factor will (1) minimize wasted space at the end of each track while (2) also minimizing space wasted in gaps. The following table shows the number of logical records per track for the file in Example 5.14 for various blocking factors. Note that bigger is not always better.

Blocking Factor	Number of Logical Records per Track
4	52
5	50
6	54
7	56
8	56
9	54
10	50
11	55
12	48
13	52

A blocking factor of *7 or 8* would be best for this file. Note that a blocking factor of 12 would be a particularly *bad* choice.

EXAMPLE 5.17   Show the effect of formatting the file in Example 5.14 in count-data format (i.e., without keys).

Without keys, the number of physical records on a 3350 track is given by the equation $19,254/(185 + DL) = 19,254/(185 + 300) = 39.6$, which is truncated to 39 physical records per track. Without blocking, 8000 logical records require $8000/39 = 205.1$, rounded to *206 tracks*. The reader will recall that the same file in count-key-data format required 243 tracks. The difference is this large because the small 8-byte key areas are followed by 82-byte gaps.

EXAMPLE 5.18   Assume the file in Example 5.14 occupies contiguous cylinders. Estimate the minimum time required to process the entire file sequentially and without head interference.

Access time:	There would be an average seek (25 ms) to position to the first cylinder, then eight minimum seeks (10 ms each) to reach the remaining eight contiguous cylinders, for a total of 105 ms.
Rotational delay:	Assuming an average rotational delay for each physical record, in the unblocked case we have $(8000 * 8.4 \text{ ms}) = 67,200 \text{ ms}$.
Data transfer:	At 1198 bytes/ms, each 300-byte physical record requires $300/1198 = 0.25$ ms. Since there are 8000 physical records, data transfer for the entire file requires $(8000 * 0.25 \text{ ms}) = 2000 \text{ ms}$.

The estimated total time for 8000 records is then $(105 + 67,200 + 2000) = 69,305 \text{ ms} = 69.305 \text{ s}$.

EXAMPLE 5.19   Show how blocking significantly reduces sequential processing time by recalculating Example 5.18 for a blocking factor of 10 (refer to the results from Example 5.15).

Access time:	There would be an average seek (25 ms) to position to the first cylinder, then five minimum seeks (10 ms each) to reach the remaining five contiguous cylinders, for a total of 75 ms.
Rotational delay:	With 10 logical records per block, there are $8000/10 = 800$ blocks. Assuming an average rotational delay for each physical record, we have $(800 * 8.4 \text{ ms}) = 6720 \text{ ms}$.
Data transfer:	At 1198 bytes/ms, each 3000-byte physical record requires $3000/1198 = 2.5$ ms. Since there are 800 physical records, data transfer for the entire file requires $(800 * 2.5 \text{ ms}) = 2000 \text{ ms}$.

The estimated total time for 8000 logical records is then $(75 + 6720 + 2000) = 8795 \text{ ms} = 8.795 \text{ s}$ (a difference of 60.51 s or 87 percent). The major savings is in reduced rotational delay.

EXAMPLE 5.20   For the unblocked file in Example 5.14 (1) show how well the file would serve an interactive application by estimating the time required to randomly access a single record, and (2) estimate the time required for a batch program to randomly access the entire file.

The following assumes that the operating system already knows the cylinder and head numbers for a desired record. In reality, extra disk accesses are often required to obtain this information, thus slowing record processing (see Problem 5.61).

(1)   To randomly access a single record for which the CCHH is already known requires (1) an average access time (25 ms), (2) an average rotational delay (8.4 ms), and (3) data transfer $300/1198 = 0.25$ ms. The I/O time required to access one record is thus *33.65 ms*.

(2)   To randomly process the entire file requires a random access as in (1) above for each record, or $(8000 * 33.65) = 269,200$ ms $= 269.2$ s. Observe that random file processing takes much longer than sequential processing.

EXAMPLE 5.21   Illustrate how blocking slightly slows random file processing by recalculating Example 5.20 for a blocking factor of 10:

(1)   Everything is the same as in Example 5.20, except that to access a single *logical* record the operating system must input or output an entire *physical* record (which actually consists of *10* logical records). Thus data transfer is $(10 * 300)/1198 = 2.5$ ms, and the I/O time is *35.9 ms* (a difference of 2.25 ms for processing a single logical record).

(2)   With random processing, it is very unlikely that the *next* logical record needed will be in the same physical record as the *current* logical record being processed (i.e., the operating system inputs an entire block, but the COBOL program usually processes only *one* logical record in that block). Thus the system will have to access a physical record for nearly every logical record in the file. The estimated file processing time is the number of logical records times the result from (1) above, or $(8000 * 35.9) = 287,200$ ms $= 287.2$ s (only 18 s slower than for the unblocked case, possibly a small price to pay for the significant savings in disk space).

5.4   File Labels and the Volume Table of Contents/Directory

Tape File Labels

Although optional, tape file labels are generally used since they help guard against operator error during tape processing. Label records are automatically created and maintained by the operating system in response to job control/command language statements.

Each tape reel has reflective strips marking the physical beginning and end of the reel. The first record following the start of a labeled tape is the *volume label*, which contains the *name* of the reel (*volume serial number*). Whenever the tape is processed, the operating system automatically checks the name in the volume label against the name specified by the programmer via job control/command language. If the names do not match, the system assumes that the operator has mounted the wrong tape in the drive. This can prevent the possibility of a costly disaster.

Each file on a labeled tape is preceded and followed by *header* and *trailer* labels containing such things as (1) the file name, (2) the logical record length, (3) the blocking factor, (4) the type of records (i.e., fixed- or variable-length), and (5) security information such as *passwords* required to access the file and an *expiration date* indicating when the file may be deleted. The trailer label also includes a count of the number of physical records in the file. Trailer labels are provided mainly because some tape drives have the capability of reading backward (in which case the trailer label is encountered first).

The operating system uses file labels to (1) position the tape to the correct file in the case of *multifile tapes* and (2) obtain descriptive information about the file to be processed. Label processing is done automatically by the operating system when a file is opened (this includes creation of file labels for a new file).

File and volume labels are separated from each other and from data records by a special character known as a *tape mark* (*TM*). Since tape drives are capable of forward and backward spacing to the next tape mark, the operating system can quickly locate any desired label on a multifile tape.

EXAMPLE 5.22   Following is the layout of a typical multifile tape (spaces shown are for readability only). Note that ⟨TM⟩ stands for a tape mark; it separates labels and marks the end of a file. G represents an interblock gap; it follows each area on the tape.

⟨reflective strip at start of reel⟩ ⟨volume label⟩ G ⟨TM⟩ G

⟨header label file 1⟩ G ⟨TM⟩ G ⟨block 1.1⟩ G ⟨block 1.2⟩ G ... G
⟨last block file 1⟩ G ⟨TM⟩ G ⟨trailer label file 1⟩ G ⟨TM⟩ G

⟨header label file 2⟩ G ⟨TM⟩ G ⟨block 2.1⟩ G ⟨block 2.2⟩ G ... G
⟨last block file 2⟩ G ⟨TM⟩ G ⟨trailer label file 2⟩ G ⟨TM⟩ G

... ⟨reflective strip at end of reel⟩

Disk File Labels and the Volume Table of Contents (Directory)

Disk file labels are always *required*. When a new disk is installed on a system, an operating system *utility program* must be run to format or initialize the pack. This utility program creates a *volume label* at a fixed location on the pack. The volume label contains the name (volume serial number) of the pack (volume) and the disk address of a special operating system file known as the *volume table of contents* (*VTOC*) or *directory*.

When a file is created on a disk, the operating system generates a new *file label* in the VTOC. The file label contains the same information found in tape file labels, plus the location and size of the file on the disk. In addition to holding a file label for every file, the VTOC also has a *free-space* label, which contains the location and size of every free area on the disk. Space for new files is allocated from this free-space entry. When a file is deleted, its file label is erased from the VTOC and the space occupied by the file is put back in the free-space entry.

Space allocated for disk files need not be *contiguous* (i.e., from adjacent tracks and cylinders). A set of contiguous tracks is known as an *extent*. The operating system always attempts to allocate contiguous space (i.e., one extent) if possible, but if not it will allocate space in separate extents. The file labels in the VTOC describe each extent allocated to each file.

When a file is *opened*, the operating system automatically creates file labels for new files and processes file labels for existing files. Since the space occupied by a file may change during file processing (as records are added and deleted), the operating system may also automatically update the file label when the file is *closed*. To *find* a file on a disk, the operating system must first find its file label in the VTOC. The file label then gives the location of the file itself.

EXAMPLE 5.23   Figure 5-6 shows the relationships between the volume label, VTOC, and user files on a typical disk pack.

5.5   File Processing Concepts

Types of File Operations

There are four basic file operations.

(1) *Creation*: Producing a brand new file and loading logical records into it.

(2) *Retrieval*: Inputting logical records from a file in order to obtain the data they hold.

(3) *Updating* or *maintenance*: Keeping the logical records in a file up to date. File maintenance consists of three separate operations on logical records:

   (*a*) Record *deletion*: Logically or physically deleting logical records from the file.

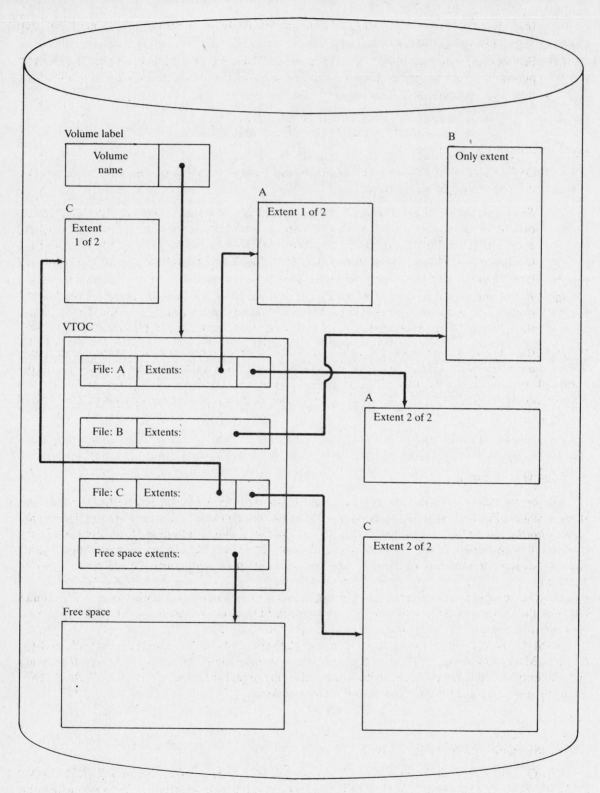

Fig. 5-6

(b) Record *insertion* or *addition*: Adding new logical records to the file (after the file has already been created).

(c) Record *change* or *updating*: Changing the contents of logical record fields to keep them current and correct.

(4) File *copying* for backup and reorganization: Making copies of a file either for backup purposes or to reorganize the file to make access more efficient and/or to reclaim space taken up by logically deleted records, etc.

File Processing (Access) Modes

COBOL is built around the concept of processing logical records *one at a time*. There are two fundamental processing or access modes:

(1) *Sequential access*: Logical records are processed one at a time, according to their physical order on the auxiliary storage device—first record first, second record second, etc. An *end-of-file* condition occurs when an attempt is made to READ a logical record *after* the last record has already been input. Files to be processed sequentially can be placed on any type of input/output or auxiliary storage device.

(2) *Random access*: Logical records are processed one at a time in an order determined by the program, e.g., 10th logical record first, 253d logical record second, 75th logical record third, etc. Files to be processed randomly must be stored on a direct access storage device.

In certain circumstances, COBOL also allows a mixture of sequential and random processing. With *dynamic access*, a program can randomly select a logical record from any position within the file, and then continue sequentially processing logical records from that point on. With this type of access, sequential and random processing can be repeated and intermixed in any desired manner.

5.6 File Organizations

File organization refers to the way in which logical records are organized within the auxiliary storage space allocated to a file. Certain file organizations also store extra information (*secondary information*) used to help locate individual logical records. File organizations differ not only in the amount of extra storage (if any) needed for secondary information but also in the types of processing (i.e., sequential or random) which they allow and in the speed with which logical records can be accessed.

The choice of file organization is a critical decision for every computer application. It determines not only the storage overhead and the processing speed but also the type of record processing (i.e., sequential or random or both) which is possible for the file.

ANSI COBOL defines three standard file organizations: (1) sequential, (2) indexed, and (3) relative. Most versions of COBOL offer these three organizations, but the way in which they are actually implemented varies. Many vendors also offer file organizations which are *extensions* to ANSI COBOL, and thus are unique to each particular vendor.

5.7 ANSI Standard File Organizations

This Outline covers the three ANSI file organizations as they are implemented in IBM OS/VS COBOL, plus several IBM OS/VS COBOL nonstandard file organizations. We first define the standard organizations.

(Physical) Sequential Organization

Sequentially organized files can be placed on any type of auxiliary storage device. They can only be processed sequentially. The file contains only logical records (no secondary information). Sequential files are often called "physical sequential" to avoid confusion with "indexed sequential files" (see below).

See *Schaum's Outline of Programming with Structured COBOL* (McGraw-Hill, 1984) for a thorough discussion of sequential file organization in COBOL.

Indexed Organization

Indexed files *must* be placed on direct access devices. They may be processed either sequentially or randomly. Sequential processing retrieves logical records in ascending order, according to a predefined *key* field which uniquely identifies each logical record (e.g., customer number, part number, etc.). Logical records are identified by the same key when processed randomly.

Indexed files contain both data records and *index records*, which associate each logical record key with the location of the corresponding logical record. Random processing involves looking up the key for a desired record in the index, which then gives the location of that particular record. The index searching can involve extra disk accesses, thus slowing random processing.

Relative Organization

Relative files are viewed as a series of fixed-length record slots (any of which may be empty or may contain a logical record) on a direct access storage device. The slots are numbered 1, 2, 3, etc., and are identified by this *record number* during random processing. Sequential processing of each slot (in record number order) is also possible.

The operating system is able to calculate the disk address directly from the record number, so relative file processing is faster than indexed file processing (which requires an index search). However, most applications naturally identify logical records by *key* (e.g., account number) rather than *record number*. Thus the use of relative file organization often requires that the programmer develop some scheme which will associate logical record key values with record number locations. Since the index of an indexed file does this automatically, indexed organization is usually chosen over relative organization (unless speed requirements absolutely dictate use of relative files).

5.8   Introduction to IBM OS/VS COBOL File Organizations

(Physical) Sequential Organization

In IBM terminology, a portion of the operating system which processes a particular file organization is known as an *access method*. Since sequential files are processed by the *Queued Sequential Access Method*, they are often referred to as *QSAM* files. QSAM implements ANSI sequential files, which are thoroughly discussed in *Schaum's Outline of Programming with Structured COBOL* (McGraw-Hill, 1984).

Indexed Sequential Organization

The access method which processes indexed sequential files is known as ISAM. *ISAM* was an earlier implementation of ANSI indexed files. In many installations it has been replaced by a newer implementation of indexed files known as VSAM (see below), but it is still sometimes used. ISAM is covered in Chapter 7.

Direct File Organization

Direct file organization is a nonstandard file organization using an access method known as *BDAM*. Direct organization is based on the concept of *key transformation*, in which the program partially calculates the disk location of a logical record as some function (a key transformation function) of the record's key. The operating system then finishes the calculation of the physical track address (i.e., cylinder and head, CCHH) and searches that track for a matching key (records are in count-key-data format).

Direct organization provides the speed of access of relative organization, while still allowing the programmer to identify logical records by key (rather than record number). It is sometimes used when speed of random processing is critical to an application. Direct organization is discussed in Chapter 6.

(Non-VSAM) Relative Organization

This is an older file organization which implements ANSI relative files. It uses the BDAM access method (the same as direct organization). IBM also offers a newer VSAM version of relative organization (see below). Neither type of relative file is used much because of the requirement that logical records be identified by record number. For those applications which *can* be adapted to use record numbers, however, relative is a very convenient organization. It is discussed in Chapter 8.

VSAM Organization(s)

VSAM (virtual storage access method) was introduced by IBM along with the virtual storage operating systems made available for IBM 370 series processors. The VSAM access method actually supports three different file organizations: (1) VSAM *Key Sequenced Data Sets* (*KSDS*) (ANSI indexed), (2) VSAM *Entry Sequenced Data Sets* (*ESDS*) (ANSI sequential), and (3) VSAM *Relative Record Data Sets* (*RRDS*) (ANSI relative). Of these, only KSDS are frequently used, and "VSAM" is usually synonymous with "VSAM Key Sequenced Data Set".

VSAM KSDS organization was developed as a replacement for the ISAM (indexed sequential) file organization. It offers considerable performance improvement and greater flexibility in processing, and many installations have converted from ISAM to VSAM. VSAM KSDS are discussed in Chapter 7.

VSAM ESDS organization was designed to implement ANSI sequential organization, while at the same time providing random file processing capabilities not available with QSAM. Most organizations have *not* adopted VSAM ESDS, however, and continue to use the older physical sequential (QSAM) organization instead. VSAM ESDS are not discussed in this Outline.

VSAM RRDS organization is a VSAM replacement for non-VSAM relative organization. The two are functionally equivalent and are both discussed in Chapter 8.

Review Questions

5.1   Why is auxiliary storage needed in addition to main memory?

5.2   Explain the relationship between I/O devices, control units, channels, and the processor.

5.3   What is meant by I/O-compute overlap?

5.4   What is cycle stealing?

5.5   What software is *directly* responsible for controlling channels, control units, and devices?

5.6   Explain the relationship between COBOL I/O verbs (such as READ and WRITE) and the operating system.

5.7   Explain the relationship between tape *volumes* and tape *drives*.

5.8   What major processing limitation is associated with magnetic tape?

5.9   In light of your answer to Problem 5.8, what is the major use of magnetic tape today?

5.10   What is meant by 9-track tape?

5.11   Explain the use of vertical and horizontal parity on tape.

5.12   Explain tape density.

5.13   What is meant by data transfer rate?

5.14   Explain the operations involved in writing on magnetic tape.

5.15   What is an interrecord gap? How is it formed?

5.16   What is meant by start/stop time?

5.17   Define blocking factor and explain the importance of blocking in determining tape capacity and processing time.

5.18   Discuss the effect of main memory availability on limiting the blocking factor for a given file.

5.19   What is meant by direct access storage device?

5.20   Compare and contrast the characteristics of hard disks and floppy disks.

5.21   Explain the difference between a track on a disk and a track on a tape.

5.22   Explain why disk space is always organized in terms of cylinders rather than surfaces.

5.23   Explain the four basic operations which must occur to access a record on disk.

5.24   What is head interference? How can it be minimized?

5.25   Explain the differences between (1) removable disk packs, (2) removable data modules, (3) fixed disks, (4) fixed head disks, and (5) combination of fixed head with movable access mechanism.

5.26   What is meant by track format?

5.27   Explain (1) fixed-block (sector) architecture and (2) conventional (variable-block) architecture.

5.28   Describe the count-data and count-key-data track formats. Include discussion of the index point, home address, track descriptor record (R0), address markers, and gaps, as well as the count, key, and data areas.

5.29   What are alternate tracks and how are they used?

5.30   Describe the use of cyclic check characters for error detection/correction on DASD.

5.31   Explain the two ways of addressing physical records stored in count-key-data format (i.e., CCHHR and CCHH-key) and tell how records are retrieved in each case.

5.32 Which conventional track format is used for sequentially processed files? randomly processed files? why?

5.33 Explain the importance of timing and storage estimates for (1) batch applications and (2) interactive applications.

5.34 Discuss why care is needed when choosing a blocking factor for disk files.

5.35 Explain the effect of blocking on (1) disk space, (2) sequential file processing, and (3) random file processing.

5.36 Explain the layout of a typical labeled multifile tape.

5.37 How are volume and file labels used in tape processing?

5.38 How are tape and disk labels created and maintained?

5.39 Explain the relationships between the volume label, volume table of contents, file labels, and files on a disk.

5.40 What actions must the operating system take to (1) create a new disk file and (2) delete an existing disk file?

5.41 What is an extent?

5.42 Discuss the four necessary types of file operations.

5.43 Discuss the two basic file processing (access) modes.

5.44 What is meant by file organization? Why is the choice of file organization important?

5.45 Explain the three ANSI standard COBOL file organizations: (1) sequential, (2) indexed, and (3) relative.

5.46 What is an access method? What are the major IBM access methods which can be invoked through COBOL?

5.47 Briefly describe the following IBM non-VSAM file organizations: (1) (physical) sequential, (2) indexed sequential, (3) direct, and (4) relative.

5.48 Briefly describe the three IBM VSAM file organizations: (1) Key Sequenced (KSDS), (2) Entry Sequenced (ESDS), and (3) Relative Record (RRDS).

Solved Problems

5.49 Compare input, processing, and output of records on systems with and without channels. Assume input requires 3 time units, processing requires 1 time unit, and output requires 4 time units. Show results for 16 time units.

Processor-controlled I/O (no channels, hence no overlap):

```
                    |--|--|--|                |--|--|--|
INPUT:              | Record 1 |              | Record 2 |

                         |--|                      |--|
PROCESS:                  R1                        R2

                      |--|--|--|--|              |--|--|--|--|
OUTPUT:               | Record # 1 |             | Record # 2 |
```

Channel-controlled I/O (assuming an input channel and output channel with I/O-compute overlap). Note the greater amount of work accomplished in the same 16 time units:

```
                 |--|--|--|--|--|--|--|--|--|--|--|--|
INPUT:           | Record 1 | Record 2 | Record 3 | Record 4 |

                    |--|       |--|       |--|       |--|
PROCESS:             R1         R2         R3         R4

                    |--|--.|--|--|--|--|--|--|--|--|--|--|
OUTPUT:             | Record # 1 | Record # 2 | Record # 3 |
```

5.50 Calculate the length of tape required to hold a file of ten thousand 163-byte logical records at 6250 BPI density. Assume 0.5-in gaps and (1) no blocking and (2) a blocking factor of 12.

(1) At 6250 BPI, a 163-byte record requires $163/6250 = 0.026$ in of tape. In an unblocked file, each logical record is followed by a 0.5-in gap, for a total of $(0.026 + 0.5)$ or 0.526 in. Ten thousand such records would require $(10,000 * 0.526)$ or 5260 in (*438.3 ft*).

(2) At 12 logical records per block, each block is $(12 * 163)$ or 1956 bytes, and each block requires $1956/6250 = 0.313$ in. With 12 logical records per block, there are $10,000/12 = 833.3$, rounded to 834 blocks. Each of these is followed by a gap, for a total of $(0.313 + 0.5)$ or 0.813 in per block. The file thus requires $(834 * 0.813)$ or 678 in (*56.5 ft*).

5.51 How much main memory must be available for buffers to process the files in Problem 5.50?

A *buffer* is an area of memory used to hold physical records during input and output. It must be large enough to hold an entire block, so 163 bytes are needed for case (1) and 1956 bytes for case (2). However, most systems allocate two buffers for sequential processing, so actually $(2 * 163) = 326$ and $(2 * 1956) = 3912$ bytes would be needed, respectively. The amount of main memory available for buffers is a limitation on the size of the blocking factor for a file.

5.52 Show what information the operating system must possess in order to program a channel to carry out the following disk operations needed to access a record (assume conventional track format): (1) seek (access arm motion), (2) head switching, (3) search (rotational delay), and (4) data transfer.

Operation	*Information Required*
Seek	Cylinder number (CC)
Head switch	Head number (HH)
Search	Either: (a) A key value, for count-key-data format or
	(b) A record number (R), for either count-data format or count-key-data format
Data transfer	No additional information is needed

5.53 What percentage of the total retrieval time for an IBM 3350 disk is consumed by access arm motion? Assume 150-byte physical records.

The average access time is 25 ms, head switching is (almost) 0 ms, the average rotational delay is 8.4 ms, and the data transfer time is $150/1198 = 0.13$ ms, for a total of $25 + 8.4 + 0.13 = 33.53$ ms. Access arm motion thus consumes $25/33.53 = 75\%$ of the total time.

5.54 In light of Problem 5.53, what can be said of fixed head disks?

Fixed head disks offer speeds which are significantly faster than disks with movable access mechanisms. They are, however, more expensive.

5.55 Why does the capacity of a disk using conventional track formats depend on the size of the physical records placed on it?

With conventional architecture, each physical record is preceded by a count area, (possibly) a key area, plus their attendant gaps. Physical record size helps determine how many physical records fit on a track, and thus how much track space is wasted in count areas, key areas, and gaps. The amount of this *overhead* space in turn affects total capacity.

5.56 Which provides superior error detection: the horizontal and vertical parity scheme used with tape or the cyclic check codes used with disk?

Cyclic check codes provide superior error-detection capability, and in some cases allow the control unit to automatically correct data transfer errors.

5.57 Given a file of ten thousand 200-byte logical records with 10-byte keys in count-key-data format on an IBM 3350 disk, calculate the number of logical records per track for blocking factors (BF) from 1 to 20.

According to IBM specifications, the number of physical records per track with 10-byte keys is given by $19,254/(185 + 82 + 10 + DL)$, where DL is the length in bytes of a physical record. By letting $DL = (BF * 200)$ for $BF = 1, 2, \ldots, 20$, we derive the number of physical records per track. The number of logical records per track is then given by (number of physical records per track) $* (BF)$. The results are:

BF	Logical Records/Track	BF	Logical Records/Track
1	40	11	77
2	56	12	84
3	63	13	78
4	68	14	84
5	75	15	75
6	78	16	80
7	77	17	85
8	80	18	72
9	81	19	76
10	80	20	80

5.58   How much space is required for the file in Problem 5.57 if the file is unblocked $(BF = 1)$?

With 40 logical records per track, 10,000 logical records will require $10,000/40 = 250$ tracks (or $250/30 = 8.3$, rounded to 9 cylinders).

5.59   How much space is required for the file in Problem 5.57 if the optimum blocking factor of 17 is used?

With 85 logical records per track, 10,000 logical records will require $10,000/85 = 117.6$, rounded to 118 tracks (or $118/30 = 3.9$, rounded to 4 cylinders).

5.60   How much I/O time will be required for (1) an interactive program to access one logical record and (2) a batch program to randomly process every logical record in the file in Problem 5.58?

To randomly access one logical record entails (1) one average seek at 25 ms, (2) one head switch at almost 0 ms, (3) one average rotational delay at 8.4 ms, and (4) data transfer of 200 bytes requiring $200/1198 = 0.17$ ms. Processing one logical record thus takes $(25 + 8.4 + 0.17) = 33.57\ ms$, and processing the whole file takes $10,000 * 33.57 = 335,700$ ms or *335.7 s*.

5.61   How accurate are the timing estimates in Problem 5.60 likely to be?

The calculations in Problem 5.60 assume that the operating system already knows the cylinder number, head number, and key (or record number) for the desired record. In reality, the way in which this information is obtained depends heavily on the file organization in use (we consider only those which support random processing):

(1) Indexed (ISAM or VSAM): The key must be known to the COBOL program. The operating system uses this key to look up the CCHH for the record in the *index* associated with the file, and then searches the indicated track for the desired key. Since the index resides on disk, this can involve several disk accesses not accounted for in the calculations in Problem 5.60.

(2) Direct (BDAM): The COBOL program must know the record's key and calculate on which track of the file (i.e., first, second, etc.) the record lies. The operating system then calculates the CCHH from this *relative track number*, and the track is searched for the desired key. Since no extra disk accesses are needed, the calculations in Problem 5.60 are accurate.

(3) Relative (VSAM or BDAM): The COBOL program must calculate the *record number* for the desired record. The operating system then calculates the desired CCHHR from this record number. No extra disk accesses are needed.

5.62   Why does the operating system try to allocate disk space in one contiguous extent, if at all possible?

If all tracks for a file are contiguous, access arm motion (the major factor in total access time) will be minimized during file processing.

5.63   Indicate your choice of file organization and access mode for the following applications:

(1) Credit-limit master file for a company that allows merchants to phone in requests for credit information

(2) Inventory master file with information about each part, used to print reports and also for interactive retrieval during order processing

(3) Master file to hold a class list of students with student numbers 1, 2, 3, etc., used to store grades and to compute and print graded class lists

(4) Accounts receivable file indicating customer balance due

(1) Organization: Indexed (key is credit card number)
    Access: Random

(2) Organization: Indexed (key is part number)
    Access: Both sequential by key (for report printing) and random (for order processing)

(3) Organization: Relative (since the student number can easily be used as a record number)
    Access: Both sequential (for reports) and random (for grade processing and inquiry)

(4) Organization: Indexed (key is customer number)
    Access: Both sequential (for reports by customer number) and random (for updating and inquiry)

Chapter 6

COBOL Direct Files

Direct file organization is an IBM extension to ANSI standard COBOL. It is not often used today because indexed file organizations offer more flexibility and convenience. However, direct organization can (if well-implemented) provide faster random processing than indexed organization. Although improvements in (1) indexed file implementation (such as IBM's transition from ISAM to VSAM), (2) operating system design, and (3) speed of direct access hardware have made this difference less and less important, direct organization is still sometimes chosen for fast random processing.

6.1   General Characteristics of Direct File Organization

Direct organization is a nonstandard file organization used when speed of random access is paramount. Direct files *must* be placed on direct access storage devices. Logical records are identified by the combination of *key* and *relative track number* (written TT). Relative track numbers are defined by numbering the tracks (occupied by the file) 0, 1, 2, etc., regardless of the actual cylinder and head numbers for each track. In COBOL terminology, the combination of key and relative track number is called the ACTUAL KEY.

The relative track number on which a given logical record is placed is determined by the COBOL program, using a *key transformation* (or *hash*) *function* which calculates a relative track number based on the logical record's key value. Many different key transformation functions are possible.

Direct files are normally created using random processing. For each logical record, the COBOL program builds the ACTUAL KEY by applying the key transformation calculation to the logical record's key field value. It then WRITEs the logical record.

When an existing direct file is accessed, the COBOL program must reconstruct the ACTUAL KEY by applying the same key transformation function to the key of the desired logical record. It can then randomly READ the record.

An ideal key transformation function spreads logical records as evenly as possible across the tracks occupied by the file. Logical records whose keys "hash" to the same relative track number are called *synonyms*. Synonyms cause no trouble so long as the track has enough free space to hold an additional record. When a logical record to be added to the file hashes to a track which is already full, however, a *collision* is said to occur.

When a collision occurs, some procedure must be used to determine an alternate location for the logical record to be added. In IBM OS/VS COBOL, *collision handling* can be dealt with by the COBOL program, or the programmer can choose to let the operating system find a track for the new record using a method called extended search (this will be discussed further in Section 6.4). In either case, the collision-handling procedure used to access logical records must be the *same* one used when the logical records were placed on the file (just as the key transformation function used to access records must be the same one used when the records were placed on the file).

6.2   A Commonly Used Key Transformation Function

One of the simplest and most frequently used key transformation functions is the *division/remainder method*, which works as follows:

(1)   Determine how many tracks are (or will be) occupied by the direct file in question.

(2)   Choose as *divisor* the number of tracks from step (1) or, optionally, the prime number closest to but not larger than the number of tracks occupied by the file. (The division/

116

remainder method works better when a prime number is used, and in most cases use of any *odd* number as divisor will produce results about as good. *Never* use an even number for the divisor.)

(3) Calculate the relative track number (TT) for a given logical record as the *remainder* produced by dividing the logical record's key by the number chosen in step (2) above. Note that the record key must be treated as a numeric field for this purpose (see Section 6.5 for handling nonnumeric keys). Note also that the mathematical properties of the remainder are such that it always lies between 0 and one less than the number of tracks (which is exactly the range of valid relative track numbers).

EXAMPLE 6.1 Assume that a directly organized file occupies 22 tracks on a disk. Use the division/remainder method to calculate the relative track numbers for logical records with keys 107, 025, 348, 072, 057, and 221.

First, choose as divisor the prime number nearest to the number of tracks occupied by the file: 19 is the largest prime less than or equal to 22. Now calculate the relative track number as TT = remainder [(logical record key)/19]:

Logical Record's Key	Relative Track Number
107	Remainder $(107/19) = 12$
025	Remainder $(25/19) = 6$
348	Remainder $(348/19) = 6$
072	Remainder $(72/19) = 15$
057	Remainder $(57/19) = 0$
221	Remainder $(221/19) = 12$

In COBOL, the DIVIDE statement always requires provision for a quotient. Thus a "dummy" work area must be defined to receive the quotient, even when it is of no interest. Suppose KEY-FIELD is defined PIC 9(3), DUMMY-FIELD is defined PIC 9(1), and RELATIVE-TRACK is defined PIC 9(2). The calculations above can be programmed in COBOL as:

```
DIVIDE KEY-FIELD BY PRIME-NUMBER-OF-TRACKS
      GIVING DUMMY-FIELD
      REMAINDER RELATIVE-TRACK
```

EXAMPLE 6.2 Identify the synonyms (if any) in Example 6.1.

Since the logical records with keys 025 and 348 are both assigned to relative track number 6, they are synonyms. Likewise, the logical records with keys 107 and 221 are both assigned to relative track number 12, so these records are also synonyms. As long as each track has room for all its synonyms, they cause no difficulty.

6.3 How Direct Organization Works

Assume we wish to create a file of unblocked fixed-length records using direct organization. Further assume that 5 tracks are allocated to the file and that each track can hold three logical records. Since direct files are created randomly, the file would initially be OPENed for OUTPUT with ACCESS RANDOM.

In IBM OS/VS COBOL, direct files are stored in count-key-data format (see Chapter 5). Opening a direct file to create it in this manner causes the entire file space to be filled with dummy records. *Dummy records* are identified by having HIGH-VALUES in the first byte of the key area on the disk. "Key area" here means the "key" of count-*key*-data format, *not* any key field which may be part of the level-01 record description (the logical record itself is placed in the "data" area of count-key-*data* format). The operating system automatically fills all tracks allocated to the file with dummy records when the file is first opened (note that if the file is large, this operation may take considerable time).

EXAMPLE 6.3 Here is an IBM OS/VS COBOL direct file after it is opened for creation ("D" indicates a dummy record written by the operating system; TT is the relative track number):

TT	Logical Records on Track		
0	D	D	D
1	D	D	D
2	D	D	D
3	D	D	D
4	D	D	D

Once the file has been filled with dummy records, actual user records may be added by replacing dummy records. The COBOL program must first construct the logical record and its ACTUAL KEY (consisting of the record's key plus the relative track number). It can then WRITE the record. The COBOL WRITE statement causes the operating system to automatically do the following:

(1) Using information about the physical location of the extents making up the file (available from the file label in the VTOC), convert the relative track number supplied by the COBOL program in the ACTUAL KEY to a physical address (cylinder and head number).

(2) Position the access mechanism to the indicated track; then, starting at the beginning of the track (i.e., at the home address), search for the first available dummy record.

(3) When a dummy record is found, replace it with the logical record written by the COBOL program.

If a dummy record cannot be found on the indicated track, the operating system will either (a) report this fact to the COBOL program, which must then itself select an alternative track on which to place the record, or (b) automatically search the next relative track (i.e., TT + 1), then the next (TT + 2), etc., for a spot in which to place the new record. Option (b) is called *extended search*; it is selected by job control/command language statements used when the file is created.

EXAMPLE 6.4 In order to create a direct file, the COBOL programmer must select (1) a key transformation function and (2) a collision-handling method. Assume that the division/remainder method is the key transformation function and that extended search is the collision-handling method used to load records into the file of Example 6.3. The keys of the logical records to be written are (in this order) 25, 17, 30, 11, 12, 10, 27, 39, and 19.

Since there are 5 tracks in the file and 5 is a prime number, use 5 as the divisor when calculating TT:

Logical Record Key	Relative Track Number (TT)
25	Remainder $(25/5) = 0$
17	Remainder $(17/5) = 2$
30	Remainder $(30/5) = 0$
11	Remainder $(11/5) = 1$
12	Remainder $(12/5) = 2$
10	Remainder $(10/5) = 0$
27	Remainder $(27/5) = 2$
39	Remainder $(39/5) = 4$
19	Remainder $(19/5) = 4$

The COBOL program would have to do the following for each logical record to be added to the file: (1) Calculate the relative track number and place it in the ACTUAL KEY, (2) move the logical record's key value into the ACTUAL KEY, (3) build the logical record to be written (i.e., place data in the level-01 record area of the FD), and then (4) WRITE the record. After adding the records in the order shown, the file would look like this (note that while there are synonyms, there have as yet been no collisions):

TT	Logical Records on Track		
0	25	30	10
1	11	D	D
2	17	12	27
3	D	D	D
4	39	19	D

Note how the logical records have been *scattered* over the available tracks. A good hash function will scatter the logical records as randomly as possible.

EXAMPLE 6.5 A major disadvantage of direct organization is the extra work involved in generating reports. If the file in Example 6.4 is accessed sequentially (as it would be to produce a report), the records are READ as follows:

25, 30, 10, 11, D(ummy), D(ummy), 17, 12, 27, D(ummy), D(ummy), D(ummy), 39, 19, D(ummy)

The logical records are *not* in sequence by key (they were, in fact, deliberately scrambled by the hash function), and dummy records are interspersed with actual data records. Thus the report-writing program must (1) remove the dummy records from the file and (2) sort the remaining records into key sequence. This extra work is not necessary for indexed files, which can be sequentially retrieved in key sequence (see Chapter 7).

EXAMPLE 6.6 Show how extended search works by adding records with the following keys to the file in Example 6.4: 47, 40, 21, and 61.

(1) Key 47 hashes to relative track 2. A search of this track yields no dummy records; thus the operating system automatically goes on to track 3, where it locates a dummy record which can be replaced with record 47:

TT	Logical Records on Track		
0	25	30	10
1	11	D	D
2	17	12	27
3	47	D	D
4	39	19	D

(2) Key 40 hashes to relative track 0. A search of track 0 reveals no available dummy records. With extended search, the operating system automatically goes on to search track 1, where it finds a dummy record to replace:

TT	Logical Records on Track		
0	25	30	10
1	11	40	D
2	17	12	27
3	47	D	D
4	39	19	D

(3) Key 21 hashes to relative track 1. A search of track 1 locates a dummy record where record 21 can be added. Note that relative track 1 contains *both* records which originally hashed to track 1, as well as records which originally hashed to track 0. Thus track 1 has filled up prematurely.

TT	Logical Records on Track		
0	25	30	10
1	11	40	21
2	17	12	27
3	47	D	D
4	39	19	D

(4) Key 61 hashes to track 1. A search of track 1 reveals no dummy records. With extended search, the operating system automatically goes on to track 2, again finding no dummy records to replace. This forces a search of the next track (TT = 3), where a dummy record is located and record 61 is finally added. The total number of tracks the operating system will examine before "giving up" during extended search is specified via job control/command language when the file is created.

TT	Logical Records on Track		
0	25	30	10
1	11	40	21
2	17	12	27
3	47	61	D
4	39	19	D

EXAMPLE 6.7 Because of the extended-search algorithm, tracks 1 and 3 in Example 6.6 contain logical records which really "belong on" (i.e., which hashed to) other tracks. This causes tracks 1 and 3 to fill up prematurely, thus increasing the probability of collisions on these tracks. Since tracks 0 and 2 are already full (which is what caused the extended search to tracks 1 and 3 in the first place), the file is developing a *cluster* of tracks, where collisions are more and more likely and where the extended search will need to examine more and more tracks (thus taking longer and longer). This phenomenon of *clustering* is a disadvantage of the extended-search method of collision handling.

EXAMPLE 6.8 Illustrate how logical records are accessed from a direct file by discussing the retrieval of records 21 and 61 from the file in Example 6.6.

In order to access a direct file, the *same* key transformation function and collision-handling method used when the file was created must again be used. The COBOL program must (1) recalculate the relative track number and place it in the ACTUAL KEY, (2) move the logical record's key value into the ACTUAL KEY area, and then (3) READ the logical record (which is input into the level-01 record area for the file).

(1) Key 21 is hashed to relative track 1 [TT = remainder (21/5) = 1]. The COBOL program places relative track number 1 and record key 21 in the ACTUAL KEY area, and then executes a READ. The operating system obtains the relative track number from the ACTUAL KEY area and converts this to a cylinder and head number (using information from the file label in the VTOC). It then positions the access mechanism to the indicated track and searches the track for a record whose key area (in count-*key*-data format) matches the key value specified in the ACTUAL KEY. Since record 21 is on relative track 1, the search is successful and the data portion of the record on the disk is placed in the level-01 record area for the file (and copied to the INTO area, if READ . . . INTO . . . is specified).

(2) Key 61 is hashed to relative track 1 [TT = remainder (61/5) = 1]. The COBOL program places relative track 1 and record key 61 in the ACTUAL KEY area, and then executes a READ. The operating system obtains the relative track number, converts it to a cylinder and head number, and positions the access mechanism. Relative track 1 is searched for a record whose key area matches that in the ACTUAL KEY. In this case the search is *not* successful. Since extended search is being used for collision handling, the operating system will automatically search the next relative track (TT = 2), just as it did when the record was first added. Since track 2 does not contain record 61 either, the operating system automatically goes on to track 3, where the record is found and input into memory in the level-01 area for the file. Observe that collisions slow file processing: only 1 track had to be searched to locate record 21; 3 tracks had to be searched to locate record 61.

EXAMPLE 6.9 Suppose the COBOL program attempts to access a logical record with key 71. Since record 71 is not in the file, extended searching will never examine a track which contains the record. The extended search will continue until the search limit (set by job control/command language statements when the file was created) is exceeded or until the end of the file is reached (whichever comes first). In this case, the operating system notifies the COBOL program that a record-not-found condition exists. The COBOL programmer is then free to deal with the error in any way which is appropriate to the application.

6.4 Restrictions on Direct Organization

The following restrictions on direct file organization must be observed in IBM OS/VS COBOL:

(1) The keys of logical records placed on the file should be *unique*. The operating system access method for processing direct files (BDAM) does not check for duplicate record keys. If logical records with duplicate keys are allowed on the file, only the record which is first on the track (or in the extended-search path, if extended search is being used) can be retrieved, thus causing serious difficulty with record processing. All programs which add records to a direct file should be designed in such a way as to prevent the possibility of duplicate record keys.

(2) Direct files must have *unblocked* records (i.e., blocking is not allowed).

(3) Direct files may have either fixed-length or variable-length records. When variable-length records are used, the tracks allocated to the file are not formatted with dummy records as described in Section 6.3. Instead, each track descriptor record (R0) is initially set to indicate that the entire track is empty. As variable-length records are added to a track, the free space represented in the track descriptor record is reduced accordingly.

(4) If variable-length records are used, they may be updated in place—but only if the change does not modify the length of the record.

(5) Dummy records may not be retrieved by the COBOL program (in fact, setting the record key portion of the ACTUAL KEY area to HIGH-VALUES, e.g., to "read" a dummy record, is *always* considered invalid).

(6) When a file is initially created and filled with dummy records (or the equivalent for variable-length records), enough space should be provided to accommodate all future additions to the file. The number of dummy records (or the equivalent) initially placed into the file determines the total number of logical records which the file can *ever* hold. The only way to increase the space available for adding records to a direct file is by re-creating the file.

6.5   Key Transformation and Efficiency Considerations

The following considerations apply to the processing of direct files in COBOL:

Packing Factor

It is usually recommended that no more than 80 to 85 percent of the space allocated to a direct file be used to hold records. This 15 to 20 percent *packing factor* helps ensure that the key transformation function spreads the records out more, thus reducing the probability of collisions. Since collisions slow direct file processing, and since direct organization is usually chosen only for applications where speed is the primary concern, it is customary to "waste" some disk space in order to improve performance. The higher the packing factor, the lower the probability of collisions.

EXAMPLE 6.10   Suppose it is estimated that the actual records to be placed on a direct file will require 200 tracks. How much space should be allocated to the file to achieve a packing factor of 20 percent?

The packing factor is the percentage of the file space which will still be unused when all records have been placed in the file. If the total number of tracks allocated to the file is called n, then $(n - 200)$ tracks will still remain unused after all records have been added. It is desired that this number of tracks represent 20 percent of the file space, which can be expressed by

$$\frac{n - 200}{n} = 20\%$$

Solving for n, we have $n - 200 = 0.20 * n$, or $n - (0.20 * n) = 200$, or $0.80 * n = 200$, or $n = 250$, the number of tracks which should be allocated to the file.

Other Key Transformation (Hash) Functions

In addition to division/remainder, there are many other hash techniques which can be used in isolation or in combination with one another. *Folding* involves breaking the key value up into pieces, and then arithmetically combining the pieces to produce a relative track number.

EXAMPLE 6.11   Illustrate how folding can be used to hash keys defined as KEY-FIELD PIC 9(7). Assume that the direct file involved occupies 309 tracks.

First define the key so that it can be broken up into pieces:

```
05    KEY-FIELD.
      10   PIECE-1   PIC 9(2).
      10   PIECE-2   PIC 9(2).
      10   PIECE-3   PIC 9(2).
      10   PIECE-4   PIC 9(1).
```

Then hash the key by "folding" the pieces together:

```
COMPUTE RELATIVE-TRACK = PIECE-1 + PIECE-2 + PIECE-3 + PIECE-4
```

Notice that RELATIVE-TRACK can be at most $(99 + 99 + 99 + 9) = 306$, and at least 0. Since the relative track numbers for the file run from 0 to 308, this is a reasonable transformation of KEY-FIELD into a relative track number (observe, however, that tracks 307 and 308 will be used only during extended searching; they can never be hashed to directly).

EXAMPLE 6.12 Illustrate the combination of *multiplicative folding* and division/remainder for keys defined as PIC 9(7). Assume there are 700 tracks allocated to the file.
    Define the key so that it can be broken up into pieces:

```
05    KEY-FIELD.
      10   PIECE-1   PIC 9(4).
      10   PIECE-2   PIC 9(3).
```

Then fold the pieces by multiplying them together:

```
COMPUTE PRODUCT-OF-PIECES = PIECE-1 * PIECE-2
```

where PRODUCT-OF-PIECES is defined PIC 9(7). Now apply division/remainder to the product (691 is the nearest prime number less than or equal to 700):

```
DIVIDE PRODUCT-OF-PIECES BY NEAREST-PRIME
       GIVING IGNORE-THE-QUOTIENT
       REMAINDER RELATIVE-TRACK
```

where NEAREST-PRIME is defined PIC 9(3) VALUE 691, IGNORE-THE-QUOTIENT is defined PIC 9(4), and RELATIVE-TRACK is defined PIC 9(3). Note that again some tracks at the end of the file are wasted in that they can only be reached by extended search, not directly by hashing (the relative track numbers run from 0 to 699, but RELATIVE-TRACK is always in the range 0 to 690; in this case, we might consider allocating only 692 or 693 tracks, instead of the full 700).

EXAMPLE 6.13 Why not allocate just 691 tracks in Example 6.12?
    If 691 tracks are allocated, there will be no tracks available for extended searching if track 691 (relative track 690) fills up. Allocating 692 or 693 tracks provides for overflow from track 691 (the last track to which records can directly hash).

There are many other key transformation techniques in use which are beyond the scope of this Outline. Some of these include (1) *digit analysis*, in which a statistical analysis of the characters in the *key set* (i.e., the set of all keys in the file) is done to determine which characters should be selected to take part in the hash function, (2) *digit extraction*, in which the relative track number is formed by selecting certain digits from the key field, and (3) *radix conversion*, in which the key value is converted to a different base number (with any excess digits being truncated), etc.

In many cases the simpler division/remainder technique performs adequately, so there is no need for more complicated functions. On the other hand, the performance of a key transformation function should always be monitored since it depends not only on the function itself but also on the key set (which is usually in constant change).

For key sets which are *static* (i.e., records are never added to or deleted from the file), there are techniques for generating a *perfect hash function* from the keys. Perfect hash functions never produce any collisions.

Handling Nonnumeric Keys

Nonnumeric keys are best handled by "tricking" the COBOL compiler into treating them as numbers. There are several techniques for accomplishing this, depending on the nature of the keys involved.

EXAMPLE 6.14 If nonnumeric keys are guaranteed to consist of only letters, digits, and/or spaces, and not to end in a space, then they may safely be treated as numbers (see Problem 6.35). If KEY-FIELD PIC X(7) meets the restrictions above, then the following is valid in IBM OS/VS COBOL:

```
05   KEY-FIELD      PIC X(7).
05   NUMERIC-KEY    REDEFINES KEY-FIELD PIC 9(7). . .

     DIVIDE NUMERIC-KEY BY PRIME-NUMBER
          GIVING IGNORED-DUMMY-FIELD
          REMAINDER RELATIVE-TRACK
```

Note that KEY-FIELD [defined PIC X(7)] is REDEFINEd as NUMERIC-KEY [PIC 9(7)]. Hence the compiler will automatically treat the PIC X(7) of KEY-FIELD as if it were PIC 9(7), for purposes of the division. This works so long as KEY-FIELD meets the restrictions indicated above.

EXAMPLE 6.15 If nonnumeric keys do not meet the restrictions in Example 6.14, the compiler can still be tricked into treating them like numbers. In order to accomplish this, we REDEFINE the nonnumeric key as a series of COMP items. The reader will recall that in IBM OS/VS COBOL, a COMP item with 1 to 4 digits takes up a halfword (2 character positions) of memory, while a COMP item with 5 to 9 digits takes up a fullword (4 character positions). Since keys with an odd number of characters obviously cannot be exactly decomposed into a series of halfwords and/or fullwords, it is necessary to *pad* them with an extra character to make the total length of the padded key *even*.

Suppose KEY-FIELD is defined as PIC X(7) but does not meet the restrictions in Example 6.14. Define PADDED-KEY as PIC X(8), and then REDEFINE it as follows:

```
05   PADDED-KEY                 PIC X(8).
05   KEY-VIEWED-AS-COMP-FIELDS  REDEFINES PADDED-KEY.
     10   PIECE-1               PIC 9(9) COMP.
     10   PIECE-2               PIC 9(9) COMP.
```

The PADDED-KEY area occupies 8 bytes. PIECE-1 and PIECE-2 of KEY-VIEWED-AS-COMP-FIELDS each occupy 4 bytes, hence the group item KEY-VIEWED-AS-COMP-FIELDS occupies 8 bytes and can correctly REDEFINE PADDED-KEY. PIECE-1 represents the first 4 bytes of PADDED-KEY interpreted as a binary number; PIECE-2 similarly represents the second half of PADDED-KEY.

The following code combines folding and division/remainder to hash KEY-FIELD:

```
MOVE KEY-FIELD TO PADDED-KEY
ADD PIECE-1 PIECE-2  GIVING FOLDED-SUM-OF-PIECES
DIVIDE FOLDED-SUM-OF-PIECES BY PRIME-NUMBER
     GIVING IGNORED-QUOTIENT-FIELD
     REMAINDER RELATIVE-TRACK
```

Since *any* bit pattern is accepted as a valid COMP number in IBM OS/VS COBOL, this technique will always work, regardless of the contents of KEY-FIELD.

EXAMPLE 6.16   Another way to handle nonnumeric keys which do not meet the restrictions in Example 6.14 is to use the INSPECT statement to *transform* the key into one which does meet the restrictions in Example 6.14, and then proceed as in that example. See Chapter 11, Example 11.18 for a discussion of the INSPECT statement.

Collision-Handling Methods

Extended search is available in IBM OS/VS COBOL as an option specified via job control/command language statements when a file is created. If room to add a new record cannot be found on the relative track to which the record's key hashes (for a WRITE), or if a record cannot be found on the track to which its key hashes (for a READ), the operating system automatically tries the *next* relative track in the file. It will continue searching, relative track after relative track, until the search is satisfied or until it either hits the end of the file or exceeds the limit (in terms of number of tracks) set by the job control/command language statements. If the search fails, the operating system reports the failure to the COBOL program. Consult an instructor or vendor manual for information on job control requirements for direct files in IBM OS/VS COBOL.

If extended search is not elected, the operating system will search only the track to which the record's key hashes. If the record (for a READ) or space to add it (for a WRITE) is not there, the system simply reports the failure to the COBOL program. The COBOL program must then contain its own collision-handling procedures. Most such techniques require a knowledge of abstract data structures and/or pseudo-random number generation, and are beyond the scope of this Outline.

With a good packing factor and a good key transformation function, extended search should perform satisfactorily for most applications.

6.6   Direct File Creation

Creating a direct file involves the ENVIRONMENT, DATA, and PROCEDURE divisions as follows:

ENVIRONMENT DIVISION Considerations

The IBM OS/VS COBOL SELECT statement for creating a direct file has the following syntax:

```
SELECT file-name
    ASSIGN TO W-ddname
    ACCESS MODE IS RANDOM
    ACTUAL KEY IS data-name
    [ TRACK-LIMIT IS integer TRACK[S] ]
```

The ASSIGN TO clause identifies the file organization ("W" indicates direct) and the name of a job control/command language statement ("ddname"), which provides further information about the file. Consult an instructor or vendor manual for information about job control requirements when creating direct files.

Direct files are normally created randomly, so ACCESS is RANDOM. The ACTUAL KEY clause names the data item (usually defined in WORKING-STORAGE) which will serve as the ACTUAL KEY area for this particular file. The ACTUAL KEY area serves as a communications area between the COBOL program and the operating system access method (called BDAM), which actually accesses the disk. The ACTUAL KEY identifies a logical record by providing its (1) relative track number and (2) record key value.

EXAMPLE 6.17   Suppose a direct file is to be created in which logical records are identified by CUSTOMER-NUMBER PIC X(7). The ACTUAL KEY area for this file might be defined as follows:

```
        SELECT CUSTOMER-MASTER-FILE
            ACTUAL KEY IS CUST-MAST-ACTUAL-KEY . . .

    WORKING-STORAGE SECTION.
    01   CUST-MAST-ACTUAL-KEY.
         05    CUST-MAST-RELATIVE-TRACK        PIC 9(5) COMP SYNC.
         05    CUSTOMER-NUMBER-VALUE           PIC X(7).
```

The ACTUAL KEY area *must* consist of two parts in the following order:

(1)   A data item to hold the relative track number assigned to a logical record. This data item must always be defined as shown [PIC 9(5) COMP or PIC S9(5) COMP, with an optional SYNCHRONIZED clause]. Use of an unsigned field eliminates the possibility of inadvertently generating a negative relative track number.

(2)   A data item to hold a logical record's key value. The definition of this item depends on the file in question (it can be any type of data item from 1 to 255 bytes in length).

The TRACK-LIMIT clause optionally defines the number of relative tracks which will be filled with dummy records (or the equivalent for variable-length records) when the file is created. It thus determines how many tracks (of the total tracks allocated to the file) can actually be used to hold records. Tracks which contain dummy records (or the equivalent) and can therefore be used to hold records are said to be *formatted*.

The final effect of the TRACK-LIMIT clause partly depends on *how* space is allocated by the job control/command language statements used when the file is created (consult an instructor or vendor manual). Since use of TRACK-LIMIT can result in tracks which are allocated to the file but which cannot be used to hold any records, and since a change in the amount of space allocated to the file would require a change to TRACK-LIMIT (and thus a change to and recompilation of the COBOL source program), it is recommended that TRACK-LIMIT *not* be used.

DATA DIVISION Considerations

Syntactically, the FD and level-01 record description for a direct file are almost the same as for a sequential file. The only difference is that since direct files must be unblocked, the BLOCK CONTAINS clause in the FD is treated as a comment and ignored (hence the BLOCK CONTAINS clause should be omitted).

It is worth noting that although the ACTUAL KEY area contains the key of a logical record to be added to the file, it is customary to also include the key value as a field in the logical record itself. Thus the level-01 record description for a direct file will usually include the key field.

If it is necessary to be able to delete logical records from a direct file (as it usually is), the record description must also include a user-defined *delete code area*. The operating system access method provides no mechanism for deleting records from direct files, hence the programmer must develop his or her own scheme for the logical deletion of records.

Logical deletion means *flagging* records to indicate whether they are *active* or *inactive* (i.e., deleted). This is usually accomplished by including a field in each logical record to indicate the record's status. The codes used to mark active versus inactive records are totally up to the programmer.

Since logical records which are flagged as deleted are not physically removed from the file, systems using direct files must be carefully designed to (1) ensure that all programs which access the file check the delete code before attempting to process a logical record (since records which are marked deleted are still physically on the file and can be input by the program) and (2) include provisions for periodically reorganizing the file to physically remove any deleted records (file reorganization produces a new copy of the file which does not include any deleted records).

EXAMPLE 6.18   The following program segment is an FD for a directly organized customer master file:

```
FD   CUSTOMER-MASTER-FILE
     LABEL RECORDS ARE STANDARD
     RECORD CONTAINS 16 CHARACTERS
     .
01   CUSTOMER-MASTER-RECORD.
     05   CUST-MAST-ID              PIC X(7).
     05   CUST-MAST-DELETE-CODE     PIC X.
          88   ACTIVE-RECORD        VALUE "A".
          88   DELETED-RECORD       VALUE "D".
     05   CUST-MAST-BALANCE         PIC S9(5)V99 COMP.
     05   CUST-MAST-CREDIT-LIMIT    PIC S9(5)V99 COMP.
```

CUST-MAST-ID is the logical record's key field. An identical field [PIC X(7)] must also appear in the ACTUAL KEY. The delete code byte is CUST-MAST-DELETE-CODE. If this field contains the value "A", the record is assumed to be active; if it contains the value "D", the record is assumed to be logically deleted and hence inactive. Programs working with CUSTOMER-MASTER-FILE must check CUST-MAST-DELETE-CODE for the value "D" *before* processing each record. Note the omission of the BLOCK CONTAINS clause from the FD.

PROCEDURE DIVISION Considerations

The logic for creating a direct file is more or less complex, depending on whether or not the creation program must check for logical records with duplicate keys. The reader will recall that the operating system access method (BDAM) does *not* check for duplicate keys when placing a record on a direct file. It simply looks for a dummy record to replace with the new record, regardless of whether or not there already is a record with the same key on the file.

Normally the records to be loaded into the direct file are taken from a *transaction file*. There are two main methods of eliminating the possibility of duplicate keys in the transaction file:

(1) If the transaction file has already been edited to ensure that duplicate keys are not present, or if the transaction file has an organization which prohibits duplicate keys, then the direct file creation program need not handle this possibility.

(2) Since direct files are usually created randomly, there is no need to sort the transaction file. However, if the transaction file is sorted by record key anyway, then a simple sequence check of the incoming transaction records will reveal the presence of any duplicate keys. This sequence check could be done within the creation program itself or by a separate edit program.

If it is decided to neither pre-edit nor sort the transaction file, then the creation program must check for the presence of a record with a duplicate key *before* attempting to add each new record. This can be done by trying to READ a record with the key value of the record about to be added. If the READ *fails*, then the program knows there is no record with that key already on the file and it is safe to add the new record. If the READ *succeeds*, then the program knows that a record with a matching key is already on the file and the new record cannot be added.

Observe that this technique requires that the creation program both READ and WRITE to the direct file, which thus must be OPENed I–O ("OPEN I–O file-name" allows a file to be used for both input and output). However, a file can only be OPENed I–O if it already exists. How, then, can a file to be created be OPENed I–O?

EXAMPLE 6.19 The following code will create a direct file filled with nothing but dummy records:

```
OPEN OUTPUT    NEW-DIRECT-FILE
CLOSE          NEW-DIRECT-FILE
OPEN I-0       NEW-DIRECT-FILE
```

The first OPEN statement opens the direct file for creation, causing the operating system to fill the file space with dummy records (or the equivalent for variable-length records). The file is then immediately closed, leaving an existing file with nothing but dummy records. Since the file now exists (and is closed), it can be opened I–O as required.

The PROCEDURE DIVISION statements relevant to creating a direct file are:

(1) <u>OPEN OUTPUT</u> file-name
When a nonexisting direct file is opened output, the operating system fills the file space with dummy records (or the equivalent) and allows the COBOL program to use the WRITE statement to add records to the file.

(2) <u>OPEN I–O</u> file-name
The file must exist to be opened I–O. I–O allows the program to use the READ, WRITE, and REWRITE statements for record processing. Only READ and WRITE are relevant to file creation.

(3) <u>CLOSE</u> file-name
The CLOSE statement completes any outstanding I/O operations for the file, makes any necessary changes to the file label in the VTOC, releases space allocated to file buffers, and generally disconnects the file from the COBOL program.

(4) <u>READ</u> file-name

```
[  INTO data-name ]
[  INVALID KEY
        imperative-statement(s). ]
```

This is the standard form of a random READ statement. The ACTUAL KEY area must contain the relative track number and the record key for the record to be retrieved before the READ is executed. In response to the READ, the operating system will: (1) convert the relative track number to a physical disk address (CCHH), (2) position the access mechanism to the indicated track, (3) search the track for a record whose key matches that given in the ACTUAL KEY, and (4) input the record (if it exists) into the level-01 record area for the file. If extended search was requested when the file was created, the search will automatically continue to succeeding relative tracks, if the record cannot be found on the track indicated in the ACTUAL KEY. If a record matching the key value given in the ACTUAL KEY cannot be found on the track (or within the limits of extended search), then the operating system turns control over to the statement(s) specified in the INVALID KEY clause. Note that the end of the INVALID KEY group of statements must be marked with a *period* (just like the AT END clause). After executing the INVALID KEY statements, the computer goes on to the next statement in the program. If the specified record *can* be found, the operating system gives control to the statement immediately following the period which marks the end of the READ statement (and the INVALID KEY clause), thus "skipping" the INVALID KEY statements. The INVALID KEY statements are executed only for a *record-not-found condition* (a special case of this also occurs when the ACTUAL KEY indicates a relative track number outside the range of the file). When a random READ fails (and INVALID KEY is executed), the contents of the ACTUAL KEY area are destroyed.

(5) <u>WRITE</u> direct-record-name

```
[  FROM data-name ]
[  INVALID KEY
        imperative-statement(s). ]
```

This is the standard form of the random WRITE statement. It is used to add a new record to a direct file. Before the WRITE statement is executed, the program must (1) construct the ACTUAL KEY area (with the relative track number and record key for the record about to be output) and (2) construct the logical record contents in the level-01 record area for the file. The INVALID KEY clause may contain one or more imperative statements, the end of which must be marked with a period. The INVALID KEY on a WRITE is executed only if (1) the relative track number in the ACTUAL KEY is outside the range of the file or (2) there is no room on the track (or set of tracks within the extended-search limit, if extended search is used) to add the record. After execution of the WRITE statement [and possibly the INVALID KEY statement(s)], normal execution continues with the next statement. In response to a WRITE statement, the operating system (1) converts the relative track number in the ACTUAL KEY to a physical disk address (CCHH), (2) positions the access mechanism to the indicated track, (3) searches the track for a dummy record (or its equivalent for variable-length records), and then (4) replaces the dummy record with the record being written.

EXAMPLE 6.20 Figure 6-1 illustrates a COBOL program which creates a direct file from a sequential transaction file. In order to minimize nonrelevant details, it is assumed that the transaction file has already been edited for everything except duplicate keys. Rather than sort the transaction file and then sequence check for duplicate keys, duplicates are detected by attempting to READ each record before adding it to the file. The following remarks pertain to the IBM OS/VS COBOL source listing in Fig. 6-1:

(1) Lines 9–13 define the sequential transaction file which holds the information to be used to construct the logical records for the direct file.

(2) Lines 14–18 define the direct file to be created. The ASSIGN TO name has the form "organization-code-ddname", where "W" indicates direct organization and "MASTER" is the name of a job control/command language statement which further defines the file. The ACTUAL KEY area is *named* here (line 17) and then *defined* in WORKING-STORAGE (lines 50–52). Note that direct files are normally created randomly (ACCESS IS RANDOM).

(3) The FD for the direct file (lines 31–38) is quite similar to the FD for the sequential transaction file (lines 21–30). The only real difference is that BLOCK CONTAINS is omitted for direct files (since they must be unblocked). Note that the level-01 record description for the direct file includes the record key field (line 35) and a special delete code field which can be used to flag records for logical deletion (line 36).

(4) The *divisor* for the division/remainder key transformation function used in this example is defined as a program constant on lines 40–42. This is not a recommended way to obtain the divisor (we do it here for simplicity only). In real life, the number of tracks occupied by the file would be subject to change, and the divisor would change accordingly. Thus the value for the divisor should be input from a special control file set up for that purpose, or should be supplied in some other manner which allows the value to be changed without having to modify and recompile the COBOL source program (e.g., with IBM OS/VS operating systems, the value for the divisor could be supplied on the job control statement which causes the execution of the COBOL object program; consult an instructor or vendor manual for information on use of the PARM field of the EXEC statement for this purpose).

(5) The ACTUAL KEY data area is defined on lines 50–52. The reader will recall that the relative track number *must* be the first part of the area and *must* be defined PIC 9(5) or PIC S9(5) COMP (with SYNC optional). Following this comes the definition of a field to hold a record key value. Note that in this example, the record key in the record is defined as PIC X(5) (line 35), while the key area in the ACTUAL KEY is defined as PIC 9(5) (line 52). This was done deliberately so that RECORD-KEY-VALUE [PIC 9(5)] could be used in the DIVIDE statement, which calculates the relative track number (IBM OS/VS COBOL syntax requires numeric operands for the DIVIDE statement). Lines 97–100 move TRANS-PROGRAMMER-ID PIC X(5) to RECORD-KEY-VALUE PIC 9(5), and then DIVIDE RECORD-KEY-VALUE BY PRIME-NUMBER-OF-TRACKS to obtain the relative track number. Note that this technique assumes that the programmer IDs meet the requirements set forth in Example 6.14 (letters, digits, and spaces only; not ending in a space).

```
00001              IDENTIFICATION DIVISION.
00002              PROGRAM-ID.  DIRECT-FILE-CREATION.

00003              ENVIRONMENT DIVISION.
00004              CONFIGURATION SECTION.
00005              SOURCE-COMPUTER.  IBM-3081.
00006              OBJECT-COMPUTER.  IBM-3081.
00007              INPUT-OUTPUT SECTION.
00008              FILE-CONTROL.

00009                  SELECT TRANSACTION-FILE
00010                      ASSIGN TO RAWDATA
00011                      ORGANIZATION IS SEQUENTIAL
00012                      ACCESS IS SEQUENTIAL
00013                      .
00014                  SELECT DIRECT-FILE
00015                      ASSIGN TO W-MASTER
00016                      ACCESS IS RANDOM
00017                      ACTUAL KEY IS ACTUAL-KEY-DATA-AREA
00018                      .

00019              DATA DIVISION.
00020              FILE SECTION.

00021              FD  TRANSACTION-FILE
00022                  LABEL RECORDS ARE STANDARD
00023                  BLOCK CONTAINS O CHARACTERS
00024                  RECORD CONTAINS 80 CHARACTERS
00025                  .
00026              01  TRANSACTION-RECORD.
00027                  05   TRANS-PROGRAMMER-ID        PIC X(5).
00028                  05   TRANS-PROJECT-ID           PIC X(8).
00029                  05   TRANS-TOTAL-HOURS          PIC 9(3)V9.
00030                  05   FILLER                     PIC X(63).

00031              FD  DIRECT-FILE
00032                  LABEL RECORDS ARE STANDARD
00033                  RECORD CONTAINS 16 CHARACTERS
                       .
00034              01  DIRECT-RECORD.
00035                  05   DIRECT-PROGRAMMER-ID       PIC X(5).
00036                  05   DIRECT-DELETE-CODE-BYTE    PIC X.
00037                  05   DIRECT-PROJECT-ID          PIC X(8).
00038                  05   DIRECT-TOTAL-HOURS         PIC 9(3)V9 COMP.

00039              WORKING-STORAGE SECTION.

00040              01  PROGRAM-CONSTANTS.
00041                  05   PRIME-NUMBER-OF-TRACKS     PIC S9(5) COMP
00042                                                  VALUE +3.
00043              01  FLAGS-AND-SWITCHES.
00044                  05   TRANS-END-OF-FILE-SW       PIC X(3).
00045                      88  MORE-TRANS-RECORDS       VALUE "NO".
00046                      88  NO-MORE-INPUT            VALUE "YES".
00047                  05   DUPLICATE-KEY-SW           PIC X(3).
00048                      88  NO-DUPLICATE             VALUE "NO".
00049                      88  DUPLICATE-KEY            VALUE "YES".

00050              01  ACTUAL-KEY-DATA-AREA.
00051                  05   RELATIVE-TRACK             PIC 9(5) COMP SYNC.
00052                  05   RECORD-KEY-VALUE           PIC 9(5).

00053              01  COPY-ACTUAL-KEY-AREA.
00054                  05   FILLER                     PIC 9(5) COMP SYNC.
00055                  05   FILLER                     PIC 9(5).

00056              01  IGNORED-QUOTIENT-FIELD          PIC S9(4) COMP SYNC.
```

Fig. 6-1

```
00057              PROCEDURE DIVISION.
00058
00059              000-EXECUTIVE-MODULE.
00060
00061                  OPEN    INPUT   TRANSACTION-FILE
00062                          OUTPUT  DIRECT-FILE
00063                  CLOSE   DIRECT-FILE
00064                  OPEN    I-O DIRECT-FILE
00065                  MOVE "NO" TO TRANS-END-OF-FILE-SW
00066                  PERFORM 010-GET-TRANSACTION-RECORD
00067                  PERFORM 020-LOAD-DIRECT-FILE
00068                      UNTIL NO-MORE-INPUT
00069                  CLOSE   TRANSACTION-FILE
00070                          DIRECT-FILE
00071                  STOP RUN
00072                  .
00073
00074              010-GET-TRANSACTION-RECORD.
00075
00076                  READ TRANSACTION-FILE
00077                      AT END
00078                          MOVE "YES" TO TRANS-END-OF-FILE-SW
00079                  .
00080
00081              020-LOAD-DIRECT-FILE.
00082
00083                  PERFORM 030-BUILD-ACTUAL-KEY
00084                  MOVE ACTUAL-KEY-DATA-AREA    TO COPY-ACTUAL-KEY-AREA
00085                  PERFORM 040-CHECK-FOR-DUPLICATE-KEY
00086                  IF NO-DUPLICATE
00087                      MOVE COPY-ACTUAL-KEY-AREA TO ACTUAL-KEY-DATA-AREA
00088                      PERFORM 050-ADD-NEW-RECORD
00089                  ELSE
00090                      DISPLAY DIRECT-PROGRAMMER-ID " ALREADY ON FILE"
00091                  .
00092                  PERFORM 010-GET-TRANSACTION-RECORD
00093                  .
00094
00095              030-BUILD-ACTUAL-KEY.
00096
00097                  MOVE TRANS-PROGRAMMER-ID TO RECORD-KEY-VALUE
00098                  DIVIDE RECORD-KEY-VALUE BY PRIME-NUMBER-OF-TRACKS
00099                      GIVING IGNORED-QUOTIENT-FIELD
00100                      REMAINDER RELATIVE-TRACK
00101                  .
00102
00103              040-CHECK-FOR-DUPLICATE-KEY.
00104
00105                  MOVE "YES" TO DUPLICATE-KEY-SW
00106                  READ DIRECT-FILE
00107                      INVALID KEY
00108                          MOVE "NO" TO DUPLICATE-KEY-SW
00109                  .
00110
00111              050-ADD-NEW-RECORD.
00112
00113                  MOVE TRANS-PROGRAMMER-ID     TO DIRECT-PROGRAMMER-ID
00114                  MOVE TRANS-PROJECT-ID        TO DIRECT-PROJECT-ID
00115                  MOVE TRANS-TOTAL-HOURS       TO DIRECT-TOTAL-HOURS
00116                  MOVE SPACE TO DIRECT-DELETE-CODE-BYTE
00117                  WRITE DIRECT-RECORD
00118                      INVALID KEY
00119                          DISPLAY "EXTENDED SEARCH REVEALED NO ROOM "
00120                              "TO ADD " TRANS-PROGRAMMER-ID
00121                  .
```

Fig. 6-1   (*cont.*)

(6) Lines 53–55 define an area to hold a copy of the ACTUAL KEY. It is convenient to have a copy because the logic of the program first builds the ACTUAL KEY (by applying the key transformation function to the transaction key) and then attempts to randomly READ a record to see if one with a duplicate key is already on file. If this READ fails, then the program goes ahead and WRITEs the new record. However, when a random READ fails, the contents of the ACTUAL KEY are destroyed. Thus the program must either (1) save a copy of the ACTUAL KEY before executing the READ and use this copy to restore the ACTUAL KEY area before executing the WRITE (to add the record to the file) or (2) recalculate the ACTUAL KEY before executing the WRITE. Since the key transformation may be complex, it is generally more efficient to save a copy of the results rather than perform the computation a second time.

(7) Line 56 defines the "dummy" field used to hold the quotient produced as a side-effect of the division/remainder method. The quotient is never actually used by the program.

(8) Lines 59–72 make up the "executive module", which controls the overall logic of the program. Observe how the direct file is (1) opened OUTPUT (line 62) to create the file and fill the tracks with dummy records (or the equivalent), then (2) immediately closed (line 63), and then (3) immediately reopened I–O (line 64). I–O is required since the method of checking for duplicate keys uses both READ and WRITE. Lines 62–63 are necessary because a file must already exist before it can be opened I–O. The file is closed for the final time in line 70.

(9) Lines 81–91 add a new logical record to the direct file (and are therefore the heart of this program). The first step is to apply the key transformation function to the incoming transaction record's key and construct the ACTUAL KEY (this is handled in 030-BUILD-ACTUAL-KEY, which is performed in line 83). Line 84 then saves a copy of the ACTUAL KEY area for later use (this eliminates the need to recalculate the relative track number). The next step is to check for an already existing record with the same key as the record to be added. This is accomplished in 040-CHECK-FOR-DUPLICATE-KEY, which sets DUPLICATE-KEY-SW (defined in WORKING-STORAGE, lines 47–49). If the switch indicates that the READ failed to locate a record with a matching key, line 87 uses the copy of the original ACTUAL KEY contents to restore the ACTUAL KEY (destroyed by the unsuccessful READ in lines 106–109). Information from the transaction record can then be moved into the direct file record area, and the record can be written to the file (handled by paragraph 050-ADD-NEW-RECORD). If a duplicate key is detected, this program simply DISPLAYs an error message. In real life, the error messages should be more complete (and should probably be formatted in a regular print file).

(10) Lines 95–101 construct the ACTUAL KEY area. The key from the incoming transaction record is moved to the record key part of the ACTUAL KEY in line 97. This value is then used to calculate the relative track number (using the division/remainder method) in lines 98–100 [see comment (5) above].

(11) Lines 103–109 carry out the check for an already existing record, with a key duplicating the one about to be added to the file. Line 105 sets DUPLICATE-KEY-SW to "YES". Lines 106–109 then attempt to randomly READ a record (remember that 030-BUILD-ACTUAL-KEY has already been executed at this point). If the record exists, the INVALID KEY routine is bypassed and DUPLI-CATE-KEY-SW remains set to "YES". If such a record does not exist, the INVALID KEY clause is executed, resetting DUPLICATE-KEY-SW to "NO". Thus if the switch is finally "YES", a duplicate key error exists; if the switch is finally "NO", it is safe to go ahead and add the new record. Remember that failure to find (READ) a duplicate record destroys the contents of the ACTUAL KEY (which must somehow be restored, e.g., as in line 87).

(12) Lines 111–121 output a new record to the direct file. First the information from the incoming transaction record is moved to the level-01 area for the direct file (lines 113–115); then the delete code byte is set to the code for an active record (line 116); and then the WRITE statement is used to output the record. Note the use of the INVALID KEY clause to cover the possibility that no room exists in which to add the record. For simplicity, the error message is just DISPLAYed. In real life, a formatted error report should be produced on a standard print file.

EXAMPLE 6.21 What happens if line 116 is omitted from the program in Fig. 6-1?

If the creation program fails to initialize the delete code field, the field contains *garbage*. If this garbage just happens to equal the code for a deleted record, then the new record will not be recognized (or processed) by any of the programs which work with the file. Moral: Always initialize the delete code.

6.7   Direct File Retrieval—Sequential

Sequential retrieval of a direct file is almost the same as retrieval from a sequential file. There are, however, two differences: (1) The operating system access method which processes direct files sequentially (BSAM) retrieves dummy and deleted records along with the active records; thus the COBOL program must be designed to *screen* these unwanted records from the input. (2) Direct file records come off the disk in physical sequence (which is random with respect to the key field; see Example 6.5); thus the COBOL program must usually be designed to sort the records into key field sequence. Both these goals can be accomplished by using the COBOL SORT verb with an INPUT PROCEDURE.

Note that key transformation is not necessary for sequential retrieval. The records are made available in their physical order on the disk.

ENVIRONMENT DIVISION Considerations

The IBM OS/VS COBOL SELECT statement for sequential retrieval of a direct file has the following syntax:

```
SELECT file-name
       ASSIGN TO D-ddname
       [ ACCESS MODE IS SEQUENTIAL ]
       [ ACTUAL KEY IS data-name ]
         .
```

The ASSIGN clause must use the file organization code "D" for sequential retrieval. The "ddname" is the programmer-defined name of a job control/command language statement which further defines the file (consult an instructor or vendor manual for the job control statements required to process direct files sequentially).

Since sequential access is the *default*, "ACCESS MODE IS SEQUENTIAL" is optional (though recommended for program documentation). The ACTUAL KEY clause is technically optional for sequential processing, but in practice it is needed to identify dummy records in fixed-length files. When the ACTUAL KEY clause is specified, the operating system access method places the relative track number and the key area from the disk into the ACTUAL KEY every time a READ is executed. Dummy records can then be identified by inspecting the first byte of the record key part of the ACTUAL KEY for HIGH-VALUES.

Since variable-length direct files use the track descriptor record (R0) rather than dummy records to identify free space on each track, programs processing variable-length direct files sequentially need not bother defining an ACTUAL KEY (dummy records do not physically exist on the file and hence are not made available to the COBOL program).

DATA DIVISION Considerations

The FD and level-01 record description are the same for sequential processing as for creation (see Section 6.6). Remember that the delete code byte must be checked to identify logically deleted records. It is useful to define a condition name for this purpose.

PROCEDURE DIVISION Considerations

One of the major purposes for retrieving direct files sequentially is to produce reports. This generally requires sorting the file into key field sequence (see Example 6.5). If the SORT verb is used with an INPUT PROCEDURE which screens dummy and deleted records, an OUTPUT PROCEDURE can then format and print the report.

The PROCEDURE DIVISION statements relevant to retrieving a direct file sequentially are:

(1)   <u>OPEN INPUT</u> file-name

(2)   <u>CLOSE</u> file-name

(3)   <u>READ</u> file-name

```
        [  INTO data-name ]
        [  AT END
                imperative-statement(s). ]
```

With the exception of testing for dummy and deleted records, direct files are treated exactly like sequential files for purposes of sequential retrieval, and the COBOL statements used are identical in syntax and function.

EXAMPLE 6.22   Figure 6-2 illustrates producing a report from the direct file created in Example 6.20. For simplicity, no headings or page breaks are included. The following remarks refer to the IBM OS/VS COBOL source listing in Fig. 6-2:

(1)   Lines 9–13 define the direct file. The organization code "D" is required for ACCESS SEQUENTIAL. The ACTUAL KEY is named on line 12 and defined in lines 51–57.

(2)   Lines 24–33 constitute the FD for the file. Note the definition of condition names for the delete code byte (lines 29–31).

(3)   The ACTUAL KEY area is defined in lines 51–57. In order to check for dummy records, the first byte of the record key area must be isolated. This is done by REDEFINEing RECORD-KEY-VALUE PIC 9(5) as the group item CHECK-FOR-DUMMY-FIELD (whose first byte is DUMMY-RECORD-FLAG PIC X). Note that a condition name for dummy records is defined on line 56.

(4)   Lines 67–74 constitute the executive module. The overall structure of the program is a SORT with INPUT and OUTPUT PROCEDUREs. The sort is ascending on the record key field (programmer ID). Some compilers do not permit INPUT and OUTPUT PROCEDURE SECTIONs to PERFORM paragraphs which lie outside the SECTION (as this example does). See *Schaum's Outline of Programming with Structured COBOL* (McGraw-Hill, 1984) if your compiler has this restriction.

(5)   Lines 76–84 are the INPUT PROCEDURE, which screens the dummy and deleted records from the sort. DIRECT-FILE is opened INPUT (line 78), an end-of-file switch is initialized (line 79), a priming READ is performed (line 80), and 040-CHECK-AND-RELEASE is then performed until the end of the file (lines 81–82). DIRECT-FILE is then closed.

(6)   Lines 98–103 show how to sequentially input from a direct file. The READ statement is exactly the same as for a sequential file, including the use of the AT END clause.

(7)   Lines 105–112 examine the direct record just input to see if it is a dummy or deleted record. Since condition names are defined for both conditions, this is easy to code (line 107). If the record is active, it is RELEASEd to the sort (lines 108–109).

(8)   The OUTPUT PROCEDURE (lines 86–94) RETURNs the sorted records, and formats and prints the report. Note that manipulation of the direct file itself is restricted to the INPUT PROCEDURE.

6.8   Direct File Retrieval—Random

The following guidelines should be considered when choosing between random and sequential processing:

(1)   Interactive applications usually dictate the use of random processing in order to provide reasonable response to terminal users.

(2)   Batch applications can typically use either approach, depending on the following:

(a)   If there is no transaction file to identify which records to access (so that *all* of the records in the file must be accessed, as when a printed report is produced), then sequential processing is indicated.

```
00001              IDENTIFICATION DIVISION.
00002              PROGRAM-ID.  DIRECT-SEQUENTIAL-RETRIEVAL.

00003              ENVIRONMENT DIVISION.
00004              CONFIGURATION SECTION.
00005              SOURCE-COMPUTER.  IBM-3081.
00006              OBJECT-COMPUTER.  IBM-3081.
00007              INPUT-OUTPUT SECTION.
00008              FILE-CONTROL.

00009                  SELECT DIRECT-FILE
00010                      ASSIGN TO D-MASTER
00011                      ACCESS IS SEQUENTIAL
00012                      ACTUAL KEY IS ACTUAL-KEY-DATA-AREA
00013                      .
00014                  SELECT REPORT-FILE
00015                      ASSIGN TO PRINTOUT
00016                      ORGANIZATION IS SEQUENTIAL
00017                      ACCESS IS SEQUENTIAL
00018                      .
00019                  SELECT SORTED-DIRECT-FILE
00020                      ASSIGN TO SORTWORK
00021                      .

00022              DATA DIVISION.
00023              FILE SECTION.

00024              FD  DIRECT-FILE
00025                  LABEL RECORDS ARE STANDARD
00026                  RECORD CONTAINS 16 CHARACTERS
                       .
00027              01  DIRECT-RECORD.
00028                  05  DIRECT-PROGRAMMER-ID          PIC X(5).
00029                  05  DIRECT-DELETE-CODE-BYTE        PIC X.
00030                      88  ACTIVE-RECORD              VALUE SPACE.
00031                      88  DELETED-RECORD             VALUE "D".
00032                  05  DIRECT-PROJECT-ID              PIC X(8).
00033                  05  DIRECT-TOTAL-HOURS             PIC 9(3)V9 COMP.

00034              FD  REPORT-FILE
00035                  LABEL RECORDS ARE STANDARD
00036                  RECORD CONTAINS 132 CHARACTERS
00037                  .
00038              01  REPORT-LINE                        PIC X(132).

00039              SD  SORTED-DIRECT-FILE
00040                  RECORD CONTAINS 16 CHARACTERS

00041              01  SORTED-RECORD.
00042                  05  SORTED-PROGRAMMER-ID           PIC X(5).
00043                  05  SORTED-DELETE-CODE-BYTE        PIC X.
00044                  05  SORTED-PROJECT-ID              PIC X(8).
00045                  05  SORTED-TOTAL-HOURS             PIC 9(3)V9 COMP.

00046              WORKING-STORAGE SECTION.

00047              01  FLAGS-AND-SWITCHES.
00048                  05  DIRECT-END-OF-FILE-SW          PIC X(3).
00049                      88  MORE-DIRECT-RECORDS        VALUE "NO".
00050                      88  NO-MORE-INPUT              VALUE "YES".

00051              01  ACTUAL-KEY-DATA-AREA.
00052                  05  RELATIVE-TRACK                 PIC 9(5) COMP SYNC.
00053                  05  RECORD-KEY-VALUE               PIC 9(5).
00054                  05  CHECK-FOR-DUMMY-FIELD          REDEFINES RECORD-KEY-VALUE.
00055                      10  DUMMY-RECORD-FLAG          PIC X.
00056                          88  DUMMY-RECORD           VALUE HIGH-VALUES.
00057                      10  FILLER                     PIC X(4).
00058              01  WS-DETAIL-LINE.
00059                  05  WS-PROGRAMMER-ID               PIC X(5).
00060                  05  FILLER                         PIC X(5) VALUE SPACES.
00061                  05  WS-PROJECT-ID                  PIC X(8).
```

Fig. 6-2

```
00062                     05  FILLER                    PIC X(5) VALUE SPACES.
00063                     05  WS-TOTAL-HOURS            PIC Z(3).9.
00064                     05  FILLER                    PIC X(104) VALUE SPACES.

00065          PROCEDURE DIVISION.
00066
00067          000-EXECUTIVE-MODULE.
00068
00069              SORT SORTED-DIRECT-FILE
00070                  ON ASCENDING KEY SORTED-PROGRAMMER-ID
00071                  INPUT PROCEDURE  IS 010-SCREEN-DIRECT-RECORDS
00072                  OUTPUT PROCEDURE IS 020-GENERATE-REPORT
00073              STOP RUN
00074              .
00075
00076          010-SCREEN-DIRECT-RECORDS SECTION.
00077
00078              OPEN    INPUT   DIRECT-FILE
00079              MOVE "NO" TO DIRECT-END-OF-FILE-SW
00080              PERFORM 030-GET-DIRECT-RECORD
00081              PERFORM 040-CHECK-AND-RELEASE
00082                  UNTIL NO-MORE-INPUT
00083              CLOSE   DIRECT-FILE
00084              .
00085
00086          020-GENERATE-REPORT SECTION.
00087
00088              OPEN    OUTPUT  REPORT-FILE
00089              MOVE "NO" TO DIRECT-END-OF-FILE-SW
00090              PERFORM 050-GET-NEXT-SORTED-RECORD
00091              PERFORM 060-PRINT-A-LINE
00092                  UNTIL NO-MORE-INPUT
00093              CLOSE   REPORT-FILE
00094              .
00095
00096          025-PERFORMED-PARAGRAPHS SECTION.
00097
00098          030-GET-DIRECT-RECORD.
00099
00100              READ DIRECT-FILE
00101                  AT END
00102                      MOVE "YES" TO DIRECT-END-OF-FILE-SW
00103              .
00104
00105          040-CHECK-AND-RELEASE.
00106
00107              IF NOT DELETED-RECORD AND NOT DUMMY-RECORD
00108                  RELEASE SORTED-RECORD
00109                      FROM DIRECT-RECORD
00110              .

00111              PERFORM 030-GET-DIRECT-RECORD
00112              .
00113
00114          050-GET-NEXT-SORTED-RECORD.
00115
00116              RETURN SORTED-DIRECT-FILE
00117                  AT END
00118                      MOVE "YES" TO DIRECT-END-OF-FILE-SW
00119              .
00120
00121          060-PRINT-A-LINE.
00122
00123              MOVE SORTED-PROGRAMMER-ID   TO WS-PROGRAMMER-ID
00124              MOVE SORTED-PROJECT-ID      TO WS-PROJECT-ID
00125              MOVE SORTED-TOTAL-HOURS     TO WS-TOTAL-HOURS
00126              WRITE REPORT-LINE
00127                  FROM WS-DETAIL-LINE
00128              .
00129              PERFORM 050-GET-NEXT-SORTED-RECORD
00130              .
```

Fig. 6-2 (*cont.*)

(*b*) If records to be accessed are identified by a transaction file, then the decision depends on (1) the percentage of records to be accessed (a low percentage favors random processing; a high percentage, sequential processing) and (2) whether or not the records need to be retrieved in sorted sequence (e.g., it may be more efficient to sort a *small* transaction file and then retrieve the indicated direct file records randomly, than it would be to sort the *large* direct file and then sequentially search for a few records; note that both of these methods retrieve the direct records by key; the difference is strictly in efficiency).

The following discussion applies when a transaction file supplies the keys of records to be retrieved randomly.

ENVIRONMENT DIVISION Considerations

The IBM OS/VS COBOL SELECT statement for random retrieval of a direct file has the following syntax:

```
SELECT file-name
    ASSIGN TO W-ddname
    ACCESS IS RANDOM
    ACTUAL KEY IS data-name
    .
```

"D" could be used in place of the organization code "W" for random retrieval (both function equivalently for this purpose). "ACCESS IS RANDOM" and "ACTUAL KEY IS ..." are both required for this purpose.

DATA DIVISION Considerations

The FD and level-01 record description are the same as for file creation and sequential retrieval. It is again useful to define a condition name for logically deleted records.

PROCEDURE DIVISION Considerations

Observe that the logic for random retrieval is exactly the logic used to check for duplicate keys in the file creation example of Section 6.6. Since the relevant PROCEDURE DIVISION statements were discussed in that section, they are only listed here:

(1) OPEN INPUT file-name

(2) CLOSE file-name

(3) READ file-name

```
[ INTO  data-name ]
[ INVALID KEY
  imperative-statement(s). ]
```

EXAMPLE 6.23 Figure 6-3 illustrates random retrieval of the direct file created in Example 6.20. Retrieval is dictated by keys provided from a transaction file. The same key transformation function used in Example 6.20 must be used again here if retrieval is to succeed. Likewise, the same collision-handling method (extended search) must be used for both programs. The following comments refer to the IBM OS/VS COBOL source listing in Fig. 6-3:

(1) Lines 9–13 define the sequential transaction file; lines 14–18 define the direct file as described above. Note that ACCESS IS RANDOM.

```
00001          IDENTIFICATION DIVISION.
00002          PROGRAM-ID.  DIRECT-RANDOM-RETRIEVAL.

00003          ENVIRONMENT DIVISION.
00004          CONFIGURATION SECTION.
00005          SOURCE-COMPUTER.  IBM-3081.
00006          OBJECT-COMPUTER.  IBM-3081.
00007          INPUT-OUTPUT SECTION.
00008          FILE-CONTROL.

00009              SELECT TRANSACTION-FILE
00010                  ASSIGN TO PROGIDS
00011                  ORGANIZATION IS SEQUENTIAL
00012                  ACCESS IS SEQUENTIAL
00013                  .
00014              SELECT DIRECT-FILE
00015                  ASSIGN TO W-MASTER
00016                  ACCESS IS RANDOM
00017                  ACTUAL KEY IS ACTUAL-KEY-DATA-AREA
00018                  .

00019          DATA DIVISION.
00020          FILE SECTION.
00021          FD  TRANSACTION-FILE
00022              LABEL RECORDS ARE STANDARD
00023              BLOCK CONTAINS O CHARACTERS
00024              RECORD CONTAINS 80 CHARACTERS
00025              .
00026          01  TRANSACTION-RECORD.
00027              05  TRANS-PROGRAMMER-ID        PIC X(5).
00028              05  FILLER                     PIC X(75).

00029          FD  DIRECT-FILE
00030              LABEL RECORDS ARE STANDARD
00031              RECORD CONTAINS 16 CHARACTERS
                   .
00032          01  DIRECT-RECORD.
00033              05  DIRECT-PROGRAMMER-ID       PIC X(5).
00034              05  DIRECT-DELETE-CODE-BYTE    PIC X.
00035                  88  ACTIVE-RECORD          VALUE SPACE.
00036                  88  DELETED-RECORD         VALUE "D".
00037              05  DIRECT-PROJECT-ID          PIC X(8).
00038              05  DIRECT-TOTAL-HOURS         PIC 9(3)V9 COMP.

00039          WORKING-STORAGE SECTION.

00040          01  PROGRAM-CONSTANTS.
00041              05  PRIME-NUMBER-OF-TRACKS     PIC S9(5) COMP
00042                                             VALUE +3.
00043          01  FLAGS-AND-SWITCHES.
00044              05  TRANS-END-OF-FILE-SW       PIC X(3).
00045                  88  MORE-TRANS-RECORDS     VALUE "NO".
00046                  88  NO-MORE-TRANSACTIONS   VALUE "YES".
00047              05  RECORD-NOT-FOUND-SW        PIC X(3).
00048                  88  RECORD-NOT-FOUND       VALUE "YES".
00049                  88  RECORD-EXISTS          VALUE "NO".

00050          01  ACTUAL-KEY-DATA-AREA.
00051              05  RELATIVE-TRACK             PIC 9(5) COMP SYNC.
00052              05  RECORD-KEY-VALUE           PIC 9(5).

00053          01  IGNORED-QUOTIENT-FIELD         PIC S9(4) COMP SYNC.

00054          PROCEDURE DIVISION.
00055
00056          000-EXECUTIVE-MODULE.
00057
00058              OPEN    INPUT   TRANSACTION-FILE
00059                              DIRECT-FILE
00060              MOVE "NO" TO TRANS-END-OF-FILE-SW
00061              PERFORM 010-GET-TRANSACTION-RECORD
00062              PERFORM 020-RETRIEVE-DIRECT-RECORDS
```

Fig. 6-3

```
00063                         UNTIL NO-MORE-TRANSACTIONS
00064                 CLOSE   TRANSACTION-FILE
00065                         DIRECT-FILE
00066                 STOP RUN
00067                 .
00068
00069          010-GET-TRANSACTION-RECORD.
00070
00071              READ TRANSACTION-FILE
00072                  AT END
00073                      MOVE "YES" TO TRANS-END-OF-FILE-SW
00074              .
00075
00076          020-RETRIEVE-DIRECT-RECORDS.
00077
00078              PERFORM 030-BUILD-ACTUAL-KEY
00079              MOVE "NO" TO RECORD-NOT-FOUND-SW
00080              READ DIRECT-FILE
00081                  INVALID KEY
00082                      MOVE "YES" TO RECORD-NOT-FOUND-SW
00083              .
00084              IF RECORD-EXISTS
00085                  IF DELETED-RECORD
00086                      MOVE "YES" TO RECORD-NOT-FOUND-SW
00087              .
00088              IF RECORD-NOT-FOUND
00089                  DISPLAY TRANS-PROGRAMMER-ID " NOT ON FILE ***"
00090              ELSE
00091                  DISPLAY DIRECT-PROGRAMMER-ID " WORKED ON PROJECT "
00092                          DIRECT-PROJECT-ID " FOR "
00093                          DIRECT-TOTAL-HOURS " HOURS"
00094
00095              PERFORM 010-GET-TRANSACTION-RECORD
00096              .
00097
00098          030-BUILD-ACTUAL-KEY.
00099
00100              MOVE TRANS-PROGRAMMER-ID TO RECORD-KEY-VALUE
00101              DIVIDE RECORD-KEY-VALUE BY PRIME-NUMBER-OF-TRACKS
00102                  GIVING IGNORED-QUOTIENT-FIELD
00103                  REMAINDER RELATIVE-TRACK
00104              .
```

Fig. 6-3 (*cont.*)

(2) Lines 34–36 define the delete code byte for direct records. Notice the use of condition names.

(3) The WORKING-STORAGE SECTION is similar to that for the creation program in Example 6.20, and the same comments apply. Major differences are that a copy of the ACTUAL KEY area is not needed here, while a *record-not-found switch* has been added (lines 47–49). Data items involved in key transformation are the same as in Example 6.20.

(4) The executive module in lines 56–67 opens both files, does a priming read of the transaction file, and then randomly retrieves direct records until there are no more transactions, at which point both files are closed.

(5) Lines 76–94 illustrate how to randomly retrieve a direct record. The paragraph 030-BUILD-ACTUAL-KEY is the same as in Example 6.20. Observe how RECORD-NOT-FOUND-SW is used to indicate whether the record was successfully READ or not. Lines 79–83 leave RECORD-NOT-FOUND-SW set to "YES" if the record is not physically present and to "NO" if a record is input. Since logically deleted records are physically present in the file, lines 84–87 check the delete code byte of records which were physically retrieved (line 84). If the record is marked deleted (line 85), RECORD-NOT-FOUND-SW is reset to "YES" (line 86). Thus records which are physically present but marked deleted are considered "not found".

(6) In real life, the error messages (line 89) and the display of file data (lines 91–93) would either be sent to a terminal (interactive system) or formatted and printed on a standard report (batch system). DISPLAY is used here to simplify nonrelevant logic.

6.9   Direct File Updating

File updating involves adding, changing, and deleting records. For direct files, it is usually done randomly. Since the operating system access method (BDAM) does not physically delete records, logical deletion must be handled by the COBOL program (by setting a *delete code byte* to mark a record as deleted). Thus deletion for direct files can be viewed as a special case of record change (i.e., changing the delete byte). Checking for duplicate keys when adding records is up to the COBOL program, as it is when a direct file is created. Finally, changes to a record may not involve changing the record's length.

ENVIRONMENT DIVISION Considerations

The syntax of a SELECT statement to update a direct file is the same as that used to create the file:

```
SELECT file-name
       ASSIGN TO W-ddname
       ACCESS MODE IS RANDOM
       ACTUAL KEY IS data-name
       .
```

DATA DIVISION Considerations

The FD and level-01 record description are the same as for file creation and retrieval.

PROCEDURE DIVISION Considerations

Incoming transaction records must contain a code identifying them as add, change, or delete transactions. The update program should classify each transaction and then perform the appropriate operation.

Adding new records to the file must be done in exactly the same way as when the file was created; i.e., the same key transformation and collision-handling methods should be used. An update program should always check for the presence of duplicate keys when adding records to a direct file. This can be done in the manner discussed in Section 6.6.

One complication of adding records to an existing file is the possibility of adding a record with a key which duplicates that of a record already on file, but marked deleted. In this case, it is *not* correct to add the new record, since this would result in two records physically on disk with the same key (so only the first one on the track to which they hash, or in the extended-search path, could ever be retrieved). The proper solution to this difficulty is to replace the logically deleted record contents with the contents of the new record and mark it active. An update program must thus distinguish between adding a brand new record and adding a record which replaces a deleted record.

Changing the fields in a logical record first involves READing the record (using the key value supplied as part of the transaction information). If an INVALID KEY results, then a record-not-found condition exists and should be handled in whatever way makes sense for the particular application.

If the record is physically input (no INVALID KEY), it must still be checked for logical deletion. If its delete byte indicates it is inactive, a record-not-found condition still exists.

If the record is physically present and active, then the changes dictated by the transaction information can be applied to the fields in the direct file's record area. When the changes are completed, the REWRITE verb is used to replace the original record contents on the disk. Note that until REWRITE is successfully executed, the disk copy of the record has not been changed.

Deleting a logical record from a direct file is a special type of change in which the delete code byte is set to indicate that the record is no longer active. This involves READing the record, checking that it is both physically and logically active, modifying the delete code value, and then REWRITEing the modified record as above.

PROCEDURE DIVISION statements relevant to updating a direct file are:

(1) <u>OPEN</u> I–O file-name

(2) <u>CLOSE</u> file-name

(3) <u>READ</u> file-name

```
[ INTO data-name ]
[ INVALID KEY
    imperative-statement(s). ]
```

(4) <u>WRITE</u> direct-record-name

```
[ FROM data-name ]
[ INVALID KEY
    imperative-statement(s). ]
```

(5) <u>REWRITE</u> direct-record-name

```
[ FROM data-name ]
[ INVALID KEY
    imperative-statement(s). ]
```

The REWRITE statement replaces the record identified by the current contents of the ACTUAL KEY with the current contents of the level-01 record area for the file. If the record cannot be found or if the relative track number in the ACTUAL KEY is outside the space allocated to the file, the INVALID KEY routine will be executed; otherwise, it will be ignored. During a direct file change or delete operation, if the update program ensures that the ACTUAL KEY for the REWRITE is identical to that used for the preceding READ, then INVALID KEY may be safely omitted (this is easily accomplished by simply not changing the ACTUAL KEY after a successful READ). The file must be OPENed I–O in order for REWRITE to be used.

EXAMPLE 6.24 Figure 6-4 illustrates a full add-change-delete update of the direct file created in Example 6.20. To eliminate nonrelevant details, it is assumed that the transaction file has been edited (note, however, that transaction field editing cannot detect record-not-found and duplicate-key errors; these can only be detected during the update itself). The following comments refer to the IBM OS/VS COBOL source listing in Fig. 6-4:

(1) Lines 9–13 and 21–34 define the sequential transaction file containing the update information. Note the TRANS-CODE (lines 27–30), which identifies the type of transaction.

(2) Lines 14–18 and 35–44 define the direct file to be updated. Note the condition names defined for the delete code byte (lines 40–42). "W" is coded in the ASSIGN TO clause, although "D" could also be used. "D" in ASSIGN TO causes the WRITE statement to function as a REWRITE statement if the record being written is the same as the last one READ, and as a WRITE statement otherwise. Since this can become confusing, the use of "D" is not recommended for file updating. With "W", WRITE always adds a new record and REWRITE always replaces an existing record. Coding "W" thus eliminates potential confusion.

(3) WORKING-STORAGE SECTION items (lines 45–65) are essentially the same as those for file creation. Lines 53–55 define a switch (RECORD-IS-THERE-SW) used to indicate whether or not a record is physically present in the file. RECORD-IS-ACTIVE-SW (lines 56–58) is used to indicate whether a record which is physically present is active or logically deleted. The reader will recall that when adding records, the update program must distinguish between (1) a record which is not physically present (in which case there is no duplicate key, and the new record can be added with WRITE), (2) a record which is physically present but marked deleted (in which case there is no duplicate key, but REWRITE should be used to replace the existing logically deleted record with the new active one, rather than add a second record with the same key), and (3) a record which is physically present and active (in which case there is a duplicate key error, and the new record cannot be added). RECORD-IS-THERE-SW and RECORD-IS-ACTIVE-SW help the program identify these three conditions.

```
00001              IDENTIFICATION DIVISION.
00002              PROGRAM-ID.  DIRECT-FILE-UPDATE.

00003              ENVIRONMENT DIVISION.
00004              CONFIGURATION SECTION.
00005              SOURCE-COMPUTER.  IBM-3081.
00006              OBJECT-COMPUTER.  IBM-3081.
00007              INPUT-OUTPUT SECTION.
00008              FILE-CONTROL.

00009                  SELECT TRANSACTION-FILE
00010                      ASSIGN TO CHANGES
00011                      ORGANIZATION IS SEQUENTIAL
00012                      ACCESS IS SEQUENTIAL
00013                      .
00014                  SELECT DIRECT-FILE
00015                      ASSIGN TO W-MASTER
00016                      ACCESS IS RANDOM
00017                      ACTUAL KEY IS ACTUAL-KEY-DATA-AREA
00018                      .

00019              DATA DIVISION.
00020              FILE SECTION.

00021              FD  TRANSACTION-FILE
00022                  LABEL RECORDS ARE STANDARD
00023                  BLOCK CONTAINS 0 CHARACTERS
00024                  RECORD CONTAINS 80 CHARACTERS
00025                  .
00026              01  TRANSACTION-RECORD.
00027                  05   TRANS-CODE                  PIC X.
00028                      88   ADD-NEW-RECORD          VALUE "A".
00029                      88   CHANGE-EXISTING-RECORD  VALUE "C".
00030                      88   DELETE-EXISTING-RECORD  VALUE "D".
00031                  05   TRANS-PROGRAMMER-ID         PIC X(5).
00032                  05   TRANS-PROJECT-ID            PIC X(8).
00033                  05   TRANS-TOTAL-HOURS           PIC 9(3)V9.
00034                  05   FILLER                      PIC X(62).

00035              FD  DIRECT-FILE
00036                  LABEL RECORDS ARE STANDARD
00037                  RECORD CONTAINS 16 CHARACTERS
                       .
00038              01  DIRECT-RECORD.
00039                  05   DIRECT-PROGRAMMER-ID        PIC X(5).
00040                  05   DIRECT-DELETE-CODE-BYTE     PIC X.
00041                      88   RECORD-DELETED          VALUE "D".
00042                      88   RECORD-ACTIVE           VALUE SPACE.
00043                  05   DIRECT-PROJECT-ID           PIC X(8).
00044                  05   DIRECT-TOTAL-HOURS          PIC 9(3)V9 COMP.

00045              WORKING-STORAGE SECTION.

00046              01  PROGRAM-CONSTANTS.
00047                  05   PRIME-NUMBER-OF-TRACKS      PIC S9(5) COMP
00048                                                   VALUE +3.
00049              01  FLAGS-AND-SWITCHES.
00050                  05   TRANS-END-OF-FILE-SW        PIC X(3).
00051                      88   MORE-TRANS-RECORDS      VALUE "NO".
00052                      88   NO-MORE-INPUT           VALUE "YES".
00053                  05   RECORD-IS-THERE-SW          PIC X(3).
00054                      88   RECORD-DOES-NOT-EXIST   VALUE "NO".
00055                      88   RECORD-EXISTS           VALUE "YES".
00056                  05   RECORD-IS-ACTIVE-SW         PIC X(3).
00057                      88   RECORD-IS-ACTIVE        VALUE "YES".
00058                      88   RECORD-IS-NOT-ACTIVE    VALUE "NO".

00059              01  ACTUAL-KEY-DATA-AREA.
00060                  05   RELATIVE-TRACK              PIC 9(5) COMP SYNC.
00061                  05   RECORD-KEY-VALUE            PIC 9(5).

00062              01  COPY-ACTUAL-KEY-AREA.
00063                  05   FILLER                      PIC 9(5) COMP SYNC.
00064                  05   FILLER                      PIC 9(5).
```

Fig. 6-4

```
00065            01  IGNORED-QUOTIENT-FIELD          PIC S9(4) COMP SYNC.

00066        PROCEDURE DIVISION.
00067
00068        000-EXECUTIVE-MODULE.
00069
00070            OPEN    INPUT   TRANSACTION-FILE
00071                    I-O     DIRECT-FILE
00072            MOVE "NO" TO TRANS-END-OF-FILE-SW
00073            PERFORM 010-GET-TRANSACTION-RECORD
00074            PERFORM 020-UPDATE-DIRECT-FILE
00075                UNTIL NO-MORE-INPUT
00076            CLOSE   TRANSACTION-FILE
00077                    DIRECT-FILE
00078            STOP RUN
00079                .
00080
00081        010-GET-TRANSACTION-RECORD.
00082
00083            READ TRANSACTION-FILE
00084                AT END
00085                    MOVE "YES" TO TRANS-END-OF-FILE-SW
00086                .
00087
00088        020-UPDATE-DIRECT-FILE.
00089
00090            IF ADD-NEW-RECORD
00091                PERFORM 050-ADD-A-RECORD
00092            ELSE IF CHANGE-EXISTING-RECORD
00093                PERFORM 070-CHANGE-A-RECORD
00094            ELSE IF DELETE-EXISTING-RECORD
00095                PERFORM 080-DELETE-A-RECORD
00096            ELSE
00097                DISPLAY "INVALID TRANS CODE: " TRANSACTION-RECORD
00098                .
00099            PERFORM 010-GET-TRANSACTION-RECORD
00100                .
00101
00102        030-BUILD-ACTUAL-KEY.
00103
00104            MOVE TRANS-PROGRAMMER-ID TO RECORD-KEY-VALUE
00105            DIVIDE RECORD-KEY-VALUE BY PRIME-NUMBER-OF-TRACKS
00106                GIVING IGNORED-QUOTIENT-FIELD
00107                REMAINDER RELATIVE-TRACK
00108                .
00109
00110        040-TRY-TO-INPUT-RECORD.
00111
00112            MOVE "YES" TO RECORD-IS-THERE-SW
00113            READ DIRECT-FILE
00114                INVALID KEY
00115                    MOVE "NO" TO RECORD-IS-THERE-SW
00116                                 RECORD-IS-ACTIVE-SW
00117                .
00118            IF RECORD-EXISTS
00119                IF RECORD-DELETED
00120                    MOVE "NO" TO RECORD-IS-ACTIVE-SW
00121                ELSE
00122                    MOVE "YES" TO RECORD-IS-ACTIVE-SW
00123                .
00124
00125        050-ADD-A-RECORD.
00126
00127            PERFORM 030-BUILD-ACTUAL-KEY
00128            MOVE ACTUAL-KEY-DATA-AREA    TO COPY-ACTUAL-KEY-AREA
00129            PERFORM 040-TRY-TO-INPUT-RECORD
00130            IF RECORD-DOES-NOT-EXIST
00131                MOVE COPY-ACTUAL-KEY-AREA TO ACTUAL-KEY-DATA-AREA
00132                PERFORM 060-WRITE-NEW-RECORD
00133            ELSE IF RECORD-EXISTS AND RECORD-IS-NOT-ACTIVE
00134                PERFORM 090-BUILD-DIRECT-RECORD
00135                REWRITE DIRECT-RECORD
00136            ELSE
00137                DISPLAY DIRECT-PROGRAMMER-ID " ALREADY ON FILE NO ADD"
00138                .
```

Fig. 6-4   (cont.)

```
00139            060-WRITE-NEW-RECORD.
00140
00141                PERFORM 090-BUILD-DIRECT-RECORD
00142                WRITE DIRECT-RECORD
00143                    INVALID KEY
00144                        DISPLAY "EXTENDED SEARCH REVEALED NO ROOM "
00145                            "TO ADD " TRANS-PROGRAMMER-ID
00146                    .
00147
00148            070-CHANGE-A-RECORD.
00149
00150                PERFORM 030-BUILD-ACTUAL-KEY
00151                PERFORM 040-TRY-TO-INPUT-RECORD
00152                IF RECORD-IS-ACTIVE
00153                    ADD TRANS-TOTAL-HOURS TO DIRECT-TOTAL-HOURS
00154                    REWRITE DIRECT-RECORD
00155                ELSE
00156                    DISPLAY TRANS-PROGRAMMER-ID " NOT FOUND FOR CHANGE"
00157                    .
00158
00159            080-DELETE-A-RECORD.
00160
00161                PERFORM 030-BUILD-ACTUAL-KEY
00162                PERFORM 040-TRY-TO-INPUT-RECORD
00163                IF RECORD-IS-ACTIVE
00164                    MOVE "D" TO DIRECT-DELETE-CODE-BYTE
00165                    REWRITE DIRECT-RECORD
00166                ELSE
00167                    DISPLAY TRANS-PROGRAMMER-ID " NOT FOUND FOR DELETE"
00168                    .
00169
00170            090-BUILD-DIRECT-RECORD.
00171
00172                MOVE TRANS-PROGRAMMER-ID    TO DIRECT-PROGRAMMER-ID
00173                MOVE TRANS-PROJECT-ID       TO DIRECT-PROJECT-ID
00174                MOVE TRANS-TOTAL-HOURS      TO DIRECT-TOTAL-HOURS
00175                MOVE SPACE TO DIRECT-DELETE-CODE-BYTE
00176                    .
```

Fig. 6-4   (*cont.*)

(4)   Lines 68–79 constitute the executive module. The direct file must be OPENed I–O in order to use READ, WRITE, and REWRITE together. Since the file already exists, this causes no difficulty.

(5)   Lines 90–98 use a *linear IF* structure to determine the type of transaction record just input. Note how easy this is with condition names. In real life, the DISPLAY statement on line 97 should be replaced with output to a formatted error report.

(6)   The paragraph 030-BUILD-ACTUAL-KEY (lines 102–108) must use exactly the same key transformation function as all other programs which randomly process this file.

(7)   Lines 125–138 constitute the routine to *add a new record*, which (1) carries out the key transformation and constructs the ACTUAL KEY (line 127), (2) saves a copy of the ACTUAL KEY contents for later use (line 128), (3) checks for a duplicate key by attempting to input a record with the key about to be added (done by performing 040-TRY-TO-INPUT-RECORD in line 129), and (4) uses a linear IF structure to determine whether a record with a duplicate key (*a*) does not exist on the file, (*b*) exists and is logically deleted, or (*c*) exists and is active (lines 130–138). If a record with a duplicate key is not on file (line 130), the program restores the ACTUAL KEY contents (which would have been destroyed by an unsuccessful READ in line 113), constructs the record in the level-01 record area, and WRITEs the new record (lines 131–132). If a record with a duplicate key exists but is marked deleted (line 133), the existing record should be replaced with the new one. This is accomplished by moving the data from the transaction record to the level-01 record area for the direct file, setting the delete code byte to "active" (done by performing 090-BUILD-DIRECT-RECORD, line 134), and then using the REWRITE verb to replace the existing (but logically deleted) record with the new active one (line 135). If a record with a duplicate key exists and is active, an error message is DISPLAYed (in real life, it should be printed on a formatted report). Note that 040-TRY-TO-INPUT-RECORD sets RECORD-IS-THERE-SW and RECORD-IS-ACTIVE-SW so that 050-ADD-A-RECORD can identify which of the three cases above applies for a particular record key.

(8) The paragraph 040-TRY-TO-INPUT-RECORD (lines 110–123) first sets RECORD-IS-THERE-SW to "YES". It then attempts to READ a record (the reader will recall that at this point, the ACTUAL KEY has already been built). If the record is not physically present (INVALID KEY), both RECORD-IS-THERE-SW and RECORD-IS-ACTIVE-SW are set to "NO". Line 118 then checks if a record was actually input. If so, the delete code must be checked to ensure that the record is active. If it is logically deleted, then RECORD-IS-ACTIVE-SW is set to "NO" (lines 118–120); if the record is active, RECORD-IS-ACTIVE-SW is set to "YES" (lines 121–122).

(9) Lines 148–157 *change an existing record* by adding the total hours from the transaction record to the total hours field in the direct file record. This involves (1) building the ACTUAL KEY, (2) trying to input the existing record (note that the input routine automatically checks the delete code byte as well; see lines 118–123), (3) if the record exists and is active, performing the addition (lines 152–153), and then (4) REWRITEing the updated version of the record. If the record cannot be found (or is marked deleted), an error message is printed.

(10) Lines 159–168 *delete an existing record* by changing its delete code byte (note the exact parallel between 070-CHANGE-A-RECORD and 080-DELETE-A-RECORD). If the record cannot be found (or is already marked deleted), an error message is printed.

6.10 Direct File Backup and Reorganization

File Backup

Backup refers to making an extra copy of a file's contents which can be used to reconstruct the original file in case it is inadvertently destroyed or corrupted. Operating system utility programs can be used to sequentially access a direct file and make a backup copy onto another disk or (more likely) a tape. Unfortunately, sequential access of a direct file will result in dummy and deleted records being copied onto the backup file (thus wasting time and space).

If it is desired to backup only active records, a simple COBOL program can be written to copy active records onto another file.

EXAMPLE 6.25 The "core" of a direct file backup program which screens dummy and deleted records is shown below. COPY-A-RECORD would be performed until the end of the file:

```
        SELECT DIRECT-FILE
            ASSIGN TO D-ddname
            ACCESS IS SEQUENTIAL
            ACTUAL KEY IS ACTUAL-KEY-DATA-AREA . . .

        OPEN INPUT    DIRECT-FILE
             OUTPUT   BACKUP-FILE . . .

    COPY-A-RECORD.
        READ DIRECT-FILE
            AT END
                MOVE "YES" TO END-DIRECT-FILE-SW
            .
        IF DIRECT-RECORD-WAS-INPUT
            IF DIRECT-RECORD-IS-NOT-A-DUMMY
                IF DIRECT-RECORD-NOT-DELETED
                    PERFORM MOVE-DIRECT-REC-TO-BACKUP-REC
                    WRITE BACKUP-RECORD
        .
```

File Reorganization

File reorganization refers to the practice of re-creating a file in order to remove logically deleted records, thereby freeing space for reuse when adding new records to the file. Direct files should be periodically reorganized by running a simple COBOL program to input the old file sequentially, screen dummy and deleted records, and create a new version of the file with only active records.

EXAMPLE 6.26   The core of a program to reorganize a direct file is shown below. Note that there is no need to check for duplicate keys when creating the new version, since the presence of duplicates on the OLD-DIRECT-FILE is presumably impossible. Hence only the WRITE verb is needed to add records to the reorganized file, and it can simply be OPENed OUTPUT (rather than I–O).

```
        SELECT OLD-DIRECT-FILE
              ASSIGN TO D-ddname
              ACCESS IS SEQUENTIAL
              ACTUAL KEY IS OLD-ACTUAL-KEY. . .
        SELECT REORGANIZED-DIRECT-FILE
              ASSIGN TO D-ddname
              ACCESS IS RANDOM
              ACTUAL KEY IS NEW-ACTUAL-KEY. . .

        OPEN INPUT    OLD-DIRECT-FILE
             OUTPUT   REORGANIZED-DIRECT-FILE

    COPY-A-RECORD.
        READ OLD-DIRECT-FILE
            AT END
                MOVE "YES" TO END-FILE-SW
            .
        IF OLD-RECORD-WAS-INPUT
            IF OLD-RECORD-NOT-DUMMY
                IF OLD-RECORD-IS-ACTIVE
                    PERFORM BUILD-NEW-ACTUAL-KEY
                    PERFORM MOVE-OLD-REC-TO-NEW-REC
                    WRITE REORGANIZED-DIRECT-RECORD
                        INVALID KEY
                            DISPLAY "NO ROOM TO ADD ..."
```

Review Questions

6.1   When is direct file organization usually used?

6.2   Define relative track.

6.3   Explain the role of a key transformation function when (1) creating and (2) accessing a direct file.

6.4   Explain the role of the ACTUAL KEY in direct file processing.

6.5   What are synonyms?

6.6   Explain the role of the collision-handling procedure when (1) creating and (2) accessing a direct file.

6.7   Explain the division/remainder key transformation function.

6.8   Distinguish between dummy and deleted records.

6.9   What really happens when a direct file WRITE is executed?

6.10   Explain the extra work involved in producing a report from a direct file.

6.11   What is clustering, and why is it undesirable?

6.12   Give six restrictions which must be observed for direct files.

6.13   Explain the importance of the packing factor for direct file processing.

6.14   Explain the key transformation technique of folding.

6.15   What is a "perfect" hash function? When can it be used?

6.16   Give two methods for handling nonnumeric keys in COBOL. Be sure to explain any restrictions associated with each method.

6.17   Explain the extended-search collision-handling algorithm available with IBM OS/VS COBOL.

6.18   Discuss the ENVIRONMENT, DATA, and PROCEDURE DIVISION considerations relevant to creating a direct file.

6.19   Discuss how records are deleted from direct files.

6.20   Give at least two methods of preventing duplicate keys when a direct file is created.

6.21   Discuss the organization of a typical program to retrieve a direct file sequentially (include ENVIRONMENT, DATA, and PROCEDURE DIVISION considerations).

6.22   Give guidelines for choosing between sequential and random retrieval of a file.

6.23   Discuss the ENVIRONMENT, DATA, and PROCEDURE DIVISION considerations relevant to random retrieval of a direct file.

6.24   Discuss procedures for (1) adding, (2) changing, and (3) deleting records during a direct file update.

6.25   Explain how backup of a direct file could be accomplished.

6.26   Why is file reorganization necessary? How could it be done for direct files?

Solved Problems

6.27   Suppose 716 tracks are required to hold the records for a direct file. How many tracks should be allocated to give a packing factor of 20 percent?

A packing factor of 20 percent means that $(100 - 20)$ or 80 percent of the file space should be used to actually hold records. If n tracks are allocated, then $(0.80 * n)$ should equal 716 tracks, or $n = (716/0.80) = 895$ tracks should be allocated.

6.28   How would the decision in Problem 6.27 be affected by choosing the division/remainder method of key transformation?

Division/remainder works best if the divisor chosen is the prime number closest to the number of tracks in the file. The largest prime number not greater than 895 is 887. If 887 is used as the divisor, however, the relative track numbers will only range from 0 to 886. If 895 tracks are actually allocated, relative tracks 887 to 894 (the 895th track of the file) cannot be hashed to directly (they will only be accessed during extended search). Thus it may be preferable to allocate only 888 or 889 tracks when using a divisor of 887. This leaves one or two tracks for extended searching beyond relative track 886, but does not waste space by allocating more than that.

6.29   For the file in Problem 6.28, give the relative track numbers for records with keys (*a*) 10729, (*b*) 53892, and (*c*) 66811.

Since the keys are numeric, use straight division/remainder, with 887 as the divisor:

(*a*)   TT = remainder (10729/887) = 85
(*b*)   TT = remainder (53892/887) = 672
(*c*)   TT = remainder (66811/887) = 286

6.30   The file label in the VTOC indicates that a direct file consists of two extents as follows: the first begins on cylinder 35, track 2 and is 8 tracks long; the second begins on cylinder 120, track 5 and is 6 tracks long. Show how the operating system could use this information to convert relative track numbers to actual cylinder and head numbers by converting (1) relative track 5 and (2) relative track 11.

Relative track 5 is actually the sixth track of the file (since relative track numbers start at 0). Since the first extent of the file is 8 tracks long, the sixth track falls in the first extent, which begins on track 2 of cylinder 35. The "sixth" track starting from track 2 is track 7; hence relative track 5 is actually on cylinder 35, track 7.

Relative track 11 is the twelfth track of the file. Since the first extent has 8 tracks, the twelfth track of the file would be the fourth track in the second extent (which consists of 6 tracks beginning on track 5 of cylinder 120). The "fourth" track starting from track 5 is track 8; hence relative track 11 is actually on cylinder 120, track 8. These computations are slightly more complicated when extents cross cylinder boundaries, but the operating system can easily convert relative track numbers to disk addresses.

6.31   Why is indexed organization often chosen over direct organization?

Indexed organization allows (1) random access by record key without the need for key transformation and (2) sequential access in sequence by record key without the need to sort and screen dummy and/or deleted records. The only disadvantage of indexed organization is that random retrieval of indexed files can be slower than for direct files. Systems analysts choose direct organization only when *forced* to do so because indexed random processing speeds are inadequate.

6.32   Why are synonyms not an immediate problem when direct organization is used?

Because logical records hash to a track of the file, and typically many records can fit on 1 track, synonyms only become a problem when a track fills up. With a good hash function and adequate packing factor, this happens infrequently.

6.33   What condition(s) can activate the INVALID KEY clause for (1) READ, (2) WRITE, and (3) REWRITE?

INVALID KEY for a *READ* or *REWRITE* is triggered when (*a*) the relative track number in the ACTUAL KEY is outside the range of the file or (*b*) a record with a key matching that in the ACTUAL KEY does not exist on the indicated track (or within the extended-search limit). INVALID KEY for a *WRITE* is triggered when (*a*) the relative track number in the ACTUAL KEY is outside the range of the file or (*b*) there is no space on the indicated track (or within the extended-search limit) in which to add the record.

6.34 What happens if a direct file update program adds a record with key 6666, then deletes it, and then adds a different record with key 6666?

This would result in *two* records with key 6666 being physically present on the file. Obviously, they would have hashed to the same relative track. The result is that only the first record with key 6666 encountered during a search of the track (or during extended search) could ever be retrieved during random processing. Both records would be retrieved during sequential processing.

6.35 In IBM OS/VS COBOL, why can nonnumeric keys which consist only of letters, digits, and/or spaces (not ending in a space) be successfully REDEFINEd as numeric for purposes of division/remainder key transformation?

In EBCDIC code, the letters are encoded (in hexadecimal) as C1–C9, D1–D9, and E2–E9; the digits as F1–F9; and the space as 40. In order to do any calculation on a field thought to be numeric, the compiler will first cause the field to be packed (i.e., converted to COMP-3). This process strips the left half-byte of each character, except the rightmost (for which the half-bytes are simply interchanged). Stripping the left half of all the codes listed above leaves a valid decimal digit (i.e., in all cases, one of the digits 0–9) in all but the rightmost position. As long as the rightmost character is not a space, interchanging the half-bytes produces a valid digit (i.e., 1–9) in the left half-byte and a valid sign code (i.e., one of the letters C, D, E, or F) in the right half-byte. The result is always a valid COMP-3 number.

6.36 Show how to hash CUSTOMER-NUMBER PIC X(5) if it is nonnumeric but meets the restrictions in Problem 6.35.

Define an area NUMERIC-CUST-NUMBER PIC 9(5) which REDEFINEs CUSTOMER-NUMBER, and then:

```
DIVIDE NUMERIC-CUST-NUMBER BY PRIME-DIVISOR
     GIVING IGNORE-THE-QUOTIENT
     REMAINDER RELATIVE-TRACK
```

6.37 Show how to hash CUSTOMER-NUMBER PIC X(5) if it is nonnumeric but does *not* meet the restrictions in Problem 6.35.

Since we need an area with an even number of bytes, define:

```
05   NUMERIC-CUST-NUMBER.          (total of 6 bytes)
     10   PIECE-1   PIC 9(9) COMP.  (5 - 9 digits COMP
                                     takes 4 bytes)
     10   PIECE-2   PIC 9(4) COMP.  (1 - 4 digits COMP
                                     takes 2 bytes)
```

Now use folding to combine the pieces before dividing:

```
MOVE CUSTOMER-NUMBER TO NUMERIC-CUST-NUMBER
ADD PIECE-1 PIECE-2 GIVING SUM-OF-PIECES
DIVIDE SUM-OF-PIECES BY PRIME-DIVISOR
     GIVING IGNORE-THE-QUOTIENT
     REMAINDER RELATIVE-TRACK
```

6.38 What is wrong with the following ACTUAL KEY definition?

```
05  ACTUAL-KEY-AREA.
    10   RECORD-KEY-VALUE      PIC X(7).
    10   RELATIVE-TRACK        PIC 9(3).
```

The relative track number must come first and must have PIC 9(5) or S9(5) COMP (with SYNC optional).

6.39 Suppose the transaction file used to create a direct file is sorted by key. Show how to sequence check the incoming transactions to eliminate the possibility of duplicate keys on the direct file.

```
        READ TRANSACTION-FILE AT END
            MOVE "YES" TO END-INPUT-SW
        .
        IF TRANSACTION-WAS-INPUT
            IF KEY-JUST-INPUT GREATER THAN PREVIOUS-KEY
                MOVE "NO"          TO DUPLICATE-KEY-SW
                MOVE KEY-JUST-INPUT TO PREVIOUS-KEY
            ELSE
                MOVE "YES"         TO DUPLICATE-KEY-SW
        .
```

PREVIOUS-KEY would be initialized to LOW-VALUES.

6.40 Write a routine to add a record to a direct file when there is no possibility of a duplicate key (e.g., as in Problem 6.39 above).

```
        ADD-A-RECORD.
            PERFORM BUILD-ACTUAL-KEY
            PERFORM MOVE-TRANS-REC-TO-DIRECT-REC
            WRITE DIRECT-RECORD
                INVALID KEY
                    DISPLAY "NO ROOM TO ADD NEW RECORD"
            .
```

6.41 Give SELECT and OPEN statements for the direct file in Problem 6.40.

```
        SELECT DIRECT-FILE
            ASSIGN TO D-ddname
            ACCESS IS RANDOM
            ACTUAL KEY IS ACTUAL-KEY-AREA. . .

        OPEN OUTPUT DIRECT-FILE
```

6.42 Why should an INPUT PROCEDURE always be used for a SORT to print a report from a direct file (i.e., why not do a USING sort)?

An INPUT PROCEDURE should always be used to eliminate dummy and deleted records from the sort operation itself. It is inefficient to include dummy and deleted records in the sorting.

6.43 How should paragraph 040-CHECK-AND-RELEASE of Fig. 6-2 be modified if the direct file consists of variable-length records?

When variable-length records are used, dummy records are not physically present on the tracks of a direct file (the system uses the track descriptor record, R0, to keep track of free space instead). Thus dummy records are not retrieved during sequential processing, and there is no need to check for their presence. It *is* still necessary to check for logically deleted records, however:

```
        IF NOT DELETED-RECORD
            RELEASE SORTED-RECORD FROM DIRECT-RECORD . . .
```

6.44   What is wrong with the following direct file retrieval program?

```
PROCESS-INQUIRY.
    PERFORM BUILD-ACTUAL-KEY
    MOVE "YES" TO RECORD-THERE-SW
    READ DIRECT-FILE
        INVALID KEY
            MOVE "NO" TO RECORD-THERE-SW
        .
    IF RECORD-THERE-SW EQUAL "YES"
        PERFORM DISPLAY-DATA-FROM-RECORD
    ELSE
        PERFORM DISPLAY-ERROR-MESSAGE
        .
```

This routine has neglected to check for a logically deleted record before responding to an inquiry transaction.

6.45   Correct the routine in Problem 6.44.

```
PROCESS-INQUIRY.
    PERFORM BUILD-ACTUAL-KEY
    MOVE "YES" TO RECORD-THERE-SW
    READ DIRECT-FILE
        INVALID KEY
            MOVE "NO" TO RECORD-THERE-SW
        .
    IF RECORD-THERE-SW EQUAL "YES"
        IF RECORD-IS-ACTIVE
            PERFORM DISPLAY-DATA-FROM-RECORD
        ELSE
            PERFORM DISPLAY-ERROR-MESSAGE
    ELSE
        PERFORM DISPLAY-ERROR-MESSAGE
        .
```

6.46   When a direct file is OPENed I–O, why does the use of "ASSIGN TO D-ddname" cause the WRITE statement to function as a WRITE (adding a new record) if the ACTUAL KEY does not match the key of the last record READ, and function as a REWRITE (replacing an existing record) if the ACTUAL KEY matches that of the last record READ?

This feature is supposed to make it easier to code an addition to the file. In particular, it eliminates the need to distinguish between a record which does not exist (and can therefore be added) and one which is physically present but marked deleted (and therefore should be replaced with the new one to be added).

6.47   Rewrite 050-ADD-A-RECORD of Fig. 6-4, assuming that ASSIGN TO D-ddname has been used instead of ASSIGN TO W-ddname.

```
050-ADD-A-RECORD.
     PERFORM 030-BUILD-ACTUAL-KEY
     MOVE ACTUAL-KEY-DATA-AREA TO COPY-ACTUAL-KEY-AREA
     PERFORM 040-TRY-TO-INPUT-RECORD
     IF RECORD-IS-ACTIVE
          DISPLAY "DUPLICATE KEY ERROR"
     ELSE
          PERFORM 090-BUILD-DIRECT-RECORD
          MOVE COPY-ACTUAL-KEY-AREA TO ACTUAL-KEY-DATA-AREA
          WRITE DIRECT-RECORD
               INVALID KEY
                    DISPLAY "NO ROOM TO ADD NEW RECORD"
```

Observe that the logic is "simpler" with code "D", since the WRITE statement itself distinguishes between a record which is not physically present and one which is physically present but not deleted. It can be argued, however, that this "hidden" logic is undesirable and that the explicit approach used in Fig. 6-4 is preferable.

6.48 How often should backup and reorganization be performed for a direct file?

It depends on the application. Usually a systems analyst will make these decisions.

Chapter 7

COBOL Indexed Files

Sequential files and direct files each offer their own unique advantages and disadvantages. *Sequential files* are typically kept sorted on a key field, allowing records to be processed sequentially in key sequence. Unfortunately, sequential files cannot be processed randomly. *Direct files* offer the capability of fast random processing by key but are inefficient to process sequentially (see Chapter 6). *Indexed file organization* is an ANSI standard file organization designed to offer the best of both worlds: (1) easy sequential access to records in key sequence plus (2) efficient random processing of records by key.

This chapter presents the details of ANSI standard indexed file organization as currently implemented in IBM OS/VS COBOL. Since indexed file organization is an ANSI standard organization, this information should apply equally well to indexed files as implemented on other systems which support the ANSI standard.

In addition, Sections 7.2–7.10 include information unique to indexed files in IBM OS/VS systems. This material is not part of the COBOL language per se but deals with (1) the concepts of indexed files as data structures and how they may be implemented and (2) information on how to use the IBM Access Method Services (IDCAMS) utility program to create, print, and delete indexed files in an IBM environment. Although the details of IBM indexed files may not exactly match those of the reader's installation, it is hoped that a thorough study of one particular indexed implementation will better prepare the reader to deal with indexed files on his or her system.

Chapter 7 is structured so that the material which directly pertains to COBOL (Sections 7.11–7.15) is all ANSI standard. The reader is urged to study the material on IBM's VSAM organization (Sections 7.2–7.10) as a detailed example of one possible indexed implementation. The reader should consult an instructor and/or vendor manual for information on the job control/command language needed to work with indexed files on his or her particular system.

7.1 General Characteristics of Indexed File Organization (ANSI Standard)

Indexed files are chosen for the master files of most business applications because they offer ease of both sequential and random processing. Indexed files *must* be placed on direct access storage devices.

The potential for both sequential and random processing of logical records is made possible by storing *secondary information* (in the form of an index) on the disk (or other DASD). Although the index takes extra space beyond that required for the data records themselves, this is usually not considered a major liability (the reader will recall that direct organization also "wastes" disk space by using a 15 to 20 percent packing factor, and that sequential files, which do not waste any space, do *not* permit random processing).

The *index* of an indexed file contains information which allows the operating system access method to relate a logical record's key field value to the physical disk address (CCHH) where the record is located. Vendors differ in the details of how the index is actually implemented, and some vendors may offer more than one implementation of indexed files. As of this writing, IBM offers two implementations of indexed file organization: (1) an older indexed file implementation known as ISAM (discussed in Problems 7.41–7.45, 7.58, and 7.71) and (2) its newer replacement, VSAM Key Sequenced Data Sets.

Regardless of the details of the file structure, the principles of indexed file operation are universal: (1) When indexed files are processed sequentially, the index is used to allow logical records to be retrieved in key sequence (the index must be used for sequential retrieval since the logical records are typically *not* in key sequence on the disk); and (2) when indexed files are processed randomly, the index is searched to locate the physical disk address of each desired logical record.

Since the index is accessed during sequential file processing, indexed files may take slightly longer to process sequentially than standard sequential files. Similarly, since the index must be searched for the key (and corresponding location) of each logical record to be retrieved randomly, indexed files *may* provide slower response than direct files (although with modern DASD hardware and modern index implementations, this difference may be negligible or nonexistent; an exact comparison depends on the size of the file, the particular index implementation and hardware used, the packing factor and key transformation considered for the direct file, etc.).

Since both the space requirements and access times of indexed files are usually satisfactory for almost all modern business applications, the flexibility of combining key sequence sequential processing with random processing makes indexed file organization the choice of most systems analysts for most business master files.

7.2   A Common Indexed File Implementation: IBM's VSAM Key Sequenced Data Sets

VSAM Key Sequenced Data Sets (hereafter called simply *VSAM*) represent IBM's latest implementation of ANSI standard indexed file organization. VSAM stores the data records themselves (called the *data component*) and the index records which constitute the index (called the *index component*) as separate files on the same or different DASDs. When viewed in combination, the data component and the index component together are called a *cluster*.

VSAM organizes all records (including both the index and data components) in terms of control intervals and control areas. A *control interval* (*CI*) is the physical unit of transfer between the DASD and main memory. VSAM always inputs and outputs complete control intervals. A *control area* (*CA*) is a group of related control intervals (see Fig. 7-3 and the discussion below).

The size of a control interval and the number of control intervals in a control area are usually automatically determined by VSAM, based on the type of DASD being used and the size of the logical records in the data component. The size of CIs and CAs can also be defined by the programmer by executing a VSAM utility program known as *Access Method Services* (or *IDCAMS*). It is usually best not to override the control interval and control area sizes picked by VSAM.

Control intervals may actually consist of one or more physical records (blocks) on a DASD. Again, the block size may be determined automatically by VSAM or dictated by the programmer via the IDCAMS utility. In either case, VSAM always inputs and outputs complete control intervals (whether or not this involves input/output of one or more physical blocks).

Organization of the Data Component

The data component (like all VSAM entities) is organized into control intervals and control areas. A data component CI normally holds several logical records. The logical records within each control interval are always kept sorted by key field.

VSAM treats all logical records as if they were variable-length (even if they are, in fact, fixed-length). VSAM keeps track of the length of logical records in a CI by using special *control information fields* placed at the end of each CI. Between the logical records themselves (at the beginning of the CI) and the control information (at the end of the CI), there is free space within the CI where new logical records can be added.

EXAMPLE 7.1   Figure 7-1 shows the layout of a typical VSAM control interval, including variable-length logical records, control information, and free space. New logical records may be added to the CI by using the free-space area.

EXAMPLE 7.2   Figure 7-2 shows the addition of a logical record to the CI in Fig. 7-1. Note that the record is inserted into the CI in key sequence (thus reorganizing the CI). When a record is added to a CI, the free space within the CI is correspondingly reduced, and the control information updated accordingly.

Logical record 1 (Key = 20)	Logical record 2 (Key = 40)	Logical record 3 (Key = 60)	Free space	Reserved for VSAM control information

Fig. 7-1 VSAM control interval

Logical record 1 (Key = 20)	Logical record 2 (Key = 30)	Logical record 3 (Key = 40)	Logical record 4 (Key = 60)	Free space	Reserved for VSAM control information

Fig. 7-2 CI showing addition of record with key 30

The control intervals in the data component are further grouped into control areas. Control areas play an important role in both sequential and random processing of logical records, as described below.

Index Component Organization—The Sequence Set

The index component is itself organized into two parts: the index set and the sequence set. The *sequence set* consists of the lowest-level index entries and is closely related to the concept of control area. There is one sequence set record for each control area in the data component. The sequence set record for a control area contains an entry for each control interval in that control area. The entry for a control interval consists of (1) the highest key of the logical records stored within that CI and (2) the physical disk address of the control interval.

The CI entries in a given sequence set record are kept sorted in ascending sequence by key. This not only facilitates searching during random processing but also allows the control intervals within a CA to be retrieved in key sequence during sequential processing—regardless of whether the CIs are actually in key sequence within the CA. Since the records within each control interval are in key sequence, if the control intervals within a control area are processed in the order dictated by the sequence set record for that particular CA, the logical records within the control area will be retrieved in key sequence.

The reader will recall that there is a sequence set record for each control area in the data component, and that each sequence set record contains an entry for each control interval within its given control area. In order to facilitate random processing, each sequence set entry consists of the highest key in its data component control interval, together with a *vertical pointer* to the control interval itself (i.e., to the disk location of the CI). The vertical pointer can be followed to retrieve any or all logical records within the CI.

In addition to the vertical pointers (to each CI within its associated CA), each sequence set record also contains a *horizontal pointer* to the next sequence set record in key sequence. The horizontal pointers are followed during sequential processing: after all logical records in a control area have been retrieved, the horizontal pointer is used to locate the sequence set record for the next control area to be processed.

EXAMPLE 7.3 Figure 7-3 shows the relationship between sequence set records and data component control intervals and control areas. The vertical pointers are used to locate CIs during both sequential and random processing. The horizontal pointers are used during sequential processing only. Note that CIs are not necessarily arranged in key sequence within their CA. This is why sequential processing must be done by following the sequence set entries (which are maintained in key sequence).

Index Component Organization—The Index Set

The second part of the index component is the *index set*. The index set consists of all higher-level

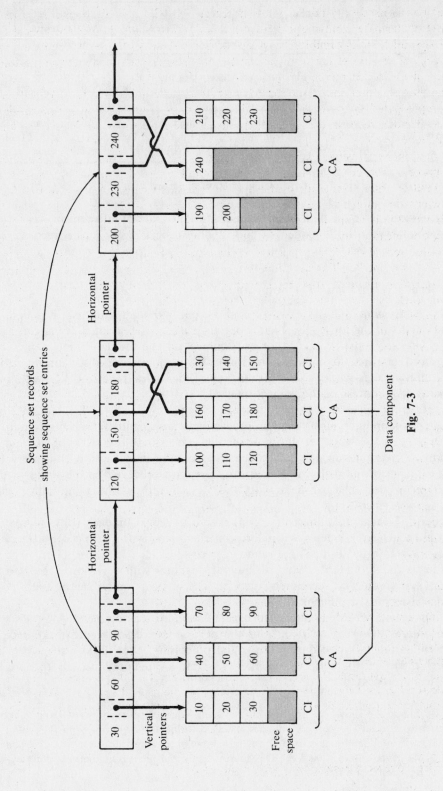

Sequence set records showing sequence set entries

Horizontal pointer

Vertical pointers

Free space

Data component

CI   CI   CA

CI   CI   CA

CI   CI   CA

Fig. 7-3

156

index entries and is used only during random processing. The purpose of the index set is to allow rapid location of the data component control interval which holds the desired logical record.

The VSAM index set is organized as a *tree* or *hierarchical* structure. There is one and only one index set record at the *top* of the tree (i.e., at the *root*). Index searching during random processing always begins at this index record.

The root and all other index set records consist of several *entries*. Each entry consists of the highest key represented in the next lower index set record, together with a pointer giving the disk location of said index record. The individual entries within an index set record are kept sorted in ascending sequence by key.

During random processing, each logical record to be accessed must first be looked up in the index. This process proceeds as follows: (1) The root index record is input, and the first entry with a key greater than or equal to the key of the desired record is located. Associated with this key value will be a downward pointer to a next lower-level index record. (2) The next lower-level index record pointed to in step (1) is input, and the first entry with a key greater than or equal to the key of the desired record is located. Associated with this key value will be a downward pointer to a next lower-level index record. (3) This process is repeated until the index record retrieved is a sequence set record. At this point, the first sequence set entry with a key greater than or equal to the key of the desired record is located. Associated with it will be a pointer to a data component control interval. Since each entry contains the highest key in its associated CI, if the desired record is in the file at all, it must be in the indicated control interval. (4) The indicated data component CI is input and searched for the desired logical record. If the record is not in *this* CI, it is not in the file (and the COBOL program is notified of the record-not-found condition).

The number of entries (and corresponding pointers to lower-level records) in an index record is known as its *fan-out*. It is clear that the greater the number of entries in an index record (i.e., the higher the fan-out), the fewer the number of index records which must be examined during an index search. VSAM automatically increases the number of index entries per index record by compressing the key values in the index entries. *Key compression* is a feature provided to limit the size of the index and thereby speed index searching. It is totally handled by VSAM and is completely transparent to the COBOL program.

The other factor that governs the speed of the index search is the number of index records that can be held (and therefore searched) in main memory, as opposed to being input from disk. If the file is small enough, the entire index component may fit in main memory, resulting in optimal random processing speed. For a large file, only a relatively small portion of the index may fit in main memory, resulting in many disk accesses during index searching and a corresponding slowdown in random processing.

EXAMPLE 7.4   Figure 7-4 shows a VSAM indexed cluster, including the index component (made up of the index set and sequence set) and the data component. The cluster is depicted as it would be immediately following the creation of a VSAM file. Observe that half of each CI in the data component has been deliberately left empty, and that one CI within each CA has also been left empty. This *distributed free space* is available to accommodate later additions to the file. The programmer controls the amount of distributed free space through the Access Method Services (IDCAMS) utility.

Initially, all CIs within each CA are in key sequence, as are the CAs themselves. This may change as records are added to the file later on, but it will not disrupt file processing because the sequence set entries are kept in key sequence, regardless of what happens with respect to the CIs themselves. Of course, the logical records within each CI are always maintained in key sequence.

7.3   How VSAM Works: Creation of VSAM Indexed Files

The Access Method Services (IDCAMS) utility program supplied with VSAM must be used to accomplish several functions before a COBOL program can actually load logical records into a VSAM indexed file. These functions are typically carried out by systems programmers, rather than by applications (i.e., COBOL) programmers. The COBOL programmer should, however, under-

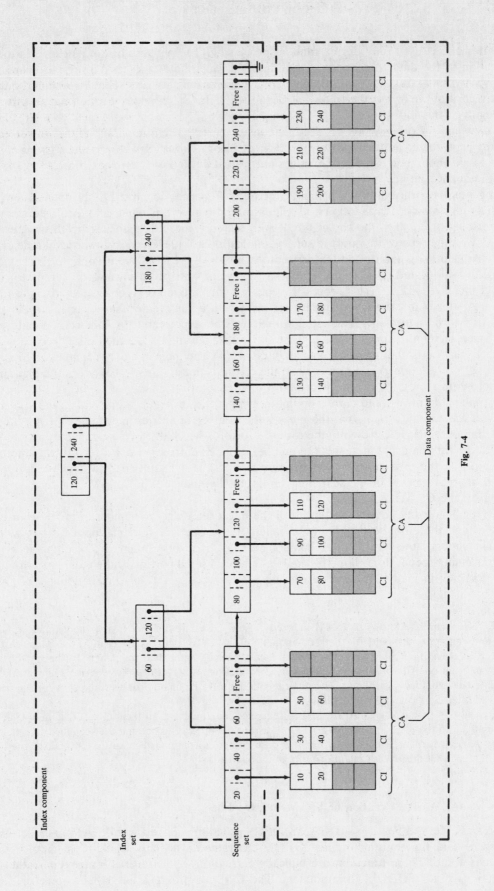

Fig. 7-4

158

stand the concepts involved in the following IDCAMS operations preparatory to executing a COBOL program to place records in a VSAM indexed file:

(1)   All VSAM files must be *cataloged* in a special file defined to the operating system as a *VSAM catalog*. A VSAM catalog essentially takes the place of the volume table of contents (VTOC) in that it holds all necessary descriptive information about the file. VSAM files are ordinarily *not* described in a VTOC, since the VSAM catalog already holds all relevant information about them. In order to create *any* VSAM file, there must first be a VSAM catalog available in which to catalog the new file. VSAM catalogs are defined by executing the IDCAMS utility program with the DEFINE MASTERCATALOG or DEFINE USERCATALOG commands. Typically, a systems programmer will be responsible for defining the VSAM catalog or catalogs at a given installation. The COBOL programmer is able to make use of these already-existing catalog(s) and need only learn the proper names and standards for their use at his or her installation. Consult an instructor or local standards manual regarding the VSAM catalog(s) available at your installation.

(2)   Usually, space for new VSAM files is allocated out of what is known as a *VSAM data space*. A data space is an area on a direct access volume (usually a disk) which has been set aside for VSAM's use. The tracks for the data space are allocated out of the free-space area (defined in the VTOC for the volume) by executing the IDCAMS utility with the DEFINE SPACE command. The VTOC then contains an entry which describes the data space itself, but does not contain information about what VSAM files reside within the data space. The files inside a VSAM data space are described, instead, in a VSAM catalog. VSAM has total control of what goes on inside a VSAM data space (i.e., within its own data spaces, VSAM controls the allocation of tracks when VSAM files are created or expanded, and the freeing of tracks when VSAM files are deleted). Typically, systems programmers are responsible for creating the VSAM data spaces to be used at a given installation. Again, the COBOL programmer need only learn the proper names and standards for using the existing data spaces at his or her shop. Consult an instructor or local standards manual regarding the rules governing VSAM data spaces at your installation.

(3)   Once a VSAM catalog and data space are available, the next step in creating a VSAM indexed file is to *define a VSAM catalog entry* for the file. One way to accomplish this is by executing the IDCAMS utility program with the DEFINE CLUSTER command (the reader will recall that the name for a VSAM index component, together with its corresponding data component, is a "cluster"). Since the COBOL programmer might be responsible for creating the catalog entry for a file, a discussion of the IDCAMS DEFINE CLUSTER command is included in Section 7.10 below. Observe that the catalog entry must be created before any records are actually placed in the file. Creation of the catalog entry also entails allocating space for the file, as dictated by the operands of the DEFINE CLUSTER command. Consult an instructor or local standards manual concerning the rules governing the use of the DEFINE CLUSTER command at your installation.

(4)   After a catalog entry has been defined (and initial file space allocated), a COBOL program can be executed to load logical records into the VSAM file. When a VSAM indexed file is created sequentially, logical records must be written in ascending sequence by key. Any records which are not in key sequence will be rejected by VSAM and not placed on the file (with the COBOL program being notified of the *sequence error*). The IDCAMS DEFINE CLUSTER command used in step (3) above can specify that a certain percentage of each control interval be left empty as records are initially loaded into the file. Likewise, DEFINE CLUSTER can dictate that a percentage of CIs within each control area be left totally empty during the initial loading of records into the file. This distributed free space will be used later on as logical records are added to the file during file maintenance. In addition to loading records into a VSAM indexed file with a COBOL program specifically written for that purpose, the IDCAMS utility REPRO command can also be used to copy

records from an existing VSAM or sequential file into the new VSAM file. This use of IDCAMS can eliminate the need to write special file creation programs in COBOL, and can be especially useful when existing non-VSAM files are being converted to VSAM organization. Consult an instructor or vendor manual regarding the use of the IDCAMS REPRO command.

EXAMPLE 7.5 Figure 7-4 shows a VSAM indexed file immediately after being created. The IDCAMS DEFINE CLUSTER command specified that 25 percent of the control intervals within each data component control area be left completely empty during creation, and that 50 percent of each utilized control interval also be left free for later additions to the file. Since records must be loaded into the file in key sequence, all CIs and CAs are initially also in key sequence. This may not remain true as records are later added to the file.

7.4 How VSAM Works: Random Retrieval of VSAM Indexed Files

When VSAM indexed files are accessed randomly, each COBOL READ statement results in a full search of the index component for the cluster. The key value for the logical record to be retrieved is first placed in the key field area associated with the level-01 record description for the file (in COBOL terminology, this field in the record description is known as the *RECORD KEY*; the RECORD KEY is named in the SELECT statement for the file). A READ statement is then executed, causing the VSAM access method to begin its index search at the highest-level (i.e., root) record in the index set.

VSAM first compares the RECORD KEY value specified by the program to the entries in the top index record. The first entry in the root record greater than or equal to the RECORD KEY is used to point to a next lower-level index set record, which is now input (if it is not already in memory). The entries in *this* index record are then compared to the RECORD KEY value. Again, the first entry greater than or equal to the RECORD KEY points to a next lower index set record, which is now input (if it is not already in memory).

This search process continues downward through the index levels until eventually an index set record entry points to a sequence set record. The first sequence set record entry which is greater than or equal to the RECORD KEY value points to a data component control interval, which must hold the record (if it is in the file). This CI is now retrieved and searched for the desired logical record. If the record is found, it is placed in the level-01 record area for the file; otherwise, the COBOL program is notified of the record-not-found condition.

EXAMPLE 7.6 VSAM carries out the following steps to randomly locate the logical record with key 90 in the file of Fig. 7-4:

(1) The COBOL program places the key value (90) in the RECORD KEY area for the file and then executes a READ statement.

(2) Execution of the READ statement causes VSAM to pick up the RECORD KEY value from the COBOL program.

(3) VSAM now retrieves the top-level record from the index set (no disk access is needed if it is already in memory; when the file was OPENed, VSAM automatically input as much of the index as possible into memory to minimize time required for disk access during index searching).

(4) The entries in the top-level index record are compared to the RECORD KEY value. Since 120 is the first entry greater than or equal to 90, the pointer (i.e., disk address) associated with key value 120 is selected as the address of the next index record to be retrieved.

(5) If it is not already in memory, the index record pointed to in step (4) is input from disk.

(6) The index record from step (5) is searched for the first entry greater than or equal to 90: 60 is skipped since it is less than 90, and the search again selects the entry associated with key 120. The pointer for this entry points to a sequence set record.

(7) The sequence set record pointed to by step (6) is input (if it is not already in memory).

(8)   The sequence set record is searched for the first key greater than or equal to 90, which in this case is the entry corresponding to key 100. This entry contains the address of a data component control interval.

(9)   The data component CI pointed to in step (8) is now input from disk.

(10) The CI input in step (9) is searched for the logical record with key 90, and this record is placed in the level-01 record area for the file (where it can be processed by the COBOL program). If no record with key 90 exists within this CI, the COBOL program is notified of the record-not-found condition.

7.5 How VSAM Works: Random Maintenance of Indexed Files—Adding Records

The COBOL program can add logical records to VSAM files by (1) moving the key of the record to be added to the RECORD KEY area which is part of the level-01 record description for the file, (2) filling in the rest of the fields in the record, and then (3) using the WRITE verb to add the record to the file.

In response to the WRITE statement, VSAM goes through a full index search to locate the data component CI in which the new record should be placed. This search is exactly the same as that used to randomly retrieve a record. Once the correct CI is located, the record is added utilizing the free space within the CI.

EXAMPLE 7.7   VSAM carries out the following steps to add a logical record with key 95 to the file in Fig. 7-4:

(1)–(9)   These are the same as in Example 7.6.

(10) After the index search locates the data component CI to which the new record should be added, that CI is input into memory. VSAM then searches through the logical records in the CI to determine where the new record should go (the reader will recall that VSAM always keeps logical records within a CI in key sequence). In this case, the new record should go between records 90 and 100.

(11) The new record is then inserted in the CI in key sequence, with other records being rearranged as necessary.

(12) The control information within the CI is updated to reflect the fact that (*a*) the available space is reduced by the length of the record just added and (*b*) there is a *new* logical record of a given length within the CI.

(13) The updated CI is rewritten back to its original location on the disk. Note that until this step is completed, the file itself has not been updated.

Figure 7-5 shows the data component CI in question *after* the addition of a logical record with key 95. Note that the free space left in the CI has been reduced by the length of the new record.

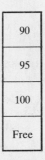

Fig. 7-5

EXAMPLE 7.8   The random addition of a logical record with key 85 to the file in Example 7.7 would proceed as follows:

(1)   The root index record is searched, and it is found that the entry for 120 is the first entry not less than 85.

(2)   The pointer for this entry is followed, and the next lower index record is retrieved; the entry for 120 is again the first entry not less than 85.

(3)   The pointer for this entry is followed, and the sequence set record pointed to is retrieved; a search of the sequence set entries discovers that entry 100 is the first entry not less than 85.

(4)   The pointer for this entry is used to input the data component CI to which record 85 should be added. The CI is rearranged as record 85 is inserted in key sequence. The control information at the end of the CI is updated to reflect the changes within the CI (note that there is no free space remaining).

(5)   The modified CI is rewritten back to its original location on disk.

Figure 7-6 shows the contents of the affected CI after the addition of logical record 85.

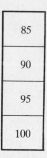

Fig. 7-6

Control Interval Splits

How does VSAM handle additions to a CI when there is not enough free space within the CI to accommodate the new record? In this case, VSAM automatically attempts to perform a *control interval split*. Splitting a control interval requires a totally empty CI within the corresponding control area. If such an empty CI exists, about half of the logical records from the full CI are moved to the empty CI. This CI split leaves the original CI only about half full, so that after the split there is plenty of room in which to add the new record. Note that the CI which was originally empty is now also only about half full, thus having space for the addition of more records.

During a CI split, VSAM must also update the sequence set record for the control area involved. In particular, the entries for the CI which was originally full and the CI which was originally empty must be changed to reflect the new status of these CIs after the split.

EXAMPLE 7.9   The addition of a record with key 87 to the file in Example 7.8 causes a control interval split as follows:

(1)   The full index search reveals that the new record should be added to the CI containing records 85, 90, 95, and 100. As Fig. 7-6 shows, this CI is full and cannot accommodate the new record.

(2)   VSAM automatically looks for an empty CI within the same CA. The sequence set record for the CA readily indicates the presence of an empty CI.

(3)   About half the logical records are copied from the full CI to the empty CI as follows:

Originally		After CI Split	
Full	Empty	Half Full	Half Full
85	Free	85	95
90	Free	90	100
95	Free	Free	Free
100	Free	Free	Free

(4)   The new record with key 87 can now be inserted into the proper CI, utilizing the free space created by the CI split. Note that the CI split has improved the situation within the file for adding new records: where formerly there was a full CI to which no new records could be added, now all CIs have at least some free space for adding new records. A CI split reduces the probability of another CI split. This is an advantage of the VSAM design.

(5)   The sequence set entries for this CA must be updated to reflect the new status of the CIs. Note that the CIs within the CA are no longer in key sequence with respect to one another after a CI split has occurred. If records are to be retrieved sequentially in key sequence, this must be done by following the sequence set entries (which are kept in key sequence), rather than physically following the data component CIs (which are no longer in key sequence).

Figure 7-7 shows the file in Figs. 7-4–7-6 after the CI split described above. The third control area in Fig. 7-7 has also been modified by the addition of records with keys 132, 134, 136, and 138.

Control Area Splits

If VSAM is attempting to perform a CI split and cannot locate an empty CI within the affected CA, then a *control area split* may occur. When the IDCAMS utility program is executed with the DEFINE CLUSTER command, the programmer can specify that VSAM may automatically acquire additional space for the file as needed. The process of obtaining more space for a file after it already exists is called *secondary allocation*.

When VSAM cannot find an empty CI with which to carry out a CI split, if secondary allocation has been provided, VSAM will automatically create a new control area for the data component (plus its associated index records in the index component). Initially, this new control area is completely empty.

Following the secondary allocation, about half the control intervals from the CA which has no empty CI are copied to the new CA just created. This leaves each CA with about half its control intervals empty. *Both* CAs can now support any control interval splits which are required (since they both have plenty of empty CIs). Again, the VSAM design is such that performing a control area split actually reduces the probability of another CA split.

The reader will recall that it is the need to perform a CI split (which cannot be carried out without an empty CI) which causes VSAM to do a CA split. After the CA split is completed, the original CI split can be carried out successfully.

EXAMPLE 7.10   Figure 7-8 shows the file in Fig. 7-7 after the addition of a logical record with key 135. The events involved in adding this record to the file are detailed below. This example also clarifies the relationship between the VSAM access method (which is part of the data management portion of the operating system) and the COBOL program. The functions carried out by VSAM are transparent to the COBOL program:

Functions Carried Out by COBOL Program

(1)   The COBOL program moves the key of the record to be added (135) to the RECORD KEY area (which is part of the level-01 record description for the file).

(2)   The COBOL program then builds the rest of the record in the record area.

(3)   Finally, the COBOL program executes a WRITE statement for the record just built.

Functions Automatically Carried Out by VSAM in Response to WRITE

(4)   VSAM picks up the key of the record to be added from the RECORD KEY area.

(5)   Using the RECORD KEY value, VSAM conducts a full index search (as in Example 7.6) to determine in which data component control interval the new record should be placed.

(6)   Having obtained the CI in which record 135 should be placed, VSAM examines the control information field at the end of the CI to determine whether there is space to add the record. In this case, the CI is already full and no space is available (see Fig. 7-7).

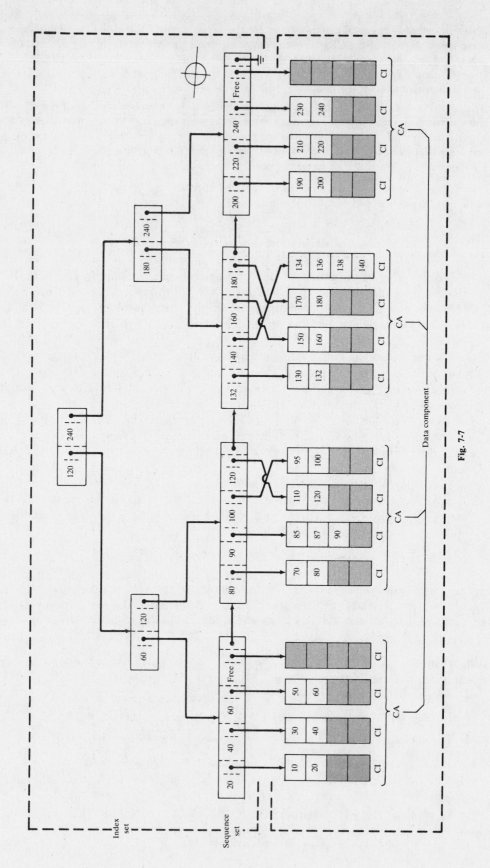

Fig. 7-7

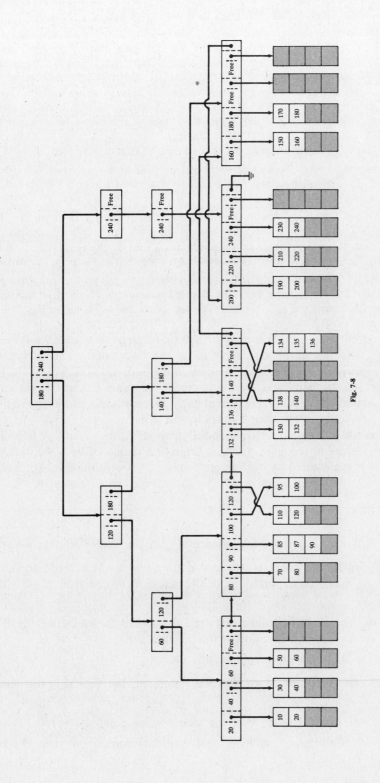

Fig. 7-8

(7) Since sufficient space to add the record is not available, VSAM attempts to perform a control interval split. This involves examining the sequence set record for the CI [already in memory because of step (5)] to locate an empty CI within the same control area.

(8) Since there are no empty CIs within the same control area, VSAM automatically attempts a control area split. This involves obtaining additional file space and creating a brand new control area, together with its associated index records. Note that creating a new CA affects not only the sequence set (which must have a new record describing the new CA) but also the entries in the index set. Conceivably, the new CA might generate modifications to index records all the way back to the top-level index set record. VSAM handles all necessary index maintenance automatically. If space to create a new CA is not available (or if secondary allocations were not provided for when the IDCAMS utility DEFINE CLUSTER command was used to create the file's catalog entry), VSAM will report to the COBOL program that the record cannot be added.

(9) Assuming that a new CA is successfully created, VSAM now copies about half the control intervals from the CA identified in step (7) to the new CA created in step (8), and the index component is updated accordingly.

(10) This leaves the original CA with about half its CIs empty, so a CI split can now be performed. About half the logical records are copied from the full CI to an empty CI, and the sequence set entries updated accordingly. Observe that whereas a CA split involves updating both the sequence set and the index set, a CI split involves changes to the affected sequence set record only.

(11) After the CI split has been carried out, there is free space available within the original CI to add the record with key 135. Record 135 is inserted in key sequence, the control information field is updated, and the CI is rewritten back to disk. This leaves the file as shown in Fig. 7-8.

Note that performing a control area split (and to a lesser extent a control interval split) entails a great deal of disk access (many index component and data component physical records are input, modified, and rewritten), and thus is a time-consuming operation. However, every time a CA or CI split is carried out, the probability of having to perform another CA or CI split goes down. Thus CA (and CI) splits are performed relatively infrequently as records are added to the file. CI splits will, of course, be necessary more often than CA splits.

CA splits also add index records to the index component, thus resulting in a slightly bigger index. However, it is important to recognize that the original structure of both the data component and the index component is maintained by both control area and control interval splits. VSAM random file processing is only slightly degraded, even if many records are added to the file.

7.6 How VSAM Works: Random Maintenance of Indexed Files—Deleting Records

Unlike direct organization, which uses *logical deletion*, VSAM indexed organization uses *physical deletion* of records. In order to randomly delete a logical record from a VSAM file, the COBOL program must:

(1) Move the key of the logical record to be deleted to the RECORD KEY area (which is part of the level-01 record description for the file).

(2) Execute a DELETE statement for the file.

In response to the execution of a DELETE statement, the VSAM access method will automatically:

(3) Pick up the RECORD KEY of the record to be deleted.

(4) Carry out a full index search to locate the data component control interval which should hold the record.

(5) Input the desired data component CI.

(6) Search the CI to locate the desired record.

(7) If the record is located, the control interval is compressed and the logical record physically deleted. The control information field for the CI is updated to indicate that the space occupied by the record has been freed. Note that since the CI is physically compressed to remove the record, the available space is always collected together at the end of the CI. If the record does not exist within the CI, the COBOL program is informed of the record-not-found condition.

(8) The CI is rewritten back to its original location on disk. If any changes to sequence set or index set entries are required because of the deletion of the record, VSAM automatically updates the index.

EXAMPLE 7.11 Figure 7-9 shows changes to the file of Fig. 7-4 caused by the deletion of logical records with keys 40 and 120. Since record 40 represents the highest key within its control interval, its deletion necessitates changes to the sequence set entry for that CI. Similarly, since record 120 represents the highest key within its control area, its deletion necessitates changes to both its sequence set entry and the index set.

The detailed operations automatically carried out by VSAM in response to the DELETE verb for record 40 are as follows:

(1) Perform a full index search to locate the CI which should hold record 40, and input that CI.

(2) Physically compress the CI to remove record 40, and update the control information field to indicate the increase in free space within the CI.

(3) Since record 40 was the highest key in its CI, modify the sequence set record for this CI to indicate the currently remaining highest key (i.e., record 30).

The detailed operations carried out by VSAM in response to the DELETE verb for record 120 are as follows:

(1)–(2) Same as above.

(3) Since 120 was the highest key in its CI, modify the sequence set record for the CI to indicate the currently remaining highest key (i.e., record 110).

(4) Since 120 was also the highest key in its CA, modify the index set record which points to the sequence set record for this CA to indicate the currently remaining highest key of 110.

(5) Modify any index set record which points to the index record updated in step (4) to replace the former highest key value of 120 with the new highest key value of 110. Continue this process until all index set records are correct.

7.7 How VSAM Works: Random Maintenance of Indexed Files—Changing Records

In order to change (update) a logical record in a VSAM indexed file, the COBOL program:

(1) Moves the key of the record to be changed into the RECORD KEY area associated with the file.

(2) Executes a READ statement for the file.

(3) If the READ statement is successful, VSAM places the current contents of the record into the level-01 record area for the file. The COBOL program can then make any desired changes to these record fields, except to the RECORD KEY field. (If the RECORD KEY field is changed, VSAM would treat this logical record as a different record because the key is different. Systems designs typically do not permit a change to a record's key.) Note that since VSAM treats all records as variable-length, the program is allowed to make changes which increase or decrease the size of the logical record.

(4) After the changes to the level-01 record area are completed, the COBOL program executes a REWRITE verb to return the modified version of the record back to the disk.

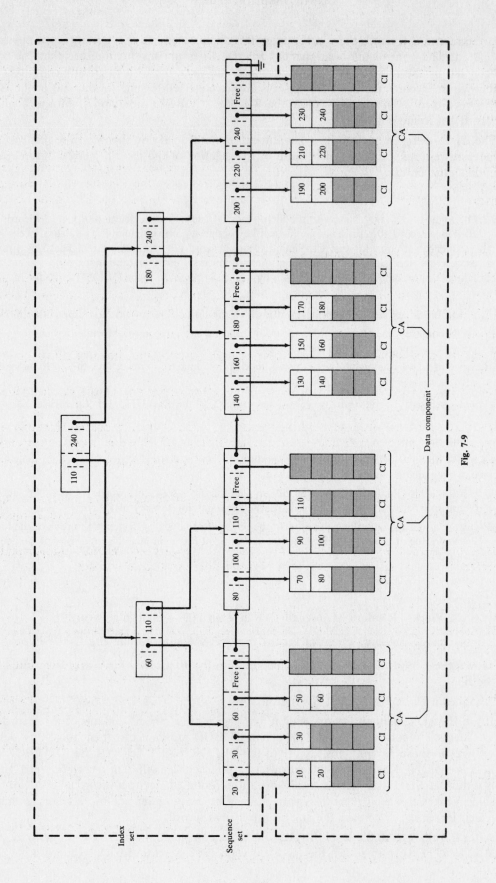

Fig. 7-9

168

In response to the COBOL program's actions, VSAM automatically does the following:

(1) In response to the READ, VSAM picks up the RECORD KEY value and does a full index search to input the correct data component CI. If the desired record is in the CI, VSAM places it into the level-01 record area for the file. Otherwise, VSAM informs the COBOL program of the record-not-found condition.

(2) In response to the REWRITE, VSAM picks up the modified record from the level-01 record area and places it back in its data component CI. If the record's length has changed, the other records in the CI are appropriately shifted, the control information within the CI is updated to indicate the new length of the record, and the free-space information is updated accordingly. VSAM then returns the updated CI to its original location on disk.

7.8 How VSAM Works: Sequential Retrieval of Indexed Files

When VSAM indexed files are processed sequentially, VSAM automatically retrieves logical records in key sequence. In order to accomplish this, VSAM must process data component CIs in the order indicated by the sequence set entries. During sequential processing, VSAM does the following:

(1) Inputs the first sequence set record from the index component.

(2) Inputs the data component CI whose address is given in the first sequence set entry of the current sequence set record.

(3) For each READ statement executed by the COBOL program, places the next logical record from the CI into the level-01 record area for the file.

(4) When all logical records in the CI have been given to the COBOL program, inputs the data component CI pointed to by the next sequence set entry in the current sequence set record.

(5) Gives the logical records within this CI to the COBOL program one at a time (as requested by the execution of READ statements).

(6) Repeats steps (4) and (5) until all CIs associated with the current sequence set record have been processed. At this time, VSAM follows the horizontal pointer in the current sequence set record to locate the next sequence set record.

(7) Repeats steps (2) through (6) until all sequence set records (and thus all data component control areas and the control intervals within them) have been processed.

EXAMPLE 7.12 The file in Fig. 7-7 is processed sequentially as follows:

(1) When the file is OPENed, VSAM inputs the first sequence set record (with entries 20, 40, 60) and then the data component CI pointed to by the first entry (20).

(2) In response to each READ statement, the COBOL program is given the next logical record in the current CI. After two READs, records 10 and 20 will have been processed.

(3) Having processed the first CI, VSAM now proceeds to the second entry in the current sequence set record (i.e., 40) and retrieves the corresponding CI. Records are now given to the COBOL program from this new CI (thus the third and fourth READs retrieve records 30 and 40).

(4) Having processed the second CI, VSAM now proceeds to process the third CI for this sequence set record, resulting in the retrieval of records 50 and 60.

(5) Since the fourth entry in the current sequence set record represents an empty CI, all CIs for this sequence set record have been processed. VSAM now follows the horizontal pointer to input the next sequence set record (with entries 80, 90, 100, 120).

(6) The first entry in the new sequence set record is used to locate the next data component CI, and records 70 and 80 are retrieved.

(7) Switching to the next entry in the current sequence set record, logical records 85, 87, and 90 are retrieved.

(8) Switching to the next entry in the current sequence set record, logical records 95 and 100 are retrieved. Note that VSAM is not processing data component CIs in their physical order. The physically next CI contains logical records 110 and 120, which are not in key sequence. It is only by following the sequence set, which is maintained in key sequence, that VSAM can retrieve records in key sequence.

(9) Switching to the last entry in the current sequence set record, VSAM will now (correctly) retrieve records 110 and 120. Since VSAM must work through the sequence set (in effect, processing the CIs within each CA in a physically random sequence), VSAM sequential processing will be slightly slower than normal sequential processing, which is done according to strict physical sequence. This is a small price to pay for the benefits provided by indexed organization.

(10) The horizontal pointer to the next sequence set record is now followed, and record retrieval continues as described above until the end of the file is encountered. The COBOL program is notified of the end-of-file condition.

7.9   How VSAM Works: Combining Sequential and Random Processing

VSAM provides the capability to mix elements of random processing with mainly sequential processing, and to mix elements of sequential processing with mainly random processing. These capabilities are supported by the use of a *current record pointer* (*CRP*), which VSAM uses to remember the current position (i.e., next logical record to be processed) in each VSAM indexed file.

Sequential Processing with the START Verb

When the SELECT statement for a VSAM indexed file specifies ACCESS IS SEQUENTIAL, the current record pointer is normally set to the first logical record (in key sequence) when the file is OPENed, and is incremented to the next logical record (in key sequence) for each READ which is executed. Logical records are thus normally processed in key sequence.

The START verb can be used at any time to randomly reset the value of the current record pointer, and sequential processing can be resumed from that point. This gives the program the capacity to "jump around" in the file during sequential processing, i.e., to sequentially process random "pieces" of the file as desired.

To randomly reset the current record pointer during SEQUENTIAL ACCESS, the COBOL program must:

(1) Move the key of the desired logical record to the RECORD KEY area for the file.

(2) Execute the START verb.

In response to the START verb, VSAM automatically does the following:

(1) Picks up the RECORD KEY value.

(2) Carries out a *full index search* to locate the desired logical record (the START feature makes use of the full index, not just the sequence set, during sequential processing).

(3) Sets the current record pointer to point to the desired logical record. This means that the next READ statement executed will input the logical record whose key is used for the START statement.

The START statement may be executed as often as desired, allowing the COBOL program to jump back and forth in the file during sequential processing. The START statement may also be executed after an end-of-file condition to reset the current record pointer to a position prior to the end of the file. Sequential processing can then be resumed without the need to CLOSE and reOPEN the file.

EXAMPLE 7.13   The following illustrates the use of the START statement while processing the file from Fig. 7-7 with ACCESS SEQUENTIAL:

Statement Executed	Record Accessed	New Current Record Pointer
1. OPEN INPUT	—	Record with key 10
2. READ	10	Record with key 20
3. READ	20	Record with key 30
4. START (key = 220)	—	Record with key 220
5. READ	220	Record with key 230
6. READ	230	Record with key 240
7. READ	240	End of file
8. READ	AT END activated	Undefined
9. START (key = 80)	—	Record with key 80
10. READ	80	Record with key 85
11. READ	85	Record with key 87
12. START (key = 60)	—	Record with key 60
13. READ	60	Record with key 70
14. START (key = 138)	—	Record with key 138
15. READ	138	Record with key 140
16. READ	140	Record with key 150
17. CLOSE	—	—

Observe that the START statement allows the COBOL program to (1) jump ahead in the file during sequential processing (statement 4 above), (2) reposition and resume sequential processing after hitting the end of the file (statement 9 above), and (3) jump backward in the file during sequential processing (statement 12 above).

Note that the first logical record retrieved after the execution of a START statement is the record identified by the RECORD KEY when the START statement is executed. The READ in statement 15 above inputs logical record 138, since the START statement in line 14 sets the current record pointer to logical record 138.

Random Processing with READ NEXT: DYNAMIC ACCESS

When VSAM indexed files are processed on a strictly random basis, the COBOL SELECT statement can specify ACCESS IS RANDOM. If it is desired to intermix sequential access with mainly random access, the SELECT statement should specify ACCESS IS DYNAMIC.

DYNAMIC ACCESS provides regular random processing in which the program moves a key into the RECORD KEY area and executes a READ; VSAM automatically carries out a full index search to locate the desired logical record.

In addition, DYNAMIC ACCESS also provides a new form of the READ statement (called *READ NEXT*), which can be used to carry out sequential processing based on the value of the current record pointer. With DYNAMIC ACCESS, the current record pointer is set as follows:

Statement	Effect on Current Record Pointer (CRP)
OPEN	Sets CRP to first logical record in file.
START	Sets CRP to logical record specified by RECORD KEY contents.
READ	When ACCESS IS DYNAMIC, a simple READ is assumed to be a random read, which sets the CRP to the logical record following (in key sequence) the one input by the READ statement itself.
READ NEXT	When ACCESS IS DYNAMIC, a sequential READ must be written as READ . . . NEXT, which sets the CRP to the logical record following (in key sequence) the one input by the READ statement itself.

The READ NEXT statement causes VSAM to first input the logical record pointed to by the current record pointer and then update the current record pointer to point to the next logical record in key sequence.

EXAMPLE 7.14 The following sequence of COBOL statements illustrates the mixture of random and sequential processing possible with ACCESS IS DYNAMIC. The file used is the one shown in Fig. 7-7.

Statement	Record Accessed	New CRP	Remarks
OPEN	—	10	OPEN positions CRP to the first logical record.
READ (key = 87)	87	90	Random READ inputs the indicated record and sets CRP to *next* record in key sequence.
READ NEXT	90	95	READ NEXT inputs the record pointed to by CRP and sets CRP to the following record (in key sequence).
START (key = 30)	—	30	START sets CRP to the indicated record.
READ NEXT	30	40	READ NEXT inputs the record pointed to by CRP and sets CRP to the next record.
WRITE (key = 175)	175	40	CRP is not changed by WRITE or REWRITE.
READ NEXT	40	50	Intervening WRITE did not affect CRP.
READ (key = 210)	210	220	Random READ inputs the indicated record and sets CRP to the next record in key sequence.
READ NEXT	220	230	READ NEXT inputs the record pointed to by CRP and sets CRP to next record in key sequence.
READ (key = 75)	—	—	READ fails since record 75 does not exist; CRP is undefined in this case.
READ NEXT	—	—	READ NEXT fails since CRP is undefined; CRP is only set by a *successful* OPEN, READ, READ NEXT, or START.

WRITE and REWRITE do not change the current record pointer, and hence have no effect on sequential processing. The logical record returned by a READ NEXT statement is determined only by the most recently successful OPEN, READ, READ NEXT, or START statement, not by any intervening WRITE or REWRITE statements.

If an OPEN, READ, READ NEXT, or START is not successful, the current record pointer is set *undefined*. Any attempt to execute a READ NEXT while the CRP is undefined results in an *unsuccessful* READ NEXT (i.e., no record is retrieved).

7.10   Using the IBM Access Method Services (IDCAMS) Utility

As discussed in Section 7.3, the Access Method Services (IDCAMS) utility must be used to define a catalog entry for a VSAM file before a COBOL program can be used to load records into the file. This section presents a rudimentary introduction to the IDCAMS "DEFINE CLUSTER" command, which can be used for this purpose, and to other IDCAMS commands which are useful when debugging COBOL programs using VSAM files.

IDCAMS is a very complex and rich utility. Consult an instructor or vendor manual for further information on how to use the IDCAMS utility at your installation.

Creating a Catalog Entry for a VSAM Indexed File

The IDCAMS DEFINE CLUSTER command is one simple way to create a catalog entry for a new VSAM indexed file. Its parameters are usually typed one entry per line, beginning in column 2 or later. Since the command typically occupies several lines, IDCAMS rules for continuation must be followed. This entails typing a blank space followed by a "-" (hyphen) at the end of each line to be continued.

EXAMPLE 7.15 The following IBM IDCAMS utility DEFINE CLUSTER command could be used to create a VSAM catalog entry for an indexed file prior to executing a COBOL program to load records into the file. Note the recommended format for typing IDCAMS commands, including the rules for continuation. Only essential parameters have been illustrated. Their meanings are discussed below.

```
DEFINE CLUSTER -
     (    NAME (SAMPLE.VSAM.INDEXED.FILE) -
          VOLUMES (VOL123) -
          KEYS (5 0) -
          FREESPACE (20 10) -
          RECORDS (2000 500) -
          RECORDSIZE (37 37)        ) -
     CATALOG (PSU.VSAMCAT)
```

As shown in Example 7.15, DEFINE CLUSTER begins with a list of parameters enclosed in parentheses. Each parameter is typed on its own line for readability, with the *name* of each parameter preceding the *value* specified for the parameter. Observe that the values of parameters are themselves enclosed in parentheses, and that every line (except the last) ends in a blank space followed by a hyphen, indicating continuation of the DEFINE CLUSTER command onto the following line.

The individual parameters and their meanings are as follows:

(1) NAME (name-of-VSAM-file)
     The NAME parameter assigns a name which will be recorded in the catalog entry for the file. This becomes the "official" name for the file, and is the name by which the file must be identified to the operating system in any job control/command language statements which refer to the file. This same name must also be used in any future IDCAMS commands which refer to the file. It has nothing to do with the name used for the file in the SELECT and FD statements in the COBOL program. Most installations have standards regarding the formation of file names used in the VSAM catalog. Consult an instructor or local standards manual for the rules governing the creation of file names at your installation.

(2) VOLUMES (name-of-disk-pack-on-which-file-is-to-be-placed)
     The VOLUMES parameter gives the name(s) of the volume(s), i.e., disk packs, on which the file is to be placed. In IBM OS/VS systems, volume names are typically 6 characters long. Most installations have standards regarding the naming and use of disk volumes. Consult an instructor or local standards manual for the rules governing the use of disk volumes for VSAM indexed files at your installation.

(3) KEYS (length-in-bytes   position-within-record)
     The KEYS parameter identifies the field within each logical record which will be used as the key field. The *key field* is used to construct the index component when records are loaded into the file. The first subparameter specifies the *length* of the key field in bytes (i.e., character positions), while the second subparameter specifies the *position* of the key field within the logical record. The first byte of the record is considered to be at position 0, the second byte at position 1, etc.

EXAMPLE 7.16 KEYS (7   3) establishes 7-byte keys beginning at the fourth byte (position 3) of each logical record.

    (4)   FREESPACE (%-of-each-CI-left-empty   %-of-each-CA-left-empty)
        The FREESPACE parameter indicates the amount of distributed free space to be left in the data component control areas (1) when the file is first *created* (i.e., when records are first loaded into it) and (2) when the file is *expanded* (as with a secondary allocation of space caused by a control area split). The distributed free space is allocated as (1) a percentage of each data component control interval which is to be initially left empty (first subparameter), and (2) a percentage of control intervals within each control area to be left completely empty when the control area is first loaded with records (second subparameter).
           Distributed free space is an important VSAM concept. It allows the programmer/analyst to plan for the future addition of logical records by reserving free space to hold these records. The distributed free space initially built into the file will postpone the time when control interval and control area splits will have to be carried out, thus improving the response time for adding records to the file. The price paid for reserving free space is, of course, that this space is initially wasted.

EXAMPLE 7.17 FREESPACE (25   50) specifies that when the file is created (and when any new control areas are added to the file later on), 50 percent of the control intervals in each data component control area should be left totally empty, and 25 percent of each control interval used should also be left empty (i.e., those CIs having any records at all will be only 75 percent full). This distributed free space will be utilized to add records to the file later on, thus forestalling the need for CI and CA splits.

    (5)   RECORDS (#-for-primary-allocation   #-for-secondary-allocation)
        The RECORDS parameter tells IDCAMS how much space to reserve for the file (1) initially (first subparameter) and (2) for a secondary allocation to be made if and when the primary allocation is filled up. Although there are other possibilities, the easiest way to request space for the file is in terms of the number of records (as shown above).

EXAMPLE 7.18 RECORDS (200   100) initially sets aside enough space to hold 200 records. If the space for the 200 records is filled up, a secondary allocation of space for 100 logical records will be made. If that space is filled up (i.e., the total primary allocation of space for 200 records plus the secondary allocation of space for 100 records), then an additional secondary allocation for 100 records will be made. VSAM is capable of making up to 128 secondary allocations of space for a given file.

        It is important to specify a secondary allocation if it is anticipated that the need for control area splits may arise. Since in general it is difficult to guarantee that the initial distributed free space will be adequate for all future additions to a file, secondary allocations are usually specified as a safety precaution.

    (6)   RECORDSIZE (average-size-in-bytes   maximum-size-in-bytes)
        The RECORDSIZE parameter indicates the size of the logical records in the file. Since VSAM treats all logical records as if they were variable-length, the record size is expressed in terms of the average size of a logical record (first subparameter), followed by the maximum size of a logical record (second subparameter).

EXAMPLE 7.19 RECORDSIZE (150   200) specifies logical records which are never more than 200 bytes in length (maximum size) and which average 150 bytes in length.

EXAMPLE 7.20 If a file has fixed-length records, the RECORDSIZE parameter should indicate that the average record size and the maximum record size are equal. Thus RECORDSIZE (175   175) indicates a file of fixed-length 175-byte logical records.

(7) CATALOG (name-of-VSAM-catalog-in-which-entry-is-to-be-made)
   The CATALOG parameter specifies the name of the VSAM catalog in which the entry describing the file is to be recorded. VSAM has one *master catalog* on each computer system. In addition, the master catalog can point to any number of VSAM *user catalogs*. VSAM files can be cataloged in either the VSAM master catalog or a VSAM user catalog.
   The VSAM master catalog is either automatically generated along with the operating system or defined by executing the IDCAMS utility with the DEFINE MASTER-CATALOG command. In either case, the generation of the VSAM master catalog is almost certainly the responsibility of a systems programmer, not a COBOL programmer.
   VSAM user catalogs are created by running the IDCAMS utility with the DEFINE USERCATALOG command. This is likewise carried out by a systems programmer. Each installation must determine what user catalogs (if any) will exist and what their names are.
   The purpose of user catalogs is to allow the entries for files to be spread out over several catalogs, so that the catalogs are smaller and catalog searching can be done more efficiently. The use of user catalogs also reduces vulnerability to loss of data, since all entries are not in one central catalog. Finally, user catalogs allow an installation to organize its VSAM files into several categories, each of which is associated with its own user catalog.
   Each installation generally establishes standards to determine where VSAM files will be cataloged. Consult an instructor and/or local standards manual to find out what VSAM catalogs are available at your installation, and how to determine in which catalog(s) the entries for your files should be recorded. Remember that every VSAM file must have a catalog entry created by running the IDCAMS utility with the DEFINE CLUSTER (or an equivalent) command, and that this must be done before a COBOL program can be used to load records into the file.

Using IDCAMS to Print the Records in a VSAM Indexed File

When debugging a COBOL program which creates or modifies a VSAM indexed file, it is useful to be able to print the contents of the file for visual inspection. Luckily, IDCAMS offers a PRINT command which allows the printing of a VSAM file without the need to code a special COBOL program for that purpose.

EXAMPLE 7.21 The following IDCAMS command prints all the logical records in the indexed file named SAMPLE.VSAM.INDEXED.FILE:

```
PRINT -
    INDATASET (SAMPLE.VSAM.INDEXED.FILE) -
    CHARACTER
```

The INDATASET parameter supplies the name of the VSAM file to be printed (this name must be the same as that used in the NAME subparameter of the DEFINE CLUSTER command used to create the catalog entry for the file).
The second subparameter specifies the format of the printed output. CHARACTER indicates that all bytes in the logical records are in DISPLAY format and are to be printed as such. If the logical records contain COMP or COMP-3 data, this parameter should be omitted, in which case the records will be printed in the same format that is used for an operating system ABEND dump.
The IDCAMS utility can be run with the PRINT command any time it is necessary to produce a hard copy of VSAM file contents.

Using IDCAMS to Delete a VSAM File

The DELETE command is used to (1) release the space occupied by a VSAM file for other use and (2) erase the catalog entry for the file, thereby removing all record of the file's existence. The simplest form of this command is useful when deleting unwanted versions of files during program debugging.

EXAMPLE 7.22 The following IDCAMS command deletes an existing VSAM file:

```
DELETE -
      (SAMPLE.VSAM.INDEXED.FILE) -
      CATALOG (PSU.VSAMCAT) -
      CLUSTER
```

The first parameter for the simple DELETE command is the name of the VSAM file to be deleted. This name must be the same as that used for the NAME parameter of the DEFINE CLUSTER command when the file was created.

The CATALOG parameter specifies the VSAM catalog in which the entry for the file resides. It must be the same catalog specified in the DEFINE CLUSTER command which created the entry. IDCAMS will automatically remove the entry for the indicated file from this catalog, thereby freeing the space occupied by the file for other use (and making it impossible to retrieve the file).

The CLUSTER parameter indicates that the entire cluster, i.e., both the index and data components, is to be deleted. Although it is possible to delete either the index component or data component separately, this is usually not done.

7.11   Creating Indexed Files in COBOL (ANSI Standard)

Creating an indexed file is much like creating a sequential file. The major difference is that whereas sequential files are usually sorted on a key field, indexed files *must* be created in ascending sequence by RECORD KEY. (Some implementations of indexed file organization, such as IBM's VSAM indexed files, allow indexed files to be created randomly; this is not recommended since it does not provide any distributed free space and may result in less efficient file processing. The random creation of indexed files is not discussed in this Outline.)

ENVIRONMENT DIVISION Considerations

The ANSI standard COBOL SELECT statement for creating an indexed file has the following syntax:

```
SELECT file-name
      ASSIGN TO external-name
      ORGANIZATION IS INDEXED
      [ ACCESS MODE IS SEQUENTIAL ]
      RECORD KEY IS name-of-key-field-in-record
      [ FILE STATUS IS name-of-status-area ]
```

The ASSIGN TO clause identifies the name of a job control/command language statement ("external-name"), which provides further information about the file to be created. The form and function of the external name vary from system to system. In IBM OS/VS COBOL, external name is the name of a job control statement which provides the name of the VSAM file as defined with the IDCAMS DEFINE CLUSTER command. It is this name from the DEFINE CLUSTER command which is used to locate the entry for the file in the appropriate VSAM catalog. Consult an instructor or vendor manual for the correct form of the external name on your system.

The ORGANIZATION clause specifies that the file has indexed organization. Note that this is a required clause.

Since indexed files are usually created sequentially, ACCESS IS SEQUENTIAL. This clause is optional, since SEQUENTIAL ACCESS is the default.

The RECORD KEY clause provides the name of a field in the level-01 record description for this file. The field named in the RECORD KEY clause is the one used to build the index for the file. If the records for the file are variable-length, the RECORD KEY field must be in the fixed-length portion of the record (typically, this would be at or near the beginning of the record, with the variable-length information coming at the end). The RECORD KEY itself must be a fixed-length alphanumeric item (an IBM OS/VS COBOL extension to the ANSI standard allows a VSAM RECORD KEY to be an unsigned DISPLAY numeric item). In systems such as IBM's VSAM indexed files, where the catalog entry for the file is defined with the IDCAMS utility program, the description of the file in the COBOL program must exactly match that in the IDCAMS DEFINE CLUSTER command (or the equivalent on other systems).

Records must be loaded into the file in ascending sequence by RECORD KEY. If the transaction file to be used to create the indexed file is not in sequence by this field, it will have to be sorted.

The FILE STATUS clause names a 2-byte area (usually defined in WORKING-STORAGE as PIC XX or PIC 99) used to provide feedback regarding the operations performed on the file. Every execution of an OPEN, CLOSE, READ, WRITE, REWRITE, START, or READ NEXT which refers to an indexed file causes a 2-character code to be placed in the file's FILE STATUS area. The FILE STATUS code can then be examined by the COBOL program to determine whether or not the corresponding operation was successful. The possible FILE STATUS codes for indexed files are part of the ANSI COBOL standard and are given in the Appendix.

Note that FILE STATUS is an optional clause. This is because the INVALID KEY clause may be used with READ, WRITE, REWRITE, START, and READ NEXT statements to obtain feedback regarding the success or failure of the operation. If INVALID KEY is used for detecting errors, then a FILE STATUS area need not be defined. However, since the FILE STATUS code provides more detailed information regarding indexed file operations than INVALID KEY, and since INVALID KEY is not activated for all errors, it is recommended that a FILE STATUS area be defined and used for every indexed file. If desired, INVALID KEY and FILE STATUS can be used together. Thus an INVALID KEY routine might test the FILE STATUS area to determine what event caused INVALID KEY to be executed (see Problem 7.75).

EXAMPLE 7.23   The following IBM OS/VS COBOL code shows how to define and use a FILE STATUS area for an indexed file:

```
          SELECT INVENTORY-MASTER
                ASSIGN TO INVENMAS
                ORGANIZATION IS INDEXED
                ACCESS IS SEQUENTIAL
                RECORD KEY IS INVENTORY-MASTER-ITEM-ID
                FILE STATUS IS INVENTORY-MASTER-STATUS. . .

      WORKING-STORAGE SECTION.
      01    INVENTORY-MASTER-STATUS PIC XX.
            88    STATUS-OK            VALUE "00".
            88    STATUS-NOT-OK        VALUE "01" THRU "99". . .

      OPEN INPUT      INVENTORY-MASTER
      IF STATUS-NOT-OK
            DISPLAY "INVENTORY MASTER OPEN FAILED -- ABORT"
            MOVE "YES" TO PROGRAM-ABORT-SW
          .
```

Since a FILE STATUS area is defined for the file, every PROCEDURE DIVISION operation on the file will cause a 2-character code to be moved to the FILE STATUS area. In ANSI standard COBOL, a STATUS CODE of zero indicates a successful operation, while a nonzero STATUS CODE (i.e., 01 through 99) indicates an unsuccessful operation. After attempting to OPEN the file, the program checks the STATUS CODE to determine whether the OPEN was successful. If not, a switch is set which will cause the program to abort execution.

DATA DIVISION Considerations

The DATA DIVISION FD and level-01 record description entries for creating an indexed file are almost the same as for a sequential file. Details which may vary from implementation to implementation are discussed below.

In IBM OS/VS COBOL, the concept of blocking has no meaning since the VSAM access method automatically controls the grouping of logical records into control intervals. BLOCK CONTAINS is thus treated as a comment (and ignored) in IBM OS/VS COBOL. Consult an instructor or vendor manual to determine the importance of BLOCK CONTAINS for your system.

In IBM OS/VS COBOL, VSAM indexed files use physical deletion when logical records are deleted, and thus need no provision for a delete code byte within the logical record. Other implementations may require the definition of a delete code field, if records are to be deleted. Consult an instructor or vendor manual to determine the rules for deleting indexed file records on your system.

EXAMPLE 7.24 A typical FD for an indexed file is shown below. Note that the data item named in the RECORD KEY clause of the SELECT statement *must* be a field in the record description for the file. The FD below is consistent with the SELECT statement in Example 7.23. In IBM OS/VS COBOL, the BLOCK CONTAINS clause is omitted and no delete code byte need be defined as part of the record:

```
FD    INVENTORY-MASTER
      RECORD CONTAINS 44 CHARACTERS
      LABEL RECORDS ARE STANDARD
      .
01    INVENTORY-MASTER-RECORD.
      05   INVENTORY-MASTER-ITEM-ID        PIC X(7).
      05   INVENTORY-MASTER-ITEM-NAME      PIC X(25).
      05   INVENTORY-MASTER-ITEM-COST      PIC S9(4)V99    COMP.
      05   INVENTORY-MASTER-ITEM-ONHAND    PIC S9(6)       COMP.
      05   INVENTORY-MASTER-ITEM-ONORDER   PIC S9(6)       COMP.
```

PROCEDURE DIVISION Considerations

The logic for sequentially creating an indexed file depends mainly on whether or not the transaction file, which supplies the input, is sorted by the RECORD KEY field. When the incoming transactions need to be sorted, an INPUT PROCEDURE can be used to validate as much of the transaction information as possible, RELEASEing to the sort only those transactions which appear to be correct. An OUTPUT PROCEDURE can then be used to WRITE records into the indexed file. The presence of duplicate keys (i.e., logical records with identical RECORD KEY fields) is automatically detected by the WRITE statement within the OUTPUT PROCEDURE as records are written to the file.

The PROCEDURE DIVISION statements relevant to creating an indexed file are:

(1) <u>OPEN</u> <u>OUTPUT</u> file-name

(2) <u>CLOSE</u> file-name

(3) <u>WRITE</u> record-name
     [<u>FROM</u> data-area]
     [<u>INVALID</u> KEY imperative-statement(s).]

The WRITE statement is used to add a record to an indexed file. The presence of duplicate keys is automatically detected as part of the execution of the WRITE. When creating an indexed file sequentially, the RECORD KEY of each record written is automatically compared (by the WRITE routine) with the key of the previous record written to ensure that the new key is greater than the previous one. If the new key is less than or equal to the previous one, the WRITE is aborted, the STATUS CODE (if defined) is set to indicate a sequence error, and the INVALID KEY routine (if specified) is executed. The WRITE is also aborted if space cannot be obtained to add the record. In this case, the STATUS CODE is again set and INVALID KEY (if present) activated. Note that since the STATUS CODE is always set to indicate error conditions, the INVALID KEY clause is not necessary when processing indexed files; errors can be detected simply by examining the STATUS CODE. Similarly, the STATUS CODE is not necessary for indexed files since the INVALID KEY routine can be used to trap errors. The use of a STATUS CODE is recommended, however, since some COBOL verbs (such as OPEN and CLOSE) do not provide for an INVALID KEY.

EXAMPLE 7.25 Figure 7-10 illustrates an IBM OS/VS COBOL program which sequentially creates an indexed file from a sequential transaction file. In order to minimize nonrelevant details, it is assumed that the transaction file has already been edited for everything except duplicate keys. It is *not* assumed that the transaction file is sorted; thus Fig. 7-10 includes a SORT. The IBM Access Method Services (IDCAMS) utility commands necessary to define the catalog entry for the file and to print and delete the file are given in Examples 7.26 and 7.27. The following comments refer to the code in Fig. 7-10:

(1) Lines 17–22 define the indexed file to be created. The ASSIGN TO clause provides the name of a job control/command language statement which will provide the name of the VSAM cluster as recorded in the VSAM catalog for the file. The ORGANIZATION IS INDEXED clause is *required*. As

```
00001              IDENTIFICATION DIVISION.
00002              PROGRAM-ID.  INDEXED-FILE-CREATION.

00003              ENVIRONMENT DIVISION.
00004              CONFIGURATION SECTION.
00005              SOURCE-COMPUTER.  IBM-3081.
00006              OBJECT-COMPUTER.  IBM-3081.
00007              INPUT-OUTPUT SECTION.
00008              FILE-CONTROL.

00009                  SELECT TRANSACTION-FILE
00010                      ASSIGN TO RAWDATA
00011                      ORGANIZATION IS SEQUENTIAL
00012                      ACCESS IS SEQUENTIAL
00013                      .
00014                  SELECT SORTED-TRANS-FILE
00015                      ASSIGN TO SORTWORK
00016                      .
00017                  SELECT INDEXED-FILE
00018                      ASSIGN TO VSAMFILE
00019                      ORGANIZATION IS INDEXED
00020                      ACCESS IS SEQUENTIAL
00021                      RECORD KEY IS INDEXED-PROGRAMMER-ID
00022                      FILE STATUS IS INDEXED-STATUS-CODE
00023                      .

00024              DATA DIVISION.
00025              FILE SECTION.
00026              FD  TRANSACTION-FILE
00027                  LABEL RECORDS ARE STANDARD
00028                  BLOCK CONTAINS 0 CHARACTERS
00029                  RECORD CONTAINS 80 CHARACTERS
00030                  .
00031              01  TRANSACTION-RECORD              PIC X(80).

00032              SD  SORTED-TRANS-FILE
00033                  RECORD CONTAINS 80 CHARACTERS
                      .
00034              01  SORTED-TRANS-RECORD.
00035                  05  SORTED-PROGRAMMER-ID        PIC X(5).
00036                  05  SORTED-PROJECT-ID           PIC X(8).
00037                  05  SORTED-TOTAL-HOURS          PIC 9(3)V9.
00038                  05  FILLER                      PIC X(63).
```

Fig. 7-10

```
00039              FD  INDEXED-FILE
00040                  LABEL RECORDS ARE STANDARD
00041                  RECORD CONTAINS 15 CHARACTERS
                         .
00042              01  INDEXED-RECORD.
00043                  05  INDEXED-PROGRAMMER-ID      PIC X(5).
00044                  05  INDEXED-PROJECT-ID         PIC X(8).
00045                  05  INDEXED-TOTAL-HOURS        PIC 9(3)V9 COMP.

00046              WORKING-STORAGE SECTION.

00047              01  FLAGS-AND-SWITCHES.
00048                  05  TRANS-END-OF-FILE-SW       PIC X(3).
00049                      88  MORE-TRANS-RECORDS      VALUE "NO".
00050                      88  NO-MORE-INPUT           VALUE "YES".

00051              01  FILE-STATUS-CODES.
00052                  05  INDEXED-STATUS-CODE        PIC XX.
00053                      88  VSAM-OPERATION-OK       VALUE "00".
00054                      88  VSAM-OPERATION-FAILED   VALUE "01" THRU "99".

00055              PROCEDURE DIVISION.
00056
00057              000-EXECUTIVE-MODULE.
00058
00059                  SORT SORTED-TRANS-FILE
00060                      ON ASCENDING KEY SORTED-PROGRAMMER-ID
00061                      USING TRANSACTION-FILE
00062                      OUTPUT PROCEDURE IS 010-LOAD-VSAM-FILE
00063                  STOP RUN
00064                      .
00065
00066              010-LOAD-VSAM-FILE SECTION.
00067
00068                  MOVE "NO" TO TRANS-END-OF-FILE-SW
00069                  OPEN    OUTPUT   INDEXED-FILE
00070                  IF VSAM-OPERATION-OK
00071                      PERFORM 030-GET-NEXT-SORTED-TRANS
00072                      PERFORM 040-OUTPUT-INDEXED-RECORD
00073                          UNTIL NO-MORE-INPUT
00074                      CLOSE   INDEXED-FILE
00075                      IF VSAM-OPERATION-OK
00076                          DISPLAY "INDEXED FILE CREATION COMPLETED"
00077                      ELSE
00078                          DISPLAY "INDEXED FILE NOT PROPERLY CLOSED"
00079                  ELSE
00080                      DISPLAY "UNABLE TO OPEN INDEXED FILE -- ABORT"
00081                      .
00082
00083              020-PERFORMED-PARAGRAPHS SECTION.
00084
00085              030-GET-NEXT-SORTED-TRANS.
00086
00087                  RETURN SORTED-TRANS-FILE
00088                      AT END
00089                          MOVE "YES" TO TRANS-END-OF-FILE-SW
00090                      .
00091
00092              040-OUTPUT-INDEXED-RECORD.
00093
00094                  MOVE SORTED-PROGRAMMER-ID    TO INDEXED-PROGRAMMER-ID
00095                  MOVE SORTED-PROJECT-ID       TO INDEXED-PROJECT-ID
00096                  MOVE SORTED-TOTAL-HOURS      TO INDEXED-TOTAL-HOURS
00097                  WRITE   INDEXED-RECORD
00098                  IF VSAM-OPERATION-FAILED
00099                      DISPLAY "DUPLICATE KEY OR SEQUENCE ERROR FOR "
00100                              SORTED-TRANS-RECORD
00101                      .
00102                  PERFORM 030-GET-NEXT-SORTED-TRANS
00103                      .
```

Fig. 7-10 (*cont.*)

recommended, the file is to be created with SEQUENTIAL ACCESS. The RECORD KEY clause *must* name a field in the record description for the file (INDEXED-PROGRAMMER-ID is defined as a part of INDEXED-RECORD in line 43). Line 22 names a STATUS CODE area for the file. INDEXED-STATUS-CODE is defined in WORKING-STORAGE as PIC XX (line 52).

(2) The FD for the indexed file (lines 39–45) closely resembles that for the sequential transaction file (lines 26–31). In IBM OS/VS COBOL, BLOCK CONTAINS is treated as comments for VSAM indexed files and is omitted.

(3) Lines 51–54 define the STATUS CODE area for the indexed file. Note the use of condition names in lines 53 and 54. In ANSI standard COBOL, the STATUS CODE is a 2-digit number, with 00 indicating a successful operation and a nonzero code indicating failure.

(4) Lines 57–64 constitute the executive module for the program, which is designed as a SORT with a USING file (the incoming transactions) and an OUTPUT PROCEDURE (the code to create the indexed file from the transactions). If the transactions were not already edited, an INPUT PROCE-DURE would be used to screen invalid transactions from participating in the sort.

(5) Lines 66–81 form the OUTPUT PROCEDURE. The indexed file is OPENed for OUTPUT in line 69. Line 70 then tests the STATUS CODE value provided by OPEN to ensure that the file was opened properly. If the OPEN failed, a message is DISPLAYed and the OUTPUT PROCEDURE termi-nates. If the OPEN succeeds, a priming read is done for the first transaction (line 71), a loop is generated to load records into the indexed file (lines 72–73), and the indexed file is then CLOSEd (line 74). Lines 75–78 examine the STATUS CODE provided by CLOSE, and DISPLAY an appropriate message. Note the use of condition names when testing the STATUS CODE.

(6) Lines 92–103 repetitively load a logical record into the indexed file and input the next transaction. Lines 94–96 move the transaction fields (including the RECORD KEY value) to INDEXED-RECORD. The WRITE statement in line 97 then attempts to add the record to the file. WRITE automatically sequence checks the records on the RECORD KEY field. In this example, failure of the WRITE statement is detected by examining the STATUS CODE in line 98. If the WRITE fails, a message is DISPLAYed in lines 99–100. Observe that the programmer has *assumed* that if the WRITE fails, it is because of a duplicate key or sequence error. This may not always be the case (e.g., the file could fill up and no space be available, there could be a hardware I/O error, etc.). If desired, the STATUS CODE could be tested to differentiate between these possible errors. In either case, no INVALID KEY clause is used (or needed) in this example.

EXAMPLE 7.26 Figure 7-11 shows the IBM OS/VS Access Method Services (IDCAMS) utility commands needed to define the catalog entry for the file in Example 7.25. Note that IDCAMS must be executed with these commands *before* the COBOL program in Example 7.25 can be executed.

```
DEFINE CLUSTER -
   ( -
   NAME (LRN.VSAM.FILE) -
   VOLUMES (CCLIB3) -
      KEYS (5 0) -
      FREESPACE (20 10) -
      RECORDS (30 15) -
      RECORDSIZE (15 15) -
   ) -
   CATALOG (PSU.VSAMCAT)
```

Fig. 7-11

It is critical that the KEYS parameter used with DEFINE CLUSTER be *consistent* with the definition of RECORD KEY in the COBOL program. KEYS (5   0) specifies that the key for the file is 5 bytes long, beginning in the first byte of the record (byte 0). This is consistent with the definition of INDEXED-PROGRAMMER-ID as PIC X(5) at the start of the record (line 43 of Fig. 7-10).

Similarly, the specification of RECORDSIZE in DEFINE CLUSTER should be consistent with the record description in the COBOL program. RECORDSIZE (15   15) specifies fixed-length 15-byte logical records to IDCAMS. This is consistent with the FD in Fig. 7-10, where RECORD CONTAINS 15 CHARACTERS (lines 39–45).

The commands in Fig. 7-11 provide for distributed free space when the file is created. FREESPACE (20   10) specifies that 20 percent of each CI be reserved for free space and that 10 percent of the CIs in each CA be left totally empty as the file is initially loaded. This free space can be used to add records to the file later on, postponing the need for CI and CA splits.

RECORDS (30   15) allocates enough DASD space to initially hold 30 records. If this space is ever filled, an additional (secondary) allocation of space for 15 records will be given. Up to 128 secondary allocations (of 15 records each) are possible with VSAM. Specification of a secondary allocation is important when the distributed free space cannot be guaranteed to handle all future additions (as is usually the case).

EXAMPLE 7.27   Figure 7-12 shows how to print the logical records in the file of Example 7.25, and then delete the file (as one might do while debugging). Note that the file name used in the PRINT and DELETE commands (i.e., LRN.VSAM.FILE) must be the same as the name used in the NAME parameter of the original DEFINE CLUSTER command.

```
PRINT -
      INDATASET (LRN.VSAM.FILE) -
      CHARACTER

DELETE -
      (LRN.VSAM.FILE) -
      CATALOG (PSU.VSAMCAT) -
      CLUSTER
```

Fig. 7-12

EXAMPLE 7.28   Redo the WRITE statement of Fig. 7-10 (lines 97–101) to use INVALID KEY instead of the STATUS CODE to check for sequence errors (i.e., duplicate keys). Although either method can be used to detect errors when processing an indexed file, STATUS CODE is recommended since the INVALID KEY routine is only activated for some, but not all, possible errors. Lines 97–101 would be replaced by:

```
WRITE INDEXED-RECORD
      INVALID KEY
            DISPLAY "DUPLICATE KEY OR SEQUENCE ERROR FOR "
                  SORTED-TRANS-RECORD
```

7.12   Sequential Retrieval of Indexed Files (ANSI Standard)

Indexed files are sequentially retrieved in key sequence, regardless of whether or not the records are physically in key sequence on the direct access device. This is possible because the index is referenced during sequential processing. Sequential retrieval of an indexed file in COBOL is almost identical to sequential retrieval of an already-sorted sequential file. This is one of the major advantages of indexed organization.

ENVIRONMENT DIVISION Considerations

The ANSI standard SELECT statement for sequential retrieval of an indexed file has the following syntax:

```
SELECT file-name
      ASSIGN TO external-name
      ORGANIZATION IS INDEXED
      [ ACCESS MODE IS SEQUENTIAL ]
      RECORD KEY IS name-of-key-field-in-record
      [ FILE STATUS IS name-of-status-area ]
```

Note that this SELECT statement is exactly the same as that used to create the file. See Section 7.11 for a discussion of the individual clauses.

DATA DIVISION Considerations

The FD and level-01 record description are exactly the same for sequential processing as for creation (see Section 7.11).

PROCEDURE DIVISION Considerations

The ease with which logical records can be sequentially retrieved from an indexed file is a major advantage of indexed organization. The relevant PROCEDURE DIVISION statements are:

(1) OPEN INPUT file-name

(2) CLOSE file-name

(3) READ file-name
     [INTO data-area-to-receive-copy-of-record]
     [AT END imperative-statement(s).]

The AT END clause is *optional* since the end of the file can also be detected by examining the STATUS CODE. Again, the use of STATUS CODE is recommended since it allows testing the success of the OPEN and CLOSE operations and also can provide feedback about errors other than the expected end-of-file condition. Example 7.29 uses only STATUS CODE for sequential retrieval of the indexed file created in Example 7.25.

EXAMPLE 7.29 Figure 7-13 shows an IBM OS/VS COBOL program to sequentially retrieve the VSAM indexed file created in Fig. 7-10. Remember that logical records are automatically retrieved in RECORD KEY sequence. The following comments pertain:

```
00001          IDENTIFICATION DIVISION.
00002          PROGRAM-ID.  INDEXED-SEQUENTIAL-RETRIEVAL.

00003          ENVIRONMENT DIVISION.
00004          INPUT-OUTPUT SECTION.
00005          FILE-CONTROL.

00006              SELECT INDEXED-FILE
00007                  ASSIGN TO VSAMFILE
00008                  ORGANIZATION IS INDEXED
00009                  ACCESS IS SEQUENTIAL
00010                  RECORD KEY IS INDEXED-PROGRAMMER-ID
00011                  FILE STATUS IS INDEXED-STATUS-CODE
00012                  .

00013          DATA DIVISION.
00014          FILE SECTION.

00015          FD  INDEXED-FILE
00016              LABEL RECORDS ARE STANDARD
00017              RECORD CONTAINS 15 CHARACTERS
                   .
00018          01  INDEXED-RECORD.
00019              05  INDEXED-PROGRAMMER-ID      PIC X(5).
00020              05  INDEXED-PROJECT-ID         PIC X(8).
00021              05  INDEXED-TOTAL-HOURS        PIC 9(3)V9 COMP.

00022          WORKING-STORAGE SECTION.

00023          01  FILE-STATUS-CODES.
00024              05  INDEXED-STATUS-CODE        PIC XX.
00025                  88  VSAM-OPERATION-OK      VALUE "00".
00026                  88  VSAM-OPERATION-FAILED  VALUE "01" THRU "99".
00027                  88  END-OF-FILE            VALUE "10".

00028          PROCEDURE DIVISION.
00029
```

Fig. 7-13

```
00030                    000-EXECUTIVE-MODULE.
00031
00032                        OPEN INPUT INDEXED-FILE
00033                        IF VSAM-OPERATION-OK
00034                            PERFORM 020-GET-NEXT-RECORD
00035                            PERFORM 030-PRINT-A-RECORD
00036                                UNTIL END-OF-FILE
00037                            CLOSE INDEXED-FILE
00038                            IF VSAM-OPERATION-OK
00039                                DISPLAY "*** SEQUENTIAL RETRIEVAL COMPLETED ***"
00040                            ELSE
00041                                DISPLAY "INDEXED FILE NOT CLOSED PROPERLY"
00042                        ELSE
00043                            DISPLAY "UNABLE TO OPEN INDEXED FILE -- ABORT"
00044                            .
00045                        STOP RUN
00046                        .
00047
00048                    020-GET-NEXT-RECORD.
00049
00050                        READ INDEXED-FILE
00051                        IF VSAM-OPERATION-FAILED
00052                            IF NOT END-OF-FILE
00053                                DISPLAY "ERROR READING INDEXED FILE -- "
00054                                    "STATUS CODE IS " INDEXED-STATUS-CODE
00055                        .
00056
00057                    030-PRINT-A-RECORD.
00058
00059                        DISPLAY INDEXED-RECORD
00060                        PERFORM 020-GET-NEXT-RECORD
00061                        .
```

Fig. 7-13   (*cont.*)

(1)   The SELECT statement in lines 6–11 is identical to that used to create the file.

(2)   The FD in lines 15–21 is identical to that used to create the file.

(3)   Lines 30–46 constitute the executive module. The indexed file is OPENed INPUT (line 32), and then the STATUS CODE is tested (line 33) to determine the success of the OPEN. If the OPEN succeeds, a priming read is performed (line 34) and a loop is generated to DISPLAY the logical records one at a time (lines 35–36). If the OPEN fails, a message is DISPLAYed (line 43) and the program aborted. Note that the STATUS CODE is also tested after the file is CLOSEd (line 37) and an appropriate message DISPLAYed (lines 38–41).

(4)   Lines 48–55 input a logical record from the indexed file. Note that instead of using the AT END clause to detect the end-of-file condition, the STATUS CODE is examined. This allows the detection of other unexpected errors (lines 51–55). If an error other than the end-of-file condition is detected, an error message is DISPLAYed with the STATUS CODE value; otherwise, processing continues as normal.

(5)   In order to eliminate nonrelevant details, the logical records are DISPLAYed rather than written to a standard print file (line 59).

7.13   Random Retrieval of Indexed Files (ANSI Standard)

Another major advantage of indexed organization is the ease with which logical records can be retrieved randomly.

ENVIRONMENT DIVISION Considerations

The ANSI standard SELECT statement for random retrieval of an indexed file has the following syntax:

```
        SELECT file-name
            ASSIGN TO external-name
            ORGANIZATION IS INDEXED
            ACCESS MODE IS RANDOM
            RECORD KEY IS name-of-key-field-in-record
            [ FILE STATUS IS name-of-status-area ]
```

The only change from the SELECT statements for sequential creation and sequential retrieval is the use of ACCESS MODE IS RANDOM. Since sequential access is the default, this clause is *required* for random processing.

DATA DIVISION Considerations

The FD and level-01 record descriptions for random retrieval are identical to those used for file creation and sequential retrieval.

PROCEDURE DIVISION Considerations

To randomly retrieve a logical record from an indexed file, the COBOL program must (1) move the key of the desired record into the RECORD KEY area for the file and then (2) execute a READ statement. Note that this is much easier than the procedure required for random retrieval from a direct file. The relevant PROCEDURE DIVISION statements are:

(1)   OPEN INPUT file-name

(2)   CLOSE file-name

(3)   READ file-name
          [INTO data-area-to-receive-copy-of-record]
          [INVALID KEY imperative-statement(s).]

Execution of the READ statement causes an automatic full index search to locate the logical record whose key matches the value currently in the RECORD KEY area for the file. If such a logical record exists, it is input into the level-01 record area. If no such logical record exists, the STATUS CODE area (if specified) is set to indicate a record-not-found condition and the INVALID KEY routine (if specified) is executed. Note that a record-not-found condition can be detected by (1) a stand-alone test of the STATUS CODE, (2) using INVALID KEY, or (3) testing the STATUS CODE within an INVALID KEY routine.

```
00001              IDENTIFICATION DIVISION.
00002              PROGRAM-ID.  INDEXED-RANDOM-RETRIEVAL.
00003              ENVIRONMENT DIVISION.
00004              CONFIGURATION SECTION.
00005              SOURCE-COMPUTER.  IBM-3081.
00006              OBJECT-COMPUTER.  IBM-3081.
00007              INPUT-OUTPUT SECTION.
00008              FILE-CONTROL.

00009                  SELECT TRANSACTION-FILE
00010                      ASSIGN TO PROGIDS
00011                      ORGANIZATION IS SEQUENTIAL
00012                      ACCESS IS SEQUENTIAL
00013                      .
00014                  SELECT INDEXED-FILE
00015                      ASSIGN TO VSAMFILE
00016                      ORGANIZATION IS INDEXED
00017                      ACCESS IS RANDOM
00018                      RECORD KEY IS INDEXED-PROGRAMMER-ID
00019                      FILE STATUS IS INDEXED-STATUS-CODE
00020                      .

00021              DATA DIVISION.
00022              FILE SECTION.
```

Fig. 7-14

```
00023        FD   TRANSACTION-FILE
00024             LABEL RECORDS ARE STANDARD
00025             BLOCK CONTAINS 0 CHARACTERS
00026             RECORD CONTAINS 80 CHARACTERS
00027             .
00028        01   TRANSACTION-RECORD.
00029             05   TRANS-PROGRAMMER-ID        PIC X(5).
00030             05   FILLER                     PIC X(75).

00031        FD   INDEXED-FILE
00032             LABEL RECORDS ARE STANDARD
00033             RECORD CONTAINS 15 CHARACTERS
             .
00034        01   INDEXED-RECORD.
00035             05   INDEXED-PROGRAMMER-ID      PIC X(5).
00036             05   INDEXED-PROJECT-ID         PIC X(8).
00037             05   INDEXED-TOTAL-HOURS        PIC 9(3)V9 COMP.

00038        WORKING-STORAGE SECTION.

00039        01   FLAGS-AND-SWITCHES.
00040             05   TRANS-END-OF-FILE-SW       PIC X(3).
00041                  88   MORE-TRANS-RECORDS    VALUE "NO".
00042                  88   NO-MORE-INPUT         VALUE "YES".

00043        01   FILE-STATUS-CODES.
00044             05   INDEXED-STATUS-CODE        PIC XX.
00045                  88   VSAM-OPERATION-OK     VALUE "00".
00046                  88   VSAM-OPERATION-FAILED VALUE "01" THRU "99".
00047                  88   RECORD-NOT-FOUND      VALUE "23".

00048        PROCEDURE DIVISION.
00049
00050        000-EXECUTIVE-MODULE.
00051
00052             MOVE "NO" TO TRANS-END-OF-FILE-SW
00053             OPEN    INPUT    INDEXED-FILE
00054                              TRANSACTION-FILE
00055             IF VSAM-OPERATION-OK
00056                 PERFORM 010-GET-NEXT-TRANS
00057                 PERFORM 020-RETRIEVE-INDEXED-RECORD
00058                     UNTIL NO-MORE-INPUT
00059                 CLOSE   INDEXED-FILE
00060                         TRANSACTION-FILE
00061                 IF VSAM-OPERATION-OK
00062                     DISPLAY "RANDOM RETRIEVAL COMPLETED"
00063                 ELSE
00064                     DISPLAY "INDEXED FILE NOT PROPERLY CLOSED"
00065             ELSE
00066                 DISPLAY "UNABLE TO OPEN INDEXED FILE -- ABORT"
00067                 CLOSE TRANSACTION-FILE
00068             .
00069             STOP RUN
00070             .
00071
00072        010-GET-NEXT-TRANS.
00073
00074             READ TRANSACTION-FILE
00075                 AT END
00076                     MOVE "YES" TO TRANS-END-OF-FILE-SW
00077
00078             .
00079        020-RETRIEVE-INDEXED-RECORD.
00080
00081             MOVE TRANS-PROGRAMMER-ID    TO INDEXED-PROGRAMMER-ID
00082             READ INDEXED-FILE
00083             IF VSAM-OPERATION-OK
00084                 DISPLAY INDEXED-PROGRAMMER-ID
00085                         SPACE
00086                         INDEXED-TOTAL-HOURS
00087             ELSE
00088                 IF RECORD-NOT-FOUND
00089                     DISPLAY "RECORD NOT FOUND FOR " TRANSACTION-RECORD
00090                 ELSE
00091                     DISPLAY "VSAM ERROR " INDEXED-STATUS-CODE
00092                             " FOR TRANSACTION " TRANSACTION-RECORD
00093             .
00094             PERFORM 010-GET-NEXT-TRANS
00095             .
```

Fig. 7-14 *(cont.)*

EXAMPLE 7.30 Figure 7-14 shows an IBM OS/VS COBOL program which randomly retrieves records from the VSAM indexed file created in Example 7.25 (Fig. 7-10). The keys of the logical records to be retrieved are supplied from a sequentially organized transaction file. The following remarks pertain to Fig. 7-14:

(1) Lines 9–13 and 23–30 define the transaction file which supplies the keys of logical records to be accessed.

(2) Lines 14–19 and 31–37 define the indexed file to be accessed. Note that except for the ACCESS IS RANDOM clause, the SELECT and FD are the same as for sequential creation or retrieval.

(3) Lines 43–47 define the FILE STATUS area for the indexed file. Note the use of condition names for each relevant condition.

(4) Lines 50–70 constitute the executive module, which OPENs the indexed file for INPUT. Note how the STATUS CODE (set by the OPEN statement in line 53) is tested in line 55. If the OPEN fails, an error message is DISPLAYed and no further processing is done (lines 65–69). If the OPEN succeeds, a priming read of the transaction file is done in line 56 and a loop established to retrieve indexed records (lines 57–58). The STATUS CODE is also tested when the indexed file is CLOSEd, and an appropriate message is DISPLAYed (lines 59–64).

(5) Random input from the indexed file is shown in lines 79–93. The record key from the transaction record is first moved to the RECORD KEY area within the indexed record (line 81), and then a READ is executed (line 82). In this example, the test for a record-not-found condition is carried out by examining the STATUS CODE area for the indexed file (lines 83–93). Observe how the use of the STATUS CODE allows the program to differentiate between a record-not-found condition and other errors (lines 88–93).

7.14 Dynamic Access of Indexed Files (ANSI Standard)

ANSI COBOL allows a mixture of sequential and random processing to be carried out simultaneously on the same indexed file. This can be accomplished in two ways.

(1) Sequential access with occasional random processing: The SELECT statement specifies ACCESS IS SEQUENTIAL, and the START verb is used to *randomly* position the current record pointer (CRP) within the file. Sequential processing then resumes with the logical record pointed to by the CRP.

(2) Random access with occasional sequential processing: The SELECT statement specifies ACCESS IS DYNAMIC, and either or both of the following occur: (*a*) the START verb is used to randomly position the current record pointer and/or (*b*) the READ verb is used to randomly input a logical record and set the CRP. In either case, READ NEXT can then be used to carry out sequential processing from the current record pointer established by the preceding START or READ.

Since the use of START with SEQUENTIAL ACCESS is the same as the use of START with DYNAMIC ACCESS, only DYNAMIC ACCESS [case (2) above] will be considered.

ENVIRONMENT DIVISION Considerations

The ANSI standard COBOL SELECT statement for DYNAMIC ACCESS has the following syntax:

```
SELECT file-name
    ASSIGN TO external-name
    ORGANIZATION IS INDEXED
    ACCESS MODE IS DYNAMIC
    RECORD KEY IS name-of-key-field-in-record
    [ FILE STATUS IS name-of-status-area ]
```

The only change is the specification of ACCESS MODE IS DYNAMIC (see Section 7.11 for a discussion of the other parameters). Note that specifying DYNAMIC ACCESS does not *require* the programmer to make use of the START verb or the READ NEXT feature; it simply provides the *option* to do so, should the need arise.

FILE STATUS is optional since errors can also be detected by specifying INVALID KEY in the appropriate PROCEDURE DIVISION statements. The use of a STATUS CODE is recommended.

DATA DIVISION Considerations

The FD and level-01 record descriptions for DYNAMIC ACCESS are the same as for SEQUENTIAL and RANDOM access, with one complication. When the START verb is to be used (with either SEQUENTIAL or DYNAMIC access), it is sometimes desirable to subdivide the RECORD KEY field. This is because the START verb can be used for either:

(1)   A *full key search*, in which the current record pointer is set to the logical record whose key is equal to that of the RECORD KEY when START is executed. If no such record exists in the file, START execution fails (with the STATUS CODE set accordingly, and the INVALID KEY routine executed, if specified) and the current record pointer is set undefined. A READ NEXT executed with the CRP undefined results in failure of the READ NEXT (with the appropriate STATUS CODE and INVALID KEY).

(2)   A *generic key search*, in which only the first *n* bytes of the RECORD KEY are used to establish the CRP. The CRP is set to the first record in key sequence whose key matches the beginning *n* bytes of the RECORD KEY. In order to do a generic key search, the RECORD KEY area must be subdivided into a *beginning portion* (on which the index searching is done) and an *ending portion* (which will not take part in the START operation). The size of the generic key thus established is determined by the definition of the first subfield of RECORD KEY.

EXAMPLE 7.31   It is common in indexed file applications to define the RECORD KEY as a *composite* of two or more subfields. Consider a file which holds customer invoice information. Each customer may have many invoices outstanding.

One approach is to design the file with just one customer record for each customer. Each customer record would hold a variable number of invoices. Since most implementations of indexed organization permit variable-length records, this is a practical approach in terms of file space. However, most of the processing against this file may focus on particular invoices. With one customer record per customer, *all* invoices will have to be input to access just one.

In order to provide more flexibility in processing (or to implement the customer invoice application on systems where indexed files are *not* allowed to have variable-length records), the designer may choose to have one record for each invoice. The RECORD KEY will consist of the customer number concatenated with the invoice number, as follows:

```
01    CUSTOMER-INVOICE-RECORD.
      05    RECORD-KEY-FIELD.
            10    CUSTOMER-ID    PIC X(4)
            10    INVOICE-ID     PIC X(5).
      05    INVOICE-INFORMATION...
```

Since the CUSTOMER-ID is the first part of the key, the logical records will be in sequence by customer number. Within each customer number, the records will be in sequence by invoice number.

If it is desired to access a *particular* invoice, the *full key* (consisting of both the customer and invoice numbers) can be specified for a random READ.

If it is desired to access all invoices for a given customer, the START verb can be used with a generic search to position the CRP to the first logical record whose CUSTOMER-ID portion of the RECORD-KEY-FIELD matches the CUSTOMER-ID specified for the START. Sequential processing (with READ NEXT) can then be carried out until the CUSTOMER-ID changes, indicating that all invoice records for the desired customer have been processed.

PROCEDURE DIVISION Considerations

The PROCEDURE DIVISION statements relevant to DYNAMIC ACCESS are as follows:

(1) OPEN INPUT file-name

(2) CLOSE file-name

(3) READ file-name
         [INTO data-area-to-receive-copy-of-record]
         [INVALID KEY imperative-statement(s).]
The READ statement functions the same for DYNAMIC ACCESS as for RANDOM ACCESS. It causes a full index search to locate and input the logical record whose key matches that in the RECORD KEY. If no such record exists, the STATUS CODE and INVALID KEY are activated appropriately. If the READ succeeds, the current record pointer is set to point to the logical record *following* (in key sequence) the one just input.

(4) READ file-name NEXT
         [INTO data-area-to-receive-copy-of-record]
         [AT END imperative-statement(s).]
The READ NEXT statement inputs the logical record pointed to by the current record pointer, and then updates the CRP to point to the *next* record in key sequence. The AT END routine is executed only when the end of the file is encountered (in which case the CRP is set undefined).

(5) START file-name
         [KEY IS   relational-operator   partial-record-key]
         [INVALID KEY imperative-statement(s).]
The START statement is used to set the current record pointer for later sequential processing. It operates in two modes: (1) When the KEY IS clause is omitted, START attempts to set the CRP to the logical record whose key matches the current contents of the RECORD KEY area (thus the RECORD KEY should be initialized before executing START); and (2) when the KEY IS clause is specified, START attempts to set the CRP to the first logical record whose key matches the partial record key. The allowable relational operators are:

(*a*) EQUAL TO

(*b*) =

(*c*) GREATER THAN

(*d*) >

(*e*) NOT LESS THAN

(*f*) NOT <

The partial record key must be a subfield of the RECORD KEY for the file and must begin at the first byte of the RECORD KEY.

EXAMPLE 7.32 The following START statements all refer to the RECORD KEY defined in Example 7.31:

```
(1)  MOVE TRANS-CUSTOMER-AND-INVOICE-ID TO RECORD-KEY-FIELD
     START CUSTOMER-INVOICE-FILE
         INVALID KEY
             MOVE "NO" TO CORRECTLY-POSITIONED-SW
```

This sets the CRP to the logical record whose full key is equal to TRANS-CUSTOMER-AND-INVOICE-ID. If no such record exists, the INVALID KEY routine is executed.

(2) MOVE TRANS-CUSTOMER-ID TO CUSTOMER-ID
     START CUSTOMER-INVOICE-FILE
          KEY IS EQUAL CUSTOMER-ID
          INVALID KEY
               MOVE "NO" TO CORRECTLY-POSITIONED-SW
     .

This sets the CRP to the first logical record in key sequence whose key *begins* with a customer ID equal to that in TRANS-CUSTOMER-ID. If no such record exists, the INVALID KEY routine is executed and the CRP is set undefined.

(3) MOVE TRANS-CUSTOMER-ID TO CUSTOMER-ID
     START CUSTOMER-INVOICE-FILE
          KEY IS NOT LESS THAN CUSTOMER-ID
     IF CUSTOMER-FILE-STATUS-CODE NOT EQUAL "00"
          MOVE "NO" TO CORRECTLY-POSITIONED-SW
     .

This sets the CRP to the first logical record in key sequence whose key *begins* with a customer ID greater than or equal to that in TRANS-CUSTOMER-ID. If no such record exists, the STATUS CODE for the file is set to indicate the record-not-found condition and the CRP is set undefined. A test of the STATUS CODE is used to detect this problem.

(4) MOVE TRANS-CUSTOMER-AND-INVOICE-ID TO RECORD-KEY-FIELD
     START CUSTOMER-INVOICE-FILE
          KEY IS NOT LESS THAN RECORD-KEY-FIELD
     IF CUSTOMER-FILE-STATUS-CODE NOT EQUAL "00"
          MOVE "NO" TO CORRECTLY-POSITIONED-SW
     .

This sets the CRP to the first logical record in key sequence whose *full* key is not less than that in TRANS-CUSTOMER-AND-INVOICE-ID. If no such record exists, the STATUS-CODE is set to indicate a record-not-found condition and the CRP is set undefined. Note that it is valid to use the RECORD KEY field as the partial record key in the START statement.

EXAMPLE 7.33 The following START statements are both *incorrect*:

(1) MOVE TRANS-INVOICE-ID TO INVOICE-ID
     START CUSTOMER-INVOICE-FILE
          KEY IS EQUAL TO INVOICE-ID . . .

The KEY IS . . . data item must be the first subfield of the RECORD KEY area for the file (or the RECORD KEY itself). In this case, only CUSTOMER-ID or RECORD-KEY-FIELD may be used for the KEY IS clause.

(2) MOVE TRANS-CUSTOMER-ID TO CUSTOMER-ID
     START CUSTOMER-INVOICE-FILE
          KEY IS LESS THAN CUSTOMER-ID . . .

LESS THAN is not an allowable relational operator for the START verb.

EXAMPLE 7.34 Figure 7-15 illustrates DYNAMIC ACCESS of the file created in Fig. 7-10. The logical records to be retrieved are identified by an incoming transaction file. For purposes of this example, the PROGRAMMER-ID which serves as the RECORD KEY for the indexed file is subdivided into an APPLI-CATION-GROUP number followed by a PROGRAMMER-NUMBER. If the transaction specifies *only* an APPLICATION-GROUP number, the program retrieves the total hours worked by *all* programmers in that

```
00001              IDENTIFICATION DIVISION.
00002              PROGRAM-ID.  INDEXED-DYNAMIC-RETRIEVAL.

00003              ENVIRONMENT DIVISION.
00004              CONFIGURATION SECTION.
00005              SOURCE-COMPUTER.  IBM-3081.
00006              OBJECT-COMPUTER.  IBM-3081.
00007              INPUT-OUTPUT SECTION.
00008              FILE-CONTROL.

00009                  SELECT TRANSACTION-FILE
00010                      ASSIGN TO RECIDS
00011                      ORGANIZATION IS SEQUENTIAL
00012                      ACCESS IS SEQUENTIAL
00013                      .
00014                  SELECT INDEXED-FILE
00015                      ASSIGN TO VSAMFILE
00016                      ORGANIZATION IS INDEXED
00017                      ACCESS IS DYNAMIC
00018                      RECORD KEY IS INDEXED-PROGRAMMER-ID
00019                      FILE STATUS IS INDEXED-STATUS-CODE
00020                      .

00021              DATA DIVISION.
00022              FILE SECTION.

00023              FD  TRANSACTION-FILE
00024                  LABEL RECORDS ARE STANDARD
00025                  BLOCK CONTAINS 0 CHARACTERS
00026                  RECORD CONTAINS 80 CHARACTERS
00027                  .
00028              01  TRANSACTION-RECORD.
00029                  05  TRANS-PROGRAMMER-ID.
00030                      10  TRANS-APPLICATION-GROUP PIC X(2).
00031                      10  TRANS-PROGRAMMER-NUMBER PIC X(3).
00032                          88  GROUP-TOTAL-QUERY   VALUE SPACES.
00033                  05  FILLER                      PIC X(75).

00034              FD  INDEXED-FILE
00035                  LABEL RECORDS ARE STANDARD
00036                  RECORD CONTAINS 15 CHARACTERS
                       .
00037              01  INDEXED-RECORD.
00038                  05  INDEXED-PROGRAMMER-ID.
00039                      10  INDEXED-APPLICATION-GROUP   PIC X(2).
00040                      10  INDEXED-PROGRAMMER-NUMBER   PIC X(3).
00041                  05  INDEXED-PROJECT-ID          PIC X(8).
00042                  05  INDEXED-TOTAL-HOURS         PIC 9(3)V9 COMP.

00043              WORKING-STORAGE SECTION.

00044              01  FLAGS-AND-SWITCHES.
00045                  05  TRANS-END-OF-FILE-SW        PIC X(3).
00046                      88  MORE-TRANS-RECORDS       VALUE "NO".
00047                      88  NO-MORE-INPUT            VALUE "YES".

00048              01  FILE-STATUS-CODES.
00049                  05  INDEXED-STATUS-CODE         PIC XX.
00050                      88  VSAM-OPERATION-OK        VALUE "00".
00051                      88  VSAM-OPERATION-FAILED    VALUE "01" THRU "99".
00052                      88  RECORD-NOT-FOUND         VALUE "23".

00053              01  WS-GROUP-TOTAL-HOURS            PIC S9(5)V9 COMP.

00054              PROCEDURE DIVISION.
00055
00056              000-EXECUTIVE-MODULE.
00057
00058                  MOVE "NO" TO TRANS-END-OF-FILE-SW
00059                  OPEN    INPUT   INDEXED-FILE
00060                                  TRANSACTION-FILE
00061                  IF VSAM-OPERATION-OK
00062                      PERFORM 010-GET-NEXT-TRANS
00063                      PERFORM 020-PROCESS-QUERY
00064                          UNTIL NO-MORE-INPUT
```

Fig. 7-15

```
00065                       CLOSE     INDEXED-FILE
00066                                 TRANSACTION-FILE
00067                       IF VSAM-OPERATION-OK
00068                           DISPLAY "DYNAMIC RETRIEVAL COMPLETED"
00069                       ELSE
00070                           DISPLAY "INDEXED FILE NOT PROPERLY CLOSED"
00071                   ELSE
00072                       DISPLAY "UNABLE TO OPEN INDEXED FILE -- ABORT"
00073                       CLOSE TRANSACTION-FILE
00074                   .
00075                   STOP RUN
00076                   .
00077
00078           010-GET-NEXT-TRANS.
00079
00080                   READ TRANSACTION-FILE
00081                       AT END
00082                           MOVE "YES" TO TRANS-END-OF-FILE-SW
00083                   .
00084
00085           020-PROCESS-QUERY.
00086
00087                   IF GROUP-TOTAL-QUERY
00088                       PERFORM 030-FIND-GROUP-TOTAL
00089                   ELSE
00090                       PERFORM 040-FIND-INDIVIDUAL-TOTAL
00091                   .
00092                   PERFORM 010-GET-NEXT-TRANS
00093                   .
00094
00095           030-FIND-GROUP-TOTAL.
00096
00097                   MOVE TRANS-APPLICATION-GROUP TO INDEXED-APPLICATION-GROUP
00098                   START INDEXED-FILE
00099                       KEY IS EQUAL INDEXED-APPLICATION-GROUP
00100                   IF VSAM-OPERATION-FAILED
00101                       DISPLAY "APPLICATION GROUP NOT FOUND FOR "
00102                               TRANS-APPLICATION-GROUP
00103                   ELSE
00104                       MOVE ZERO TO WS-GROUP-TOTAL-HOURS
00105                       PERFORM 050-READ-NEXT-INDEXED-RECORD
00106                       PERFORM 060-ACCUMULATE-GROUP-TOTAL
00107                           UNTIL TRANS-APPLICATION-GROUP NOT EQUAL
00108                                 INDEXED-APPLICATION-GROUP
00109                       DISPLAY TRANS-APPLICATION-GROUP " (GROUP) "
00110                               WS-GROUP-TOTAL-HOURS
00111                   .
00112
00113           040-FIND-INDIVIDUAL-TOTAL.
00114
00115                   MOVE TRANS-PROGRAMMER-ID   TO INDEXED-PROGRAMMER-ID
00116                   READ INDEXED-FILE
00117                   IF VSAM-OPERATION-OK
00118                       DISPLAY INDEXED-PROGRAMMER-ID
00119                               SPACE
00120                               INDEXED-TOTAL-HOURS
00121                   ELSE
00122                       IF RECORD-NOT-FOUND
00123                           DISPLAY "RECORD NOT FOUND FOR " TRANSACTION-RECORD
00124                       ELSE
00125                           DISPLAY "VSAM ERROR " INDEXED-STATUS-CODE
00126                                   " FOR TRANSACTION " TRANSACTION-RECORD
00127                   .
00128
00129           050-READ-NEXT-INDEXED-RECORD.
00130
00131                   READ INDEXED-FILE NEXT
00132                       AT END
00133                           MOVE SPACES TO INDEXED-APPLICATION-GROUP
00134                   .
00135
00136           060-ACCUMULATE-GROUP-TOTAL.
00137
00138                   ADD INDEXED-TOTAL-HOURS TO WS-GROUP-TOTAL-HOURS
00139                   PERFORM 050-READ-NEXT-INDEXED-RECORD
00140                   .
```

Fig. 7-15   *(cont.)*

particular group (this operation illustrates the use of the START and READ NEXT statements). If the transaction specifies a *full* key (i.e., APPLICATION-GROUP and PROGRAMMER-NUMBER), then the program retrieves the total hours worked by that programmer (illustrating a random READ). The following comments pertain:

(1) Lines 14–19 and 34–42 define the indexed file. The only differences from previous examples are (*a*) the specification of ACCESS IS DYNAMIC in line 17 and (*b*) the treatment of RECORD KEY INDEXED-PROGRAMMER-ID as a group item consisting of an applications group number followed by a programmer number (lines 38–40).

(2) Note the use of condition names for the STATUS CODE area (lines 48–52).

(3) Lines 56–76 make up the executive module in which the files are OPENed (lines 59–60), the indexed file STATUS CODE tested (line 61), the queries from the transaction file processed (lines 62–64), the files CLOSEd (lines 65–66), and the STATUS CODE for the CLOSE tested and an appropriate message DISPLAYed (lines 67–70). If the OPEN fails, the program prints an error message and STOPs (lines 71–75).

(4) 030-FIND-GROUP-TOTAL (lines 95–111) illustrates sequential processing from a randomly selected point within the file. The TRANS-APPLICATION-GROUP value is first moved to the INDEXED-APPLICATION-GROUP field, which begins the RECORD KEY area (line 97). A START statement is then used to position the CRP to the first logical record in the file with its application group portion of the key *equal* to TRANS-APPLICATION-GROUP (lines 98–99). The STATUS CODE is then used to test whether the START operation is successful. If so, the group total is zeroed and a loop established to input the records for *all* programmers within the group (lines 104–108). If the START fails to locate a record whose application group field matches TRANS-APPLICATION-GROUP, an error message is DISPLAYed in lines 101–102.

(5) 060-ACCUMULATE-GROUP-TOTAL (lines 136–140) adds the total hours for the current record to an accumulator, and then inputs the next logical record by performing 050-READ-NEXT-INDEXED-RECORD (lines 129–134).

(6) The important feature of 030-FIND-GROUP-TOTAL is that it must position the CRP to the *first* record for an applications group (via the START statement in line 98), and then continue to sequentially input records (via the READ NEXT in line 131) until the application group number changes. This is handled by performing 060-ACCUMULATE-GROUP-TOTAL until the INDEXED-APPLICATION-GROUP field from the indexed file fails to equal the TRANS-APPLICATION-GROUP field on the transaction record (lines 106–108).

(7) An interesting problem occurs if the READ NEXT statement hits the end of the file *before* the INDEXED-APPLICATION-GROUP field changes value. This is handled by having an AT END clause set the INDEXED-APPLICATION-GROUP to SPACES at the end of the file (lines 131–133), thus halting the execution of the PERFORM statement in lines 106–108. The reader should study this logic carefully, since it illustrates the essence of START with READ NEXT.

(8) If 020-PROCESS-QUERY (lines 85–93) discovers that the transaction specifies a full key, 040-FIND-INDIVIDUAL-TOTAL (lines 113–127) is performed. Here the full key is moved from the transaction record to the RECORD KEY area, and a random READ used to input the desired programmer record so INDEXED-TOTAL-HOURS can be DISPLAYed. Note the use of STATUS CODE to detect any record-not-found conditions or other errors (lines 117–127).

7.15 Random Updating of Indexed Files (ANSI Standard)

Indexed files may be updated either sequentially or randomly. Sequential updates require that the transaction file be sorted by the RECORD KEY field, and are only efficient if most of the records in the file are to be changed (see Problem 7.70). If a file is OPENed I–O with ACCESS SEQUENTIAL, the REWRITE verb can be used to replace an existing logical record and the DELETE verb can be used to delete an existing record. In both cases, a successful READ for the record in question *must* precede the REWRITE or DELETE (this rule does not apply to a random update; see below).

When ACCESS IS SEQUENTIAL, records can only be added to the *end* of an indexed file. This implies that the keys of the records to be added are all greater than those currently in the file. The file must be OPENed EXTEND, and the additional records written in key sequence just as when the file was initially created.

Since there are restrictions on the effective use of sequential updating, most modern applications update indexed files randomly. It is relatively easy to randomly add, change, and delete logical records in indexed files, as discussed below.

ENVIRONMENT DIVISION Considerations

The ANSI COBOL SELECT statement for randomly updating an indexed file has the following syntax:

```
SELECT file-name
     ASSIGN TO external-name
     ORGANIZATION IS INDEXED
     ACCESS MODE IS { RANDOM | DYNAMIC }
     RECORD KEY IS name-of-key-field-in-record
     [ FILE STATUS IS name-of-status-area ]
```

The notation "{ RANDOM | DYNAMIC }" indicates that either RANDOM or DYNAMIC access can be used.

DATA DIVISION Considerations

The FD and level-01 record description(s) are the same as for RANDOM and DYNAMIC access.

PROCEDURE DIVISION Considerations

The PROCEDURE DIVISION must include code to add, change, and delete logical records, as well as to detect possible duplicate key and record-not-found conditions. The relevant statements for each operation are as follows:

General

(1)   OPEN I–O file-name
      Full add, change, and delete capability requires that the file be OPENed "I–O". This allows the file to be used for *both* input *and* output. In particular, READ, WRITE, and REWRITE are all valid verbs for a file opened I–O.

(2)   CLOSE file-name

(3)   IF status-code-area NOT EQUAL "00" . . .
      The best way to detect errors following any indexed file operation is to test the STATUS CODE associated with the file. In ANSI standard COBOL, a nonzero status code indicates some type of error.

Adding Logical Records

(4)   WRITE record-name
      [FROM data-area]
      [INVALID KEY imperative-statement(s).]

Execution of a WRITE statement automatically causes a full index search to locate the position (based on the RECORD KEY) where the new record should be added. As part of this process, WRITE also checks for the presence of a record with a duplicate key. If necessary, control interval and control area splits (or their equivalent on a non-IBM/ VSAM system) are carried out to make room for the addition. If the record to be added is a duplicate key or if space cannot be obtained in which to write the record, the STATUS CODE is set to the appropriate value and the INVALID KEY clause (if specified) is executed. Note that all of the considerable amount of work involved in adding a record to an indexed file is automatically carried out by the WRITE statement, thus freeing the COBOL programmer to concentrate on the details of the application.

EXAMPLE 7.35 The following illustrates random addition of a record to an indexed file:

```
MOVE TRANSACTION-KEY-VALUE          TO RECORD-KEY-AREA
PERFORM MOVE-TRANS-INFO-TO-INDEXED-REC
WRITE INDEXED-RECORD
IF FILE-STATUS-AREA NOT EQUAL VALUE-FOR-SUCCESS
    PERFORM ERROR-ANALYSIS-ROUTINE
.
```

Changing Logical Records

(5)   <u>READ</u> file-name
     [<u>INTO</u> data-area]
     [<u>INVALID</u> KEY imperative-statement(s).]

The random READ does a full index search and attempts to bring the logical record specified by the RECORD KEY contents into the level-01 record area for the file. If such a record cannot be located, the STATUS CODE is set and the INVALID KEY routine (if specified) is executed.

(6)   <u>REWRITE</u> record-name
     [<u>FROM</u> data-area]
     [<u>INVALID</u> KEY imperative-statement(s).]

The REWRITE statement uses the current contents of the level-01 record area for the file to *replace* the logical record on disk whose key matches the current contents of the RECORD KEY. If no such record exists, the STATUS CODE is set to indicate the record-not-found condition and the INVALID KEY clause (if specified) is executed. The file must be OPENed I-O when REWRITE is used. In ANSI COBOL, the *length* of a record may not be changed by REWRITE. With IBM OS/VS COBOL VSAM indexed files, this restriction is relaxed. Note that a record can be replaced with REWRITE without having been READ first. In actual practice, however, the information already present in the record is usually needed before changes can be made. In this typical case, the record is first input with READ, the changes are made (using transaction information), and then the updated record is written back to its original disk location with REWRITE. Note that the permanent (disk) copy of the record is not updated until the REWRITE is completed.

EXAMPLE 7.36 The following illustrates random change(s) to a logical record in an indexed file:

```
MOVE TRANSACTION-KEY-VALUE TO RECORD-KEY-AREA
READ INDEXED-FILE
IF FILE-STATUS-CODE NOT EQUAL "00"
    PERFORM RECORD-NOT-FOUND
ELSE
    PERFORM MAKE-CHANGES-TO-INDEXED-REC
    REWRITE INDEXED-RECORD
    IF FILE-STATUS-CODE NOT EQUAL VALUE-FOR-SUCCESS
        PERFORM ERROR-ANALYSIS-ROUTINE
.
```

Note that the only error anticipated for the REWRITE would be a hardware error (or change in record length on a system which did not allow such change). It is assumed that ERROR-ANALYSIS-ROUTINE would test the FILE-STATUS-CODE and take appropriate action.

Deleting Logical Records

(7)   <u>DELETE</u> file-name [RECORD]
          [<u>INVALID</u> KEY imperative-statement(s).]

The DELETE statement automatically does a full index search to locate the record whose key matches the current contents of the RECORD KEY for the file. This record is then "removed" from the file. (The exact method of removal depends on the indexed file implementation; see Problem 7.71. In IBM OS/VS COBOL VSAM indexed implementation, logical records are *physically* removed and their space is immediately available for future additions.) If no such record exists, the STATUS CODE is set to indicate a record-not-found condition and the INVALID KEY clause (if specified) is executed. The file must be OPENed I–O when DELETE is used.

EXAMPLE 7.37   The following illustrates deleting a logical record from an indexed file:

```
MOVE TRANSACTION-KEY-VALUE TO RECORD-KEY-AREA
DELETE INDEXED-FILE RECORD
IF FILE-STATUS-CODE NOT EQUAL "00"
    PERFORM RECORD-NOT-FOUND
```

EXAMPLE 7.38   Figure 7-16 illustrates the random update of the IBM OS/VS COBOL indexed file created in Fig. 7-10. Additions, changes, and deletions are supplied via a sequentially organized transaction file. For simplicity, it is assumed that the transaction file has *already* been validated, so that only duplicate key and record-not-found errors remain. The following comments apply to Fig. 7-16:

(1)   Lines 9–12 and 23–36 define the already validated transaction file. Note the condition names defined for the three possible types of transactions (lines 29–32).

(2)   Lines 14–19 and 37–43 define the indexed file to be updated. Note that ACCESS IS RANDOM (line 17).

(3)   A status code area has been defined for the indexed file (lines 19, 50–54). Note the use of condition names to identify the most likely errors during a file update (i.e., duplicate key and record-not-found condition).

(4)   Lines 57–77 constitute the executive module, which (a) OPENs the indexed file I–O (required for REWRITE and DELETE), (b) tests the STATUS CODE to determine the success of the OPEN (line 61), printing an error message and aborting the program if the OPEN fails (lines 72–76), (c) does a priming read of the transaction file and then loops to process each transaction (lines 63–65), and (d) CLOSEs the files and tests the STATUS CODE, DISPLAYing an appropriate message (lines 66–71).

(5)   020-UPDATE-INDEXED-FILE (lines 86–98) examines the incoming transaction code and performs the appropriate update operation. This module is the "transaction center" discussed in Chapter 2.

(6)   030-ADD-A-RECORD (lines 100–110) adds a new record to the indexed file. First it moves all fields (including the RECORD KEY field) from the transaction record to the indexed record by performing 090-BUILD-INDEXED-RECORD (lines 131–136). Having established all fields in INDEXED-RECORD, the record is then added to the file by executing the WRITE verb in line 103. The STATUS CODE is used to detect any failure in the WRITE operation (lines 104–110). Note that this illustrates the superiority of testing the STATUS CODE over using INVALID KEY, since in this example the program can detect not only the anticipated duplicate key error but also any other unanticipated errors which might actually occur.

```
00001              IDENTIFICATION DIVISION.
00002              PROGRAM-ID.  INDEXED-FILE-UPDATE.

00003              ENVIRONMENT DIVISION.
00004              CONFIGURATION SECTION.
00005              SOURCE-COMPUTER.  IBM-3081.
00006              OBJECT-COMPUTER.  IBM-3081.
00007              INPUT-OUTPUT SECTION.
00008              FILE-CONTROL.

00009                  SELECT TRANSACTION-FILE
00010                      ASSIGN TO CHANGES
00011                      ORGANIZATION IS SEQUENTIAL
00012                      ACCESS IS SEQUENTIAL
00013                      .
00014                  SELECT INDEXED-FILE
00015                      ASSIGN TO VSAMFILE
00016                      ORGANIZATION IS INDEXED
00017                      ACCESS IS RANDOM
00018                      RECORD KEY IS INDEXED-PROGRAMMER-ID
00019                      FILE STATUS IS INDEXED-STATUS-CODE
00020                      .

00021              DATA DIVISION.
00022              FILE SECTION.

00023              FD  TRANSACTION-FILE
00024                  LABEL RECORDS ARE STANDARD
00025                  BLOCK CONTAINS 0 CHARACTERS
00026                  RECORD CONTAINS 80 CHARACTERS
00027                  .
00028              01  TRANSACTION-RECORD.
00029                  05   TRANS-CODE                PIC X.
00030                       88  ADD-NEW-RECORD        VALUE "A".
00031                       88  CHANGE-EXISTING-RECORD  VALUE "C".
00032                       88  DELETE-EXISTING-RECORD  VALUE "D".
00033                  05   TRANS-PROGRAMMER-ID       PIC X(5).
00034                  05   TRANS-PROJECT-ID          PIC X(8).
00035                  05   TRANS-TOTAL-HOURS         PIC 9(3)V9.
00036                  05   FILLER                    PIC X(62).

00037              FD  INDEXED-FILE
00038                  LABEL RECORDS ARE STANDARD
00039                  RECORD CONTAINS 15 CHARACTERS
                       .
00040              01  INDEXED-RECORD.
00041                  05   INDEXED-PROGRAMMER-ID     PIC X(5).
00042                  05   INDEXED-PROJECT-ID        PIC X(8).
00043                  05   INDEXED-TOTAL-HOURS       PIC 9(3)V9 COMP.

00044              WORKING-STORAGE SECTION.

00045              01  FLAGS-AND-SWITCHES.
00046                  05   TRANS-END-OF-FILE-SW      PIC X(3).
00047                       88  MORE-TRANS-RECORDS    VALUE "NO".
00048                       88  NO-MORE-INPUT         VALUE "YES".

00049              01  FILE-STATUS-CODES.
00050                  05   INDEXED-STATUS-CODE       PIC XX.
00051                       88  VSAM-OPERATION-OK     VALUE "00".
00052                       88  VSAM-OPERATION-FAILED  VALUE "01" THRU "99".
00053                       88  RECORD-NOT-FOUND      VALUE "23".
00054                       88  DUPLICATE-KEY         VALUE "22".

00055              PROCEDURE DIVISION.
00056
00057              000-EXECUTIVE-MODULE.
00058
00059                  OPEN     INPUT   TRANSACTION-FILE
00060                           I-O     INDEXED-FILE
00061                  IF VSAM-OPERATION-OK
00062                      MOVE "NO" TO TRANS-END-OF-FILE-SW
00063                      PERFORM 010-GET-TRANSACTION-RECORD
```

Fig. 7-16

```
00064                        PERFORM 020-UPDATE-INDEXED-FILE
00065                            UNTIL NO-MORE-INPUT
00066                        CLOSE   TRANSACTION-FILE
00067                                INDEXED-FILE
00068                        IF VSAM-OPERATION-OK
00069                            DISPLAY "INDEXED FILE UPDATE COMPLETED"
00070                        ELSE
00071                            DISPLAY "INDEXED FILE NOT PROPERLY CLOSED"
00072                    ELSE
00073                        DISPLAY "UNABLE TO OPEN INDEXED FILE -- ABORT"
00074                        CLOSE TRANSACTION-FILE
00075                    .
00076                    STOP RUN
00077                    .
00078
00079            010-GET-TRANSACTION-RECORD.
00080
00081                    READ TRANSACTION-FILE
00082                        AT END
00083                            MOVE "YES" TO TRANS-END-OF-FILE-SW
00084                    .
00085
00086            020-UPDATE-INDEXED-FILE.
00087
00088                    IF ADD-NEW-RECORD
00089                        PERFORM 030-ADD-A-RECORD
00090                    ELSE IF CHANGE-EXISTING-RECORD
00091                        PERFORM 040-CHANGE-A-RECORD
00092                    ELSE IF DELETE-EXISTING-RECORD
00093                        PERFORM 080-DELETE-A-RECORD
00094                    ELSE
00095                        DISPLAY "INVALID TRANS CODE: " TRANSACTION-RECORD
00096                    .
00097                    PERFORM 010-GET-TRANSACTION-RECORD
00098                    .
00099
00100            030-ADD-A-RECORD.
00101
00102                    PERFORM 090-BUILD-INDEXED-RECORD
00103                    WRITE INDEXED-RECORD
00104                    IF VSAM-OPERATION-FAILED
00105                        IF DUPLICATE-KEY
00106                            DISPLAY "DUPLICATE KEY FOR " INDEXED-PROGRAMMER-ID
00107                        ELSE
00108                            DISPLAY "VSAM ERROR NUMBER " INDEXED-STATUS-CODE
00109                            " FOR " INDEXED-PROGRAMMER-ID
00110                    .
00111
00112            040-CHANGE-A-RECORD.
00113
00114                    MOVE TRANS-PROGRAMMER-ID TO INDEXED-PROGRAMMER-ID
00115                    READ INDEXED-FILE
00116                    IF VSAM-OPERATION-OK
00117                        ADD TRANS-TOTAL-HOURS TO INDEXED-TOTAL-HOURS
00118                        REWRITE INDEXED-RECORD
00119                    ELSE
00120                        DISPLAY TRANS-PROGRAMMER-ID " NOT FOUND FOR CHANGE"
00121                    .
00122
00123            080-DELETE-A-RECORD.
00124
00125                    MOVE TRANS-PROGRAMMER-ID TO INDEXED-PROGRAMMER-ID
00126                    DELETE INDEXED-FILE
00127                    IF VSAM-OPERATION-FAILED
00128                        DISPLAY TRANS-PROGRAMMER-ID " NOT FOUND FOR DELETE"
00129                    .
00130
00131            090-BUILD-INDEXED-RECORD.
00132
00133                    MOVE TRANS-PROGRAMMER-ID     TO INDEXED-PROGRAMMER-ID
00134                    MOVE TRANS-PROJECT-ID        TO INDEXED-PROJECT-ID
00135                    MOVE TRANS-TOTAL-HOURS       TO INDEXED-TOTAL-HOURS
00136                    .
```

Fig. 7-16   (cont.)

(7) 040-CHANGE-A-RECORD (lines 112–121) modifies an existing logical record. First the RECORD KEY value is moved from the current transaction record to the RECORD KEY area. The READ verb is then used to input the existing record. Line 116 uses the STATUS CODE to determine whether the record was successfully obtained (if not, an error message is DISPLAYed). If a record matching the transaction is found, the hours from the transaction are added to the total hours field in the master record (line 117) and the updated version of the record is written back to its original location in the file with REWRITE. Note that the program assumes that no unanticipated errors will occur during the REWRITE. If desired, the STATUS CODE could have been tested after the REWRITE to detect any unexpected errors (see Problem 7.72).

(8) 080-DELETE-A-RECORD (lines 123–129) deletes a logical record. First the RECORD KEY value from the transaction is moved to the RECORD KEY area (line 125), and then the DELETE verb is executed in line 126. The STATUS CODE is then examined to determine whether the deletion was successfully accomplished (again, if desired, the simple STATUS CODE test shown could be replaced with a more sophisticated test, as in lines 104–110).

Review Questions

7.1 Why are indexed files so popular for business applications?

7.2 Explain the role of the index during (1) sequential processing and (2) random processing.

7.3 Explain the relationship between a VSAM data component, index component, and cluster.

7.4 Define the concepts of control interval and control area.

7.5 Give the layout of a data component control interval (with specific reference to the sequence of logical records within the CI).

7.6 What is the sequence set? Explain its role in sequential processing.

7.7 What is the structure of a VSAM index component?

7.8 Explain the role of the index component during random access.

7.9 Explain the role of VSAM catalogs.

7.10 What is a VSAM data space?

7.11 How is a VSAM catalog entry for a file created?

7.12 Explain the four steps which must be carried out in order to create a VSAM file.

7.13 Explain the role of distributed free space as a file is created.

7.14 Give a detailed explanation of how a record in a VSAM file is randomly accessed.

7.15 Give a detailed description of control interval splits and the circumstances under which they are needed.

7.16 Give a detailed description of control area splits and the circumstances under which they are needed.

7.17 Explain in detail the steps involved in randomly deleting a record from a VSAM file.

7.18   Explain in detail the steps involved in randomly changing a record in a VSAM file.

7.19   Explain in detail the steps involved in accessing a VSAM file sequentially. Be sure to include the role of the sequence set.

7.20   Explain how the START statement allows some random capabilities to be introduced into normal sequential processing.

7.21   Explain the function of START and READ NEXT with DYNAMIC ACCESS.

7.22   Explain the role of the IDCAMS utility DEFINE CLUSTER command when creating a VSAM file.

7.23   Explain the syntax and use of the following DEFINE CLUSTER parameters: (1) NAME, (2) VOLUMES, (3) KEYS, (4) FREESPACE, (5) RECORDS, (6) RECORDSIZE, (7) CATALOG.

7.24   Explain the syntax and use of the IDCAMS utility PRINT command.

7.25   Explain the syntax and use of the IDCAMS utility DELETE command.

7.26   Discuss the ENVIRONMENT DIVISION requirements when creating an ANSI indexed file sequentially.

7.27   Why should a FILE STATUS area be defined and used (instead of INVALID KEY) for indexed files?

7.28   What, if any, are the differences between an FD for a sequential file and an FD for an indexed file?

7.29   Discuss the PROCEDURE DIVISION logic needed to sequentially create an ANSI indexed file.

7.30   Explain the relationship between (1) the KEYS and RECORDSIZE parameters of the IDCAMS DEFINE CLUSTER command and (2) the FD in the COBOL program.

7.31   Discuss the PROCEDURE DIVISION logic needed to sequentially retrieve an ANSI indexed file in key sequence.

7.32   Discuss the PROCEDURE DIVISION logic needed to randomly retrieve records from an ANSI indexed file.

7.33   Discuss the file processing capabilities available with DYNAMIC ACCESS.

7.34   Explain the difference between START with a full key versus a generic key.

7.35   Explain the use of a composite key for indexed files and the processing flexibility provided by such a design.

7.36   Discuss the PROCEDURE DIVISION logic involved in retrieving a *group* of records with START and READ NEXT.

7.37   Discuss how to add logical records to an ANSI indexed file during a random update.

7.38   Discuss how to change records in an ANSI indexed file during a random update.

7.39   Discuss how to delete records in an ANSI indexed file during a random update.

Solved Problems

7.40　Why are logical records in a VSAM indexed file not necessarily physically in key sequence?

Control interval and/or control area splits may cause control intervals to be physically out of key sequence. This does not matter since sequential retrieval is done through the sequence set entries, which *are* maintained in key sequence.

7.41　Prior to the announcement of VSAM, IBM provided an earlier implementation of indexed files known as ISAM. How does the ISAM index structure differ from that of VSAM's index set and sequence set?

An ISAM index is built around the concept of disk cylinders. ISAM file space must be allocated from the VTOC in cylinder units. The first track of each cylinder is used for the *track index*. The track index has an entry for each track of its cylinder. Each entry contains the highest key on its associated track, together with the disk address of the track (CCHH). The cylinders which hold the track indexes and their associated data records are called the *prime area*. The logical records on the tracks of each prime cylinder are maintained in ascending sequence by key.

In addition to the prime area, an ISAM file consists of an *index area* which has an entry for each prime cylinder in the file. The entries in this *cylinder index* contain the highest key in each prime cylinder, along with the disk address of the track index for that cylinder (CCHH).

The entries in both the cylinder index and all track indexes are kept in ascending sequence by key.

Random retrieval for an ISAM file begins at the cylinder index, which is searched sequentially, entry by entry, until the first key greater than or equal to the desired key is found. Associated with this index entry is the address of the track index for the cylinder which holds the record. This track index is now searched sequentially for the first entry with a key greater than or equal to the desired key. Associated with this track index entry is the address of the *prime track* which holds the record. This track can now be searched to locate the desired record.

7.42　Why does VSAM usually outperform ISAM for random processing?

As described in Problem 7.41, the ISAM cylinder and track indexes are searched sequentially, entry by entry. For large files, the indexes may be quite large, and this type of searching becomes relatively inefficient.

The VSAM index set is organized as a tree and is searched as a tree. As the file becomes larger and larger, the tree search becomes more and more effective when compared to a sequential index search.

7.43　How does ISAM accommodate additions to a file?

When a record is to be added to an ISAM file, the cylinder and track indexes are first searched to locate the prime track on which the record belongs. The logical record is placed on the track in key sequence, necessitating reorganization of the track. Typically, the addition of a new record to the track forces the (formerly) last record off the track. This record is then placed into an *overflow area*.

If possible, ISAM will place the "bumped" record into an area reserved for this purpose at the bottom of the prime cylinder in question. Such an area is called *cylinder overflow*. If cylinder overflow has not been provided for or is full, the bumped record will be placed into an *independent overflow area* on a separate cylinder.

ISAM keeps track of logical records in cylinder and independent overflow via the track index entries. Each track index entry points to the first record (in key sequence) bumped off that track into an overflow area. Each logical record in overflow has a *chaining field* added to it which contains the address of the next logical record in key sequence. This *chain* of overflow records (technically a linked list data structure) is maintained in key sequence.

The only way to locate records in overflow is to start at the track index entry and sequentially search through the *overflow chain* of records. This can be quite time-consuming as the chains grow long and as records are placed on separate cylinders in independent overflow (necessitating disk access arm movement).

7.44   How is VSAM's method of handling additions superior to ISAM's?

VSAM accommodates additions by providing (1) distributed free space, (2) control interval splitting, and (3) control area splitting. The first two techniques introduce no inefficiencies with respect to processing speed, and each CA split adds only one record to the index set, thereby minimally slowing index searching. An old VSAM file with many additions will perform almost as well as when it was first created.

ISAM's use of overflow chains can significantly slow both sequential and random processing as the number of additions grows larger.

7.45   How do indexed file implementations such as ISAM deal with the inefficiencies introduced by adding records?

ISAM and similar indexed files must be periodically reorganized. *File reorganization* involves reading the file sequentially and using the logical records thus obtained to create a brand new version of the file. Since the new version will have no records in overflow chains, it can be processed more efficiently than the old version. File reorganization is typically carried out by an operating system utility program designed for that purpose.

7.46   List (in order) the four operations involved in creating a VSAM indexed file and state how they are accomplished and who is typically responsible.

(1)   Create VSAM catalog: This is done either during operating system generation or with the IDCAMS DEFINE USERCATALOG command. It is typically the responsibility of a systems programmer.

(2)   Create VSAM data space: This is done by executing the IDCAMS DEFINE SPACE command. It is typically the responsibility of a systems programmer.

(3)   Create a VSAM catalog entry for the file: This is done by executing the IDCAMS DEFINE CLUSTER command. It may be handled either by a systems programmer or by the COBOL programmer.

(4)   Load records into the file: This is done either by executing a COBOL program to place records in the file or by executing the IDCAMS REPRO command to copy records from another file. It is typically the responsibility of an applications programmer.

7.47   Suppose the index records of an ANSI indexed file with a tree-structured index (such as VSAM) have a fan-out of n (i.e., each index record contains n keys and n pointers to lower-level index records). What is the maximum number of index records which must be input and examined to randomly locate a record (assume that the data records are evenly distributed throughout the file)?

If the data records are evenly distributed, following a particular pointer from the highest-level index record eliminates all but $1/n$ of the records from consideration. Similarly, following a particular pointer from the next lowest index record eliminates $1/n$ of these (or $1/n * 1/n$ of the total). After k index records have been processed during the index search, all but $1/n^k$ records have been eliminated from consideration. If there are t bottom-level groupings of data records in the file (e.g., t VSAM data component control intervals), this can occur at most $\log_n t$ times, which is the maximum number of index records which need be examined.

7.48   Show how the four control intervals of the first control area in Fig. 7-4 would appear after the addition of logical records with keys 16, 18, and 12 (in that order).

The addition of the three records would result in a control interval split, leaving the CA as follows:

CI-1	CI-2	CI-3	CI-4
10	30	50	18
12	40	60	20
16	Free	Free	Free
Free	Free	Free	Free

Note that the records are no longer *physically* in key sequence.

7.49 Show what would happen if records with keys 14 and 11 are added to the control area in Problem 7.48.

The addition of these two records would cause a control area split, thus creating a new control area in addition to the one shown in Problem 7.48. First, 14 is added to CI-1, causing it to become full. Since 11 should also go in CI-1 (which is full), a CI split is attempted. Since there are no empty CIs with which to carry out a CI split, a CA split is carried out, leaving the file as follows:

Original CA				New CA Created by Split			
CI-1	CI-2	CI-3	CI-4	CI-1	CI-2	CI-3	CI-4
10	Free	Free	18	30	50	Free	Free
12	Free	Free	20	40	60	Free	Free
14	Free	Free	Free	Free	Free	Free	Free
16	Free	Free	Free	Free	Free	Free	Free

After the CA split shown above, the CI split to add record 11 can be carried out and record 11 added, leaving the file as follows:

Original CA				New CA Created by Split			
CI-1	CI-2	CI-3	CI-4	CI-1	CI-2	CI-3	CI-4
10	14	Free	18	30	50	Free	Free
11	16	Free	20	40	60	Free	Free
12	Free	Free	Free	Free	Free	Free	Free
Free	Free	Free	Free	Free	Free	Free	Free

7.50 Why is it preferable for an indexed file implementation to use physical deletion (as with IBM's VSAM indexed organization) rather than logical deletion (as with IBM's direct organization)?

When physical deletion is used, the space occupied by deleted records is immediately made available for reuse when adding new records to the file. Also, since deleted records are not physically present in the file, COBOL programs which process the file need not be concerned with recognizing (and ignoring) deleted records.

When logical deletion is used, files must be periodically reorganized (i.e., the active records input from an old file are used to create a new "clean" version of the file) in order to recover the space occupied by deleted records.

7.51 Describe the actions automatically taken by VSAM to sequentially retrieve the file shown in Fig. 7-3.

Sequential retrieval begins at the CI pointed to by the first sequence set entry in the first sequence set record (i.e., entry 30). As the COBOL program executes READ statements, VSAM moves each record from this CI into the level-01 record area for the file. After records 10, 20, and 30 have been READ, VSAM proceeds to the CI pointed to by the next sequence set entry (i.e., 60), retrieving records 40, 50, and 60, in turn. VSAM then again proceeds to the CI pointed to by the next sequence set entry (90) and retrieves records 70, 80, and 90, in that order.

Having exhausted all sequence set entries (and their associated data component CIs) in the current sequence set record, VSAM follows the horizontal pointer to the next sequence set record (entries 120, 150, and 180) and works through the CI pointed to by the entry for 120. Following this, VSAM proceeds to the next entry (150) and retrieves the records from the corresponding CI (records 130, 140, and 150). Note that VSAM is at this point not processing data component CIs in their physical order.

After retrieving record 150, VSAM switches to the CI pointed to by the next sequence set entry (180) and retrieves records 160, 170, and 180 from that CI.

This exhausts the current sequence set record, so VSAM again follows the horizontal pointer to the next sequence set record (entries 200, 230, 240) and begins processing the CI pointed to by the first entry (200), thus retrieving records 190 and 200. The next sequence set entry directs VSAM to the CI with records 210, 220, and 230. The final sequence set entry in Fig. 7-3 causes VSAM to retrieve record 240. Assuming this is the last record in the file, the READ executed after record 240 has been input will result in an end-of-file condition.

7.52 Fill in the "Record Accessed" and "New CRP" columns in the chart below. Use the file in Fig. 7-3 with ACCESS SEQUENTIAL:

Statement	Record Accessed	New CRP
OPEN		
READ		
START (key = 230)		
READ		
READ		
READ		
START (key = 120)		
READ		
READ		

Statement	Record Accessed	New CRP
OPEN	—	10
READ	10	20
START (key = 230)	—	230
READ	230	240
READ	240	End of file
READ	AT END activated	Undefined
START (key = 120)	—	120
READ	120	130
READ	130	140

7.53 Fill in the "Record Accessed" and "New CRP" columns below for the file in Fig. 7-3. Assume ACCESS IS DYNAMIC.

Statement	Record Accessed	New CRP
OPEN		
START (key = 230)		
READ NEXT		
READ (key = 150)		
READ NEXT		
WRITE (key = 25)		
READ NEXT		
READ (key = 80)		
REWRITE (key = 80)		
READ NEXT		
START (key = 120)		
READ NEXT		

Statement	Record Accessed	New CRP
OPEN	—	10
START (key = 230)	—	230
READ NEXT	230	240
READ (key = 150)	150	160
READ NEXT	160	170
WRITE (key = 25)	25	170
READ NEXT	170	180
READ (key = 80)	80	90
REWRITE (key = 80)	80	90
READ NEXT	90	100
START (key = 120)	—	120
READ NEXT	120	130

7.54 Give an IBM Access Method Services (IDCAMS) command to create a VSAM catalog entry for a VSAM indexed file named AR.MASTER. The file currently has 8000 fixed-length 130-byte records, but file growth should be provided for in the form of 500-record secondary allocations. The file should be placed on disk volume VOL739 and should be cataloged in a VSAM user catalog named FINANCE.CAT. The RECORD KEY for the file is a 6-byte field beginning in the fourth column of each record. Reserve 10 percent of each data component CA and 20 percent of each data component CI for distributed free space.

```
DEFINE CLUSTER -
  ( -
    NAME (AR.MASTER) -
    VOLUMES (VOL739) -
    KEYS (6  3) -
    FREESPACE (20  10) -
    RECORDS (8000  500) -
    RECORDSIZE (130  130) -
  ) -
  CATALOG (FINANCE.CAT)
```

7.55 Give an IDCAMS command to print the VSAM indexed file from Problem 7.54. Assume all record fields are DISPLAY.

```
PRINT -
    INDATASET (AR.MASTER) -
    CHARACTER
```

7.56 Redo Problem 7.55 if some record fields are COMP or COMP-3.

```
PRINT -
    INDATASET (AR.MASTER)
```

7.57 Suppose that during debugging it is desired to delete the current version of the file from Problem 7.54. Give an IDCAMS command to accomplish this.

```
DELETE -
    (AR.MASTER) -
    CATALOG (FINANCE.CAT) -
    CLUSTER
```

7.58 How is record deletion handled in IBM's earlier implementation of indexed files (ISAM)?

Records are logically deleted by setting the first byte of the record to HIGH-VALUES (which serves as a delete code). This usually entails defining a delete byte of PIC X at the beginning of an ISAM record description.

7.59 Which COBOL statements must be altered to convert a program which sequentially retrieves a sorted sequential file to one which sequentially retrieves an indexed file?

Only the SELECT statement need be changed (to specify ORGANIZATION IS INDEXED). Since both sequential organization and indexed organization support the use of STATUS CODE and/or INVALID KEY, the PROCEDURE DIVISION need not be changed at all. In both cases, records are retrieved in key sequence.

7.60 Give a COBOL paragraph to load a record into an ANSI indexed file during creation. Your solution may PERFORM paragraphs and use data items you do not define, so long as they are given descriptive names.

```
LOAD-A-RECORD.
    MOVE RECORD-KEY-VALUE TO RECORD-KEY-FIELD
    PERFORM MOVE-OTHER-DATA-TO-INDEXED-REC
    WRITE INDEXED-RECORD
    IF STATUS-CODE-AREA NOT EQUAL SUCCESS-CODE
        DISPLAY "SEQUENCE ERROR AND/OR DUPLICATE KEY"
    .
```

7.61 Give a COBOL paragraph to sequentially retrieve a record from an ANSI indexed file.

```
GET-A-RECORD.
    READ INDEXED-FILE
    IF STATUS-CODE-AREA NOT EQUAL SUCCESS-CODE
        IF STATUS-CODE-AREA EQUAL END-OF-FILE-CODE
            MOVE "YES" TO END-OF-FILE-SW
        ELSE
            DISPLAY "UNEXPECTED ERROR"
    .
```

7.62 Redo 020-RETRIEVE-INDEXED-RECORD (lines 79–95 of Fig. 7-14) to use INVALID KEY instead of STATUS CODE.

```
020-RETRIEVE-INDEXED-RECORD.
    MOVE TRANS-PROGRAMMER-ID TO INDEXED-PROGRAMMER-ID
    MOVE "YES" TO GOT-A-RECORD-SW
    READ INDEXED-FILE
        INVALID KEY
            MOVE "NO" TO GOT-A-RECORD-SW
    .
    IF GOT-A-RECORD-SW EQUAL "YES"
        DISPLAY INDEXED-PROGRAMMER-ID INDEXED-TOTAL-HOURS
    ELSE
        DISPLAY    "RECORD NOT FOUND FOR "
                    TRANS-PROGRAMMER-ID
    .
```

Note that with INVALID KEY, there is no way to distinguish between a record-not-found error and other types of errors (as can be done when STATUS CODE is used; see Fig. 7-14).

7.63   Give a COBOL paragraph to randomly input a record from an ANSI indexed file.

```
RANDOM-GET-A-RECORD.
    MOVE DESIRED-KEY-VALUE TO RECORD-KEY-FIELD
    READ INDEXED-FILE
    IF STATUS-CODE-AREA NOT EQUAL SUCCESS-CODE
        IF STATUS-CODE-AREA EQUAL RECORD-NOT-FOUND-CODE
            DISPLAY "RECORD NOT FOUND"
        ELSE
            DISPLAY "UNEXPECTED ERROR"
    .
```

7.64   It is desired to keep information on an indexed file regarding each salesperson and the
client(s) he or she services. Most accesses to the file will require data on a particular client of a
given salesperson, but occasionally it will be desired to collect summary information about all
clients of a given salesperson. Give a SELECT statement and FD to randomly access such an
indexed file [assume salesperson IDs are PIC X(4), client IDs are PIC X(5), and the
remaining fields consist of CLIENT-DATA PIC X(100)].

This problem could be solved by designing a file with key field salesperson ID. Records would be
variable-length, with a variable-length table which would hold the client ID and CLIENT-DATA for
each client. In order to access a particular client for a salesperson, the entire record for that salesperson
would be input and the table searched for the desired client (assume no more than 25 clients per
salesperson).

```
SELECT SALESPERSON-FILE
    ASSIGN TO SALEFILE
    ORGANIZATION IS INDEXED
    ACCESS IS RANDOM
    RECORD KEY IS SALESPERSON-ID
    FILE STATUS IS SALES-STATUS-AREA. . .

FD  SALESPERSON-FILE
    LABEL RECORDS ARE STANDARD
    .
01  SALESPERSON-RECORD.
    05   SALESPERSON-ID      PIC X(4).
    05   NUMBER-OF-CLIENTS   PIC 99     COMP.
    05   CLIENT-TABLE OCCURS 1 TO 25 TIMES
              DEPENDING ON NUMBER-OF-CLIENTS
              INDEXED BY CLIENT-INDEX.
        10   CLIENT-ID     PIC X(5).
        10   CLIENT-DATA   PIC X(100).
```

7.65   To eliminate having to input large variable-length records to retrieve data on just one client,
redesign the file in Problem 7.64 to use fixed-length records, each holding data about one
client, with a composite key consisting of salesperson ID followed by client ID.

```
SELECT SALESPERSON-FILE
    ASSIGN TO SALEFILE
    ORGANIZATION IS INDEXED
    ACCESS IS DYNAMIC
    RECORD KEY IS SALES-CLIENT-ID
    FILE STATUS IS SALES-STATUS-AREA. . .
```

```
FD    SALESPERSON-FILE
      LABEL RECORDS ARE STANDARD
      .
01    SALESPERSON-RECORD.
      05    SALES-CLIENT-ID.
            10    SALESPERSON-ID          PIC X(4).
            10    CLIENT-ID               PIC X(5).
      05    CLIENT-DATA                   PIC X(100).
```

Note the use of ACCESS DYNAMIC in the SELECT statement.

7.66 Show how to retrieve the CLIENT-DATA for TRANS-SALESPERSON-ID and TRANS-CLIENT-ID using the file design in Problem 7.64.

```
OPEN INPUT SALESPERSON-FILE . . .

MOVE TRANS-SALESPERSON-ID TO SALESPERSON-ID
READ SALESPERSON-FILE
IF SALES-STATUS-AREA EQUAL SUCCESS-CODE
    SET CLIENT-INDEX TO 1
    SEARCH CLIENT-TABLE
        AT END DISPLAY "CLIENT NOT FOUND ..."
        WHEN CLIENT-ID (CLIENT-INDEX) EQUAL TRANS-CLIENT-ID
            DISPLAY CLIENT-DATA (CLIENT-INDEX)
ELSE
    DISPLAY "SALESPERSON NOT FOUND ..."
    .
```

7.67 Redo Problem 7.66 using the file design from Problem 7.65. Which is easier and more efficient?

The following code inputs a smaller record and eliminates the need for a SEARCH; thus for this type of query, separate records with a composite key provide better performance. Observe the important role played by file design in determining the complexity of PROCEDURE DIVISION logic.

```
OPEN INPUT SALESPERSON-FILE . . .

MOVE TRANS-SALESPERSON-ID TO SALESPERSON-ID
MOVE TRANS-CLIENT-ID      TO CLIENT-ID
READ SALESPERSON-FILE
IF SALES-STATUS-AREA EQUAL SUCCESS-CODE
    DISPLAY CLIENT-DATA
ELSE
    DISPLAY "SALESPERSON/CLIENT NOT FOUND ..."
    .
```

7.68 Show how to DISPLAY *all* CLIENT-DATA for TRANS-SALESPERSON-ID. Use the file design from Problem 7.64 (the reader will recall that ACCESS IS RANDOM).

```
OPEN INPUT SALESPERSON-FILE . . .

MOVE TRANS-SALESPERSON-ID TO SALESPERSON-ID
READ SALESPERSON-FILE
IF SALES-STATUS-AREA NOT EQUAL SUCCESS-CODE
    DISPLAY "SALESPERSON NOT FOUND ..."
```

```
            ELSE
                  PERFORM DISPLAY-CLIENT-DATA
                        VARYING CLIENT-INDEX
                        FROM 1 BY 1
                        UNTIL CLIENT-INDEX GREATER THAN NUMBER-OF-CLIENTS
            .
            .
            .

      DISPLAY-CLIENT-DATA.
            DISPLAY CLIENT-DATA (CLIENT-INDEX)
            .
```

7.69 Show how to DISPLAY *all* CLIENT-DATA for TRANS-SALESPERSON-ID. Use the file design from Problem 7.65 (the reader will recall that ACCESS IS DYNAMIC). Compare this solution to that in Problem 7.68.

```
            OPEN INPUT SALESPERSON-FILE . . .

            MOVE TRANS-SALESPERSON-ID TO SALESPERSON-ID
            START SALESPERSON-FILE
                  KEY IS EQUAL SALESPERSON-ID
            IF SALES-STATUS-AREA NOT EQUAL SUCCESS-CODE
                  DISPLAY "SALESPERSON NOT FOUND ..."
            ELSE
                  PERFORM READ-NEXT-RECORD
                  PERFORM DISPLAY-AND-READ
                        UNTIL TRANS-SALESPERSON-ID NOT EQUAL
                              SALESPERSON-ID
            .
            .
            .

      READ-NEXT-RECORD.
            READ SALESPERSON-FILE NEXT
                  AT END
                        MOVE SPACES TO SALESPERSON-ID
            .

      DISPLAY-AND-READ.
            DISPLAY CLIENT-DATA
            PERFORM READ-NEXT-RECORD
            .
```

When all CLIENT-DATA for a given salesperson is packed into one variable-length record (as in Problem 7.64), it is easier and more efficient to access *all* CLIENT-DATA for that salesperson. When each CLIENT-DATA value is packaged as a separate logical record with a composite key, it is easier and more efficient to access *one* particular piece of CLIENT-DATA. The "best" file design for this problem thus depends on the relative frequencies of these two kinds of requests.

7.70 Suppose the transaction file for the update program in Fig. 7-16 is already sorted by RECORD KEY value, and that only change transactions are to be performed. If under these circumstances a high percentage of the records in the file are to be changed, it is probably more efficient to update the file sequentially rather than randomly (if only a low percentage of records were to be changed, random processing would probably be more efficient, even though the transactions are already sorted). Show how to carry out a *sequential update in place* by sequentially updating the file in Fig. 7-16. Note that typically there may be more than one transaction per indexed file master record.

```
                    .
                    .
                    .
00042          WORKING-STORAGE SECTION.
                    .
                    .
                    .
00043          01  FLAGS-AND-SWITCHES.
00047              05  INDEXED-RECORD-CHANGED-SW    PIC X(3).
00048                  88  INDEXED-RECORD-MODIFIED VALUE "YES".
00049                  88  INDEXED-RECORD-THE-SAME VALUE "NO".
                    .
                    .
00054          PROCEDURE DIVISION.
00055
00056          000-EXECUTIVE-MODULE.
00057
00058              OPEN    INPUT   TRANSACTION-FILE
00059                      I-O     INDEXED-FILE
00060              IF VSAM-OPERATION-OK
00061                  MOVE "NO" TO TRANS-END-OF-FILE-SW
00062                  PERFORM 010-GET-TRANSACTION-RECORD
00063                  PERFORM 030-GET-MASTER-RECORD
00064                  MOVE "NO" TO INDEXED-RECORD-CHANGED-SW
00065                  PERFORM 020-UPDATE-INDEXED-FILE
00066                      UNTIL NO-MORE-INPUT
00067                  PERFORM 060-REWRITE-CURRENT-REC
00068                  CLOSE   TRANSACTION-FILE
00069                          INDEXED-FILE
00070                  IF VSAM-OPERATION-OK
00071                      DISPLAY "INDEXED FILE UPDATE COMPLETED"
00072                  ELSE
00073                      DISPLAY "INDEXED FILE NOT PROPERLY CLOSED"
00074              ELSE
00075                  DISPLAY "UNABLE TO OPEN INDEXED FILE -- ABORT"
00076                  CLOSE TRANSACTION-FILE
00077                  .
00078              STOP RUN
00079              .
00080
00081          010-GET-TRANSACTION-RECORD.
00082
00083              READ TRANSACTION-FILE
00084                  AT END
00085                      MOVE "YES" TO TRANS-END-OF-FILE-SW
00086              .
00087
00088          020-UPDATE-INDEXED-FILE.
00089
00090              IF CHANGE-EXISTING-RECORD
00091                  PERFORM 040-CHANGE-A-RECORD
00092              ELSE
00093                  DISPLAY "INVALID TRANS CODE: " TRANSACTION-RECORD
00094                  .
00095              PERFORM 010-GET-TRANSACTION-RECORD
00096              .
00097
00098          030-GET-MASTER-RECORD.
00099
00100              READ INDEXED-FILE
00101                  AT END
00102                      MOVE HIGH-VALUES TO INDEXED-PROGRAMMER-ID
00103              .
00104
00105          040-CHANGE-A-RECORD.
00106
00107              PERFORM 050-FIND-MATCHING-MASTER
00108              IF TRANS-PROGRAMMER-ID EQUAL INDEXED-PROGRAMMER-ID
00109                  ADD TRANS-TOTAL-HOURS TO INDEXED-TOTAL-HOURS
00110                  MOVE "YES" TO INDEXED-RECORD-CHANGED-SW
00111              ELSE
```

Fig. 7-17

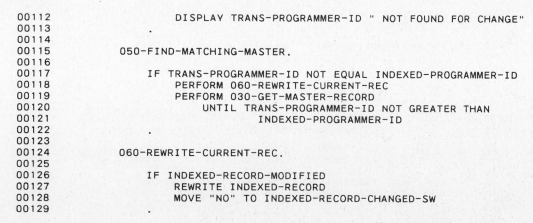

```
00112                    DISPLAY TRANS-PROGRAMMER-ID " NOT FOUND FOR CHANGE"
00113                .
00114
00115          050-FIND-MATCHING-MASTER.
00116
00117              IF TRANS-PROGRAMMER-ID NOT EQUAL INDEXED-PROGRAMMER-ID
00118                  PERFORM 060-REWRITE-CURRENT-REC
00119                  PERFORM 030-GET-MASTER-RECORD
00120                      UNTIL TRANS-PROGRAMMER-ID NOT GREATER THAN
00121                              INDEXED-PROGRAMMER-ID
00122                .
00123
00124          060-REWRITE-CURRENT-REC.
00125
00126              IF INDEXED-RECORD-MODIFIED
00127                  REWRITE INDEXED-RECORD
00128                  MOVE "NO" TO INDEXED-RECORD-CHANGED-SW
00129                .
```

Fig. 7-17   (*cont.*)

See Fig. 7-17 for a possible solution (and Problem 7.76 for a variation). The DATA and ENVIRONMENT DIVISIONs (not shown) are the same as in Fig. 7-16, except ACCESS IS SEQUENTIAL for the indexed file. The following comments pertain to the PROCEDURE DIVISION:

(1) The executive module is modified to also input the first indexed file record and initialize a switch indicating whether or not the current master record has been changed (lines 63–64). INDEXED-RECORD-CHANGED-SW is defined in WORKING-STORAGE (lines 47–49).

(2) 020-UPDATE-INDEXED-FILE (lines 88–96) has been modified to accept only change transactions.

(3) A module has been added to *sequentially* input the next indexed file record (lines 98–103).

(4) For each transaction, 040-CHANGE-A-RECORD (lines 105–113) is executed. It begins by attempting to find an indexed record whose RECORD KEY matches that of the transaction. This is handled by 050-FIND-MATCHING-MASTER (lines 115–122) which keeps reading indexed records until the transaction record's key value is less than or equal to that of the current indexed record.

(5) Note that 050-FIND-MATCHING-MASTER begins by checking the current transaction record's key field against the current master record's key field. If the keys are equal, we already have a matching master record and the paragraph ends without doing anything. If the keys are not equal, 060-REWRITE-CURRENT-REC is called to see if the current indexed file record was modified (and, therefore, should be rewritten), and then the indexed file is READ repetitively until the transaction key is less than or equal to the current indexed file record's key. If this indexed record's key is greater than that of the transaction there was no matching indexed record for the current transaction and a message is DISPLAYed indicating the record-not-found error (lines 111–112).

(6) If a master record is found to match the transaction, 040-CHANGE-A-RECORD adds the transaction hours to the master record hours and then sets INDEXED-RECORD-CHANGED-SW to indicate that the master record was updated (lines 108–110).

(7) 060-REWRITE-CURRENT-REC is called before each indexed file record is READ. It checks to see if the current master record was modified (line 126), and if so, it REWRITEs the record (line 127). Note that immediately after a modified record is rewritten, the record-changed switch is reset to indicate no modification. This eliminates the wasteful REWRITEing of records which actually were not modified.

(8) Verify that in order for this logic to work, a priming read of both the transaction and the master files must be carried out (as in lines 62–63).

7.71 Illustrate the differences in syntax between IBM's older ISAM implementation of indexed files and IBM's newer VSAM implementation of indexed files by recoding the random file update program in Fig. 7-16 to use ISAM.

```
00001          IDENTIFICATION DIVISION.
00002          PROGRAM-ID.  ISAM-FILE-UPDATE.

00003          ENVIRONMENT DIVISION.
00004          CONFIGURATION SECTION.
00005          SOURCE-COMPUTER.  IBM-3081.
00006          OBJECT-COMPUTER.  IBM-3081.
00007          INPUT-OUTPUT SECTION.
00008          FILE-CONTROL.

00009              SELECT TRANSACTION-FILE
00010                  ASSIGN TO CHANGES
00011                  ORGANIZATION IS SEQUENTIAL
00012                  ACCESS IS SEQUENTIAL
00013                  .
00014              SELECT ISAM-FILE
00015                  ASSIGN TO DA-I-ISAMFILE
00016                  ACCESS IS RANDOM
00017                  RECORD KEY IS ISAM-PROGRAMMER-ID
00018                  NOMINAL KEY IS ISAM-KEY-AREA
00019                  .

00020          DATA DIVISION.
00021          FILE SECTION.

00022          FD  TRANSACTION-FILE
00023              LABEL RECORDS ARE STANDARD
00024              BLOCK CONTAINS 0 CHARACTERS
00025              RECORD CONTAINS 80 CHARACTERS
00026              .
00027          01  TRANSACTION-RECORD.
00028              05  TRANS-CODE                PIC X.
00029                  88  ADD-NEW-RECORD          VALUE "A".
00030                  88  CHANGE-EXISTING-RECORD  VALUE "C".
00031                  88  DELETE-EXISTING-RECORD  VALUE "D".
00032              05  TRANS-PROGRAMMER-ID       PIC X(5).
00033              05  TRANS-PROJECT-ID          PIC X(8).
00034              05  TRANS-TOTAL-HOURS         PIC 9(3)V9.
00035              05  FILLER                    PIC X(62).

00036          FD  ISAM-FILE
00037              LABEL RECORDS ARE STANDARD
00038              RECORD CONTAINS 16 CHARACTERS
                   .
00039          01  ISAM-RECORD.
00040              05  DELETE-BYTE               PIC X.
00041                  88  RECORD-NOT-ACTIVE       VALUE HIGH-VALUES.
00042              05  ISAM-PROGRAMMER-ID        PIC X(5).
00043              05  ISAM-PROJECT-ID           PIC X(8).
00044              05  ISAM-TOTAL-HOURS          PIC 9(3)V9 COMP.

00045          WORKING-STORAGE SECTION.

00046          01  FLAGS-AND-SWITCHES.
00047              05  TRANS-END-OF-FILE-SW      PIC X(3).
00048                  88  MORE-TRANS-RECORDS      VALUE "NO".
00049                  88  NO-MORE-INPUT           VALUE "YES".
00050              05  RECORD-EXISTS-SW          PIC X(3).
00051                  88  RECORD-EXISTS           VALUE "YES".

00052          01  NOMINAL-KEY-AREA.
00053              05  ISAM-KEY-AREA             PIC X(5).

00054          PROCEDURE DIVISION.
00055
00056          000-EXECUTIVE-MODULE.
00057
00058              OPEN    INPUT   TRANSACTION-FILE
00059                      I-O     ISAM-FILE
00060              MOVE "NO" TO TRANS-END-OF-FILE-SW
00061              PERFORM 010-GET-TRANSACTION-RECORD
00062              PERFORM 020-UPDATE-ISAM-FILE
00063                  UNTIL NO-MORE-INPUT
00064              CLOSE   TRANSACTION-FILE
00065                      ISAM-FILE
00066              STOP RUN
00067                  .
```

Fig. 7-18

212

```
00068
00069              010-GET-TRANSACTION-RECORD.
00070
00071                  READ TRANSACTION-FILE
00072                      AT END
00073                          MOVE "YES" TO TRANS-END-OF-FILE-SW
00074                      .
00075
00076              020-UPDATE-ISAM-FILE.
00077
00078                  IF ADD-NEW-RECORD
00079                      PERFORM 030-ADD-A-RECORD
00080                  ELSE IF CHANGE-EXISTING-RECORD
00081                      PERFORM 040-CHANGE-A-RECORD
00082                  ELSE IF DELETE-EXISTING-RECORD
00083                      PERFORM 080-DELETE-A-RECORD
00084                  ELSE
00085                      DISPLAY "INVALID TRANS CODE: " TRANSACTION-RECORD
00086                      .
00087                  PERFORM 010-GET-TRANSACTION-RECORD
00088                      .
00089
00090              030-ADD-A-RECORD.
00091
00092                  PERFORM 090-BUILD-ISAM-RECORD
00093                  MOVE TRANS-PROGRAMMER-ID TO ISAM-KEY-AREA
00094                  WRITE ISAM-RECORD
00095                      INVALID KEY
00096                          DISPLAY "DUPLICATE KEY FOR " ISAM-PROGRAMMER-ID
00097                      .
00098
00099              040-CHANGE-A-RECORD.
00100
00101                  MOVE TRANS-PROGRAMMER-ID TO ISAM-KEY-AREA
00102                  MOVE "YES" TO RECORD-EXISTS-SW
00103                  READ ISAM-FILE
00104                      INVALID KEY
00105                          MOVE "NO" TO RECORD-EXISTS-SW
00106                      .
00107                  IF RECORD-EXISTS
00108                      IF RECORD-NOT-ACTIVE
00109                          MOVE "NO" TO RECORD-EXISTS-SW
00110                      .
00111                  IF RECORD-EXISTS
00112                      ADD TRANS-TOTAL-HOURS TO ISAM-TOTAL-HOURS
00113                      REWRITE ISAM-RECORD
00114                  ELSE
00115                      DISPLAY TRANS-PROGRAMMER-ID " NOT FOUND FOR CHANGE"
00116                      .
00117
00118              080-DELETE-A-RECORD.
00119
00120                  MOVE TRANS-PROGRAMMER-ID TO ISAM-KEY-AREA
00121                  MOVE "YES" TO RECORD-EXISTS-SW
00122                  READ ISAM-FILE
00123                      INVALID KEY
00124                          MOVE "NO" TO RECORD-EXISTS-SW
00125                      .
00126                  IF RECORD-EXISTS
00127                      IF RECORD-NOT-ACTIVE
00128                          MOVE "NO" TO RECORD-EXISTS-SW
00129                      .
00130                  IF RECORD-EXISTS
00131                      MOVE HIGH-VALUES TO DELETE-BYTE
00132                      REWRITE ISAM-RECORD
00133                  ELSE
00134                      DISPLAY TRANS-PROGRAMMER-ID " NOT FOUND FOR DELETE"
00135                      .
00136
00137              090-BUILD-ISAM-RECORD.
00138
00139                  MOVE "A"                 TO DELETE-BYTE
00140                  MOVE TRANS-PROGRAMMER-ID  TO ISAM-PROGRAMMER-ID
00141                  MOVE TRANS-PROJECT-ID     TO ISAM-PROJECT-ID
00142                  MOVE TRANS-TOTAL-HOURS    TO ISAM-TOTAL-HOURS
00143                      .
```

Fig. 7-18 *(cont.)*

Figure 7-18 shows a possible solution. The changes needed to convert the VSAM version to ISAM are as follows:

SELECT Statement

(1) In IBM OS/VS COBOL, the ASSIGN TO clause (line 15) must be of the form "DA-I-externalname" for an ISAM file. The "externalname" refers to a job control language statement which further defines the ISAM file.

(2) In addition to the RECORD KEY clause in the SELECT statement, ISAM random processing requires the naming of a NOMINAL KEY area (line 18). The NOMINAL KEY is usually defined in WORKING-STORAGE (lines 52–53) and should have the same PICTURE and USAGE as the RECORD KEY item. ISAM picks up the key of the logical record to be read or written from the NOMINAL KEY area, not the RECORD KEY area. The RECORD KEY area is still required as part of the record description, since it is used to identify logical records for random retrieval.

(3) The ORGANIZATION IS INDEXED clause must not be specified for ISAM. ISAM organization is indicated by the "I" in ASSIGN TO DA-*I*-externalname.

(4) The FILE STATUS area is not supported by ISAM and is thus omitted.

FD and Record Description

(5) Although blocking has not been specified in Fig. 7-18, ISAM permits the use of the BLOCK CONTAINS clause (which VSAM ignores).

(6) If logical records are to be deleted, ISAM requires the definition of a delete byte character in the first position of the logical record (lines 40–41). Deleted records are specified by placing HIGH-VALUES in this byte. ISAM uses a combination of logical and physical deletion. Initially, records are logically deleted by REWRITEing them with HIGH-VALUES in the first byte. These records remain in the file until they are bumped off a track to make room for the addition of a new record. Deleted records which are bumped off a track are not moved into overflow (see Problem 7.43 for a discussion of how ISAM adds records to a file) and are hence physically removed from the file. Deleted records may thus remain physically present for an indefinite amount of time.

WORKING-STORAGE

(7) No FILE STATUS area should be defined for ISAM.

(8) The ISAM NOMINAL KEY is typically defined in WORKING-STORAGE (lines 52–53).

PROCEDURE DIVISION

(9) Since OPEN (lines 58–59) and CLOSE (lines 64–65) do not set a FILE STATUS code, it is impossible to test for the success or completion of these operations with ISAM. If either ISAM operation fails, the COBOL program simply ABENDs. Note that with VSAM, the program can recover from such a failure since the program does not ABEND and the STATUS CODE is set.

(10) Lines 90–97 illustrate how to randomly add a record to an ISAM file. The record fields are first moved from the transaction record to the ISAM record by performing 090-BUILD-ISAM-RECORD (lines 137–143). Line 93 then moves the key value from the transaction record to the NOMINAL KEY area for the ISAM file. Finally, the WRITE verb is executed to add the record to the file. ISAM automatically detects a duplicate key condition as part of the execution of the WRITE, and activates the INVALID KEY routine if such a condition exists.

(11) Lines 99–116 illustrate how to randomly change a record in an ISAM file. First the transaction key value is moved to the NOMINAL KEY area and a switch initialized to indicate that the desired record exists (lines 101–102). Next a random READ is executed (automatically causing a full index search to locate and input the record whose RECORD KEY value matches the NOMINAL KEY value). If a record-not-found condition exists, the INVALID KEY routine is executed, causing the RECORD-EXISTS-SW to be reset to "NO" (lines 103–105). It is possible that the record may physically exist but have HIGH-VALUES in its delete byte, marking it as inactive. If the record physically exists, its delete byte is tested; if HIGH-VALUES are present, the RECORD-EXISTS-SW is reset to "NO" (lines 107–110). If RECORD-EXISTS-SW is still "YES", the changes are made to the ISAM record and the record is rewritten (lines 111–113). If a record-not-found condition exists, a message is DISPLAYed (lines 114–115).

(12)   Lines 118–135 illustrate how to randomly delete a record from an ISAM file. Since ISAM uses a delete byte, record deletion must be handled as a special type of change (i.e., changing the delete byte to HIGH-VALUES). First, an attempt is made to retrieve the record as in (11) above (see lines 120–129). If the record physically exists and is not already deleted (checked in lines 126–128), HIGH-VALUES are moved to the delete byte and the record is rewritten (lines 130–132). If the record does not physically exist or is already marked deleted, a message is DISPLAYed (line 134).

7.72   The REWRITE statement in line 118 of Fig. 7-16 assumes that the REWRITE will always work correctly. Recode 040-CHANGE-A-RECORD (lines 112–121) to check the STATUS CODE for unexpected I/O errors.

```
MOVE TRANS-PROGRAMMER-ID TO INDEXED-PROGRAMMER-ID
READ INDEXED-FILE
IF VSAM-OPERATION-OK
    ADD TRANS-TOTAL-HOURS TO INDEXED-TOTAL-HOURS
    REWRITE INDEXED-RECORD
    IF VSAM-OPERATION-FAILED
        DISPLAY "UNEXPECTED VSAM ERROR ..."
    ELSE
        NEXT SENTENCE
ELSE
    DISPLAY "RECORD NOT FOUND FOR CHANGE ..."
```

7.73   ANSI indexed files provide for the creation and use of more than one index. This allows indexed file records to be sequentially or randomly retrieved using more than one key field. The RECORD KEY for such a file is known as the *primary key*, and the index associated with it is called the *primary index*. Other key fields are known as *ALTERNATE KEY*s, and their associated indexes are known as *alternate indexes*. Illustrate the use of ALTERNATE KEYs for ANSI indexed files by modifying the random retrieval program of Fig. 7-14 to retrieve records either by programmer ID or by project ID. Programmer ID will be the RECORD (primary) KEY, while project ID will be the only ALTERNATE KEY.

Figure 7-19 shows an IBM OS/VS COBOL program using an ALTERNATE KEY. The changes to the original random retrieval program in Fig. 7-14 are as follows:

(1)   The SELECT statement (lines 14–21) includes a new clause to name the ALTERNATE KEY(s). The syntax of the new clause is as follows:

```
ALTERNATE RECORD KEY IS name-of-secondary-key-in-record
    [ WITH DUPLICATES ]
```

As many ALTERNATE KEYs as needed may be defined. If the values of an ALTERNATE KEY are unique (i.e., if the ALTERNATE KEY, like the RECORD KEY, uniquely identifies each record), then the WITH DUPLICATES subclause is omitted. If different records may have the same value in the ALTERNATE KEY field, then WITH DUPLICATES must be specified. Each ALTERNATE RECORD KEY must be a field in the level-01 record description for the file and must follow the same rules of formation as the RECORD KEY field.

(2)   If, as in this case, DUPLICATES are permitted for an ALTERNATE RECORD KEY, it may be useful to specify ACCESS IS DYNAMIC (line 17). This allows the use of a random READ to retrieve the first record with a given ALTERNATE RECORD KEY value, to be followed by multiple READ NEXTs which retrieve the remaining records matching the given ALTERNATE RECORD KEY (see lines 111–131).

```
00001              IDENTIFICATION DIVISION.
00002              PROGRAM-ID.  ALTERNATE-INDEX-RETRIEVAL.

00003              ENVIRONMENT DIVISION.
00004              CONFIGURATION SECTION.
00005              SOURCE-COMPUTER.  IBM-3081.
00006              OBJECT-COMPUTER.  IBM-3081.
00007              INPUT-OUTPUT SECTION.
00008              FILE-CONTROL.

00009                  SELECT TRANSACTION-FILE
00010                      ASSIGN TO PROGIDS
00011                      ORGANIZATION IS SEQUENTIAL
00012                      ACCESS IS SEQUENTIAL
00013                      .
00014                  SELECT INDEXED-FILE
00015                      ASSIGN TO VSAM
00016                      ORGANIZATION IS INDEXED
00017                      ACCESS IS DYNAMIC
00018                      RECORD KEY IS INDEXED-PROGRAMMER-ID
00019                      ALTERNATE RECORD KEY IS INDEXED-PROJECT-ID
00020                          WITH DUPLICATES
00021                      FILE STATUS IS INDEXED-STATUS-CODE
00022                      .

00023              DATA DIVISION.
00024              FILE SECTION.

00025              FD  TRANSACTION-FILE
00026                  LABEL RECORDS ARE STANDARD
00027                  BLOCK CONTAINS 0 CHARACTERS
00028                  RECORD CONTAINS 80 CHARACTERS
00029                  .
00030              01  TRANSACTION-RECORD.
00031                  05   TRANS-PROGRAMMER-ID        PIC X(5).
00032                      88   PROJECT-INQUIRY        VALUE SPACES.
00033                  05   TRANS-PROJECT-ID           PIC X(8).
00034                  05   FILLER                     PIC X(67).

00035              FD  INDEXED-FILE
00036                  LABEL RECORDS ARE STANDARD
00037                  RECORD CONTAINS 15 CHARACTERS
                       .
00038              01  INDEXED-RECORD.
00039                  05   INDEXED-PROGRAMMER-ID      PIC X(5).
00040                  05   INDEXED-PROJECT-ID         PIC X(8).
00041                  05   INDEXED-TOTAL-HOURS        PIC 9(3)V9 COMP.

00042              WORKING-STORAGE SECTION.

00043              01  FLAGS-AND-SWITCHES.
00044                  05   TRANS-END-OF-FILE-SW       PIC X(3).
00045                      88   MORE-TRANS-RECORDS      VALUE "NO".
00046                      88   NO-MORE-INPUT           VALUE "YES".

00047              01  FILE-STATUS-CODES.
00048                  05   INDEXED-STATUS-CODE        PIC XX.
00049                      88   VSAM-OPERATION-OK       VALUE "00".
00050                      88   VSAM-OPERATION-FAILED   VALUE "01" THRU "99".
00051                      88   RECORD-NOT-FOUND        VALUE "23".
00052                      88   DUPLICATE-ALTERNATE-KEY VALUE "02".
00053                      88   FOUND-PROJECT-ID        VALUE "00" "02".

00054              PROCEDURE DIVISION.
00055
00056              000-EXECUTIVE-MODULE.
00057
00058                  MOVE "NO" TO TRANS-END-OF-FILE-SW
00059                  OPEN    INPUT   INDEXED-FILE
00060                                  TRANSACTION-FILE
00061                  IF VSAM-OPERATION-OK
```

Fig. 7-19

```
00062                         PERFORM 010-GET-NEXT-TRANS
00063                         PERFORM 020-RETRIEVE-INDEXED-RECORD
00064                             UNTIL NO-MORE-INPUT
00065                     CLOSE   INDEXED-FILE
00066                             TRANSACTION-FILE
00067                     IF VSAM-OPERATION-OK
00068                         DISPLAY "RANDOM RETRIEVAL COMPLETED"
00069                     ELSE
00070                         DISPLAY "INDEXED FILE NOT PROPERLY CLOSED"
00071                 ELSE
00072                     DISPLAY "UNABLE TO OPEN INDEXED FILE -- ABORT"
00073                     CLOSE TRANSACTION-FILE
00074                     .
00075                 STOP RUN
00076                 .
00077
00078         010-GET-NEXT-TRANS.
00079
00080             READ TRANSACTION-FILE
00081                 AT END
00082                     MOVE "YES" TO TRANS-END-OF-FILE-SW
00083                 .
00084
00085         020-RETRIEVE-INDEXED-RECORD.
00086
00087             IF PROJECT-INQUIRY
00088                 PERFORM 040-RETRIEVE-BY-PROJECT
00089             ELSE
00090                 PERFORM 030-RETRIEVE-BY-PROGRAMMER
00091             .
00092             PERFORM 010-GET-NEXT-TRANS
00093             .
00094
00095         030-RETRIEVE-BY-PROGRAMMER.
00096
00097             MOVE TRANS-PROGRAMMER-ID   TO INDEXED-PROGRAMMER-ID
00098             READ INDEXED-FILE
00099             IF VSAM-OPERATION-OK
00100                 DISPLAY "PROGRAMMER " INDEXED-PROGRAMMER-ID
00101                         " IS ASSIGNED PROJECT "
00102                         INDEXED-PROJECT-ID
00103             ELSE
00104                 IF RECORD-NOT-FOUND
00105                     DISPLAY "PROGRAMMER NOT FOUND " TRANSACTION-RECORD
00106                 ELSE
00107                     DISPLAY "VSAM ERROR " INDEXED-STATUS-CODE
00108                             " FOR TRANSACTION " TRANSACTION-RECORD
00109             .
00110
00111         040-RETRIEVE-BY-PROJECT.
00112
00113             MOVE TRANS-PROJECT-ID TO INDEXED-PROJECT-ID
00114             READ INDEXED-FILE
00115                 KEY IS INDEXED-PROJECT-ID
00116             IF FOUND-PROJECT-ID
00117                 DISPLAY "PROGRAMMERS ASSIGNED TO " TRANS-PROJECT-ID
00118                 PERFORM 050-GET-NEXT-PROGRAMMER
00119                     UNTIL INDEXED-PROJECT-ID NOT EQUAL
00120                         TRANS-PROJECT-ID
00121             ELSE
00122                 DISPLAY "PROJECT NOT FOUND " TRANS-PROJECT-ID
00123             .
00124
00125         050-GET-NEXT-PROGRAMMER.
00126
00127             DISPLAY "   " INDEXED-PROGRAMMER-ID
00128             READ INDEXED-FILE NEXT RECORD
00129                 AT END
00130                     MOVE SPACES TO INDEXED-PROJECT-ID
00131             .
```

Fig. 7-19   (*cont.*)

(3) The STATUS CODE area for this file is defined in lines 47–53. For indexed files, the STATUS CODE is set to 00 when a record is successfully retrieved by ALTERNATE RECORD KEY and is the only record with that ALTERNATE KEY value; the STATUS CODE is set to 02 when a record is successfully retrieved by ALTERNATE KEY, but other records exist having the same ALTERNATE KEY value (this situation is indicated by the alternate index entry).

(4) The transaction records have been modified (lines 25–34) to specify either a programmer ID (in which case the project assigned to that programmer is retrieved by accessing the file through the RECORD KEY INDEXED-PROGRAMMER-ID) or a project ID [in which case the programmer(s) assigned to that project are retrieved by accessing the file through the ALTERNATE RECORD KEY INDEXED-PROJECT-ID].

(5) Paragraph 020-RETRIEVE-INDEXED-RECORD (lines 85–93) identifies the type of transaction (i.e., a programmer inquiry or a project inquiry) and calls the appropriate inquiry processing module.

(6) The logic for randomly accessing a record by the primary key INDEXED-PROGRAMMER-ID is the same as in Fig. 7-14 (see 030-RETRIEVE-BY-PROGRAMMER, lines 95–109).

(7) 040-RETRIEVE-BY-PROJECT (lines 111–123) accesses all records having a given value of INDEXED-PROJECT-ID (an ALTERNATE RECORD KEY). It begins by moving the project ID from the transaction record to the ALTERNATE RECORD KEY area (line 113) and then executing a READ statement of the following form:

```
READ file-name RECORD
    [ INTO data-area-to-receive-copy-of-record ]
    KEY IS name-of-alternate-or-primary-key-to-be-used
    [ INVALID KEY imperative-statement(s). ]
```

The KEY IS . . . clause must name either a RECORD KEY or an ALTERNATE RECORD KEY for the file. The key named in the KEY IS . . . clause becomes the current *key of reference* for the file. Any subsequent READ NEXT statements will retrieve records in key sequence for the current key of reference. If a READ statement omits the KEY IS . . . clause, the current key of reference is assumed to be the RECORD KEY for the file. Once set, the key of reference remains unchanged until another READ statement is executed to reset it. Note that READ NEXT statements, although controlled by the current key of reference, do not change it. The READ in lines 114–115 specifies the ALTERNATE RECORD KEY INDEXED-PROJECT-ID.

(8) In this example, there may be more than one programmer associated with a given project. After the random READ in lines 114–115 is used to retrieve the first record with a matching project ID, a title is printed and a loop is established to retrieve other records with the same project ID (lines 117–120). If a record with the given project ID cannot be found, a message is printed and no further processing is carried out for this transaction (lines 121–122).

(9) 050-GET-NEXT-PROGRAMMER repeatedly DISPLAYs the programmer ID and READs the NEXT record until either the AT END is activated or the INDEXED-PROJECT-ID no longer matches the project ID in the transaction (lines 118–120; note how AT END is handled in lines 129–130 to guarantee that INDEXED-PROJECT-ID changes for the end of the file). This allows the program to retrieve all records whose ALTERNATE RECORD KEY matches the project ID from the transaction. Note that the current key of reference for the READ NEXT statement in line 128 has been established as the ALTERNATE RECORD KEY INDEXED-PROJECT-ID by the READ statement with KEY IS INDEXED-PROJECT-ID in lines 114–115.

(10) Note that by omitting the KEY IS . . . clause, the READ statement in line 98 changes the current key of reference back to the RECORD KEY INDEXED-PROGRAMMER-ID (which is what is desired within 030-RETRIEVE-BY-PROGRAMMER).

7.74 Does the IDCAMS utility play a role in defining ALTERNATE KEYs for IBM VSAM indexed files?

Yes. The following IDCAMS commands must be used:

(1) DEFINE CLUSTER must be used to create the catalog entry for the *base cluster* (i.e., the original indexed file).

(2) Then a COBOL program can be used to load records into the file.

(3) Then the DEFINE ALTERNATEINDEX command is used to define a VSAM catalog entry for the alternate index to be created.

(4) Then the DEFINE PATH command is used to associate the new alternate index with its base cluster. A VSAM path specifies the index to be used when accessing a file. More than one path may be open at the same time for the same file (as in Fig. 7-19).

(5) Finally, the BLDINDEX command is used to actually create the alternate index. After this last step, the program in Fig. 7-19 could finally be executed.

Clearly alternate indexes are a complicated topic. Consult an instructor or vendor manual for further information on alternate indexes/keys on your system.

7.75 Illustrate how to combine the use of INVALID KEY with a FILE STATUS area by doing a random retrieval from INDEXED-CUSTOMER-FILE (the RECORD KEY is INDEXED-CUSTOMER-ID, and the FILE STATUS area is INDEXED-STATUS-CODE).

```
        MOVE TRANSACTION-CUSTOMER-ID TO INDEXED-CUSTOMER-ID
        READ INDEXED-CUSTOMER-FILE
            INVALID KEY
                PERFORM ERROR-ANALYSIS-ROUTINE

              .

              .
              .
              .

    ERROR-ANALYSIS-ROUTINE.
        IF INDEXED-STATUS-CODE EQUAL VALUE-FOR-NOT-FOUND
            PERFORM RECORD-NOT-FOUND-ROUTINE
        ELSE IF INDEXED-STATUS-CODE EQUAL VALUE-FOR-DATA-ERROR
            PERFORM PERMANENT-I-O-ERROR-ROUTINE
        ELSE
            PERFORM OTHER-I-O-ERROR-ROUTINE

              .
```

Note that the linear IF statement could not be placed directly in the INVALID KEY clause since INVALID KEY must consist of only imperative statements. This problem is circumvented by placing the analysis of INDEXED-STATUS-CODE in a PERFORMed paragraph.

7.76 The indexed file update program in Problem 7.70 sequentially READs through the indexed file looking for a record whose key matches that of the current transaction. Improve this solution by recoding paragraph 050-FIND-MATCHING-MASTER to use the START statement to position the current record pointer to the desired record. By taking advantage of the existing index, the START statement can randomly position the CRP to the record matching the current transaction, thus eliminating unnecessary READs of indexed records which have no matching transactions.

```
        050-FIND-MATCHING-MASTER.
            IF TRANS-PROGRAMMER-ID NOT EQUAL INDEXED-PROGRAMMER-ID
                PERFORM 055-POSITION-CRP
                IF INDEXED-PROGRAMMER-ID NOT EQUAL SPACES
                    PERFORM 030-GET-MASTER-RECORD
              .
        055-POSITION-CRP.
            MOVE TRANS-PROGRAMMER-ID TO INDEXED-PROGRAMMER-ID
            START INDEXED-FILE
                INVALID KEY
                    MOVE SPACES TO INDEXED-PROGRAMMER-ID
              .
```

Chapter 8

COBOL Relative Files

Relative organization is an ANSI standard file organization providing fast and convenient random processing for those applications meeting certain restrictions. Unfortunately, most applications do not readily meet these restrictions, and relative files are not often used. Relative organization generally achieves *faster* random access than indexed organization, however, and should always be considered to see if it is applicable.

8.1 General Characteristics of Relative File Organization

Relative files are built on the concept of *relative record number*. They must reside on direct access storage devices. The direct access space occupied by a relative file is viewed as a series of fixed-length *slots*, each of which can hold one logical record. Each slot in the file is assigned a relative record number which uniquely identifies it. Relative record numbers run 1, 2, 3, etc.

The slot corresponding to any given relative record number may be empty or may hold a logical record. Empty record slots contain *dummy records* with a special code identifying the slot as empty.

EXAMPLE 8.1 Here is a conceptual view of a relative file, showing record slots and their relative record numbers. Note that some slots are empty ("empty" slots contain a special code value which identifies them as "dummy" or inactive records). Empty slots can be used to add new records to the file.

Relative Record Number	Contents of Record Slot in File
1	—
2	Logical record a
3	—
4	Logical record b
5	Logical record c
6	—
7	—
8	—
9	Logical record d
10	—

8.2 How Relative Organization Works

Sequential Processing

When relative files are accessed sequentially, logical records are retrieved in the order of their relative record numbers. During SEQUENTIAL ACCESS, dummy records (i.e., empty record slots) are automatically skipped by the operating system file management routines and are never given to the COBOL program, which need not be aware of their presence. The START statement may be used during SEQUENTIAL ACCESS to cause sequential retrieval to "skip" to the relative record number identified in the START statement.

EXAMPLE 8.2 Relative files, like indexed files, maintain a *current record pointer* (*CRP*) during SEQUEN-TIAL or DYNAMIC ACCESS. The following illustrates sequential access of the file in Example 8.1. "RR#" indicates the relative record number:

COBOL Statement	Accesses	New CRP	Comments
OPEN INPUT	—	RR# 1	OPEN positions file to first relative record number
READ	Record a	RR# 3	Operating system access method routine automatically skips over the dummy record in slot 1, then retrieves active record in slot 2, then sets new CRP to next slot (i.e., 3).
READ	Record b	RR# 5	Operating system skips dummy record in slot 3, retrieves active record in slot 4, sets CRP to next slot (5).
READ	Record c	RR# 6	System retrieves active record in slot 5 and sets CRP to next slot.
READ	Record d	RR# 10	Operating system skips dummy records in slots 6–8, retrieves active record from slot 9, and sets CRP to slot 10.
READ	—	Undefined	AT END routine is executed since there are no more active records in file.
START (RR# = 9)	—	RR# 9	START positions SEQUENTIAL ACCESS to indicated record slot. START must indicate active record in order to successfully reset CRP.
READ	Record d	RR# 10	SEQUENTIAL READ attempts to access record pointed to by CRP; the active record in slot 9 is retrieved, and CRP is set to next slot (10).
READ	—	Undefined	AT END routine is activated as above.

Random Processing

RANDOM ACCESS of a relative file is done by relative record number. The SELECT statement names a RELATIVE KEY data area (usually defined in WORKING-STORAGE) into which the program moves the relative record number of the logical record to be read or written. DYNAMIC ACCESS is also allowed for relative files, as shown below.

EXAMPLE 8.3 The following illustrates DYNAMIC ACCESS of the file in Example 8.1:

COBOL Statement	Accesses	New CRP	Comments
OPEN I–O		RR# 1	OPEN positions file to slot 1.
READ (RR# = 5)	Record c	6	Random READ inputs record in indicated slot and sets CRP to next slot (6).
READ NEXT	Record d	10	Empty slots 6–8 are automatically skipped; active record in slot 9 is retrieved, and CRP is set to next slot (10).

COBOL Statement	*Accesses*	*New CRP*	*Comments*
READ (RR# = 3)	—	Undefined	Random READ attempts to access an empty slot; STATUS CODE is set to indicate record-not-found condition, and INVALID KEY is activated (if specified); CRP is set undefined.
READ NEXT	—	Undefined	READ NEXT with CRP undefined fails; STATUS CODE is set to indicate an error.
START (RR# = 7)	—	Undefined	START attempts to position CRP to an empty record slot; STATUS CODE is set to indicate record-not-found condition, and INVALID KEY is activated. CRP is set undefined.
START (RR# = 2)	—	RR# 2	START positions CRP to active record in slot 2.
READ NEXT	Record a	RR# 3	READ NEXT attempts to input record at current CRP; since slot 2 is active, this is successful and CRP is set to next slot.
READ (RR# = 4)	Record b	RR# 5	Random READ inputs active record at indicated slot and sets CRP to next slot.
READ NEXT	Record c	RR# 6	READ NEXT inputs active record at current CRP and sets CRP to next slot.
READ NEXT	Record d	RR# 10	READ NEXT automatically skips empty slots 6–8 and inputs next active record from slot 9; CRP is set to next slot.
WRITE (RR# = 7)	Record e	RR# 10	Random WRITE adds a new record to the file in the indicated slot (which must be empty); WRITE does *not* change the CRP.
WRITE (RR# = 4)	—	RR# 10	An attempt to add a record to a slot which is already occupied results in a duplicate key error, setting the STATUS CODE and activating INVALID KEY. WRITE does not affect the CRP
DELETE (RR# = 2)	Record a	RR# 10	The record in slot 2 is logically deleted from the file. Slot 2 is now available to add a new record. DELETE does not affect the CRP.
DELETE (RR# = 6)	—	RR# 10	Since slot 6 is empty, the STATUS CODE is set to indicate a record-not-found condition and INVALID KEY is activated. Only *active* records may be successfully deleted.
REWRITE (RR# = 5)	Record c	RR# 10	The active record in slot 5 is replaced with the current contents of the level-01 record area for the file. REWRITE does *not* affect the CRP.
REWRITE (RR# = 6)	—	RR# 10	Since slot 6 is empty, the STATUS CODE is set to indicate a record-not-found condition and INVALID KEY is activated. Only *active* records may be successfully rewritten.

As the above examples show, relative file processing and indexed file processing are quite similar. Relative files, in fact, act like indexed files in which the "key" is the relative record number.

In terms of implementation, however, relative files work by having the operating system access method routines calculate the physical disk address of a given record as a function of its relative record number. In most cases, this calculation can be done faster than an index can be searched. Although the COBOL *syntax* and *logic* for relative and indexed files are similar, relative organization may perform much faster than indexed organization for some applications (actual results will depend on the size of the file, the structure of the index, the percentage of the index which can be searched in main memory, and the details of how relative record numbers are converted to physical disk addresses). Relative files should be considered as an effective alternative to indexed files for certain applications.

8.3　Restrictions on Relative File Organization

The major obstacle to the use of relative files is the need to identify logical records by relative record number. Since most business applications require that records be identified by *key* (not relative record number, which is generally meaningless to the *users* of a system), a means must be created to transform record keys into relative record numbers. Unfortunately, it is frequently difficult to come up with an effective key transformation (hash) function.

If the *key set* (i.e., the set of key field values) for a file consists of closely spaced numbers, then it is easy to calculate the relative record number from the key field. If the key set is not numeric or is not closely spaced, then it becomes difficult to find an effective key transformation function.

EXAMPLE 8.4　Suppose a file of records for 500 inventory items has part numbers between 98013 and 98543. This satisfies the criteria that the key field values be (1) numeric and (2) closely spaced. It is then easy to transform a part number into a relative record number using the following key transformation function:

$$RR\# = (\text{part-number}) - (98012)$$

According to the above hash function, the following records would be assigned the indicated slots in a relative file:

Part Number		RR Number
98013	1	(98013 − 98012)
98543	531	(98543 − 98012)
98427	415	(98427 − 98012)

Note that the record numbers produced by the above formula range between 1 and 531. This wastes 31 slots since there are only 500 records in the file, but such a small amount of wasted space (6 percent) is usually acceptable.

EXAMPLE 8.5　Suppose the part numbers for the 500 items in Example 8.4 are randomly scattered within the range 00027 to 98543. The approach taken in Example 8.4 no longer works because it creates an unacceptable amount of wasted space. If the relative record number is calculated as

$$RR\# = (\text{part-number}) - (26)$$

the relative record numbers range from 1 to 98517. This means that 98517 slots would have to be allocated to hold only 500 actual records—clearly an unacceptable waste of space (99 percent).

Obviously, more sophisticated key transformation functions would solve the problem of wasted space illustrated in Example 8.5. However, there is a more subtle problem which typically resists solution—that of key *synonyms*. The reader will recall from Chapter 6 that synonyms are records whose keys hash to the same address. With the direct files in Chapter 6, this was not a serious problem because keys were hashed to a relative track number, and many records typically fit on a track. If k records fit per track of a direct file, each track can hold k synonyms without the need for any special collision-handling procedures.

Since relative file records must hash to a relative record number (i.e., a slot number), and since each slot can hold only one logical record, the *first* synonym created by a given hash function requires special collision-handling procedures to find an alternate location in which to place the record. Since ANSI relative files provide no "built-in" method of collision handling, this procedure must be designed by the programmer and coded into the COBOL program.

Technically, there are many ways to solve the problem of synonyms (consult any text on abstract data structures and/or direct access file organizations), but in an age when programmers' time is at a premium, it is usually more cost-effective to switch to indexed file organization than to tie up applications programmers designing and writing collision-handling routines for relative files. Thus relative files are usually a practical choice only when a key transformation function which never produces synonyms can be found.

EXAMPLE 8.6   The key transformation function in Example 8.4 produces a *unique* relative record number for each part number; i.e., there are never any synonyms. Thus this file could effectively be implemented as a relative file.

EXAMPLE 8.7   Consider the key set from Example 8.5. A possible key transformation function (which will not waste space) is the division/remainder method discussed in Chapter 6. For 500 actual records, one could use the function

$$RR\# = [\text{remainder }(\text{part-number}/500)] + 1$$

Since the remainder upon division by 500 lies between 0 and 499, one more than the remainder lies in the range 1 to 500—the exact range of relative record numbers needed for 500 records (with *no* wasted space).

Unfortunately, this key transformation function is not guaranteed to eliminate synonyms; e.g., both part numbers 06785 and 40285 are assigned to relative record number 286 by this hash function. Hence the COBOL programmer would have to design and code a collision-handling procedure which could select alternate locations for record 40285 and any subsequent synonyms. It is probably better in such a situation simply to use indexed rather than relative organization.

EXAMPLE 8.8   The *best* key transformation function for a relative file is *none at all*. This is possible when the analyst and/or programmer has control over the design of the key set for the file. If the inventory file in Example 8.4 had not existed prior to the development of this application, the analysts/programmers might have been able to design the part numbers for the 500 items to run from 1 to 500. In this case, the record's key field could have directly served as the relative record number for the record, eliminating the need for a hash function.

Since numeric keys which are closely spaced do not occur "ready-made" in many applications, one of the major uses of relative organization occurs when the analyst/programmer has the chance to determine the key set for a file. By choosing numeric keys which run from 1 to n, the analyst/programmer creates a file deliberately tailored for ease of implementation as a relative file.

Another disadvantage of relative files is that in order for the operating system access method routines to be able to calculate the physical disk location of a record from its relative record number, the record slots in the file must be fixed-length.

Some implementations of relative file organization enforce this by requiring the use of only fixed-length records. Other implementations allow variable-length records but still allocate fixed-length slots equal to the maximum record size. The variable-length records are placed into the fixed-length slots, giving the equivalent of fixed-length records in terms of space utilization. In this case, much disk space is wasted if the average record size is below the maximum record size. Consult an instructor or vendor manual for more information on variable-length records in relative files on your system.

8.4   A Common Relative File Implementation:
   IBM'S VSAM Relative Record Data Sets

Just as IBM offers an older indexed file organization (ISAM) and a newer replacement (VSAM indexed files), so IBM offers an older relative file organization (non-VSAM relative) and a newer version (VSAM relative). The differences between VSAM relative and non-VSAM relative are minimal (see Problem 8.34), so we will discuss the newer VSAM relative files.

VSAM relative files permit variable-length records but allocate fixed-length record slots equal in size to the maximum record size (so no space savings are achieved over fixed-length records).

Just as the IDCAMS utility program must be run to define a VSAM catalog entry for an indexed file *before* a COBOL program can actually load records into the file, so the IDCAMS utility must be run to define a VSAM catalog entry for a relative file *before* a COBOL program can place any records in the file. The use of IDCAMS for relative files is quite similar to its use for indexed files. See Sections 7.3 and 7.10 for further discussion of the IBM IDCAMS utility.

The syntax of a minimal IDCAMS DEFINE CLUSTER command to define a catalog entry for a relative file is as follows.

```
DEFINE CLUSTER -
    ( -
      NAME (name-of-vsam-file) -
      VOLUMES (name-of-disk-volume-on-which-file-is-to-go) -
      NUMBERED -
      RECORDS (#-for-primary  #-for-secondary) -
      RECORDSIZE (average-record-size  maximum-record-size) -
      ) -
      CATALOG (name-of-vsam-catalog-in-which-entry-is-to-be-made)
```

The DEFINE CLUSTER command for a relative file is simpler than that for an indexed file. NAME is the name to be recorded in the catalog. This is the name which will be used to refer to the file in other IDCAMS commands and in job control/command language statements.

VOLUMES specifies the name of the disk pack on which the file is to be placed. NUMBERED indicates that this is a *relative* file. RECORDS specifies the number of record slots to be allocated initially (primary allocation) and the number of additional record slots (secondary allocation, if any) to be allocated if the initial allocation is filled up or if a relative record number outside the current bounds of the file is added (so that the file must be expanded up to the new highest relative record number).

RECORDSIZE specifies the average length and the maximum length of a logical record. Remember that VSAM relative organization allocates record slots equal to the maximum size. Logical records less than the maximum size thus waste space when they are packaged into the maximum size slots.

CATALOG specifies the VSAM catalog in which the entry describing the new file is to be made.

EXAMPLE 8.9   Figure 8-1 shows an IBM IDCAMS utility DEFINE CLUSTER command for a relative version of the programmer file used in Chapters 6 and 7. The meanings of the individual parameters are similar to those for indexed files, although fewer parameters are required. Remember that a catalog entry must be defined *before* any COBOL program can manipulate the file.

```
DEFINE CLUSTER -
  ( -
    NAME (LRN.VSAM.RELATIVE) -
    VOLUMES (CCLIB3) -
    NUMBERED -
    RECORDS (30 15) -
    RECORDSIZE (15 15) -
  ) -
    CATALOG (PSU.VSAMCAT)
```

Fig. 8-1

EXAMPLE 8.10   Figure 8-2 shows how to use IDCAMS to print and then delete the relative file defined in Fig. 8-1. PRINT...CHARACTER assumes that all record fields are DISPLAY. Note that the PRINT and DELETE commands are *exactly* the same as those for indexed files (see Examples 7.21, 7.22, and Fig. 7-12 for further discussion of PRINT and DELETE).

```
PRINT -
    INDATASET (LRN.VSAM.RELATIVE) -
    CHARACTER
DELETE -
    (LRN.VSAM.RELATIVE) -
    CATALOG (PSU.VSAMCAT) -
    CLUSTER
```

Fig. 8-2

8.5   Creating Relative Files in COBOL (ANSI Standard)

Relative files can be created with either ACCESS SEQUENTIAL or ACCESS RANDOM. When a relative file is created *sequentially*, the operating system access method routines place the logical records in ascending record slots, beginning with relative record number 1. Thus the first logical record written goes in slot 1, the fifth logical record written goes in slot 5, the forty-seventh goes in slot 47, etc.

Since random retrieval of relative file records requires that some relationship be established between a record's key field and its relative record number, sequential creation of relative files is usually not practical (since records are simply placed into the file in the order in which they are written). Accordingly, this Outline will discuss only *random* creation of relative files.

When relative files are created randomly, the COBOL program indicates the relative record number at which a given record is to be placed by moving this record number into a special RELATIVE KEY area before writing the record. The RELATIVE KEY data item must be an unsigned numeric integer item which is *not* part of the level-01 record description for the file. It is usually defined in WORKING-STORAGE.

If the RELATIVE KEY specifies a record number which is greater than the previous highest in the file, the operating system access method routines automatically write enough dummy records to fill in record slots between the previous highest slot and the new one. This is done as part of the execution of the WRITE statement and is transparent to the COBOL program. The empty slots thus created can be used to add other records to the file.

If a WRITE statement uses a RELATIVE KEY value for an already-existing record slot which is not empty, the record will not be added and the STATUS CODE will be set to indicate a duplicate key error (and INVALID KEY will be activated, if specified).

As with direct file organization, the secret to randomly creating a relative file is to have a good key transformation function which can map logical record keys into relative record numbers. This same function will then have to be used for all future random processing against the file.

ENVIRONMENT DIVISION Considerations

The ANSI standard COBOL SELECT statement for randomly creating a relative file has the following syntax:

```
SELECT file-name
    ASSIGN TO external-name
    ORGANIZATION IS RELATIVE
    ACCESS MODE IS RANDOM
    RELATIVE KEY IS name-of-area-to-hold-relative-record-#
    [ FILE STATUS IS name-of-status-area ]
```

The ASSIGN TO clause identifies the name of a job control/command language statement ("external-name"), which provides further information about the file to be created. Since the form and function of the external name differ from system to system, consult an instructor or vendor manual regarding the ASSIGN TO clause for relative files on your system.

The ORGANIZATION IS RELATIVE clause specifies relative file organization. Since sequential organization is the default, this is a required clause.

Similarly, since sequential access is the default, random creation requires the use of ACCESS IS RANDOM. The FILE STATUS clause is optional, but its use is always recommended.

The RELATIVE KEY clause names a data area to be used to hold the relative record number of the record to be accessed. It must be an unsigned numeric integer item which is not a field in the records for the file (it is usually defined in WORKING-STORAGE). The random WRITE statement will add a record to the file in the slot identified by the RELATIVE KEY.

DATA DIVISION Considerations

The FD and level-01 record description for a relative file are similar to that for an indexed file. LABEL RECORDS is usually required in most implementations, but blocking may or may not be permitted (e.g., for IBM VSAM relative files, the BLOCK CONTAINS clause is ignored and treated as a comment; therefore, it is usually omitted).

The RELATIVE KEY (as described above) and FILE STATUS areas are usually defined in WORKING-STORAGE. It is helpful to use condition names for the most frequently occurring FILE STATUS codes.

PROCEDURE DIVISION Considerations

The main factor in creating relative files randomly is choosing a key transformation function which is guaranteed not to produce any synonyms (or, even better, arranging the key set so that no key transformation is needed). Once such a function is found, each logical record is placed in the file by:

(1) Applying the key transformation (if any) to the record's key field to derive a relative record number

(2) Moving the relative record number from step (1) to the RELATIVE KEY area

(3) Moving needed data items into the level-01 record area for the file

(4) Using the WRITE verb to add the record

The relevant PROCEDURE DIVISION statements are:

(1) OPEN OUTPUT file-name

(2) CLOSE file-name

(3) WRITE record-name
    [FROM data-area]
    [INVALID KEY imperative-statement(s).]

   The WRITE statement causes the operating system access method routines to automatically do the following:

   (a) Retrieve the relative record number from the RELATIVE KEY area.

   (b) Calculate the physical disk address of the record from the RELATIVE KEY value.

   (c) Attempt to retrieve the record at that physical disk address. If the record exists and is already active, the WRITE operation fails with a duplicate key error. The STATUS CODE and INVALID KEY are activated accordingly.

(d) If the RELATIVE KEY value lies outside the current bounds of the file, enough dummy records are written to bring the number of slots in the file up to the record number in the RELATIVE KEY. If sufficient space is not available to do this, the WRITE fails, with STATUS CODE and INVALID KEY treated accordingly. Note that this process *may* result in automatic secondary allocations of space to the file.

(e) At this point, there must be an empty slot matching the record number in RELATIVE KEY. This slot is filled with a copy of the logical record in the level-01 record area for the file, and the STATUS CODE is set to indicate successful completion.

EXAMPLE 8.11 Figure 8-3 shows an IBM OS/VS COBOL program which randomly creates the programmer file from Chapters 6 and 7 as a relative file. Again, the master file is created from a sequential transaction file which is assumed to be already validated. It is also assumed that the key field (programmer ID) has been deliberately designed so that the programmer IDs run from 1 up to the current number of programmers. This eliminates the need for a hash function to convert the key field to a relative record number (since the unchanged key field can serve directly as the relative record number). The following comments apply:

(1) The SELECT statement in lines 14–19 specifies ORGANIZATION IS RELATIVE and ACCESS IS RANDOM. Line 18 names the RELATIVE KEY data item, which is actually defined in WORKING-STORAGE (lines 49–50). Note that RELATIVE-RECORD-NUMBER is an unsigned numeric item, as required.

(2) Lines 33–39 form the FD and record description for the file. They are exactly the same as for an indexed file. Note that for IBM VSAM relative files, BLOCK CONTAINS is treated as a comment and is therefore omitted. The *key field*, which is part of and uniquely identifies each record, is RELATIVE-PROGRAMMER-ID (line 37). The key field (RELATIVE-PROGRAMMER-ID) should not be confused with the RELATIVE KEY field (RELATIVE-RECORD-NUMBER), which may not be part of the record. The RELATIVE KEY field is used to hold the relative record number at which a record is to be placed; the key field within the record uniquely identifies the record. In this program, the relative record number for each record is made equal to the key field, but in some cases a more complicated key transformation from key field to relative record number may be necessary.

```
00001              IDENTIFICATION DIVISION.
00002              PROGRAM-ID.  RELATIVE-FILE-CREATION.

00003              ENVIRONMENT DIVISION.
00004              CONFIGURATION SECTION.
00005              SOURCE-COMPUTER.   IBM-3081.
00006              OBJECT-COMPUTER.   IBM-3081.
00007              INPUT-OUTPUT SECTION.
00008              FILE-CONTROL.

00009                  SELECT TRANSACTION-FILE
00010                      ASSIGN TO RAWDATA
00011                      ORGANIZATION IS SEQUENTIAL
00012                      ACCESS IS SEQUENTIAL
00013                      .
00014                  SELECT RELATIVE-FILE
00015                      ASSIGN TO RELFILE
00016                      ORGANIZATION IS RELATIVE
00017                      ACCESS IS RANDOM
00018                      RELATIVE KEY IS RELATIVE-RECORD-NUMBER
00019                      FILE STATUS IS RELATIVE-STATUS-CODE
00020                      .

00021              DATA DIVISION.
00022              FILE SECTION.

00023              FD  TRANSACTION-FILE
00024                  LABEL RECORDS ARE STANDARD
00025                  BLOCK CONTAINS O CHARACTERS
00026                  RECORD CONTAINS 80 CHARACTERS
00027                  .
```

Fig. 8-3

```
00028              01   TRANSACTION-RECORD.
00029                   05    TRANS-PROGRAMMER-ID        PIC 9(5).
00030                   05    TRANS-PROJECT-ID           PIC X(8).
00031                   05    TRANS-TOTAL-HOURS          PIC 9(3)V9.
00032                   05    FILLER                     PIC X(63).


00033              FD   RELATIVE-FILE
00034                   LABEL RECORDS ARE STANDARD
00035                   RECORD CONTAINS 15 CHARACTERS
                        .
00036              01   RELATIVE-RECORD.
00037                   05    RELATIVE-PROGRAMMER-ID     PIC 9(5).
00038                   05    RELATIVE-PROJECT-ID        PIC X(8).
00039                   05    RELATIVE-TOTAL-HOURS       PIC 9(3)V9 COMP.


00040              WORKING-STORAGE SECTION.
00041              01   FLAGS-AND-SWITCHES.
00042                   05    TRANS-END-OF-FILE-SW       PIC X(3).
00043                         88    MORE-TRANS-RECORDS   VALUE "NO".
00044                         88    NO-MORE-INPUT        VALUE "YES".


00045              01   FILE-STATUS-CODES.
00046                   05    RELATIVE-STATUS-CODE       PIC XX.
00047                         88   RELATIVE-OPERATION-OK      VALUE "00".
00048                         88   RELATIVE-OPERATION-FAILED  VALUE "01" THRU "99".


00049              01   RELATIVE-KEY-AREA.
00050                   05    RELATIVE-RECORD-NUMBER     PIC 9(5).


00051              PROCEDURE DIVISION.
00052
00053              000-EXECUTIVE-MODULE.
00054
00055                   MOVE "NO" TO TRANS-END-OF-FILE-SW
00056                   OPEN    OUTPUT   RELATIVE-FILE
00057                           INPUT    TRANSACTION-FILE
00058                   IF RELATIVE-OPERATION-OK
00059                       PERFORM 010-GET-NEXT-TRANS
00060                       PERFORM 020-OUTPUT-RELATIVE-RECORD
00061                           UNTIL NO-MORE-INPUT
00062                       CLOSE    RELATIVE-FILE
00063                                TRANSACTION-FILE
00064                       IF RELATIVE-OPERATION-OK
00065                           DISPLAY "RELATIVE FILE CREATION COMPLETED"
00066                       ELSE
00067                           DISPLAY "RELATIVE FILE NOT PROPERLY CLOSED"
00068                   ELSE
00069                       DISPLAY "UNABLE TO OPEN RELATIVE FILE -- ABORT"
00070                       CLOSE TRANSACTION-FILE
00071                   .
00072                   STOP RUN
00073                   .
00074
00075              010-GET-NEXT-TRANS.
00076
00077                   READ TRANSACTION-FILE
00078                       AT END
00079                           MOVE "YES" TO TRANS-END-OF-FILE-SW
00080                   .
00081
00082              020-OUTPUT-RELATIVE-RECORD.
00083
00084                   MOVE TRANS-PROGRAMMER-ID     TO RELATIVE-PROGRAMMER-ID
00085                                                   RELATIVE-RECORD-NUMBER
00086                   MOVE TRANS-PROJECT-ID        TO RELATIVE-PROJECT-ID
00087                   MOVE TRANS-TOTAL-HOURS       TO RELATIVE-TOTAL-HOURS
00088                   WRITE    RELATIVE-RECORD
00089                   IF RELATIVE-OPERATION-FAILED
00090                       DISPLAY "DUPLICATE KEY FOR "
00091                               TRANSACTION-RECORD
00092                   .
00093                   PERFORM 010-GET-NEXT-TRANS
00094                   .
```

Fig. 8-3   (*cont.*)

(3) The executive module (lines 53–73) is *exactly* the same as that used for creating the indexed version of the file (see Fig. 7-10). As in Fig. 7-10, the STATUS CODE (defined in lines 45–48) is used to check for successful completion of OPEN and CLOSE.

(4) 020-OUTPUT-RELATIVE-RECORD (lines 82–94) is the heart of the creation program. Since in this file a record's key is used as its relative record number, the transaction key value is moved to the RELATIVE KEY area unchanged (lines 84–85). The rest of the transaction fields are moved to the level-01 record area, and then the WRITE statement in line 88 is used to add the record to the file. WRITE causes the operating system access method routine to calculate the physical disk address of the record slot corresponding to the current value in the RELATIVE KEY. This slot is then examined to see if it already holds an active record. If so, the WRITE is aborted and the STATUS CODE set to indicate a duplicate key (and INVALID KEY is activated, if specified). Otherwise, the current contents of the level-01 record area are placed into the empty slot on the disk. If the slot number in RELATIVE KEY exceeds the highest slot in the file prior to the WRITE, dummy records are automatically added to the file to bring the number of record slots up to that in RELATIVE KEY (if space is not available to do this, the WRITE statement fails, with the appropriate STATUS CODE and INVALID KEY).

8.6 Sequential Retrieval of Relative Files (ANSI Standard)

Relative files are retrieved sequentially in order of relative record number, which is in effect the *physical* sequence of the records on the disk. The only exception is that dummy records (i.e., empty record slots) are automatically skipped during sequential processing (and are not made available to the COBOL program).

The START statement may be used to position (and reposition) the current record pointer during SEQUENTIAL retrieval. The only consideration is that the START verb must indicate an *active* record slot in order for the CRP to be reset (if START indicates a dummy record slot, it fails, with a record-not-found STATUS CODE and INVALID KEY).

ENVIRONMENT DIVISION Considerations

The ANSI COBOL SELECT statement for sequential retrieval of a relative file has the following syntax:

```
SELECT file-name
    ASSIGN TO external-name
    ORGANIZATION IS RELATIVE
    [ ACCESS MODE IS SEQUENTIAL ]
    [ RELATIVE KEY IS name-of-area-to-hold-relative-record-# ]
    [ FILE STATUS IS name-of-status-area ]
```

The only differences between this and the SELECT statement used to randomly create the file are that (1) ACCESS IS SEQUENTIAL (now optional, since it is the default) and (2) the RELATIVE KEY is optional, since it is only needed if START is to be used.

DATA DIVISION Considerations

The FD and level-01 record description are the same as those used for creating the file. The RELATIVE KEY area is usually not needed (unless START is to be used).

PROCEDURE DIVISION Considerations

Sequential retrieval of a relative file is *almost* like retrieving a sequential file. The major difference is that the logical records are input in relative-record-number order. If a key transformation function has been used to assign relative record numbers, the relative record number order may not be in key sequence. Depending upon the circumstances, a SORT may, therefore, be required.

The relevant PROCEDURE DIVISION statements are:

(1) <u>OPEN</u> <u>INPUT</u> file-name

(2) <u>CLOSE</u> file-name

(3) <u>READ</u> file-name
    [<u>INTO</u> data-area]
    [AT <u>END</u> imperative-statement(s).]

The sequential READ statement causes the operating system access method routines to automatically locate the next record slot containing an active logical record (any dummy records encountered are simply skipped over and ignored). This record is then placed into the level-01 record area for the file. If a READ is executed and there are no more active records in the remaining record slots, the STATUS CODE is set to indicate the end of the file and the AT END routine is executed. Remember that sequential access inputs *only active* records *in record number sequence*.

EXAMPLE 8.12 Figure 8-4 shows an IBM OS/VS COBOL program which sequentially accesses the file created in Fig. 8-3. Since for this particular file the relative record number for a record *is* the record's key, the records just happen to come off in key sequence (i.e., record number sequence is also key sequence for this file). In general, this may not be the case, and a SORT may be required. Comments:

(1) The SELECT statement (lines 6–11) specifies ORGANIZATION IS RELATIVE and ACCESS IS SEQUENTIAL (optional, since it is the default). The specification of RELATIVE KEY is not required for sequential access, but if specified, the relative record number of the logical record just read is placed in this area by the READ statement. This program DISPLAYs each logical record followed by its relative record number (see line 61), so RELATIVE KEY is specified to obtain the desired record number information.

(2) The executive module (lines 32–48) OPENs the relative file for INPUT, loops to READ and DISPLAY each record, and then CLOSEs the file. Note the use of STATUS CODE to check the success of OPEN and CLOSE.

(3) Actual sequential retrieval of logical records is done in 020-GET-NEXT-RECORD (lines 50–57). Note the use of STATUS CODE to check for unexpected errors other than the end of the file (lines 53–57). If an unexpected error occurs, an error message is DISPLAYed; otherwise, processing proceeds as if the error had not happened (not always appropriate, depending on the application).

(4) Since the RELATIVE KEY was named for sequential access, the slot number for each record is placed in the RELATIVE KEY area by the READ. The relative record number for each record can then be DISPLAYed in line 61, along with the record.

```
00001          IDENTIFICATION DIVISION.
00002          PROGRAM-ID.   RELATIVE-SEQUENTIAL-RETRIEVAL.

00003          ENVIRONMENT DIVISION.
00004          INPUT-OUTPUT SECTION.
00005          FILE-CONTROL.

00006              SELECT RELATIVE-FILE
00007                  ASSIGN TO RELFILE
00008                  ORGANIZATION IS RELATIVE
00009                  ACCESS IS SEQUENTIAL
00010                  RELATIVE KEY IS RELATIVE-RECORD-NUMBER
00011                  FILE STATUS IS RELATIVE-STATUS-CODE
00012                  .

00013          DATA DIVISION.
00014          FILE SECTION.

00015          FD  RELATIVE-FILE
00016              LABEL RECORDS ARE STANDARD
00017              RECORD CONTAINS 15 CHARACTERS
                   .
```

Fig. 8-4

```
00018          01  RELATIVE-RECORD.
00019              05  RELATIVE-PROGRAMMER-ID      PIC 9(5).
00020              05  RELATIVE-PROJECT-ID         PIC X(8).
00021              05  RELATIVE-TOTAL-HOURS        PIC 9(3)V9 COMP.

00022          WORKING-STORAGE SECTION.

00023          01  FILE-STATUS-CODES.
00024              05  RELATIVE-STATUS-CODE         PIC XX.
00025                  88  FILE-OPERATION-OK        VALUE "00".
00026                  88  FILE-OPERATION-FAILED    VALUE "01" THRU "99".
00027                  88  END-OF-FILE              VALUE "10".

00028          01  RELATIVE-KEY-AREA.
00029              05  RELATIVE-RECORD-NUMBER       PIC 9(5).

00030          PROCEDURE DIVISION.
00031
00032          000-EXECUTIVE-MODULE.
00033
00034              OPEN INPUT RELATIVE-FILE
00035              IF FILE-OPERATION-OK
00036                  PERFORM 020-GET-NEXT-RECORD
00037                  PERFORM 030-PRINT-A-RECORD
00038                      UNTIL END-OF-FILE
00039                  CLOSE RELATIVE-FILE
00040                  IF FILE-OPERATION-OK
00041                      DISPLAY "*** SEQUENTIAL RETRIEVAL COMPLETED ***"
00042                  ELSE
00043                      DISPLAY "RELATIVE FILE NOT CLOSED PROPERLY"
00044              ELSE
00045                  DISPLAY "UNABLE TO OPEN RELATIVE FILE -- ABORT"
00046                  .
00047              STOP RUN
00048                  .
00049
00050          020-GET-NEXT-RECORD.
00051
00052              READ RELATIVE-FILE
00053              IF FILE-OPERATION-FAILED
00054                  IF NOT END-OF-FILE
00055                      DISPLAY "ERROR READING RELATIVE FILE -- "
00056                              "STATUS CODE IS " RELATIVE-STATUS-CODE
00057                  .
00058
00059          030-PRINT-A-RECORD.
00060
00061              DISPLAY RELATIVE-RECORD " IS AT " RELATIVE-RECORD-NUMBER
00062              PERFORM 020-GET-NEXT-RECORD
00063                  .
```

Fig. 8-4 (*cont.*)

8.7 Random Retrieval of Relative Files (ANSI Standard)

The steps involved in randomly retrieving a logical record from a relative file are as follows:

(1) Apply the key transformation function (if any) to the key of the desired record to produce the relative record number of the slot at which the record is stored. The *same* function which was used to create the file must be used when processing the file.

(2) Move the relative record number to the RELATIVE KEY area.

(3) Execute a random READ statement. The operating system access method routine will automatically convert the RELATIVE KEY value to the disk address for the record slot and retrieve the contents. If the record is active, it is placed in the level-01 record area for the file; otherwise, the STATUS CODE is set to indicate a record-not-found condition, and INVALID KEY is activated.

ENVIRONMENT DIVISION Considerations

The SELECT statement for random retrieval is exactly the same as for random creation (see Section 8.5). ORGANIZATION IS RELATIVE, ACCESS IS RANDOM, and RELATIVE KEY are all required clauses for this purpose.

DATA DIVISION Considerations

The FD and level-01 record descriptions are the same as for random creation (see Section 8.5).

PROCEDURE DIVISION Considerations

The relevant PROCEDURE DIVISION statements for random retrieval are:

(1)　OPEN INPUT file-name

(2)　CLOSE file-name

(3)　READ file-name
　　　　[INTO data-area-to-receive-copy-of-record]
　　　　[INVALID KEY imperative-statement(s).]

The random READ statement attempts to access the logical record in the slot whose record number matches the current contents of the RELATIVE KEY area. If the slot is empty or if no such slot exists in the file, the STATUS CODE is set to indicate a record-not-found condition and INVALID KEY is activated. If the slot contains an active record, the record is placed in the level-01 record area for the file.

```
00001              IDENTIFICATION DIVISION.
00002              PROGRAM-ID.   RELATIVE-RANDOM-RETRIEVAL.

00003              ENVIRONMENT DIVISION.
00004              CONFIGURATION SECTION.
00005              SOURCE-COMPUTER.   IBM-3081.
00006              OBJECT-COMPUTER.   IBM-3081.
00007              INPUT-OUTPUT SECTION.
00008              FILE-CONTROL.

00009                  SELECT TRANSACTION-FILE
00010                      ASSIGN TO PROGIDS
00011                      ORGANIZATION IS SEQUENTIAL
00012                      ACCESS IS SEQUENTIAL
00013                      .
00014                  SELECT RELATIVE-FILE
00015                      ASSIGN TO RELFILE
00016                      ORGANIZATION IS RELATIVE
00017                      ACCESS IS RANDOM
00018                      RELATIVE KEY IS RELATIVE-RECORD-NUMBER
00019                      FILE STATUS IS RELATIVE-STATUS-CODE
00020                      .

00021              DATA DIVISION.
00022              FILE SECTION.

00023              FD  TRANSACTION-FILE
00024                  LABEL RECORDS ARE STANDARD
00025                  BLOCK CONTAINS 0 CHARACTERS
00026                  RECORD CONTAINS 80 CHARACTERS
00027                  .
00028              01  TRANSACTION-RECORD.
00029                  05  TRANS-PROGRAMMER-ID        PIC 9(5).
00030                  05  FILLER                     PIC X(75).
```

Fig. 8-5

```
00031          FD  RELATIVE-FILE
00032              LABEL RECORDS ARE STANDARD
00033              RECORD CONTAINS 15 CHARACTERS
                   .
00034          01  RELATIVE-RECORD.
00035              05  RELATIVE-PROGRAMMER-ID      PIC 9(5).
00036              05  RELATIVE-PROJECT-ID         PIC X(8).
00037              05  RELATIVE-TOTAL-HOURS        PIC 9(3)V9 COMP.

00038          WORKING-STORAGE SECTION.

00039          01  FLAGS-AND-SWITCHES.
00040              05  TRANS-END-OF-FILE-SW        PIC X(3).
00041                  88  MORE-TRANS-RECORDS      VALUE "NO".
00042                  88  NO-MORE-INPUT           VALUE "YES".

00043          01  FILE-STATUS-CODES.
00044              05  RELATIVE-STATUS-CODE        PIC XX.
00045                  88  FILE-OPERATION-OK       VALUE "00".
00046                  88  FILE-OPERATION-FAILED   VALUE "01" THRU "99".
00047                  88  RECORD-NOT-FOUND        VALUE "23".

00048          01  RELATIVE-KEY-AREA.
00049              05  RELATIVE-RECORD-NUMBER      PIC 9(5).

00050          PROCEDURE DIVISION.
00051
00052          000-EXECUTIVE-MODULE.
00053
00054              MOVE "NO" TO TRANS-END-OF-FILE-SW
00055              OPEN    INPUT   RELATIVE-FILE
00056                              TRANSACTION-FILE
00057              IF FILE-OPERATION-OK
00058                  PERFORM 010-GET-NEXT-TRANS
00059                  PERFORM 020-RETRIEVE-RELATIVE-RECORD
00060                      UNTIL NO-MORE-INPUT
00061                  CLOSE   RELATIVE-FILE
00062                          TRANSACTION-FILE
00063                  IF FILE-OPERATION-OK
00064                      DISPLAY "RANDOM RETRIEVAL COMPLETED"
00065                  ELSE
00066                      DISPLAY "RELATIVE FILE NOT PROPERLY CLOSED"
00067              ELSE
00068                  DISPLAY "UNABLE TO OPEN RELATIVE FILE -- ABORT"
00069                  CLOSE TRANSACTION-FILE
00070
                       .
00071              STOP RUN
00072                       .
00073
00074          010-GET-NEXT-TRANS.
00075
00076              READ TRANSACTION-FILE
00077                  AT END
00078                      MOVE "YES" TO TRANS-END-OF-FILE-SW
00079                  .
00080
00081          020-RETRIEVE-RELATIVE-RECORD.
00082
00083              MOVE TRANS-PROGRAMMER-ID    TO RELATIVE-RECORD-NUMBER
00084              READ RELATIVE-FILE
00085              IF FILE-OPERATION-OK
00086                  DISPLAY RELATIVE-PROGRAMMER-ID
00087                          SPACE
00088                          RELATIVE-TOTAL-HOURS
00089              ELSE
00090                  IF RECORD-NOT-FOUND
00091                      DISPLAY "RECORD NOT FOUND FOR " TRANSACTION-RECORD
00092                  ELSE
00093                      DISPLAY "VSAM ERROR " RELATIVE-STATUS-CODE
00094                              " FOR TRANSACTION " TRANSACTION-RECORD
00095                  .
00096              PERFORM 010-GET-NEXT-TRANS
00097                  .
```

Fig. 8-5 *(cont.)*

EXAMPLE 8.13   Figure 8-5 shows an IBM OS/VS COBOL program to randomly access the file created in Fig. 8-3. Again, since the key set runs 1, 2, 3, and is closely spaced, the key of each logical record serves as its relative record number. This eliminates the need for any type of key transformation function. In this case, the PROCEDURE DIVISION logic for manipulating a relative file is almost identical to that used for an indexed file:

(1)   The SELECT statement, FD, and level-01 record description (lines 14–19, 31–33, and 34–37) are the same as for random creation. The RELATIVE KEY and ACCESS IS RANDOM clauses are required for random retrieval.

(2)   The executive module (lines 52–72) is exactly the same as for random creation and sequential retrieval: The file is OPENed, the STATUS CODE checked, all transactions are processed, the file is CLOSEd, and the STATUS CODE checked again.

(3)   020-RETRIEVE-RELATIVE-RECORD (lines 81–97) illustrates random access of a logical record in a relative file. Since no key transformation function is required for this file, the programmer ID from the transaction record is copied unchanged (line 83) into the RELATIVE KEY area, where it will serve as the relative record number to access the record (the reader will recall that this exact technique was used when the file was created). The random READ in line 84 causes the operating system to calculate the physical disk address of a record slot using the record number in the RELATIVE KEY area. If such a slot does not exist or if it contains a dummy record (i.e., is empty), the STATUS CODE is set to indicate a record-not-found condition and INVALID KEY is activated. If the slot contains an active record, this record is placed in the level-01 record area for the file. In order to keep the example as simple as possible, the information from the record is just DISPLAYed.

(4)   Note how the STATUS CODE is used for extensive error checking in lines 89–94.

8.8   Dynamic Access of Relative Files (ANSI Standard)

Dynamic access of relative files is almost identical to dynamic access of indexed files. The only difference is in the use of the START statement:

```
START file-name
    [ KEY IS   relational-operator   relative-key-area ]
    [ INVALID KEY imperative-statements(s). ]
```

Valid relational operators are "EQUAL TO", " = ", "GREATER THAN", " > ", "NOT LESS THAN", and "NOT < ". Note that for relative files, the optional KEY IS . . . clause must name the RELATIVE KEY area for the file. The START operation is *always* done by matching a particular record slot to the condition specified in the START statement. The SELECT statement must, of course, specify ACCESS IS DYNAMIC and name a RELATIVE KEY area.

EXAMPLE 8.14   The following are valid START statements for the file in Fig. 8-5:

```
(1)   MOVE 83 TO RELATIVE-RECORD-NUMBER
      START RELATIVE-FILE
            INVALID KEY
                PERFORM RECORD-NOT-FOUND-ROUTINE
          .
```

This positions the CRP to record slot 83. If slot 83 does not exist or is empty, RECORD-NOT-FOUND-ROUTINE is executed and the CRP is undefined. If the KEY IS clause is omitted, the RELATIVE KEY area is assumed to contain the relative record number to which the CRP is to be set (note that typically the record number would be input, not hard-coded).

```
(2)   MOVE DESIRED-SLOT-NUMBER TO RELATIVE-RECORD-NUMBER
      START RELATIVE-FILE
            KEY IS NOT LESS THAN RELATIVE-RECORD-NUMBER
      IF RELATIVE-STATUS-CODE NOT EQUAL "00"
            PERFORM ERROR-ANALYSIS-ROUTINE
          .
```

This positions the CRP to the first slot containing an active record whose slot number is greater than or equal to DESIRED-SLOT-NUMBER. If no such slot exists, ERROR-ANALYSIS-ROUTINE is executed.

8.9   Random Updating of Relative Files (ANSI Standard)

Relative files, like indexed files, may be updated either sequentially or randomly. Since a sequential update would require that the transactions be sorted in relative-record-number order, sequential updates are not often used. The following procedures are used to randomly update a relative file:

(1)   Adding a new record during updating is the same as adding a record during random creation. It entails:

    (a)   Applying the key transformation function being used (if any) to the record's key field to obtain a relative record number.

    (b)   Moving the relative record number to the RELATIVE KEY area.

    (c)   Moving all necessary data into the level-01 record area for the file.

    (d)   Using the WRITE verb to add the record. If the record slot derived in (a) already holds an active record, the WRITE statement automatically recognizes this situation and raises INVALID KEY, with the STATUS CODE set to indicate a duplicate key error.

(2)   Deleting an existing record entails:

    (a)   Applying the key transformation function being used (if any) to the record's key field to obtain a relative record number.

    (b)   Moving the relative record number to the RELATIVE KEY area.

    (c)   Using the DELETE verb to logically remove the record from the file, thus freeing the record's slot for future use (logically deleted records, in effect, become empty record slots). If the record slot derived in (a) does not contain an active record, the DELETE statement automatically recognizes the record-not-found condition.

(3)   Changing an existing record entails:

    (a)   Applying the key transformation function being used (if any) to the record's key field to obtain a relative record number

    (b)   Moving the relative record number to the RELATIVE KEY area.

    (c)   Using a random READ to bring the record into the level-01 record area for the file. If the slot number in the RELATIVE KEY does not exist or is empty, the READ will set the STATUS CODE and INVALID KEY will be executed (if specified). The following steps would be carried out only if the READ is successful.

    (d)   Using transaction information to make any necessary changes to relative record fields.

    (e)   Using REWRITE to place the (modified) record contents back in the original record slot on the disk.

PROCEDURE DIVISION logic and syntax for randomly updating a relative file are quite similar to those for randomly updating an indexed file.

ENVIRONMENT DIVISION Considerations

The SELECT statement for a random update is exactly the same as for random creation and random retrieval (see Sections 8.5 and 8.7).

DATA DIVISION Considerations

The FD and level-01 record description for a random update are also the same as for random creation and random retrieval. A random update requires the definition of the RELATIVE KEY area (usually in WORKING-STORAGE).

PROCEDURE DIVISION Considerations

The logic for randomly updating relative files is discussed in Problems 8.40–8.42. The relevant PROCEDURE DIVISION statements are discussed below:

General File Operations:

(1) OPEN I–O file-name
     Use of the DELETE and REWRITE verbs requires that the file be OPENed I–O. This allows the file to be used for both input and output.

(2) CLOSE file-name

(3) IF status-code-area NOT EQUAL code-for-successful-completion
     The best way to detect errors following a relative file operation is to test the STATUS CODE.

Adding a New Logical Record

(4) WRITE record-name
         [FROM data-area]
         [INVALID KEY imperative-statement(s).]
     Execution of the WRITE statement causes the operating system access method routines to access the record slot associated with the relative record number whose value is currently in the RELATIVE KEY area. If this slot number exceeds the bounds of the file, enough empty slots are automatically added to bring the total up to the indicated number. If sufficient space cannot be obtained to create the required slots, the WRITE is aborted, with the appropriate STATUS CODE and INVALID KEY (if specified). If the slot being accessed already contains an active record, the WRITE is also aborted and the STATUS CODE and INVALID KEY indicate duplicate key. If the indicated slot is empty (i.e., was never used or the record in it was DELETEd), it is filled with the current contents of the level-01 record area for the file and the STATUS CODE is set to indicate successful completion of the WRITE.

Changing an Existing Logical Record

(5) READ file-name [RECORD]
         [INTO data-area]
         [INVALID KEY imperative-statement(s).]
     The random READ causes the current value of RELATIVE KEY to be used to calculate the physical disk address of a record slot. If the slot does not exist or if it is empty, the STATUS CODE is set for a record-not-found condition and the INVALID KEY routine (if specified) is executed. If an active record is in the slot, it is input into the level-01 record area.

(6) REWRITE record-name
         [FROM data-area]
         [INVALID KEY imperative-statement(s).]
     REWRITE causes the current value of RELATIVE KEY to be used to calculate the physical disk address of a record slot. If this slot does not exist or if it is empty, the STATUS CODE is set to indicate a record-not-found condition and INVALID KEY (if specified) is executed. If the slot contains an active record, this record is replaced by the current contents of the level-01 record area for the file.

Deleting an Existing Logical Record

(7)   <u>DELETE</u> file-name [<u>RECORD</u>]
      [<u>INVALID</u> KEY imperative-statement(s).]
      DELETE causes the current value of RELATIVE KEY to be used to calculate the physical
      disk address of a record slot. If this slot does not exist or if it is empty, the STATUS CODE
      is set to indicate a record-not-found condition and INVALID KEY (if specified) is
      executed. If the slot contains an active record, this active record is replaced with a dummy
      record, thereby marking the slot as empty. It can then be used to add a new record later
      on. Note that this is actually a form of logical deletion, with the dummy record serving as a
      flag to mark the slot as available.

EXAMPLE 8.15   Figure 8-6 shows an IBM OS/VS COBOL program which randomly updates the relative file
created in Fig. 8-3. No key transformation function is used for this file; the key field (programmer ID) runs 1, 2,
3, etc., and so can serve as the relative record number. Add, change, and delete transactions are input from a
sequentially organized transaction file, which has already been validated. The following comments apply:

(1)   The SELECT statement (lines 14–19) is exactly the same as that used to create and randomly retrieve
      the file. ORGANIZATION IS RELATIVE, ACCESS IS RANDOM, and RELATIVE KEY are all
      required clauses.

(2)   The FD and level-01 record description (lines 37–43) are the same as for Figs. 8-3–8-5.

(3)   The file must be OPENed I–O since DELETE and REWRITE will be used (lines 61–62).

(4)   The success of OPEN and CLOSE is checked by testing the STATUS CODE, and appropriate
      messages are DISPLAYed (lines 63–77). Since any VSAM operation in IBM OS/VS COBOL will
      never cause a program to ABEND, it is imperative that each operation be tested for successful
      completion. Consider what might happen if the OPEN failed but the program did not know it; *all* the
      transactions would appear to fail (because they would be applied to an unopened file), when the real
      problem is that the file is not open.

(5)   030-ADD-A-RECORD (lines 102–113) shows how to randomly add a record to a relative file. Line
      104 performs 090-BUILD-RELATIVE-RECORD (lines 134–139), which fills in all the fields of the
      level-01 record area for the relative file. Line 105 then moves the transaction programmer ID (the key
      field) to the RELATIVE KEY area (in a more complex situation, a key transformation function might
      have to be used here instead of a simple MOVE). The WRITE statement is then used to attempt to
      add the record to the file, and the STATUS CODE tested to check for errors (lines 106–113). The
      reader will recall that the WRITE statement may add dummy (empty) record slots to the file if the
      value in RELATIVE KEY exceeds the number of already existing record slots. If RELATIVE KEY
      points to an active record slot, the WRITE is aborted.

(6)   040-CHANGE-A-RECORD (lines 115–124) begins by moving the relative record number (which for
      this file is the programmer ID key field) to the RELATIVE KEY area and then using a READ to
      attempt to input the current record. If the record slot identified by RELATIVE KEY has an active
      record, it is placed into the level-01 record area, where it can be updated (line 120). After the record
      is modified, REWRITE is used to return it to its original record slot (line 121). Note that the value in
      RELATIVE KEY is the same for the execution of both the READ and the REWRITE.

(7)   080-DELETE-A-RECORD (lines 126–132) moves the transaction key value to the RELATIVE KEY
      area (line 128) and then executes a DELETE statement (line 129). If the record slot identified by
      RELATIVE KEY holds an active record, this record is replaced by a special code indicating a dummy
      record (in effect, logically deleting the original record and making the slot available for future
      additions to the file). Otherwise, the STATUS CODE is set to indicate a record-not-found condition,
      and INVALID KEY (if specified) is executed. In Fig. 8-6, errors are checked by testing the STATUS
      CODE rather than using INVALID KEY.

```
00001              IDENTIFICATION DIVISION.
00002              PROGRAM-ID.  RELATIVE-FILE-UPDATE.

00003              ENVIRONMENT DIVISION.
00004              CONFIGURATION SECTION.
00005              SOURCE-COMPUTER.   IBM-3081.
00006              OBJECT-COMPUTER.   IBM-3081.
00007              INPUT-OUTPUT SECTION.
00008              FILE-CONTROL.

00009                  SELECT TRANSACTION-FILE
00010                      ASSIGN TO CHANGES
00011                      ORGANIZATION IS SEQUENTIAL
00012                      ACCESS IS SEQUENTIAL
00013                      .
00014                  SELECT RELATIVE-FILE
00015                      ASSIGN TO RELFILE
00016                      ORGANIZATION IS RELATIVE
00017                      ACCESS IS RANDOM
00018                      RELATIVE KEY IS RELATIVE-RECORD-NUMBER
00019                      FILE STATUS IS RELATIVE-STATUS-CODE
00020                      .

00021              DATA DIVISION.
00022              FILE SECTION.

00023              FD  TRANSACTION-FILE
00024                  LABEL RECORDS ARE STANDARD
00025                  BLOCK CONTAINS 0 CHARACTERS
00026                  RECORD CONTAINS 80 CHARACTERS
00027                  .
00028              01  TRANSACTION-RECORD.
00029                  05  TRANS-CODE                PIC X.
00030                      88  ADD-NEW-RECORD          VALUE "A".
00031                      88  CHANGE-EXISTING-RECORD  VALUE "C".
00032                      88  DELETE-EXISTING-RECORD  VALUE "D".
00033                  05  TRANS-PROGRAMMER-ID       PIC 9(5).
00034                  05  TRANS-PROJECT-ID          PIC X(8).
00035                  05  TRANS-TOTAL-HOURS         PIC 9(3)V9.
00036                  05  FILLER                    PIC X(62).

00037              FD  RELATIVE-FILE
00038                  LABEL RECORDS ARE STANDARD
00039                  RECORD CONTAINS 15 CHARACTERS
                       .
00040              01  RELATIVE-RECORD.
00041                  05  RELATIVE-PROGRAMMER-ID    PIC 9(5).
00042                  05  RELATIVE-PROJECT-ID       PIC X(8).
00043                  05  RELATIVE-TOTAL-HOURS      PIC 9(3)V9 COMP.

00044              WORKING-STORAGE SECTION.

00045              01  FLAGS-AND-SWITCHES.
00046                  05  TRANS-END-OF-FILE-SW      PIC X(3).
00047                      88  MORE-TRANS-RECORDS      VALUE "NO".
00048                      88  NO-MORE-INPUT           VALUE "YES".

00049              01  FILE-STATUS-CODES.
00050                  05  RELATIVE-STATUS-CODE       PIC XX.
00051                      88  VSAM-OPERATION-OK       VALUE "00".
00052                      88  VSAM-OPERATION-FAILED   VALUE "01" THRU "99".
00053                      88  RECORD-NOT-FOUND        VALUE "23".
00054                      88  DUPLICATE-KEY           VALUE "22".

00055              01  RELATIVE-KEY-AREA.
00056                  05  RELATIVE-RECORD-NUMBER    PIC 9(5).

00057              PROCEDURE DIVISION.
00058
00059              000-EXECUTIVE-MODULE.
00060
00061                  OPEN    INPUT   TRANSACTION-FILE
00062                          I-O     RELATIVE-FILE
00063                  IF VSAM-OPERATION-OK
00064                      MOVE "NO" TO TRANS-END-OF-FILE-SW
```

Fig. 8-6

```
00065                               PERFORM 010-GET-TRANSACTION-RECORD
00066                               PERFORM 020-UPDATE-RELATIVE-FILE
00067                                   UNTIL NO-MORE-INPUT
00068                               CLOSE   TRANSACTION-FILE
00069                                       RELATIVE-FILE
00070                               IF VSAM-OPERATION-OK
00071                                   DISPLAY "RELATIVE FILE UPDATE COMPLETED"
00072                               ELSE
00073                                   DISPLAY "RELATIVE FILE NOT PROPERLY CLOSED"
00074                           ELSE
00075                               DISPLAY "UNABLE TO OPEN RELATIVE FILE -- ABORT"
00076                               CLOSE TRANSACTION-FILE
00077                           .
00078                       STOP RUN
00079                       .
00080
00081               010-GET-TRANSACTION-RECORD.
00082
00083                   READ TRANSACTION-FILE
00084                       AT END
00085                           MOVE "YES" TO TRANS-END-OF-FILE-SW
00086                   .
00087
00088               020-UPDATE-RELATIVE-FILE.
00089
00090                   IF ADD-NEW-RECORD
00091                       PERFORM 030-ADD-A-RECORD
00092                   ELSE IF CHANGE-EXISTING-RECORD
00093                       PERFORM 040-CHANGE-A-RECORD
00094                   ELSE IF DELETE-EXISTING-RECORD
00095                       PERFORM 080-DELETE-A-RECORD
00096                   ELSE
00097                       DISPLAY "INVALID TRANS CODE: " TRANSACTION-RECORD
00098                   .
00099                   PERFORM 010-GET-TRANSACTION-RECORD
00100                   .
00101
00102               030-ADD-A-RECORD.
00103
00104                   PERFORM 090-BUILD-RELATIVE-RECORD
00105                   MOVE TRANS-PROGRAMMER-ID TO RELATIVE-RECORD-NUMBER
00106                   WRITE RELATIVE-RECORD
00107                   IF VSAM-OPERATION-FAILED
00108                       IF DUPLICATE-KEY
00109                           DISPLAY "DUPLICATE KEY FOR " RELATIVE-PROGRAMMER-ID
00110                       ELSE
00111                           DISPLAY "VSAM ERROR NUMBER " RELATIVE-STATUS-CODE
00112                           " FOR " RELATIVE-PROGRAMMER-ID
00113                   .
00114
00115               040-CHANGE-A-RECORD.
00116
00117                   MOVE TRANS-PROGRAMMER-ID TO RELATIVE-RECORD-NUMBER
00118                   READ RELATIVE-FILE
00119                   IF VSAM-OPERATION-OK
00120                       ADD TRANS-TOTAL-HOURS TO RELATIVE-TOTAL-HOURS
00121                       REWRITE RELATIVE-RECORD
00122                   ELSE
00123                       DISPLAY TRANS-PROGRAMMER-ID " NOT FOUND FOR CHANGE"
00124                   .
00125
00126               080-DELETE-A-RECORD.
00127
00128                   MOVE TRANS-PROGRAMMER-ID TO RELATIVE-RECORD-NUMBER
00129                   DELETE RELATIVE-FILE
00130                   IF VSAM-OPERATION-FAILED
00131                       DISPLAY TRANS-PROGRAMMER-ID " NOT FOUND FOR DELETE"
00132                   .
00133
00134               090-BUILD-RELATIVE-RECORD.
00135
00136                   MOVE TRANS-PROGRAMMER-ID    TO RELATIVE-PROGRAMMER-ID
00137                   MOVE TRANS-PROJECT-ID       TO RELATIVE-PROJECT-ID
00138                   MOVE TRANS-TOTAL-HOURS      TO RELATIVE-TOTAL-HOURS
00139                   .
```

Fig. 8-6 *(cont.)*

Review Questions

8.1   Why should relative file organization be considered as an alternative to indexed organization?

8.2   Why is indexed organization usually used instead of relative organization?

8.3   Explain the concept of relative record number.

8.4   Explain how sequential processing works for relative files.

8.5   Explain how random processing works for relative files.

8.6   Discuss the similarities between relative file processing and indexed file processing.

8.7   Compare the manner in which the operating system access method routines locate a record in a relative file with the way in which records are located in an indexed file. Which is likely to be faster?

8.8   What is the major obstacle to using relative organization?

8.9   What is meant by key set?

8.10   Give restrictions on a file's key set which make it easy to use relative organization.

8.11   Why are synonyms such a problem when a key transformation function must be used with a relative file?

8.12   If a key transformation function which does not produce synonyms cannot be found, what choice is usually made?

8.13   Why are collision-handling routines for relative files usually not developed?

8.14   What is the best key transformation function for a relative file? How is the use of such an approach made possible?

8.15   Some implementations allow the use of variable-length records for relative files. Why is this illusory?

8.16   Discuss the use of the IDCAMS utility for IBM VSAM relative files.

8.17   What are the major parameters for the IDCAMS DEFINE CLUSTER command for a relative file?

8.18   Discuss the use of IDCAMS to delete and print a copy of an IBM VSAM relative file.

8.19   Why are relative files usually created randomly rather than sequentially?

8.20   Discuss the syntax of the ANSI COBOL SELECT statement for relative file processing.

8.21   Discuss the logic for randomly creating a relative file.

8.22   Discuss the logic for sequential retrieval of a relative file.

8.23   Discuss how to use the START verb with a relative file.

8.24   Discuss the logic for random retrieval of a relative file.

8.25   Why are relative files usually not updated sequentially?

8.26   Discuss the logic for the following random update operations on a relative file: (1) adding a record, (2) changing a record, and (3) deleting a record.

Solved Problems

8.27 Show the effect of a random WRITE with RELATIVE KEY set to 8, adding record C to the following file:

Relative Record Number	Slot Contents
1	Empty
2	A
3	Empty
4	B

A random WRITE with RELATIVE KEY beyond the current end of the file automatically causes the operating system access method routine to add enough dummy records to bring the number of slots up to the value in the RELATIVE KEY. In this case, there are 4 slots in the file when the WRITE is executed. Since the RELATIVE KEY is 8, dummy records must be written for slots 5, 6, and 7 before the new record can be added in slot 8:

Relative Record Number	Slot Contents
1	Empty
2	A
3	Empty
4	B
5	Empty
6	Empty
7	Empty
8	C

8.28 Show the *cumulative effects* of the following COBOL statements when applied to the relative file below. Also indicate the record accessed and the new value of the current record pointer. Assume ACCESS IS DYNAMIC. The notation used to describe the file is "relative-record-number = slot-contents", where "*" signifies a dummy record (i.e., empty slot) and "^" is used to mark a modified record. Originally the file is $1 = *, 2 = a, 3 = *, 4 = b$.

Statement	Accesses	New CRP	New File Contents
OPEN I–O	—	RR# = 1	$1 = *, 2 = a, 3 = *, 4 = b$
READ (RR# = 2)			
READ NEXT			
READ NEXT			
START (RR# = 2)			
READ NEXT			
WRITE c (RR# = 3)			
WRITE d (RR# = 7)			
REWRITE a^ (RR# = 2)			
READ NEXT			
WRITE e (RR# = 4)			
DELETE (RR# = 4)			
WRITE e (RR# = 4)			
DELETE (RR# = 1)			
READ (RR# = 1)			
REWRITE f^ (RR# = 1)			
START (RR# = 1)			
WRITE g (RR# = 9)			
WRITE h (RR# = 5)			

Statement	Accesses	New CRP	New File Contents
OPEN I–O	—	RR# = 1	1 = *, 2 = a, 3 = *, 4 = b
READ (RR# = 2)	a	RR# = 3	Unchanged
READ NEXT	b	RR# = ?	Unchanged
READ NEXT	—	RR# = ?	Unchanged; AT END is activated
START (RR# = 2)	—	RR# = 2	Unchanged
READ NEXT	a	RR# = 3	Unchanged
WRITE c (RR# = 3)	c	RR# = 3	1 = *, 2 = a, 3 = c, 4 = b
WRITE d (RR# = 7)	d	RR# = 3	1 = *, 2 = a, 3 = c, 4 = b, 5 = *, 6 = *, 7 = d
REWRITE a^ (RR# = 2)	a^	RR# = 3	1 = *, 2 = a^, 3 = c, 4 = b, 5 = *, 6 = *, 7 = d
READ NEXT	c	RR# = 4	Unchanged
WRITE e (RR# = 4)	—	RR# = 4	Unchanged; WRITE fails since 4 is not empty.
DELETE (RR# = 4)	b	RR# = 4	1 = *, 2 = a^, 3 = c, 4 = *, 5 = *, 6 = *, 7 = d
WRITE e (RR# = 4)	e	RR# = 4	1 = *, 2 = a^, 3 = c, 4 = e, 5 = *, 6 = *, 7 = d
DELETE (RR# = 1)	—	RR# = 4	Unchanged; DELETE fails since 1 is empty.
READ (RR# = 1)	—	RR# = ?	Unchanged; READ fails since 1 is empty.
REWRITE f^ (RR# = 1)	—	RR# = ?	Unchanged; REWRITE fails since 1 is empty.
START (RR# = 1)	—	RR# = ?	Unchanged; START fails since 1 is empty
WRITE g (RR# = 9)	g	RR# = ?	1 = *, 2 = a^, 3 = c, 4 = e, 5 = *, 6 = *, 7 = d, 8 = *, 9 = g
WRITE h (RR# = 5)	h	RR# = ?	1 = *, 2 = a^, 3 = c, 4 = e, 5 = h, 6 = *, 7 = d, 8 = *, 9 = g

8.29 It is proposed to implement a file of 2000 employee records using employee last name as the key field. Should relative organization be used?

Since the keys are nonnumeric, a key transformation function would have to be used to generate a relative record number from a last name. Since it is likely that any such key transformation function will produce synonyms, it is probably best to implement this file as an indexed file rather than spend time designing and coding collision-handling procedures.

8.30 Suppose the employee file in Problem 8.29 were to use social security number (instead of name) as the key field.

Now the keys are numeric, but a 9-digit social security number is used for only 2000 records. Since the social security numbers in the key set are likely to be scattered randomly throughout the 9-digit range, it will again be difficult to find a key transformation function which will map social security numbers into relative record numbers without producing synonyms. It is probably better to use indexed organization than to create the necessary collision-handling procedures.

8.31   Suppose the employee file in Problem 8.29 were to use employee badge number as the key field. When the company first started, badge numbers were assigned by personnel, beginning with badge number 1000. Since that time, badge numbers have been reassigned when possible and new badge numbers created only when necessary. As a result, the badge numbers for the 2000 employees range from 1000 to 3208.

This file could be implemented with relative organization using the following key transformation function:

$$\text{relative-record-number} = \text{badge-number} - 1000 + 1$$

This function produces relative record numbers in the range 1 to 2209 for 2000 employees, thus wasting 209 slots (only 10 percent). Since it would be wise to allocate some extra space for new employees anyway, this is a practical solution.

8.32   Why does the use of variable-length records *not* save space for relative files?

In order to calculate the physical disk address of a record slot from its slot number, the operating system must know that each slot in the file is exactly the same length. Hence variable-length records, even if permitted, must still be packaged into fixed-length slots. This makes them equivalent to fixed-length records.

8.33   How might an operating system calculate a disk address from a relative record number?

Since the file consists of fixed-length slots, the system can figure exactly how many slots fit on a track. It can then divide the number of slots per track into the relative record number. The quotient of this division gives the relative track number (starting from 0) on which the record slot resides. The remainder of this division gives the number of the slot (starting from 0) on the indicated track. The operating system can use the information from the file label (either in the disk's volume table of contents or, in the case of VSAM, in the VSAM catalog entry for the file) to convert the relative track number to an actual cylinder and head number (CCHH). See Problem 6.30 for a discussion of how to convert a relative track number to a cylinder and head number. Since the slot number on the track is also known, it is then simple to produce a full disk address of the form CCHHR (cylinder number, head number, and record number).

8.34   IBM offers two implementations of relative file organization: an older non-VSAM relative and the newer VSAM relative. Discuss the differences in COBOL syntax between non-VSAM relative and VSAM relative.

The differences between IBM VSAM relative files and non-VSAM relative files are as follows:

ENVIRONMENT DIVISION

(1)   The SELECT statement for non-VSAM relative has the form:

```
SELECT file-name
     ASSIGN TO DA-R-externalname
     ACCESS IS [ SEQUENTIAL | RANDOM ]
     NOMINAL KEY IS area-to-hold-relative-record-#
```

"DA-R" in the ASSIGN TO clause identifies the file organization as non-VSAM relative. The ORGANIZATION IS RELATIVE clause is *not allowed* for non-VSAM relative. ACCESS can be either SEQUENTIAL or RANDOM, but DYNAMIC access is *not allowed*. There is *no RELATIVE KEY* for non-VSAM relative. In its place, the SELECT statement must name a NOMINAL KEY field, which plays the same role as the RELATIVE KEY; i.e., it holds the relative record number of the slot to be accessed. The NOMINAL KEY is usually defined in WORKING-STORAGE and must be defined as PIC S9(8) COMP.

(2)   Non-VSAM relative files *must* consist of fixed-length unblocked records.

(3)   The first byte of a non-VSAM logical record is used as a delete code byte. Records are deleted from a non-VSAM relative file by placing HIGH-VALUES in the first byte of the record. The DELETE verb *cannot be used* with non-VSAM relative files. Deleted records are automatically skipped by the operating system access method routines during sequential retrieval. However, deleted records are retrieved during random processing. Hence when ACCESS IS RANDOM, the user must test the first byte of a logical record before allowing any processing on that record.

(4)   Non-VSAM relative files *must* be created sequentially. The NOMINAL KEY must be used to indicate the slot in which each record is to be placed, with the system automatically creating any necessary dummy records between successive values of the NOMINAL KEY. This is quite different from VSAM relative sequential creation, in which the system always places the records in ascending record slots (i.e., 1, 2, 3, etc.). With non-VSAM relative sequential creation, the records must still be written in ascending sequence by NOMINAL KEY.

(5)   Random creation is not allowed for non-VSAM relative files.

(6)   Sequential retrieval is exactly the same for both VSAM and non-VSAM relative files. The system automatically skips over any dummy records in the file.

(7)   Random retrieval is the same, except that NOMINAL KEY is used instead of RELATIVE KEY and the COBOL program must test the first byte of each record accessed to determine whether it contains HIGH-VALUES and should, therefore, be ignored.

(8)   Random deletion of logical records is done by REWRITEing the record with HIGH-VALUES in the first byte. The DELETE verb is not used.

(9)   Random additions are done by REWRITEing a record to the slot indicated by the NOMINAL KEY. The *WRITE verb is not allowed for non-VSAM relative files accessed randomly*. Records are added by replacing empty record slots, using the REWRITE verb. The COBOL program should input the contents of the slot and test for an active record before executing REWRITE; otherwise, a new record could be placed over the top of an already-existing record by mistake.

(10)   Random changes to existing records are done by first READing the desired record (using NOMINAL KEY to point to the appropriate slot), then making the necessary changes to record fields, and then REWRITEing the record. It is also possible to completely replace an existing record without reading it by setting the NOMINAL KEY and then doing a REWRITE without a preceding READ.

(11)   STATUS CODE is not available with non-VSAM relative files. The INVALID KEY clause is activated for a WRITE during sequential creation if space is not available to write the record. During random processing, INVALID KEY is activated if the contents of the NOMINAL KEY are beyond the boundaries of the file.

8.35   Give the logic needed to place a record into an ANSI (e.g., VSAM) relative file during random creation. Transaction information is available in TRANS-RECORD.

```
OPEN OUTPUT SAMPLE-RELATIVE-FILE ...

PERFORM MOVE-TRANS-INFO-TO-RECORD-AREA
PERFORM HASH-TRANS-KEY-TO-RELATIVE-KEY
WRITE RELATIVE-RECORD
IF RELATIVE-STATUS-CODE NOT EQUAL CODE-FOR-SUCCESS
    DISPLAY "DUPLICATE KEY ERROR"
```

8.36   Show how to sequentially retrieve a logical record from an ANSI (e.g., VSAM) relative file.

```
OPEN INPUT SAMPLE-RELATIVE-FILE ...

READ SAMPLE-RELATIVE-FILE
    AT END
        MOVE "YES" TO END-OF-FILE-SW
```

8.37   Show how to randomly retrieve a logical record from an ANSI (e.g., VSAM) relative file.

```
OPEN INPUT SAMPLE-RELATIVE-FILE ...

PERFORM HASH-TRANS-KEY-TO-RELATIVE-KEY
READ SAMPLE-RELATIVE-FILE
IF RELATIVE-STATUS-CODE NOT EQUAL CODE-FOR-SUCCESS
    DISPLAY "RECORD NOT FOUND ERROR"
.
```

8.38   Show how to position the file in Problem 8.36 to TRANS-STARTING-SLOT for subsequent sequential retrieval.

```
OPEN INPUT SAMPLE-RELATIVE-FILE

MOVE TRANS-STARTING-SLOT TO RELATIVE-KEY-FIELD
START SAMPLE-RELATIVE-FILE
IF RELATIVE-STATUS-CODE NOT EQUAL CODE-FOR-SUCCESS
    DISPLAY "RECORD NOT FOUND ERROR"
.
```

8.39   Modify Problem 8.38 to position the file to the first slot greater than or equal to TRANS-STARTING-SLOT.

```
OPEN INPUT SAMPLE-RELATIVE-FILE

MOVE TRANS-STARTING-SLOT TO RELATIVE-KEY-FIELD
START SAMPLE-RELATIVE-FILE
    KEY IS NOT LESS THAN RELATIVE-KEY-FIELD
    INVALID KEY
        DISPLAY "RECORD NOT FOUND FOR START"
.
```

8.40   Show how to add a logical record to an ANSI (e.g., VSAM) relative file during a random update.

The logic is exactly the same as that used during random file creation. See Problem 8.35.

8.41   Show how to randomly delete a record from an ANSI relative file.

```
OPEN I-O SAMPLE-RELATIVE-FILE ...

PERFORM HASH-TRANS-KEY-TO-RELATIVE-KEY
DELETE SAMPLE-RELATIVE-FILE
IF RELATIVE-STATUS-CODE NOT EQUAL CODE-FOR-SUCCESS
    DISPLAY "RECORD NOT FOUND ERROR"
.
```

8.42 Show how to randomly change a record in an ANSI relative file.

```
OPEN I-O SAMPLE-RELATIVE-FILE ...

PERFORM HASH-TRANS-KEY-TO-RELATIVE-KEY
READ SAMPLE-RELATIVE-FILE
IF RELATIVE-STATUS-CODE NOT EQUAL CODE-FOR-SUCCESS
    DISPLAY "RECORD NOT FOUND ERROR"
ELSE
    PERFORM MAKE-CHANGES-WITH-TRANS-INFO
    REWRITE RELATIVE-RECORD
    IF RELATIVE-STATUS-CODE NOT EQUAL CODE-FOR-SUCCESS
        PERFORM UNEXPECTED-ERROR-ANALYSIS
```

Chapter 9

The COPY Statement and
the Source Program Library

The ANSI COBOL COPY facility has been designed to save time when coding standard sequences of statements such as FDs and level-01 record descriptions. In a typical business computer application, *many* COBOL programs will need to access the *same* file(s). COBOL has been designed to allow prewritten sequences of COBOL statements (such as FDs and record descriptions) to be permanently stored on a disk file called a *source program library*. The COPY verb can then be used to literally *copy* these prewritten statements from the source program library into a particular COBOL source program.

9.1 Types of Libraries and Their Uses

A *library* is a disk file which is designed to hold many subfiles (usually called *members*) in such a way that each member can be quickly located and retrieved individually. This is accomplished by having the library file consist of two parts: (1) a *directory*, which is a sorted list of the names of all members in the library, together with their locations on the disk, and (2) the members themselves. Each member can be retrieved individually and processed as a separate file. The purpose of the library is to allow many similar files (members) to be collected together in such a way that rapid retrieval of each individual file (member) is possible. Libraries are particularly useful for storing programs or parts of programs.

EXAMPLE 9.1 In IBM OS/VS systems, libraries are also called *partitioned data sets* (*PDS*). The structure of an IBM PDS is shown in Fig. 9-1. Observe that while the names of members in the directory are kept sorted for efficient directory searching, the members themselves can be in any order within their portion of the library. The operating system can quickly retrieve individual members by looking them up in the directory (which gives the physical disk address of each member).

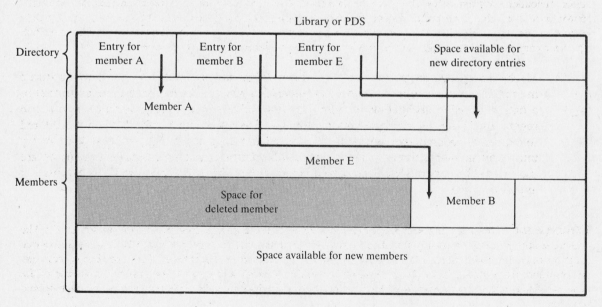

Fig. 9-1

Although implementations vary, most systems supply some sort of library facility. Consult an instructor or vendor manual for information on libraries (or their equivalent) for your system. Libraries, or their equivalent, are extremely useful for storing the following kinds of information:

(1) Source program libraries store programs or parts of programs in their original source language form (e.g., COBOL). Each SELECT statement, FD, record description, paragraph, or routine is typically stored as a separate member.

EXAMPLE 9.2   A COBOL COPY library is an example of a source program library. Individual members might consist of pieces of COBOL source programs such as (1) SELECT statements for files which must be accessed by more than one program, (2) FDs for such files, (3) level-01 record descriptions for such files, and (4) PROCEDURE DIVISION paragraphs or isolated routines for tasks which must be carried out by more than one program. Programs which require such ENVIRONMENT or DATA DIVISION entries need not include the statements in the source program, for the programs can COPY the desired members from the source program library. Likewise, a programmer who must carry out a task which has already been coded and stored in the source program library need not *re*write the required statements, for he or she can simply COPY the appropriate member(s) from the source program library.

(2) *Object program libraries* (also known as *subroutine libraries*) store programs or subroutines in machine language form. Typically, each subroutine is stored as a separate member. Programs known as *linkage editors* or *linking loaders* can combine machine language subroutines from object program libraries with the programs which call them. The resulting machine language programs are then ready for execution. In an IBM environment, programs which have been linked and are ready for execution are called *load modules*. See Chapter 10 for a more extensive discussion of subroutines, linking, and object program libraries.

EXAMPLE 9.3   The IBM OS/VS COBOL compiler deliberately does not produce a full translation of a typical COBOL source program. Rather, it is designed to translate certain COBOL statements into *calls* on prewritten subroutines. These prewritten subroutines, however, are not inserted into the object program by the compiler. The object program produced by the COBOL compiler is thus *not executable* (if execution is attempted, the program "blows up" when it reaches the point of actually calling one of the subroutines which is not yet available).

Object programs produced by IBM OS/VS COBOL compilers must be processed by either the linkage editor or loader program before they can be executed. The linkage editor (or loader) obtains the "missing" subroutines from the appropriate object program (subroutine) library and inserts them into the machine language code. It is only after this *linking* process is completed that the program can be successfully executed. The necessary machine language subroutines are, of course, stored in a *COBOL subroutine library*.

(3) Machine language programs which have been linked and are ready for execution are stored in *load libraries* (sometimes known as *production libraries*). Load libraries are important to a data processing installation because they hold all the executable programs which are in regular use. Each such program is typically stored as a separate member. When it is desired to execute a program, the operating system inputs a copy of the code from the load library into main memory, where it is executed. Job control/command language statements are used to tell the operating system *which* member(s) of the load library are to be executed at any given time.

EXAMPLE 9.4   The following four steps are required to make a change to a production program: (1) The original source program (probably stored in a source program library) must be modified, (2) the modified source program must be recompiled, (3) the resulting object program must be relinked (i.e., combined with any missing subroutines stored in an object program subroutine library), and then (4) the production version of the program stored in the appropriate load library must be replaced with the final (linked) version of the modified program.

Observe that step (1) involves a maintenance programmer's time, while steps (2) through (4) involve not only personnel but also computer runs. Anything which streamlines the maintenance process will clearly pay dividends in terms of lower costs. Intelligent use of libraries is one way to cut maintenance costs.

The exact mechanisms for creating libraries and creating, changing, and deleting individual members vary from system to system and are beyond the scope of this Outline. Consult an instructor or vendor manual for the job control/command language statements and/or utility programs needed to work with program libraries on your system. Mastery of these topics will allow the student to take full advantage of the important COBOL COPY facility.

9.2 Accessing Source Program Libraries with the COBOL COPY Verb

Once a source program library has been created and meaningful sequences of COBOL statements stored as separate members, each COBOL programmer can and should take advantage of the code in the library. The COPY statement directs the COBOL compiler to retrieve a designated member from a source program library and insert the statements making up the member into the COBOL program at the point where the COPY verb appears. The statements thus "copied" into the COBOL program are then treated just as if the programmer had actually written them out.

The syntax for the ANSI COBOL COPY statement is:

```
COPY member-name
     [ IN library-name ]
     [ SUPPRESS ]
     [ REPLACING   string-1 BY string-2
                  [ string-3 BY string-4 ] ...]
```

The COPY statement must be preceded by a blank space and *must end with a period followed by a space*.

"Member-name" is the name of the library member to be copied into the COBOL source program. It must follow the rules for a PROGRAM-ID (see *Schaum's Outline of Programming with Structured COBOL*, McGraw-Hill, 1984). In IBM OS/VS COBOL, the member name should be further restricted so that it conforms to the rules for naming members of partitioned data sets (1–8 characters consisting of letters, digits, $, #, or @, the first of which is a letter, $, #, or @). The entire member is copied from the disk library and inserted into the COBOL program at the point where the COPY statement appears. The COPY statement is logically replaced with the member from the library.

If more than one source program library is accessible to the COBOL compiler, the IN . . . clause must be used to name the particular library from which this COPY statement is to obtain the desired member. Usually the library(s) available to the compiler are defined via job control/command language statements when the compiler is executed. Consult an instructor and/or vendor manual for information on how to specify accessible source program libraries to the COBOL compiler on your system. Normally the IN clause is not needed, since the compiler automatically searches the default library specified for the compiler.

If the SUPPRESS option is *not* specified, the compiler will print the statements copied from the library on the source listing. Such statements are identified on the listing with a "C". The COPY statement itself is *always* printed on the listing, although it is not itself translated into the object program (it is the statements which the COPY statement brings in from the library which are actually translated into the object program).

If the SUPPRESS option is specified, then only the COPY statement itself appears on the listing. The statements which are copied from the library, although they are actually part of both the source and object programs, are *not* printed on the source listing. Use of SUPPRESS is *not recommended*, since the printed version of the source program and the actual source program are no longer identical when SUPPRESS is used.

The REPLACING option allows the version of the member placed into the COBOL program to differ from the permanent version of the member as stored in the library. This transformation is effected by *replacing* one or more strings as they appear in the library version with strings specified in the REPLACING clause. Use of the REPLACING option is *not recommended*, since it defeats the purpose of using a COPY library in the first place.

"String-1" and "string-2" can be either (1) any data name from the DATA DIVISION, (2) any valid literal (or figurative constant), (3) any single reserved word from the COBOL language, or (4) pseudo-text, which is any string of characters enclosed in double equal signs, as in "= = string = =".

EXAMPLE 9.5 The following are valid COPY statements:

(1) COPY ARFILEFD.
     This copies the member named "ARFILEFD" from the default source program library into the COBOL program in which the COPY statement appears. The period following the member name is *required* to end the COPY statement. The statements copied from member ARFILEFD will be printed on the source listing (marked with a "C").

(2) COPY ARFILEFD
        IN MYOWNLIB
        SUPPRESS.
     This copies the member named ARFILEFD from the source program library named "MYOWNLIB". MYOWNLIB must be properly defined via job control/command language statements when the compiler is executed. Since SUPPRESS is coded, the statements copied from ARFILEFD will *not* be printed on the listing (although they are actually part of the source program and will, of course, be translated into the object program).

EXAMPLE 9.6 Suppose the member ARRECORD in the source program library available to the compiler consists of the following statements:

```
01    AR-CUSTOMER-RECORD.
    05    AR-CUSTOMER-ID      PIC X(5).
    05    AR-CUSTOMER-NAME    PIC X(30).
    05    AR-CUSTOMER-BAL     PIC S9(5)V99.
```

If the following COPY statement is used in a program:

```
COPY ARRECORD
    REPLACING    AR-CUSTOMER-ID      BY AR-CUST-NUMBER
                 AR-CUSTOMER-BAL     BY AR-AMOUNT-OWED
        .
```

then the sequence of statements inserted into the program as a result of the COPY statement will be:

```
01    AR-CUSTOMER-RECORD.
    05    AR-CUST-NUMBER      PIC X(5).
    05    AR-CUSTOMER-NAME    PIC X(30).
    05    AR-AMOUNT-OWED      PIC S9(5)V99.
```

Each occurrence of the data name "AR-CUSTOMER-ID" from the library member is replaced by the data name "AR-CUST-NUMBER" to produce the version of the statements for the COBOL program. Similarly, each occurrence of "AR-CUSTOMER-BAL" which appears in the member will be replaced by "AR-AMOUNT-OWED" to produce the version of the statements in the source program. The member in the library is unchanged by the REPLACING operation; only the copy of the statements brought into the source program is changed. It is the programmer's responsibility to ensure that the final version of the source program is syntactically correct.

EXAMPLE 9.7 Suppose the library member ARRECORD is as in Example 9.6 above. The COPY statement:

```
COPY ARRECORD
     SUPPRESS
     REPLACING ==AR-CUSTOMER== BY ==CUST-MAST==
.
```

will insert the following statements into the source program:

```
01   CUST-MAST-RECORD.
     05   CUST-MAST-ID      PIC X(5).
     05   CUST-MAST-NAME    PIC X(30).
     05   CUST-MAST-BAL     PIC S9(5)V99.
```

Since the SUPPRESS option is specified, these statements will *not* be printed on the source listing (hence the exact effects of the REPLACING option will not be visible to the programmer). *Never do this*, as it needlessly confuses debugging and maintenance.

The pseudo-text specifies that all occurrences of the string "AR-CUSTOMER" in the library member should be replaced by the string "CUST-MAST" to produce the version of the statements brought into the COBOL program. The library member itself remains unchanged.

EXAMPLE 9.8 Suppose the library member ARRECORD is as in Example 9.6 above. The COPY statement:

```
COPY ARRECORD
     IN MYOWNLIB
     REPLACING PIC        BY PICTURE
               ==AR-==    BY ====
.
```

will insert the following statements into the source program:

```
01   CUSTOMER-RECORD.
     05   CUSTOMER-ID      PICTURE X(5).
     05   CUSTOMER-NAME    PICTURE X(30).
     05   CUSTOMER-BAL     PICTURE S9(5)V99.
```

Every occurrence of the COBOL reserved word "PIC" from the library member has been replaced by the reserved word "PICTURE" in the program.

Note that the pseudo-text for "string-2" is allowed to be the *empty string*, i.e., a string with *0* characters (how many characters are between the opening delimiter "= =" and the closing delimiter "= =" in the string "= = = ="?). Thus every occurrence of the string "AR-" from the library member has been replaced by the empty string. This effectively removes all occurrences of "AR-" from the copied member.

Note, too, that any number of original/replacement string pairs can be specified in the REPLACING clause. There are two such pairs in this example: "PIC"/"PICTURE" and "AR-"/"empty string".

EXAMPLE 9.9 Figure 9-2 shows the IBM OS/VS COBOL program in Fig. 7-14 revised to use the COPY facility. The FD and level-01 record description for the programmer/project file used in Chapters 6–8 were first placed in an IBM OS/VS source program library (with the member name "MASTERFD"), using a utility program (consult an instructor or vendor manual to learn how to create library members on your system). The PROCEDURE DIVISION statements necessary to input a transaction record for this program were also placed in the source program library as a separate member (with the name "GETTRANS").

Having created the desired source program library, the program in Fig. 7-14 was then revised so that it did not contain the COBOL statements for the FD or the transaction input function. These statements were instead COPYed into the program as needed.

Line 39 contains the statement "COPY MASTERFD." which causes the contents of the member MASTERFD to be copied unchanged from the source program library into the program. The source listing

```
00001              IDENTIFICATION DIVISION.
00002              PROGRAM-ID.  INDEXED-RANDOM-RETRIEVAL.

00003              ENVIRONMENT DIVISION.
00004              CONFIGURATION SECTION.
00005              SOURCE-COMPUTER.  IBM-3081.
00006              OBJECT-COMPUTER.  IBM-3081.
00007              INPUT-OUTPUT SECTION.
00008              FILE-CONTROL.

00009                  SELECT TRANSACTION-FILE
00010                      ASSIGN TO PROGIDS
00011                      ORGANIZATION IS SEQUENTIAL
00012                      ACCESS IS SEQUENTIAL
00013                      .
00014                  SELECT INDEXED-FILE
00015                      ASSIGN TO VSAMFILE
00016                      ORGANIZATION IS INDEXED
00017                      ACCESS IS RANDOM
00018                      RECORD KEY IS INDEXED-PROGRAMMER-ID
00019                      FILE STATUS IS INDEXED-STATUS-CODE
00020                      .

00021              DATA DIVISION.
00022              FILE SECTION.

00023              FD  TRANSACTION-FILE
00024                  LABEL RECORDS ARE STANDARD
00025                  BLOCK CONTAINS O CHARACTERS
00026                  RECORD CONTAINS 80 CHARACTERS
00027                  .
00028              01  TRANSACTION-RECORD.
00029                  05  TRANS-PROGRAMMER-ID          PIC X(5).
00030                  05  FILLER                       PIC X(75).
00031
00032              **********************************************
00033              *  NOTE USE OF COPY STATEMENT TO BRING FD AND LEVEL-01
00034              *  RECORD DESCRIPTION FOR INDEXED FILE INTO COBOL PROGRAM
00035              *  FROM SOURCE STATEMENT LIBRARY.   STATEMENTS COPIED FROM
00036              *  SOURCE STATEMENT LIBRARY ARE MARKED WITH "C"
00037              **********************************************
00038
00039              COPY MASTERFD.
00040 C            FD  INDEXED-FILE
00041 C                LABEL RECORDS ARE STANDARD
00042 C                RECORD CONTAINS 15 CHARACTERS.
00043 C            01  INDEXED-RECORD.
00044 C                05  INDEXED-PROGRAMMER-ID       PIC X(5).
00045 C                05  INDEXED-PROJECT-ID          PIC X(8).
00046 C                05  INDEXED-TOTAL-HOURS         PIC 9(3)V9 COMP.
00047
00048              WORKING-STORAGE SECTION.

00049              01  FLAGS-AND-SWITCHES.
00050                  05  TRANS-END-OF-FILE-SW         PIC X(3).
00051                      88  MORE-TRANS-RECORDS       VALUE "NO".
00052                      88  NO-MORE-INPUT            VALUE "YES".

00053              01  FILE-STATUS-CODES.
00054                  05  INDEXED-STATUS-CODE          PIC XX.
00055                      88  VSAM-OPERATION-OK        VALUE "00".
00056                      88  VSAM-OPERATION-FAILED    VALUE "01" THRU "99".
00057                      88  RECORD-NOT-FOUND         VALUE "23".
00058              PROCEDURE DIVISION.
00059
00060              000-EXECUTIVE-MODULE.
00061
00062                  MOVE "NO" TO TRANS-END-OF-FILE-SW
00063                  OPEN    INPUT   INDEXED-FILE
00064                                  TRANSACTION-FILE
00065                  IF VSAM-OPERATION-OK
00066                      PERFORM 010-GET-NEXT-TRANS
```

Fig. 9-2

```
00067                    PERFORM 020-RETRIEVE-INDEXED-RECORD
00068                        UNTIL NO-MORE-INPUT
00069                    CLOSE   INDEXED-FILE
00070                            TRANSACTION-FILE
00071                    IF VSAM-OPERATION-OK
00072                        DISPLAY "RANDOM RETRIEVAL COMPLETED"
00073                    ELSE
00074                        DISPLAY "INDEXED FILE NOT PROPERLY CLOSED"
00075                ELSE
00076                    DISPLAY "UNABLE TO OPEN INDEXED FILE -- ABORT"
00077                    CLOSE TRANSACTION-FILE
00078                    .
00079                STOP RUN
00080                    .
00081
00082            010-GET-NEXT-TRANS.
00083
00084            ************************************************
00085            *    COPY CAN ALSO BE USED IN PROCEDURE DIVISION
00086            ************************************************
00087
00088                COPY GETTRANS.
00089 C              READ TRANSACTION-FILE
00090 C                  AT END
00091 C                      MOVE "YES" TO TRANS-END-OF-FILE-SW
00092 C              .
00093 C
00094
00095            020-RETRIEVE-INDEXED-RECORD.
00096
00097                MOVE TRANS-PROGRAMMER-ID    TO INDEXED-PROGRAMMER-ID
00098                READ INDEXED-FILE
00099                IF VSAM-OPERATION-OK
00100                    DISPLAY INDEXED-PROGRAMMER-ID
00101                        SPACE
00102                        INDEXED-TOTAL-HOURS
00103                ELSE
00104                    IF RECORD-NOT-FOUND
00105                        DISPLAY "RECORD NOT FOUND FOR " TRANSACTION-RECORD
00106                    ELSE
00107                        DISPLAY "VSAM ERROR " INDEXED-STATUS-CODE
00108                            " FOR TRANSACTION " TRANSACTION-RECORD
00109                    .
00110                PERFORM 010-GET-NEXT-TRANS
00111                    .
```

Fig. 9-2 *(cont.)*

shows that, in fact, lines 40–46 were imported from the source program library in response to this statement. Note that COPYed statements are marked in the listing with a "C" following the line number.

The code for the paragraph 010-GET-NEXT-TRANS (lines 82–93) is also COPYed into the program from the source program library (via "COPY GETTRANS." in line 88). Again, the statements brought in from the library are marked with a C in the listing.

The statements marked with C were not actually part of the source program as written by the programmer. They were automatically inserted into the program by the compiler in response to the COPY statements, thus saving the programmer the time and effort required to design and code them. If these statements ever require change, the copy in the library can be changed and the program recompiled. The compiler will automatically copy the revised statements without the need for any manual changes to the program itself.

The use of the SUPPRESS and/or REPLACING options is *never recommended*, since they undercut the major advantages derived from using the COPY statement in the first place. See Problems 9.29 and 9.30 for other difficulties with SUPPRESS and REPLACING.

9.3 Applications and Advantages of the COPY Feature

The use of the COPY facility with a source program library has the following applications/advantages:

(1) Programmers' time is saved since COBOL statements which might be used in more than one program need only be written *once*, and then placed in the source program library. Any other programmer requiring these particular statements need not "reinvent the wheel", for he or she can simply COPY the statements from the already existing source program library.

EXAMPLE 9.10   Consider the programs in Figs. 7-10, 7-13, 7-14, 7-15, 7-16, and 7-19, all of which access a master file named INDEXED-FILE. The FD and level-01 record description for this file are *exactly the same* in all these programs. If the FD and level-01 record description are developed and placed in a source program library, then the DATA DIVISION entry for this file need not be recoded for each program; it can simply be COPYed from the source program library each time it is needed, thus saving time and wasted effort. See Example 9.9 above.

(2) Potential mistakes and/or misunderstandings regarding the PICTUREs, USAGEs, and layouts of file records are avoided. Many different programmers working on many different programs all use one and the same FD and level-01 record description for shared files, namely, the FD stored in the source program library and COPYed into each individual program.

EXAMPLE 9.11   When the COPY facility is not used, great care must be taken that each program accessing a given file uses the correct FD and record layout information. Since many programmers may be involved in writing many such programs, ensuring proper communication between the human beings working on a project can become a difficult task. Clearly if one program describes a given field as DISPLAY while a different program describes the same field as COMP, or if one program describes it as PIC 9(4) and the other as PIC 9(5), or if the two programs place the field in different positions within the record, the system of programs as a whole cannot work together correctly. Agreement on the definition of shared data items is one of the major hurdles to successfully completing a large project. This is why low coupling is desirable in systems designs (see Chapter 2) and why the COPY facility can be so useful in real life.

(3) Names of files and record fields are standardized from one program to another (since all programs use the names COPYed from the source program library), making development and maintenance of programs easier.

EXAMPLE 9.12   Suppose in the program of Fig. 7-16 (which updates the programmer indexed file in Chapter 7) the field which holds the total hours a given programmer worked on a given project is named INDEXED-TOTAL-HOURS, while in the program of Fig. 7-14 (which randomly retrieves the total hours field), this same field is named PROJECT-HOURS-WORKED. A maintenance programmer working on the system 3 years after it was developed is likely to be confused by the use of two different names for the same thing. There would be no confusion if the COPY facility had been used to COPY one and the same set of DATA DIVISION statements into *both* programs. Use of COPY guarantees not only the same names but also the same PICTUREs, USAGEs, and record layout, thus eliminating many potential sources of errors.

(4) Use of COPY makes system maintenance easier, since only *one* version of an FD, record description, etc., need be changed (namely, the version in the source program library). All programs affected by the change can then be recompiled without any direct modification to the source program. The COBOL compiler will automatically copy the *changed* version of the code from the source program library into each program being recompiled.

EXAMPLE 9.13   Suppose the INDEXED-FILE in Chapter 7 must be modified so that INDEXED-PROJECT-ID is PIC X(9) instead of PIC X(8). If the programs in Figs. 7-10, 7-13, 7-14, 7-15, 7-16, and 7-19 (all of which access INDEXED-FILE) did *not* use the COPY facility and so included their own individual versions of the FD and record description for the file, *all six programs* would have to be modified by a maintenance programmer before being recompiled. Conversely, if the programs had used the COPY verb to copy the FD and record description from the source program library, only *one* version of the FD and record description would have to be changed (the copy in the library). The six programs could then be recompiled (which must be done in either case), and the compiler would automatically copy the new version of the FD and record description into each individual program. The use of the COPY facility can often save a maintenance programmer considerable time, since changes need be made only to the library member in question; the COPY verb will then automatically bring the changed version into each program as it is recompiled.

(5) The COPY library can be used to store relatively static tables which are initialized with the VALUE clause. Such table definitions can be COPYed into any program which needs them. If the table has to be changed, the member in the source program library can be modified and all the programs using the table recompiled (automatically bringing the new version of the table into each program without the need to actually make manual changes).

EXAMPLE 9.14 There are three basic approaches to defining tables for COBOL programs:

(a) Place the table *values* in a file, and then load the COBOL table by inputting the values from the file. If the table values need to be changed, the file can be modified using an interactive editor or a utility program. The COBOL program(s) themselves need not be changed, recompiled, or relinked. This approach allows the table to be changed with the least amount of effort and is generally most efficient.

(b) Place the table definitions (with VALUE clauses) in a source program library and COPY them into all appropriate programs. If the table values need to be changed, the library member holding the table definition can be modified and the appropriate programs recompiled and relinked. This requires more work than approach (1) in that the affected programs must be recompiled and relinked. However, the maintenance programmer still need only make the changes in *one* place.

(c) The table definition (with VALUE clauses) can be *hard-coded* into each relevant COBOL program. This means that the necessary COBOL statements are repeated in each separate program. If table values need to be changed, each separate program must be modified, recompiled, and relinked. This is obviously the least desirable approach.

EXAMPLE 9.15 Suppose a business has many geographically distributed locations, and that transaction file and master file records contain a LOCATION-CODE PIC X(2) which identifies a particular location. For reports, however, it is desired to expand the 2-byte code to a LOCATION-NAME PIC X(30). This could be done by keeping LOCATION-CODE values together with their corresponding LOCATION-NAMEs in a table. It is expected that such a table would change (as locations were closed and new locations opened), but that change would occur relatively infrequently (perhaps once a year on average).

If the table were stored on a disk file, table maintenance would be easy (see Example 9.14), but each program needing the table would have to OPEN and CLOSE the file and input the table values each time the program was executed. This results in extra execution-time overhead.

Since the table changes so infrequently, it might be more desirable to place the table definition in a source program library and then COPY the table definition into each program which needs it. A change to the table would now require not only changing the actual data but also recompiling and relinking every program which COPYs it (see Example 9.14). On the other hand, since the table would be compiled into each program, the overhead involved in reading table values from a file would be saved. Since table maintenance is done only once a year, the extra effort required for maintenance may be worthwhile in the long run. See Problems 9.32 and 9.33.

(6) Use of the COPY feature can standardize solutions to common programming tasks. This makes sure that all programs using such routines will agree on things such as how to handle errors, whether to round or not (or when), etc. Such standardization can also be accomplished by using external subroutines kept in a subroutine library (see Chapter 10).

EXAMPLE 9.16 A short list of common COBOL routines which every installation needs and which, therefore, might be placed in a source program library includes such things as (1) routines to convert from Julian dates to standard MM/YY/DD form and back; (2) routines for doing frequent calculations such as federal, state, and local taxes, FICA deductions, employee medical plans, credit unions, etc.; (3) routines for converting time information from one representation to another (e.g., military to nonmilitary time, etc.); and (4) validation routines for time, date, and other standard fields. Any given installation will find many more routines which appear again and again in different programs and are, therefore, candidates for a source statement library.

Review Questions

9.1   What is the reason for having a COBOL COPY facility?

9.2   What is a library?

9.3   What is a directory?

9.4   What is a member?

9.5   What is another name for libraries in IBM OS/VS systems?

9.6   What is meant by a source program library?

9.7   What is the purpose of an object program (or subroutine) library?

9.8   What is the function of linkage editors and linking loaders?

9.9   Why are IBM OS/VS COBOL object programs *not* executable until after they have been linked?

9.10   What is the purpose of load libraries?

9.11   Explain the purpose of job control/command language statements with respect to load libraries.

9.12   Explain the four steps typically involved in modifying a program which is in production.

9.13   What does the COPY statement do?

9.14   Give the syntax for the ANSI COBOL COPY statement.

9.15   Discuss the SUPPRESS option of COPY and why it should not be used.

9.16   Discuss the REPLACING option of COPY and why it should not be used.

9.17   Discuss the use of the IN option for COPY and why it is often not needed.

9.18   Explain how COPY can save programmers' time and effort.

9.19   Explain how the COPY facility can eliminate potential mistakes involving shared files and data items.

9.20   Explain how COPY can standardize names of data items and why this is desirable.

9.21   Explain how COPY can eliminate needless duplication of effort during program maintenance.

9.22   Explain the advantages and disadvantages of COPY for static tables.

9.23   Discuss the three possible approaches for handling static table definitions in COBOL.

Solved Problems

9.24 Why does a typical installation have *several* program libraries instead of just one?

Different libraries are used to store programs in different stages of development:

(1) Source program libraries store programs in their original source language (e.g., COBOL).

(2) Object program (subroutine) libraries store programs which have been compiled (and are, therefore, in machine language form) but which have not yet been linked.

(3) Load libraries store programs which have been both compiled and linked and are, therefore, ready for execution.

Also, different source, object, and load libraries may be used to hold programs for different applications, programmer teams, individual programmers, etc. In short, the programs at an installation can be grouped according to any convenient criteria and stored in separate libraries.

9.25 What is the function of a linkage editor or linking loader?

In most languages (including COBOL, see Chapter 10) a program can call *external subroutines* which have been separately written and separately compiled and are, therefore, not part of the calling program itself. The translation of the call statement will include all the code needed to branch to the subroutine except the address of the subroutine (clearly the compiler, when translating the call, does not know the address of the subroutine, since the external subroutine is not part of the calling program which is being translated). The compiler must leave a place for the address in the calling program, but cannot actually fill in the correct value.

The missing subroutine address must be filled in by a linkage editor or linking loader, which (1) combines the machine language of the call*ing* program and the machine language of the call*ed* routine into one machine language package (called a load module) and (2) fills the (now known) address of the call*ed* program into the place left for it in the call*ing* program.

A typical linkage editor or linking loader will be capable of automatically searching for missing subroutines in an object program (subroutine) library. This allows any programmer to "call" on any subroutine(s) which are available in public subroutine libraries. Such sharing of routines can greatly enhance the productivity of a programming staff.

9.26 What kinds of programs are kept in load libraries?

Load libraries contain programs which are ready for execution. Such libraries typically include (1) operating system programs such as compilers, linkers, etc., (2) operating system utility programs (such as IBM's VSAM utility, IDCAMS), (3) program packages which have been purchased by an installation (such as word processors, spreadsheets, statistical and graphics packages, etc.), and (4) applications programs which have been purchased or developed by the installation and which are "in production". Programs are executed from load libraries by job control/command language statements which request that the operating system load and execute them.

9.27 If a program needs to be changed, why is it advantageous to change it as early in its history as possible?

If changes can be made before the program goes into production, some (or all) of the four steps in Example 9.4 can be skipped. If a change is made before a program has been keyed into the system (i.e., during design or early implementation), then no effort is wasted. Once a program is compiled, linked, and placed in a load library, all these steps must be repeated in order to make a change.

9.28 What, if anything, is wrong with the following:

```
FD    MASTER-FILE
      COPY MASTERFD
FD    TRANSACTION-FILE ...
```

The COPY statement *must end with a period* followed by a space. It should read:

```
FD    MASTER-FILE
      COPY MASTERFD.
FD    TRANSACTION-FILE ...
```

9.29 Suppose member MASTREC of the default source program library available to the compiler contains:

```
01    MASTER-RECORD.
      05    MASTER-IDENTIFIER    PIC X(5).
      05    MASTER-NAME          PIC X(25).
      05    MASTER-BALANCE       PIC S9(5)V99.
      05    MASTER-STATUS        PIC X(5).
```

It is desired to change the status information from PIC X(5) to PIC X(6). What, if anything, is wrong with the following approach?

```
FD    MASTER-FILE ...
      COPY MASTREC
            REPLACING ==PIC X(5)== BY ==PIC X(6)==.
```

First, the REPLACING option pseudo-text specifies that *all* occurrences of "PIC X(5)" be replaced by "PIC X(6)", thus incorrectly changing the definition of MASTER-IDENTIFIER as well as MASTER-STATUS. Since the REPLACING option works strictly with the *text* of the member (and not its *meaning*), care must be taken when using this option.

Second, it is recommended that the REPLACING option *never* be used since it defeats the standardization, which is one of the major reasons for using COPY in the first place. The correct approach to this problem is, of course, to change the definition of MASTER-STATUS *in the library*; then the COBOL program could be written simply:

```
FD    MASTER-FILE ...
      COPY MASTREC.
```

and would *require no changes itself*.

9.30 Suppose MASTREC is a member of a source program library as in Problem 9.29. It is desired to change "MASTER" to just "MAST" in the version copied into a program. Although this is not recommended, as an exercise tell what, if anything, is wrong with the following attempt:

```
COPY MASTREC
      REPLACING ==ER== BY ====.
```

Although this seems, at first glance, to be a clever way to convert "MASTER" to "MAST" (by replacing "ER" with the empty string), it will cause errors since the string "ER" also appears at the end of "MASTER-IDENDIFI*ER*", which will be changed to "MAST-IDENTIFI". It is easy to make this type of error when using REPLACING (another reason not to use it).

9.31 As an exercise, correct the error in Problem 9.30.

```
COPY MASTREC
      REPLACING ==MASTER-== BY ==MAST-==.
```

9.32 Show how a source program library can be used to help implement static tables by giving the contents of a library member for the table in Example 9.15.

```
01    LOCATIONS-TABLE-AREA.
      05    LOCATIONS-TABLE-VALUES.
            10    FILLER          PIC X(2)  VALUE "A7".
            10    FILLER          PIC X(30) VALUE "PHILADELPHIA".
            10    FILLER          PIC X(2)  VALUE "A9".
            10    FILLER          PIC X(30) VALUE "NEW YORK-1".
            10    FILLER          PIC X(2)  VALUE "B3".
            10    FILLER          PIC X(30) VALUE "NEW YORK-2".
      05    LOCATIONS-TABLE REDEFINES LOCATIONS-TABLE-VALUES
                            OCCURS 3 TIMES.
            10    LOCATION-CODE   PIC X(2).
            10    LOCATION-NAME   PIC X(30).
```

· If the table values need to be changed, the VALUE clauses in the above definition can be changed in the library. All programs using the table would then need to be recompiled (and relinked) to COPY the new version of the table into the program.

9.33 Suppose the library member name for the table in Problem 9.32 is LOCTAB. Show how to copy the table into a program's WORKING-STORAGE SECTION.

```
WORKING-STORAGE SECTION.
COPY LOCTAB.
      .
      .
      .
```

Chapter 10

External Subprograms

Up until now, modules have been implemented as COBOL paragraphs, and calls on other modules have been implemented with PERFORM statements. A module which is called by another module is known as a *subprogram*. Of course, subprograms can call other subprograms, which in turn can call still other subprograms, etc.

A subprogram implemented as a PERFORMed paragraph is known as an *internal subprogram*, since it is inside the same PROCEDURE DIVISION as the calling module. COBOL also provides for *external subprograms*, in which the called module is in a different COBOL program than the calling module.

Since external subprograms are in separate PROCEDURE DIVISIONs, they must be compiled separately from the calling program. One compiler run must be made to compile the calling program, and a second compiler run must be made to compile the subprogram. Each compiler run produces a machine language program, usually called an *object module*, creating one object module for the calling program and a separate object module for the external subprogram.

The object modules for the calling program and its external subprogram(s) must then be combined into one program unit before execution can be attempted. The task of combining object modules into one executable program unit (often called a *run unit* or *load module*) is usually carried out by computer programs known as *linkage editors* or *linking loaders*.

10.1 Subprogram Libraries and the Linking Function

Linking Object Programs Together

As was discussed in Chapter 9, a linkage editor or linking loader is a program capable of inputting two or more object modules and combining them into one executable program unit (called a load module or run unit). Basically, the *linking function* involves (1) determining which external subprogram(s) are missing from the object module(s) which were input, (2) finding the object module(s) for these subprograms, (3) combining the object module(s) for the missing external subprograms with the object modules which were originally input, and (4) putting the address(es) of the external subprogram(s) into the calling sequence(s) of the calling program(s).

EXAMPLE 10.1 Figure 10-1 illustrates an IBM OS/VS COBOL main program, together with an external subprogram. The main program and external subprogram are compiled in separate compiler runs to produce two separate object modules. These object modules are then input to a linkage editor program supplied as part of the operating system. The linkage editor combines the two object modules into one executable program unit called a load module.

Observe that the original object module for the main program contains an area to hold the starting address of the external subprogram, but that this address is not filled in by the compiler (which does not know at compilation time what the address will be). The address of the external subprogram is filled in by the linkage editor as it combines the two object programs into one load module. This process of combining calling programs with the needed external subprograms and filling in missing addresses is known as *resolving external references*. It is the main function of a linkage editor or linking loader.

Notice that in addition to combining the user-written main program with its user-written external subprogram, the linkage editor also obtains any system subprograms deliberately left out of the object program by the compiler. By leaving some of the work of producing a final machine language translation of a COBOL program to the linkage editor, the COBOL compiler can be made simpler and more efficient. The system subprograms needed by COBOL object programs are kept in a *COBOL subroutine library*, which is made available to the linkage editor via job control/command language statements. The COBOL subroutine library is supplied by the vendor as part of the COBOL compiler package.

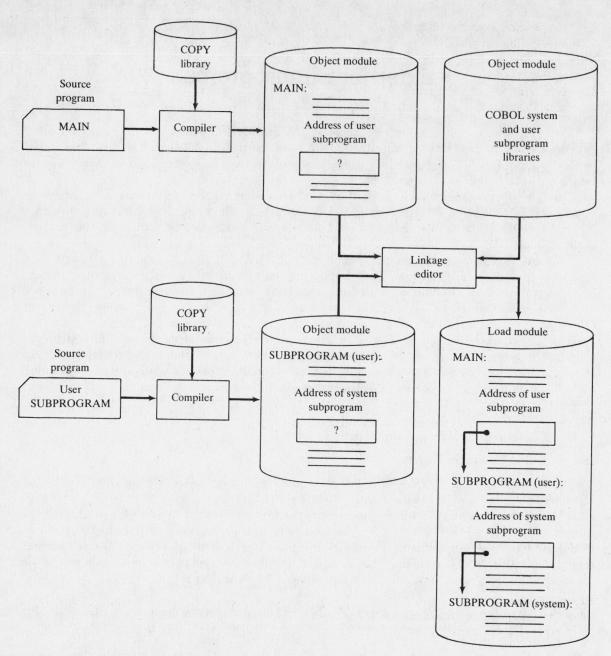

Fig. 10-1

Subprogram Libraries

As Example 10.1 illustrates, there are two types of subprograms in use: (1) *user-written subprograms*, which are written by applications programmers in a language such as COBOL, and (2) *system subprograms*, which come with a given compiler and/or operating system.

System subprograms are generally stored in object program libraries in machine language form. They are ready to be linked with other programs by the linkage editor, and the system is generally set up so that these subprograms are automatically available to the linkage editor or its equivalent. This means that any programmer can call an external system subprogram, and the linkage editor will automatically obtain the necessary object code and *link* it to the user's program.

User-written external subprograms may or may not be placed in a publicly available external subprogram library. If a programmer writes an external subprogram which might be used by more than one program, it is useful to put the external subprogram in a public object program library accessible to the linkage editor. This allows *any* programmer to call the external subprogram without special effort. When the calling program is linked, the linkage editor automatically inserts the external subprogram from the subprogram library into the calling program.

EXAMPLE 10.2   Here is a list of external subprograms which may be useful in a public object program library:

(1)   Date conversions (e.g., Julian to mm/dd/yy and back)

(2)   Time conversions (e.g., military to standard and back)

(3)   Date and time validation routines

(4)   Routines for various payroll calculations (e.g., taxes, FICA, etc.)

(5)   Routines for accessing records in commonly used master files

(5)   Routines for interfacing with interactive terminals or data base management software

(5)   Key transformation routines for direct or relative files

10.2   How to Write a Calling Program: The CALL Statement

While the PERFORM statement is used to call an internal subprogram (i.e., a paragraph in the same PROCEDURE DIVISION as the calling paragraph), a special CALL statement is used to call an external subprogram (i.e., a COBOL program which has been separately compiled and is to be linked with the calling program). The simplest form of the CALL statement is:

```
CALL "program-id"
```

where "program-id" is the PROGRAM-ID of the *called* program. In IBM OS/VS COBOL, the external PROGRAM-ID should be limited to 1–8 letters or digits, the first of which is a letter.

When the CALL statement is executed, it results in the immediate execution of the called program (beginning at the first statement in the called PROCEDURE DIVISION). When the called program is finished executing, control is automatically returned to the statement following the CALL statement in the calling program (see Section 10.3 for details on how to write the called program).

EXAMPLE 10.3   The code below illustrates a calling program, together with a separately compiled external subprogram. The linkage is effected with the simplest version of the CALL statement (and is somewhat unrealistic; see Section 10.3 for more information on writing external subprograms).

```
          Calling Program                    External Subprogram
     PROGRAM-ID.  UPDATE.                PROGRAM-ID.  COUNTREC.
          .                                   .
          .                                   .
          .                                   .
     PROCEDURE DIVISION.                 PROCEDURE DIVISION.
          .                                   ADD 1 TO   RECORD-COUNTER
          .                                              TOTAL-LOGGED
          .                                   SUBTRACT 1 FROM NOT-ACTIVE
     CALL "COUNTREC"                          .
     MOVE TRANS-KEY TO MAST-KEY          RETURN-TO-CALLER.
          .                                   EXIT PROGRAM
          .                                   .
          .
```

The CALL statement in UPDATE names the external subprogram to be invoked. The linkage editor (or the equivalent) must be used to link the external subprogram COUNTREC to the calling program UPDATE before UPDATE can be executed. When the CALL statement is executed, control is transferred to the *first* statement in the PROCEDURE DIVISION of the external subprogram named COUNTREC (ADD . . . in the example). The EXIT PROGRAM statement is used in an external subprogram to cause control to return to the calling program (see Section 10.3). Control remains in the external subprogram until an EXIT PROGRAM (or the equivalent) is executed. Control returns to the statement immediately following the CALL (MOVE TRANS-KEY TO MAST-KEY in the example).

The external subprogram in Example 10.3 is unusual in that it exhibits no coupling with the calling module. Typically, when an external subprogram is called, it must access data items passed from the calling program. Data items passed from the calling program to the external subprogram are known as *arguments*.

When a calling program passes only elementary items to an external subprogram, this implements the lowest (most desirable) form of coupling known as *data coupling* (see Chapter 2). When a calling program passes some or all group items to an external subprogram, this implements the next lowest form of coupling known as *stamp coupling*. These two most desirable forms of coupling can be implemented in COBOL only when external subprograms are used.

Passing Arguments with the CALL Statement

The general form of the CALL statement when arguments must be passed to the external subprogram is:

```
CALL "program-id-of-subprogram"
     [ USING name-of-argument-1 [name-of-argument-2] ... ]
```

As before, the CALL statement names the PROGRAM-ID of a separately compiled external subprogram.

The USING clause names one or more arguments to be passed to the external subprogram. The argument(s) must be level-01 (or level-77) items and can come from anywhere in the DATA DIVISION (i.e., they may be defined in the FILE SECTION, WORKING-STORAGE SECTION, etc.). An IBM OS/VS COBOL extension to ANSI COBOL allows the data item(s) to be at *any* level.

When the CALL statement is executed, the data item(s) named in the USING list are made available to the external subprogram (see Section 10.3). Any changes made to the contents of these items in the subprogram will, of course, still apply after control is returned to the calling program. Thus an external subprogram may modify the value(s) of the argument(s) passed to it.

EXAMPLE 10.4   The following CALL statement illustrates how to pass arguments to an external subprogram:

```
PROGRAM-ID.  CALLING.

DATA DIVISION.

FILE SECTION.
FD   SOME-FILE ...
01   ANY-RECORD ...

WORKING-STORAGE SECTION.
01   ANY-DATA-ITEM ...
01   SOME-OTHER-ITEM ...

PROCEDURE DIVISION.

     CALL "EXTSUB"
          USING  ANY-DATA-ITEM
                 ANY-RECORD
                 SOME-OTHER-ITEM
```

In IBM OS/VS COBOL, the name of the external subprogram should be limited to 8 characters, as is EXTSUB. The linkage editor must be used to combine the object modules for the calling program (CALLING) and EXTSUB in order for this CALL statement to execute successfully (consult an instructor or vendor manual regarding the linking function at your installation).

The arguments passed to the external subprogram come from *both* the FILE SECTION and the WORKING-STORAGE SECTION. Observe that the order of the items in the USING clause need have no relationship to the order in which the items are defined in the DATA DIVISION. Following the ANSI standard, all the USING items are at level-01 (IBM OS/VS COBOL would allow some or all of the items to be at *any* level).

The order of the data items in the USING clause determines how the external subprogram must be written to correctly "pick up" the argument values (see Section 10.3). Thus it will be important for the author of the external subprogram to know that the order of the items is ANY-DATA-ITEM, ANY-RECORD, and then SOME-OTHER-ITEM. Since this ordering is totally up to the programmer, good communication and documentation between programmers are necessary to the successful use of external subprograms.

10.3 How to Write an External Subprogram

There are four major considerations when writing a COBOL program to be called as an external subprogram.

The PROGRAM-ID for an External Subprogram

The PROGRAM-ID of the external subprogram must be the same as that used in the CALL statement when the subprogram is invoked. In IBM OS/VS COBOL, the PROGRAM-ID is truncated by the compiler to 8 characters; hence it is best not to exceed this limit.

Just as it is important to make up paragraph names which describe the paragraph's function, so it is important to make up PROGRAM-IDs which describe the function of an external subprogram. Typically, if an external subprogram is stored in a public subprogram library, the PROGRAM-ID will also be used as the member name in the library.

Picking Up Arguments: The PROCEDURE DIVISION Header

If, as is usually the case, an external subprogram is designed to process one or more arguments, the PROCEDURE DIVISION header must include a USING clause similar to the USING clause in the corresponding CALL statement:

```
PROCEDURE DIVISION
     [ USING name-of-argument-1 [name-of-argument-2] ...].
```

The optional USING clause names one or more arguments which must be defined in the LINKAGE SECTION of the DATA DIVISION for the external subprogram (see page 266). ANSI standards dictate that each item in the USING list must be a level-01 (or a level-77) item (there is no IBM extension to this standard for the PROCEDURE DIVISION header; i.e., USING items here *must* be level-01 or 77).

The argument names in the CALL statement USING list and the argument names in the PROCEDURE DIVISION USING list should agree as follows: (1) There should be the same number of data items in both USING lists; (2) the data items in the CALL list should match up with the data items in the subprogram PROCEDURE DIVISION header strictly on the basis of their positions within the lists; i.e., the first item in the CALL list corresponds to the first item in the subprogram header list, the second item in the CALL list corresponds to the second item in the subprogram header, etc.; and (3) data items which correspond because they occupy the same positions in the CALL list and the subprogram PROCEDURE DIVISION header list must have the same descriptions in terms of PICTURE, USAGE, etc.; they need not, however, have the same names.

EXAMPLE 10.5 The following shows a calling program, together with a separately compiled external subprogram.

Calling Program

```
PROGRAM-ID.  CALLING.


DATA DIVISION.


FILE SECTION.
FD  SOME-FILE ...
01  ANY-RECORD.
  05  FIELD-1  PIC X(5).
  05  FIELD-2  PIC 9(7).


WORKING-STORAGE SECTION.
01  NUMERIC-DATA-ITEM   PIC 99.
01  ALPHABETIC-DATA-ITEM PIC AA.


PROCEDURE DIVISION.
       .
       .
       .
    CALL "EXTSUB"
       USING NUMERIC-DATA-ITEM
             ANY-RECORD
             ALPHABETIC-DATA-ITEM
       .
       .
       .
```

External Subprogram

```
PROGRAM-ID.  EXTSUB.


DATA DIVISION.


LINKAGE SECTION.


01   ANY-RECORD-LINKAGE-AREA.
     05   FIELD-A     PIC X(5).
     05   FIELD-B     PIC 9(7).


01   ALPHA-ITEM-AREA   PIC AA.


01   NUMERIC-DATA-ITEM PIC 99.


PROCEDURE DIVISION
     USING  NUMERIC-DATA-ITEM
            ANY-RECORD-LINKAGE-AREA
            ALPHA-ITEM-AREA
       .
       .
       .
```

The CALL statement lists three data items, so the PROCEDURE DIVISION header must name three items. These items match up strictly on the basis of their positions in the respective USING lists. Thus NUMERIC-DATA-ITEM matches up with NUMERIC-DATA-ITEM (in this case, the names are the *same*), ANY-RECORD corresponds to ANY-RECORD-LINKAGE-AREA (in this case, the names are *different*; the important factor is not the name but the *position* in the list), and ALPHABETIC-DATA-ITEM corresponds to ALPHA-ITEM-AREA (different names, but they are both third in their USING lists).

Corresponding data items must have equivalent definitions. Data items passed to the subprogram from the calling program must be defined in a special DATA DIVISION LINKAGE SECTION in the subprogram (i.e., all items in the subprogram PROCEDURE DIVISION USING list *must* be defined in the LINKAGE SECTION, which is described below). NUMERIC-DATA-ITEM is defined as PIC 99 in both the calling program and the subprogram. ANY-RECORD consists of a PIC X(5) field followed by a PIC 9(7) field in the calling program. The corresponding ANY-RECORD-LINKAGE-AREA also consists of a PIC X(5) field followed by a PIC 9(7) field. Note that although the record names and the subfield names may be different, the definitions must be equivalent. Thus ALPHABETIC-DATA-ITEM (PIC AA in the calling program) correctly corresponds to ALPHA-ITEM-AREA (PIC AA in the subprogram).

Defining Arguments: The LINKAGE SECTION

As Example 10.5 illustrates, all arguments passed to an external subprogram are defined in a special DATA DIVISION section of the subprogram called the LINKAGE SECTION. The LINKAGE SECTION must follow the WORKING-STORAGE SECTION within the DATA DIVISION (i.e., FILE SECTION, then WORKING-STORAGE SECTION, and then LINKAGE SECTION).

Each item named in the PROCEDURE DIVISION header of the subprogram *must* be defined as a level-01 (or level-77) item in the LINKAGE SECTION. LINKAGE SECTION items are different from other DATA DIVISION items in that the compiler does not allocate storage for

LINKAGE SECTION items. LINKAGE SECTION definitions provide names and descriptions for data items which do not really exist in the subprogram itself, but which exist in the calling program and are passed to the subprogram. The critical thing about LINKAGE SECTION items is that they match the descriptions of the corresponding actual items back in the calling program.

When arguments are passed to an external subprogram, it is actually the *addresses* of the arguments which are given to the subprogram. The machine language instructions in the subprogram can then manipulate the arguments directly in memory (since their locations are now known to the subprogram). This means that any change to a LINKAGE SECTION item made in the subprogram will actually change the value of the corresponding data item back in the calling program.

EXAMPLE 10.6 Consider the following PROCEDURE DIVISION for the LINKAGE SECTION and CALL in Example 10.5:

```
PROCEDURE DIVISION
     USING   NUMERIC-DATA-ITEM
             ANY-RECORD-LINKAGE-AREA
             ALPHA-ITEM-AREA
     .
     MOVE 12       TO NUMERIC-DATA-ITEM
     MOVE "AB"     TO ALPHA-ITEM-AREA
     MOVE SPACES   TO FIELD-A
     MOVE ZERO     TO FIELD-B
     .
RETURN-TO-CALLING-MODULE.
     EXIT PROGRAM
     .
```

Since NUMERIC-DATA-ITEM in the subprogram corresponds to NUMERIC-DATA-ITEM in the calling program, any change to NUMERIC-DATA-ITEM in the subprogram will actually change NUMERIC-DATA-ITEM back in the calling program. After the subprogram executes the EXIT PROGRAM statement and returns to the calling program, NUMERIC-DATA-ITEM will contain the value 12 (back in the calling program). Any previous value of NUMERIC-DATA-ITEM will have been destroyed.

ALPHA-ITEM-AREA corresponds to ALPHABETIC-DATA-ITEM back in the calling program. Hence moving "AB" to ALPHA-ITEM-AREA is in reality moving "AB" to ALPHABETIC-DATA-ITEM in the calling program. When the subprogram returns, ALPHABETIC-DATA-ITEM will contain "AB" and any previous contents will be lost.

Moving SPACES to FIELD-A of ANY-RECORD-LINKAGE-AREA is in reality moving SPACES to the first 2 bytes (FIELD-1) of ANY-RECORD back in the calling program (since ANY-RECORD-LINKAGE-AREA and ANY-RECORD are in corresponding positions in their USING lists). Likewise, moving 0 to FIELD-B of ANY-RECORD-LINKAGE-AREA is actually moving 0 to FIELD-2 (the second 2 bytes) of ANY-RECORD back in the calling program. The previous contents of ANY-RECORD are thus destroyed by the subprogram, and upon return from the subprogram, ANY-RECORD will contain the values determined by the subprogram.

EXAMPLE 10.7 It is helpful to think of LINKAGE SECTION items as names which represent the actual data items in the CALL statement, whatever they may be. If an external subprogram is CALLed more than once, the LINKAGE SECTION items may refer to different actual arguments.

Suppose the subprogram from Example 10.6 is called by:

```
CALL "EXTSUB"
        USING   ANOTHER-NUMERIC-ITEM
                ANOTHER-RECORD
                ANOTHER-ALPHA-ITEM
```

For this CALL statement, NUMERIC-DATA-ITEM corresponds to ANOTHER-NUMERIC-ITEM back in the calling program; while ANY-RECORD-LINKAGE-AREA corresponds to ANOTHER-RECORD, and

ALPHA-ITEM-AREA corresponds to ANOTHER-ALPHA-ITEM. This particular CALL on the subprogram will thus set ANOTHER-NUMERIC-ITEM to 12, ANOTHER-ALPHA-ITEM to "AB", and ANOTHER-RECORD to 2 bytes of SPACES followed by 2 bytes of ZEROS.

It is quite common to CALL the same external subprogram from more than one place in a program, perhaps passing different arguments for each different CALL.

EXAMPLE 10.8   Show how the arguments from the calling program in Example 10.7 would have to be defined in order for the CALL to work properly.

```
DATA DIVISION.
FILE-SECTION.
FD   ANOTHER-FILE ...
01   ANOTHER-RECORD.
     05   FIRST-FIELD         PIC X(5).
     05   SECOND-FIELD        PIC 9(7).
WORKING-STORAGE SECTION.
01   ANOTHER-ALPHA-ITEM       PIC XX.
01   ANOTHER-NUMERIC-ITEM     PIC 99.
```

The definitions of the items in the calling program must be *compatible* with the definitions of the corresponding items in the external subprogram's LINKAGE SECTION. The names of the items do not have to match.

Note that ANOTHER-ALPHA-ITEM is defined PIC XX in the calling program, while ALPHA-ITEM-AREA is defined as PIC AA in the subprogram. Although not identical, these two definitions are compatible with one another and will not cause any problems. Defining ANOTHER-ALPHA-ITEM as PIC S9(7)V99 COMP, for example, *would* result in incompatibility between the calling and called programs.

EXAMPLE 10.9   Assuming the definitions in Examples 10.8 and 10.6, what is wrong with the following CALL?

```
CALL "EXTSUB"
     USING     ANOTHER-NUMERIC-ITEM
               ANOTHER-ALPHA-ITEM
               ANOTHER-RECORD
```

This CALL illustrates a common error when using external subprogram linkages: the USING list in the CALL statement is incompatible with the USING list in the external subprogram. In this case, the definitions of the items are consistent but the order is different in the CALL list and the PROCEDURE DIVISION header list. This causes ANOTHER-ALPHA-ITEM in the calling program to correspond with ANY-RECORD-LINKAGE-AREA in the subprogram, and ANOTHER-RECORD in the calling program to correspond with ALPHA-ITEM-AREA in the subprogram. The results are clearly not what is needed.

The subprogram statement 'MOVE "AB" TO ALPHA-ITEM-AREA' will actually change ANOTHER-RECORD back in the calling program, and 'MOVE SPACES TO FIELD-A ... MOVE ZERO TO FIELD-B' will actually change ANOTHER-ALPHA-ITEM back in the calling program. Since the PICTUREs and USAGEs of these corresponding items are *not* compatible, unpredictable results will occur (resulting in either a fatal or nonfatal logic error). The programmer must ensure that the CALL USING list exactly matches the PROCEDURE DIVISION USING list in the external subprogram with respect to the number, order, PICTUREs, and USAGEs of items.

Returning to the Calling Program: EXIT PROGRAM, STOP RUN, etc.

When a called program is ready to return to its calling program, it can do so with the ANSI standard EXIT PROGRAM statement. EXIT PROGRAM must be the *only* statement in its own paragraph. It causes execution to resume with the statement immediately following the CALL statement back in the calling module.

EXAMPLE 10.10 The calling program below begins by invoking an external subprogram to initialize some data items. The CALL statement passes two group items as arguments (thus implementing stamp coupling). The PROGRAM-ID in the CALL statement is identical to the PROGRAM-ID of the subprogram.

The PROCEDURE DIVISION header in the subprogram names two group items whose definitions in the LINKAGE SECTION exactly match the definitions of the corresponding items in the CALL statement. When the subprogram MOVEs ZEROS to L-COUNTER-A, it is actually moving 0 to COUNTER-1 back in the calling program; when the subprogram MOVEs SPACES to L-SWITCH-A, it is actually moving spaces to SWITCH-1 back in the calling program, etc.

After initializing the required items, the subprogram returns to the calling program by executing the EXIT PROGRAM statement. EXIT PROGRAM must be the only statement in its own paragraph. In this example, a paragraph named RETURN-TO-CALLING-MODULE is defined specifically to satisfy this rule. When EXIT PROGRAM is executed, control returns to the DISPLAY "ANYTHING" statement immediately following the CALL statement back in the calling program. Normal execution of the calling program resumes from this point.

```
           Calling Program              Separately Compiled External Subprogram
        PROGRAM-ID. CALLING.             PROGRAM-ID. INITSUB.
        DATA DIVISION.                   DATA DIVISION.
        WORKING-STORAGE SECTION.         LINKAGE SECTION.
        01    COUNTERS.                  01   LINKAGE-SWITCHES.
          05   COUNTER-1  PIC 9.           05   L-SWITCH-A    PIC X.
          05   COUNTER-2  PIC 99.          05   L-SWITCH-B    PIC XX.
          05   COUNTER-3  PIC 999.       01   LINKAGE-COUNTERS.
        01    SWITCHES.                    05   L-COUNTER-A   PIC 9.
          05   SWITCH-1   PIC X.           05   L-COUNTER-B   PIC 99.
          05   SWITCH-2   PIC XX.          05   L-COUNTER-C   PIC 999.

        PROCEDURE DIVISION.              PROCEDURE DIVISION
                                             USING    LINKAGE-COUNTERS
                                                      LINKAGE-SWITCHES
        CALL "INITSUB"                       .
             USING    COUNTERS            MOVE ZEROS TO  L-COUNTER-A
                      SWITCHES                           L-COUNTER-B
        DISPLAY "ANYTHING"                                L-COUNTER-C
             .                           MOVE SPACES TO L-SWITCH-A
             .                                          L-SWITCH-B
             .                               .

                                         RETURN-TO-CALLING-MODULE.
                                             EXIT PROGRAM
                                             .
```

The EXIT PROGRAM statement may also be used in a *main program* (the program unit directly invoked by the operating system), in which case it is ignored and execution proceeds normally with the statement immediately following EXIT PROGRAM; i.e., if EXIT PROGRAM is executed by a program unit *not* under the control of a CALL statement, EXIT PROGRAM is ignored.

This feature allows a programmer to write a program unit which can function either as a main program or as an external subprogram (depending on whether it is invoked by the operating system as a main program or by another program unit via the CALL statement).

EXAMPLE 10.11 Suppose the following program is invoked directly by the operating system as a main program. Execution of the EXIT PROGRAM statement, in this case, will *not* result in a return to the system. Instead, EXIT PROGRAM is ignored and normal execution continues with the statement(s) following EXIT PROGRAM (i.e., PERFORM DO-MAIN-STUFF, ADD . . . , DISPLAY . . . , etc.):

```
PROGRAM-ID.  MAIN.

PROCEDURE DIVISION.

    PERFORM DO-SOMETHING
    MOVE ...

MAYBE-RETURN-TO-CALLER.
    EXIT PROGRAM.

STUFF-TO-DO-IF-MAIN-PROGRAM.
    PERFORM DO-MAIN-STUFF
    ADD ...
    DISPLAY ...
```

When used within a subprogram or a main program, STOP RUN terminates execution of the entire run unit. Execution of a STOP RUN always results in the termination of not only the program in which it is executed but also the entire run unit. Thus if STOP RUN is executed in a subprogram, control never returns to the calling program(s).

Structured programming principles dictate that only one STOP RUN should be used in a run unit. Even though COBOL allows a run unit to be terminated within a subprogram, this would be poor programming style, and in general a subprogram should *always return* to its calling program. Thus STOP RUN should only be executed in a main program.

EXAMPLE 10.12 Suppose main program A CALLs external subprogram B, which in turn calls external subprogram C:

$$A \xrightarrow{\text{CALL B}} B \xrightarrow{\text{CALL C}} C$$

If C executes an EXIT PROGRAM, control will return to program B at the point immediately following the CALL "C" statement in program B. If B then executes an EXIT PROGRAM, control will return to A (at a point immediately following the CALL "B" statement in program A). Since A is the main program, if A executes an EXIT PROGRAM statement, it will be ignored. A should, therefore, execute a STOP RUN statement to terminate execution of the entire run unit.

EXAMPLE 10.13 Suppose in Example 10.12 that instead of executing an EXIT PROGRAM statement, program C issues a STOP RUN. In this case, control does not return to program B (or to program A). Instead, execution of the entire run unit (consisting of programs A, B, and C) ceases immediately; i.e., the operating system receives control and removes the run unit consisting of A, B, and C from the system. Note that this violates principles of structured programming.

EXAMPLE 10.14 Suppose in Example 10.12 that C returns to B with an EXIT PROGRAM, and then B executes a STOP RUN. In this case, control never returns to program A, since the STOP RUN in B terminates execution of the entire run unit at that point. Again, this violates principles of structured programming.

IBM OS/VS COBOL offers an extension to ANSI standard COBOL for returning to a calling program. The IBM OS/VS COBOL GOBACK statement may appear *anywhere* in a PROCEDURE DIVISION (it need not be placed in a separate paragraph). When executed, it *always* causes control to return to the calling program.

If a GOBACK is executed in a program which was CALLed by another, then the GOBACK effects a return to the CALLing program (same as EXIT PROGRAM). If a GOBACK appears in a main program, the "calling program" is considered to be the operating system and the GOBACK causes a return to it, which results in the termination of the run unit.

EXAMPLE 10.15   The following is a revision of Example 10.6 which uses the IBM OS/VS COBOL GOBACK statement instead of the ANSI standard EXIT PROGRAM. Note that GOBACK need not be placed in a separate paragraph.

```
PROCEDURE DIVISION
     USING  NUMERIC-DATA-ITEM
            ANY-RECORD-LINKAGE-AREA
            ALPHA-ITEM-AREA
         .
     MOVE 12       TO NUMERIC-DATA-ITEM
     MOVE "AB"     TO ALPHA-ITEM-AREA
     MOVE SPACES   TO FIELD-A
     MOVE ZERO     TO FIELD-B
     GOBACK
         .
```

EXAMPLE 10.16   Figure 10-2 shows an IBM OS/VS COBOL main program which calls an external subprogram named BUILDMSG. In order to focus on subprogram linkage considerations, the subprogram does nothing more than format a trivial user message describing exceptional conditions. The CALLing program then DISPLAYs the message. CALL statements appear on lines 80, 86, 92, 119, and 125.

Note that BUILDMSG must be designed to receive three arguments, since each CALL statement lists three data items in its USING list. Note, too, that while the PICTUREs and USAGEs of the three arguments are always the same, the arguments themselves vary from CALL to CALL (e.g., the CALL on line 80 passes USERS-MESSAGE, RUN-COMPLETED-MSG, and BLANK-TRANS-RECORD; while the CALL on line 119 passes USERS-MESSAGE, RECORD-NOT-FOUND-MSG, and TRANSACTION-RECORD).

The purpose of the external subprogram is to fill in the ERROR-TEXT and ERROR-RECORD subfields of USERS-MESSAGE with the information provided by the second and third arguments, respectively. Note that the first argument is a group item (USERS-MESSAGE, the same for all CALLs), while the second and third arguments are elementary items which *vary* from one CALL to the next.

Finally, note how a *blank* record area (BLANK-TRANS-RECORD, defined on lines 64–65) is passed to the subprogram when the error in question does not actually involve a transaction record. This is necessary because the subprogram is designed to *receive* three arguments, and hence must always be *passed* three arguments. By passing BLANK-TRANS-RECORD for the third argument when there is no transaction record involved in the message to be constructed, the ERROR-RECORD portion of USERS-MESSAGE will be set blank, and so will not appear on the DISPLAYed output.

EXAMPLE 10.17   Figure 10-3 shows the IBM OS/VS COBOL external subprogram BUILDMSG CALLed in Fig. 10-2. As is common, the DATA DIVISION of the called program has nothing more than a LINKAGE SECTION in which the arguments are described. Note how the LINKAGE SECTION items are named in the PROCEDURE DIVISION header in lines 16–20. Care must be taken that the LINKAGE SECTION descriptions of the arguments and their order in the USING list exactly match the descriptions and order in the CALL statement USING list of the calling program(s).

Note, too, how the subprogram returns to the calling program after formatting the desired message (lines 26–29). This subprogram has been deliberately kept simple to better show linkage details.

10.4 Dynamic Linkage Versus Static Linkage

When an external subprogram is separately compiled and the resulting object module is link edited with the calling program to produce an executable load module, the linkage between the calling and called program is said to be *static*. In *static linkage*, the calling and called programs are linked (by a linkage editor or the equivalent) prior to execution. Observe that with static linkage the external subprogram is part of the load module (and hence occupies memory space during execution) whether or not it is ever called.

ANSI COBOL provides a second type of linkage in which the subprogram is not link edited into the calling program's load module, but rather is linked and stored as a separate load module on a

```
00001          IDENTIFICATION DIVISION.
00002          PROGRAM-ID.  CALLING-PROGRAM.

00003          ENVIRONMENT DIVISION.
00004          CONFIGURATION SECTION.
00005          SOURCE-COMPUTER.  IBM-3081.
00006          OBJECT-COMPUTER.  IBM-3081.
00007          INPUT-OUTPUT SECTION.
00008          FILE-CONTROL.

00009              SELECT TRANSACTION-FILE
00010                  ASSIGN TO PROGIDS
00011                  ORGANIZATION IS SEQUENTIAL
00012                  ACCESS IS SEQUENTIAL
00013              .
00014              SELECT INDEXED-FILE
00015                  ASSIGN TO VSAMFILE
00016                  ORGANIZATION IS INDEXED
00017                  ACCESS IS RANDOM
00018                  RECORD KEY IS INDEXED-PROGRAMMER-ID
00019                  FILE STATUS IS INDEXED-STATUS-CODE
00020              .

00021          DATA DIVISION.
00022          FILE SECTION.

00023          FD  TRANSACTION-FILE
00024              LABEL RECORDS ARE STANDARD
00025              BLOCK CONTAINS O CHARACTERS
00026              RECORD CONTAINS 80 CHARACTERS
00027              .
00028          01  TRANSACTION-RECORD.
00029              05  TRANS-PROGRAMMER-ID        PIC X(5).
00030              05  FILLER                     PIC X(75).

00031          FD  INDEXED-FILE
00032              LABEL RECORDS ARE STANDARD
00033              RECORD CONTAINS 15 CHARACTERS
                   .
00034          01  INDEXED-RECORD.
00035              05  INDEXED-PROGRAMMER-ID      PIC X(5).
00036              05  INDEXED-PROJECT-ID         PIC X(8).
00037              05  INDEXED-TOTAL-HOURS        PIC 9(3)V9 COMP.
00038          WORKING-STORAGE SECTION.

00039          01  FLAGS-AND-SWITCHES.
00040              05  TRANS-END-OF-FILE-SW       PIC X(3).
00041                  88  MORE-TRANS-RECORDS     VALUE "NO".
00042                  88  NO-MORE-INPUT          VALUE "YES".

00043          01  FILE-STATUS-CODES.
00044              05  INDEXED-STATUS-CODE        PIC XX.
00045                  88  VSAM-OPERATION-OK      VALUE "00".
00046                  88  VSAM-OPERATION-FAILED  VALUE "01" THRU "99".
00047                  88  RECORD-NOT-FOUND       VALUE "23".

00048          01  WS-USERS-MESSAGE-AREA.
00049              05  USERS-MESSAGE.
00050                  10  ERROR-TEXT             PIC X(30).
00051                  10  FILLER                 PIC X(3) VALUE SPACES.
00052                  10  ERROR-RECORD           PIC X(80).
00053              05  TEXT-AREA.
00054                  10  RUN-COMPLETED-MSG      PIC X(30)
00055                          VALUE "RETRIEVAL COMPLETED".
00056                  10  FILE-NOT-CLOSED-MSG    PIC X(30)
00057                          VALUE "INDEXED FILE NOT CLOSED".
00058                  10  FILE-NOT-OPEN-MSG      PIC X(30)
00059                          VALUE "UNABLE TO OPEN INDEXED FILE".
00060                  10  RECORD-NOT-FOUND-MSG   PIC X(30)
00061                          VALUE "RECORD NOT FOUND".
00062                  10  UNEXPECTED-ERROR-MSG   PIC X(30)
00063                          VALUE "UNEXPECTED VSAM ERROR".
```

Fig. 10-2

```
00064                      10   BLANK-TRANS-RECORD        PIC X(80)
00065                                   VALUE SPACES.

00066          PROCEDURE DIVISION.
00067
00068          000-EXECUTIVE-MODULE.
00069
00070              MOVE "NO" TO TRANS-END-OF-FILE-SW
00071              OPEN    INPUT    INDEXED-FILE
00072                               TRANSACTION-FILE
00073              IF VSAM-OPERATION-OK
00074                  PERFORM 010-GET-NEXT-TRANS
00075                  PERFORM 020-RETRIEVE-INDEXED-RECORD
00076                      UNTIL NO-MORE-INPUT
00077                  CLOSE   INDEXED-FILE
00078                          TRANSACTION-FILE
00079                  IF VSAM-OPERATION-OK
00080                      CALL "BUILDMSG" USING
00081                          USERS-MESSAGE
00082                          RUN-COMPLETED-MSG
00083                          BLANK-TRANS-RECORD
00084                      DISPLAY USERS-MESSAGE
00085                  ELSE
00086                      CALL "BUILDMSG" USING
00087                          USERS-MESSAGE
00088                          FILE-NOT-CLOSED-MSG
00089                          BLANK-TRANS-RECORD
00090                      DISPLAY USERS-MESSAGE
00091              ELSE
00092                      CALL "BUILDMSG" USING
00093                          USERS-MESSAGE
00094                          FILE-NOT-OPEN-MSG
00095                          BLANK-TRANS-RECORD
00096                      DISPLAY USERS-MESSAGE
00097                  CLOSE TRANSACTION-FILE
00098                  .
00099              STOP RUN
00100                  .
00101
00102          010-GET-NEXT-TRANS.
00103
00104              READ TRANSACTION-FILE
00105                  AT END
00106                      MOVE "YES" TO TRANS-END-OF-FILE-SW
00107                  .
00108
00109          020-RETRIEVE-INDEXED-RECORD.
00110
00111              MOVE TRANS-PROGRAMMER-ID    TO INDEXED-PROGRAMMER-ID
00112              READ INDEXED-FILE
00113              IF VSAM-OPERATION-OK
00114                  DISPLAY INDEXED-PROGRAMMER-ID
00115                          SPACE
00116                          INDEXED-TOTAL-HOURS
00117              ELSE
00118                  IF RECORD-NOT-FOUND
00119                      CALL "BUILDMSG" USING
00120                          USERS-MESSAGE
00121                          RECORD-NOT-FOUND-MSG
00122                          TRANSACTION-RECORD
00123                      DISPLAY USERS-MESSAGE
00124                  ELSE
00125                      CALL "BUILDMSG" USING
00126                          USERS-MESSAGE
00127                          UNEXPECTED-ERROR-MSG
00128                          TRANSACTION-RECORD
00129                      DISPLAY USERS-MESSAGE
00130                  .
00131              PERFORM 010-GET-NEXT-TRANS
00132                  .
```

Fig. 10-2   (cont.)

```
00001               IDENTIFICATION DIVISION.
00002               PROGRAM-ID.  BUILDMSG.

00003               ENVIRONMENT DIVISION.
00004               CONFIGURATION SECTION.
00005               SOURCE-COMPUTER.  IBM-3081.
00006               OBJECT-COMPUTER.  IBM-3081.

00007               DATA DIVISION.

00008               LINKAGE SECTION.

00009               01  LINKAGE-USERS-MESSAGE.
00010                   10  USERS-MESSAGE-TEXT        PIC X(30).
00011                   10  FILLER                    PIC X(3).
00012                   10  USERS-MESSAGE-RECORD      PIC X(80).
00013               01  LINKAGE-ERROR-TEXT            PIC X(30).
00014               01  LINKAGE-ERROR-RECORD          PIC X(80).
00015
00016               PROCEDURE DIVISION
00017                   USING  LINKAGE-USERS-MESSAGE
00018                          LINKAGE-ERROR-TEXT
00019                          LINKAGE-ERROR-RECORD
00020                   .
00021
00022                   MOVE    LINKAGE-ERROR-TEXT    TO USERS-MESSAGE-TEXT
00023                   MOVE    LINKAGE-ERROR-RECORD TO USERS-MESSAGE-RECORD
00024                   .
00025
00026               RETURN-TO-CALLING-PROGRAM.
00027
00028                   EXIT PROGRAM
00029                   .
```

Fig. 10-3

load module (execution) library. The external subprogram is not initially loaded into memory with the calling program. If the calling program never actually calls the subprogram, the subprogram never gets loaded (thus conserving memory for other uses). If the calling program *does* execute a CALL on the subprogram, then the operating system will, when the CALL is executed, automatically load a copy of the external subprogram from its load library into memory and establish the necessary linkage between the subprogram and the calling program.

Advantages and Disadvantages of Static and Dynamic Linkage

A CALL in which the subprogram is automatically loaded into memory and linked to the calling program by the operating system at the time the CALL is executed is said to be a *dynamic CALL* and illustrates *dynamic linkage*. Dynamic linkage has a major advantage in that a subprogram need not take up memory until and unless it is actually CALLed. The major disadvantage of dynamic linkage is that it takes more time to execute a dynamic CALL (which requires that the subprogram be input from a load library and linkage established with the calling program) than a static CALL (where the subprogram is already part of the calling program's load module and is, therefore, already in memory along with the calling program, and where linking has already been performed prior to execution by a linkage editor or the equivalent).

Static linkage executes faster than dynamic linkage, although it requires more advance preparation in that the subprogram must be linked to the calling program in advance by a linkage editor or the equivalent. Static linkage is best suited for external subprograms which tend to be heavily used.

EXAMPLE 10.18 The following subprograms would probably be called frequently during execution and, therefore, should probably be CALLed using static linkage:

(1) A subprogram to validate incoming transactions

(2) A subprogram to apply changes to master records during a master file update

(3) A subprogram to format a print line for a report program

(4) A subprogram to calculate employee withholding during a payroll run

Dynamic linkage is best suited for external subprograms which will be called infrequently or sometimes not at all. In this case, the extra time involved in dynamic linkage will be relatively small, while the memory savings may be significant.

EXAMPLE 10.19   Real-life error-handling routines tend to be large in size but (hopefully) infrequently needed, and are usually good candidates for dynamic linkage. Examples of subprograms which might be CALLed using dynamic linkage include:

(1)   A subprogram to deal with overtime hours that exceed the company's limit during a payroll run

(2)   A subprogram to deal with an uncorrectable I/O error during a file update

(3)   A subprogram to process an inquiry transaction which can only be input from two terminals restricted to top-level management

(4)   A subprogram to truncate a new customer name which exceeds the size of the CUSTOMER-NAME field in the appropriate master file

Implementing Dynamic Linkage in ANSI COBOL

The choice of dynamic versus static linkage to an external subprogram is determined in ANSI COBOL by three things: (1) the job control/command language statements used when the calling and called programs are both compiled and linked, (2) the job control/command language used when the main (calling) load module is executed, and (3) the type of CALL statement used in the COBOL program. Items (1) and (2) are beyond the scope of this Outline. Consult an instructor and/or vendor manual for the job control/command language needed to implement dynamic linkage on your system.

The ANSI standard CALL statement used for dynamic linkage has the form:

```
CALL name-of-data-item-containing-program-id-of-subprogram
    [ USING name-of-argument-1 [name-argument-2] ... ]
    [ ON OVERFLOW imperative-statement(s). ]
```

The name of the subprogram to be invoked is placed in an alphanumeric data item (usually defined in WORKING-STORAGE) before the CALL is executed. The fact that a data item is used (instead of a literal) to indicate the name of the subprogram tells the compiler that this is to be a dynamic CALL. The external subprogram is written in exactly the same way for both static and dynamic calls.

The USING clause lists the names of data items to be passed to the subprogram as arguments (same as for static CALLs).

The ON OVERFLOW clause consists of a set of imperative statements to be executed if and only if there is not sufficient memory for the operating system to load the CALLed subprogram. Clearly in this case, the CALL statement cannot be executed. Dynamic CALLs should always be written with the ON OVERFLOW clause to cover this (otherwise disastrous) possibility. Note that ON OVERFLOW follows the pattern of AT END and INVALID KEY in that *it must end with a period*.

EXAMPLE 10.20   Show how to modify the CALL on lines 119–122 of Fig. 10-2 to be a dynamic call:

```
MOVE "BUILDMSG" TO NAME-OF-EXTERNAL-SUBPROGRAM
CALL NAME-OF-EXTERNAL-SUBPROGRAM
    USING USERS-MESSAGE
          RECORD-NOT-FOUND-MSG
          TRANSACTION-RECORD
    ON OVERFLOW
        MOVE "YES" TO NOT-ENOUGH-MEMORY-ABORT-SW
```

The data item NAME-OF-EXTERNAL-SUBPROGRAM would be defined in WORKING-STORAGE as PIC X(8). When the CALL is executed, the current contents of NAME-OF-EXTERNAL-SUBPROGRAM are passed to the operating system, which searches available load libraries for the necessary subprogram. Upon finding BUILDMSG, the operating system attempts to load a copy of the subprogram into memory and establish the linkage (including the passing of arguments) with the calling program. If there is not enough memory available to hold the subprogram, the operating system does *not* load it and immediately returns to the calling program's ON OVERFLOW routine.

If the subprogram has been successfully loaded, control returns to the statement immediately following the period marking the end of the ON OVERFLOW routine (back in the calling program) when the subprogram executes its EXIT PROGRAM (or GOBACK). Note that a period *must* be used to mark the end of the ON OVERFLOW routine. The use of ON OVERFLOW is always recommended for dynamic calls.

If the indicated subprogram cannot be found, or if memory is not available and ON OVERFLOW was not specified, the CALLing program will ABEND.

Use of the CANCEL Statement for Dynamic Calls

When an external subprogram is CALLed dynamically, it is loaded into memory only when (and *if*) it is actually needed. The CANCEL statement provides a means to remove a dynamically called external subprogram from memory, thus freeing memory for other uses (including the loading of other dynamically called external subprograms).

The ANSI standard CANCEL statement has the form:

```
CANCEL { "program-id" | data-item-containing-program-id } . . .
```

Execution of the CANCEL statement causes a dynamically CALLed subprogram to be released from memory, thus freeing memory resources. The name of the subprogram to be CANCELed may be supplied either as a nonnumeric literal or as the contents of a data item. If the subprogram being CANCELed has already been CANCELed or has never been CALLed, the CANCEL statement simply does nothing (note that this does *not* cause an error).

EXAMPLE 10.21   The following are valid CANCEL statements:

   (1) CANCEL "BUILDMSG"

   (2) CANCEL "BUILDMSG"
             "VALIDATE"

   (3) MOVE   "BUILDMSG" TO NAME-OF-SUBPROGRAM-AREA
       CANCEL "VALIDATE"
             NAME-OF-SUBPROGRAM-AREA

When a subprogram is dynamically CALLed, the copy brought into memory stays in memory until it is CANCELed. After a subprogram is CANCELed, it may be CALLed again. When this happens, a fresh copy of the subprogram is loaded from the operating system load library into memory. This mechanism can be useful not only to control memory utilization but also to control whether a *fresh* copy or an *old* copy of the subprogram is executed.

EXAMPLE 10.22   Given the following subprogram:

```
PROGRAM-ID.  DYNAM.

WORKING-STORAGE SECTION.
01   CALL-COUNTER   PIC 9 VALUE ZERO.

PROCEDURE DIVISION.
     DISPLAY CALL-COUNTER
     ADD 1 TO CALL-COUNTER
     .
RETURN-TO-CALLER.
     EXIT PROGRAM.
```

explain what is output by the following series of CALLs:

```
MOVE "DYNAM" TO NAME-OF-SUBPROGRAM
CALL NAME-OF-SUBPROGRAM                          (1)
CALL NAME-OF-SUBPROGRAM                          (2)
CANCEL NAME-OF-SUBPROGRAM
CALL NAME-OF-SUBPROGRAM                          (3)
```

The first CALL statement causes the operating system to load an initial copy of the external subprogram named DYNAM into memory for execution. Since DYNAM initializes CALL-COUNTER to 0 with the VALUE clause, this initial execution of DYNAM DISPLAYs the value 0 and then increments CALL-COUNTER to 1.

The second CALL does *not* load a fresh copy of DYNAM into memory since there is already an active copy of the subprogram available. Thus the second CALL executes exactly the same copy of the subprogram as the first CALL. This means that CALL-COUNTER will contain the value 1 (as left by the first execution) at the beginning of the second execution. Thus the second CALL causes the value 1 to be DISPLAYed and increments CALL-COUNTER to 2.

The CANCEL statement removes the active copy of subprogram DYNAM from memory, thus freeing the storage it occupied for other use.

Since a CANCEL for subprogram DYNAM was issued before the third CALL, the third CALL will cause the operating system to load a *fresh* copy of the subprogram from the system load library. This fresh copy off the disk library will, of course, have CALL-COUNTER initialized to 0 (because of the VALUE clause), so that the third execution is equivalent to the first, DISPLAYing 0 and incrementing CALL-COUNTER to 1. Any subsequent CALL (without an intervening CANCEL) would find CALL-COUNTER equal to 1.

Great care must be taken when using dynamic linkage to ensure that data items defined in the WORKING-STORAGE SECTION of the subprogram are properly initialized. If the subprogram initializes items with PROCEDURE DIVISION statements, then the same copy of the subprogram can be used repeatedly. If the subprogram relies on the VALUE clause to initialize items whose values change as the program executes, then CANCEL must be used to ensure that a fresh copy of the subprogram is brought in for each CALL.

Clearly it is more efficient if dynamic subprograms avoid using the VALUE clause for data items which might change during execution (see *Schaum's Outline of Programming with Structured COBOL*, McGraw-Hill, 1984). This allows the same copy of the subprogram to be used by several CALLs, thus saving the time required to load the subprogram from the system load library.

EXAMPLE 10.23 The following dynamic subprogram finds the average of two arguments passed to it, placing the result in a third. It is designed as an exercise in dynamic linkage and is otherwise unrealistic.

```
PROGRAM-ID. DYNAMAVG.

WORKING-STORAGE SECTION.
01   SUM-OF-ARGS    PIC S9(5) COMP VALUE ZERO.

LINKAGE SECTION.
01   FIRST-NUM      PIC S9(5) COMP.
01   SECOND-NUM     PIC S9(5) COMP.
01   AVERAGE        PIC S9(5) COMP.

PROCEDURE DIVISION
     USING    FIRST-NUM
              SECOND-NUM
              AVERAGE

     .
     ADD FIRST-NUM TO  SUM-OF-ARGS
     ADD SECOND-NUM TO SUM-OF-ARGS
     DIVIDE SUM-OF-ARGS BY 2 GIVING AVERAGE

     .
RETURN-TO-CALLER.
     EXIT PROGRAM.
```

The following sequence of dynamic CALLs would *not* work correctly:

```
MOVE "DYNAMAVG" TO NAME-OF-SUBPROGRAM
CALL NAME-OF-SUBPROGRAM
        USING      NUMBER-IS-2
                   NUMBER-IS-4
                   FIRST-AVERAGE
        ON OVERFLOW
            PERFORM NOT-ENOUGH-MEMORY
         .
CALL NAME-OF-SUBPROGRAM
        USING      NUMBER-IS-6
                   NUMBER-IS-8
                   SECOND-AVERAGE
        ON OVERFLOW
            PERFORM NOT-ENOUGH-MEMORY
         .
```

The first call passes the numbers 2 and 4 to the subprogram, which adds them to SUM-OF-ARGS; SUM-OF-ARGS thus contains the value 6. Since there is no CANCEL between the first and second CALLs, the second CALL invokes the *same* copy of the subprogram as the first. Thus when the second CALL passes the numbers 6 and 8, they are added to the 6 left in SUM-OF-ARGS by the previous CALL (giving a result of 20). This causes the second CALL to produce an *incorrect average* of 10 (instead of 7).

EXAMPLE 10.24   The problem illustrated in Example 10.23 could be corrected in either of two ways:

(1)   Redesign the *calling* program to execute a CANCEL "DYNAMAVG" statement in between the two CALLs. This would cause the second CALL to bring in a fresh copy of the subprogram, with SUM-OF-ARGS again initialized to 0.

(2)   Redesign the *subprogram* so that it does not use the VALUE clause to initialize SUM-OF-ARGS, i.e.:

```
PROCEDURE DIVISION USING ...
    MOVE ZERO TO SUM-OF-ARGS
    ADD ...
    ADD ...
    DIVIDE ...
```

If SUM-OF-ARGS is initialized with a MOVE statement, then the *same copy* of the subprogram can be correctly used by both CALL statements without the need for an intervening CANCEL operation. Note that this second solution is more efficient with respect to overall execution time (since the "expensive" CANCEL and reloading operations are eliminated). Although this example is trivial, the principles illustrated should be carefully understood.

10.5   COPY Versus CALL Libraries

A routine (module) which may be needed by several different COBOL programs or at several places within the same COBOL program can be implemented in four different ways:

(1)   The routine may be *hard-coded* into each COBOL program at each spot where it is needed. This is a poor choice because it results in duplication of effort by the programmer(s) involved, produces many different copies of the same routine (thus taking up extra memory), and creates maintenance difficulties since each copy of the routine must be located and changed separately.

(2)   The routine may be hard-coded once into each program which needs it and then PERFORMed as an internal subprogram as many times as appropriate within each program. This is a slightly better approach which saves memory, since each program has

only one copy of the common module. Maintenance is also slightly easier since the code need only be changed at one point within each program. Each program's copy of the code would have to be changed separately, however, and each program recompiled and relinked.

(3) Place the routine in a COPY (source program) library. The routine could then be COPYed once into each program which needs it during compilation. If a given program needs to use the routine at several different points, it would PERFORM the single copy as an internal subprogram.

This approach saves memory since each program contains only one copy of the module. It also makes maintenance easier since only one copy of the module need be modified (the copy in the source program library). Each program using the module would, however, have to be recompiled and relinked to obtain the updated version of the module.

(4) Compile the module and place it in an object module (subroutine) library. Design each program which uses the module to CALL it as an external subprogram wherever needed.

This approach saves memory if static CALLs are used, since only one copy of the module is linked (by the linkage editor) to the calling program. If dynamic CALLs are used, possibly *no copy* of the module will actually be loaded (if a CALL statement is never executed for the module).

This approach also minimizes maintenance because not only does just *one* copy of the code have to be changed but only the module itself needs to be recompiled (and the updated object program placed in the appropriate subroutine library). If static calls are used, each calling program will have to be relinked to pick up the updated version of the module, but not recompiled (thus saving maintenance effort). If dynamic calls are used, the calling program(s) will not even have to be relinked. The operating system will automatically load the updated subprogram module from the system load library during dynamic CALL execution.

Summary of Approaches

The first approach is viable only for trivial routines of at most a few lines. The second approach may be attractive for routines which appear in only one program. Routines which are used by more than one program should be handled using either the third or fourth approach.

If COPY libraries are used as in (3), then there is no concern regarding the passing of arguments.

If CALL libraries are used as in (4), then great care must be taken to ensure that the arguments actually passed by the CALLing programs match the descriptions of those items in the subprogram's LINKAGE SECTION. Sometimes it is useful in this case to establish COPY library entries for the data items appearing in the USING lists of the CALLs and subprogram PROCEDURE DIVISION headers. If standard argument descriptions are COPYed from a library, many "coupling" difficulties are eliminated. In either case, approach (4) calls for good communication between all people involved in writing, maintaining, and CALLing library modules.

Review Questions

10.1   Differentiate between internal and external subprograms.

10.2   Explain what is meant by a load module or run unit.

10.3   What functions does a linkage editor or linking loader carry out?

10.4 Distinguish between system subprograms and user-written subprograms. What is the purpose of system subprograms?

10.5 How is an internal subprogram called?

10.6 How is an external subprogram called?

10.7 Explain the function of the CALL statement.

10.8 Explain the function of the EXIT PROGRAM statement.

10.9 Explain the rules which the calling program must follow when passing arguments to an external subprogram.

10.10 Explain the rules which the subprogram must follow in order to correctly access arguments passed from a calling program.

10.11 Explain the considerations involved in making up a PROGRAM-ID for an external subprogram.

10.12 Explain the rules which must be followed to achieve a correct combination of the USING list in a CALL statement with the USING list in the subprogram's PROCEDURE DIVISION header.

10.13 Explain how changes to LINKAGE SECTION items in a subprogram actually change corresponding data items back in the calling program.

10.14 Explain how it is possible that LINKAGE SECTION items do not actually take up any memory space in the subprogram.

10.15 Explain how the "meaning" of a LINKAGE SECTION item may change from one CALL to the next.

10.16 Explain what happens if the USING list in a CALL is incompatible with the USING list in a subprogram PROCEDURE DIVISION header.

10.17 What happens if EXIT PROGRAM is executed by a main program (i.e., the program directly invoked by the operating system)?

10.18 Explain the difference between STOP RUN and EXIT PROGRAM.

10.19 Discuss the use of the IBM OS/VS COBOL GOBACK statement.

10.20 Explain the difference between static and dynamic linkage.

10.21 What are the advantages of static linkage and when should it be used?

10.22 What are the advantages of dynamic linkage and when should it be used?

10.23 Discuss the differences in the syntax of an ANSI COBOL CALL statement for static linkage and dynamic linkage.

10.24 What is the purpose of the ON OVERFLOW clause for a dynamic CALL?

10.25 Discuss the function and use of the CANCEL statement for dynamic linkage.

10.26 What happens if multiple dynamic calls to a subprogram are made without an intervening CANCEL?

10.27 Discuss some restrictions on dynamic subprograms which are called multiple times without being CANCELed.

10.28 Why should dynamically called subprograms use the VALUE clause only for items whose value never changes?

10.29 Discuss the four different ways to implement routines used by more than one program, and compare and contrast them with respect to (1) efficiency of execution and (2) ease of maintenance.

Solved Problems

10.30 What is the difference between a linkage editor and a linking loader?

A linkage editor links together one or more object modules plus any user or system library subprograms that they call, placing the result (usually called a load module) in a *load library* on a direct access device. When it is desired to execute the load module, it can be loaded from the load module library into main memory for execution. Since a *permanent* copy of the load module is produced, there is no need to relink the modules each time they are executed.

Use of a linkage editor results in the fastest possible execution of debugged programs, since they need only be copied into memory and executed. A linkage editor is inefficient during debugging, however, because each time a change is made to a program, the modules must be relinked and placed in a disk load library, only to be immediately reloaded into memory for testing. Further, since the load module usually has bugs, it needs to be deleted from the load library after the test run.

A linking loader links together one or more object modules plus any user or system library subprograms that they call, placing the result directly in main memory where it is executed immediately. This system is ideal for debugging (when a permanent copy of an undebugged load module is usually not desired) and is faster than using a linkage editor since the load module is not placed out on disk only to be immediately reloaded.

Once a program is debugged, however, the final version should be linked with the linkage editor to produce a permanent load module in a load library. Use of a linking loader for a debugged program is wasteful since the program would have to be relinked every time it is executed.

10.31 Differentiate between system subprograms and user-written subprograms.

System subprograms are supplied with the operating system and/or with particular compilers. They perform functions which have been found to be useful to all installations or which are needed for the proper functioning of the object programs produced by the compilers. They typically are not designed to meet the needs of business applications.

User-written subprograms are external subprograms either written by in-house programming staff or purchased from outside software companies. In either case, they are designed to solve specific problems of given business applications.

Both types of subprograms may be placed in object module (subprogram) libraries and made publicly available to all programmers at an installation for either static or dynamic CALLs.

10.32 Illustrate how external subprograms can in turn CALL *other* external subprograms by redesigning the subprogram in Fig. 10-3 to call an external subprogram named LEFTJUST (which ensures that USERS-MESSAGE-TEXT is left-justified).

```
        IDENTIFICATION DIVISION.
        PROGRAM-ID.  BUILDMSG.

        DATA DIVISION.
        LINKAGE SECTION.
```

```
01   LINKAGE-USERS-MESSAGE.
     05   USERS-MESSAGE-TEXT        PIC X(30).
     05   FILLER                    PIC X(3).
     05   USERS-MESSAGE-RECORD      PIC X(80).
01   LINKAGE-ERROR-TEXT            PIC X(30).
01   LINKAGE-ERROR-RECORD          PIC X(80).

PROCEDURE DIVISION
     USING    LINKAGE-USERS-MESSAGE
              LINKAGE-ERROR-TEXT
              LINKAGE-ERROR-RECORD
     .
     MOVE LINKAGE-ERROR-TEXT TO USERS-MESSAGE-TEXT
     CALL "LEFTJUST"
          USING    USERS-MESSAGE-TEXT
     MOVE LINKAGE-ERROR-RECORD TO USERS-MESSAGE-RECORD
     .
RETURN-TO-CALLING-PROGRAM.
     EXIT PROGRAM
     .
```

BUILDMSG, itself an external subprogram, can validly CALL still other subprograms (which can in turn CALL yet other subprograms, etc.). Note that the argument passed in the CALL on LEFTJUST is itself a LINKAGE SECTION item passed to BUILDMSG from *its* calling program. This is perfectly legal.

When LEFTJUST executes its EXIT PROGRAM, control will return to the MOVE LINKAGE-ERROR-RECORD . . . statement immediately following CALL "LEFTJUST" . . . in BUILDMSG.

10.33 Some versions of COBOL allow an ENTRY statement to be used to define multiple external subprograms *within the same PROCEDURE DIVISION* (in strict ANSI COBOL, the entire PROCEDURE DIVISION is always one big external subprogram). Illustrate the use of the ENTRY statement by writing an IBM OS/VS COBOL subprogram to perform the following operations on a sequential file: (1) open the file, (2) close the file, and (3) input a record from the file. Different entry points in the program may use different arguments, as defined in the USING clause of the ENTRY statement. The ENTRY statement also assigns a *name* to the entry point (this name must be used in the CALL statement which invokes the entry point). Note that each entry point routine is indeed written as a separate subprogram. In particular, each entry point ends with its own GOBACK or EXIT PROGRAM. The format of the ENTRY statement is:

```
ENTRY "name-of-entry-point"
     [ USING name-of-argument-1 [name-of-argument-2] ... ]
```

The following program illustrates the use of the ENTRY statement.

```
IDENTIFICATION DIVISION.
PROGRAM-ID.  MULTIPLE-ENTRY-POINTS-EXAMPLE.
ENVIRONMENT DIVISION . . .
     SELECT SAMPLE-FILE
          ASSIGN TO EXTNAME
          ORGANIZATION IS INDEXED
          ACCESS IS SEQUENTIAL
          RECORD KEY IS KEY-AREA
          FILE STATUS IS STATUS-AREA
     .
DATA DIVISION.
FILE SECTION.
FD   SAMPLE-FILE
     LABEL RECORDS ARE STANDARD.
```

```
01   SAMPLE-RECORD.
     05    KEY-AREA               PIC X(5).
     05    FILLER                 PIC X(95).
WORKING-STORAGE SECTION.
01   STATUS-AREA                  PIC XX.
LINKAGE SECTION.
01   AREA-TO-HOLD-RECORD          PIC X(100).
01   I-O-ERROR-SWITCH             PIC X(3).
PROCEDURE DIVISION.

     ENTRY "OPENFILE"
         USING  I-O-ERROR-SWITCH.
           OPEN INPUT SAMPLE-FILE
           IF STATUS-AREA NOT EQUAL "00"
               MOVE "YES" TO I-O-ERROR-SWITCH
           ELSE
               MOVE "NO"  TO I-O-ERROR-SWITCH

           .
           GOBACK.

     ENTRY "CLOSEFIL"
         USING  I-O-ERROR-SWITCH.
           CLOSE SAMPLE-FILE
           IF STATUS-AREA NOT EQUAL "00"
               MOVE "YES" TO I-O-ERROR-SWITCH
           ELSE
               MOVE "NO"  TO I-O-ERROR-SWITCH

           .
           GOBACK.

     ENTRY "READREC"
         USING  AREA-TO-HOLD-RECORD
                I-O-ERROR-SWITCH.
           READ SAMPLE-FILE
           IF STATUS-AREA NOT EQUAL "00"
               MOVE "YES" TO I-O-ERROR-SWITCH
           ELSE
               MOVE "NO"  TO I-O-ERROR-SWITCH
               MOVE SAMPLE-RECORD TO AREA-TO-HOLD-RECORD

           .
           GOBACK.
```

10.34 Show how to use the entry points in Problem 10.33 by writing CALLs to open the file, input a record, and then close the file.

```
CALL "OPENFILE"
    USING ERROR-SWITCH
IF ERROR-SWITCH EQUAL "NO"
    CALL "READREC"
        USING WS-AREA-WHERE-SUBPGM-PUTS-REC
              ERROR-SWITCH
    IF ERROR-SWITCH EQUAL "NO"
        DISPLAY WS-AREA-WHERE-SUBPGM-PUTS-REC

.
CALL "CLOSEFIL"
    USING ERROR-SWITCH
IF ERROR-SWITCH EQUAL "YES"
    DISPLAY "SOMETHING IS WRONG HERE"

.
```

10.35 Given the following subprogram:

```
PROGRAM-ID.  ASUB.

LINKAGE SECTION.
01   ARG-1              PIC XXX.
01   ARG-2              PIC 999.
01   ARG-3.
     05   SUB-FIELD-1   PIC 9.
     05   SUB-FIELD-2   PIC 99.
PROCEDURE DIVISION
     USING ARG-1 ARG-2 ARG-3.
          MOVE "ABC" TO ARG-1
          MOVE 123   TO ARG-2
          MOVE 4     TO SUB-FIELD-1
          MOVE 56    TO SUB-FIELD-2
              .
RETURN-TO-CALLER.
     EXIT PROGRAM.
```

What is accomplished by the following CALL?

```
WORKING-STORAGE SECTION.
    01   ALPHA          PIC XXX.
    01   BETA           PIC 999.
    01   GAMMA.
         05   GAMMA-1   PIC 9.
         05   GAMMA-2   PIC 99.
    PROCEDURE DIVISION.
         CALL "ASUB"
              USING ALPHA GAMMA BETA
```

Inspecting the USING lists, we see that ARG-1 in the subprogram corresponds to ALPHA in the calling program, ARG-2 in the subprogram corresponds to GAMMA in the calling program, and ARG-3 corresponds to BETA. Thus setting ARG-1 to "ABC" actually sets ALPHA to "ABC".

BETA is defined PIC 999 but corresponds to ARG-3, which is defined as the two subfields SUB-FIELD-1 (PIC 9) and SUB-FIELD-2 (PIC 99). In effect, it is as if *ARG-3 REDEFINES BETA*. Hence moving 4 to SUB-FIELD-1 is the same as moving 4 to the first byte of BETA, and moving 56 to SUB-FIELD-2 is the same as moving 56 to the second and third bytes of BETA. Since all data is USAGE DISPLAY, this has the effect of setting BETA (PIC 999) to the value 456.

Finally, GAMMA (composed of two subfields, PIC 9 and PIC 99, respectively) corresponds to ARG-2 PIC 999. Again, it is as if ARG-2 REDEFINES GAMMA. Thus when 123 is moved to ARG-2, the 1 is actually moved to GAMMA-1 and the 23 is actually moved to GAMMA-2.

10.36 Is the CALL in Problem 10.35 in error?

Technically, no. If the results produced by the CALL are anticipated and desired, then it is a correct CALL. If the intent was to match arguments exactly, then the *order* of the arguments should have been

```
CALL "ASUB" USING ALPHA BETA GAMMA
```

However, the order ALPHA GAMMA BETA does not produce any incompatibilities between the data definitions, and the subprogram can execute and produce the results described above.

This problem illustrates that data items in the CALL USING list and the subprogram USING list do not have to be defined identically. They must, however, be consistent in terms of data length and the way the data is used. The best way to check the correspondence is to ask whether the subprogram argument could *successfully* (and *meaningfully*) REDEFINE the item passed from the CALLing program. If the answer is yes, then the CALL should work correctly.

10.37 Will the following CALL work for the subprogram in Problem 10.35?

```
CALL "ASUB" USING GAMMA BETA ALPHA
```

Probably not. When the subprogram returns, GAMMA will have the value "ABC" stored in it (setting GAMMA-1 to "A" and GAMMA-2 to "BC"). If the calling program attempts to use these fields in calculations, the results will be incorrect and may lead to ABEND (since the fields are defined as numeric but do not contain numeric data). This is a case where the PIC XXX field in the subprogram cannot meaningfully REDEFINE the numeric subfields in the calling program.

10.38 Three programs (A, B, and C) call the *same* module (D). Depict the amount of work which must be done to change module D if the system is implemented (1) by hard-coding D into each program, (2) by COPYing D into each program, (3) by having each program CALL D statically, and (4) by having each program CALL D dynamically.

(1) D is hard-coded into each program:

Module	Modified	Recompiled	Relinked
A	×	×	×
B	×	×	×
C	×	×	×
D	(meaningless since D is part of A, B, and C)		

(2) D is COPYed into each program:

Module	Modified	Recompiled	Relinked
A		×	×
B		×	×
C		×	×
D	×		

(3) D is statically CALLed by each program:

Module	Modified	Recompiled	Relinked
A			×
B			×
C			×
D	×	×	

(4) D is dynamically CALLed by each program:

Module	Modified	Recompiled	Relinked
A			
B			
C			
D	×	×	×

10.39 Suppose a program is attempting to randomly input a record from an indexed file. Show how to dynamically CALL an error-handling subprogram named IOERROR if the status code indicates an error condition. IOERROR uses one argument: the indexed file STATUS CODE. Design the solution to ensure that a *fresh* copy of IOERROR is executed every time it is called.

```
READ SOME-INDEXED-FILE
IF INDEXED-STATUS-CODE NOT EQUAL CODE-FOR-SUCCESS
    MOVE "IOERROR" TO NAME-OF-MODULE
    CANCEL NAME-OF-MODULE
    CALL NAME-OF-MODULE
        USING INDEXED-STATUS-CODE
```

Chapter 11

Advanced Verbs:
Character Manipulation

Although not primarily designed for character manipulation, ANSI COBOL provides some powerful verbs which allow the following operations on strings of characters:

Verb	Operation Supported
INSPECT	*Counting* the occurrences of a given character string within another character string.
INSPECT	*Replacing* specified substrings of a given character string with a new value. This can be thought of as a translate operation in which a set of characters is "translated" into a different set of characters.
STRING	*Joining* the contents of two or more separate character strings to produce a single combined string.
UNSTRING	*Separating* a single string into one or more substrings which are placed into distinct receiving fields.

In addition to the ANSI standard statements for character manipulation, this chapter also discusses the nonstandard TRANSFORM statement, which allows easy translation of one set of characters into another.

11.1 Counting Characters—INSPECT . . . TALLYING

The TALLYING option of the INSPECT statement is used to count (tally) the number of times a given character or string of characters occurs within a specified data item. The count is placed in a numeric item named in the TALLYING clause. The syntax for this form of the INSPECT statement is:

```
INSPECT  name-of-data-item-to-be-examined
     TALLYING name-of-numeric-item-to-hold-count
     FOR { {ALL|LEADING} {data-item|literal}|CHARACTERS }
     [ {BEFORE|AFTER} INITIAL {data-item|literal} ] ...
```

The notation $\{a \mid b\}$ means that either *a* or *b* must be selected. The notation [*a*] means that *a* is optional. The ". . ." indicates that the FOR clause may be repeated more than once. Similarly, there may be more than one TALLYING clause specified in a single INSPECT statement.

The field to be inspected may be a group or elementary item but must have USAGE DISPLAY. The TALLYING field(s) must be elementary numeric field(s) without decimal points. For efficiency, it is best to make the TALLYING item(s) COMP (or COMP-3). It is the programmer's responsibility to initialize the TALLYING field(s) (typically to 0) before executing INSPECT.

The following examples illustrate valid INSPECT . . . TALLYING statements with their applications. To avoid confusion, the notation "b" is sometimes used to explicitly indicate a blank space.

EXAMPLE 11.1 INSPECT . . . TALLYING is often useful for *validating input fields*. Suppose a social security number is supposed to be entered in the form xxx-xx-xxxx. INSPECT can be used to check that the correct number of "-" is present in the field. Note that the programmer must initialize the TALLYING item NUMBER-OF-HYPHENS, and that it is defined with USAGE COMP.

```
05    SSN-TO-LOOK-AT       PIC X(11).
05    NUMBER-OF-HYPHENS    PIC S9 COMP.

MOVE ZERO TO NUMBER-OF-HYPHENS
INSPECT SSN-TO-LOOK-AT
      TALLYING NUMBER-OF-HYPHENS
      FOR ALL "-"
```

Contents of SSN Field	Tally in NUMBER-OF-HYPHENS
111-22-3333	2
111--2-3333	3
111b22b3333	0
11-12-2-3--	5

EXAMPLE 11.2 The following example determines how many decimal points are present in INPUT-FIELD, another validating operation. Note how TALLY pinpoints invalid input:

```
05    INPUT-FIELD      PIC X(6).
05    NUMBER-DECIMALS  PIC S9 COMP.

MOVE ZERO TO NUMBER-DECIMALS
INSPECT INPUT-FIELD
      TALLYING NUMBER-DECIMALS
      FOR ALL "."
```

Contents of INPUT-FIELD	Tally in NUMBER-DECIMALS
bb1.23	1
000123	0
001.23	1
0.1.23	2

EXAMPLE 11.3 Suppose an input field may have a leading minus sign. The following INSPECT statement uses the BEFORE INITIAL option to count the number of characters (hopefully none) in front of the first "−" (if any). "FOR CHARACTERS" specifies that *all* characters are to be counted. "BEFORE INITIAL . . ." specifies that *only those characters to the left of the initial occurrence of the specified value* are to be INSPECTed.

```
05    INPUT-NUMBER     PIC S999V99
                       SIGN IS LEADING SEPARATE CHARACTER.
05    MINUS-SIGN-COUNT PIC S9 COMP.
MOVE ZERO TO MINUS-SIGN-COUNT
INSPECT INPUT-NUMBER
      TALLYING MINUS-SIGN-COUNT
      FOR CHARACTERS
          BEFORE INITIAL "-"
```

INPUT-NUMBER	Tally in MINUS-SIGN-COUNT	
−12345	0	(No characters are *before* the first "−".)
b12345	0	(There is no initial "−".)
−00123	0	
bb − 123	2	(A blank space counts as a character.)
−bb123	0	(Spaces still make this field NOT NUMERIC.)
b1234−	5	
−123 − 5	0	(The second "−" is not an *initial* "−"; hence characters to the left of it are *not* counted; i.e., this test is not foolproof.)

EXAMPLE 11.4 INSPECT can also be used to test for a valid trailing sign. This involves counting the number of characters (hopefully none) following the minus sign. The FOR CHARACTERS AFTER INITIAL "−" clause counts the number of characters to the right of the first occurrence of a minus sign (if any).

```
05    INPUT-NUMBER        PIC S999V99
                          SIGN IS TRAILING SEPARATE CHARACTER.
05    MINUS-SIGN-COUNT    PIC S9 COMP.


MOVE ZERO TO MINUS-SIGN-COUNT
INSPECT INPUT-NUMBER
      TALLYING MINUS-SIGN-COUNT
      FOR CHARACTERS
          AFTER INITIAL "-"
```

INPUT-NUMBER	Tally in MINUS-SIGN-COUNT	
00123b	0	
00123−	0	(No characters are *after* the first "−".)
123 − bb	2	(Blanks count as characters.)
−12345	5	
bb−2bb	3	(Blanks count as characters.)
1 − 23 − 4	4	(*All* characters *after* the *initial* minus sign are counted, including the second "−".)

EXAMPLE 11.5 Suppose a reply typed by a terminal operator may or may not be left-justified. It is desired to count the number of blank spaces (if any) preceding the first nonblank character. This can be accomplished with the FOR LEADING . . . option, which counts the number of leftmost occurrences of the specified value. Any occurrences of the given value *not* at the extreme left of the INSPECTed field are *not* counted.

```
05    TERMINAL-REPLY     PIC X(15).
05    NUMBER-OF-BLANKS   PIC S9(2) COMP.


MOVE ZERO TO NUMBER-OF-BLANKS
INSPECT TERMINAL-REPLY
      TALLYING NUMBER-OF-BLANKS
          FOR LEADING SPACES
```

TERMINAL-REPLY	Tally in NUMBER-OF-BLANKS	
bbbbYESbbbbbbbb	4	(Only *leading* spaces are counted.)
YESbbbbbbbbbbbb	0	(These spaces are *not leading*.)
bNObbbbbbbbbbbb	1	(Only one space is a *leading* space.)
bbbbbbbbbbbbbbb	15	(*All* spaces are leading.)

EXAMPLE 11.6 INSPECT may also be used to count occurrences of a *group* of characters. Suppose it is desired to count the number of times the word "and" is used in a memo:

```
05    MEMO       PIC X(200).
05    AND-COUNT  PIC S9(3) COMP.


MOVE ZERO TO AND-COUNT
INSPECT MEMO
      TALLYING AND-COUNT
      FOR ALL " AND "
```

Note that the string actually being tabulated is "bANDb". The blanks preceding and following the desired word are necessary in order to keep such occurrences as the "AND" in "H*AND*Y" from being counted incorrectly.

	MEMO		*Tally in AND-COUNT*
TELL BILL AND SUE AND SANDY		2	
TELL SANDY		0	("AND" would match "S*ANDY*"; "b*AND*b" does not.)

EXAMPLE 11.7 Variables may also be used in INSPECT statements in place of literals. Note, however, that the following statement can only count words which are *exactly* 8 characters long (the length of WORD-TO-COUNT). It is assumed that a value has somehow been placed in WORD-TO-COUNT before the following is executed:

```
05   MEMO              PIC X(200).
05   WORD-TO-COUNT     PIC X(8).
05   WORD-COUNTER      PIC S9(3) COMP.


MOVE ZERO TO WORD-COUNTER
INSPECT MEMO
      TALLYING WORD-COUNTER
      FOR ALL WORD-TO-COUNT
```

EXAMPLE 11.8 The following example illustrates multiple tallying with one INSPECT statement:

```
05   MEMO              PIC X(200).
05   WORD-COUNTERS.
     10   AND-COUNT    PIC S9(3) COMP.
     10   OR-COUNT     PIC S9(3) COMP.
     10   NOT-COUNT    PIC S9(3) COMP.


MOVE ZEROS TO  AND-COUNT
               OR-COUNT
               NOT-COUNT
INSPECT MEMO
   TALLYING
      AND-COUNT
           FOR ALL " AND "
      OR-COUNT
           FOR ALL " OR "
      NOT-COUNT
           FOR ALL " NOT "
```

The reserved word "TALLYING" appears only *once*. The name of the data item to hold the count (together with its associated FOR clause) may be repeated as often as desired. In this case, there are three separate counters used to tally the number of times the words "AND", "OR", and "NOT" appear in MEMO.

EXAMPLE 11.9 Use an INSPECT statement to check that the hyphen is properly positioned in a telephone number of the form xxx-xxxx.

```
05   TELEPHONE-NUMBER          PIC X(8).
05   VALIDATION-COUNTERS.
     10   CHARACTERS-BEFORE-HYPHEN  PIC S9 COMP.
     10   TOTAL-HYPHENS             PIC S9 COMP.


MOVE ZEROS TO  CHARACTERS-BEFORE-HYPHEN
               TOTAL-HYPHENS
INSPECT TELEPHONE-NUMBER
```

```
            TALLYING
                TOTAL-HYPHENS
                    FOR ALL "-"
                CHARACTERS-BEFORE-HYPHEN
                    FOR CHARACTERS
                        BEFORE INITIAL "-"
        IF TOTAL-HYPHENS EQUAL 1 AND
            CHARACTERS-BEFORE-HYPHEN EQUAL 3
                MOVE "YES" TO VALID-SW
        ELSE
            MOVE "NO" TO VALID-SW
```

11.2   Replacing Characters—INSPECT . . . REPLACING

The ANSI COBOL INSPECT statement can also be used to replace a given character or string of characters in the INSPECTed field with a specified character or string of characters. This facility can be useful for *character translation* applications, where data prepared on one system is to be processed on a system using a different character code (e.g., it is sometimes necessary to translate from ASCII to EBCDIC or vice versa). The REPLACING option can also be useful for certain *editing* applications.

The syntax of INSPECT . . . REPLACING is either:

```
INSPECT name-of-data-item-to-be-inspected
    REPLACING CHARACTERS
        BY replacement-value
    [ { BEFORE|AFTER } INITIAL starting-string-value ] ...
```

or

```
INSPECT name-of-data-item-to-be-inspected
    REPLACING  { ALL|LEADING|FIRST } value-to-be-replaced
        BY replacement-value
    [ { BEFORE|AFTER } INITIAL starting-string-value ] ...
```

Both the INITIAL clause and the REPLACING clause can be repeated more than once in the same INSPECT statement.

The value to be replaced and the replacement value must be the same length. If data items are used to indicate either value, they *must* have USAGE DISPLAY. All data items are treated by the INSPECT statement as if they were REDEFINEd as alphanumeric. Thus care must be taken when applying INSPECT to data items which are *not* PIC X. If literals or figurative constants are used for either the value to be replaced or the replacement value, they must be *nonnumeric* (with the exception of the figurative constant "ALL literal", which is not allowed).

If more than one value-to-be-replaced/replacement-value pair is specified, the replacements are carried out in the order in which they are written in the INSPECT statement.

EXAMPLE 11.10   A social security number is stored in the form PIC X(9). Show how to edit it for printing in the form xxx-xx-xxxx.

```
05   SSN-FROM-A-FILE       PIC X(9).
05   SSN-TO-PRINT          PIC XXXBXXBXXXX.

MOVE SSN-FROM-A-FILE TO SSN-TO-PRINT
INSPECT SSN-TO-PRINT
    REPLACING ALL SPACES BY "-"
```

Since COBOL has no PICTURE editing characters to insert hyphens, the social security number is first moved to a field which uses the B editing character to insert SPACES in the positions where the hyphens will eventually go. INSPECT is then used to replace all the spaces in the output field with the desired hyphens.

Suppose SSN-FROM-A-FILE contains "111223333". After the MOVE, SSN-TO-PRINT will contain "111 22 3333"; and after the INSPECT, it will contain "111-22-3333", as desired.

EXAMPLE 11.11 The NUMERIC class test will not accept a field which contains spaces. Thus "bbb123" in a PIC 9(6) field would be considered NOT NUMERIC. The INSPECT statement can be used to convert such fields into valid numeric fields as follows:

```
05   INPUT-FIELD        PIC 9(6).

INSPECT INPUT-FIELD
     REPLACING LEADING SPACES BY ZEROS
IF INPUT-FIELD NOT NUMERIC . . .
```

The field to be INSPECTed *must* have USAGE DISPLAY. If it is not an alphabetic (PIC A) or alphanumeric (PIC X) field, it is treated for purposes of the INSPECT as if it were REDEFINEd as alphanumeric.

The LEADING option specifies that *only leading* characters are to be replaced.

Original Contents INPUT-FIELD	*Contents after INSPECT*
bbb123	000123
123456	123456
bb12bb	0012bb (Only *leading* spaces are REPLACEd.)

EXAMPLE 11.12 What would be wrong with specifying

```
INSPECT INPUT-FIELD
     REPLACING ALL SPACES BY ZEROS
```

in Example 11.11?

Replacing *nonleading* spaces with 0s would result in modifying the value of the number. If INPUT-FIELD originally contains "bb12bb", then REPLACING ALL SPACES BY ZEROS would produce "001200", a value of 1200 instead of 12.

The INSPECT should be done as in Example 11.11. This produces the value "0012bb", which will be caught as an invalid field by a NUMERIC class test.

EXAMPLE 11.13 Suppose it is desired to remove a leading sign from an input field. The INSPECT statement can be used as follows:

```
05   INPUT-FIELD        PIC X(7).

INSPECT INPUT-FIELD
   REPLACING
     FIRST "-" BY SPACE
     FIRST "+" BY SPACE
```

Original INPUT-FIELD Contents	*INPUT-FIELD after INSPECT*
bb − 1234	bbb1234
bb − 123−	bbb123− (Only the *first* "−" is replaced.)
bb + 1234	bbb1234
bb1234 +	bb1234b
bbb1234	bbb1234 (No "+" or "−" to replace.)

The REPLACING FIRST option replaces *only the first occurrence* (if any) of the specified character(s).

EXAMPLE 11.14 The REPLACING CHARACTERS option replaces *all* characters specified by the BEFORE/AFTER INITIAL clause. One possible use is to remove the cents portion of a dollar amount to be printed:

```
05    AMOUNT-TO-PRINT          PIC Z,ZZZ,ZZ9.99.

INSPECT AMOUNT-TO-PRINT
     REPLACING CHARACTERS BY ZERO
          AFTER INITIAL "."
```

Original Contents of AMOUNT-TO-PRINT	*After INSPECT*
bbbb1,234.56	bbbb1,234.00

Note that a numeric edited item (such as AMOUNT-TO-PRINT) may be used in an INSPECT statement. For this purpose, it is treated as if it were REDEFINEd alphanumeric.

EXAMPLE 11.15 The INSPECT statement can also be used to isolate the *cents* portion of a numeric field:

```
05    AMOUNT-TO-PRINT          PIC 999.99.

INSPECT AMOUNT-TO-PRINT
     REPLACING CHARACTERS BY ZEROS
          BEFORE INITIAL "."
```

Original Contents of AMOUNT-TO-PRINT	*After INSPECT*	
123.45	000.45	
123456	123456	(No replace since there is no initial ".")

EXAMPLE 11.16 Suppose a customer mailing list is purchased on magnetic tape. The tape encodes customers as frequent buyers (code "A" on the tape), moderate buyers ("B"), or low-volume buyers ("C"). It is desired to recode the mailing information with numeric codes as follows: code "3"—preferred customers (old code "A"); code "2"—general sales (old "B"); code "1"—seasonal only (old "C"). The following INSPECT statement could be used:

```
01    MAILING-TAPE-RECORD.
      05    CUSTOMER-NAME      PIC X(30).
      05    TYPE-OF-CUSTOMER   PIC X.
      05    OTHER-FIELDS . . .

INSPECT TYPE-OF-CUSTOMER
     REPLACING
          ALL "A" BY "3"
          ALL "B" BY "2"
          ALL "C" BY "1"
```

EXAMPLE 11.17 Suppose the CUSTOMER-NAME in Example 11.16 has the following form: lastname space firstname space initial space(s). The following INSPECT statements will replace the original spaces with commas as delimiters between the names:

```
INSPECT CUSTOMER-NAME
     REPLACING FIRST SPACE BY ","
INSPECT CUSTOMER-NAME
     REPLACING FIRST SPACE BY ","
```

Initial CUSTOMER-NAME:	"GETZbDAVIDbHbbbbbbbbbbbbbbbbbbbbb"
After first INSPECT:	"GETZ,DAVIDbHbbbbbbbbbbbbbbbbbbbb"
After second INSPECT:	"GETZ,DAVID,Hbbbbbbbbbbbbbbbbbbbb"

Note that REPLACING ALL SPACES BY "," would *not* achieve the desired result since it would also replace any trailing spaces, producing strings such as "GETZ,DAVID,H,,,,,,,,,,;,,,,,,,,," instead of "GETZ, DAVID,Hbbbbbbbbbbbbbbbbbbbb".

EXAMPLE 11.18 Suppose nonnumeric keys are used with a direct or relative file. The INSPECT statement can be used to transform a nonnumeric key into a key which can be operated on by a hash function such as division/remainder. Let KEY-FIELD PIC X(7) be composed of characters from the set 0 through 9, /, -, #, @, and blank space. The following INSPECT will transform such a key into a valid numeric field (the assignment of nonnumeric characters to digits is arbitrary):

```
INSPECT KEY-FIELD
   REPLACING
      ALL "/" BY "1"
      ALL "-" BY "2"
      ALL "#" BY "3"
      ALL "@" BY "4"
      ALL SPACES BY "5"
```

Original KEY-FIELD	After INSPECT
12-34#5	1223435
1-23/#7	1223137
1-2/3bb	1221355
#89bbbb	3895555

Although the INSPECT statement is quite powerful, it is also time-consuming. Programs which put a premium on execution time should avoid using INSPECT when other solutions to a task are available.

EXAMPLE 11.19 The problem in Example 11.10 (inserting hyphens in a social security number) can also be solved without using INSPECT. The solution which follows, although less elegant, will execute faster on most computers:

```
05   SSN-FROM-A-FILE.
     10   FIRST-PART-IN      PIC X(3).
     10   SECOND-PART-IN     PIC X(2).
     10   THIRD-PART-IN      PIC X(4).

05   SSN-TO-PRINT.
     10   FIRST-PART-OUT     PIC X(3).
     10   FILLER             PIC X VALUE "-".
     10   SECOND-PART-OUT    PIC X(2).
     10   FILLER             PIC X VALUE "-".
     10   THIRD-PART-OUT     PIC X(4).

MOVE FIRST-PART-IN  TO FIRST-PART-OUT
MOVE SECOND-PART-IN TO SECOND-PART-OUT
MOVE THIRD-PART-IN  TO THIRD-PART-OUT
```

11.3   Combining TALLYING and REPLACING in One INSPECT Statement

It is possible to combine one or more tallying operations with one or more replacing operations in a single INSPECT statement. When TALLYING and REPLACING are both specified, the TALLYING is done *first*, using the *original* value of the data item being INSPECTed. After the tally has been completed, the REPLACING operation proceeds as described in Section 11.2 above.

EXAMPLE 11.20 Suppose a number is typed right-justified in INPUT-FIELD PIC X(7). It is desired to replace any leading spaces with 0s and also to determine how many significant digits are in the number. Both these tasks can be carried out by a single INSPECT statement:

```
05   NUMBER-SIGNIFICANT-DIGITS     PIC S9 COMP.
05   NUMBER-LEADING-SPACES         PIC S9 COMP.

MOVE ZERO TO NUMBER-LEADING-SPACES
INSPECT INPUT-FIELD
     TALLYING NUMBER-LEADING-SPACES
          FOR LEADING SPACES
     REPLACING ALL LEADING SPACES
          BY ZEROS
SUBTRACT NUMBER-LEADING-SPACES FROM 7
     GIVING NUMBER-SIGNIFICANT-DIGITS
```

Field before INSPECT	Tally	Field after INSPECT	(7 − Tally)
bbb1234	3	0001234	4
bb123bb	2	00123bb	5
bbbbbb9	6	0000009	1
9bbbbbb	0	9bbbbbb	7

Note that this method only produces correct results when INPUT-FIELD is indeed *right*-justified (see Problems 11.22–11.24).

EXAMPLE 11.21 Suppose a dollar amount is to be keyed by a terminal operator into a field named AMOUNT-FIELD PIC X(7). Use the INSPECT statement to (1) determine whether or not a sign is present and, if so, whether the amount is negative, (2) remove any sign, replacing it with 0s, *and* (3) replace any leading spaces with 0s. Nonleading spaces should remain in the field, which should be checked with a NUMERIC class test. If the value is correct, place it in a field called FINAL-VALUE.

```
05   NUMBER-OF-MINUS-SIGNS     PIC S9 COMP.
05   FINAL-VALUE               PIC S9(7).

MOVE ZERO TO NUMBER-OF-MINUS-SIGNS
INSPECT AMOUNT-FIELD
   TALLYING NUMBER-OF-MINUS-SIGNS
      FOR ALL "-"
   REPLACING
      LEADING "-" BY ZERO
      LEADING "+" BY ZERO
      LEADING SPACES BY ZEROS
IF NUMBER-OF-MINUS-SIGNS NOT GREATER THAN 1
      IF AMOUNT-FIELD NUMERIC
          MOVE AMOUNT-FIELD TO FINAL-VALUE
      .

IF NUMBER-OF-MINUS-SIGNS EQUAL 1
      COMPUTE FINAL-VALUE = - FINAL-VALUE
      .
```

Original AMOUNT-FIELD	Tally "−"	AMOUNT-FIELD after INSPECT
bbbb123	0	0000123
bbb − 123	1	0000123
bb − 123−	2	000123− (NOT NUMERIC)
bbb + 123	0	0000123
bb − 123+	1	000123+ (NOT NUMERIC)
bb − 12bb	1	00012bb (NOT NUMERIC)

11.4 Joining Separate Data Items—STRING

The STRING statement takes the contents (or partial contents) of two or more data items and joins them together, placing the result in a receiving data item. The general syntax of the ANSI COBOL STRING statement is:

```
STRING    sending-field-1 [sending-field-2] ...
              DELIMITED BY delimiter-value
          [ sending-field-3 [sending-field-4] ...
              DELIMITED BY delimiter-value ] ...
      INTO data-item-to-receive-result
      [ WITH POINTER name-of-numeric-integer-item ]
      [ ON OVERFLOW imperative-statement(s). ]
```

Each *sending field* may be a data item with USAGE DISPLAY or a nonnumeric literal. Each *delimiter value* may be either (1) a data item with USAGE DISPLAY, (2) a nonnumeric literal, or (3) the reserved word SIZE. A delimiter value serves to mark the *logical end* of its corresponding sending field(s), as described below.

STRING execution causes the contents of the sending field(s) to be copied to the INTO . . . field. If WITH POINTER . . . is specified, the *POINTER value* indicates the starting position within the *receiving field* (beginning with 1) where the sending-field characters are to be placed. It is the programmer's responsibility to initialize the POINTER item before executing the STRING statement. If WITH POINTER . . . is omitted, an *implicit pointer* is automatically assigned to the STRING statement by the compiler. This implicit pointer is always initialized to 1, so copying begins at the first position of the receiving field.

The sending field(s) are copied into the receiving field in the order in which they appear in the STRING statement. Each sending-field value is treated as an alphanumeric field for purposes of the copying operation, and is copied left to right, character by character. As each character is copied into the receiving field, the POINTER value (either explicit or implicit) is incremented by 1. After the STRING is completed, the POINTER will point one character position beyond the last character actually copied into the receiving field. This allows one STRING statement to pick up where the previous one left off.

The DELIMITED BY option specifies the logical end of its sending field as follows:

(1) "DELIMITED BY data-item" causes the copying of this particular sending field to end when the current contents of the data item are encountered within the sending field. The DELIMITED BY value itself is *not* copied to the receiving field. If the DELIMITED BY value is not present in the sending field, then the *entire* sending field is copied.

(2) "DELIMITED BY nonnumeric-literal" causes the copying of this particular sending field to end when the literal is encountered within the sending field. The literal itself is *not* copied to the receiving field.

(3) "DELIMITED BY SIZE" causes the *entire* sending field to be copied into the receiving field.

The optional ON OVERFLOW clause specifies one or more imperative statements to be executed if and only if at any point during STRING statement execution (1) a character is about to be moved into the receiving field and (2) the value in the POINTER item (either explicit or implicit) is less than 1 or greater than the length of the receiving field. If this happens, the sending field(s) have literally "overflowed" the receiving field. Note that an OVERFLOW does *not* occur if the sending field(s) and receiving field are the same length (in this case, STRING execution ends with the POINTER item 1 greater than the length of the receiving field, but since the sending field is also exhausted at this point, no attempt is made to move a character into this position). Note also that the ON OVERFLOW clause *must* end with a period (same as AT END, INVALID KEY, etc.).

EXAMPLE 11.22 Suppose it is desired to construct a name field for a mailing label from three separate fields stored in a record as follows:

```
05   MASTER-RECORD-NAME.
     10   MASTER-LAST-NAME        PIC X(15).
     10   MASTER-FIRST-NAME       PIC X(10).
     10   MASTER-MIDDLE-INITIAL   PIC X.

05   MAILING-LABEL-NAME          PIC X(26).

STRING   MASTER-FIRST-NAME
              DELIMITED BY SIZE
         MASTER-MIDDLE-INITIAL
              DELIMITED BY SIZE
         MASTER-LAST-NAME
              DELIMITED BY SIZE
     INTO MAILING-LABEL-NAME
```

If MASTER-LAST-NAME contains "GETZbbbbbbbbbbb", MASTER-FIRST-NAME contains "MARIEbbbbb", and MASTER-MIDDLE-INITIAL contains "H", then after the STRING statement, MAILING-LABEL-NAME will contain "MARIEbbbbbHGETZbbbbbbbbbbb". Observe that the STRING statement above has *not* provided for space between the first name and the middle initial or for space between the middle initial and the last name. Also, any "extra" spaces in each name field have been copied into the receiving field, since DELIMITED BY SIZE was used to copy the *entire* sending field in each case.

EXAMPLE 11.23 The following STRING statement corrects the deficiencies in Example 11.22 by adding "literal" sending fields to insert a space between the first name and the middle initial, and a period followed by a space between the middle initial and the last name. Also, the DELIMITED BY clause is used to pick up only the *nonblank* portion of each part of the name. Note that this technique assumes the names are left-justified within their respective fields:

```
MOVE SPACES TO MAILING-LABEL-NAME
STRING   MASTER-FIRST-NAME
              DELIMITED BY SPACE
         SPACE
              DELIMITED BY SIZE
         MASTER-MIDDLE-INITIAL
              DELIMITED BY SPACE
         ".b"
              DELIMITED BY SIZE
         MASTER-LAST-NAME
              DELIMITED BY SPACE
     INTO MAILING-LABEL-NAME
```

The STRING statement (unlike the MOVE statement) does *not* pad the receiving field with spaces if the sending field values do not completely fill the receiving field. Since DELIMITED BY SPACE is used here to remove unwanted spaces from the sending fields, the actual number of characters copied may not fill the receiving field. Whenever this situation is possible, the receiving field should be cleared with a MOVE statement prior to executing the STRING statement (as in "MOVE SPACES TO receiving field").

Since the DELIMITED BY item is *not* copied into the receiving field, spaces to separate the various parts of the name must be supplied with the STRING statement. When a figurative constant is used as a sending field or delimiter, it is always assumed to have a *length of 1*. Thus "SPACE DELIMITED BY SIZE" represents a sending field of exactly 1 blank space. Note, too, the use of a nonnumeric literal to insert a period and a space after the middle initial.

If sending values are as in Example 11.22, MAILING-LABEL-NAME will contain "MARIEbH.bGETZbbbbbbbbbbbbbbbbb" after the above STRING is executed.

EXAMPLE 11.24 Suppose PROGRAMMER-RECORD contains a table of projects assigned to a given programmer:

```
05   PROGRAMMER-RECORD.
     10   PROGRAMMER-ID      PIC X(3).
     10   NUMBER-OF-PROJECTS PIC S9 COMP.
     10   PROJECT-LIST       OCCURS 1 TO 10 TIMES
                             DEPENDING ON NUMBER-OF-PROJECTS.
          15   PROJECT-ID    PIC X(3).
          15   PROJECT-NAME  PIC X(20).
```

It is desired to construct a print line containing a programmer ID and as many project names as possible. Project names should have rightmost spaces stripped away and should be placed next to one another in a 120-character area. They should be separated from one another by a comma followed by a space. The following data areas and PROCEDURE DIVISION code could be used to build the print line:

```
01   PROGRAMMER-WORK-LOAD-LINE.
     05   OUT-PROGRAMMER-ID      PIC X(3).
     05   FILLER                 PIC X(3) VALUE ":bb".
     05   OUT-PROJECT-LIST       PIC X(120).

01   POINTERS-AREA.
     05   NEXT-AVAILABLE-POSITION  PIC S9(3) COMP.
     05   TABLE-ENTRY              PIC S9(2) COMP.
     05   LAST-STARTING-POSITION   PIC S9(3) COMP.

     MOVE PROGRAMMER-ID  TO OUT-PROGRAMMER-ID
     MOVE SPACES         TO OUT-PROJECT-LIST
     MOVE 1              TO NEXT-AVAILABLE-POSITION
     STRING    PROJECT-NAME (1)
                    DELIMITED BY "bb"
          INTO OUT-PROJECT-LIST
          WITH POINTER NEXT-AVAILABLE-POSITION
     PERFORM BUILD-OUTPUT-LIST
          VARYING TABLE-ENTRY
               FROM 2 BY 1
               UNTIL TABLE-ENTRY GREATER THAN NUMBER-OF-PROJECTS

BUILD-OUTPUT-LIST.
     MOVE NEXT-AVAILABLE-POSITION TO LAST-STARTING-POSITION
     STRING    ",b"
                    DELIMITED BY SIZE
               PROJECT-NAME (TABLE-ENTRY)
                    DELIMITED BY "bb"
          INTO OUT-PROJECT-LIST
          WITH POINTER NEXT-AVAILABLE-POSITION
          ON OVERFLOW
               PERFORM MUST-START-NEW-LINE
```

OUT-PROJECT-LIST must be cleared to spaces *before* any STRING statements are executed to copy project names into it. NEXT-AVAILABLE-POSITION is used to keep track of where the STRING statements are placing data into OUT-PROJECT-LIST. It is initialized to 1, and then automatically incremented each time a STRING statement copies a character into the receiving field. Since it is never reinitialized, NEXT-AVAILABLE-POSITION always points to the character slot where the next sending-field character should be placed.

Since a single space may appear as part of a PROJECT-NAME, the DELIMITED BY clause specifies a *double space* to mark the logical end of PROJECT-NAME.

In order to avoid an extra comma after the last project in the list, an initial STRING statement is used to copy the first project name from the PROJECT-LIST table into the output area. Subsequent STRING statements (in paragraph BUILD-OUTPUT-LIST) each insert a comma, then a space, and then the next PROJECT-NAME into OUT-PROJECT-LIST. There is thus no dangling comma after the last PROJECT-NAME in the list.

If the second or a subsequent STRING statement causes NEXT-AVAILABLE-POSITION to exceed the length of OUT-PROJECT-LIST, the ON OVERFLOW routine will be executed. It is assumed that paragraph MUST-START-NEW-LINE will output the current PROGRAMMER-WORK-LOAD-LINE and restart the execution of BUILD-OUTPUT-LIST with an empty OUT-PROJECT-LIST (see Problem 11.25; the work area LAST-STARTING-POSITION is used by this routine).

Given the following names in the PROJECT-LIST table:

(1) SALESbANALYSISbbbbbb

(2) INVENTORYbCONTROLbbb

(3) PAYROLLbbbbbbbbbbbbb

(4) ACCOUNTSbRECEIVABLEb

OUT-PROJECT-LIST is built step by step as follows. The "^" identifies the contents of NEXT-AVAILABLE-POSITION *after* the execution of each STRING statement:

(1) SALESbANALYSIS^

(2) SALESbANALYSIS,bINVENTORYbCONTROL^

(3) SALESbANALYSIS,bINVENTORYbCONTROL,bPAYROLL^

(4) SALESbANALYSIS,bINVENTORYbCONTROL,bPAYROLL,bACCOUNTSbRECEIVABLEb^

11.5 Distributing Pieces of a Single String into Several Data Items—UNSTRING

The UNSTRING statement is used to separate a *single* alphanumeric data item into pieces which are distributed among *several* different data items. The sending field is broken up into subfields according to the positions of delimiter characters defined in the UNSTRING statement. UNSTRING also provides capabilities for counting the number of characters in each piece of the original sending field and for saving the delimiter character(s) which define each particular subfield. The general syntax of the ANSI COBOL UNSTRING statement is:

```
UNSTRING name-of-alphanumeric-sending-field
    [ DELIMITED BY [ALL] delimiter-value
        [ OR [ALL] delimiter-value ] ... ]
    INTO receiving-field
        [ DELIMITER IN area-to-hold-delimiter-used ]
        [ COUNT IN characters-examined-counter ]
        [ receiving-field
            [ DELIMITER IN area-to-hold-delimiter-used ]
            [ COUNT IN characters-examined-counter ] ] ...
    [ WITH POINTER sending-field-starting-position-value ]
    [ TALLYING IN number-of-receiving-fields-used-counter ]
    [ ON OVERFLOW imperative-statement(s). ]
```

The delimiter value(s) must be alphanumeric data items, figurative constants, or literals. When data items or literals are used, the delimiter value may consist of more than 1 character. If ALL is not specified, *each* occurrence of the delimiter value acts as a delimiter. This means that 2 consecutive delimiter values in the sending field are recognized as delimiting the *null string* (i.e., a string with *0 characters*). A null string in the sending field causes the corresponding receiving field to be filled with either SPACES or ZEROS (depending on the definition of the receiving field).

If DELIMITED BY ALL . . . is specified, consecutive occurrences of the delimiter value in the sending field are treated as only 1 delimiter (i.e., contiguous delimiter values after the first one are simply ignored).

More than 1 delimiter value may be specified in the DELIMITED BY . . . clause. The reserved word OR *must* appear between delimiter values when more than 1 is listed. The delimiter values are compared against the sending field in the order in which they are written in the UNSTRING statement.

EXAMPLE 11.25   The following indicates the action of DELIMITED BY . . . options on various sending fields:

(1)   DELIMITED BY "/"
Sending field "AB/CDE//FG///H"
Subfields recognized (in order):

AB
CDE
Null string   (Two "//" define the null string when ALL is not specified.)
FG
Null string
Null string   (Three delimiter values define 2 null strings.)
H

(2)   DELIMITED BY ALL "/"
Sending field "AB/CDE//FG///H"
Subfields recognized (in order):

AB
CDE
FG   (When ALL is used, consecutive delimiters are treated as just *1* delimiter.)
H

(3)   DELIMITED BY "/" OR ALL "R2" OR ALL ","
Sending field "AB/CR2DE//FG,,HI,JKR2R2LMN"
Subfields recognized (in order):

AB   ("/" recognized as the delimiter.)
C   ("R2" recognized as the delimiter; the delimiter itself is not part of the subfield.)
DE   ("/" acts as the delimiter, itself not included in the subfield.)
Null   (ALL not specified for "/" delimiter; hence 2 delimiters in a row define the null string.)
FG   ("," acts as the delimiter. Since ALL is specified, consecutive occurrences of "," are treated as just one "," and no null string is recognized.)
HI   ("," acts as the delimiter.)
JK   ("R2" acts as the delimiter. Since ALL is specified, consecutive occurrences of "R2" are treated as just one "R2" and no null string is recognized.)
LMN   (Last subfield proceeds to the end of the sending field.)

(4)   DELIMITED BY ALL "AB" OR ALL "BC" OR ALL "AB4"
Sending field "12ABC3AB456"
Subfields recognized (in order):

12	(Both "AB" and "BC" serve as delimiter values, but the UNSTRING statement examines the sending field on a left-to-right basis; hence "AB" is found and recognized as a delimiter before "BC" is encountered.)
C3	(Having recognized the delimiter value "AB", UNSTRING skips over the delimiter characters "AB" and continues scanning the sending field at "C". The next possible delimiter value is either "AB" or "AB4". In this case, UNSTRING recognizes the delimiter value which appears *first* in the UNSTRING list. Since "AB" is listed first, *it* is used as the next delimiter value and skipped over. Scanning continues with the "4" immediately following the delimiter "AB".)
456	(Scanning continues until the end of the sending field.)

UNSTRING places the subfield(s) defined by the DELIMITED BY clause into the receiving field(s) listed in the UNSTRING statement, first subfield into the first receiving field, second subfield into the second receiving field, etc. If the receiving field is shorter than its corresponding subfield, UNSTRING simply truncates the subfield (on the right). If the receiving field is *longer* than the subfield, UNSTRING does *not* pad the receiving field with SPACES (as would MOVE). If this is desired, the programmer must initialize the receiving field(s) to SPACES before executing UNSTRING.

If the DELIMITER IN . . . clause is used for a given receiving field, UNSTRING also places the delimiter value marking the end of the corresponding subfield into the area-to-hold-delimiter-used item. If the end of the subfield is marked by the end of the sending field (rather than by a delimiter), then the DELIMITER IN . . . item is set to SPACES. DELIMITER IN . . . items *must* be alphanumeric.

If the COUNT IN . . . clause is used for a given receiving field, UNSTRING also places a count of the number of characters examined in the corresponding sending field (i.e., the number of characters between delimiters) into the COUNT IN . . . item. This count does *not* include the delimiter character(s) themselves. If the subfield copied into the receiving field is the null string, the COUNT IN . . . item is set to 0. COUNT IN . . . items must be numeric integer items. COUNT IN . . . can be used to determine if a sending-field string is larger than the receiving field (see Example 11.27).

The WITH POINTER . . . option allows the programmer to control where scanning of the sending field begins. If the user does not supply a POINTER, the compiler automatically generates an implicit pointer which always starts at position 1. The POINTER is incremented by 1 each time UNSTRING examines a character in the sending field. After UNSTRING execution, an explicit POINTER will point to the character position following the last character actually examined. This allows an UNSTRING statement to pick up where a previous UNSTRING left off. The POINTER item must be a numeric integer item. It is the programmer's responsibility to initialize any explicit pointer *before* executing UNSTRING.

If used, the TALLYING IN . . . item must also be a numeric integer item initialized by the programmer. UNSTRING increments the TALLYING item by 1 for each receiving field which actually receives a substring (or null string) from the sending field. Since it is possible for the sending field to be exhausted before all receiving fields actually receive a substring, the TALLYING value is not necessarily equal to the number of receiving fields originally given in the UNSTRING statement. TALLYING allows the programmer to determine how many receiving fields actually hold data after completion of the UNSTRING.

ON OVERFLOW . . . specifies a routine to be executed if and only if either (1) an explicit POINTER is used with a value less than 1 or greater than the length of the sending field or (2) during UNSTRING execution, all receiving fields have received a substring but more characters remain to be examined in the sending field (i.e., sending field is not exhausted). This situation may or may not be a problem, depending on the application. ON OVERFLOW—like AT END, INVALID KEY, etc.—*must* end with a period.

EXAMPLE 11.26 Here is a complete UNSTRING statement:

```
01    SENDING-STRING               PIC X(14).

01    SUBFIELD-AREAS.
      05    SUBFIELD-1             PIC X(5).
      05    SUBFIELD-2             PIC X(5).
      05    SUBFIELD-3             PIC X(5).
      05    SUBFIELD-4             PIC X(5).
01    DELIMITER-AREAS.
      05    DELIM-1                PIC X.
      05    DELIM-2                PIC X.
01    COUNTER-AREAS.
      05    COUNTER-1              PIC S9(3) COMP.
      05    COUNTER-3              PIC S9(3) COMP.


MOVE SPACES TO SUBFIELD-1 SUBFIELD-2 SUBFIELD-3 SUBFIELD-4
MOVE ZEROS  TO COUNTER-1 COUNTER-3
UNSTRING SENDING-STRING
      DELIMITED BY "/"
      INTO SUBFIELD-1
              DELIMITER IN DELIM-1
              COUNTER IN COUNTER-1
           SUBFIELD-2
              DELIMITER IN DELIM-2
           SUBFIELD-3
              COUNTER IN COUNTER-3
           SUBFIELD-4
```

Suppose SENDING-STRING contains "AB/CDE//FG///H" before the UNSTRING. The results after UNSTRING will be as follows:

```
SUBFIELD-1:     ABbbb
   DELIM-1:          /     ("/" serves as delimiter value for first subfield)
   COUNTER-1:       2     (Two characters moved to receiving field)
SUBFIELD-2:     CDEbb
   DELIM-2:          /
SUBFIELD-3:     bbbbb     (Null string defined by "//" causes
                           SPACES to be moved to, receiving field.)
   COUNTER-3:       0     (Null string contains 0 characters.)
SUBFIELD-4:     FGbbb
```

Since there are still unexamined characters left in the sending field, an OVERFLOW condition exists. If ON OVERFLOW . . . had been specified, it would be executed. Since it was *not* specified, execution continues with the statement immediately following UNSTRING.

Note that it is necessary to initialize the SUBFIELD-*n* and COUNTER-*n* areas *before* executing the UNSTRING statement, since UNSTRING does not initialize or pad these areas.

EXAMPLE 11.27 Suppose a mailing list has been purchased on tape. It is necessary to reformat the records to suit the purchaser's programs and to remove any records duplicating those already on the purchaser's files.

The MAILING-LABEL-NAME field from the tape contains names in the form "first i. last", with only one space between each part of the name ("i" denotes middle initial). It is desired to separate the names into three fields for purposes of sorting and comparing with names already on file. The following UNSTRING statement is one way to accomplish this task:

```
        05    NAME-FROM-TAPE           PIC X(34).

01    CUSTOMER-MAILING-RECORD.
        05    CUST-LAST-NAME           PIC X(15).
        05    CUST-FIRST-NAME          PIC X(15).
        05    CUST-INITIAL             PIC X.

01    COUNTER-AREA.
        05    LENGTH-LAST-NAME         PIC S9(2) COMP.
        05    LENGTH-FIRST-NAME        PIC S9(2) COMP.
        05    LENGTH-INITIAL           PIC S9(2) COMP.
        05    NUMBER-OF-FIELDS         PIC S9(2) COMP.

        MOVE SPACES TO CUST-LAST-NAME
                       CUST-FIRST-NAME
                       CUST-INITIAL
        MOVE ZEROS  TO LENGTH-LAST-NAME
                       LENGTH-FIRST-NAME
                       LENGTH-INITIAL
                       NUMBER-OF-FIELDS
        MOVE "NO" TO ERROR-IN-TAPE-NAME
        UNSTRING NAME-FROM-TAPE
                 DELIMITED BY ALL SPACES
                          OR ALL ".b"
              INTO CUST-FIRST-NAME
                      COUNT IN LENGTH-FIRST-NAME
                   CUST-INITIAL
                      COUNT IN LENGTH-INITIAL
                   CUST-LAST-NAME
                      COUNT IN LENGTH-LAST-NAME
              TALLYING IN NUMBER-OF-FIELDS
              ON OVERFLOW
                   MOVE "YES" TO ERROR-IN-TAPE-NAME
        .
        IF ERROR-IN-TAPE-NAME EQUAL "NO"
           IF NUMBER-OF-FIELDS NOT EQUAL 3
              OR (LENGTH-FIRST-NAME ZERO OR GREATER THAN 15)
              OR (LENGTH-LAST-NAME ZERO OR GREATER THAN 15)
              OR (LENGTH-INITIAL ZERO OR GREATER THAN 1)
                   MOVE "YES" TO ERROR-IN-TAPE-NAME
        .
```

Note how extensive error checking can be carried out with the feedback provided from UNSTRING execution.

EXAMPLE 11.28 Suppose a list of project names is stored in PROJECT-LIST PIC X(100). Each name (except the last) is followed immediately by a comma followed by a space. It is desired to place the project names in the table:

```
01    PROJECT-TABLE-AREA.
        05    NUMBER-ACTIVE-ENTRIES    PIC S9(2) COMP.
        05    PROJECT-NAME             OCCURS 20 TIMES
                                       PIC X(10).
```

The following code will accomplish the desired task:

```
01    UNSTRING-WORK-AREAS.
        05    POSITION-TO-SCAN         PIC S9(3) COMP.
        05    KEEP-SCANNING-SW         PIC X(3).
```

```
            MOVE 1 TO POSITION-TO-SCAN
            MOVE ZERO TO NUMBER-ACTIVE-ENTRIES
            MOVE "YES" TO KEEP-SCANNING-SW
            PERFORM SCAN-AND-MOVE-NEXT-SUBFIELD
                 UNTIL    KEEP-SCANNING-SW EQUAL "NO"
                      OR  NUMBER-ACTIVE-ENTRIES EQUAL 20
            IF KEEP-SCANNING-SW EQUAL "YES"
                 PERFORM TABLE-TOO-SMALL-ERROR
            .
            . . .

        SCAN-AND-MOVE-NEXT-SUBFIELD.
            ADD 1 TO NUMBER-ACTIVE-ENTRIES
            MOVE SPACES TO PROJECT-NAME (NUMBER-ACTIVE-ENTRIES)
            MOVE "NO" TO KEEP-SCANNING-SW
            UNSTRING PROJECT-LIST
                      DELIMITED BY ",b"
                 INTO PROJECT-NAME (NUMBER-ACTIVE-ENTRIES)
                 WITH POINTER POSITION-TO-SCAN
                 ON OVERFLOW
                      MOVE "YES" TO KEEP-SCANNING-SW
```

The POINTER POSITION-TO-SCAN is initialized to 1 and automatically incremented each time UNSTRING moves a character into a receiving field or skips over a delimiter value. Hence after each execution of UNSTRING, POSITION-TO-SCAN is left pointing to where the *next* execution of UNSTRING should begin.

Note how the switch KEEP-SCANNING-SW is reset to "NO" just before the UNSTRING is executed. If the UNSTRING does not scan all the characters in PROJECT-LIST, ON OVERFLOW will be executed and set the switch back to "YES". If all characters have been scanned, ON OVERFLOW is not executed and the switch remains "NO". The switch thus indicates whether the UNSTRING statement should be executed again or not.

Note, too, that the PERFORM statement repeating the UNSTRING also guards against table overflow. If NUMBER-ACTIVE-ENTRIES becomes 20 but KEEP-SCANNING-SW is still "YES", not all fields in the PROJECT-LIST will fit in the table (i.e., the table is too small).

Finally, each table entry must be cleared to SPACES before UNSTRING is executed, since UNSTRING does *not* pad the receiving field.

11.6   TRANSFORM—A Nonstandard Verb for Character Translation

IBM OS/VS COBOL provides a nonstandard statement which is easier to use than the ANSI standard INSPECT statement for purposes of translating from one set of characters to another. The TRANSFORM statement has the following syntax:

```
        TRANSFORM name-of-string-to-be-modified CHARACTERS
            FROM original-character-values
            TO   replacement-character-values
```

EXAMPLE 11.29 The following statement converts all occurrences of the indicated special characters in RELATIVE-FILE-KEY-FIELD to ZEROS:

```
        TRANSFORM RELATIVE-FILE-KEY-FIELD
            FROM "@#$&*+-,./:="
            TO   ZEROS
```

Any character in RELATIVE-FILE-KEY-FIELD equal to any of the characters in the FROM string will be replaced by a single ZERO, as specified in the TO string. The double quotes in the FROM string mark the beginning and end of the string and are *not* considered part of the string itself.

EXAMPLE 11.30   The following TRANSFORM statement will convert the decimal digits 1 through 9 to the letters A through I, respectively.

```
TRANSFORM SOME-ALPHANUMERIC-FIELD
    FROM "123456789"
    TO   "ABCDEFGHI"
```

The translation scheme is determined by the *order* of the characters in the FROM and TO strings. Each occurrence of the first FROM character ("1") in SOME-ALPHANUMERIC-FIELD is translated into the first TO character ("A"), each occurrence of the second FROM character ("2") is translated into the second TO character ("B"), etc.

Review Questions

11.1   What basic character string operations are supported by ANSI COBOL and what statements are used to program each?

11.2   What is the function of the nonstandard TRANSFORM statement?

11.3   Discuss the syntax and operation of INSPECT with the TALLYING option.

11.4   Give several applications using INSPECT . . . TALLYING.

11.5   Discuss the syntax and operation of INSPECT with the REPLACING option.

11.6   Give several applications using INSPECT . . . REPLACING.

11.7   Tell how INSPECT can be used as part of a hash function for nonnumeric keys.

11.8   Why should INSPECT not be used if there is another reasonably simple way to accomplish the same task?

11.9   Explain what happens when TALLYING and REPLACING are used in the *same* INSPECT statement.

11.10   Discuss the syntax and operation of the STRING statement.

11.11   Give several applications using STRING.

11.12   Discuss the syntax and operation of the UNSTRING statement.

11.13   Give several applications using UNSTRING.

11.14   Explain the actions of the various DELIMITED BY options for UNSTRING.

11.15   Discuss the syntax and operation of the nonstandard TRANSFORM statement.

11.16   Give several applications using TRANSFORM.

Solved Problems

11.17 Use INSPECT to count the number of sentences in a memo (assume that each sentence ends with a period followed by at least one space).

```
05   NUMBER-OF-SENTENCES      PIC S9(4) COMP.


MOVE ZERO TO NUMBER-OF-SENTENCES
INSPECT MEMO
       TALLYING NUMBER-OF-SENTENCES
             FOR ALL ".b"
```

11.18 Use INSPECT to fully validate NUMERIC-FIELD PIC X(8) of the form −xxxx.xx. The leading minus is optional and, if present, should be replaced by a 0. The number should be right-justified but need not be zero-filled (this should be done as part of the validation). There should always be two decimal places as indicated.

```
05   NUMBER-OF-MINUS-SIGNS       PIC S9 COMP.
05   NUMBER-OF-DECIMAL-POINTS    PIC S9 COMP.
05   NUMBER-OF-DECIMAL-PLACES    PIC S9 COMP.


MOVE ZEROS TO  NUMBER-OF-MINUS-SIGNS
               NUMBER-OF-DECIMAL-POINTS
               NUMBER-OF-DECIMAL-PLACES
INSPECT NUMERIC-FIELD
       TALLYING  NUMBER-OF-MINUS-SIGNS
                      FOR ALL "-"
                 NUMBER-OF-DECIMAL-POINTS
                      FOR ALL "."
                 NUMBER-OF-DECIMAL-PLACES
                      FOR CHARACTERS
                          AFTER INITIAL "."
       REPLACING
             LEADING SPACES BY ZEROS
             ALL "-" BY ZEROS
IF NUMBER-OF-MINUS-SIGNS GREATER THAN 1
     MOVE "NO" TO NUMBER-IS-VALID-SW
ELSE IF NUMBER-OF-DECIMAL-POINTS NOT EQUAL 1
     MOVE "NO" TO NUMBER-IS-VALID-SW
ELSE IF NUMBER-OF-DECIMAL-PLACES NOT EQUAL 2
     MOVE "NO" TO NUMBER-IS-VALID-SW
ELSE
     MOVE "YES" TO NUMBER-IS-VALID-SW
```

11.19 The solution in Problem 11.18 replaces any minus signs and leading spaces with 0s, but does not check that only valid digits are left after the REPLACING operation is completed. Continue the solution in Problem 11.18 to test for invalid characters (after 11.18, the field should only contain digits and the decimal point).

```
05    NUMBER-VALID-CHARACTERS        PIC S9 COMP.


IF NUMBER-IS-VALID-EQUAL "YES"
        MOVE ZERO TO NUMBER-VALID-CHARACTERS
        INSPECT NUMERIC-FIELD
          TALLYING NUMBER-VALID-CHARACTERS
            FOR  ALL "0"  ALL "1"  ALL "2"  ALL "3"  ALL "4"
                 ALL "5"  ALL "6"  ALL "7"  ALL "8"  ALL "9"
                 ALL "."
        IF NUMBER-VALID-CHARACTERS NOT EQUAL 8
            MOVE "NO" TO NUMBER-IS-VALID
```

11.20 Continue the solution in Problem 11.19 by using UNSTRING to move valid numbers into:

```
05    VALID-NUMBER              PIC S9999V99.
05    NUMBER-PARTS REDEFINES VALID-NUMBER.
      10    INTEGER-PART         PIC 9999.
      10    FRACTION-PART        PIC 99.
```

The solution is

```
IF NUMBER-IS-VALID-SW EQUAL "YES"
        UNSTRING NUMERIC-FIELD
                DELIMITED BY "."
            INTO INTEGER-PART
                 FRACTION-PART
        IF NUMBER-OF-MINUS-SIGNS EQUAL 1
            COMPUTE VALID-NUMBER = - VALID-NUMBER
```

11.21 A company has decided to eliminate certain types of discounts. All CUSTOMER-DISCOUNT-CODE fields (PIC XX) containing any of "A7", "B5", or "**" are to be changed to "C1". Write an INSPECT statement to accomplish this task.

```
INSPECT CUSTOMER-DISCOUNT-CODE
    REPLACING ALL "A7" BY "C1"
              ALL "B5" BY "C1"
              ALL "**" BY "C1"
```

11.22 An integer is keyed by a terminal operator somewhere within the field INPUT-NUMBER PIC X(9). Write code to place the number, *right-justified* and *zero-filled* (i.e., leading positions filled with 0s), in RIGHT-FIELD PIC X(9). You may assume that the field consists of 0 or more spaces, followed by a series of digits, followed by 0 or more spaces.

One solution uses the following steps: (1) Use INSPECT to REPLACE all leading spaces with 0s, (2) use UNSTRING to copy all characters up to the first space into a WORK-AREA (use the COUNTER IN . . . option to obtain the length of the number), (3) calculate at what position in RIGHT-FIELD the number must be placed in order to be right-justified (the correct starting position is one more than the length of RIGHT-FIELD, minus the length of the number), and (4) use STRING to copy the number from the WORK-AREA into this position of RIGHT-FIELD (fill RIGHT-FIELD with 0s before the STRING so that unused leftmost positions will contain leading 0s):

```
01    WORK-AREAS-AND-COUNTERS.
      05    WORK-AREA                     PIC X(9).
      05    WHERE-NUMBER-SHOULD-BEGIN     PIC S9 COMP.
      05    LENGTH-OF-NUMBER              PIC S9 COMP.
```

```
INSPECT INPUT-NUMBER
        REPLACING LEADING SPACES BY ZEROS
MOVE ZERO TO LENGTH-OF-NUMBER
MOVE SPACES TO WORK-AREA
UNSTRING INPUT-NUMBER
            DELIMITED BY ALL SPACE
        INTO WORK-AREA
            COUNT IN LENGTH-OF-NUMBER
COMPUTE WHERE-NUMBER-SHOULD-BEGIN =
        9 - LENGTH-OF-NUMBER + 1
MOVE ZEROS TO RIGHT-FIELD
STRING WORK-AREA
            DELIMITED BY SPACE
        INTO RIGHT-FIELD
        WITH POINTER WHERE-NUMBER-SHOULD-BEGIN
```

Suppose INPUT-NUMBER originally contains "bbb123bbb". After the INSPECT statement, leading spaces are replaced with 0s, and INPUT-NUMBER contains "000123bbb". WORK-AREA is then cleared to spaces and LENGTH-OF-NUMBER zeroed. The UNSTRING statement scans INPUT-NUMBER until the delimiter value SPACE is encountered (at the seventh position), copying characters preceding the space into the WORK-AREA and placing a count of the number of characters copied into LENGTH-OF-NUMBER. After the UNSTRING, WORK-AREA contains "000123bbb" and LENGTH-OF-NUMBER contains 6. The position where the number in WORK-AREA should be placed in RIGHT-FIELD is then calculated as 9 − length + 1, which gives 4 for WHERE-NUMBER-SHOULD-BEGIN. RIGHT-FIELD is then filled with ZEROS (since STRING does not pad), and STRING is used to copy the number from the WORK-AREA into RIGHT-FIELD. Since WHERE-NUMBER-SHOULD-BEGIN is used as the WITH POINTER . . . option, the copy begins at *position* 4 of RIGHT-FIELD, thus producing "000000123" in RIGHT-FIELD as the final result.

11.23 Although pedagogically satisfying because it uses INSPECT, STRING, and UNSTRING, the solution in Problem 11.22 can be accomplished more easily without UNSTRING. Show how.

The INSPECT statement can be used simply to count the length of the number in the INPUT-AREA after leading spaces have been replaced by 0s. STRING can then be used to copy the number into RIGHT-FIELD as in Problem 11.22.

```
01    WORK-AREAS-AND-COUNTERS.
      05    WHERE-NUMBER-SHOULD-BEGIN       PIC S9 COMP.
      05    LENGTH-OF-NUMBER                PIC S9 COMP.

INSPECT INPUT-NUMBER
        REPLACING LEADING SPACES BY ZEROS
MOVE ZERO TO LENGTH-OF-NUMBER
INSPECT INPUT-NUMBER
        TALLYING LENGTH-OF-NUMBER
            FOR CHARACTERS BEFORE INITIAL SPACE
COMPUTE WHERE-NUMBER-SHOULD-BEGIN =
        9 - LENGTH-OF-NUMBER + 1
MOVE ZEROS TO RIGHT-FIELD
STRING INPUT-NUMBER
            DELIMITED BY SPACE
        INTO RIGHT-FIELD
        WITH POINTER WHERE-NUMBER-SHOULD-BEGIN
```

11.24 Why can't the two INSPECT statements in Problem 11.23 be combined into one as follows:

```
        MOVE ZERO TO LENGTH-OF-NUMBER
        INSPECT INPUT-NUMBER
             TALLYING LENGTH-OF-NUMBER
                   FOR CHARACTERS BEFORE INITIAL SPACE
             REPLACING LEADING SPACES BY ZEROS
```

They cannot be combined because the TALLYING operation is carried out *before* the REPLAC-ING operation. In this application, it is imperative to REPLACE leading spaces with 0s *before* doing the TALLY.

11.25 Write paragraph MUST-START-NEW-LINE from Example 11.24.

MUST-START-NEW-LINE is faced with a situation where the last table entry has overflowed the end of OUT-PROJECT-LIST. The program segment first erases any partial version of the last project name copied before the OVERFLOW by STRINGing SPACES into OUT-PROJECT-LIST at the LAST-STARTING-POSITION before the OVERFLOW. It can then output the current line. Before STRINGing other table entries into OUT-PROJECT-LIST, it must also (1) clear OUT-PROJECT-LIST to SPACES, (2) reset NEXT-AVAILABLE-POSITION to 1, and (3) decrement TABLE-ENTRY so that the *current* entry (which caused the OVERFLOW and was erased from the line) can be reprocessed with the next execution of BUILD-OUTPUT-LIST.

```
        05    ALL-SPACES          PIC X(21) VALUE SPACES.

MUST-START-NEW-LINE.
        STRING ALL-SPACES
                   DELIMITED BY SIZE
             INTO OUT-PROJECT-LIST
             WITH POINTER LAST-STARTING-POSITION
        WRITE REPORT-LINE
             FROM PROGRAMMER-WORK-LOAD-LINE
             AFTER ADVANCING 1 LINES
        MOVE SPACES     TO OUT-PROJECT-LIST
        MOVE 1          TO NEXT-AVAILABLE-POSITION
        SUBTRACT 1 FROM TABLE-ENTRY
        .
```

11.26 Use STRING to construct an address line for a mailing label from separate data items holding the street address, city, and state. Place two spaces between the street and city, and a comma and a space between the city and state.

```
        05    ADDRESS-LINE              PIC X(36).

01    MAILING-LABEL-DATA.
        05    STREET                    PIC X(20).
        05    CITY                      PIC X(10).
        05    STATE                     PIC XX.

        MOVE SPACES TO ADDRESS-LINE
        STRING    STREET
                       DELIMITED BY "bb"
                  "bb"
                       DELIMITED BY SIZE
                  CITY
                       DELIMITED BY "bb"
                  ",b"
                       DELIMITED BY SIZE
                  STATE
                       DELIMITED BY SIZE
             INTO ADDRESS-LINE
```

11.27 Given ADDRESS-LINE as created in Problem 11.26, use UNSTRING to place the data in ADDRESS-LINE into the separate fields STREET, CITY, and STATE.

```
MOVE SPACES TO STREET CITY STATE
UNSTRING ADDRESS-LINE
        DELIMITED BY ALL "bb"
                  OR ALL ",b"
    INTO STREET
         CITY
         STATE
    ON OVERFLOW
         PERFORM ADDRESS-LINE-IS-INVALID
```

11.28 The TRANSFORM statement in Example 11.30 is *not* available in strict ANSI COBOL. Show how to accomplish the same translation (i.e., digits 1 through 9 to letters A through I) with the ANSI standard INSPECT statement.

```
INSPECT SOME-ALPHANUMERIC-FIELD
    REPLACING ALL "1" BY "A"
              ALL "2" BY "B"
              ALL "3" BY "C"
              ALL "4" BY "D"
              ALL "5" BY "E"
              ALL "6" BY "F"
              ALL "7" BY "G"
              ALL "8" BY "H"
              ALL "9" BY "I"
```

11.29 Give a TRANSFORM statement equivalent to the INSPECT statement in Example 11.18.

```
TRANSFORM KEY-FIELD CHARACTERS
    FROM "/-#@b"
    TO   "12345"
```

Chapter 12

ANS COBOL X3.23-1985
Language Changes

Beginning in 1960, the American National Standards (ANS) Committee on Computers and Information Processing (called the X3 Committee) established a series of subcommittees to define and publish a standard version of the COBOL programming language. To date, there have been three major revisions of the COBOL programming language developed and published by the ANS COBOL Subcommittee (known as X3.23): (1) ANS COBOL X3.23-1968, (2) ANS COBOL X3.23-1974, and now (3) ANS COBOL X3.23-1985.

This Outline (and its companion *Schaum's Outline of Programming with Structured COBOL*, McGraw-Hill, 1984) presents the COBOL language as defined by the 1974 standard ANS COBOL X3.23-1974. As of this writing, ANS COBOL X3.23-1985 has just been approved. Although most compilers in use today adhere to the ANS 1974 standards, compiler developers will certainly move quickly to implement the changes defined by ANS COBOL X3.23-1985. This chapter discusses most (but not all) of the *major* changes to be expected with forthcoming COBOL compilers.

12.1 General Language Changes

(1) When supported by the host computer system, lowercase letters may be used in character strings. They are equivalent to the corresponding uppercase letters (except within non-numeric literals, where "A" is not equal to "a", etc.; for example, "CAT" is not equal to "CaT", "Dog" is not equal to "dog", etc.).

(2) A table may now have up to seven dimensions instead of the previous three (i.e., OCCURS clauses may be nested up to a maximum of seven). This provides for up to seven subscripts and/or indexes, up to seven VARYING/AFTER clauses in the PERFORM . . . VARYING . . . AFTER . . . statement, etc.

(3) *All* DIVISIONs within a COBOL program are now *optional*.

(4) The data item named in an OCCURS . . . DEPENDING ON . . . clause may now have a 0 value. Thus the minimum number of entries in a variable-length table is now *0*.

(5) It is now possible for the COBOL programmer to control the way in which arguments are passed to a called program. With CALL . . . BY REFERENCE, any changes to LINK-AGE SECTION items in the called program are transferred back to the corresponding items in the USING list of the CALL statement; with CALL . . . BY CONTENT, changes to LINKAGE SECTION items in the called program do not affect the corresponding actual arguments back in the calling program. If the type of call is not given explicitly, CALL . . . BY REFERENCE is assumed.

EXAMPLE 12.1   Following is an example of the correct use of the new CALL statement options:

```
CALL ANY-SUBPROGRAM USING
            BY REFERENCE   RECORD-COUNTER
                           TOTAL-ERRORS
            BY CONTENT     INPUT-RECORD
                           VALID-CODES-TABLE
```

Subprogram changes to LINKAGE SECTION items corresponding to RECORD-COUNTER and TOTAL-ERRORS will automatically change RECORD-COUNTER and TOTAL-ERRORS back in the calling program. Subprogram changes to LINKAGE SECTION items corresponding to INPUT-RECORD and VALID-CODES-TABLE will *not* change these fields back in the calling program.

(6)   COBOL-85 introduces several changes to the SORT statement. Files to be sorted may now contain variable-length records, and USING and/or GIVING files may now have either indexed or relative organization (as well as the earlier sequential organization). Finally, a WITH DUPLICATES IN ORDER clause has been added, specifying that in the case of duplicate sort keys the records should remain in the same sequence as in the original input to the sort. In COBOL-74, the ultimate sequence of records with duplicate sort keys was unspecified.

EXAMPLE 12.2   Here is a syntactically correct COBOL-85 SORT statement:

```
SORT SOME-SORT-FILE
    ON ASCENDING  KEY MAJOR-CONTROL-FIELD
    ON DESCENDING KEY MINOR-CONTROL-FIELD
    WITH DUPLICATES IN ORDER
    USING  AN-INDEXED-FILE
    GIVING A-RELATIVE-FILE
```

(7)   There are two new class conditions. The ALPHABETIC-UPPER test is true for upper-case letters and the space character; the ALPHABETIC-LOWER test is true for lowercase letters and the space character. The old ALPHABETIC test still exists, and is now true for uppercase letters, lowercase letters, and the space character.

EXAMPLE 12.3   The following program segment illustrates the correct use of the new class conditions:

```
IF INPUT-ITEM IS ALPHABETIC-UPPER
    PERFORM ALL-CAPS-ROUTINE
ELSE IF INPUT-ITEM IS ALPHABETIC-LOWER
    PERFORM ALL-LOWER-CASE-ROUTINE
ELSE IF INPUT-ITEM ALPHABETIC
    PERFORM MIXED-UPPER-AND-LOWER-ROUTINE
ELSE
    PERFORM ERROR-ROUTINE
```

(8)   New FILE STATUS codes have been specified in the 1985 standard. See the Appendix for a full list of these codes.

(9)   The following elements have been placed in the *obsolete language element list*. Obsolete language elements are not removed from the COBOL-85 standard, but they probably will be removed in later revisions of COBOL. Some of the more important features in the COBOL-85 obsolete element list include (1) AUTHOR, INSTALLATION, DATE-WRITTEN, DATE-COMPILED, and SECURITY paragraphs in the IDENTIFICATION DIVISION (this information can and should be supplied by comment lines instead), (2) the LABEL RECORDS clause, (3) the DATA RECORDS clause (of the FD), (4) the "STOP literal" statement, and (5) the WITH DEBUGGING MODE capability and the USE FOR DEBUGGING DECLARATIVE capability, including DEBUG-ITEM (it is felt that modern operating systems and interactive COBOL debugging packages provide much more efficient debugging facilities than these COBOL features). The programmer should discontinue use of items (1) through (5), since they ultimately will be removed from the standard version of the language.

12.2 Changes to the IDENTIFICATION and ENVIRONMENT DIVISIONs

(10) The CONFIGURATION SECTION and SOURCE-COMPUTER and OBJECT-COMPUTER paragraphs, required in COBOL-74, have been made *optional* in COBOL-85.

(11) The SPECIAL-NAMES paragraph may include user-defined names for SYMBOLIC CHARACTERS, which may be used anywhere figurative constants may be used.

EXAMPLE 12.4 The following illustrates the definition and use of SYMBOLIC CHARACTERS:

```
SPECIAL-NAMES.
     SYMBOLIC CHARACTERS
         LEFT-PARENTHESIS
         RIGHT-PARENTHESIS
       ARE
         77
         93 . . .

WORKING-STORAGE SECTION.
01   END-OF-PHRASE  PIC X VALUE RIGHT-PARENTHESIS . . .
PROCEDURE DIVISION.

     IF INPUT-CHARACTER EQUAL LEFT-PARENTHESIS . . .
```

The values 77 and 93 are the numeric integer equivalents of the EBCDIC codes for the characters "(" and ")", respectively. The symbolic names given in the SYMBOLIC CHARACTERS list correspond to the characters whose numeric code values are specified, the first name corresponding to the first code value, the second name corresponding to the second code value, etc. SYMBOLIC CHARACTERS may be used anywhere figurative constants may be used, e.g., in VALUE clauses, PROCEDURE DIVISION statements, etc.

(12) A new clause has been added to the PROGRAM-ID paragraph:

```
PROGRAM-ID.  program-name IS INITIAL PROGRAM.
```

This permits the specification of external subprograms which are to be reinitialized to their starting state each time they are CALLed (thus providing the equivalent of the CANCEL statement when dynamic linkage is not being used).

EXAMPLE 12.5 Each time the following (sub)program is CALLed, all WORKING-STORAGE items will be reset to their specified VALUEs before execution begins:

```
PROGRAM-ID.  EXTERNAL-SUB IS INITIAL PROGRAM.
```

(13) A new clause in the SPECIAL-NAMES paragraph allows user-defined CLASS names, which can be used as conditions in IF and PERFORM . . . UNTIL . . . statements. A CLASS name condition is true if all characters in the data item being tested come from the set of characters associated with the specified CLASS name.

EXAMPLE 12.6 Here is the correct definition and use of a CLASS name:

```
SPECIAL-NAMES.
     CLASS VALID-PART-NUMBER IS    "0" THROUGH "9"
                                   "@#$"
                                   "A" THROUGH "Z"

PROCEDURE DIVISION.

     IF INPUT-PART-NUMBER IS VALID-PART-NUMBER . . .
```

The condition in the above IF statement is *true* if and only if INPUT-PART-NUMBER consists of characters only from the set 0 through 9, @, #, $, and A through Z.

12.3 Changes to the DATA DIVISION

(14) The decimal point and comma may be specified as the rightmost character of a PICTURE character string. In COBOL-74, this was not permitted.

EXAMPLE 12.7 The following PICTURE will edit the value + 001234 as "bb1,234.":

```
05   OUTPUT-NUMBER  PIC ZZZ,ZZ9..
```

The period ending the COBOL sentence must immediately follow the rightmost "." in the PICTURE string.

(15) The omission of BLOCK CONTAINS no longer defaults to an unblocked file. It now defaults to whatever blocking factor is specified by the operating system and any relevant job control/command language statements. In order to specify an unblocked file, "BLOCK CONTAINS 1 RECORDS" must now be used.

(16) The LABEL RECORDS clause is now *optional*. When omitted, LABEL RECORDS ARE STANDARD is assumed.

(17) The reserved word FILLER is now *optional* in a data description entry. FILLER may also be used to name a group item or an item which REDEFINES another.

EXAMPLE 12.8 The following record description is now valid:

```
01   CUSTOMER-REPORT-LINE.
     05   CUSTOMER-NAME        PIC X(30).
     05                        PIC X(5) VALUE SPACES.
     05   CUSTOMER-ADDRESS     PIC X(40).
     05                        PIC X(5) VALUE SPACES.
     05   CUSTOMER-PHONE       PIC X(8).
```

Observe that the omission of the (now) optional name FILLER makes the entire record description much more readable.

(18) The size of a data item which REDEFINES another may now be *less than* or equal to the size of the original item. In COBOL-74, the original and REDEFINEing items had to be the same length.

(19) Two new data types have been added to the USAGE clause. USAGE IS BINARY specifies that a numeric data item is to be represented in binary (base 2) notation. The details of this representation are left to the compiler implementer. Similarly, USAGE IS PACKED-DECIMAL specifies that a numeric data item is to be represented in decimal (base 10) notation. Again, the details of this representation are left to the compiler implementer. Note that USAGE IS PACKED-DECIMAL will standardize (and replace) the current USAGE IS COMP-3 (an IBM OS/VS COBOL extension to the COBOL-74 standard).

(20) The VALUE clause may now be used with or subordinate to an OCCURS clause, in which case every associated table entry is initialized to the specified value.

EXAMPLE 12.9 The VALUE clause may now be used to initialize table entries as follows:

```
01    INVENTORY-TABLE.
   05    INVENTORY-ITEM       OCCURS 200 TIMES.
      10    PART-NUMBER          PIC X(7).
      10    QUANTITY-ON-HAND     PIC S9(5) PACKED-DECIMAL
                                      VALUE ZERO.
      10    PART-NAME            PIC X(20) VALUE SPACES.
```

Each of the 200 table entries will initially have QUANTITY-ON-HAND set to 0 and PART-NAME set to spaces. Note also the use of the new data type PACKED-DECIMAL. PART-NUMBER fields will *not* be initialized to any particular value.

12.4   Changes to the PROCEDURE DIVISION

(21)   The maximum length of a nonnumeric literal (120 in COBOL-74) is increased to 160 characters in COBOL-85.

(22)   Relative subscripting, in which a subscript is followed by a " + " or " − " followed by an integer, is now allowed for *both* subscripts and indexes.

EXAMPLE 12.10   The following is supported in COBOL-85:

```
05    SUBSCRIPT-VALUE     PIC S9(4) COMP.

MOVE SAMPLE-TABLE (SUBSCRIPT-VALUE + 3) TO OUTPUT-AREA
```

Previously, relative table addressing was restricted to use with indexes.

(23)   Indexes and subscripts may be mixed when identifying a multidimensional table entry. In COBOL-74, multidimensional table entries have to be identified either with all subscripts or with all indexes.

EXAMPLE 12.11   The following is now legal:

```
MOVE SAMPLE-TABLE (INDEX-NAME SUBSCRIPT-VALUE) TO SOMEWHERE
```

(24)   *Reference modification* provides a method of specifying a substring of any data item with USAGE DISPLAY. The substring is defined by specifying a beginning character position and the length of the substring:

```
data-name ( starting-position : [length] )
```

"Starting-position" and "length" can both be any valid arithmetic expression. The *first* character in the data item is assumed to be at position *1*. If length is omitted, the substring begins at the indicated starting position and continues to the end of the data item.

EXAMPLE 12.12   Given the definition DISPLAY-ITEM PIC X(7) VALUE "ABCDEFG", reference modification yields the following results (assume START-HERE contains 5 and HOW-MANY contains 2):

Reference Modification Item	Corresponding Characters
DISPLAY-ITEM (2:3)	BCD
DISPLAY-ITEM (4:2)	DE
DISPLAY-ITEM (2:)	BCDEFG
DISPLAY-ITEM (4:)	DEFG
DISPLAY-ITEM (START-HERE:HOW-MANY)	EF

(25)   The *optional* word THEN is now allowed to begin the true part of an IF statement.

EXAMPLE 12.13 The following program segment illustrates the use of THEN in an IF statement:

```
IF   AN-ITEM EQUAL ANOTHER-ITEM
     THEN
           ADD 1 TO A-COUNTER
     ELSE
           SUBTRACT 1 FROM ANOTHER-COUNTER
END-IF
```

(26) New *scope terminators* have been added to COBOL to mark the end of various statements. In previous versions, the end of a READ with an INVALID KEY or AT END clause is marked with a period, the end of an IF statement is marked with a period, etc. The use of structured periods helps clarify the scope of such statements, but often poor printers or cheap quality paper produces periods which are difficult to identify. The following new scope terminators eliminate these difficulties: END-ADD, END-CALL, END-COMPUTE, END-DELETE, END-DIVIDE, END-EVALUATE, END-IF, END-MULTIPLY, END-PERFORM, END-READ, END-RECEIVE, END-RETURN, END-REWRITE, END-SEARCH, END-START, END-STRING, END-SUBTRACT, END-UNSTRING, END-WRITE. Note that the new scope terminators *supplement* the period, which still serves to mark the end of a statement.

EXAMPLE 12.14 The following are all valid statements:

(*a*)
```
READ SOME-INPUT-FILE
     INTO SOME-DATA-AREA
     AT END
           MOVE "YES" TO EOF-SW
END-READ
MOVE SPACES TO ...
```

(*b*)
```
IF VALID-DATA
     MOVE INPUT-DATA TO OUTPUT-AREA
     WRITE INDEXED-RECORD
           INVALID KEY
                 MOVE "YES" TO DUPLICATE-KEY-SW
     END-WRITE
ELSE
     PERFORM PRINT-ERROR-REPORT
END-IF
ADD 1 TO ...
```

Note that the above code could not be implemented in COBOL-74 since the period necessary to end the INVALID KEY clause of the WRITE statement would also be considered to end the IF statement (thus the WRITE statement would have to be removed to its own paragraph and PERFORMed from within the IF).

(*c*)
```
IF INPUT-DATA-CODE EQUAL "A"
     MOVE SPACES TO ...
     ADD INPUT-FIELD TO TOTAL-AREA
         ON SIZE ERROR
               PERFORM TOTAL-AREA-OVERFLOW
     END-ADD
END-IF
PERFORM ...
```

(27) Two new relational operators have been added to the language: (1) IS GREATER THAN OR EQUAL TO (or " > = ") is equivalent to IS NOT LESS THAN (or "NOT < "), and (2) IS LESS THAN OR EQUAL TO (or " < = ") is equivalent to IS NOT GREATER THAN (or "NOT > ").

(28) "ACCEPT numeric-data-item FROM DAY-OF-WEEK" places an integer between 1 and 7 (where 1 represents Monday) into the specified numeric data item.

(29) "TO" is now allowed in the following form of the ADD statement:

```
ADD { data-item ¦ literal} TO { data-item ¦ literal}
    GIVING data-item
```

The GIVING field receives the sum of the other two fields, which remain unchanged.

(30) The ON SIZE ERROR, AT END, AT END-OF-PAGE, and INVALID KEY clauses are supplemented with clauses that provide routines for the opposite conditions: NOT ON SIZE ERROR, NOT AT END, NOT AT END-OF-PAGE, and NOT INVALID KEY.

EXAMPLE 12.15 Here is the correct use of NOT AT END and NOT INVALID KEY:

(*a*)
```
READ SEQUENTIAL-INPUT-FILE
      AT END
            PERFORM END-OF-FILE
      NOT AT END
            PERFORM PROCESS-DATA
END-READ
```

(*b*)
```
PERFORM FORMAT-INDEXED-RECORD
WRITE INDEXED-RECORD
      INVALID KEY
            PERFORM DUPLICATE-KEY-ERROR
      NOT INVALID KEY
            PERFORM FORMAT-NEW-RECORD-LINE
            PERFORM PRINT-NEW-RECORD-LINE
END-WRITE
```

(31) COBOL-85 provides a new statement to implement the case structure discussed in Chapter 3.

EXAMPLE 12.16 The following illustrates the simplest version of the EVALUATE statement. It could be used in a transaction center module to identify the type of transaction and invoke the proper processing. INPUT-TRANSACTION-CODE is PIC X(3):

```
EVALUATE INPUT-TRANSACTION-CODE
      WHEN "ADD"
            PERFORM ADD-NEW-RECORD
            PERFORM LOG-TO-NEW-RECORD-LIST
      WHEN "DEL"
            PERFORM DELETE-EXISTING-RECORD
      WHEN "CHA"
            PERFORM CHANGE-EXISTING-RECORD
      WHEN "INQ"
            PERFORM PROCESS-USER-INQUIRY
      WHEN OTHER
            PERFORM INVALID-TRANSACTION-ID
END-EVALUATE
```

INPUT-TRANSACTION-CODE is compared to each WHEN value in turn. If at any point a match is found, the corresponding statement(s) are executed and normal execution resumes following END-EVALUATE. If INPUT-TRANSACTION-CODE does not match any of the WHEN values, then the WHEN OTHER routine is executed.

(32) The new INITIALIZE statement permits one or more specified data items to be set to selected values.

EXAMPLE 12.17 The following are both valid INITIALIZE statements:

(*a*) INITIALIZE   NUMERIC-ITEM
                  ALPHANUMERIC-ITEM

If no initial values are specified as part of the INITIALIZE statement, then all numeric and numeric edited items specified in the list of data items to be initialized are set to 0, and all alphabetic, alphanumeric, and alphanumeric edited items in the list are set to spaces.

(*b*) INITIALIZE   GROUP-ITEM
            REPLACING ALPHANUMERIC DATA BY ALL "*"
                  NUMERIC DATA BY ZEROS

All alphanumeric data items subordinate to GROUP-ITEM are set to ALL "*", all numeric data items subordinate to GROUP-ITEM are set to 0s, and any other type of field subordinate to GROUP-ITEM is left unchanged. If GROUP-ITEM is defined:

```
01   GROUP-ITEM.
     05   FIELD-1       PIC X(4).
     05   FIELD-2       PIC 9(4).
     05   FIELD-3       PIC Z,ZZ.99.
     05   FIELD-4       PIC X(3).
```

then FIELD-1 and FIELD-4 are set to ALL "*", FIELD-2 is set to 0s, and FIELD-3 is unchanged. The possible choices for data types in the INITIALIZE statement are ALPHABETIC, ALPHANUMERIC, NUMERIC, ALPHANUMERIC-EDITED, and NUMERIC-EDITED.

(33) The capabilities provided by the nonstandard TRANSFORM statement discussed in Chapter 11 have been standardized as a new version of the INSPECT statement.

EXAMPLE 12.18 Redo Problem 11.29 using the COBOL-85 INSPECT statement instead of the nonstandard TRANSFORM statement:

```
INSPECT KEY-FIELD
     CONVERTING     "/-#@b"
     TO             "12345"
```

The CONVERTING . . . TO . . . option causes each character in KEY-FIELD which occurs in the CONVERT-ING . . . string to be *replaced* by the corresponding character in the TO . . . string. The CONVERTING and TO strings must be the same length so that the correspondence is one-to-one. The above statement converts "/" to "1", "-" to "2", "#" to "3", etc. An optional "BEFORE/AFTER INITIAL {data-item | literal}" clause can also be specified to restrict the conversion process to just a beginning (or ending) piece of a data item (see Problem 12.45).

(34) A numeric edited item may now be MOVEd to a numeric (i.e., nonedited) item. This type of MOVE *undoes* the editing.

EXAMPLE 12.19 If NUM-1 PIC ZZ,ZZZ.99 contains b9,876.53 and NUM-2 is defined PIC 9(5)V99, then "MOVE NUM-1 TO NUM-2" places 0987653 (with two decimal places assumed) in NUM-2, thus "de-editing" the contents of NUM-1.

(35) Variable-length records can now be processed with the INTO option of READ and RETURN. In COBOL-74, READ . . . INTO . . . and RETURN . . . INTO . . . could only be used with fixed-length records.

(36) The REWRITE statement is allowed to replace the original record *with a record of a different length* for both indexed and relative files. In COBOL-74, it was only possible to REWRITE a same-length record.

(37) The SORT and MERGE statements now allow INPUT and/or OUTPUT PROCE-DURES to be *paragraphs* as well as SECTIONs. In COBOL-74, an INPUT or OUTPUT PROCEDURE name must be a SECTION name.

(38) The INPUT and OUTPUT PROCEDUREs of a SORT or MERGE statement may now contain transfers of control to points *outside* the INPUT or OUTPUT PROCEDURE (e.g., an INPUT or OUTPUT PROCEDURE may PERFORM a paragraph which is outside the INPUT or OUTPUT PROCEDURE itself). Some compilers, such as IBM OS/VS COBOL, have already implemented this feature as an extension to the COBOL-74 standards, while others have not.

(39) A new version of the PERFORM statement allows what is called an *in-line PERFORM*, in which the statements to be PERFORMed are physically placed between the PERFORM statement itself and the (new) END-PERFORM terminator. The statements appearing in an in-line PERFORM must be imperative statements, but COBOL-85 defines an impera-tive statement as either (*a*) an unconditional statement or (*b*) a conditional statement delimited by an explicit scope terminator (such as END-READ, END-IF, etc.). This second definition allows the inclusion of any statement (if written with a scope terminator) in an in-line PERFORM.

EXAMPLE 12.20   The following illustrates a correct in-line PERFORM:

```
SOME-PARAGRAPH.
    MOVE SPACES TO SOME-FIELD
    MOVE "YES" TO KEEP-GOING-SW
    PERFORM UNTIL KEEP-GOING-SW EQUAL "NO"
        ADD 1 TO SOMETHING
        IF SOMETHING EQUAL ANYTHING
            MOVE SOMETHING TO SOMEWHERE
        END-IF
        PERFORM ROUTINE-CAN-SET-SW-TO-NO
        READ A-FILE
            INVALID KEY
                MOVE SOMETHING-ELSE TO SOMEWHERE-ELSE
        END-READ
    END-PERFORM
    ADD 1 TO SOMETHING-ELSE
```

An in-line PERFORM is signaled by the lack of a paragraph (or SECTION) name in the PERFORM statement (e.g., "PERFORM UNTIL . . . " instead of "PERFORM paragraph-name UNTIL . . . "). The rules for PERFORMing the statements between PERFORM and END-PERFORM are the same as they would be if the statements were placed in a separate paragraph (say SEPARATE-PARA) and the following were used:

```
PERFORM SEPARATE-PARA
    UNTIL KEEP-GOING-SW EQUAL "NO"
```

(40) PERFORM . . . UNTIL . . . has been expanded to allow specification of whether the UNTIL condition should be tested *before* or *after* the indicated statements or paragraph(s)

are PERFORMed. In COBOL-74, the test is always done before the paragraph(s) are ever PERFORMed; thus if the UNTIL condition is initially true, the specified paragraph(s) are not PERFORMed at all. In COBOL-85, WITH TEST BEFORE is the *default* (i.e., same as the 1974 standard), but WITH TEST AFTER may also be coded.

EXAMPLE 12.21   The following examples illustrate proper use of the new WITH TEST AFTER clause for PERFORM...UNTIL. Note that WITH TEST AFTER effectively implements the structured programming DOUNTIL structure presented in Chapter 3.

(*a*)
```
PERFORM SOME-PARAGRAPH
     WITH TEST AFTER
     UNTIL END-FILE-SW EQUAL "YES"
```

Specification of WITH TEST AFTER causes the UNTIL condition to be tested *after* the indicated paragraph is PERFORMed the first (and subsequent) time(s). This guarantees that the indicated paragraph will be PERFORMed at least once, even if the UNTIL condition is initially true. PERFORM...WITH TEST AFTER thus implements the DOUNTIL structure discussed in Chapter 3.

(*b*)
```
PERFORM
     WITH TEST AFTER
     UNTIL WE-ARE-DONE
          MOVE A TO B
          ADD C TO D
          PERFORM SET-SWITCH-IF-DONE
          COMPUTE ...
END-PERFORM
```

The WITH TEST AFTER clause may be used with in-line PERFORMs.

EXAMPLE 12.22   The following illustrate proper use of the WITH TEST BEFORE clause. Remember that WITH TEST BEFORE is the COBOL-74 standard and is still the default in COBOL-85.

(*a*)
```
PERFORM SAMPLE-PARAGRAPH
     WITH TEST BEFORE
     UNTIL SWITCH-SAYS-QUIT
```

When WITH TEST BEFORE is specified, the UNTIL condition is tested *before* the first execution of the indicated statement(s). If the condition is initially true, SAMPLE-PARAGRAPH will not be PERFORMed at all. PERFORM...WITH TEST BEFORE thus implements the DOWHILE structure presented in Chapter 3.

(*b*)
```
PERFORM SAMPLE-PARAGRAPH
     UNTIL SWITCH-SAYS-QUIT
```

Since WITH TEST BEFORE is the default, this is equivalent to (*a*) above.

(*c*)
```
PERFORM
     WITH TEST BEFORE
     UNTIL STOP-IT-SWITCH EQUAL "YES"
          MOVE A TO B
          ADD X TO Y
          PERFORM SOME-ROUTINE
          DISPLAY A-MESSAGE
END-PERFORM
```

WITH TEST BEFORE can also be used with an in-line PERFORM.

(41) When a variable-length field with an OCCURS . . . DEPENDING ON . . . clause acts as a *receiving field*, the maximum possible value of the DEPENDING ON item is used to determine the effective length of the receiving field. In COBOL-74, it is the current value of the DEPENDING ON item which determines the effective length of the receiving field (see Problem 12.47). The *sending-field* length is always determined by the current value of its DEPENDING ON item.

(42) COBOL-85 defines an imperative statement as either (*a*) an unconditional statement or (*b*) a conditional statement delimited by an explicit scope terminator. This allows conditional statements to be used in contexts which are not allowed by COBOL-74 (see Problem 12.46).

Review Questions

12.1 Name the three major revisions of ANS standard COBOL.

12.2 Which version of standard COBOL is in use at your installation?

12.3 Discuss the general language changes introduced in COBOL-85.

12.4 Distinguish between CALL BY CONTENT and CALL BY REFERENCE.

12.5 Discuss the COBOL-85 changes to the SORT/MERGE features.

12.6 What is the significance of the WITH DUPLICATES IN ORDER clause when doing a SORT?

12.7 Explain the new class conditions available in COBOL-85.

12.8 What is the purpose of the COBOL-85 obsolete element list?

12.9 List some features named as obsolete elements in the COBOL-85 standard.

12.10 Why should programmers discontinue use of obsolete language elements?

12.11 Discuss the use of SYMBOLIC CHARACTERS.

12.12 Discuss the use of the INITIAL PROGRAM phrase in the PROGRAM-ID paragraph.

12.13 Discuss the use of the user-defined CLASS name feature in COBOL-85.

12.14 Discuss the difference in effect when BLOCK CONTAINS is *omitted* in (1) COBOL-74 and (2) COBOL-85.

12.15 What DATA DIVISION items have become optional in COBOL-85?

12.16 Discuss the two new data types available in COBOL-85.

12.17 Discuss the new application of the VALUE clause for initializing tables.

12.18 Explain the use of relative subscripting.

12.19 Explain the use of reference modification.

12.20 Give several examples of the correct use of the new COBOL-85 scope terminators.

12.21   What are two new relational operators in COBOL-85?

12.22   What does ACCEPT . . . FROM DAY-OF-WEEK do?

12.23   Discuss the use of NOT ON SIZE ERROR, NOT AT END, NOT AT END-OF-PAGE, and NOT INVALID KEY.

12.24   Explain the use of the new EVALUATE statement.

12.25   Explain the use of the new INITIALIZE statement.

12.26   Discuss the use of INSPECT . . . CONVERTING.

12.27   Explain how the MOVE statement can now be used to "un-edit" an edited data item.

12.28   Discuss the changes for READ . . . INTO . . . and RETURN . . . INTO . . . with respect to variable-length records.

12.29   Discuss the relaxation of record length restrictions for REWRITE.

12.30   Discuss any significant changes to the SORT/MERGE capability.

12.31   Explain the use of in-line PERFORM.

12.32   Explain the use of the new WITH TEST BEFORE/AFTER clause of the PERFORM . . . UNTIL-. . . statement.

12.33   Discuss the impact of the change to the default length of a variable-length table from the current value of the DEPENDING ON item to the maximum value of the DEPENDING ON item.

Solved Problems

12.34   Give the contents of ARG-1 through ARG-4 as displayed by the program below:

```
PROGRAM-ID. CALLING.              PROGRAM-ID. SUBPGM.

WORKING-STORAGE SECTION.          LINKAGE SECTION.
01  ARG-1 PIC X VALUE "A".        01  ITEM-1 PIC X.
01  ARG-2 PIC X VALUE "B".        01  ITEM-2 PIC X.
01  ARG-3 PIC X VALUE "C".        01  ITEM-3 PIC X.
01  ARG-4 PIC X VALUE "D".        01  ITEM-4 PIC X.

PROCEDURE DIVISION.               PROCEDURE DIVISION
                                       USING     ITEM-1 ITEM-2
    CALL "SUBPGM" USING                          ITEM-3 ITEM-4.
        BY REFERENCE
            ARG-1                     MOVE "W" TO ITEM-1
            ARG-2                     MOVE "X" TO ITEM-2
        BY CONTENT                    MOVE "Y" TO ITEM-3
            ARG-3                     MOVE "Z" TO ITEM-4
            ARG-4                 RETURN-TO-CALLER.
    DISPLAY ARG-1 ARG-2               EXIT PROGRAM.
            ARG-3 ARG-4
    STOP RUN.
```

Since ARG-1 and ARG-2 are passed BY REFERENCE, changes to the corresponding LINKAGE SECTION items in the subprogram result in changes to ARG-1 and ARG-2 back in the calling program. Since ARG-3 and ARG-4 are passed BY CONTENT, subprogram changes to the corresponding items ITEM-3 and ITEM-4 do *not* affect ARG-3 and ARG-4 back in the calling program. Thus ARG-1 becomes "W", ARG-2 becomes "X", ARG-3 remains "C", and ARG-4 remains "D", which are the values DISPLAYed.

12.35 The numeric code values for the characters "#" and "@" in the EBCDIC code are 123 and 124, respectively. Show how to define and use SYMBOLIC CHARACTERS for these characters.

```
SPECIAL-NAMES.
    SYMBOLIC CHARACTERS
        POUND-SIGN
        AT-SIGN
    ARE
        123
        124...

    MOVE POUND-SIGN TO OUTPUT-AREA
    IF INPUT-AREA EQUAL AT-SIGN ...
```

12.36 Define CLASS names which can be used to test (1) if an input social security number consists of only digits and hyphens and (2) if an input balance due amount consists of only digits, decimal points, and possible minus signs.

```
SPECIAL-NAMES.
    CLASS VALID-SOC-SECURITY-NUMBER IS "0" THROUGH "9"
                                        "-"
    CLASS VALID-BALANCE IS   "0" THRU "9"
                             "-."
```

12.37 What, if anything, is wrong with the following:

```
01   AN-ITEM   PIC X(6).
01   ANOTHER-ITEM REDEFINES AN-ITEM.
    05   SUB-FIELD-1   PIC X(3).
    05   SUB-FIELD-2   PIC X(4).
```

While a redefining item may be *less than* the original item in size, it may not be *greater* than the original item.

12.38 Define a table to hold programmer ID's and hours worked. Initially, each programmer ID should contain spaces, and each hours-worked field should be 0.

```
01  PROGRAMMER-DATA-TABLE.
    05  PROGRAMMER-ENTRY   OCCURS 100 TIMES.
        10  PROGRAMMER-ID  PIC X(5)  VALUE SPACES.
        10  HOURS-WORKED   PIC S9(3) COMP VALUE ZERO.
```

12.39 Suppose N is defined PIC S9(3) COMP VALUE +50. Show how to DISPLAY the fifty-seventh PROGRAMMER-ID from Problem 12.38 using N as a subscript.

```
DISPLAY PROGRAMMER-ID (N + 7)
```

12.40 Suppose it is known that the first name of a customer begins in position 12 of CUSTOMER-NAME PIC X(40) and is 15 characters long. Using reference modification, move the first name into FIRST-NAME PIC X(20).

```
MOVE CUSTOMER-NAME (12 : 15) TO FIRST-NAME
```

12.41 After the MOVE in Problem 12.40, the first name will be left-justified and padded with spaces on the right of FIRST-NAME. Using INSPECT and reference modification, show how to copy the name into RIGHT-NAME PIC X(20), *right*-justified and padded with spaces on the *left*.

```
MOVE ZERO TO NUMBER-CHARS
INSPECT FIRST-NAME
     TALLYING NUMBER-CHARS
          FOR CHARACTERS
               BEFORE INITIAL SPACE
MOVE SPACES TO RIGHT-NAME
MOVE FIRST-NAME (1 : NUMBER-CHARS) TO
  RIGHT-NAME (20 - NUMBER-CHARS + 1 : NUMBER-CHARS)
```

Note that both the sending field and the receiving field of the MOVE can involve reference modification, which is permitted anywhere a DISPLAY-type data item can appear.

12.42 Rewrite the following code as one paragraph using the COBOL-85 scope terminators:

```
PARA-1.
    IF A EQUAL B
        PERFORM GET-A-RECORD
        ADD 1 TO A-COUNTER
    ELSE
        PERFORM ADD-TO-FILE
    .
    ADD 1 TO RECORDS-INPUT
    .
GET-A-RECORD.
    READ INPUT-FILE
        AT END
            MOVE "YES" TO EOF-SW
    .
ADD-TO-FILE.
    WRITE OUTPUT-RECORD
        INVALID KEY
            MOVE "YES" TO DUPLICATE-KEY-SW
    .
    ADD 1 TO RECORDS-ADDED
    .
```

The paragraphs above can be combined in COBOL-85 as follows:

```
PARA-1.
    IF A EQUAL B
        READ INPUT-FILE
            AT END
                MOVE "YES" TO EOF-SW
        END-READ
        ADD 1 TO A-COUNTER
```

```
                      ELSE
                          WRITE OUTPUT-RECORD
                              INVALID KEY
                                      MOVE "YES" TO DUPLICATE-KEY-SW
                          END-WRITE
                          ADD 1 TO RECORDS-ADDED
                      END-IF
                      ADD 1 TO RECORDS-INPUT
                          .
```

12.43 An inquiry code for an online student information system dictates whether a program is to display a student's phone number (code 1), grade average (code 2), or semester standing (code 3). Write an EVALUATE statement to process an incoming INQUIRY-CODE PIC 9.

```
            EVALUATE INQUIRY-CODE
                WHEN 1
                        PERFORM SHOW-PHONE-NUMBER
                WHEN 2
                        PERFORM CALCULATE-GPA
                        PERFORM SHOW-GPA
                WHEN 3
                        PERFORM SHOW-STANDING
                WHEN OTHER
                        PERFORM SHOW-ERROR-SCREEN
            END-EVALUATE
```

12.44 GROUP-ITEM consists of some alphabetic fields (PIC A), some numeric fields, and some alphanumeric fields (PIC X). Show how to initialize all alphabetic fields to spaces, all alphanumeric fields to all "*", and all numeric fields to 0s.

```
            INITIALIZE GROUP-ITEM
                    REPLACING ALPHABETIC DATA       BY SPACES
                              ALPHANUMERIC DATA     BY ALL "*"
                              NUMERIC DATA          BY ZEROS
```

12.45 Redo Example 11.30 with the new version of the INSPECT statement. Modify the problem so that only characters before the first "/" (if any) are translated.

```
            INSPECT SOME-ALPHANUMERIC-FIELD
                CONVERTING      "123456789"
                TO              "ABCDEFGHI"
                BEFORE INITIAL "/"
```

12.46 Implement the following COBOL-74 code as one READ statement, illustrating how the COBOL-85 scope terminators and in-line PERFORM allow what were formerly conditional statements to be treated as imperative statements:

```
            READ A-FILE
            INVALID KEY
                PERFORM ERROR-ANALYSIS
                .
```

```
ERROR-ANALYSIS.
    IF A-SWITCH EQUAL "YES"
        ADD 1 TO A-COUNTER
    ELSE
        ADD 2 TO A-COUNTER
    .
    MOVE "YES" TO I-O-ERROR-SW
    .
```

The above can be written as a single READ in COBOL-85 as follows:

```
READ A-FILE
    INVALID KEY
        PERFORM
            IF A-SWITCH EQUAL "YES"
                ADD 1 TO A-COUNTER
            ELSE
                ADD 2 TO A-COUNTER
            END-IF
            MOVE "YES" TO I-O-ERROR-SW
        END-PERFORM
END-READ
```

Note that PERFORM and END-PERFORM could be removed from this solution without affecting the logic.

12.47 Given the following table definitions:

```
01  TABLE-AREA.
    05  NUMBER-ENTRIES    PIC S9(5) BINARY.
    05  VALID-CODE        PIC X(4)
                          OCCURS 1 TO 20 TIMES
                          DEPENDING ON NUMBER-ENTRIES.
01  COPY-TABLE-AREA.
    05  COPY-NUMBER       PIC S9(5) BINARY.
    05  COPY-CODE         PIC X(4)
                          OCCURS 1 TO 20 TIMES
                          DEPENDING ON COPY-NUMBER.
```

show how to move TABLE-AREA to COPY-TABLE-AREA in (1) COBOL-74 and (2) COBOL-85.

(1) In COBOL-74, the active length of the receiving table is controlled by its DEPENDING ON item, which must be set before the rest of the table is copied (to avoid the truncation which would occur if, say, NUMBER-ENTRIES were 10 but COPY-NUMBER were 5):

```
MOVE NUMBER-ENTRIES TO COPY-NUMBER
MOVE TABLE-AREA TO COPY-TABLE-AREA
```

(2) In COBOL-85, the active length of the receiving table is always the *maximum* possible length, so the truncation problem described above never occurs (and it is not necessary to move the DEPENDING ON item separately):

```
MOVE TABLE-AREA TO COPY-TABLE-AREA
```

Chapter 13

COBOL in an Interactive Environment

In the past, almost all business applications were developed as *batch processing systems*. In a batch processing system, users prepare information in the form of *source documents* which are collected ("batched") over a period of time. The length of time depends on the application. The batch of source documents is then sent to a centralized data entry department, where it is keyed onto a machine-readable medium (e.g., key-to-tape or key-to-disk), producing a file of transaction records.

The transaction file is eventually processed by a batch program designed to input and process the entire file, one record at a time. Output goes directly to printers and/or auxiliary storage devices.

13.1 Characteristics of Batch Systems

There is no way for the users who prepare the original source documents (or the data entry personnel who key them) to interact with a batch program while it is executing. A batch program is controlled solely by the data placed in its input file(s) *before* the program runs; thus all input must be prepared ahead of time. The user cannot provide input, make corrections, abort particular actions, select options, etc., while the program is running. After submitting the original source documents, the user of a batch system becomes a spectator, unable to do anything except await the receipt of printed reports *after* the program finishes executing.

There are many applications where batch processing provides an efficient and effective way to meet users' needs, and batch processing is still heavily used in business and industry. There are other applications, however, where batch processing does not serve the users so well. In general, batch processing fails when users need results immediately, when files must constantly be kept current and accurate, or when users need the flexibility of interacting with a program while it is executing.

One problem with batch systems is that information is always outdated. Transactions do not update master files when the transactions actually occur. Instead, they are collected until it is time to run the next batch of transactions. Since master files do not reflect the transactions in the batch currently being collected, they are never up to date. Batch processing is *delayed* processing.

EXAMPLE 13.1 Suppose a batch inventory system collects inventory transactions all day and runs the inventory file updates overnight. The printed inventory listing produced Tuesday night will not reflect the inventory activity occurring between the opening of business Wednesday morning (say 9:00 a.m.) and the time the report is used (say 4:30 p.m. Wednesday). Since Wednesday's transactions have not yet been used to update inventory files or produce reports, both the files and the reports grow more and more inaccurate throughout the day (as more and more inventory transactions occur but are not yet processed). Depending on the nature of the business, this can be a serious problem (e.g., a salesperson cannot immediately answer a customer's telephoned question regarding the availability of a given item).

Another disadvantage of batch systems is the method of handling errors. If a batch program finds an error in a transaction, it prints an error message and ignores the record. After the program finishes executing, the user must read the error report, make the corrections on a source document, and resubmit the corrected document to data entry to be included in the next batch of transactions. The error cannot be corrected *when it is discovered* since the user is unable to interact with the program.

EXAMPLE 13.2 For the batch inventory system in Example 13.1, suppose an error is found during Tuesday night's update runs. The error report printed Tuesday night is available to an inventory clerk first thing Wednesday morning. The clerk prepares a corrected source document and includes it with Wednesday's batch of inventory transactions. The correction is processed by data entry and run Wednesday night. The results of this (corrected) transaction are not available until inventory reports are distributed Thursday morning, 2 days after the transaction actually occurred.

13.2   Interactive Versus Batch Processing

Applications which do not fit the batch processing model are typically implemented as *interactive* or *online* systems. An interactive program is designed to communicate with a user at a video display (or equivalent) terminal while the program is executing, literally allowing the user to *interact* with the running program. Interactive systems implement a *conversational* relationship between the program and the user: the user enters data from the terminal's keyboard, the data is processed immediately, and the results are displayed (typically within seconds) on the terminal's video screen.

EXAMPLE 13.3 An interactive program typically implements the following dialogue with a user at a video display terminal (CRT):

(1) A transaction (such as a sale or customer inquiry) occurs during normal business operation. The user immediately inputs the transaction information, using a terminal keyboard.

(2) When the user hits the ENTER key, the program processes the transaction immediately.

(3) If transaction processing involves no errors, the program displays the results of processing on the user's terminal (typically in a matter of seconds) and invites the user to enter another transaction.

(4) If an error is discovered, error information is displayed on the terminal and the user is allowed to make immediate corrections to the transaction. Processing then continues with step (2) above.

EXAMPLE 13.4 Suppose the inventory system in Example 13.1 is implemented as an interactive system. Then:

(1) As each order is placed or shipment received, a salesperson or inventory control clerk enters the transaction from a terminal. The program processing the transaction will immediately update the appropriate master files, thus keeping inventory information constantly up to date.

(2) Anyone needing to know current inventory status can enter an inquiry transaction from a terminal and receive an immediate, up-to-the-minute response.

(3) If an error is made entering any type of transaction, the processing program's editing routines will detect the error immediately and prompt the terminal user to make the appropriate correction(s). The user still gets immediate results even when mistakes are made (because they are corrected immediately).

13.3   The Hardware Environment for Interactive Systems

A major consideration for interactive systems is *response time* (i.e., the time between the user's hitting the last key to enter a transaction and the receipt of the corresponding results on the terminal's video screen). The need for reasonable response times (typically measured in seconds) dictates that the files used by interactive applications be kept on direct access storage devices (which allow random retrieval of records in tens of milliseconds). Since files on direct access devices are said to be "online", interactive applications are often called *online applications*.

In addition to direct access hardware, interactive systems must also support many terminals. Terminals (typically video display or CRT terminals) may be connected to the host computer system by in-house cable or may be remotely located and connected via telecommunications facilities. There are several types of specialized hardware needed to support the many terminals typically required by interactive applications.

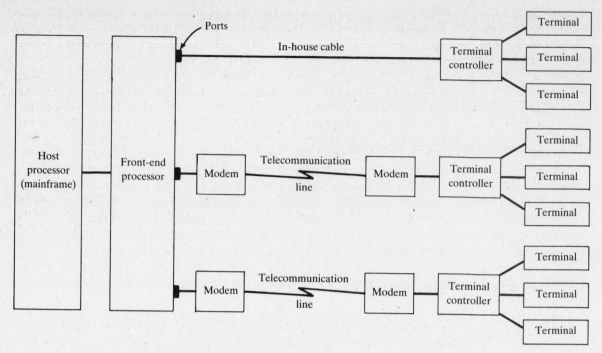

Fig. 13-1

EXAMPLE 13.5   Figure 13-1 shows a typical hardware connection between a remote terminal and a host computer system. Each element in the sequence from the user to the host computer system is discussed below:

(1)   At the user end, *terminals* come in a variety of styles and capabilities. Typically, the terminal's input medium is a keyboard (although other possibilities, such as light pens, exist), and the terminal's output medium is a video display screen (again other possibilities, such as hard copy, exist). Video displays differ in whether or not they can provide color, graphics, *reverse video* (i.e., light characters on a dark background versus dark characters on a light background), multiple brightness levels (*highlighting*), etc.

(2)   Several terminals are often connected by in-house cable to a *terminal controller*. The controller allows multiple terminals to share the same communication pathway to the host computer system, thereby significantly reducing network costs (especially if long distances are involved). The controller directs the operation of each terminal connected to it. Terminal controllers are also called *cluster controllers*.

(3)   Terminals can be connected (via their controllers) to the host end of the communication network in one of two ways. If the distances involved are short enough (e.g., within the same building), the terminal controller can be connected via *in-house cable*.

(4)   When longer distances are involved, terminal controllers must be connected to the host end via *telecommunications lines*. Telecommunications lines may be (1) *private* (installed, owned, and operated by the company owning the computer network), (2) *leased* (installed, owned, and operated by a common carrier such as the telephone company but, for a monthly fee, permanently dedicated to the use of the company owning the computer network), or (3) *dial-up* (temporary connections established by dialing the host computer's telephone number as for a normal voice telephone call, and billed in the same manner).

(5)   If telecommunications lines are used, they may be analog or digital. *Digital* lines are designed to carry data in the same binary form in which it is stored within the terminal and host processor. *Analog* lines are designed to carry voice communications, and cannot handle the binary (on/off) type of signal used within the terminals and host. When analog lines are used, devices called *modems* must be installed between the terminal controller and the telecommunications line at the user end, and between the telecommunications line and the host's front-end processor at the host end. A modem ("modulator/demodulator") converts (modulates) digital (binary) data from a terminal or controller to a form of

analog signal suitable for transmission over an analog line to the host. Similarly, a modem converts (demodulates) analog signals coming from the host's modem to digital signals, which it passes along to the terminal (via the terminal controller). The use of digital lines eliminates the need for analog modems within the network and can provide higher transmission speeds.

(6) At the host end, in-house cables or lines coming from modems are attached to *ports* on a *front-end processor*. A port is simply the physical point of attachment for an incoming communication line. The front-end processor is typically a programmable mini- or microcomputer with software to control the communications lines attached to its ports. The use of a front-end processor to control the communications lines frees the host processor from this burden, allowing it to spend more time actually processing data. Less sophisticated front-end processors are often called *communications controllers*. Note that the maximum number of ports on the front-end processor is a limiting factor on the possible size of the network.

(7) The host processor is typically a mainframe which runs the user operating system, together with all user application programs. The host carries out the major *processing* of data within the entire system, and all necessary files and data bases must be available on direct access devices attached (via channels) to the host.

13.4 The Software Environment for Interactive Systems

The front-end processor typically runs software which controls communication with all terminals. The software in the front-end processor is responsible for implementing the *protocols* (i.e., rules for proper communication) used by the devices attached to the front-end's ports. Under control of this software, the front-end receives data from terminals and/or terminal controllers, interprets and reformats the data according to the proper protocol, and passes it along to the host. It also receives data from the host and routes it to the proper destination terminal using the proper protocol. In addition, the front-end software is responsible for the detection and correction (by retransmission if necessary) of any errors in data transmission.

Data coming from the front-end processor is received in the host under the control of a part of the operating system known as a *telecommunications access method*. Just as operating systems have data management routines called file access methods for handling the details of transferring records to and from files, so operating systems have specialized access methods for handling the details of input/output to terminals attached to the front-end processor.

EXAMPLE 13.6 In an IBM installation, the operating system file access methods QSAM, BDAM, ISAM, VSAM, etc., handle the physical details of transferring records to and from files on regular input/output and auxiliary storage devices. Similarly, there are several operating system telecommunications access methods specifically designed to handle the physical details of transferring data to and from terminals. The three major IBM telecommunications access methods are (1) VTAM (Virtual Telecommunications Access Method), (2) TCAM (Telecommunications Access Method), and (3) BTAM (Basic Telecommunications Access Method). The various telecommunications access methods differ in their power, flexibility, and ease of use.

In addition to the operating system and its telecommunications access methods, the host processor also runs user applications programs. The major difference between a typical batch application and a typical interactive application is the interactive program's need to receive input from a terminal keyboard and send output to a terminal screen. Whereas a batch COBOL program can directly call an operating system file access method (such as VSAM) with a READ or WRITE statement, interactive applications programs generally do *not* directly interface with a telecommunications access method when it is desired to send/receive data to/from a terminal.

Installations implementing interactive systems typically use a *teleprocessing monitor* program to interface between the operating system telecommunications access methods and the user application programs. The teleprocessing monitor (also called *telecommunications monitor* or *communications control program*) is responsible for (1) accepting data from an application program and formatting it for proper transmission to its destination terminal, (2) passing the user message (along with any necessary control information) to the appropriate operating system telecommunications access method which will handle the physical details of sending the message to the terminal, (3) receiving data originating at the terminal from the operating system telecommunications access method which handled the physical details of input from the terminal, (4) reformatting the terminal data to a form suitable for use by the application program, and (5) passing the reformatted data to the application program.

A typical teleprocessing monitor also carries out many of the functions normally performed by the operating system for batch programs, including (1) recognizing that a terminal user needs to execute a particular application program, (2) obtaining main memory in which to load the desired program, (3) loading and executing the application, (4) recognizing the termination of the application program and releasing all program resources (including memory) for reuse, and (5) interfacing between the operating system file-handling access methods and the application program's requests for access to files on input/output and auxiliary storage devices.

Note that item (5) implies that a typical interactive COBOL program does *not* contain the normal READ, WRITE, and REWRITE statements for file processing. Input, output, and updating of records are handled, instead, by requesting these services from the teleprocessing monitor (which in turn passes the requests along to the operating system file-handling access methods).

EXAMPLE 13.7 Figure 13-2 shows the relationship between two interactive COBOL application programs, a batch application program, a teleprocessing monitor program, and the operating system. Observe that:

(1) The batch application interfaces *directly* with the operating system file access methods (via READ, WRITE, and REWRITE statements) to access records in files.

(2) The interactive applications do *not* directly interface with the operating system access methods. Instead, they pass requests for both file I/O and terminal I/O services to the teleprocessing monitor. The teleprocessing monitor checks the requests for validity, reformats them, and passes them along to the appropriate operating system access method, which actually carries out the desired I/O service.

(3) The operating system access methods pass input data and control information to the teleprocessing monitor in response to its input service requests. The teleprocessing monitor then reformats this file and terminal input and passes the data along to the interactive application program for processing.

(4) Although not apparent from the diagram, the batch application was loaded into memory for execution under the direct control of the operating system. The interactive applications, however, were loaded into memory for execution by the teleprocessing monitor.

(5) From the point of view of the interactive application program, the teleprocessing monitor has taken over many of the critical service functions normally performed by the operating system.

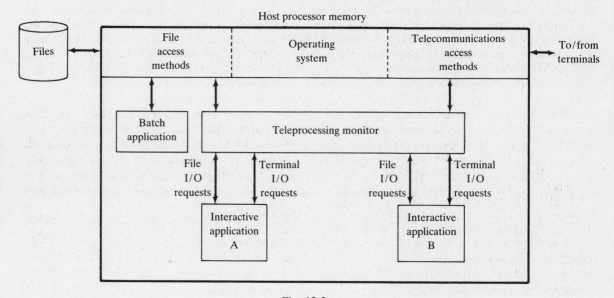

Fig. 13-2

13.5   Services Provided by Teleprocessing Monitors

Why are teleprocessing monitors used to "insulate" COBOL applications programs from direct control of the operating system telecommunications and file-handling access methods, and from those portions of the operating system which schedule and initiate programs for execution? The answer lies in the fact that in an interactive environment with many users, it frequently happens that several *different* terminal users need to execute the *same* interactive application program. If the application is given direct control of critical operating system facilities, the following serious problems can arise:

EXAMPLE 13.8   Suppose 10 different terminal users wish to execute the same application program at the same time. It is clearly wasteful of memory to load a separate copy of the program for each terminal. On the other hand, if the 10 terminal users are to share the same single copy of the program, then (1) the object code must be designed in such a way that this is feasible (such programs are said to be *reentrant*) and (2) the execution of the single copy of the program for different users must be supervised to ensure proper transition from one user to the next. The responsibility for overseeing the sharing of interactive applications between users is usually given to the teleprocessing monitor.

EXAMPLE 13.9   What if two or more terminal users running the same or different programs decide to update the same record in the same file at the same time? Suppose an inventory record currently indicates 100 items in stock and user A inputs the record and adds 10 to the total. Before user A's program rewrites the record, however, user A loses control of the CPU to user B, who also inputs the inventory record (still indicating 100 items in stock, since the *disk* copy of the record has not yet been changed). User B adds 20 to the total and rewrites the record placing the value 120 on the disk. User A's program then regains control of the processor and rewrites user A's version of the record with the total of 110 items (erasing the current disk value of 120). After this scenario, the disk record indicates 110 items in stock (instead of the correct value of 130).

Since all requests for file access must pass through the teleprocessing monitor (see Fig. 13-2), it is in a position to *lock* records so that the above type of error cannot occur. Thus when user A's program inputs the record for purposes of updating it, the monitor assigns a "locked" status to the record. If user B's program then attempts to input the record, the monitor detects the lock on the record and will not give it to user B's program until user A's program is finished with it. It is the teleprocessing monitor's responsibility to deal with such problems of *concurrent processing*, thus freeing the applications programmer to concentrate on the application.

EXAMPLE 13.10   Communicating with a terminal directly through an operating system telecommunications access method requires the specification of vast amounts of detail which are peculiar to the particular terminal involved. Suppose, as frequently happens, new terminals are added to a system or existing terminals are replaced with a new model. If each interactive application deals directly with the telecommunications access method, then each program will have to be changed.

Conversely, if each program passes terminal output data to the teleprocessing monitor and allows the teleprocessing monitor to deal with the telecommunications access methods, then changes to terminal hardware or software will not necessitate changes to the applications programs (but only to the teleprocessing monitor itself, and then only if the monitor does not already include the desired capabilities). The use of a teleprocessing monitor thus makes interactive applications independent of particular terminal characteristics.

EXAMPLE 13.11   In a batch environment, the ability to execute programs and manipulate data requires access to I/O devices in the computer operations center. Thus security considerations involve mainly the physical security of the machine room and control of the batches of data sent to and from the data entry department.

In an interactive environment, users are able to execute programs and manipulate data from many terminals spread throughout the organization (or from anywhere in the world, if dial-in lines are available). This presents far more serious security problems, and teleprocessing monitors typically provide features which help an installation maintain the security of its interactive applications.

One such feature is the *logon* procedure, in which a terminal user must correctly identify himself or herself to the teleprocessing monitor and provide a *password* which authorizes the user to access certain programs and/or files within the system. Only *selective access* to programs and files may be provided on the basis of the *user ID* and password entered.

EXAMPLE 13.12   If a batch application fails because of a hardware or software error, it is often relatively easy to restart program execution (either from the beginning or from an appropriate *checkpoint* at which the program is designed to be restarted). Even though restart is inconvenient because it requires extra machine time, recovery from a batch system failure is fairly straightforward.

In an interactive environment, where many terminal users may be simultaneously engaged in transactions affecting several files, a hardware or software failure can cause more serious problems. Since different terminals may be in different stages of execution of the same or different programs, there is no definable single "program" to "restart" in case of failure.

Teleprocessing monitors must include facilities for recovering from hardware and software failures in a controlled and orderly manner, enabling terminal users to continue with their work with as little loss of data and as little interruption as possible.

Teleprocessing monitors should also be relatively immune to failure themselves (i.e., *robust*), since if the teleprocessing monitor goes down, *all* terminal users go down with it.

EXAMPLE 13.13   After an interactive user logs onto a terminal, some means must be provided to allow the user to begin executing the desired application program. Teleprocessing monitors typically allow users to enter a *transaction identifier*, which specifies that a particular application program is to be executed. The teleprocessing monitor then (1) finds the auxiliary storage location of the object program associated with the given transaction identifier, (2) assigns a memory area to hold the object program, (3) loads the object program into memory, and (4) initiates the execution of the object program. If a copy of the desired object program is *already* in memory (because some other terminal is executing it), then steps (1) through (3) can be bypassed and the new user simply allowed to share access to the existing copy of the application.

The loading and execution of application programs in response to transaction identifiers entered by the user provides a simple mechanism by which the user can control the processing carried out at his or her terminal.

EXAMPLE 13.14   Response time is a critical characteristic of interactive systems. A teleprocessing monitor must provide rapid response to application program requests for file access and terminal I/O services so that the application program can, in turn, provide fast response to the user.

The teleprocessing monitor must also implement *multitasking*; i.e., it must ensure that each of the many user programs gets a fair and reasonable chance to execute on the CPU. This means that the teleprocessing monitor must supervise the execution of user applications and require that they "take turns" executing in such a manner that no one user can consume CPU resources at the undue expense of other users (e.g., it is usually unacceptable to give 2 users response times of 1 s, while 12 other users must wait 5 min).

13.6   Interfacing with a Typical Teleprocessing Monitor—CICS

In order to develop a feel for working with COBOL in an interactive environment, some considerations for interfacing with CICS are presented. CICS (Customer Information Control System) is a popular teleprocessing monitor developed by IBM for its 370-series computers.

Before an applications programmer can begin to code and test an interactive COBOL program which interfaces with CICS, the following steps must be carried out:

(1)   Either the applications programmer or a CICS systems programmer must define to CICS all the screen layouts (maps) to be used by the application program. This includes definition of all input and output screens as they should appear at the terminal. The actual coding of such *mapset definitions* is done in assembler language and is beyond the scope of this Outline. The mapset (i.e., screen format) definitions are stored on direct access storage.

(2)   A CICS systems programmer must update CICS tables (kept on direct access storage) which describe each file to be processed by the application program. These tables contain the information necessary for CICS to carry out the application program's requests for access to these files.

(3)   A CICS systems programmer must update CICS tables which describe the application program itself—the disk location of the machine language program, the spelling of the transaction identifier(s) which, when entered at a terminal, will cause CICS to load and execute the program, etc. All these functions require advanced knowledge of CICS and are beyond the scope of this Outline.

Once the screen, file, and program definitions have been coded, processed, and placed on direct access storage, the applications programmer is ready to code and test the necessary interactive COBOL programs.

An interactive COBOL program calls CICS when it needs the teleprocessing monitor to perform some service. It does this by calling CICS as an external subprogram. There are two ways for a COBOL programmer to code a request for file access and terminal I/O services from CICS:

(1) The programmer can code WORKING-STORAGE and LINKAGE SECTION definitions of the data areas which must be passed back and forth between CICS and the COBOL program, and then code the PROCEDURE DIVISION "CALL ... USING ... " statements necessary to request services of CICS. Since the amount of information which must be passed to CICS to describe a desired service is considerable, and since the format of the information is rigidly fixed by CICS requirements, coding the DATA DIVISION entries and the CALL ... USING ... statements is time-consuming and error-prone. Hence most applications do not invoke CICS with this method.

(2) The programmer can code CICS *commands* into the source program to invoke CICS services. CICS commands are statements which are not part of the standard COBOL language, but which readily define particular CICS services. In addition, if the screen formats have been defined in such a way as to permit it, most WORKING-STORAGE and LINKAGE SECTION data areas needed to communicate with CICS can simply be COPYed into the DATA DIVISION from a source program library created during the mapset definition procedure. COBOL programs written in this manner are said to use *command-level CICS*. Most interactive programs are written using command-level CICS.

The Role of the CICS Command-Level Translator

Since command-level CICS programs include commands which are not part of the COBOL language, they cannot be properly translated by the COBOL compiler. In order to make a command-level program syntactically correct, the CICS commands must be removed from the program and replaced with the equivalent CALL ... USING ... statements which link to CICS as an external subprogram. The task of translating syntactically unacceptable CICS commands into syntactically correct CALL ... USING ... statements is carried out by a special program available with the CICS system known as the *CICS command-level translator* (or *precompiler*).

After a command-level program has been processed by the precompiler, it contains only valid COBOL statements and can be input to the standard COBOL compiler for translation into machine language in the normal manner.

EXAMPLE 13.15 Figure 13-3 shows the use of the CICS command-level precompiler to translate a command-level COBOL program into machine language. First, the original source program (including any CICS commands) is input to the precompiler. The output of this step is a syntactically correct COBOL program in which all CICS commands have been translated into the equivalent CALL ... USING ... statements.

Next, the output of the precompiler (still a COBOL source program, but now containing only valid COBOL statements) is input by the standard COBOL compiler, which translates it into machine language. The machine language object program produced by the COBOL compiler is then ready for linking and execution.

The precompiler is designed in such a way as to ensure that the object program produced by this process has reentrant characteristics (i.e., the same copy can be shared by more than one terminal user).

13.7   Sample Command-Level CICS COBOL Routines

Some of the most important terminal and file operations are illustrated below, using CICS command-level COBOL.

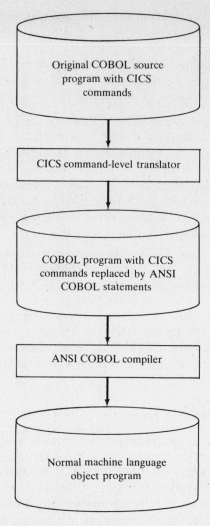

Fig. 13-3

EXAMPLE 13.16 The following CICS PROCEDURE DIVISION command will input data keyed by a terminal operator:

```
EXEC CICS
      RECEIVE   MAP      ('PRICMP1')
                MAPSET   ('PRICMS1')
                INTO     (ITEM-PRICING-MAP-AREA)
END-EXEC
```

"EXEC CICS" and "END-EXEC" mark the beginning and end of each CICS command. They serve as delimiters for the precompiler, which only processes statements inside the EXEC CICS/END-EXEC pair (all other statements are assumed to be valid COBOL and are left to the standard compiler).

The map "PRICMP1" and the mapset "PRICMS1" must be defined to CICS *prior* to the precompiling of this program. COPY statements in the DATA DIVISION (not shown) will result in the definition of data areas corresponding to the indicated map and mapset. The reader will recall that "map" and "mapset" are CICS terms referring to the predefined descriptions of the screens used by a program.

The INTO parameter tells CICS where to place a copy of the data coming from the terminal. Remember that CICS first reformats the data to remove any control characters, etc., putting the data in a form suitable for use by the COBOL program.

EXAMPLE 13.17 The following CICS command outputs a screenful of information to a terminal:

```
EXEC CICS
    SEND MAP      ('PRICMP1')
         MAPSET   ('PRICMS1')
         FROM     (ITEM-PRICING-MAP-AREA)
         ERASE
         CURSOR
    END-EXEC
```

Again, the map and mapset are the names of the precoded assembler modules which define the logical and physical characteristics of the terminal and the screen layouts to CICS. The FROM parameter identifies the data area into which the program has placed the data to be output to the terminal screen.

The ERASE option specifies that the previous contents of the screen are to be erased before sending out this screen (i.e., a totally new screen is sent). CURSOR specifies that the cursor is to be positioned to a screen field specified by the programmer prior to issuing the SEND MAP command.

EXAMPLE 13.18 The following CICS command illustrates how a COBOL program can randomly retrieve a record from a file:

```
EXEC CICS
    READ DATASET   ('PRICMAST')
         INTO      (PRICING-MASTER-RECORD)
         RIDFLD    (PRICING-ITEM-ID)
         UPDATE
    END-EXEC
```

This command inputs a record from a file named "PRICMAST". The key of the record to be input is in data area PRICING-ITEM-ID. If the record exists, CICS will place a copy of the record into PRICING-MASTER-RECORD. Both these areas can be defined in WORKING-STORAGE. The UPDATE option specifies that CICS should *lock* the record so that no other program is allowed to access it (until the record is released by rewriting it or explicitly unlocking it with a CICS command). The PRICMAST file must be defined to CICS in a special *file control table* before applications accessing the file can be run.

EXAMPLE 13.19 The routine on page 336 combines several CICS commands with standard COBOL statements to change the price for an item in the PRICMAST pricing master file. This module is not a good example of interactive design (see Section 13.8); it is oversimplified to better show the relationship between normal COBOL statements and CICS commands in a command-level program. Numbers in the right margin are for ease of reference and are not part of the program itself.

Statement (1) is a CICS command which outputs a screen to the terminal. This screen would contain messages (called *prompts*) instructing the user to enter the item ID and new price for an item in the PRICMAST file. ITEM-PRICING-SCREEN-AREA contains whatever variable data makes up this screen. When the SEND MAP command is executed, CICS will pick up this information, combine it with whatever constant information is specified in the screen definitions found in PRICMP1 and PRICMS1, and then add whatever control characters are necessary for the particular terminal in use. It then sends the screenful of data to the terminal via the appropriate operating system telecommunications access method.

The terminal user then enters the needed information at the terminal keyboard. This information is made available to the application program when it executes the RECEIVE MAP command in statement (2). CICS reformats the input data according to the screen definitions in PRICMP1 and PRICMS1 and places it into the fields of ITEM-PRICING-SCREEN-AREA.

At point (3), the program processes the data input from the terminal. If the data is valid, the item ID from the terminal is copied to an area which holds the record key for the pricing master record. If the data is not valid, a paragraph is called to build a screen with an appropriate error message. Note the use of a GO TO statement to then transfer control back to the beginning of the CHANGE-ITEM-PRICE paragraph. The use of GO TO, although discouraged within batch programs, is quite common within interactive programs using CICS (see Section 13.8).

Statement (4) calls CICS to randomly input the pricing master file record whose key is in PRICING-

MASTER-ITEM-ID. A CICS systems programmer must have created an entry for "PRICMAST" in a special CICS file control table prior to the execution of this program. The READ command causes CICS to call the appropriate operating system file access method to actually input the record, and then pass a copy of the record to the COBOL program by placing it in the PRICING-MASTER-RECORD field. The key of the desired record is available to CICS in the RIDFLD (record *ID* field) PRICING-MASTER-ITEM-ID. Since the UPDATE parameter has been specified, CICS will also lock this record so that no other program will be allowed access to it until after it has been rewritten.

One of the unrealistic things about this example is that it does not handle the possible record-not-found condition. Handling of errors and exceptional conditions under CICS is beyond the scope of this Outline.

Assuming that the desired pricing record has been read successfully, the program goes on, in statement (5), to move the new price value input from the terminal into the pricing master record.

Statement (6) then rewrites the pricing master record with the updated price. The REWRITE command must have been preceded by a successful READ command with the UPDATE option. REWRITE replaces the record on auxiliary storage with the current contents of PRICING-MASTER-RECORD (the FROM area in the command). Successful completion of the REWRITE command also unlocks the record being rewritten so that other programs can again access it.

```
        PROCEDURE DIVISION.
            .
            .
            .

        CHANGE-ITEM-PRICE.

            PERFORM BUILD-ITEM-PRICING-SCREEN

            EXEC CICS                                               (1)
                SEND      MAP        ('PRICMP1')
                          MAPSET     ('PRICMS1')
                          FROM       (ITEM-PRICING-SCREEN-AREA)
                          ERASE
                          CURSOR
            END-EXEC

            EXEC CICS                                               (2)
                RECEIVE   MAP        ('PRICMP1')
                          MAPSET     ('PRICMS1')
                          INTO       (ITEM-PRICING-SCREEN-AREA)
            END-EXEC

            PERFORM EDIT-SCREEN-INPUT                               (3)
            IF SCREEN-INPUT-IS-VALID
                MOVE SCREEN-AREA-ITEM-ID TO PRICING-MASTER-ITEM-ID
            ELSE
                PERFORM BUILD-SCREEN-AREA-ERROR-MESSAG
                GO TO CHANGE-ITEM-PRICE
            .

            EXEC CICS                                               (4)
                READ      DATASET    ('PRICMAST')
                          INTO       (PRICING-MASTER-RECORD)
                          RIDFLD     (PRICING-MASTER-ITEM-ID)
                          UPDATE
            END-EXEC
                                                                    (5)
            MOVE NEW-PRICE-FROM-TERMINAL TO PRICING-MASTER-PRICE-FIELD
            EXEC CICS                                               (6)
                REWRITE   DATASET    ('PRICMAST')
                          FROM       (PRICING-MASTER-RECORD)
            END-EXEC
```

13.8 Changes in Design Philosophy for an Interactive Environment

The overriding design consideration for interactive systems is fast response time. The need for good response can dictate that interactive programs follow different (and sometimes opposite!) design principles than batch programs. This section lists some of the more important design considerations for interactive systems.

(1) Most interactive programs are designed to be pseudo-conversational rather than conversational. A conversational program remains active while waiting for the terminal operator to enter data. A pseudo-conversational program deactivates itself by returning to the teleprocessing monitor while waiting for an operator action. This allows the teleprocessing monitor to assign memory occupied by the inactive task to tasks which can make immediate use of it, thereby allowing the teleprocessing monitor to support more simultaneous users. Pseudo-conversational program logic is usually *the* most important efficiency technique for interactive programs.

EXAMPLE 13.20 Consider the amount of real time which could elapse between the execution of statement (1) and statement (2) in Example 13.19 (which is designed as a conversational program). Since the RECEIVE MAP command cannot be completed until the user hits the ENTER (or an equivalent) key on the terminal, the program must wait for this operator action. If the user goes to lunch in the middle of a transaction, this could be several hours. Since the program remains active and in memory all this time, it is tying up resources and could prevent other users from logging on and executing their programs.

Since pure conversational programs waste valuable resources by remaining active until the user terminates program execution, CICS allows programs to be designed as pseudo-conversational. Pseudo-conversational programs return control to the teleprocessing monitor whenever they must wait for operator action. This frees processor resources during those times when the user is thinking, typing, etc., thereby making room for other programs which are *not* waiting on the user and are immediately ready to execute. Since interactive programs spend most of their time waiting on the terminal user, a given processor can accommodate many more simultaneous users if the applications are designed as pseudo-conversational rather than conversational.

The teleprocessing monitor automatically restarts an inactive pseudo-conversational program when the user hits the ENTER key. A discussion of how to design and code pseudo-conversational programs is beyond the scope of this Outline, but the reader should be aware that pseudo-conversational logic is different from standard batch processing logic, and that interactive programs are almost always written using pseudo-conversational logic.

(2) A given teleprocessing monitor may not allow the use of certain ANS COBOL PROCEDURE DIVISION verbs. For example, CICS does not support any of the file processing verbs (e.g., OPEN and READ), STOP RUN, GOBACK, SORT (or any related statements such as RELEASE), INSPECT, UNSTRING, and others. If this is the case, interactive applications must be designed *without* these features.

(3) Processor memory is a critical resource in an interactive environment because it determines how many simultaneous users can be logged onto the system. Many interactive program design techniques, therefore, attempt to limit memory usage. When command-level CICS is used, the precompiler automatically generates the object program in such a way that the same copy of the PROCEDURE DIVISION can be *shared* by several users. Thus even if 15 users are running the same interactive program, only *one* copy of the PROCEDURE DIVISION need be in memory.

(4) While CICS shares PROCEDURE DIVISION code between users, it gives *each* user a separate copy of the WORKING-STORAGE SECTION of the program. The programmer can, therefore, save memory by making the WORKING-STORAGE SECTION as small as possible.

EXAMPLE 13.21 In a batch program, one tries to keep literals out of the PROCEDURE DIVISION and instead use program constants in WORKING-STORAGE. In an interactive program, the design should be exactly opposite; the programmer should try to use PROCEDURE DIVISION literals instead of constants in WORKING-STORAGE (e.g., use MOVE "INVALID ITEM NUMBER" TO SCREEN-MESSAGE-AREA instead of MOVE RECORD-NOT-FOUND-MESSAGE TO SCREEN-MESSAGE-AREA). This saves memory since the WORKING-STORAGE SECTION will be duplicated for each user, but users will all share a single copy of the PROCEDURE DIVISION.

(5)   Care should be taken not to overdo modularity in interactive programs. This means writing more *straight-line code* and using fewer PERFORM and CALL statements (and any other linkage facilities which may be provided by the teleprocessing monitor). The reason for this involves the concept of working set. The *working set* consists of those portions of an object program which are actually needed in memory for the program to be able to execute.

EXAMPLE 13.22   Suppose a program consists of 50 paragraphs. If the fifteenth paragraph is currently being executed, and if it contains a PERFORM . . . UNTIL . . . invoking the fortieth paragraph 500 times, then the working set consists of just the fifteenth and fortieth paragraphs; i.e., the only pieces of the program which *must* be in memory at this time are the fifteenth and fortieth paragraphs.

Modern *virtual storage* operating systems are designed to more effectively manage memory by keeping only a program's current working set in real storage at any given time, thus freeing memory to hold the working set of programs for other users. Virtual storage systems do this by arbitrarily breaking programs up into chunks called *pages*, and then placing in memory only those pages which are needed to make up the working set. Note that since page is a physical concept (e.g., a typical page size is 4096 bytes), memory may still be wasted if the working set is spread over many pages.

EXAMPLE 13.23   Suppose the working set consists of 100 bytes. If the 100 bytes fall in one page of a program, then the working set takes only one page (4096 bytes) of memory. If the 100 bytes are composed of 25 bytes from each of 4 different pages, then the working set takes 4 pages (4 * 4096 bytes) of memory.

EXAMPLE 13.24   In Example 13.22, since paragraph 15 and paragraph 40 are far apart in the program, they are likely to fall in different pages. Thus the working set in Example 13.22 would occupy two pages of memory.

If the program in Example 13.22 were redesigned to eliminate the use of the PERFORM (e.g., by placing a copy of the code from paragraph 40 directly in paragraph 15), then it is likely that the working set would fall in one page of memory, thus cutting memory requirements to execute this portion of the program in half. The memory thus freed could be used to hold the working set for another active program, thus increasing the number of possible interactive users logged onto the system.

Note that implementing the *repetitive* execution of the paragraph 15 code *within* paragraph 40 may well require the use of a GO TO statement for COBOL-74 (which does not support the COBOL-85 in-line PERFORM). Design considerations such as these often result in the use of GO TO statements within interactive COBOL-74 programs.

There are many other interactive design factors which are beyond the scope of this Outline. The purpose of this chapter has simply been to make the reader aware that there are significant differences between batch and interactive systems.

Review Questions

13.1   Describe the major characteristics of a traditional batch processing system.

13.2   Describe some important disadvantages of batch systems.

13.3   Describe the major characteristics of an interactive or online system.

13.4   Give some advantages of interactive systems.

13.5   Define the term "response time".

13.6   Why are interactive systems often called online systems?

13.7   Diagram and explain the hardware used in most interactive systems.

13.8   Explain the role of a terminal controller.

13.9   Distinguish between private, leased, and dial-up telecommunications lines.

13.10 Distinguish between analog and digital telecommunications lines.

13.11 Explain the role of modems when analog lines are used.

13.12 Explain the functions of a front-end processor.

13.13 What is a port?

13.14 What is a telecommunications access method?

13.15 Describe the major functions of a teleprocessing monitor.

13.16 Contrast the relationship between a batch program and the operating system access methods and an interactive program and the operating system access methods.

13.17 What functions provided by a teleprocessing monitor are normally provided by the operating system? Why have such functions been moved into the teleprocessing monitor?

13.18 Describe several reasons why teleprocessing monitors are used to interface between interactive application programs and the operating system.

13.19 Why are teleprocessing monitors designed to enforce record locking?

13.20 How can teleprocessing monitors help with the security of an interactive system?

13.21 In a CICS environment, what must be done *before* a programmer can test an interactive COBOL program?

13.22 Explain the concept of command-level CICS, including the role of the CICS command-level translator.

13.23 Describe the major CICS commands and explain their functions.

13.24 Differentiate between conversational and pseudo-conversational programs.

13.25 Explain the importance of pseudo-conversational program logic for interactive applications.

13.26 Explain the importance of saving memory when designing an interactive program.

13.27 Explain the concept of working set.

13.28 Why might too much modularity in a program design be inefficient in an interactive environment?

Solved Problems

13.29 What is meant by online batch processing?

     In online batch systems, data is entered and edited using online (i.e., interactive) programs. The data entry and editing programs do *not*, however, process the data. They simply collect the data on disk files for later processing by traditional batch programs. The system as a whole, then, appears to be a combination of online and batch processing, whence the name.

13.30 Which of the following systems could be implemented as batch and which as interactive systems?

(1)   An airline reservations system

(2)   An order entry system for a catalog sales company that takes 90 percent of its orders through the mail

(3)   An order entry system for a catalog sales company that takes 90 percent of its orders over the phone

(4)   A banking system for processing monthly mortgage payments

(5)   A banking system supporting teller processing of savings account deposits and withdrawals

(6)   A system allowing retail stores to phone in credit checks on charge card customers

(1)   Must be interactive because of the need for immediate, up-to-the-minute information.

(2)   Probably batch, since interactive is not needed and batch is usually cheaper to install and operate.

(3)   Must be interactive if the telephone customer is to be given information about availability of items ordered; if this is not the case, then the system could be batch.

(4)   Probably batch for the same reason as (2) above.

(5)   Must be interactive if balances are to be updated immediately and customers given immediate feedback; if transactions are simply recorded on paper and collected by each teller for later processing, then a batch system would suffice. Many banks actually use online batch systems for this particular application. If a customer needs to know the new balance, it is specially calculated by a program which reads the account master file (not yet updated), then reads the file containing the as-yet-unprocessed transactions, and then figures the new balance using this information.

(6)   An interactive system is needed to give immediate response to telephone inquiries.

Appendix

ANS COBOL-1985 Indexed File Status Codes

ANS COBOL-1985 specifies more codes than were defined in the previous (1974) ANS version of COBOL. Codes which are included in the 1985 standard but which were *not* part of the 1974 standard are marked with an "*".

Group 1: Successful Completion

Note that the first digit of all codes indicating successful completion is 0. This provides a simple mechanism to test for successful completion when the more detailed information provided in the second digit of the code is not of interest. Codes beginning with a nonzero digit indicate *unsuccessful* completion.

Code	Meaning
00	Successful completion
02	Successful completion, but with a duplicate key detected (must be using ALTERNATE RECORD KEY with DUPLICATES specified)
04*	Successful READ, but logical record input contains more (or fewer) characters than the maximum (or minimum) specified for the file
05*	Successful OPEN for OPTIONAL file, but file is not present
07*	Successful CLOSE, but a NO REWIND, REEL/UNIT, or FOR REMOVAL clause is specified for a device which did not support the clause; the clause is ignored

Group 2: Unsuccessful Completion because of AT END

Code	Meaning
10	End-of-file condition
14*	A sequential READ for a relative file attempts to input a record whose relative record number is too large to fit in the RELATIVE KEY data item

Group 3: Unsuccessful Completion because of INVALID KEY Condition

Code	Meaning
21	Sequence error for sequentially accessed file
22	Duplicate key for WRITE or REWRITE
23	Record-not-found condition—attempt to randomly access a logical record which does not exist in the file
24*	Attempt to write beyond the boundaries of the file; exact meaning of this error depends on the particular system

Group 4: Unsuccessful Completion because of Permanent I–O Error

Code	Meaning
30	Permanent I–O error; no further information is available
35*	OPEN with INPUT, I–O, or EXTEND for a file which is not present
37*	OPEN for a file which must be on a direct access device, but which is not

Code	Meaning
38*	Attempt to OPEN a file previously CLOSEd with LOCK
39*	OPEN fails because of conflict between information in file label (or equivalent) and information given in the COBOL program

Group 5: Unsuccessful Completion because of Logic Error

Code	Meaning
41*	Attempt to OPEN an already open file
42*	Attempt to CLOSE a file which is not open
43*	During sequential access, a DELETE or REWRITE fails because it was not preceded by a successful READ
44*	Attempt to WRITE or REWRITE a logical record whose size is invalid
46*	Sequential READ fails because current record pointer is undefined (because preceding START or READ failed)
47*	READ or START to file not opened for INPUT or I–O
48*	WRITE to file not opened for OUTPUT, I–O, or EXTEND
49*	DELETE or REWRITE to file not opened for I–O

Group 6: Codes Reserved for Particular Implementations

The codes 90–99 may be assigned different meanings by different compiler developers. Consult an instructor or vendor manual for the meanings of these codes at your installation.

Index

Catalog

If you are interested in a list of SCHAUM'S
OUTLINE SERIES send your name
and address, requesting your free catalog, to:

SCHAUM'S OUTLINE SERIES, Dept. C
McGRAW-HILL BOOK COMPANY
1221 Avenue of Americas
New York, N.Y. 10020